THE HOLY WA

A PRIMORDIAL SYMBOL IN HINDU MYTHS

The Book:

How can we be indifferent to our surroundings? Embedded in us lies an awareness of the sacred. It is expressed through myths and symbols by an attitude of harmonious oneness with the world.

Such myths and symbols show the reality of a single cosmic manifestation. They also suggest a common core of humanity, untrammelled by any difference of race, religion or culture. That may be an encouraging thought. We, in our modern technological times, still remain trapped in discrimination of various kinds.

Awareness of the sacred presents us with the gift and the challenge of myths and symbols of liberation, unity, harmony, and peace. The symbol of the Sacred Waters in the Vedic and later Hindu tradition in India is singularly attractive. It invites people from all over the world to India's holy waters.

The author brings together 250 "happenings of the Sacred Waters" in a chain of symbolism. It links diverse aspects of the universe with our daily experiences, our human condition. Typical of the Vedic and Hindu tradition is that we, human beings, should not claim an undeserved position of importance on the earth. We are her inhabitants, but that only as guests.

The author explores our willingness to acknowledge mythical thinking as an original constituent of our person. The author finds that we are called upon to evolve in ourselves the myths and symbols of the sacred. They are there. While undergoing revolutionary changes, our perception of the universe cannot avoid commitment to the maintenance or restoration of the loss of its integrity and harmony. A tree, a river, a bird, a mountain, the atmosphere and one's chosen deity are as much part of the universe as we are. What then do the myths and symbols of the sacred tell us, human beings? An Indian myth calls us "the protectors of the world."

***

The Author:

Frans Baartmans (1936) is a member of the London-based International Society of Mill Hill. After his seminary studies in The Netherlands and the United Kingdom, he lived and worked almost ten years with the Kenyah and Kayan people in the interior of Sarawak, Malaysia, at a time when their traditional longhouse culture came under pressure from large-scale timber industry.

He became deeply involved in efforts by the local population to preserve their traditional cultural heritage and protect it against multinational timber corporations.

He graduated in Anthropology of Religion and Ethnic Theology from the University of Nijmegen, The Netherlands. In 1979 he came to Varanasi, India, to study Indian Philosophy and Religion. In 1985 he received a Ph.D. degree from Banaras Hindu University. He is currently engaged in research and community development in Varanasi.

THE HOLY WATERS

A PRIMORDIAL SYMBOL IN HINDU MYTHS

Frans Baartmans

B.R. Publishing Corporation
[A Division of BRPC (India) Ltd.]
Delhi-110035

Distributed by:
BRPC (India) Ltd.
4222/1, Ansari Road, Darya Ganj,
New Delhi-110002
Ph.: 3259196, 3259648
Fax: 3201571
E-Mail: *info@brpcltd.com*

First published in 1990 with the title "Āpaḥ—The Sacred Waters: An Analysis of a Primordial Symbol in Hindu Myths."

Second Edition in 2000 with the title "The Holy Waters: A Primordial Symbol in Hindu Myths."

ISBN 81-7646-151-2

Published by:
B.R. Publishing Corporation
[A Division of BRPC (India) Ltd.]
3779, Ist Floor,
Kanhaiya Nagar, Tri Nagar,
Delhi-110035
Phones: 7152140
E-Mail: *info@brpcltd.com*

Printed at:
PRAJA Offset
Delhi-110033

PRINTED IN INDIA

THIS BOOK

I

DEDICATE TO MY PARENTS

ACKNOWLEDGEMENTS

While preparing this book, I have received wholehearted support and encouragement from Prof. Dr. N.S.S. Raman. He provided me, moving in the midst of myth, with a matter-of-fact guidance. Prof. Raman's guidance also enabled me to complete the work in time. Were it not for his guidelines, I might not have been able to find the balance between mythical time and space and that allotted to me by circumstance.

From Mr. Om Prakash Sharma and his wife and children I learnt to acquaint myself with Indian family life. I am indebted to them for many graces needing no elaboration here.

The book has been written in India's holy city of Banaras. Many travelling young people from the West and elsewhere, in their backpacks their myths, encouraged and helped me to write in exchange for my promise to let their anguish about senseless destruction of environment be known.

FRANS BAARTMANS

FOREWORD TO THE FIRST EDITION

I have great pleasure in introducing Frans Baartmans' book on a theme which has attracted very little attention from the students and scholars of comparative religions and philosophy of religion. Students of Hinduism have in the past studied either only its superficial aspects or one of its various philosophies such as Advaita Vedanta. Dr. Baartmans has in a very painstaking and commendable study taken up the mythical, the symbolic aspects of Hinduism, concentrating mainly on the myths of the Waters as part and parcel of the consciousness of the sacred. The relation of the various myths and symbols to human existence and their relevance with regard to religious experience are quite appropriately examined in great detail and depth. In so far as the symbol of the Waters is concerned, its ramifications in the cosmic, the ethical and the socio-political contexts have been analysed in an impressive manner. I am confident that Dr. Baartmans' phenomenology of religious experience will prove to be a most valuable contribution to the progress of comparative religion as a rigorous discipline.

Muthos as an original direction of the human spirit must be recognized in any comprehensive understanding of man's existence and his relations to the Universe. Philosophers of religion in the past have overemphasized the logos-aspect at the expense of the muthos. In any understanding of religious consciousness, it is essential that we explore the profundity of symbolic expressions including those of myth and ritual. One recalls here the basic distinction which Blaise Pascal made long ago between what he called logic of reason and logic of heart. If a balance has to be restored in the study of Hinduism as a philosophy and religion, it is of fundamental importance that philosophers devote attention to a comprehensive study of myth and ritual as partly constituting the beliefs and values of that religion. It is from this standpoint that I regard Dr. Frans Baartmans' work as a significant and original contribution to the study of Hinduism.

Laying too much stress on the logos-aspect of religion would only dissolve reality into a set of logical relations, however exhaustive such an exercise may be. Hence, side by side with an understanding of the rational, the philosopher of religion would do well to delve deeper into the configurations of myth and symbol and the values they proclaim. This Frans Baartmans has done in ample measure and I congratulate him wholeheartedly on his achievement.

Water symbolism does play a prominent role in the complex myths and symbols of Hinduism. Water represents not only an inexhaustible reservoir of meanings, it is also pregnant with suggestions concerning the end, the goal of human endeavour in the realm of man's cosmic existence — or his 'cosmic pilgrimage', as Dr. Baartmans describes it. Thus the symbol of water manifests itself overwhelmingly in man's psyche in many ways, a description of which would be limitless. From creation to destruction, from man's birth to his death and the dissolution of his ashes, water is an inseparable companion in man's existence. As the author eloquently puts it: it is in the experience of the happening of *Āpaḥ*, the Waters, that man intends to gain a foothold in the totality of Being. Such an effort is truly characterized by the author as a karmic, a cosmic pilgrimage, an attempt to cover the distance between man and God.

The present work exhibits deep study and penetrative meditation not ordinarily available in a scholar. Dr. Baartmans' book is commended to all students of philosophy and religion, in particular to the students of Hinduism, who will no doubt find in it a source of inspiration to the authentic study of that religion.

N.S.S. Raman

FOREWORD TO THE SECOND EDITION

It gives me great pleasure to welcome the second edition of Frans Baartmans' commendable study of a revered symbol in the Hindu tradition, that of the Sacred Waters. There is a need for a study of this kind for the benefit of both students and scholars of Philosophy and religion, and of comparative religion. The author has given an authentic exposition of the significance of myths and symbols in the Hindu tradition. Hindu religion is Vedic religion, Sanatana Dharma. It cannot be understood unless one studies in depth its myths and symbols. In fact, mythical and symbolic thought permeates the whole of Sanatana Dharma.

Cosmology is an essential component of Indian Mythology. It is Hindu Dharma's belief that creation of the universe evolves from the five elements. Of these, Hindu Cosmology awards primordial status to the waters rather than to any of the other elements. It is from the waters that the universe first emerged. Greek cosmology shares this belief. Hindu tradition hinges on Advaita Vedanta which declares: "sarvam khalvidam brahma." The sacred, the divine is present, not only in the human being but in the entire universe: its air, oceans, mountains, sky, birds, animals, plants, galaxies, stars, sun and moon. Hinduism cherishes a holistic approach to the universe. Reality within and without is one and the same. It is here that the elements, the world as we experience it, is transformed into spirituality.

Hindu Dharma's spirituality attributes the greatest importance to the waters when on our way to godliness: "devo bhutva devam upaset." The waters at once purify and enable us to engage in upasana, worship and contemplation of The Highest.

Today, a study of the Sacred Waters is of still greater relevance when their very symbol, the river Ganga, is being polluted. Pollution endangers the well-being of the whole universe. Unless we control it, pollution poses a serious threat to the very existence of the earth.

Pollution threatens not only the world outside. More harmful and threatening still, is pollution of the world inside, pollution of the heart. The heart is in constant need of purification through the Sacred Waters.

Dr. Baartmans' detailed and original work on the profound symbol of the waters in the Hindu tradition deserves admiration. I congratulate him on the occasion of the second edition of his book, and wish him to come with further comprehensive studies of the wealth of myths, symbols and ritual of Hindu Dharma.

Professor Rewati Raman Pandey
Head, Department of Philosophy and Religion,
Banaras Hindu University,
Varanasi

CONTENTS

ABBREVIATIONS

AA	Aitareya Āraṇyaka
AB	Aitareya Brāhmaṇa
AGS	Āśvalāyana Gṛhya Sūtra
AP	Agni Purāṇa
AU	Aitareya Upaniṣad
AV	Atharva Veda
BG	Bhagavad Gītā
BGB	Bhagavad Gītā Bhāṣya
BhagP	Bhāgavata Purāṇa
BhavP	Bhavisyottara Purāṇa
BP	Brahmāṇḍa Purāṇa
BrahbU	Brahmabindu Upaniṣad
BrhadP	Bṛhaddharma Purāṇa
BrahmavaiP	Brahmavaivarta Purāṇa
Brh. Sri	Bṛhat Śrīkrama
BU	Bṛhadāraṇyaka Upaniṣad
CU	Chāndogya Upaniṣad
DbhP	Devībhāgavata Purāṇa
DhyanabU	Dhyānabindu Upaniṣad
Gorak. S	Gorakśasiddhāntasaṃgraha
HevT	Hevajra Tantra
Hath Ypr	Hatha Yogapradīpikā
HaU	Haṁs Upaniṣad
HGS	Hiraṇyakeśī Gṛhya Sūtra
IsU	Iśa Upaniṣad
JaimB	Jaiminīya Brāhmaṇa
JaimUB	Jaiminīya Upaniṣad Brāhmaṇa
KathU	Kaṭha Upaniṣad
KausB	Kauśitakī Brāhmaṇa
KausU	Kauśitaki Upaniṣad
KKh	Kāśī Khaṇda
KP	Kūrma Purāṇa
KR	Kāśī Rahasya
KS	Kotirudra Saṃhitā
Kulac. Nig	Kulacūḍāmani Nigama
KularT	Kularṇava Tantra
LP	Liṅga Purāṇa
MahaU	Mahā Upaniṣad
MahanarU	Mahānārāyaṇa Upaniṣad
MahanT	Mahānirvaṇa Tantra
MaiS	Maitrāyana Saṃhitā

MaitraU	Maitrāyana Upaniṣad
MaiU	Maitrī Upaniṣad
MandU	Māṇḍūkya Upaniṣad
MaP	Mārkaṇḍeya Purāṇa
MaSm	Manu Smṛti
Mhb	Mahābhārata
MP	Matsya Purāṇa
MU	Muṇḍaka Upaniṣad
NU	Nārāyaṇa Upaniṣad
PGS	Praskara Gṛhya Sūtra
PP	Pādma Purāṇa
PranagniU	Prāṇāgnihotra Upaniṣad
PranU	Pranava Upaniṣad
PrasnU	Praśna Upaniṣad
R	Rāmāyaṇa
RS	ṚgVeda (Sāyana)
RutU	Rāma-Uttara-Tāpanīya Upaniṣad
RV	ṚgVeda
SCN	Sāt Çakra Nirupaṇa
SB	Śatapatha Brāhmaṇa
SGS	Sāṅkhyāyana Gṛhya Sūtra
SkP	Skanda Purāṇa
SmC	Smṛti Chandrikā
SP	Śiva Purāṇa
SS	Śiva Saṃhitā
SSS	Śāṅkhyāyaṇa Śrauta Sūtra
SU	Śvetāśvatara Upaniṣad
TA	Taittirīya Āraṇyaka
TB	Taittirīya Brāhmaṇa
TMB	Tāṇḍya Mahā Brāhmaṇa
TS	Taittirīya Saṃhitā
VaikS	Vaikhānas-smarta Sūtra
VajS	Vājasaneyi Saṃhitā
VaP	Vāyu Purāṇa
VaSa	Vāmana Saromāhātmya
VDhS	Viṣñu Dharma Sūtra
VDS	Vaśiṣṭha Dharma Sūtra
VmP	Vāmana Purāṇa
VP	Viṣñu Purāṇa
YogkU	Yogakuṇḍalinī Upaniṣad
YogS	Yogasāra Saṃgraha
YS	Yoga Sūtra
YT	Yoginī Tantra
YUp	Yogatattva Upaniṣad
YV	Yajur Veda

Plate 1: Pilgrims bathing at Dasaswamedh Ghat, Varanasi, during Shivaratri festival (Photo by Peter Harrap)

Plate 2: A pilgrim in Varanasi reciting the Gayatri mantra facing the rising sun. The sun represents the Absolute, Brahman.
(Photo by Peter Harrap)

Plate 3: Salutation to the sun at dawn. The watervessel symbolizes the generative womb of the Divine. (Photo by Peter Harrap)

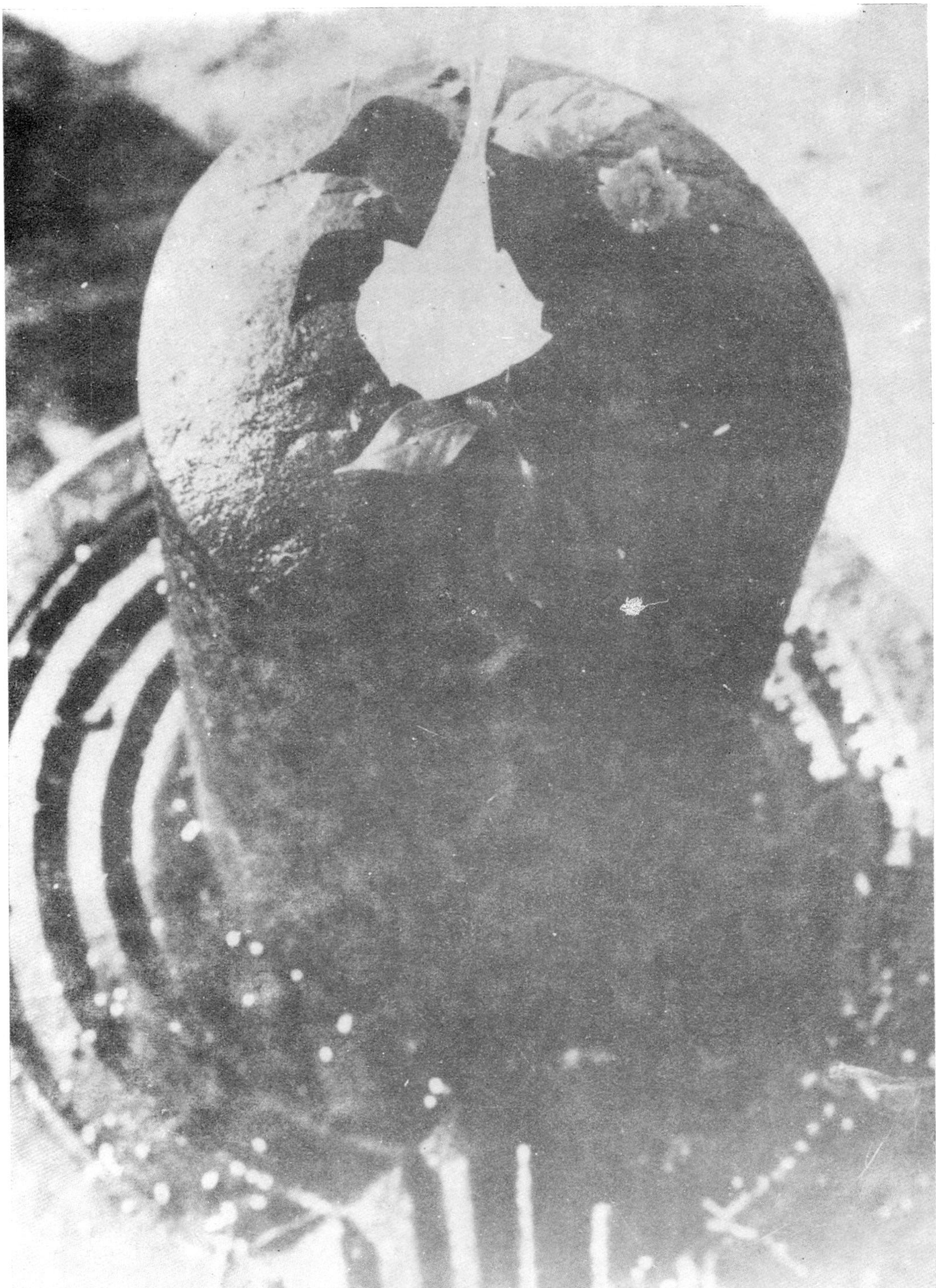

Plate 4: Lingam – Yoni adorned with datura flower. (*Datura Stramonium* of the *Solanaceae genus*). (Photo by Peter Harrap)

Plate 5: After her morning bath in the Ganges an elderly woman pours water over a lingam– yoni at Assi Ghat, Varanasi. (Photo by Peter Harrap)

Plate 6: Dawn over the waters of the Ganges, Varanasi. (Photo by Peter Harrap)

Plate 7: Sadhus chanting the Kirtan in boat in the Ganges.
(Photo by Mirjam Letsch)

Plate 8: After morning bath people are offering prayers to the Ganges.
(Photo by Hans de Clercq)

Plate 9: A man worshipping the Peepal tree.

Plate 10: Kashi, The City of Light. (Photo by Hans de Clercq)

INTRODUCTION

In this book I have attempted an analysis of a primary symbol in living Indian mythical awareness: that of *Āpaḥ*, the Waters. Such an undertaking seems to me one of the needs of not only philosophy, but also of analytical psychology and of theology. For, in both a theoretical and a practical sense, it is very hard for those who have not experienced the reality of a primary symbol by undergoing analysis to understand what depth it reveals.

What is that depth a primary symbol reveals? We must not forget that the symbolic manifestation as a *thing* is a matrix of symbolic meanings as *thought words*. We have never ceased — to restrict ourselves to our chosen primary model of the Waters — to find meaning in water. It is the same thing to say that water *manifests* birth, growth, decay and destruction and to say that it *signifies* the whole of potentiality: the immense, the unity of things in their diversity, the crisis of fragmentation, and the synthesizing comfort of understood orderly flux. The manifestation through the water-"thing" is like the condensation of an infinite discourse. The water-"thing" is the counterpart of the overcharge of its inexhaustible meaning which has ramifications in the cosmic, the ethical and the socio-political. Thus the symbol-"thing" water is the potentiality of innumerable spoken symbols which are knotted together in a single cosmic manifestation. In our case that cosmic manifestation will come to us, I hope, through the primary symbol of the Cosmic Waters.*

How do the Waters relate to human existence? The question betrays an intention. There is no problem at the cosmic end. At that end there is nothing but ultimate harmony. The *problem* of human existence enters where mere reason fails to discover the cosmic connection. One might say that the *problem* of human existence offers at the same time the most considerable challenge to *think and feel* the cosmic connection and the most deceptive invitation to talk nonsense, as if the *problem* were inherited by us from the Cosmos, the Universe.

The contradiction felt between the destination of man, projected in the image of primordial innocence and final perfection, and the actual situation of man when acknowledged and confessed to, gives rise to a gigantic "Why?" at the centre of the experience of existing. There is indeed a problem. A periodic immersion into the Waters, not once but daily only to emerge re-created, might make the "Why?" more bearable, if not intelligible.

Like all other humans, the Indian is engaged in a constant quest for harmony between finitude and that which is *other* than finitude. On the human level, finitude is readily experienced unlike its posing *other*. The locus of the quest for harmony

*Throughout I have used the term "primordial symbol", "primary symbol", "primary model" or "exemplary model" rather than the term "archetype". True, "archetype" is a mythical motif. However, it may easily lead to confusion to use a term which plays a role of primary importance in Jung's psychology with regard to the effects of the archetype manifested in processes that take place both in the unconscious and between the unconscious and consciousness. Unless I expressly refer to those realms, the term "archetype" has been avoided.

between the two is man's life as a human being in between those opposites. The quest reminds the Indian of the battle of *Kurukṣeira* where the concord between finitude and non-finitude turned out to be indissolubly linked with the problem of good and evil. It is, however, not only once that Lord *Kṛiṣña* approached *Arjuna* and joined him on the chariot stationed between the two camps. *Kurukṣetra* is a daily experience involving the simple question: "What ought I to do?", and the not always simple answer.

While being maintained and supported between *nirguṇa* and *saguṇa* during *sthiti*, the "in-between", the Indian is well aware of his existential predicament as a creature endowed with intellect, the sumtotal of *vāc*, *prāṇa* and *manas*. The quest for harmony and synthesis in life receives its significant accent in two sets of values which seem to be opposed, one to the other: *Pravṛtti* and *Nivṛtti*. Contrary to *Pravṛtti*—"rolling onward, act of turning around"— *Nivṛtti* means "act of turning back, returning". Each concept and the practical lifestyle symbolized by it, if taken seriously, is discernible in the meaning of the words. While alive on *bhūmi*, the earth as man's home, man experiences both forces, each with its justified claims. The fact that man is at the same time an inhabitant of and a guest in this world creates a tension which is conspicuously present.

In trying to come to terms with both *pravṛtti* and *nivṛtti*, the Indian transposes all *anthropological* dualism by appealing to the Vedic *Dhī*, visionary insight and perception.[1] *Dhī* has laid down the groundrules for human existence. The Vedic *Dhī* has subsequently been reviewed, meditated on, and thought about. That resulted at times in agonizing and hairsplitting metaphysical and epistemological argumentation. Ultimately, however, both the crisis and the consoling discoveries concerned the values of *pravṛtti* and *nivṛtti*.

The first chapter of Part II attempts to provide a pictorial of the Indian effort to come to grips with *pravṛtti* and *nivṛtti* values. The effort has continued till the present day. Philosophical curiosity has led me to ask the Indian to take me to his "Origin", perceived through *Dhī*. Possible existential doubt and feeling of relief are better understood when man knows where he comes from by analysing his cultural memory. The second chapter of Part II, therefore, provides a glimpse into the Indian Prestige of Origin, the Origin of the Beginnings. I restrict myself as much as possible to accounts of "the beginnings". By limiting myself to that cycle of accounts I hope to be repaid with a more rigorous understanding of what happens *now* in the world of man through close proximity to what happened *then*, at *that time*.

The Indian Prestige of Origin is formidable and impressive. It has particular characteristics which are of interest, not only for academic philosophical exercise, but also for one's personal edification. That is of course all the more true for the researcher whose cultural memory has originated in an *other* source and *other* origin. That is why sympathetic participation in the course of the book will not go unnoticed.

---

1. *Dhī* is with the Vedic poet-sages more than a mere "modification of the thinking principle" (*citta-vṛtti-nirodhah* : *Patañjali's* definition in *Yoga-Sūtra* 1.2). *Dhī* contacts supersensuous realms (*RV.* 1.36.4), is multivalent and encompasses various kinds of perception. It is a definite exercise in mental activity and is in *RV.* 10. 67.1 described as having seven aspects to it, *sapta-śīrsñim* (seven headed). It originates in *ṛta*, the realm of truth where cosmic harmony resides : *imām dhiyaṃ saptaśirṣñim pūta na ṛta prajātāṃ bṛhatim avindat.*

My origin is embedded in the Greek vision of reality. That vision is an *other* of philosophy. By circumstance of history that Greek philosophy encountered—a living meeting, therefore—, the so-called historical revelation of the Hebrew god Jahweh and the later revelation of the Saviour, Jesus Christ. Athens and Jerusalem shaped my first European memory. The scientific-critical method since Descartes and Newton added a further memory at the close of the European Middle Ages. I must, therefore, know and feel where my principle of orientation becomes a principle of limitation when meeting another cultural memory. An excellent maxim for any philosopher. Had the Indian not told me, I would not have known of Mount *Kailāśa* or Mount Meru, a mount different from the Olympus and from Mount Calvary in Jerusalem. *Śiva's* eternal embrace of *Pārvatī*, the daughter of the mount, seems an antithetic image of *Śiva Sthānu*, the motionless. But *Pārvatī* is *Prakṛti*, the eternal female half of the one all-encompassing essence and, therefore, in itself still. The eternal embrace is the image of inherent cosmic satisfaction (*nivṛtti*) on the level of myth which would, unless activated (*pravṛtti*), not result in creation. (see Part III, no. 207.)

What strikes me in the Hindu's Perfection of Origin is that at no point there seems to be a "fatal flaw", an inherent existential doubt. The Origin provides security. One is *in Brahman*, *Brahman* is *in* everything created.[2]

Thus the Indian Origin has not given occasion to fall into the snare of antagonism between "scire" and "credere", belief as *against* knowledge. After the death of the Christian Saviour, when the Greek "logos" in a manner unique in itself, slowly severed heaven and earth on Europe's soil, Europe lost some of its "cosmological moment". If in every European language "myth" came to mean—until very recently—a fable, it is because the Greeks' "thinking thought" (res cogitans) left the myth more or less demystified. The encounter with the Semitic adamic myth where Adam is banished and condemned to earth, had already been a foreboding.

The Indian's transposition of his anthropological dualism is basically extremely simple even to the degree of embarrassment to the so-called thinker. *Advaita* is the general secure conviction in Indian belief. "As high as an inch in size", the *Puruṣa*, dwells here in the body. The lord of the past and the future : One, who knows him, does not feel alarmed at anything anymore. Truly, this is that (*KathU* 4.12). What else is more secure than to know that "this whole world is *Brahman*"—(*sarvam khalvidam brahmā*) (*CU* 3.14.1).

The believer is part of *Brahman*, morphologized in *Puruṣa*, the Cosmic Man. *Manuṣa*, small man "as big as a thumb", is the instance, the place where the difference between soul and body is "forgotten", "abolished". Where the difference does make itself felt, "remembered", it is again "forgotten" by speaking of and acting out the totality of the cosmos in myth and ritual. That is as such nothing special of India. All myth-narration and ritual attempt an *aimed-at* restoration of wholeness by a constant "forgetting" and "remembering". Wholeness, in the case of man having been created, is always lost to some extent. That loss I call the "fault" of creation. The Indian too, experiences that "fault". When *Prajāpati*, the Lord of Generation, was about to shed

2. *BU*. 2.3.6 calls *Brahman* the "Real of the real"—*atha namadheyam satyasya satyamiti*. It is the Real behind all appearances. The fact that *Brahman* is *"neti, neti"*— "not this, not this" —negates not everything, but everything that is not *Brahman*: *tasmādbrahmāvasāno'yam pratisedho nābhāvāsāna ityadhyavasyā-maḥ*. (*Brahmasūtra Śankara Bhāṣya*, 3.2.22).

his seed into *Uṣas*, the goddess Dawn and daughter of *Prajāpati*, the gods tried to prevent it. Once the seed did fall on earth, the gods said : "*ma-dūṣa*", "pollute not". Hence *manuṣa*, the human, is affected by some form of pollution.

It is the experience of "fault"—any time when the Uncreated breaks into created— that gave rise to the quest for harmony between *pravṛtti* and *nivṛtti*. It is here that I wish to present India's surprise-gift of its mythical consciousness of the sacred *Āpaḥ*, the Waters. In the history of religion India is known for its plunge into the Waters with a view to awareness of man's ambiguous circumstance in the world. When doubts beset him, when the temptation of over-asking becomes almost irresistable, man is advised to go into the Waters. They are man's ambience when new thought must be engendered with regard to *pravṛtti* and *nivṛtti*. The totality of the Waters suggest the beachline with the land, the world of man, and a choice may be made. The Waters offset the danger of settling all too comfortably on the land. They provide a true perspective and present a possibility of escape from ignorance (*avidyā*). They tell one who one is and who one is not. *Āpaḥ* in the Indian *Dhī* reveal the veil of existence which would surely be an illusion (*māyā*) if one were to take the veil as the ultimate.

No pure rational thought will reveal the Waters. It is not meant to reveal these. The Waters are being confessed to by the mind receptive of the sacred. Intellectualized formations of the receptive consciousness are inadequate with regard to the perception of the Waters. Intellectualized rational thought will simply overlook the Waters or not even think that they exist. Part III attempts to show the all-pervading *Āpaḥ*, the Waters, entering into the whole life of a man, a woman, a child, an animal, a plant, a stone, the seasons etc., participants as they all are in the throb of the Universe. To try and systematize the Waters is like asking whether *Brahman* is god or God. The answer to that question can be, like the question, only rhetorical. The Waters resist classification. Every authentic symbol brackets the "thing" which set it into motion. From the point of view of the Waters, intellectualization will destroy them and burn them up. The symbol *Āpaḥ* beams into all directions at once, like any true symbol. For the symbol does not say what the symbol-thing says. Once the symbol-thing is *spoken, thought*, therefore, the thing as a cosmic fragment recedes and its concrete limits get lost in innumerable meanings. Symbols, therefore, are formative and can be learnt. So can their derivatives. Anyone prepared to confess to the Waters will find no difficulty in relating the one instance, confessed to in Part III, to another or more of the instances of *Āpaḥ*. The interwovenness and relatedness of all 250 instances of *Āpaḥ* which I have presented are all aspects of finite and infinite existence as a total experience, like the Waters themselves. Here and now the Waters are all-encompassing. In that sense the term "pregnance" in the title of Part III is justified. If the Waters envelop both creation (*sṛṣṭi*), maintenance and support (*sthiti*) as well as decay and destruction (*pralaya*), only to give rise to new creation, it follows that man's doings are part of a continuum. *Karma*, therefore, is not a crippling fate, but rather the conscious acceptance of the Universe's totality which man is called upon to complete from his end as a pilgrim covers the whole length of the road— inevitably— in order to reach the goal, already there. That is why I have discussed *karma* as a "cosmic pilgrimage" in the last chapter of Part III.

In the conspectus and conclusion in Part IV I have tried to listen to the mind of the Waters as an exemplary model for living in the world. But no one could force the

Waters on someone else. The Waters reveal themselves or one looks for them. How can one interpret the Waters? Probably not at all. Avoiding the risk of destructive interpretation— and who is not aware of the dangers lurking in any hermeneutic? — I have taken recourse to an attempt at creative exploration and exposition of what the Waters *say*. The Waters think and, like any true symbol, have an opinion. That is why symbols make us too think.

That then would be a general outline of the book except that I have not yet explained Part I on myth in general. Myth is an expression by man's consciousness of "what there is more in the Universe than himself". Mythical consciousness attempts to gather the surplus of cosmic totality which there of itself is. From man's end it is indeed a surplus since he, as I observed earlier, *is not* that totality. The Universe expressed meaning long before man came to know about it. That meaning is gathered and expressed by man through mythical awareness. That awareness is closely related to the consciousness of the sacred which is not a title for only psychological structures. It rather is an *other* edge of man's awareness that life itself in the world has meaning, being, and truth, as *believed*. It is held dear, hence sacred. Basically all men, women and children are in myth for each one of us holds persons, and things, and ideas dear and sacred. The most common language of human kind—that of love-relationships—speaks language of the sacred, of surprise. We even keep it on a private level for its very sacrality. That attitude in us, humans, which is affective and receptive, the attitude of confession whether it be love or hate etc., is simultaneous and concomitant with the attitude of rational reasoning in the form of syllogism. But the latter must of necessity always turn back to the former, to myth therefore, to understand human culture. Because love for the ratio is already affection and confession.

Another reason why I begin our inquiry with a general discourse on myth is the thorny question of its analysis, its hermeneutic. Is it at all possible to understand someone else's myth? I have already referred to the *other* of philosophy in, for example, the case of India and Europe.

In the cross-cultural context there would appear to be no other way of understanding and appreciating someone else's myth than by what I have called the *incarnational dialectics of myth*. I must first live my own myth of the *possibility* of human communication without the trimmings and fetters of cultural misgivings, before I can even begin to understand something of someone else's myth. The first part of the book, therefore, takes us through—all the way—a confession of the consciousness of the sacred. That confession is necessary first of all for myself, a Westerner, if I wish to come anywhere near the Indian mind. It would be necessary for any one in whatever distance from any other culture when its mythical receptive awareness of the sacred is concerned. Apart from episodic efforts by individuals or by groups of individuals, Europe has thus far not yet come in soul-contact with the *other* of Indian thought. The same holds good the other way round.

Be it as it is, with regard to the contours and the contents of his cultural heritage, the Indian ought to *keep* confessing to his receptivity. For, as anyone would agree, it is not too difficult to overstress one or the other of *pravrtti* and *nivṛtti* and thereby (lose) the balance. It is still true to say, in the words of the *Katha Upaniṣad*, 4.14-15, that the synthesis underlying the whole of totality is perceived in The Pure Water of Understanding (*Yathodakam śuddham*):

"As water descending on mountain crags
wastes its energies among the gullies,
so he who views things as separate
wastes his energies in their pursuit.
But as pure water poured into pure,
becomes the selfsame—wholly pure,
so too becomes the self of the silent sage,
of the one, O Gautama, who has understanding".

Part I : Myth

If here is where I ought to produce, like a juggler, a working definition of myth I cannot do that. The whole book is the podium I try to build for myth to show us its true wonders. To train our mind and heart for the mythical, the reader should be warned that we shall try and extract from ourselves two confessions : the confession of receptivity and the confession of the sacred.

Shall we be astonished or even scandalized by the memory of our *whole* awareness? I mean, the inescapable moment of surprise. To put it differently: it takes an inveterate scepticist not to be moved by the majestic splendour of the Himalayas or by a child running away like a human torch from a scene of napalm-bombing. Those are extremes. There are more frequent and ordinary extremes in our daily lives when we feel as if we are being done a world of good, or harm. Surprise implies a surplus. When the moment of surprise in any relationship between men and women, children and their parents, erodes, the relationship is reduced to a mere minimum of tolerance, if at all the relationship must be rescued by convention. Surprise is an indelible part of human existence. Since human existence concerns philosophy, surprise inhabits the history of philosophy itself. Surprise breaks the sequence of continued argument by the springing up of bubbles unforeseeable. It is always in the midst of discontinued *expression* that the rationality of *impression* must be detected. That too is an excellent maxim for any philosopher. It is equal to the one I alluded to earlier: the principle of orientation becomes at one moment the principle of limitation. A no-man's-land of "pure objectivity" does not exist. We would at the most know and see everything but understand nothing.

The Vedic and later Indian attitude towards the Universe and the world is one of surprise. The absence of an attempt to *dominate* is conspicuous. One fails to discover an attitude of connivance, conspiracy against the Universe and the earth. In fact, *dīkṣā*, dedication, primarily means an attitude by which something is converted into a bit of "world" or rather into "human world". How could one live in collision with one's own "human world"? Vedic man calls his surrounding a Person, *Puruṣa*. Rudeness and vulgarity with regard to the Universe and the earth was unknown to Vedic man.

The Vedic quest for the significance of the world (*abidhā lakṣya*) has blessed posterity with a singularly sympathetic integration of utilitarian instinct and reflexive vision by its intellectual manner of looking at surrounding (*manomaya*). Vedic man with his attitude of *dīkṣā* "ordered", things "made" them (*prativihita*) of things already fashioned. The Vedic hymn of the Earth, *Bhūmi Śūkta*, reveals, besides a feeling of full participation, an attitude of distance taken as if by a pilgrim, an onlooker, a traveller not claiming the stream until he has found the source. Aware of an entire circuit of forces, the Vedic seer (*ṛṣi*) is a round-about-seer (*paridraṣṭr*). The theme of his participation in the Universe and the world is that of expectation and surprise. That theme constitutes the vision of Vedic man's "significant situation" in reality, his condition of consciousness of participation.

A figure, representing undetermined potentiality in that consciousness of participation, are *Āpaḥ* , the Waters. They are an immeasurable reservoir of significance of reality with their own history running its course beyond the time and space of man. The release of the waters by *Indra* is an emptying out of the hollows (*khāni*) conceived of as shut up from within. At the instance "of the beginning" the Waters roar forth as a limitless sea of universal potency. They give rise to the flow of words and inspirations of the Vedic visionary poet *as of* the Waters. Thus the Waters enter into space (*ākāśa*). *Ākāśa* however is not primarily physical space, it is an ideal and principled space without dimension.

Like Indra "opens the closed spaces" (*RV*. 4. 28. 1), so the Self awakens this rational cosmos from that space.[3] With an astonishing sense of non-exploitation the Vedic vision places the locus of that space "within you".[4] Thus inspiration and an integrated intelligence, able to grasp the *idea* of cosmic unity, became to the Vedic poet-seer, as F.B.J. Kuiper says : an opening of the door of the mind which was on a level with the opening of the doors of the primordial hill."[5] The author finds the same concept expressed in the *kha*, the aperture, the well, opened by *Agni* " to give free course to Inspiration from the *hṛdaya-samudra,* the primordial Waters in Man's heart.[6] The "space in the heart" is the locus where is deposited in secret all that is already ours or may be ours on any plane of experience. The intelligible plenitude inherent in what already is but not yet manifest, becomes so when the rock of the mind opens and the Waters flow.

What Vedic man read *on* the Universe and the world, *on* some element of it such as water, manifested itself *in* his psyche. Thus an authentic symbol created authentic words and hence an authentic surrounding. By careful shifts between their psyche and the earth on which they lived and the Universe they grasped, the Vedic poet-sages accomplished metaphysically, through the Waters, an actual construction of familiarity with the Universe without claiming an all too privileged position for man:

"Whatever I dig up of you, O Earth, may you of that
have quick replenishment!
O purifying One, may my thrust never reach
right into your vital points, your heart!
Heaven and Earth and the space in between
have set me in a wide expanse!
Fire, the Sun, the Water, the Gods,
have joined to give me inspiration."[7]

---

3. *MaiU*. 6. 17 : *ākāśāt eṣa khalu idam cetāmatram dobhyati.*
4. *MaiU*. 7. 11 : *tat svarūpam nabhasaḥ khe antarbhūtasya yat param tejaḥ*—what is the intrinsic aspect of expansion is the fiery energy in the vacant place of the inner man.
5. F.B.J. Kuiper, *Ancient Indian Cosmogony, Essays selected and introduced by John Irwin*, Vikas Publishing House, Ghaziabad, India, 1983, p. 182f.
6. Op. cit., p. 183.
7. *AV*. 12. 35. 53. tr. Raimundo Panikkar, *The Vedic Experience, Mantramañjari. An Anthology of the*

Their discovery of a design in the Universe relates Vedic-Indian society to it in a "significant situation" of being, meaning, and truth. Why? They encounter an eventful universum by the accent of mutual receptivity and proximity between the totality of the universe and themselves. Their statements are no mere statements. They are acclamations, acknowledgements of the movement and the forces of life.

What is the Vedic and later Indian vision for us, so-called "moderns"? Nothing possibly, if we have lost the sense of surprise of the cycle of days and nights, droughts and floods, the flight of our planet and the circle of seasons. If we think that "modern man"—especially Western "modern man" at present—with all his gadgets and machinations is more than Man, then indeed the Vedic-Indian vision may seem to us a worn-out dress only to be shed. But if we think that Man is more than our own particular nook in the vast space of the Universe's history, we might find in the Vedic-Indian non-aggressive attitude towards the Universe and the world some explanation of our roots. And if we claim to want to be "secular", then the "saeculum", the "*āyus*" the circle of seasons in the Universe, must be taken all the more seriously. The Universe and the world of man cannot be bought over by the offer of a unilateral pact.

"Whether, when I repose on you, O Earth,
I turn upon my right side or my left,
or whether, extended flat upon my back,
I meet your pressure from head to foot,
be gentle, Earth; You are the couch of all ![8]

The affective Vedic-Indian relationship towards the cosmos, resulting from a receptive acceptance of a surplus of cosmic totality more than the mind and the heart can encompass, betrays a general impulse in humanity towards reality. The *one* stream of the possibility of discovering cosmic plenitude in and through our consciousness—for the Universe meant something long before man began to know what it meant—is tempered by *another* stream in our awareness of not *being* that total cosmic plenitude. Hence we realize that cosmic wholeness is not merely given to us. It must be looked for, *aimed-at*. The search is justified by the argument of its own reasonability. For as "something-somebody" we reject the thought of being in "nothing". Traditions call that "chaos". Any human culture, whether on the personal level or on the level of the group, claims some time "before time" when somebody—whether it be god, God, or man, speaking animals or plants, or rivers—began giving names to things and putting order into them. In India that order is *Ṛta*, cosmic harmony and intelligibility.

The *aimed-at* restoration of cosmic perfection, the speaking of it and acting it out in imitation by man as the "perfection of the beginnings", what is that? Shall we call that the myth-narration and ritual? Broadly speaking then, myth-narration and ritual are of the widest possible distribution. It is important to take note of that because often, when myth is concerned, it is made into a sitting duck: easy to laugh at, scorn, a

Vedas for Modern Man and Contemporary Celebration, edited and translated with introductions and notes by Raimundo Panikkar. All India Books Pondicherry, India, 1983, pp. 126, 128.

8. *AV*. 12. 34. in : op. cit., p. 126.

good target. Myth is treated with suspicion. Yet, when men and women in love have suffered disagreement and try to restore "the beginnings", they are in the myth. The offer of an apology or a bouquet of flowers is the narration of it. All love is mirrored against some "perfection" of it beyond its concreteness in this love or that.

In an essay on myth the word itself must occur somewhere and preferably as soon as possible. Delaying its appearance too long could mean a betrayal to myth's immediate presence in any human awareness in any culture. It is there from the most archaic level of human history, back in time as far as we know it, to the present-day archaic level of awareness in us. Myth makes us contemporaries of people long ago. Psychology owes to that fact its first inspiration. I intend to show later that an ill-conceived conception of "modernity", often thinking light of myth, cannot explain away the presence of myth.

"Myth" is derived from the Greek "muthos". It is embarrassing but perhaps characteristic of "muthos" that we can claim till today no satisfactory etymology of the word. We know more about the Greek "muthos" by paying attention to what the Greeks themselves eventually came to consider its opposite, the "logos". Under the Greek "logos", the "muthos", involving a confession to gods and their doings, eventually emerged radically demystified. After centuries of erosion, "myth" finally was considered to be "an untrue story", a fable. Not only was myth emptied of its etiological content, the form of thought of "muthos" too was discredited. Its final erosion as a traceable fact took place at the close of the European Middle Ages. When Cartesian-Newtonian scientific critical thought gained the upperhand, myth was finally forgotten as capable of saying anything true. That implied that it also lost the contours of the sacred, the latter being confused with forms that religions take in human cultures. Such is the opinion with regard to myth on the level of ordinary experience of most Western people, the greater part of whom still cling to the Cartesian-Newtonian mentality that scientific-rational thought says "more truth" than does myth. In fact, Western formal education and that in other parts of the world where it was imported, is based on just that opinion. The non-linear movement of the Universe has been practically altogether forgotten. The often disastrous results with regard to unbridled industrialization and mechanization, the dislocation of ecological balance and the loss of a sense of meaning in life on the part of a considerable number of modern youths, appear to begin to cast doubts on the West's naive optimism. It would seem that present-day celebrated physicists are more aware of the Universe's personality than are the average minister of education, university professor, college teacher, business man, physician or pastor.

Mythical consciousness however is indelible. "Living as a human being" as one of the basic tenets of mythical thinking, continues to be expressed in terms of secularized myth in the West. Secularized myth is, everything notwithstanding, myth. Likewise, dialectical materialism strives after a "perfection".

Cultures take different forms. When the Greeks posed the persistent and normal question "ti tō ōn ?" — "what is being ?" —, the Indians did the same. When Aristotle posed his question concerning reality, *Gārgi* the daughter of *Vaçaknu* in the *Bṛhadāraṇyaka Upaṇisad* did the same, asking the great master *Yājñavalkya*: "But then, what is it in which the worlds of *Brahman* are interwoven lengthwise and crosswise?" And he said : "O *Gārgi*, do not question further (*mā ati prākṣīh*) so that your head should not burst". Indians followed *Yājñavalkya's* advice and stayed with and in *Brahman* whereas the Greeks and later Europe continued the question. As I said, Europe lost some of its "cosmological moment". In exchange a flowering of individuality arose in Europe which certainly has been amazing and which has not gone without its benefits. It remains to be seen, however, whether a secularized culture is able to produce a civilization. Within a span of fifty years Europe burnt out twice.

Mythical consciousness is closely related to the consciousness of the sacred. The sacred is not of necessity linked with organized religion. Religion is too limited a concept to accommodate the manifestations of the sacred. These are inexhaustible and transcend dogmatic definition and systematized belief in God, god or ghosts. The idea of the sacred, linked with the confession by receptive awareness, creates an attitude of "muthos" which unfolds a "significant situation" of man in the Universe.

Analysis of myth in a given culture happens whenever the question "Why?" is being asked, which is, therefore, always. The content of one myth-narration may be examined as to its rendering of the Perfection of Origin and new elements may be added. Nothing is of course added to the Perfection but to the exploratory value of the narration. Myth's inherent illumination is untouchable, it passes in the coming. The logos of the myth-narration is re-examined and then re-mythicized by reading the myth anew. That creates advance in speculation. Such processes within a given culture I have called morphological and diachronical modernity. A culture lives by and through those modernities. They make a culture viable. A third modernity is the diatopical one. It is the analysis of one particular culture's myth done from the distance of an *other* philosophy. Diatopical modernity is a cross-cultural adventure. I have already indicated how harassing that analysis can be. Uptil now most diatopical adventures of analysis of myth have been done by the distant European mind with regard to another culture under observation. A surreptitious Western superiority-complex is still discernible in many an analysis of other cultures' myths. Many mythical cultures exist contemporaneous with Western culture and it will probably depend on scholars belonging to the former to correct mistakes made by the latter.

Analysis of the Indian myth then should be done through an effort to extend, to deepen, my own cultural memory by opening up to that of India. I must stand with "logos" under the illumination of the Indian Word, the Womb: *Vāc*. Its fourth quarter, says the Vedic seer, is *Vaikhāri*, human speech. It is truly a quarter, for the other three are hidden above it in secrecy. Man's quarter, *vaikhāri*, however, has on its inside, the inside of human language, the "footprint", *pada*, of the three quarters above. Thus I am given the opportunity to learn to be receptive of surprise. Am I not perhaps more *being spoken by the Universe* than speaking? I discover that I must stand in the elements, in water, fire, ether, air and wind, for of those I am built up.

What is all that for philosophy? The relationship between myth and philosophy becomes strained when we try and present to philosophy the most "philosophic-looking" expressions of myth. That would be a betrayal to both myth and philosophy. For myth need not be rescued. We must present to philosophy myth's *least philosophic-looking language*. That language is symbolic language. Philosophy will then be asked how it is to take up that language in its discourse because philosophy is concerned with all utterance about reality. Philosophy cannot be flippant about myth's utterance for it deals with what for myth is reality.

Must we distinguish between myth and symbol? I shall always understand by symbol the most primary meaning of it. Man first reads the sacred *on* the Universe, *on* the world, *on* some element of it. In the speaking of it, in the acting it out, the concrete fragment loses its limits and gets charged with innumerable meanings, gathering the greatest possible amount of human experience as part and parcel of the cosmos. Myths then are a species of symbols, condensed in narrative and ritual. Myths, therefore, are no allegories. The relationship between myth and psychology is intense but it is one of a mutually agreed understanding.

If myth is a problem for the scientist and the philosopher of "pure reason" insofar as it expresses an original direction of the human spirit, an independent configuration of man's consciousness with regard to his understanding of himself in the Universe, then the problem is not for myth but for what is *not* myth. Myth would seem to burst the bond of philosophy as a phenomenology of the spirit. Anyone aiming at a comprehensive system of human culture has, of necessity, turned to myth.

By living in myths man experiences the solace of being able to move in at least one possible *whole* world without being beleaguered by threats of rules and regulations at political, racial, national, religious or economic frontiers.

Part II : The Quest for Harmony, *Pravṛtti* and *Nivṛtti*

In preparing for an experience of the Indian *Āpaḥ*, the Waters, I now attempt to put up a fitting décor. We shall see how the Indian world-view tries to come to terms with man's condition between finitude and non-finitude. Both withdrawal from and involvement in the whole vortex of wordly life are *believed* to be true facts of human life, but they are *valued* differently. Many Indian texts would argue that, if two ideas clash, both may be true.

Śaṅkarāchārya's commentary to the *Bhagavad Gītā* begins with the account of a two-fold *dharma* by the Lord Creator who wished to establish order. "This two-fold religion, leading directly to liberation and prosperity, has long been practised by all castes and religious orders (*varṇa-āśrama*)". Only the most recent demands of present-day modern industrialization and technology seem to slowly undermine the ancient Indian system of *āśrama*, the four stages of life literally enacting *pravṛtti* and *nivṛtti* values. The polemics between the two sets of values have been sedulously commented upon in the epics and in the *Purāṇas* where *Brahmā*, *Viṣṇu* and *Śiva* portray man's efforts to come to terms with those apparent opposite forces. Significant in the two-fold value-system underlying Indian myth, is the relationship of each god with asceticism somehow or another. However, by an inversion of the ascetics-theme by means of a pictorial of its exaggeration often leading to disaster, the myths point to the need for balance. Especially *Śiva* time and again appears on the scene of paradox. He is a master in portraying truth in disguise. Not only the gods, the elements too appear swayed between participation and renunciation. Among the elements *Āpaḥ*, the Waters, are much in the foreground. Thus, for example, the *Liṅga Purāṇa* gives an account of *Śiva's* seed placed in *Viṣṇu's* womb from where all the ascetics appeared. In a myth denying that, *Brahmā* who is often *Viṣṇu*, lifts the veil off

Sati's face during her marriage with *Śiva*. *Brahmā*, unable to control himself, spilt his seed in lust and was consequently exiled by *Śiva*. The seed became the thunderous rainclouds. They suggest the rainwater which must of necessity flow if procreation is to continue. Hence, seedless asceticism when overdone becomes sterile rather than creative. *Pravṛtti* and *nivṛtti* are sometimes being played out against each other in a note of absurdity, both losing thereby their sharp edges. Throughout, both sets of values claim their defenders and decry their opponents. *Yudhiṣṭhira* in the *Mahābhārata* proclaims the excellence of renunciation whereas *Bhimasena* ridicules it.

The antithetical element in a mythical cycle dealing with a particular theme, rests on the characteristic of myth able to go back not to a similarity of efficacy but to an original identity of essence. In terms of cosmic totality both *pravṛtti* and *nivṛtti* are of equal value. In fact, the one cannot dispense with the other without losing the totality. Myth knows no functional space, as mathematics does. Its space is structural. In the spacial aspect of myth, *pravṛtti* belongs as much to *Puruṣa*, Cosmic Man, as does *nivṛtti*. Symbiosis is obtained when structure supersedes function. That idea is contained in the Indian concept of *lokasaṁgraha*, in which the cosmos, gods, and men are related. The desired result is *svadharma* which is reflected in a genuine interest in serving a prospering earth.

Myth, therefore, creates its own unique civilizing sense of order. It answers the question "either—or" by reducing all fundamental form of thought into structures as of *bodies*. Mythical time corresponds to the idea of body in that it is not an immediate intuition but a growth, a "becoming" as a life in time such as the rhythms of the cosmos unfolding a cycle of birth, sustenance, death and re-birth. Thus time becomes for myth a cosmic potency. For myth there is no moment of time wholly fulfilled in itself. Even a lifetime of asceticism, therefore, or an active involvement in matters of the world, has no necessary value of truth when considered by itself. Any form of spirituality, whether it be ascetic or socalled non-ascetic, must by virtue of its symbolic meaning include integrated appreciation of both life-styles. Such an appreciation would be devotion, *bhakti*, to which I shall presently return. As such the *varṇa-āśramadharma*, four bodily stages representing in one life both values, scores perfect mythical success. Whether that success will become true in one's individual life will depend on the degree of one's devotion and dedication. That, as such, is not a matter to be decided by myth but more a matter of spirituality. The *āśrama* system rose to the idea of a temporal order as a universal order of destiny and purpose.

It must be remembered that mythical consciousness distinguishes itself from rational thought which—true to its aim and function—dissolves reality into relations and then attempts to grasp that same reality through and by means of the discovered relations. Mythical consciousness proves its value in matters of the spirit.

From the outset the celebrated *āśrama*-system encountered a serious problem with regard to the important metaphysical position in a man's life of the individuating principle, *ahaṁkāra*, the "I". The total renouncer, making a move symbolic of the unblemished state of pre-creation—often accentuated by a literal withdrawal into the jungles or any other form of seclusion—, turns away from the symbiotic relationships governing day-to-day society. The renouncer's true essence, however, the *ātman*, he shares with all others. Renouncing society and its incumbent obligations might rather hurt than heal. On the other hand, *pravṛttidharma* runs the risk of ego-inflation, equally disfiguring the universal *ātman* residing in the performer as well as in his *ātman*-fellow-citizens. As time went by, *Upaniṣads* realized the increasing need for a solution. It was sought in the interiorization of both *pravṛtti* and *nivṛtti* values rather than in the status quo of orthopraxis. Some myths would seem to reveal historical power-struggles with a philosophical-theological edge when Brahmins attempted to keep their control over society. Part of the problem, was the fact that low-castes and non-castes were advised to strive after the loftiest but were forbidden to practise *nivṛtti* for reasons of economy. A certain contempt with regard to *nivṛtti*—possibly artificially induced—is noticeable in the Indian Middle Ages. Brahmins were keeping a close watch over possible outbreaks of overenthusiastic withdrawal. Mythical instances too seem to point in that direction. Yogis and other deviants were often loaded with scorn. A law regulating the exercise of asceticism was promulgated by *Kauṭilya* and the status of householder, *girhasthyāśrama*, extolled. Myths were re-infused with a bias towards "normalcy".

Indian metaphysics attempts to secure a sound hankering after *Brahman* beyond the absolutes of *Sat-Cit-Ānanda*, formulated by our consciousness. Being part of the *Svarūpa* of the Self, man is already free, the oddity being that he might not be conscious of it. It is therefore in the unconditioned turn towards the *Svarūpa* that illusory action is avoided. "See the Self—*ātma va are draśtavyāh*"— is the keynote of all Indian philosophical schools. *Nivṛtti* is man's metaphysical quality but its execution in daily life is a matter of spiritual and moral balance which cannot validly disregard surrounding as if it were no part of the totality of life.

Efforts at a satisfactory reconciliation between the two value-systems are in the myths portrayed by the cycle of action and non-action. Such myths introduce their psychological perspicuity by their agility in neutralizing opposites. That is often done by giving many versions of the same situation without necessarily saying anything new. The pungency of the polemic is thus played down. Tension is released. Myth succeeds in toning down extreme positions by only *imagining* them with a view to show that the positions taken are untenable. The catharctic function of myth—providing a sense of impunity in the midst of ambiguity—is one of myth's abilities to reconcile conflicting moral injunctions. It is the humour of myth.

The most gratifying reconciliation between *pravṛtti* and *nivṛtti* is *bhakti*. It is a compelling love for (the) God transcending rational barriers. I have called *bhakti* an "irrational" solution which is different from saying that it is unreasonable. *Bhakti* is a late solution in the sense that man is inclined first to reason his existence and its meaning. Then, finding himself at a loose end, he makes explicit a tendency which was already there. He appeals to emotion to transcend the polemic. *Bhakti* is almost an excuse. It has in India created admirable religious stimulants giving rise to high spiritual rhapsody.

The Indian search for balance between *pravṛtti* and *nivṛtti* corroborates the claim by mythical thought to *aim at* restoration of universal totality. What I referred to earlier must now be said with emphasis and a little more elaborately. For here *Āpaḥ*, the Waters, are appearing on the scene where loss of totality and its restoration are acted out in a manner which only the excellence of a primary symbol is capable of. What *Āpaḥ*, the Waters, say, could not possibly be said by me. What they say I have tried to put together as best as I could in Part III. What the Indian *Āpaḥ,* the Waters, reveal is the mysterious truth that the *aimed-at restoration of totality, although aimed-at, is possible*. The Waters do heal.

I am here referring to what I have already called the necessary "flaw" there is in the break from the Uncreated into the created. I have failed to observe in the Vedic-Indian mythical accounts of *the beginnings* a "flaw" or "fault" which would have the connotation of being fatal. The myths do not suggest a banishment by a fatal indisposition towards *The Origin* which then consequently would have shed or shaken off the human being. The myths do not show a fatal disobedience, a ruinous revolt. The transpositon of his anthropological dualism has saved the Indian from an indissoluble complicity, a plot, against *The Origin*. That again leads to my contention that there is no ethical terror observable in the Vedic-Indian myths of *the beginnings*. One is not faced with anonymous wrath, a faceless violence of retribution. Living without eternal vengeance hovering over him, the Indian human world is not written in letters of existential absurdity. *Saṁsāra* would, therefore, not be what it is all too easily said to be by non-Indian analysts of Indian myth: suffering. The evil of suffering is synthetically linked with the evil of plotted creational fault. I would oppose the translation of *saṁsāra* by the mere word "suffering" by an interpretation of it as the painfully felt necessity of creational flux by man and the delay of its removal in ultimate reunion in the Self while man lives on earth. A reign of terror follows from existential defilement which would be best fought by hoping for nothing in order to fear nothing. Psychology teaches us that ethical terror is close to obsessional neurosis. I do not think one can discover much of that in ordinary Indian religious life, whether it be in the home, in the temple or anywhere. Why I ask then to be introduced to the Indian *Perfection of Origin* is my curiosity how the absence of terror has come about. Myths in other philosophies show a parting between gods and men. The plot by Prometheus in Greece, for example, at the primordial sacrifice at Mekone, initiated such a parting. Prometheus offered to Zeus the bones instead of the flesh of the sacrificed bull. The Greeks eventually escaped the terror of Moira, Fate, the wrathful god, by declaring Mount Olympus their own mount of human excellence, thus turning the sacred towards a striving after human optimal performance and in that sense being like god. Likewise, the Hebrew god Jahweh inspired fear and terror and the adamic myth is a fatal one. Although in the biblical creation-account a promise of salvation is given, it needed a New Testament through the revelation of the god-man Jesus where ethics could be entered through the door of love instead of fear.

Returning to the Indian *Perfection of the Beginning*, the myths of origin do not shy away from stammering but can equally tell marvels without a blush. India's primal creation strikes one as of quiet dawns of movement. Even Indra' struggle with *Vṛtra* took place in view of quietude.

The Indian primal creation offers to human quest a singularly beautiful mythical-speculative concept. That concept is *tapas*. *Tapas*, warmth, heat, concentration, austerity, plays an important part in the creation-myths. With the thrust from the Uncreated into creation, a result of *Prajāpati's tapas*, *tapas* flowed into human existence. Man is in need of *tapas*, intelligent concentration, when handling his human situation and organizing it according to what *dharma* and *ṛta* suggest with regard to life. For, ultimately, the nature of the phenomenal world, *saṁkleśa*, is identical with that of the Absolute, *vyavadāna*. *Tapas* in man is a form of intelligent assault on chaos which man rejects as meaningless.

Part III: The symbolic pregnance of *Āpaḥ*, the Waters

Archaic man, be it in temporal time or in the archaic depth of his psyche, is already a man of division. Hence the myth can only be an intentional restoration or reinstatement and in this sense already symbolical. To gather scattered fragmentation into some wholeness, man needs, as I observed earlier when referring to the *Kathaka Upaniṣad*, "The Pure Waters of Understanding", *yathodakam śuddham*. To see things as separate is to waste one's energies. The experience of *Āpaḥ* is a sacred experience, not a philosophical one. The Waters of course have no intention of antagonizing the philosopher but only respectfully insist that creation out of them, maintenance by them, immersion into and emergence from them require a particular *dīkṣā*, initiation, which is not that of rational-critical argumentation. We may be tempted to apply a hermeneutic and try to "explain" the Waters. That is impossible. The Waters rather explain us. The experience of the Waters ratifies and confirms man's understanding of himself as struggling at this end of all intentionality, *idam*, as distinct from *tat* at the other end, the surplus of cosmic totality beyond man. The Waters explain to man that his experience of a tension between *pravṛtti* and *nivṛtti* is a *normal* experience from the point of view of his human condition. Man is a *double entity, but one reality* of eternal *jñāna* and fleeting *māyā*. The Greek "exiled" and "straying" soul would be hard to find in the Indian myth. If an analogue must be found in as far as the concept of alienation is concerned, it would have to be in the realms of *māyā* and *avidyā*. But they involve, in the Indian myth, the whole of the human being. In the dialectic between the uncreated and the created, Indian thought is free to search for the union of both. The union can be achieved, be it conditioned, in the experienced created human condition by the attainment of consciousness of *Brahman*.

If, in the Indian world-view, "*Brahman* is this whole world"—"*sarvam khalvidam brahmā*"—, human existence comes to express an already moral purification—katharsis— by the understanding acceptance of the *reasonability* of body and soul—finitude and its "other"— for the simple fact that man *is* body and soul. Man cannot be guilty of what he constitutionally is nor can he be made to suffer moral blemish or stigma on account of it. In as far as myth can be said to be the self-representation of man, the Indian mythical view of man does not consider him as just "soul" nor does it reduce him to the dead weight of just "body". The *possibility* of an understood lived balance between *pravṛtti* and *nivṛtti* is successfully shown by the primary symbol of *Āpaḥ*, the Waters, perceived by the receptive consciousness of the sacred. Consciousness of *Āpaḥ* and its symbolism in the Vedic-Indian mind is the other complementary side of its rational intellectual admission that the fundamental law of the Universe cannot be arrived at through only the rational mind. In saying this I have stated my working hypothesis.

For the self-representation of Vedic-Indian man as portrayed in the myth we will turn to myth's *exploratory* power. That power will be turned in the direction that follows it. That is possible because I have treated the myth as a rehandling of the fundamental symbols elaborated in man's living experience in this world and the Universe. The myth *anticipates speculation* because it is already *word*, an interpretation, a hermeneutic of the primary symbols in which the prior consciousness of loss of and yearning for totality gave itself form. With regard to philosophical speculation, therefore, we must now recall our earlier professed maxim: at one point our principle of orientation becomes a principle of limitation. We ought now to suspend our theorizing. In other words: uptil now we have thought about myth, now myth will think about and for us.

Is there then nothing for philosophy in *Āpaḥ*, the Waters? The approach to absolute truth by *receptively wishing* to be created, maintained, enveloped and again created by *Āpaḥ* through the mythical awareness, is *corroborated* by the metaphysical endeavour of Indian philosophy. The Sankarite School does not reduce change and flux of life to a pure illusion of the senses. It admits constant change as a particular type, order or level of reality: a pragmatic type of reality, *vyavahāric sattvā*, but real from the point of view of primal ignorance, *māyā* or *avidyā*. Creation cannot be said to fool man. It is man's home, a place of culture and civilization in the making.

"Being", in Indian philosophic thought, is on the one hand indeterminable, *nirguṇa*, and on the other the creative source of all determination, *saguṇa* : Being is all-encompassing and total. It is in the experience of the happenings of *Āpaḥ*, the Waters, that man intends to gain a foothold in that totality of Being. The indeterminable silence and the creative eloquence are two equally real dimensions of ultimate reality. Man is the most unique word of the creative eloquence of Being and it is both in philosophy and in myth that man attempts his ultimate reply. Because this work deals with that reply on the part of myth, I may be justifiedly allowed to show not a bias towards myth at the cost of rational argumentation, but a stress on myth as the rational argumentation's fellow thinker. That, in our case, will be done under the primary symbol of *Āpaḥ* as perceived by the Indian mythical awareness.

> "O Waters, source of happiness,
> pray give us vigor so that we
> may contemplate the great delight.
> You like loving mothers are
> who long to give to children dear.
> Give us of your propitious sap.
> You Waters who rule over precious things
> and have supreme control of men,
> we beg you, give us healing balm
> Now I have come to seek the Waters.
> Now we merge, mingling with the sap.
> Come to me, Agni, rich in milk !
> Come and endow me with your splendor ![9]

Unable to think outside space and time, man finds he is *given* an expanse where limits seem to disappear. That expanse is the symbol. For our setting in which to locate the symbol of water, the Indian concept of *ākāśa*, space, offers an excellent suggestion as it is derived from the root "*kās*", to shine. It implies an active movement, vibration or

---

9. *RV.* 10.9.1.2.5.9. tr. Raimundo Panikkar, *The Vedic Experience*, pp. 119-120.

radiation. Even in its negative definition, the idea of movement is instinctively associated with the concept of space as the "non-existence of obstruction or hindrance". That is the expanse in which the Waters move and which they *are*. The typical Indian attitude to affirm by negation provides the Waters their multivalence.

Better than any other element, water conveys of itself the idea of non-existence of obstruction and it responds to the needs in the depths of man's psyche to be allowed to think and feel in freedom. Its work is to precede creation and take it again to itself. It can never get beyond its own mode of existence. It can never express itself in *forms* because it is always in the condition of *potential*, of seeds and hidden powers. Everything that has form is manifested beneath or in the waters as separated from it. On the other hand, as soon as "form" has separated itself from water its potentiality is lost. It will fall under the law of time and life; it will become limited, enter history, share in the universal law of change and decays. It would finally altogether cease to exist were it not again to go through a flood and be re-created. What the Waters reveal on their course is a logic of direction different from the inorganic logic of material, three-dimensional extension. What results is dynamic instead of statics. A statically conceived Universe has no reality *behind* it. It is, in Indian thought, an illusion. The world must be grasped as it "moves about".

Because the world is grasped as "moving about", it touches the mythical-religious spirit in its deepest root which is embedded, not in the world of ideas, but in the realm of feeling and will. In accounts of the primordial beginnings there is no distinction between language and being, between word and meaning. By the power of the word the majesty of *Prajāpati* said : "*Bhūḥ*", "earth!!", and the earth was". The creative will and feeling flowed with creation into man's actual existence, into his human condition. It became a constitutive part of it. Such is the setting for a chapter on *karma* as the cosmic pilgrimage. *Karma* is not a fate, a deadening pre-destination but that "what is to be done" as the necessary and valid human existential reply to the Creator's will and intention.[10] "I am the doer" and "I am the non-doer" are equally an illusion if the agent does not put himself in a true perspective with regard to his being part and parcel of the cycles of the Universe and with regard to the claim he makes concerning the fruits of what he does or does not. That perspective has been mythically painted in what happened to *Maṅkaṇaka,* roaming the world in search of truth. Once, when hurting his finger in the forests, he was amazed to see plant-juice instead of blood dripping from the wound. Celebrating his realized cosmic identity, he exulted in a dance. For his evolution into involution was not a statement of formation—which is the way a Western contemporary of *Maṅkaṇaka* would have conceived of the change—, but an *explanation* of his being. The universal Energy of which he was part had now broken through. Until *Śiva* appeared on the scene. Striking his thumb, ashes pale as snow flowed from the wound. Ashes are the utterly purified result of the burning of all *kāma*, lust and desire. It is ashes suspended in water that makes one a free roamer of the Universe, and ready to do what is to be done.

Water *and* ashes are the condition for *karma* and true kārmic action. That is a far cry from the general Western misinterpretation of *karma* as re-incarnation and

---

10. "What is to be done" or "having done what was to be done" : *krtakṛtya, kata karaniya, katakicca.*

survival of the identical individuality. The promise of "my" survival and physical re-appearance is the great lure! *Karma*, however, is not "my" survival, but the restoration of the Universal Totality asked from me. In India too, many misunderstand the theory of *karma*. Those given the boon of a bearable existence prefer to keep it for themselves, attributing their luck to the workings of *karma*. The next-door neighbour, battling with poverty, equally appeals to *karma* as the hope for a "better" incarnation. True *karma* is based on the *pañçamahā-yajña* the, five debts to be paid, covering all the essentials of an authentic participation in the Universe's existence. None of those essentials allows for the idea as if my ego were the owner of my life.

Man's mythical awareness attributes to the Creator's utterance of names the simultaneous appearance of the worlds. Between "let the earth be" and "the earth was" there is no temporal succession of events. The point is that, if *karma* is the cause and dynamic of this world as a possible replica of "that world", man is responsible for covering any unjustified "distance" of events in this world so that it might resemble "that world" as best as possible. Hence man's karmic cosmic pilgrimage is the attempt to cover the distance between him and (the) God, between justice and injustice, peace and violence, poverty and wealth and between oneself and the neighbour

Part IV: Conspectus: The exemplary history of *Āpaḥ*, the Waters

We shall meet an initial difficulty. How can the immediacy of the symbol and the mediation of thought be held together? This will be possible if we succeed in finding an interpretation that respects the symbol's original enigma. Neither the symbol nor the myth can be moralized. They can be said to give rise to thought because they are *already* thought.

One thing we may have acquired, at the end of our exercise, is a conviction that the myths of origin reveal the ethical dimension of the myth of tension in man's awareness of his dual status as guest and as inhabitant of the world. For indeed we have discovered a new myth—or better to say, uncovered an old truth—the myth of tension. Man's dual status as guest and as inhabitant in the world and the Universe is his only valid existential tension and it is the sole truth about man.

At the end then of our double approach through the abstract description of that tension and its re-enactment in the experience of *Āpaḥ*, the Waters, as origin, maintenance, destruction and again origin, the question arises: How shall we continue?

All through our inquiry the *whole* of man has been our postulate. To screen off one constituent of human experience and its expression *as human* leads to pseudo-philosophy, an offence against the rational-critical instinct. For the mythical awareness to screen off one ingredient of man is impossible. To avoid both pseudo-philosopy and an unbearable burden on myth, we must remind ourselves of our promise to shape mind and heart together in rationally untranslated receptivity and thus find ourselves in a state which may be equalled to the silence of expectation. In that way we condition ourselves to the *irruption* of existence into consciousness rather than looking back on it through a compartmentalized introduction by rational-critical thought. The pattern of our thought will now receive a particular colour: not that of the observer's model of control and prediction over the world—dangerously proximate to domination—, but that of a *mood* rather. The evil we experience will then be a painful drama and the good a celebration.

And here we may find an answer to our question: How do we continue? We continue by volitional action with regard to the original enigma of the primary symbol such as that of *Āpaḥ*, the Waters, by *promoting* its meaning in our psyche, thereby evoking commitment. Our volitional action will not concern the stress on the opposition between *pravṛtti* and *nivṛtti* but their mutual complementarity. In other words: we continue, not as obsessed by the inherent tension in our dual status of guest and inhabitant, but as humans set free.

The Vedic-Indian mind discovered the Waters held up from within in *Vṛtram*, the monstrous mountain, and their release by *Indra*. What the Vedic-Indian mind read *on* the Universe in the symbol—"thing" water, it realized as manifested *in* the human psyche. Any unwarranted tension engendered by man's possible misunderstanding of *pravrtti* and *nivrtti* is to be released by the apprehension of them as mutually complementary.

Complementarity induces surprise. It unites where initially unity seemed impossible. Surprise, therefore, includes involvement. It thrusts towards both celebration and drama. Thus we may experience celebration about the splendour of the forests while their ruthless felling by greed, the world-poison rising from the ocean of man's mind, may bring tears to our eyes.

The Indian mythical world view of universal plenitude, made up of manifested fragmentation, cannot be caught in the net of appropriative logic or utilitarian greed, *bhogin*, with regard to the treasures of gathered meaningfulness of the Universe. That would be incongruity, *viruddhatva*, the reverse of concordance and sense of surprise, *sādhāraṇya*.

Notes

Throughout the work I have cited an abundance of mythical material. Even so, selection has been necessary. My choice may be said to be arbitrary in the sense that each myth might be replaced by similar or corresponding examples. Arbitrary selection is not without its risks. Not only do myths and their themes select themselves but they also develop in the course of time. A seemingly similar myth may stress a different point or lean towards an other cycle of myths. I have applied only those themes which seemed relevant to the particular topic under discussion. This may seem to be begging the question: to choose one theme and then to say that it is important. I have tried to justify this by the selection of the sources. I selected the one particular mythical theme for the fact that it *is* important.

The work of arranging and developing the material in Part III — The symbolic pregnance of *Āpaḥ*, the Waters — is based on the views and the history of the Indian people in Part II. The second part takes a closer look at what makes a Hindu a Hindu. The presentation is fairly extensive. I felt I was preparing the ground for the central theme of the waters in living Indian experience and I could hardly avoid an elaborately documented essay. To me it seemed necessary. Perhaps I should have shifted the chapter on *karma*, now in Part III, to the second part. *Karma* is a central and much debated concept in Indian thought. However, from the point of view I assume when discussing *Karma — Karma*, a cosmic pilgrimage — I decided it fitted better in Part III after our cosmic journey guided by the primary symbol of *Āpaḥ*, the Waters.

The reader who is less interested in the complex and possibly even tedious matter in Parts I and II may prefer to begin with Part III. The Waters, encompassing so many aspects and sentiments of our human life, provide, I hope, an interesting picture. I do, however, not wish to imply that the earlier parts of the book are addressed to a restricted circle.

I have rendered the relevant texts, especially in Part III, in full. We are after all listening to what the myths have to say. The concatenation of 250 serially numbered instances of the Waters, or concepts and happenings related to that symbol, I consider to be a minimum for my inquiry to be acceptable as a substantial contribution to the study of the experienced reality of the Waters. The Waters pour into all directions, times and spaces in the cosmos and into all of man's experiences in his human condition. A mere one hundred Water-events, for example, would not have satisfactorily covered at least the most central of all these areas. One's curiosity, moreover, for more of the Waters might not have been aroused.

The question has arisen if the phenomenology of the Waters as I have presented it, should either be reshaped into one running essay or else be divided into three chapters under the headings Creation-*Sṛṣṭi*, Support-*Sthiti* and Destruction-*Pralaya*. For these are three clearly distinct potentialities of *Āpaḥ*. A running essay might also have enhanced the style of the presentation and made more pleasant reading. After seriously considering these valuable suggestions, I chose the original arrangement. *Sṛṣṭi*, *sthiti* and *pralaya* are forces simultaneously and contemporaneously at work. They bear one another in the mythical awareness a special relationship of interaction. A neat trilogy would hardly do justice to that interaction.

The concatenation of the events of the living Waters should not be looked upon as a chain-symbolization in the sense that a chain's link is of necessity tied to its next and where the strongest point of the chain lies in its weakest link. That logic would irritate the mythical symbol. The chain-symbolization here presented is one of interchangeable links. Symbols resist being pinned down to one or two of their many functions and fields of operation. An example may be clarifying. No. 138 carries the myth of *Rudra's* attempt at preventing the incestuous approach by the creator-god *Prajāpati* to his daughter *Uṣas*, Dawn. The god's seed was spilt nonetheless and creation resulted. This "fault" in creation is later taken up in the myth of *Śiva* and *Pārvatī* when her touch makes *Śiva's* seed fall on *Shambu's* forehead. The "drop of copious water" referred to in the myth becomes "the liquid of passion". *Śiva* opposes incestuous relationship, that is, overattachment to creation, by injuring his son. His son *Andhaka* is born blind. The following number 139 considers that liquid of passion which now in its turn and in this particular instance refers to excess-energy of over-emphasized *pravṛtti*, involvement in the things of creation. *Śiva's* feelings of passion as a symbol of uncontrolled *pravṛtti* must now be tempered by immersion into the Waters. No. 140 features *Pārvatī* longing for ordered desire both sexual and otherwise. The sequence is logical. Although nothing is mentioned about the Waters, the theme can be retraced to *Śiva's* immersion in the preceding instance. As a contrast to *Pārvatī's* valid and orderd desire and her sound view of things, we meet in No. 141 *Brahma's* vicious and intentional infusion of lust into *Pārvatī*, showing the destructive side of createndness and through it the problem of a balanced involvement in things of earth. No. 141 might just as well and with equal validity have followed No. 139, depending on the theme and the myth one wishes to introduce first. The concatenation shows the multivalence of the primary symbol of the Waters and that of its secondary and derived symbols.

At the back of the book the reader will find an index interlinking the names and themes occurring in the water-myths in Part III. It will of course be understood that the 250 moments of the Waters I have presented by no means exhaust their presence.

Banaras, on the feast of Makar Saṅkrānti,
The Sun's return.
January 14th, 1990

PART I

MYTH

Chapter 1

BREAKING THE BOUNDARIES

A Phenomenology of "Chaos"

We are guests on earth. At the same time we are her inhabitants. This experience creates a tension between ourselves and the earth. The tension is conspicuously present, for without it would there have been any poetry, art, philosophy or religious quest?

Vedic man's relationship with his surrounding shows no attempt to dominate it. His familiarity with the earth and the universe is attractive for its friendly and harmonious cooperation with them. The earth and the universe were as close to him as his skin. One is moved by the absence of any conspiracy against the earth and the universe in the mind of Vedic man. There is no evidence of exploitative or fraudulent transactions. Vedic man made no unilateral decisions with regard to his surrounding. Living in a singularly endearing fellowship with the earth and the universe, he created a world. How could one live in collision with one's world?

Vedic man calls his surrounding a Person, *Puruṣa*. Rudeness and vulgarity towards the earth and the universe were unknown to him. His was an attitude of communion and consecration (*Dīkṣā*). One is struck by the constant sparks of surprise and wonder about things.

Not that Vedic man shied away from a utilitarian outlook *(vyāpāra-mātra)*. The vegetative mode of life *(annamāya)* called for expediency and practical sense.

"The Earth on whom are ocean, river, and all waters,
on whom have sprung up food and ploughman's crops,
on whom moves all that breathes and stirs abroad,
Earth, may she grant to us the long first draught!
Earth, may she grant us cattle and food in plenty."[1]

The Vedic quest for the significance of the world (*abidhā lakṣya*) has blessed posterity with a singularly sympathetic integration of utilitarian instinct and reflexive vision by its intellectual manner of looking at surrounding (*manomaya*).

The hymn to the Earth *(Bhūmi Sūkta)* in the *Vedas* reveals, besides a feeling of full participation, an attitude of distance. Distance taken by a pilgrim, an onlooker, a traveller not claiming the stream until he has found its source. Aware of an entire condensed circuit of forces, the Vedic seer (*Ṛṣi*) is a "round-about-seer" *(paridraṣṭr)*.[2] The vision of his "significant situation" proceeds for the Vedic participant in

1. *Bhūmi Sūkta*, *AV*. 12.3-4, tr. by Raimundo Panikkar, *The Vedic Experience, Mantramañjarī An Anthology of the Vedas for Modern Man and Contemporary Celebration,* Pondicherry, 1983, p. 123.
2. *RV*. 1.164.44-45: We are told of four layers of understanding in *Vāc*, the Word. Three are hidden and the fourth, human language, is able to provide a picture of simultaneity, "overlooking everything" – *viśvam... abhicaṣṭe*. I shall return to this under "Vāc and Vaikhāri" and "Vāco Bhāgam" when I look for an orientation in the cross-cultural perspective.

creation from a condition of consciousness whereby he is fully identified with a particular theme of participation. That theme is participation in expectation. With respect to the consumer (*bhogin*) and spectator (*draṣṭṛ*), the Vedic vision inserts, between the two, the protective experience of an intellectual-ecstatic mode of being (*ānanda-cinmaya*) which is self-manifested (*svaprakāśa*) like a flash of light. The Vedic vision discloses relish and gusto, not only by means of an ideal sympathy with surrounding, but also by consent (*sādhāraṇya*) as a passionate response to the theme and rhythm inherent in everything that surrounds man and resounds within him. The unction that life is, the surprise, is evident.

> "Instill in me abundantly that fragrance,
> O Mother Earth, which emanates from you
> and from your plants and waters, that sweet perfume
> that all celestial beings are wont to emit,
> and let no enemy every wish us ill!
>
> Your fragrance which adheres to human beings,
> the good cheer and the charm of women and men,
> that which is found in horses and in warriors,
> that which is in wild beasts and in the elephant,
> the radiance that shines about a maiden –
> O Earth, steep us too in that fragrance,
> and let no enemy ever wish us ill!"[3]

A figure, representing undetermined potentiality of manifest existence are *Āpaḥ*, the Waters. Their renewal, support and ultimate purifying power, be it at times in sudden frenzies of storm and flood (*laya*) are an immeasurable reservoir of significance of reality. That reservoir has its own history, running its course beyond man's time and space. *Āpaḥ*, the Waters, stretch far beyond the limits of man's horizon.

> "Of this universe, it is in truth the Waters that were made first. Hence, when the Waters flow, then everything here, whatsoever exists, is produced."[4]

When *Indra* opens the closed or hidden naves or rocks,[5] seven rivers of Life are released. As reservoirs of *possibility* they are *Aditi*, the mothers, and equal in number to the seven famous "worlds" or planes of being where *Viṣṇu* strides, "the all pervading and encompassing".[6]

---

3. *Bhūmi Sūkta, AV.* 12.23.25, tr. Panikkar, *The Vedic Experience,* p. 125.
4. *SB.* 7.4.1.6; tr. Panikkar, *The Vedic Experience,* p. 118.
5. *RV.*4.28: *apihitā. . . khāni* (verse I); *apihitām aśna* (verse 5). Mircea Eliade characterizes the most popular of the Vedic gods, *Indra,* as "embodying all the exuberance of life, of the cosmic and biological energies; he unloosens the waters and opens the clouds, quickens the circulation of the sap and the blood, governs all moistures and ensures all fecundities. All the attributes of *Indra* are of a piece and all the domains he rules are complimentary . . . we are being continually presented with an epiphany of the forces of life . . . a wonderful expression of the profound unity that underlies all the abounding manifestations of life", in: *Myths, Dreams and Mysteries, The Encounter between contemporary faiths and archaic realities,* Harper Torchbooks, 1975, p. 139.
6. *RV.* 1.22.16 – 17: "The Gods be gracious unto us even from the place where *Viṣñu* strode. Through the seven regions of the earth! (*pṛthivya sapta-dhamabhiḥ*). Through all this creation strode *Viṣñu*; thrice his foot he planted, and the whole was gathered in his footstep's dust". tr. R.T.H. Griffith, *The Hymns of the ṚgVeda,* Motilal Banarsidass, reprint, Delhi, 1976, p. 12f. Although not in the

The release of the Waters by *Indra* is an emptying out of the hollows (*khāni*) conceived of as shut up within "before the beginning". At the instant "of the beginning" the Waters roar forth from a common ground, rock or mountain. Within this limitless sea of universal potency flow the words, the inspirations, of the Vedic visionary poet *as of* the Waters.[7] Thus the Waters enter into space (*ākāśa*). *Ākāśa* is not primarily physical space but an ideal and principled space without dimension.[8]

While reflecting in the company of his friends about the world, *Pravāhana* explains in the *Chandogya Upaniṣad*:

> "It is the *Ākāśa* out of which all these beings arise and in which they again disappear.[9] The *Ākāśa* is older than all of them, the *Ākāśa* is the final startingpoint."[10]

In the same *Upaniṣad ākāśa* is the name of the cause permitting individual integration:

> "It is the space which extends the names and forms separate; wherein both these are it is the *Brahman*"

Like *Indra* "opens the closed spaces",[11] so the Self[12] awakens this rational cosmos from that space".[13] With an astonishing sense of non-exploitative participation, the Vedic vision places the locus of this space "within you".[14]

Inspiration and an integrated intelligence, able to grasp the idea of cosmic unity, became to the Vedic seer-poet, as Kuiper says:

---

foremost rank of Vedic deities, *Viṣñu* appears closely related to *Indra* and *Varuṇa*, keeping the worlds together as a guardian of "*skambha*", the world axle, cosmic pillar or centre. The idea of a centre evokes the reality of totality and plenitude. In his book, *Ancient Indian Cosmogony*, Vikas Publishing House, India, reprint, 1983, F.B.J. Kuiper would seem to guard against a lack of appreciation of *Viṣñu's* role in the Vedic pantheon. He writes:" The mythological meaning of the centre has long been known: it represents the totality of the parts distributed over the four quarters. So we are driven to the conclusion that at an early date *Viṣñu* occupied a more *central* (Kuiper) position than either *Indra* or *Varuṇa*, who are the protagonists of the opposed groups of *Devas* and *Asuras* and thus stand each for one of the moieties only. In contrast with them *Viṣñu* must consequently represent the unity of the two antagonistic parties, upper world and nether world. He stands for and *is* (*K*) each of the two worlds just as later he is, in a way, the heavenly bird *Garuḍa* and the serpent of the subterranean waters, *Śeṣa*, but under the aspect of their unity, like *Prajāpati*. In *AthS*. 10.10.30 the cosmic cow is said to be Heaven and Earth (i.e. the totality of the universe), *Viṣñu* and *Prajāpati*", p. 48. For "*Prajāpati*, the Lord of Generation", see Part II:5:4. in this book. References to *Aditi, Bhūmi, Viṣñu, Varuṇa* etc. can be found in the index at the back, enumerating the numbers under which each name and theme has been dealt with in Part III:7." An experience of *Āpaḥ*, the Waters, inspired by Vedic and Hindu myth".

7. *RV*. 10.89.4: "I will send forth my songs in flow unceasing like water from the ocean's depth, to *Indra*", see Griffith, *The Hymns of the ṚgVeda*, p. 601.
8. As matrix of dimension "*Ākāśa*" is the physical space which is "above" the earth.
9. *CU*. 1.9.1: *Ākāśa samapadyanta – ākāsaṃ pratyastaṃ yānti.* See Paul Deussen, *Sixty Upaniṣads of the Veda*, Motilal Banarsidass, first Indian ed., Delhi, 1980, 2 vols., vol. I, p. 80.
10. Op. cit.; startingpoint – *parāyaṇam*, p. 80.
11. *CU*. 8.14: *ākāśo vai nāma nāmarupayor nirvahitā.*
12. *RV*. 4.28.1: *apihitā khāni.*
13. *MaiU*. 6.127: *ākāśat eṣa khalu idam cetāmātram dobhyati*, in: R.E. Hume, (ed), *The Thirteen Principal Upaniṣads*, 2nd ed., London, 1931.
14. *MaiU*. 7.11: *tat svarūpam nabhasah khe antarbhūtasya yat param tejaḥ* – what is the intrinsic aspect of expansion is the fiery energy in the vacant place of the inner man. In the *Bhagavad Gītā* 7.8–10 it is said: "The savour in the waters am I, the light in the moon and the sun. I am the *OM* in all Vedas, the sound in space, in men vigour. I am the sweet fragrance of earth and of fire the brilliance. I am the life within all beings, the fervour in ascetics."

"an opening of the door of the mind which was on a level with the opening of the doors of the primordial hill."[15]

The author finds the same concept expressed in the *"kha"*, the aperture, the well, opened by *Agni*,

"to give free course to Inspiration from the *hṛdayasamudra*, the primordial Waters in Man's heart"[16]

The "space in the heart" is the locus where is deposited in secret all that is already ours or may be ours on any plane of experience.[17] Kuiper's observation with regard to *Agni* is the *Agni* "before the beginning". It is intelligent plenitude inherent in what already is but not yet manifest until the rock opens so the Waters flow.

The Vedic rock is a centre without place. Hence when the Waters have come forth, that is, when the cosmos has come to be and has been "seen" as such by man's intellect and heart, we ask :

"Far have they gone, the first of all these waters, the waters that flowed forth when *Indra* sent them. Where is their spring? Where now, you Waters, is your inmost centre?"[18]

The *Vedas* speaks its own language. Language is a revelation of the Spirit. It is not known how long it took for Vedic man to put words together to become a language discovering a new perspective for looking at reality. Each word and the tone in which it is spoken is the physical and metaphysical crystallization of long human experience. Authentic words create an authentic world and an authentic fellowship among men and between man and his environment. By careful shifts between their psyche and the earth on which they lived and the universe they grasped, the Vedic poet-sages accomplished, metaphysically, through the Waters, an actual construction of familiarity with the universe without claiming an all too privileged and exceptional position for man:

"Whatever I dig up of you, O Earth, may you of that
have quick replenishment!
O purifying One, may my thrust never reach
right into your vital points, your heart!
Heaven and Earth and the space in between
have set me in a wide expanse!
Fire, the Sun, the Waters, the Gods,
have joined to give me inspiration."[19]

---

15. Kuiper refers to *RS*. 9.10.6: *"āpa dvārā matinām pratnā ṛnvanti kāravaḥ" and 6.51.2: "vy ū vrajasya tāmaso dvāro chantir-av-ran-chucayah pāvakaḥ"*. Mention is made by the author of *Agni* as the child of the Cosmic Waters, who as a guest among men brings them knowledge of the cosmic Truth, wisdom, insight and inspiration. *Agni* is called "the inventor of resplendent speech", see Kuiper, *Ancient Indian Cosmogony,* p. 182f.
16. Op. cit., p. 183. With regard to *Agni*, see Part II:5:4 (i) *"Agni*: Sacrifice of fire and intelligence".
17. *CU*. 8.1.3.: "Truly, this space inside the heart is as great as this world-space; in it are resolved both, the heaven and the earth—both the fire and the wind, both the sun and the moon, the lightning and the stars and what one below here possesses and does not possess, everything is resolved therein."
18. *RV*. 10.111.8
19. *AV*. 12.35.53 : *Bhūmi Sūkta*, hymn to the Earth.

What is the Vedic vision for us, moderns, a few thousand years later? Nothing possibly, if we consider the days and nights, droughts and floods, high tide and low tide, the flight of our planet and the seasons as having come and passed for ever. If we think that "modern man" with all his gadgets and machinations is more than Man, then indeed the Vedic vision may seem to us a worn-out dress only to be shed. If we think that Man is more than our particular nook in the vast space of the universe's history we might find in the Vedic dedication some explanation of our roots. And if we claim to want to be "secular", then the "saeculum", the *āyus*, the circle of seasons in the universe must be taken seriously. Otherwise "modern man" will be swallowed up by his own machinery and, indeed, precisely by the mechanism of cosmic processes which we might think we can tamper with at will. Man has never been able to buy over the universe by offering a unilateral pact. It is the universe and the earth in it that cling to man and offer him protection from nothingness:

> "Whether, when I repose on you, O Earth,
> I turn upon my right side or my left,
> or whether, extended flat upon my back,
> I meet your pressure from head to foot,
> be gentle, Earth! You are the couch of all!"[20]

If meaning, *artha*, and significance is created by the revolution of the seasons and rhythms of the year of the universe and the earth, it has neither place nor date. It cannot be thought of as the private property of anyone or of any one culture. One who identifies himself with any meaning or idea, and hence finding it at its very source within himself, is equally "original" with those who long ago found it in the circling of the seasons.[21]

Shall we say, then, that the universe witnesses to meaning which it of itself has? That the liquid chaos of the Waters "before the beginning" shut up from within, turned into fresh salubrious waters by their own inherent potency of an overcharge of significance? Their significance is the radiance and effulgence of the visible universe. Through their soul-language the Vedic *ṛṣis* recognized a realm of reference.[22] Their reflexive proximity to the astonishing transition from Unform into form has taken the Vedic seers – with the elegance of a receptive mind – to the acknowledgement of things not dead, but of things alive. "Alive" in the sense that, if man were to try and overrule the inherent liveliness of form, he would create his own flood which, instead

20. *AV.* 12.34: *Bhūmi Sūkta*, Hymn to the Earth.
21. *RV.* 10.101.1: "Wake with one mind, my friends, and kindle *Agni*, you are many and dwell together", tr. Griffith, p.614. I shall later refer to archaism in time and that in the psychic depth of man.
22. "Soul-language" reveals a state where the dichotomy between subject and object is less pronounced. The question is debatable. The psychological functions chiefly involved in the outward-turned, "objective" order of cognition, "common to all men", are sensation and thinking. Feeling and intuition, on the other hand, lead inward, to private spheres. As Jung declares: "The pain-pleasure reaction of feeling marks the highest degree of subjectivation of the object; whereas intuition is that mode of perception which includes the apprehension of subliminal factors: "the possible relationships to objects not appearing in the field of vision, and the possible changes, past and future, about which the object gives no clue. Intuition is an immediate awareness of relationships that could not be established by the other three functions at the moment of orientation.", in: C.G. Jung, *The Structure and Dynamics of the Psyche*, tr. R.F.C. Hull, Bolingen Series XX. 8, New York: Pantheon Books 1960, pp. 123-124.

of the separation of the Waters in the creative act, would reduce all things back to primitive chaos. He would cause the fury of uncreation, locked up in itself in a monstrous incommunicative mountain. That mountain would be man himself. Some part of our lives is guided by reality which is of itself a stir, oscillation, fermentation, regress and progress. The secret of the universe is its own inbuilt, although not easily discoverable, design.

What is that for philosophy? I shall return to this question on more than one occasion. What I may at this stage ask is: philosophy, is it prepared to accept moments of suspense? Can we accept the fact that we do not *know* everything? Reality, when analyzed, resists a constant narrative, dressed in pure rational syllogism. It resists enclosure in mere rational concepts as much as it rejects disclosure into fragmentation, into mere crumbs of its own "whole" and – not to forget – its "wholesomeness".

Hence, in our understanding of reality, "pure reason" might have to be suspended or bracketed as soon as we realize the moment when the principle of orientation becomes the principle of limitation. Suspension or bracketing, therefore, of "pure" reasoned syllogism implies the transition from statement to acclamation or, at least, acknowledgement. I am here referring to the whole man's conviction of the symbolic character of every human manifestation, particularly the linguistic one. Is there not an awareness of the impossibility of presenting "pure" word-for-word translation of what is in man and the whole gamut of experience of being in this world ? No *more* elaborate and explicative paraphrasing of that which is *unsayable* will be able to make it more *sayable*.[23]

Shall we be astonished, then, or even scandalized by the memory of our *whole* consciousness? To put it in other words: it takes an inveterate scepticist not to be moved by the majestic splendour of the Himalayas or by a child running away as a human torch from a scene of napalm-bombing. These are extremes. But we know of more frequent and ordinary "extremes" in our daily lives when we feel as if we are being done a world of good, or harm.

What is our *whole* consciousness? It would certainly include the inescapable moment of surprise. Surprise and amazement imply a surplus. When the moment of

23. I am aware of the risk of my wording when the science of epistemology is concerned. The question is: what could be said to be "reason". From the point of view of phenomenology, "reason" as an abstraction from the flux of life would seem to make an incision into the wholeness of man's experience. Goethe has declared:

"The Godhead is effective in the living and not in the dead, in the becoming and the changing, not in the become and the set-fast; and therefore, accordingly, reason (Vernunft) is concerned only to strive toward the divine through the becoming and the living, and the understanding (Verstand) only to make use of the become and the set-fast", in: Johann Peter Eckermann, *Gespräche mit Goethe in den letzten Jahres seines Lebens*, 1823-1832, Berlin, Deutsches Verlagshaus, 1916, vol.1, p. 251 (Feb. 13, 1829). Transl. by Charles Francis Atkinson, in Oswald Spengler, *The Decline of the West*, tr. C.F. Atkinson, London, New York: Alfred A. Knopf, 1928, vol. 1, p. 49.

Waking Consciousness, which is outward-turned, is called the common-to-all-men in Indian tradition (see *Mand. Upaniṣad*). Its objects are of gross matter and separate from each other: a is not b. Perceived by the senses, named by the mind, and experienced as desirable or fearful, they compose the world of, what Goethe called, "the become and the set-fast: the dead" of which the understanding (Verstand) "only makes use". This is the aspect of experience that Mefistopheles comprehends and controls: the world of empirical man, his desires, fears and duties, laws, statistics, economics and "hard facts" which may be syllogized and reasoned as being the whole truth about man in intellectual abstraction.

surprise in any relationship, such as that between a man and a woman or children and their parents, erodes, the relationship is reduced to a mere minimum of tolerance, if at all the relationship must be rescued by convention. Surprise is an indelible part of human existence. Because human existence concerns philosophy, *surprise inhabits the history of philosophy itself*. It breaks the sequence of continued syllogism by the springing up of bubbles unforeseeable. It is always in the midst of discontinued *expression* that the rationality of *impression* must be detected.[24]

What the Vedic philosophers discovered and, consequently, believed of the universe, relates them to it in a "significant situation" of being, meaning and truth. It is when the centre of our individual being coincides with the entire circuit of manifest cycles in the universe that an intricate network is discovered. Instead of attempting to handle the universe, the Vedic poet-*ṛṣis meet* the universe.[25] Indeed, it is difficult to imagine how the human mind could function without the conviction that there is something irreducibly real and significant in the world. There is more to it than meets the eye. Man's meeting the world as *event* has been expressed in terms of cosmic intelligence:

> "The universe meant something long before man began to know what it meant...; it signified from the beginning the totality of what humanity might expect to know about it."[26]

The universe, therefore, extends an invitation to man to discover and unfold it. However, the universe has no structure other than its own. Both mind and matter are part of it. The invitation, therefore, receives an accent of mutuality through which we feel ourselves in proximity to what we feel ourselves *in*. Thus arises the paradox of man being both "near to" and "far from" the universe.

Now, the affective relationship of an *intention* to discover, as we see it in the Vedic mind and, for that matter, in the mind of present day scientists, betrays an impulse of personal fervour. This, as the study of human behaviour in culture reveals,

---

24. Anyone who wishes to escape this fact of encounter and stand apart in the no-man's-land of "objectivity" would at the most think he knows everything but we may ask whether he, in fact, would understand anything.
25. It is of interest to note that their proximity to the deepest secrets of the physical universe brings not a few present day celebrated physicists to the conclusion that mechanistic hypotheses are of no help in understanding the universe. Nature speaks in riddles, now wave, now particle. The man who upset the mechanomorphic model was Albert Einstein. His contemporary, Werner Heisenberg writes: "(in modern physics) one has divided the world not into different objects but into different groups of connections. What can be distinguished is the kind of connection which is primarily important in a certain phenomenon. The world thus appears as a complicated tissue of events, in which the connections of different kinds alternate or overlap or combine and thereby determine the texture of the whole", in: W. Heisenberg, *Physics and Philosophy*, Allen and Undwin, London, 1963, p. 69. With the discovery of matter as a form of energy, the suggestion of the presence of an order and consciousness in the universe is increasingly attracting attention. From various corners comes the thought that in place of the reductionist view something closer to the ecological and mystical must be considered. The limits of science and language are admitted and paradox recognized, as in poetry. Later in this chapter I shall refer to the development of the new so-called "systems-philosophy" referring to the universe as a network of interrelated systems. The question is, in any case, that science without a soul is increasingly considered to be unscientific.
26. Levi-Strauss in G. Gusdorf, *Mythe et Metaphysique*, Paris, 1953, p. 45. (tr. F.B.). cf. the similarity in content between Levi-Strauss' observation and that of the *Chandogya Upaniṣad*: see note 17.

is a particular human attitude towards reality and towards man.[27] The *one* stream in our consciousness of cosmic plenitude, totality, is tempered – to the point of possible experienced darkness – by the *other* stream in our consciousness of not *being* that total plenitude. The cosmic wholeness is not simply given to us, it must be looked for, aimed at. It is only in intention that we restore some wholeness. And what is more, if we are true to our awareness we apparently cannot escape the intention. A meaningful world for us results because we cannot live in "nothing" which, so traditions call it, is chaos. Experiencing ourselves and others as "something-somebody", we reject the thought of being in "nothing", "chaos", as both metaphysically absurd and emotionally unbearable. For we know that around us, as well as in us, exists the cosmic plenitude present from before we humans began to breathe. The Waters shut up from within and spilling over into "being universe" were there before we came to be. Man's psyche and that of the universe are indissolubly related.[28] The aimed-at restoration of wholeness, therefore, is an unavoidable result of our rejection of chaos, meaninglessness. It is because we ourselves have lost total wholeness – by what I shall later call the "fault" of creation – that we attempt the restoration of it by re-enacting and imitating the totality of the beginnings. We are able to do so in speaking of them and acting them out. Precisely because, as I said, the totality is not merely *given* to us.

Now, if I said that speaking of the beginnings and the re-enacting of them is man's attempt at restoration of cosmic totality and restoration of himself, I would have referred to what is called the myth-narration and ritual. This would be a part-description of myth and ritual but in any case, in my opinion, acceptable. Do myth-narrations strike us in a particular way? The language, for example, is different. There is no trace of what is called rational critical syllogism or argumentation of any kind. The logic of myth, as we shall see, is different.[29]

---

27. The question of fervour, heat, concentration etc. is a frequently occuring theme in creation-thought and the idea of "unfolding". In my inquiry after the Indian "Prestige of Origin" I have elaborated at length the concept of "*tapas*" under the title "*Tapas*: Discernment and intelligent concentration" in the conclusion to Part II, ch.2.

28. It is from here that Sigmund Freud attempted to develop his theories on the human psyche. In his early paper on "The Psychopathology of Everyday Life" (1904), Freud writes: "I believe that a large portion of the mythological conception of the world which reaches far into the most modern religions, is nothing but psychology projected to the outer world. The dim perception (the endo-psychic perception, as it were) of psychic factors and relations of the unconscious was taken as a model in the construction of a transcendental reality, which is destined to be changed again by science into psychology of the unconscious. We venture to explain in this way the myths of paradise and the fall of man, of God, of good and evil, of immortality and the like – that is, to transform metaphysics into meta-psychology", in: *The Psychopathology of Everyday Life*, tr. A.S. Brill in, *The Basic Writings of Sigmund Freud,* New York: The Modern Library, 1938, pp. 164-165. From a certain point of view psychology is right. It is indeed possible to homologize the function of the Figures and the results of the Events upon the parallel planes of unconscious activity and of religion and mythology. It has been Freud's genius to set depth-psychology at work for decades. However, as Mircea Eliade comments: "It is when the psychologist "explains" a mythological Figure or Event by reducing it to the process of the unconscious that the historian of religion – and perhaps not he alone – hesitates to follow him." in: *Myths, Dreams and Mysteries, The Encounter between contemporary faiths and archaic realities*, Harper Torchbooks, 1975, p. 14. Whereas Freud rejected the religious realm, Jung was impressed by transpersonal, universal forces that were working towards for Jung the most important archetype, that of the Self. Jung made a careful study of archaic and oriental religions to shape his depth-psychological theories.

29. It is embarrassing, but perhaps characteristic of myth itself that uptil now no etymology of the

On the most archaic levels of human culture back in temporal time, living as a human being has always been protected against the anxiety of its possible destruction by relating it to the consoling idea of the perfection of the beginnings. On the archaic level of the depth of our psyche the perfection of the beginnings manifests itself in everyday life. Thus it is that the love that husband and wife bear each other is mirrored against and intended to be the replica of "some" perfect love. When failure occurs, the rite of restoration may take various forms. Its aim is to avoid the chaos or the nothingness of loveless love. Broadly speaking, then, mythical attitude, myth-narration and ritual are of the widest possible distribution. They underlie all further speculation and discourse. Why? Because myth-narration and ritual are already *word*, be it that they belong to the aesthetic field rather than the critical rational.

It is when myth-narration and ritual concerns itself with gods and the ideal of the sacred that difficulties arise with regard to secular man. Likewise, group-thought, inspired by myth as against individual endeavour, appears to cause obstacles. The present day world offers a spectacle of contemporary societies divided in what are called traditional and modern societies. The idea of "secular" man as well as the stress on personal and individual endeavour are features particularly applicable to post-medieval Western society. The history of myth or perhaps better to say, the myth of history has taken a different turn in the West. The consequences for myth and the mythical consciousness in the West as well as for traditional societies touched by it especially through colonialism, have been significant. I shall later pay special attention to particular features resulting from this cross-cultural contact. Rather than taking an antagonistic position with regard to myth from the point of view of "secular man", I would prefer to try and avoid unnecessary dispute and misunderstanding by the observation that man can survive on earth and develop his humanity, both as a species and as a person, only if he pays careful attention to precisely everything secular. As a preliminary to the widest possible understanding of the nature of myth and the mythical consciousness, an inquiry into the idea of the sacred may provide us with a better perspective.

The Idea of the Sacred

It is unfortunate that we do not have at our disposal a better, a more precise word than "religion" to clarify the experience of the sacred.[30] Religion has a long

---

Greek word "muthos" has proved satisfactory. At one stage in the Greek cultural memory, "muthos" came to signify something in opposition to "Logos", the reasoned word. Is "Logos" the true and valid word, muthos is an untrue story, a fable. But it was not always like that. It is striking that we do not know the origin of the word "muthos". Stalin in his, Theologisches *Wörterbuch zum Neuen Testament*, vol. IV, 1948, p. 772, attempts to derive the word from the root "meudh – mudh", which would mean "to remember, to long for, to be homesick". "Muthos", then, would first mean "thought". Stalin finally arrives at "News, information, history – rumour, telling, fairytale, fable, myth". Myth, then, would, as to the truth of its content, come under severe stress. Over the past few decades an increasing number of Western classical philologists appear not only to give "myth" the benefit of the doubt, but to attribute to "muthos" the authority of truth. If "muthos" originally meant "thought", why should it not be true and real thought? Walter Otto, an authority on the Greek heritage, holds, as does his pupil Karl Kerenyi, that myth is "the word which transmits happenings, the authoritative word". See: Jan de Vries, *Forschungsgeschichte der Mythologie*, Verlag Karl Alber, Freiburg/Munchen, 1961, p. 305.

30. For the present it will be sufficient to observe that the word "sacred" is derived from the Latin "sacer" meaning something set apart or different from the profane.

history. Culturally it is rather limited. Looking at the various manifestations of it in human history, beyond the paleolythic age of which, moreover, we have as yet little knowledge, one wonders how "religion" can be indiscriminately applied to ancient Egypt or China, the Sumerians, Islam, Buddhism, Christianity, Hinduism, Judaism and so-called animism or shamanism of primitives as well as numerous religious movements mushrooming in the modern West.[31]

It is useful to remember that "religion" does not necessarily imply belief in God, gods or ghosts. In Mircea Eliade's opinion, the religious phenomenon seems to draw sharper contours round at least one aspect of it, namely, the *experience of the sacred*. It manifests itself as something different from the profane, the ordinary, the natural. We must, however, not forget that Cosmos and Psyche are the two poles of the selfsame *expressivity* of the total *possibility* of expression. One cannot express more than there is in the plenitude of the cosmos. I express myself in expressing the world. But in as far as the universe, the world, is something *not* made by me physically, it has a significance other than my own, a greater significance. That significance is in need of expression, a name protecting it from vulgarization and indeed from possible appropriation by man. The study of man's language has proved that the term *sacred* is used to signify that in which there is more than man himself, the surplus of being beyond man. The manifestations of the sacred seem inexhaustible. The variety of its expression is for the student practically unmanageable. It covers both cosmic and psychic manifestations.[32] Mircea Eliade gives an excellent description of its manifold expression. A haphazard handling of the idea of the sacred is quite out of place when studying human culture.

> "We are faced with rites, myths, divine forms, sacred and venerable objects, symbols, cosmologies, theologoumena, consecrated men, animals and plants, sacred places, and more. And its category has its own morphology – of a branching and luxurious richness. We have to deal with a vast and ill-assorted mass of material, with a Mesopotamian cosmogony myth, or a Brahmin sacrifice having as much right to our considerations as the mystical writings of a St. Theresa or a Nichiren, an Australian totem, a primitive initiation rite, the symbolism of the Borubudur temple, the ceremonial costumes and dances of Siberian shaman, the sacred stones to be found in so many places, agricultural ceremonies, the myths and rites of the Great Goddesses, the enthroning of an ancient king or the superstitions attached to precious stones. Each must be considered as a hierophany in as much as it expresses in some way some modality

---

31. By "the modern West" is not meant contemporary Western society only. The term also designates a certain state of mind which has been formed by successive deposits since the Western Renaissance and Reformation and carried by expansive Western colonialism to other parts of the world. The active urban classes in Africa, Asia and Latin America are "modern" in the sense that they have been formed by norms prevalent in Western education and official culture. An excellent quarterly studying new religious movements in the sense that they are outside the mainstream of traditional religions is: "Update, a quarterly on New Religious Movements" published by The Dialog Centre, Klvermarksvej 4, DK-8200 Aarhus, Denmark.

32. In the two phenomenologies which I have presented in the second chapter, viz., "the confession of receptivity" and the "confession of the sacred", we shall try and "draw" ourselves through this double expressivity – cosmic and psychic – in order to put ourselves at "the origin of the speaking being "where we discover a third modality of expression – the symbol – to express that which there is more than we ourselves. This third modality we shall follow, in the Indian context, under the primary symbol of *Āpaḥ*, the Waters.

of the sacred and some moment in its history; that is to say, some one of the many kinds of experience of the sacred man has had. Each is valuable for two things it tells us: because it is a hierophany, it reveals some modality of the sacred; because it is a historical incident, it reveals some attitude man has towards the sacred. For instance, the following Vedic text addressing a dead man: "Crawl to your Mother, Earth: May she save you from the void "(*RV.* 10.18.10). This text shows the nature of earth-worship; but it also shows one given stage in the history of Indian religion, the moment when Mother Earth was valued – at least by one group – as a protectress against the void, a valuation which was to be done away with by the reform of the *Upaniṣads* and the preaching of *Buddha*."[33]

From Eliade's description it is clear that man's awareness of a reality as distinct from ordinary reality, need not necessarily be belief in a personal God. The term "God" is confusing. "God" cannot be known unless through the faculty of the sacred, a concept larger than that of "religion" which may be "making" God or "unmaking" God by possible limitations of a particularized theological concept. In Eliade's view the history of religions is constituted by a number of hierophanies, manifestations of the sacred, which amounts to saying that religion is not first and foremost a code of beliefs to be adhered to. In his famous work, *The Idea of the Holy*, Rudolph Otto analyses the modalities of religious experience rather than the ideas of God and religion. He does not touch on the question of myth and mythical thought but concentrates on the non-rational side or religion. For Otto the sacred is the feeling of terror, the numinous, the awe-inspiring.

"The feeling of it", he writes, "may at times come sweeping like a gentle tide, pervading the mind with a tranquil mood of deepest worship. It may pass over into a more set and lasting attitude of the soul, continuing, as it were, thrillingly vibrant and resonant, until at last it dies away and the soul resumes its "profane", non-religious mood of everyday experience. It may burst in sudden eruption up from depths of the soul with spasms and convulsions, or lead to the strangest excitements, to intoxicated frenzy, to transport, and to ecstasy. It has its wild and demonic forms and can sink in an almost grisly horror and shuddering. It has its crude, barbaric antecedents, and early manifestations, and again it may be developed into something beautiful and pure and glorious. It may become the hushed, trembling, and speechless humility of the creature in the presence of – whom or what? In the presence of that which is a Mystery inexpressible and above all creatures."[34]

If religion refers to the experience of the sacred it follows that it is related to the experience of a revelation which need not necessarily fall within the binding framework of dogma and organized religion. The experience of the sacred is one of its own kind. It is lost when identified with this or that conceptualized deity. No one can be taught it nor can it be explained to anyone who has not known it. That what it reveals for the person struck by it, is the only valid revelation of reality. The experience of the sacred is related to the ideas of being, meaning truth. Its experience unfolds a dimension not apprehended by theoretical reflection alone. Its content is too

33. Mircea Eliade, *Patterns in Comparative Religion*, Sheed and Ward, London, 1958, p. 2.
34. Rudolf Otto, *Das Heilige*, Breslau, 1917, English translation John W. Harvey, *The Idea of the Holy*, Penguin Books, London, 1959, pp. 12-13.

tender and fragile to be left at the mercy of circumscriptive conversation or parlour-speech.[35] Phenomena of the sacred and religious phenomena can best be understood on their own plane of reference. There is, however, no such thing as a purely religious fact. It will also have social, psychological and historical implications. Every religious event is, in the final analysis, also a human event. Less obvious perhaps is that religious phenomena deserve to be interpreted in religious terms. They ought to be taken for what they pretend to be, that is, manifestations or revelations of the sacred. Besides his social, political, economic and historical dimension, the human also has a religious dimension. Humanity has traditionally demonstrated that it must relate itself to an *other* sphere of reality *in order to be human*. Although things of the sacred obviously meet social, psychic and historic needs and functions, they also claim to transcend these horizontal factors. In fact, the sacred claims to underlie these factors. But how does one study the sacred as being such? The question does not elicit a simple answer. To be receptive of the sacred one needs to be open to things mysterious and unusual. Die-hard critics at times call that attitude naive or childlike. The temptation to reduce a manifestation of the sacred to more easily manageable cause-and-effect interpretations must be resisted. The sacred represents a non-objectifiable vision of the universe and the world. It implies a conviction that not everything non-objectifiable would hence be exhausted of its meaning. Without letting ourselves be taken too far we may look at the sacred from yet another viewpoint.

The idea of the sacred prevents us from falling into chaos and nothingness, thus drawing the sacred into the realm of universal human experience as does the rejection of chaos. Limiting ourselves to the Vedic hymn of creation, the *Nāsadīya Sūkta*, there were in the beginning two kinds of darkness.[36] The first darkness is the creator, the primordial principle himself (*Svayambhū*). That primordial principle is masculine. It refers to the Waters shut up from within and incapable of birth. Birth of the Waters takes place when their inherent fertility is being freed and creation (*parameṣṭhi*) emanates. That creation is feminine and fecund. Thus chaos, nothingness, is transformed and fashioned into meaningfulness by the interaction and combination of extremes. These extremes are in mythical language, where the androgyne is an important personality, often expressed under sexual symbols. The response from man's end to what of the Universe is of itself total and whole and replete, is man's idea of the sacred. That idea makes him relate and combine all fragmented oppositions into a single reservoir of meaning. Its singleness is at once its perfection.[37]

Passing from psyche to cosmos we would not do well by opposing the manifestations of the sacred described by the phenomenologist of religion to the ideas of Freudian and Jungian psychoanalysis.[38] The manifestation *on* the cosmos and *in* the psyche are the same thing. Immersion in our psychic cosmos is an immersion of

35. The *Śatapatha Brāhmaṇa* 3.2.1.23 speaks of "*Asura's* gibberish" referring to a dual possibility of applying the Voice to the statement of truth or falsehood. The Voice is called the double-tongued (*SB*. 3.2.4.16). One application is that of *pratirūpa*, reflection, imitation. The other is that of speech at random without ground.
36. See Part II:5:4: (iii): "The Perfection of the Beginnings: *Sat – Asat*".
37. See V.S. Agarwala, *Vision in Long Darkness*, Vārāṇasī, Bhargava Bhushan, 1963.
38. At least those ideas which, by Freud's own admission, go beyond the projections of individual history and beneath the private archeology of a subject into the common representations of a culture, or into the common cultural heritage of humanity as a whole.

ourselves in the common thought of humanity. This regression, in as far as we thereby also identify ourselves with earlier humanity, may well be a discovery regarding ourselves. We may have *forgotten* concerning the cosmos and ourselves. The danger of losing memory's potentiality, all potentiality in fact, is a characteristic of the human condition.[39] It would seem, however, that reductionism of the experience of the sacred as expressed, for example, in myth and ritual, to particular psychic, economic and socio-political conditions is becoming untenable. Freud's reductionism stimulated the student of religion and forced him to have a closer look at the psyche and the psychological presuppositions of religious manifestations.[40] The symbol came once again into focus and the discussion regarding myth intensified. It was none other than Freud's disciple, Carl Jung, who through his postulate of the collective unconscious manifesting itself through "archetypes", drew the attention to the presence of transpersonal universal forces in the depth of the psyche.[41] Jung arrived at his postulate through the discovery of the striking similarities between myths, symbols and mythological figures of widely separated peoples and civilizations. Contrary to Freud who despised religion and the experience of the sacred, Jung was convinced that religious experience has meaningful goals which cannot be simply explained away by reductionism. Jung's most important archetype is that of the Self, the wholeness of man. The self of Jung is not the *Ātman* of Indian thought nor is it the idea of a personal God.[42] Van der Leeuw has had considerable influence in pointing

39. Heinz Hartmann, "Ego Psychology and the Problem of Adaptation", 1939, in: David Rapaport, *Organization and Pathology of Thought*, Columbia University Press, 1951.

40. From the middle of the nineteenth century Western historiography has at times shown an obsession with the quest of "origins". The origin of language, of institutions, art, the Indo-Aryan races etc. occupied the attention of scholars. The origin of religion was always a point of hot debate. Max Müller thought that the *RgVeda* reflects a primordial phase of Aryan religion and consequently is one of the most archaic stages of religious beliefs and mythological creations. In the early 1870's Abel Bergaigne proved that the Vedic hymns, far from being the spontaneous and naive expression of a naturalistic religion, were the product of a highly sophisticated class of priests. Andrew Lang in his, *Custom and Myth* (1883) and *Modern Mythology* (1897) discredited Müller's ideas with the aid of Tylor's theories who found the origin of religion in animism. Lang himself rejected that theory later and based his arguments on the presence of a belief in High Gods found among some very primitive peoples in Australia and the Andaman Islands. It has been especially Nietzsche who, through his mouthpiece Zarathustra, made an impact by his proclamation of the death of God. It announced the radical end of Christianity – of religion – and prophesied that modern man must live henceforth in an exclusively immanent, godless world. In Nietzsche's concept, after the death of the Judeo-Christian God, man has to live by himself, alone, in a radically desacralized world. But this immanent world is the world of history. Whatever be the case, we are confronted with a new idea by men as Nietzsche, Lang and others: the responsibility of history in the degradation, the oblivion and untimely "death" of God.

41. Jung has defined the concept of the "archetype" as a structural abstract concept signifying "eternal presence". See C.G. Jung," On the Nature of the Psyche" in: *the Structure and Dynamics of the Psyche*, Coll. Works, vol. 8, New York and London, 1960. Other definitions by Jung are "patterns of behaviour" or propensities that are part of human nature.

42. C.G. Jung, *Psychology and Religion: West and East*, Bollingen Series, New York, 1958, vol. 2, p. 502: "In Eastern texts, the "Self" represents a purely spiritual idea, but in Western psychology the "self" stands for a totality which comprises instincts, physiological and semi-physiological phenomena." Thus the Indian Cosmic Self is different from the European earlier mythical self, the "weird". See also: *Archetypes and the Collective Unconscious*, p. 173: "The deeper "layers" of the psyche loose their individual uniqueness as they retreat farther and farther into darkness. "Lower down" that is to say, as they approach the autonomous functional systems, they become increasingly collective untill they are universalized and extinguished in the body's materiality, i.e., in chemical substances. The body's carbon is simply carbon. Hence, "at bottom" the psyche is simply "world".

out the irreducibility of religious representations to social, psychological and other rational functions. Later I shall have occasion to refer to Durkheim and the French sociological school. To try and explain the experience of the sacred by something other than itself is, as I said, a risky endeavour.[43]

The concept of "religion" must be critically viewed when the idea of the sacred is concerned. Religion, especially in its institutionalized form, is exposed to the dangers of a despotic power-elite and dogmatism obscuring rather than clarifying the sacred.[44]

The Juices of *Saptadvīpas*, the Seven Islands

When, in Indian mythical tradition, *Priyavrata,* son of *Svāyambhū Manu*, ruled the country for a period of eleven *arbudas,* a hundred million years, his strength of mind and body never weakened. He saw the sun travelling on the first side of the earth, and began to think: "When the sun is walking on one side of the earth, the other side must naturally be dark. Will it happen so in our times? In all places at all times it should be bright and there should be darkness". Thinking thus he climbed a chariot as bright as the sun and travelled round the earth seven times. During these travels the wheels of the chariot made seven furrows on the earth. These furrows became the seven seas and the beds between the furrows became seven islands, the lands of people.[45] And the *Liṅga Purāṇa* adds to this episode in the *Devī Bhāgavata* that all people cherished similar ideals and they all had the lustre of the lotus flower on their faces.[46]

On that same earth of ours things appear not as ideal as *Priyavrata* meant them to be. But the myth-narrator was aware that the banality of discrimination and war between races, countries and neighbours could hardly be the original intention of the earth, feeding all, and of the sun spreading its light and warmth over all lands. The myth is aware of the sacred. It gathers the surplus of the universe and the world beyond man. That surplus is sacred. It is not at once detectable in everyday life unless we make a conscious effort at the restoration of it in ourselves. That effort is myth and ritual portraying at once reality. Mythical awareness, therefore, is the attitude of confession to a surplus, a surprise. The awareness of surplus, surprise and expectation – the sacred in fact—is, as I said, not a title for psychological structures only. It reveals an other edge of man's consciousness that life in the universe is of itself meaningful and true as *believed*. Myths *say* something. By what they *say* one is made to look retrogressively ahead. The reason is the surplus myth uncovers and

43. G. Van der Leeuw, *Religion in Essence and Manifestation,* 2 vols., Harper Torch Books, New York, 1963.
44. Western man's longing for the "origins" and the "primordial" has forced him into an encounter with history. In itself, the irreducibility of history—man is always a historical being— is not a negative, sterilizing experience. It has, however, given way to relativistic and historicistic ideologies. A salutory effect of Western man's quest has been the discovery of himself on the same level with every other man. He is no longer the unique creator of a high culture, no longer the master of the world, and culturally menaced by extinction. This profound humiliation has opened roads to a better cross-cultural perspective.
45. *DbhP., Skandha* 8 in: Vettam Mani, *Purāṇic Encyclopaedia,* Motilal Banarsidass, reprint, 1979, pp. 690-691.
46. *LP* 52. 35-39 in: *The Liṅga-Purāṇa*, tr. A Board of Scholars, 2 vols., Ancient Indian Tradition and Mythology Series, Motilal Banarsidass, 1973, vol. 1, p. 203.

which is all around and in man. That surplus is as such indivisible in functional provinces or measurements of past, present and future. Myth knows two territories of being: a common and generally accessible territory and another cordoned off, sacred and protected against the common surrounding. Nevertheless, the mythical consciousness manifests a universal direction and function. The mythical worldview effects a construction of space and time which, although far from being identical in content, is analogous in form to the construct of geometrical space and time and its framework of empirical objective "nature". The mythical edge in man operates also as a ferment. The most diversive elements, at first sight utterly incommensurate, are made to correlate one with another. In the idealist view, objective knowledge rests essentially on the reduction of all mere and immediate sense distinctions to pure distinctions of space and magnitude. In the mythical view, one finds a similar representation. It "copies" in space what is intrinsically unspatial. Lands, races, faces, and the amazing variety of manifest creation are for myth but one reality of the same truth. For that is what it is, one platform in a common bond. Racism, discrimination, exploitation and the denial of earth's blessings by one to another are to the mythical consciousness utterly inconceivable and despicable. It is fraud. All continents are indeed the result of one and the same chariot's wheels furrowing the earth. The suggestion that conferences dealing with well known scandals in our modern world be begun with the reading of a relevant myth is not as naive as it may sound. The myth is both soothing, provocative and creative.

Dare we say that all men, women and children are in myth? Each of us has treasures and secrets, known and unknown, which we hold dear and sacred, mirroring them in some ideal wherein we wish to share. When at times things cannot be said bluntly they can be spoken robed in the language of myth. A common language of the human species is that of the wide variety of love relationships. It speaks the language of dearness, treasure and surprise, relating them to a perfection beyond. Its very dearness and vulnerability face to face with the mediocre and the commonplace leads us to keep our love language private as if not of this world. No one should cast a net over our treasures.

This affective and receptive disposition in us—the attitude of confession— is simultaneous and concomitant with another attitude: the rational critical thought. The latter must of necessity turn to the former — to myth therefore— to understand the human thrust. Love of the ratio already is confession and affection.

Should we be brave enough, take a shortcut and at once admit myths to be gems, the glitter of the luxury of creational surplus? Totality and wholeness are from the point of view of the Universe its property. For us mortals they are, if we succeed in gathering them, precisely that: a luxury.

The Universe's very order and harmony is called *Rta* in Indian thought. Under the tutelage of myth itself we cannot disturb that thought's stylistic sequence without destroying it. A frequent error is the effort to divest the myth of its miraculous and supposedly "fanciful" and "poetic" elements. It is precisely in these marvels that the deepest truths of myth inhere. The marvels *are* the myth and they are not being questioned.

"The myth is transparent like the light and the mythical story — mythologoumenon

— is only the form, the garment in which the myth happens to be expressed, enwrapped, illumined."[47]

Under the light of myth itself we catch a glimpse of *that* crack between darkness and light through which an order or reality appears entirely different from that of mere rational critical syllogism and debate. If, for example, in one lovely mythical instance in Indian thought, "the lotus provides a ground, the earth, as a means of our support (*pratiṣṭhā*) in the midst of the boundless waters of the possibilities of existence"[48] we would lose that very support by rationalizing the lotus and merely see its frail delicacy. Standing on that lotus we would indeed forthwith sink with it.

The moment between darkness and light—the myth—reveals how people think differently of the world in different places. They have different customs, different gods and different post-mortem fates. People's presuppositions differ. What is amazing is that people do not want the moment between dark and light to be screened off. They cannot be fooled by those whose task it is to repeat, enforce and elucidate mere clichés, shut up from within and hence merely announcing "chaos" rather than harmony. Where reality must, at all cost, be patterned by assumed authority, not emergent from life as it is read on the universe, people sooner or later resist. They fear the terror of the wasteland, meaninglessness.[49]

47. R. Panikkar, *Myth, Faith and Hermeneutics, Cross-Cultural Studies*, Asian Trading Corporation, Bangalore, 1983, p. 4. We shall later see how the mythologoumenon as symbol cannot be appropriated by a particular history without becoming decadent. It must remain a "luxury". Once symbols are appropriated by a limited quantity, they loose their meaning. Thus, for example, we should find a way, with regard to the present arms race, to convince nations that no nation can be "the most powerful" one. The weapon as symbol, amassed in quantity, destroys the notion of power.

48. *Sāyana* on *RV*. 6.16.3: (*agni puṣkarat*): *puṣkara-parṇyāsa svargajagaddhārakatva*.

49. A striking contemporary example would be the reaction of the Njemps, Tugen and Pokot peoples in Kenya, Africa. They reacted in stupefaction and moral anguish — but to no avail — to the intrusion of Western and local government patronized ore-mining industry in their pastoral grounds in the semi-arid area of Baringo. Even the building of a road caused them anguish. They asked me to explain why the intruders offered no sacrifice or at least an apology before digging like wild beasts into the earth which, in Baringolanguage, is called, "the skin of God". See: F. Baartmans, *Tradition and Transition in Black Africa's tribal and family-systems. A quest for human well-being round Lake Baringo, Kenya*", unpublished "doctoraal-scriptie" for the University of Nijmegen, The Netherlands, May 1977. Who is not aware of similar contemporary wastelands being created e.g. among the Latin American Indians by modern industry and mercantilist-minded intrepreneurs in the name of "progress" and gain. Merely to repeat, enforce, and elucidate clichés is the property of those usurping power over the universe whether it be in traditional mythical societies or modern mythical secular societies. Authority for its own sake destroys its complementary symbol, that of service and solidarity. When speaking of the Wasteland of Europe at the turn of the century, Nietzsche writes a shattering criticism with regard to his own land but also implying other Western countries. I quote from Joseph Campbell, *Creative Mythology, The Masks of God*, Penguin Books, reprint, 1982, p. 373f, who introduces Nietzsche's writing by saying that the Wasteland is "where there is no poet's eye to see, no adventure to be lived, where all is set for all and forever: Utopia! It is the land where poets languish and priestly spirits thrive and this blight of the soul extends today from the cathedral close to the university campus." "Nietzsche", he writes, "made the point almost a century ago: "Here and there I come in touch with German universities (Nietzsche wrote in his Twilight of the Idols, 1888): what an atmosphere prevails among the scholars, what a spiritual desert, how lukewarm and complacent! It would be a profound misunderstanding to bring up German science against me on this point—and a proof, besides, that not a single word I have written had been read. For I have been calling attention for the past seventeen years, untiringly, to the *despiritualizing* (F.N.) influence of our present day science industry. The hard helotism to which the prodigious range of the contemporary sciences condemns every individual scholar is the main reason why the fuller, richer, more *profoundly* (F.N.) endowed of our students can no longer find appropriate education

The various continents, the furrows left by the chariot's wheels when *Priyavrata* travelled seven times round the earth, have each, in the midst of the oceans, their own peculiar luxury adding up to the most exquisite mixture of juices imaginable. While each has its own flavour together they make up the most nectarine of Waters, viz., the whole of the universe.

"The seven islands are *Jāmbudvīpa*, *Plaksadvīpa*, *Śālmalidvīpa*, *Kuśadvīpa*, *Krauñcaddvīpa*, *Śākadvīpa*, and *Puṣkaradvīpa*. Each of these islands is surrounded by the sea. The sea that surrounds *Jāmbudvīpa* is the *Lavaṇasea*, the salt sea, the *Plaksadvīpa* is surrounded by the sea of sugarcane-juice, *Śālmalidvīpa* by the sea of liquor, *Kuśadvīpa* by the sea of clarified butter, *Krauñcadvīpa* by the sea of curd, *Śākadvīpa* by the sea of milk and *Puskaradvīpa* by the sea of pure water. In the centre of all lies the *Jāmbudvīpa* and in the centre of this island is standing the golden mountain *Meru*".[50]

The mythical worldview of universal plenitude, made up of manifested fragmentation, cannot be caught in a net of rational, critical logic or merely utilitarian greed, *bhogin*. That would belie the treasures of gathered *significance* of the universe in mankind's cultural memory. It would mean, in the Indian aesthetic vocabulary *viruddhatva*, incongruity, the reverse of concordance and the sense of surprise, *sādhāraṇya*.

From the universe's point of view the myth is the universe's own single totality and reality. From man's end the myth-narration reveals a plurality of form and thought through divergent cultures and traditions. Together they are the *one* totality of perfection of all that the universe has to say. Hence, mythical consciousness does not lay claim to the full totality in a particularized narration of the cosmic perfection. What is perhaps more important to realize is the invalidity of a denial of another man's or another culture's mythical effort to try and recapture cosmic wholeness. The on-going myth-formation, that is, the speculation within the mythical view, keeps giving rise to new surprise and wonder. Whereas the universe itself is its own tranquil fullness, the tellings and doings about it by man display a bustling activity.

Man's many-sided consciousness is the inescapable reality for philosophy. It is for the philosopher to make room among the groundrules of his word game for both the bubble of wondering surprise and the statement of critical rational thought. Both are part of the revelation of the whole of reality. Where the language of receptivity, suspense and surprise would not be able to get a word in edgeways, the reality which man believes that he thinks is true, would be done injustice to. Belief in dearness and the sacred has its own mode of reality. Being part of the mythical narrative, they make

or *educators* (F.N.). There is nothing from which this culture suffers more than from superabundance of pretentious corner-watchers and fragments of humanity; and the universities, *against* (F.N.) their will are the real hot houses of this kind of stunting of the spiritual instincts. All of Europe has already a realization of this; no one is fooled by our high politics. Germany is regarded, more and more, as Europe's Flatland." (Friedrich Nietzsche, "Gotzen-Dämmerung", *Werke*, Leipzig: Alfred Kroner Verlag, 1919, vol. 8, pp. 110-111.) Campbell comments: "the only correction I can find needed for a translation of this murderous criticism to our own mid-twentieth century would be a change of the word "against" to "with all". . . There is no time, no place, no permission — let alone encouragement for *experience* (J.C.).

50. *VP. Aṁśa* 2, ch. 2: in: Vettam Mani, *Purāṇic Encyclopaedia*, p. 690. Mount *Meru*, the centre of Indian mythical reality where *Śiva* resides, will be discussed in the following paragraph. See also Part III on the symbol of *Āpaḥ*, passim.

the myth primarily a deposit of spirit. Faced with "pure reason" it would not be overcome. It would rather keep silent.

Athens, Jerusalem, and Mount *Kailāśa*

The re-enactment of the perfection of the beginnings in myth-narrative and cult is celebrated at a level of man's consciousness *other* than that of his rational-critical awareness. What does that imply with regard to philosophy? I suspended that question.[51] We shall now take it up with a view to the problem of analysis of myth, presented in the following chapter.[52] While discussing the nature of myth, we now slowly approach our actual encounter with a particular mythical world view, the Indian one. We ought to prepare ourselves to meet personally the Indian mythical situation and condition of man.

To understand the problem of analysis of myth, we must consider some essential preliminaries. We are not yet seeking a philosophy of myth.[53] We shall, for the present, first be looking for a "place" where it remains possible to permit the mythical consciousness to speak without destroying it by rational-critical argument. This does not at all mean that we should neglect, let alone despise, the value of such thought and ignore the realm and the right of the "logos". To allow myth to speak means that man cannot be reduced to mere "logos", the rationally-critically reasoned word, nor can his awareness be shortened to mere rational reflexive consciousness. In the words of Paul Ricoeur:

> "Myth is already logos, but it still has to be taken up into *philosophic* (P.R.) discourse. . . . The philosopher adopts provisionally the motivations and intentions of the believing soul. He does not "feel" them in their first naivete, he "re-feels" them in a neutralized mode, in the mode of "as if."[54]

First, then, there *are* myths; we encounter them, we find them. People simply know the difference between fables, fairytales and myths. We should be prepared to admit that it will not be possible to try and answer the question "what is being?" without the knowledge that there are myths, and that there is ritual. A philosophy without presuppositions, therefore, is not possible. The reality as it is seen by the mythical consciousness ought to be taken up into the discourse if we are to be true to what we find. Our philosophic orientation receives from the start a limitation. An excellent maxim for any philosopher. With regard to myth, the question is: even if we *knew* them, do we *understand* them? Is it possible to understand my own and someone else's myth? The problem ultimately centres round the question whether an analysis of myth is at all possible without destroying it. Not only is each one's situation in the

51. If the myth has a protective, integrating role against the domination of "chaos" and meaninglessness, one cannot hold, as G. Gusdorf does in, *Mythe et Metaphysique*, Paris, 1953, that it is "the spontaneous form of being in the world". An overestimation of the mythical consciousness comes from the forgetfulness of the distance between *experienced conciliation* and *aimed-at re-conciliation*. It would be difficult to understand how the mythical consciousness, if it were the spontaneous form of being in the world, would give itself up to a different form of consciousness, often in opposition to what is understood by mythical consciousness.
52. See Part I.3: "Analysis of myth-Problem and Method".
53. A phenomenology of myth by means of the confessions of receptivity and that of the sacred will be presented later in this chapter.
54. Paul Ricoeur, *The Symbolism of Evil*, tr. Emerson Buchanan, Beaconpress, Boston, 1969, p. 19.

universe limited, also the cultural origin of the philosophical question itself is limited. This fact deserves emphasis. Analysis of myth has been drawn into the history of philosophy ever since philosophy encountered the mythical consciousness at the dawn of the origin of the human race. Myth and philosophy are simultaneous and contemporaneous.

Here I shall occupy myself with a particular segment of that history. I limit myself to the analysis of myth since the onset of Western colonial expansion. By doing so, I also draw myself, a Westerner, more personally into the discussion. Colonial expansion by the West began at an early stage with the crusades against Islam in the European Middle Ages and the first voyages of discovery of lands. What, for the West, became a quantitative increase of the knowledge of peoples had its repercussions also on philosophy. Avoiding details, it may be said that analysis of myth was more or less appropriated and inspired by the so-called enlightened and modern European mind in search of a new humanism during and after the Western Renaissance.[55]

Europe's philosophy, like any philosophy, is situated. It is Greek by birth. I am not yet speaking of Europe's outlook, a discussion on which would be incomplete without considering the presence of Christianity on its soil. It may be said, however, that the European mind has its philosophic and cultural memory in the Greek "Logos"[56] Heraclitus was the first, in the European philosophical memory, to propose his Greek "logos" as a principle of purifying gods and as the agent of grasping reality.[57] Cassirer writes:

> "At first sight the concept of the logos as it first appears in Greek speculation seems closely related to the mythical view of the dignity and omnipotence of the heavenly word. For here too the word is eternal and imperishable; here too the unity and permanence of reality are built upon the unity and understructability of the word. For Heraclitus the lögus is "the helmsman of the cosmos". Like the cosmos which it governs it was created by god and no man, but always was and always will be. Yet, though Heraclitus still speaks the language of myth, an entirely new tone is discernible within it. For the first time the mythical view of the cosmic process is clearly and consciously confronted by the fundamental philosophical speculative idea that the universe is subordinate to a unified and indivisible law."[58]

In Greece the doubt, the "why?" caused a crisis between the gods and man. "The sun will not transgress his measures: otherwise the Furies, ministers of justice, will find him out", proclaimed Heraclitus.[59]

55. Mircea Eliade, *The Quest, History and Meaning in Religion*, The University of Chicago Press, 1969, pp. I-II.
56. See Ernst Cassirer, *The Philosophy of Symbolic Forms*, 3 Vols. tr. Ralph Manheim, New Haven and London, reprint, 1977, Vol. 2, *Mythical Thought*, preface and introduction where Cassirer takes this fact for granted. See also: Paul Ricoeur, *The Symbolism of Evil*, p. 211 - 231.
57. Jan de Vries, *Forschungsgeschichte der Mythologie*, p. 5: De Vries is of opinion that Heraclitus' "logos" may be translated as "Worldmind" - "Weltvernunft".
58. Ernst Cassirer, *The Philosophy of Symbolic Forms*, Vol. I, *Language*, p. 119.
59. Heraclitus, Fragment 94, in: H. Diels, *Die Fragmente der Vorsokratiker*, tr. Kathleen Freeman in Ancilla to the Pre-Socratic Philosophers, Cambridge, Harvard Univ. Press, 1948. Later in this

The second important limiting situation of the European mind, influencing and shaping its philosophic and cultural memory, is the "historical revelation" of the Hebrew god Jahweh and the equally stressed "historical revelation" of the Redeemer Jesus Christ in the Christian tradition.

A third philosophical location of the European memory is the general belief in scientific rational thought, engendered in Europe's first Renaissance. This location immensely influenced the European understanding of man and reality.[60] Other customs, gods, presuppositions and worldviews came under severe criticism by the West, once it hit upon them by its colonial expansion.

Both the Greek question "ti tō ōn?"-"what is being?"-and the Hebrew-Jewish and later Christian historical revelation of The Highest Being would have contained nothing exceptional among all other cultural memories in the world of human cultures when seen by some imaginary eye outside the universe. What, in the history of human cultures, known and experienced by man himself *in* the world, became a new and impressive cultural memory among all other already existing memories (e.g. the Sumerian, the Akkadian, the Zoroastrian, the Buddhist, the Vedic-Hindu, the Aztecs and the then completely unknown but surely existing memories in Africa) was the encounter and intersection of the Greek memory and that of the Hebrew-Jewish and later Christian memory on European soil. European existence and its whole cultural physiology finds its first and deepest layer in this encounter. All its presuppositions stem from it. All its doubts, ecstasies, modes of thought, forms of art, poetry, its life of myths, economic, political, social and religious inspiration have their root in that encounter. It is Europe's undeniable identity, its very existence and point of reference. The pre-Greek and the pre-Christian mythical consciousness of Europe was either absorbed or rejected by the newly arisen spirit or they eroded by themselves, unable to serve any longer as pointers. We cannot stray too far and we must limit ourselves to Europe's situational philosophical locus with regard to the problem of analysis of myth.

The history of European consciousness, textured by the intersection between Athens and Jerusalem and subsequently grounded in the scientific rational approach when the European Middle Ages came to an end, can now be typified for our purpose by attributing to it two elements relevant to our discussion. These elements are the *deflation* of the sacred by the Greek proclamation of human excellence symbolized by Mount Olympus and the *inflation* of facticity as the only kind of history inspired by the historical revelation of the Saviour Jesus and his historical death on Mount Calvary in Jerusalem.[61] The stress on history as *fact* must be linked to the impact of the scientific-rational approach since the beginning of the sixteenth century.

Official European scientific and Christian culture came to deny all other myths except its own newly found one: the myth of believed factual history as the only kind

---

chapter I shall return to this crisis with regard to Prometheus.

60. In quick succession very significant and totally revolutionary discoveries and visions saw the daylight. Copernicus (1473-1543), Galileo (1564-1642): the discovery of the heliocentric universe. Descartes (1591-1650) and Newton (1642-1727): the marriage between scientific discovery and rational critical thought.

61. I shall elaborate on these topics when dealing with some specific elements of the Greek mythical consciousness at the end of the following chapter.

of history, history as the incontestability of facts.[62] Post-colonial non-Western scholars now not infrequently begin to criticize the Western view on history. Panikkar writes:

> "History is the landmark to which (the West) refers to incontestability of facts and in terms of which it criticizes other myths. For Western man historical facts are the hard and inescapable reality."[63]

Cultures with memories other than the European look upon historical facts rather as mere events that have not yet reached their full maturity.[64] This is an embarrassing thought to the modern Western mind. Other and different cultural memories exist contemporaneously with that of the West till today. One of the striking differences between Western man and people of other cultures is western man's contention that sacred history would not be needed by him to know his whole history. He appears to dispense with it. Hence the West's attitude of grave suspicion, also of myth and its awareness. Thereby the West looses some of its "cosmological moment". However, as I observed earlier, myth and ritual continue to live and are visible to the trained eye in many European instances. For example, in the slogans and codes of arms of movements, universities and colleges. Later I shall have occasion to refer to the new conceptual framework of ecological thought and that of the modern peace movements which clearly show the mythical drive. Perhaps it will depend on scholars of the new nations, more than on those of the West, to show that the Western peoples are no longer the only ones to "make history". With myth's presence "history cannot be limited to empirical and utilitarian language".[65]

---

62. See W.T. Stevenson, *History as Myth*, New York: Seabury Press, 1969, and his article: "History and Myth: Some Implications for History and Theology", Cross Currents (Winter, 1970) XX I; 15-28. Here we find an example of the flourishing of this idea in the West.
63. R. Panikkar, *Myth, Faith and Hermeneutics*, p. 99. Over the past decades efforts to counteract the historicist-view have been made in the West itself. Mention should be made here of Christopher Dawson, Arnold Toynbee and Oswald Spengler who attempt a philosophy of history seeking to interpret it in a total context and sometimes even use language of "muthos". Spengler in his, *Decline of the West*, tr. Charles Francis Atkinson, vol. 2, p. 55, writes, referring to "destiny-making readiness for life": "What a wealth there is (in history) of psychology, in all the seeking, resisting, choosing and interpreting, misunderstanding, penetrating and revering—not only as between cultures in immediate contact with each other, whether in mutual admiration or in strife, but also as between a living culture and the world of forms of one dead, whose remains still stand visible on the landscape! And how poor and thin are the conceptions, then, that historians bring to all this with such verbal formulae as "influence", "continuity" and "effect". Such labeling is merely nineteenth century. What is sought is merely a chain of cause and effects".
64. Panikkar in op. cit., p. 100 refers to assertions made by Levi Strauss in his *La Pensée sauvage*, 1962: "... dans le système de Sartre, l'histoire joue tres précisement le role du mythe" (p. 336). "Peut-être cet age d'or de la conscience historique est-il déja revolu" (p. 337). . . and he makes note of "une sorte de cannibalisme intellectuel de la 'raison historique', see notes p. 173. In the field of the history of religions Pettazoni deserves mention for his attempt at an all-encompassing historico-religious interpretation.
65. Mircea Eliade, *The Quest*, p. 2. Panikkar in op. cit., p. 39 says "The so-called Renaissance neither introduced nor re-introduced myth to the European world; it only provoked a more or less rational reflection on it. Thus that hybrid and even selfcontradictory science of mythology was born. In fact, as soon as one approaches mythos with the instrument of the logos, myth can only disappear just as darkness is no longer darkness after light penetrates." The comparison is well chosen. In myth there is an element of enigma and obscurity which is part of an intuition of reality not to be further broken up and explained but rather to be taken as such or believed. The scientific temper is highly prosaic, even antimythical, and it is only during the past hundred years that we have become interested in probing into the nature of myth. This is, for the involved student of myth easy to

A true analysis of myth cannot but deal with the central values in the culture of the participants. One may ask if such an exercise would not require more than just academics. Objectivity of science, does it have, with a view to mythical consciousness, an opinion and a situation? Objectivity cannot equalize cultures except by neutralizing their values. Is it possible for "objectivity" to think what someone else thinks? Is it aware of the situation in which thoughts and feelings arise? Such questions should serve to put us on our guard when analysis of myth is concerned. When discussing the domination of life by rational critical thought and scientific empirical knowledge, Fritjof Capra writes:

> "The division between mind and matter led to a view of the universe as a mechanical system consisting of disparate objects, which in turn were reduced to fundamental material building-blocks whose properties and interactions were thought to completely determine all natural phenomena. This Cartesian view of nature was further extended to living organisms, which were regarded as machines constructed from separate parts. . . such a mechanistic conception of the world is still at the bases of most of our sciences and continues to have a tremendous influence on many aspects of our lives. It has led to the well-known fragmentation in our academic disciplines and government agencies and has served as a rationale for treating the natural environment as if it existed of separate parts, to be exploited by different interest groups."[66]

The Greek "logos", continuing to be a cultural force in the West, can rightfully boast astonishing results. It will nevertheless remain unequal to the concrete universality of "value" as long as no serious encounter brings the West into the field of other cultures' experience. This encounter has not yet really taken place. Over the past four centuries the West's efforts to extend its cultural physiology has been, and still is, limited to more or less individual efforts of some men and women and groups.[67] But they have remained episodic for the West's culture as a whole. African, Asian and Latin American "memories" are unknown to most Westerns. From the point of view of the West's economic influence and domination, this disparity can be most harmful to the value systems of other civilizations. One could well ask whether the average highpowered business executives have any idea what situation of culture they travel to if it is not a particular place merely defined in terms of economic profit and loss. The *other* of philosophy in different cultures is unknown to most Westerners.[68]

---

understand. Rational-scientific thought is not everything of man. Presentday education-policies in the West do not yet seem to aim at extending the cultural memory of students by drawing attention to what has become increasingly known about cultures and philosophies other than the West's. Policies keep being directed at a utilitarian outlook without, for example, paying attention to the cultures of former colonized people who now live in the West, It is all too easily said that they must "adapt". On the global scale much misunderstanding with regard to the so-called North-South dialogue may be attributed to cultural negligence regarding rightful demands.

66. Fritjof Capra, *The Turningpoint, Science, Society and the Rising Culture*, Fontana Paperbacks, 1982, p. 21.
67. Paul Ricoeur, *The Symbolism of Evil*, p. 23 who observes that we, unless there is a real encounter, cannot imagine what that is to mean for the categories of Western ontology and for the reading of the pre-Socratics, Greek tragedy, and the Bible.
68. The Western colonization period, which in the eyes of many new nations is far from bygone, has extended its cultural memory from the point of view of mainly the economic aspect. Mercantilism,

We must now return to the problem of analysis of myth and the mythical consciousness from the cross-cultural perspective. In the third chapter I attempt a method of analysis which would seem to be a round-about one. For, unless I seek and cultivate my own myth of the *possibility* of trans-syllogistic human communication, I cannot possibly even begin to understand someone else's myth. Hence, more than mere academic exercise is needed. As I shall explain later in the method of analysis which I have proposed, something not very far from love is needed. I must know, try and feel and be prepared to be told where my principle of orientation becomes a principle of limitation. If the mounts which have shaped my European cultural memory—Mount Olympus and Mount Calvary—have for me and also other Europeans become the central axles, through and round which my cultural being has been patterned, then I should presuppose, on the grounds that there is only one species of humanity, that other and different "world-centres" will probably be there. I must leave my own centre — I cannot forget it, and I ought not to — and venture into the unknown, hoping to find something similar to what I know to be the axis of my own European cultural memory.

Thus it is that India reveals to me Mount *Kailāśa* where *Śiva* lies in eternal embrace with *Pārvatī*, the daughter of *Parvata*, the mountain. It seems an antithetic image of *Śiva Sthānu*, the motionless, the one beyond all flux, *Śiva Jīmūtaketu*, the one far away from man's doings, "having a cloud as his banner."[69] But *Pārvatī* is *Prakṛti*, the eternal female half of the all-encompassing essence. The eternal embrace is the image of eternal inherent cosmic satisfaction, *nivṛtti*, which, on the level of myth, would not result in procreation unless activated, *pravṛtti*.[70]

A source of neo-formation in my culturally limited situation must come then from a modification of the "distance" between my European source and the Indian source. I shall try and bridge the distance between these two sources by placing myself near the womb of the Indian Word, *Vāc*. I shall try and hear "the whole end of the Voice" (*kṛtsnam vāgārtham*). That Voice has been a revelation of the meaningfulness of being *(padārthā-bhinaya)* for innumerable people in India since time immemorial. Simultaneously I also accept the invitation to stand in the midst of the elements. The world and its elements are the first manifestation, the primordial revelation to man. It is not individual things that first stir his imagination. Indeed, the division between matter and spirit may be said to be artificially drawn and that only for practical purposes. The elements are symbols communicating the ultimate constituents of reality.

---

along with commercialization, industrialization and use of technology, has always been written large in the Western banner. Presentday theories of so-called development could often be subjected to severe criticism when it comes to defining the gain obtained by whom. Capra writes in, *The turningpoint*, p. 22: "Our (Western) culture takes pride in being scientific; our time is referred to as the Scientific Age. It is dominated by rational thought, and scientific knowledge is often considered the only acceptable kind of knowledge".

69. *VmP*. 1. 11-30. In the second and third part of the book we will often turn to Mount *Kailāśa*, in Indian mythical thought also called Mount *Meru* or Mount *Parvata*.

70. Mount *Kailāśa*, a shimmering mountain of twenty thousand feet, lies beyond the high Himalayas in the vast reaches of the Tibetan plateau. As such it seems less a place than a state of mind, constellated with the dreams and aspirations of millions of pilgrims who shall never make the journey except in their hearts. In some of the ancient writings — Hindu, Buddhist, even Chinese and Tibetan — *Kailāśa* is also the home of *Gaṅgā*, flowing from its slope, dividing into four streams and gracing the world of men. Near the foot of *Kailāśa* lies *Mānassarovar*, the Lake of the Mind, another supposed source of the *Gaṅgā*.

Vāc and _Vaikhāri_: The Word and Human Speech

The poet-sage of Vedic times, wakeful before the sun arrives, felt himself alone at times among those on earth.

> "He was born here together with many; they were found sleeping when the Eastern hemisphere was opened. . ."[71] And he said:
> "That Sacred Word which was first born in the East the Seer has revealed for the shining horizon. He discloses its varied aspects, high and low, the womb of both the existent and the non-existent."[72]

In each of us there is an East: a horizon, an orient which we may never reach, a dimension of hope, a dimension of transcendence, the path of life ahead which, instead of hope and fulfilment, may also turn the day as though visited by divinities of a furious kind, into an ordeal of the dark, brutal and implacable aspects of nature and that of human nature. But each sunrise is meant to be a further completion of each man, woman and child and all there is in the world. Both the burden and the ease at the end of our day are said in words behind words. Words which are not connected by elements of only linguistic and synthetical form. Burden and ease are not explained by concepts inspired by exclusively rational curiosity. The best things — even when they are bad — cannot be easily told. The effusion of unbounded force that Life is, makes words fall short of communication unless they are infused by the strength of that selfsame Life-force.

Early Vedic man has left us with a priceless heritage of a science of linguistics which has held him to what is "East" in man. It is the opening up of visions and perspectives outlining the contours of creation. Likewise, Vedic man discovered the "West" in human existence when the values we have gathered shape themselves into mature concreteness of what reality is and man in it.

Is there something which does not come from man as involution or development but which falls upon him as a revolution, a surprise? Is man not primarily a spoken rather than a speaking reality? A spoken rather than a speaking word, a receiver rather than a giver, a creature rather than a creator?

Once, so we are told in the *Śatapatha Brāhmaṇa*, there was a dispute between the spirit and the word as to who was the greater. Both equally claimed supremacy. Unable to settle the dispute, they approached *Prajāpati* for a solution. He spoke in favour of the spirit, saying to the word:

> "The spirit is certainly better, because you only imitate and follow what the spirit is doing; and he who is imitating and following what another does is undoubtedly inferior."[73]

The ground rules of our philosophic word-games may, at times, have little to do with the native sense and active life-force of the spirit circulating from the East to the West and from the West to the East in the daily experiences of men, women and children. Who can exactly pinpoint what is in man? Whether in Europe, the Near East or the

71. *AV*. 4.6.
72. *AV*. 4.1.
73. *SB*. 1.4.5.8. - 11.

Far East, some have always doubted whether philosophy or, for that matter, theology, would ever be able to initiate, to cut, or even force, a passage to the spirit by the purely cerebral discourse. In the seventeenth century the theory of Epicurus of "natural sounds" underwent a renewal. Especially Giambattista Vico (1668-1744) presented words and language as an expression of emotion within the realm of a general metaphysic of the spirit. Vico attacked the notion of human nature as stereotype, invariant from age to age, and the idea of language as a mere perpetual convention. Radical divergence of outlook in the human being also brings about a spirit-inspired word. In fact, holds Vico, language can only be critically grasped by a critical interpretation of cultural phenomena.[74] George Hamann followed his master Vico by declaring that revelation of reality happens through symbolic metaphysic and a symbolic view of history where poetry is regarded as the mothertongue of the human race. Not as something to be replaced by a "better" language but as an autonomous human expression of reality and truth.[75] The Vedic way of speaking kept close to intuition and feeling, underlying the expressive and participating human word.

In the Western discussion on language, contemporary philosophers keep insisting on what they claim must be language's necessary feature of facticity. Bertrand Russell summarized his and Ludwig Wittgenstein's idea of language in one sentence:

"The essential business of language is to assert or deny facts."[76]

This tombstone spirit appears to me a far cry from a more usual business of language. Is language not there to motivate action and, to this end, to excite fear, rage, desire, love, laughter, smiles and tears, to indoctrinate, intimidate, brainwash, console, strengthen and praise and so on? To merely assert or to deny just facts seems the very last thing language has ever been used for. Of course language states facts, everything may be called a fact, even an un-fact is a fact. For the positivist all the other business of language I mentioned is "emotive" and hence "nonsensical". But then, the fervour with which Russell defends his vision is emotive too!

No more wording about words! The primordial principle at the origin of everything in the Indian vision, we shall now see.

***Vāco Bhāgam*: Sharing in the womb of the Word**

Vāc, the Word, so the Vedic poet-sage says, is not affected by *Prajāpati's* decision in favour of the Spirit. For the Spirit is the Creator Himself, *Prajāpati*, and how can He be without Her, *Vāc*? She is the "womb of the universe", *Vāgvisarga*. She is, says the *ṚgVeda*:

"The Word, measured in four quarters,
The Wise who possess insight know these four divisions.
Three quarters, concealed in secret,
cause no movement,
The fourth is the quarter spoken by men."[77]

---

74. Ernst Cassirer, *The Philosophy of Symbolic Forms*, vol. 2, *Language*, p. 149 - 150.
75. Ernst Cassirer. op. cit., ibidem.
76. Bertrand Russell, "Introduction" to Ludwig Wittgenstein, *Tractatus Logico-Philosophicus*, tr. D.F. Pears and B.F. McGuinness, Routledge and Kegan Paul, New York: The Humanities Press, 1961, p. X.
77. *RV*. 1.164.15. "*Vāgvisarga*": see *AB*. 2.38; 10.6.

The fourth quarter, then, *vaikhāri*, is the immediate medium through which we make our days' and nights' experiences resound: it is the precariousness of words, their lucidity and invigoration but also their clumsiness and unwieldiness. Words are a risk. "To know that when men say "no", *neti*, the gods may say "yes", *om iti*, and the other way round.[78] And so men do among themselves. So that, when the conflict becomes too serious, we may prefer to keep silent. For we know that our speech, bound by "yes" and "no" or by "either-or", does not always convey in full depth the "indestructible syllable" of our experiences, the *akṣara*. That "indestructible syllable" through which things of experience can really be explained and worded, lies above man, in the secrecy and stillness of the three quarters of the Word beyond.

The Word is not a possession to be manipulated at will. On the contrary, one can only speak meaningfully when one is constantly attentive, aware, and possesses "quickness of mind", that is, when one is endowed with *manojeveṣu*, quick intuitions. People differ in this respect:

> "Friends, though endowed alike with sight and hearing may yet in quickness of mind be quite unequal. Some are like ponds that reach to mouth and shoulder while others resemble lakes deep enough for bathing."[79]

The four quarters of the Word are parallel to the divisions of *Puruṣa*, the primordial Man. Together, all divisions of *Puruṣa* and all divisions of the Word, each equally having four parts, make up that what is said in the whole of the universe.[80] When we utter the right words, we utter the universe, we help it being created.

The fourth quarter, *vaikhāri,* the words of man's daily life, receives a touch of mystery — which the Vedic seer knew to be there — when we think that the word for "quarter" — *pada* — originally meant "footprint". It is the Vedic technical term to designate the fourth part of a *mantra.*[81] A *mantra* is a "thought instrument": representation of some deity through basic sounds, a sacred evocation or incantation. Man is, in his speech, not alone. It would be a fatal illusion of man to think that he can boss over his speech when he wishes to define and name things and situations. The idea of *pada* is a consolation. Man has no worry to think that he is bound hand and foot to the arguments, a-priori's and categories that other men have written over the face of nature.[82] What the Zen master says: "Show

---

78. *AB.* 2.2.
79. *RV.* 10.71.7.
80. For "*Puruṣa*" see Part II:5:4(vi): "In praise of man's Origin: *Puruṣa Sūkta*".
81. See Panikkar, *The Vedic Experience,* p. 103, note 45.
82. Sigmund Freud has described as a process of introjection the psychological mechanism by which, in infancy, parental commands are imprinted indelibly on the motivating centres of the will. The study of the Eastern way of thought has helped him thereby as it did his disciple, Carl Jung. The well-known comparative linguist Benjamin Lee Whorf has demonstrated through a number of detailed comparisons to what extent the language, learnt in infancy, determines not only the manner in which one's thoughts and feelings have to be expressed, but also the very patterns of those thoughts and feelings themselves. In the light of Freud and Whorf the categories according to which our experiences become conscious even to ourselves have been supplied to us by our society and are shared by everybody in it. The idea of a "collective faith" however must be seen together with the safeguarding of personal, private experience, falling within one's own circle. The really private experiences do not occur until the categories are dissolved; and then communication emerges that will not immediately drag the whole discourse — and one's life itself — into the accepted social patterns. Whorf is careful not to include into his "everyman's" formed language that of scientists

me the face you had before you were born" may also be: "Speak to me the Word you spoke before you were born".

Hence, in the joys and ecstasies we experience, in the solitude and vastness that befalls us as we move from morning to evening and again to morning, the *pada*, the footprint of *something* beyond us, is imprinted on the inside of our speech.

And now we might be struck by the thought that in the case of the *shared* language we speak with the three quarters above, *vāco bhāgam*, an immediate secret language of signs and symbols arises from which the rational-critical syllogism, if construed without awareness of the *pada*, the footprint, would be automatically excluded. Here we come into the realm of the language of myth and that of sacred language. In that genetic zone of intentional language we need not be worried any longer about human convention of how things ought to be said. The unconventionality of prophetic language in its widest sense, including that of the demonstrator who claims his human rights against obvious maltreatment, has its origin here. Likewise, it is here that manifestos with regard to ecology, the nuclear arms-race, women's movements etc. begin. They speak language unknown to the conventional speech of the powers that be.

The ascent, then, from our measured, limited language by means of the *pada* has, by Vedic man, been carefully termed. It is the ascent from *śabda*, limited, to *sphoṭa*, unlimited. This then is man's seemingly paradoxical and precarious situation: he enters from below into the universal Womb, The Word, *Vāc*.[83]

The ascent to the summit of believing the good sense of what we see and experience takes place via the gates of increasing secrecy and speechlessness, culminating in The Silence. In the quarter just above man, the middle quarter, *madhyama*, an increased flash of awareness of totality brings man to *paṣyanti*, the quarter of the illumined word in the close vicinity of *Vāc*, the womb of the universe. In the "seeing" word, which cannot but be creative, man's language and his moves change from possible sterility and conventionality to fecundity and originality. In his words, then, man discovers that he is more than he might have thought he was, down in *vaikhāri*, the language of habitual speech of daily life.

Man, when illumined in the womb of the word, begins to "eat other words" says the Indian tradition. These words will be different from those of the metabolism of a critical-rational argumentation.

Having thus far covered at least *some* of the "distance" between my Western cultural memory of the logos and the Indian reality of *Vāc*, the Womb-Word, I may be better equipped for a method of analysis of myth in order to personally meet the Hindu mythical view of the world.

---

and philosophers whose infancy language may have little to do with their theories. See: Benjamin Lee Whorf: "The Relation of Habitual Thought and Behaviour to Language", *Language, Culture and Personality*, Menasha, Wisconsin, 1941, pp. 75-93 in: "International Journal of American Languages", Vol. 16, no. 2 (April 1950).

83. Indian art portrays the womb of the universe showing the world goddess seated on her spouse who is underneath her in two aspects: one upward-turned uniting with her, the other turned-downward and away. The first is the consciousness of The Source, *yoni*, the Generative Womb. Here the world is consciously being created, the *Śiva-Śakti*. The other is called *Śava*, the "corpse" and is Consciousness transcendent, the highest portion of the Self, symbolized in the Silence. See: *MandU.* 5-6.

Conclusion

Myth and the mythical consciousness, then, pronounce a judgment of signification and meaning. They are capable of apprehending and evaluating reality. If, in the attempt to discover "being", empirical thought is essentially directed towards establishing unequivocal relation between *specific* cause and *specific* effect, mythical consciousness has a much more fluid and fluctuating character. Mythical thinking has a free selection of causes at its disposal.[84] Mythical thought distinguishes itself from a purely theoretical worldview not only by its concept of causality but also by its notion of the object. The content, no matter how commonplace, of the mythical consciousness emphasizes a specific ideal relation rather than a specific objective property. Its basic credential is that of the sacred. It is not limited to specific objects or clusters of objects. On the contrary, any content, however variable, can suddenly be summoned to participate.

Thus myth becomes a problem for the scientist and the philosopher of "pure reason" insofar as it expresses an original direction of the human spirit, an independent configuration of man's consciousness. Myth would seem to burst the bonds of philosophy as a "phenomenology of the spirit". I propose that we draw ourselves through this experience in the following chapter. Receptiveness will be the password. Anyone aiming at the comprehensive system of human culture has, of necessity, to turn to myth.

The following chapter aims at making ourselves available to some central features of mythical thinking. Perhaps we will have to get used to some of its ways. Suspicion of myth or antagonism or the wish to eliminate the miraculous would be of no help if we are to emerge from our exercise successfully. Our endeavour to understand and appreciate the mythical awareness will be often supported by what the Indian myths say. For it is these myths which have captured my imagination.

84. One reason for this could be said to be myth's Memory. It is a latent knowledge but does not "pose" as such nor does it make conspicuous claims to be recognized as such. This "fund" of knowing corresponds to the Indian *alayavijñāna*, a treasurehouse of discernment to be distinguished from all specific, singular discernments and identified with the *vijñāna-ghana* of the *Upaniṣads*. Memory is a recovering or re-experience, *pratynubhū* (*Prash. Up.* 4.5). It is evidently not the outer aesthetic self but an inner and immanent power, higher than that of the senses, that remembers or fore-knows with the kind of knowledge that is rather "prior" with respect to all empirical means of knowing than merely "being ahead" with respect to future events. That which remembers, or rather which is aware always of all things, must be a principle always present to, *anubhū*, all things and therefore itself unaffected by the duration of things. It is clear from the Indian way of thought that this Memory is the Self, co-existent and inexistent in all things as their-selves, ultimately being the true Self. In this sense liberation and omniscience are potentially inherent in our memory when we are aware of Memory.

Chapter 2

RECEPTIVE OF THE SACRED

Myths are no Allegories

If myths were allegories one would not be able to account for their persistence as meaningful for all times. Efforts to explain myths by reducing them to utterings trying to clarify phenomena of nature have been known from the earliest Greeks. Ernst Cassirer writes:

> "Thus, sharply as the mere *probability (E.C.)* of myth is distinguished from the truth of strict science, this very distinction creates a close methodological tie between the world of myth and that world which we call the empirical reality of phenomena, the reality of nature. Here the meaning of myth is quite beyond anything merely material: it is conceived as a specific *function* (*E.C.*)—necessary in its place—of man's way of knowing the world. Thus understood it could become a truly creative and formative force in the development of Plato's philosophy. This profound view, to be sure, was not always sustained in the subsequent course of Greek thought. The Stoics and Neoplatonists went back to the old speculative-allegorical interpretation of myths, and through them this method was handed down to the (Western) Middle Ages and Renaissance. . . As opposed to this objectivizing hypostasis of mythical figures in Neoplatonic speculation, modern philosophy has in this point turned more and more to man's subjectivity."[1]

Myth and its narrative, engendered by the awareness of the sacred, is a means of being emerging from man's search and yearning for totality. All human cultures, bundled together as a *whole*, show the single calling of man to re-integrate into cosmic awareness beyond him. Within man this calling is *aimed-at* and *intentioned*. In myth, therefore, man responds to his needs and to his status of a true inhabitant of the world, *kāṛayitu*, a true consumer, *bhogin*, and a true spectator, *draṣṭr*. That is not a negligible feat of myth. The expression by the mythical consciousness is directed to an end over and beyond the *fact* of expression. The surplus of the universe's significance is there "as such". And we take it for granted. It is our daily presupposition that, for example, the sun will appear and the earth will yield crops. Dare we say that the surplus is there as though patterned and preconceived, *dhyāta*, *nirmāta*? Should we not admit to the universe's surplus as its own inherent quality?

Lacking mere words to make the design speak, man uses constructs of image to aim at the universe's intelligible aspect, *sattva, jñana-rūpa*. It is the "lack" of the "clear word" which has made myth into a sitting duck: easy to attack, injure, even made a

1. Ernst Cassirer, *The Philosophy of Symbolic Forms*, vol 2: *Mythical Thought*, p. 3. See also: Jan de Vries, *Forschungsgeschichte der Mythologie*, pp. 128-134.

laughingstock of, a good target. It is not difficult to maltreat myth with the slingstone of the critical-rational word or the request for that word.

Making myth into an allegory—which may be considered as giving myth the benefit of the doubt—equally takes from myth the inherent truth of its own awareness. Allegories are already hermeneutic. What is primarily signified in an allegory—namely, its literal meaning—and what is signified secondarily, is symbolic but sufficiently external to be directly understood without leaving an enigma. But enigma is characteristic of myth.

An important function of myth is its embrace of mankind as a *whole* in one ideal history: that of totality and perfection. By means of a time which represents all times, man is manifested, in myth, as a concrete universal. Traditions condense this "man-being" into a type such as, for example, Adam or Marduk or, in India, *Puruṣa*. In the myth the human type is recapitulated and summed up.

Man's universality, manifested to himself through the myth, receives its concrete character from the *movement* introduced into human experience by saying something about it in the narration and by doing something about it in the ritual. It endowes human experience with an orientation, with quickening tension. Hence, more fundamentally, myth tries to get at the enigma of human existence and the human condition. These are ponderables for man. There is an experienced discordance between the fundamental reality of the prime beginning and the actual modality of man. It is, as I said earlier, the experience of not *being* the totality. Myth and ritual disclose the attempt at *some* restoration.[2]

An interesting illustration of this I witnessed among the little known contemporary society of the semi-nomad Kakus-Punan people in Sarawak, Malaysia, inhabiting the greater district of Bintulu. An analysis of the Punan prayers and rituals at the death of a member of their society, shows how the element earth, soil, symbolizes the lack of participation in the totality of things in those present round the deceased, now "spread out in the universe". The living get the truth literally rubbed in by being besmeared with mud and soil while the deceased, dressed up festively and strung to a ladder for all to see, is meticulously kept clean and hailed as "grown", "fulfilled".[3]

Myth and ritual have an ontological bearing. They punctuate the intersection of man's essential being and his historical being as "not so perfect". By a three-fold function of concrete universality, orientation in time and ontological opinion, myth and ritual reveal things only indirectly translatable.

It can now be guessed how far we are removed from giving to myth an allegorical interpretation. What an allegory shows can be said directly in a

2. "At *some* restoration": if myth is intimately linked with the experience of the sacred, the full experience of the sacred in mystical experience will give the mystic a sense of complete integration of totality. Such experiences have been known—and still are—in human cultures and religious practices.

3. F. Baartmans, "Kakus Punan Mud Healing Rites", *Sarawak Museum Journal*, Vol. XIV, Nos. 28-29 (New Series), reprint, 1966. The Punan word "mud" (pronounced like the English "mood") means "healing, restoration etc". Since I was the only one on the spot and little research on Punan-life had been done at that time, the responsibility for my findings would rest completely with me. My findings, however, were carefully scrutinized by the then curator of the Sarawak Museum, Mr. Tom Harrison.

face-to-face statement verifiable by history in the physical, economic, social, political or religious realm. An allegory "tries to secure a one-to-one fit between two areas of discourse" as I.T. Ramsey explains.[4] Once, through a distance of time, the allusions which used to provide a basis of interpretation of an allegory, are lost, the allegory may become unintelligible. The listener or reader may not be able to relate the signs to the significant personages and events in the allegory. What myth reveals is not transportable to any translation into clearer language. Myth is already clear by virtue of its own consciousness.[5] The myth does not, like the allegory, deal with objective events of history, political manoevres and economic disasters. Nor is the myth, like the allegory, "dropped" once the fulfilment of the translation to the analogous event has taken place. The allegory is also called a riddle. Until the major correspondences are given, the story is no more than an idle tale. To those who have not been initiated into the particular sign-language used, an allegory is no more than a puzzle. While the figures used in the allegory are appropriate representations, their inner meaning is an arbitrary one in the manner of mere sign. The esoteric signs of allegory are often used in the context of persecution and oppression. The authors are able to speak freely about such matters. The content, which otherwise might be regarded as seditious by the authorities, remains a secret.

Comprehension of myth is achieved only by letting it open up. Myths are not fulfilled like an allegory or a prophecy. Through the mythical awareness they are themselves fulfilment of understanding and revelation. While allegories are bound to the confusion of tongues and linked to a peculiar and particularized time and place, myths transcend these by their functions typified in their symbolic language. They are self-operative.

When making ourselves, in the following paragraphs, available to myth and its consciousness, we will of ourselves meet the symbol. Myth is embedded in the living experience of *aimed-at* totality. The beginnings, the perfection of Origin, we do not simply find; they are not simply given to us. The point of departure must be *reached*, it must be *won*. To achieve that, it is necessary for thought to inhabit the fullness of language. That, precisely, is the symbol. It may at times be a harassing backward flight of thought and more harassing still: the symbol does not allow for presuppositions.

The Confession of Receptivity: A First Phenomenology

To remind ourselves, we are in search of reality. How shall I now, with a view to myth and its consciousness, present the problem of human thought and reality?

---

4. In: Thomas Fawcett, *The Symbolic Language of Religion, An Introductory Study*, SCM Press Ltd., 1970, pp. 39-40: the author gives an example of an allegory by referring to the passage of the Biblical Ezechiel (17. 1-5) in the Jewish *Old Testament*: "A great eagle comes to Libanon, takes the young twigs from the top of the cedar and carries them to the city of merchants, takes the seed of the land and plants it to become a low spreading vine". Its translation: The king of Babylon comes to Jerusalem, takes its king and princes and deports them to Babylon, takes a royal prince and makes a treaty with him allowing Israel the role of a subject kingdom. Such an event actually happened in Jewish history but the allegory was not understood until the events "cleared" the allegory.
5. In the following paragraphs we shall see how myth is autonomous and immediate and means what it says. It has been especially Schelling who, when myth was much under fire in the West, has shown and defended this quality of the myth.

Cautiously, no doubt. For no one would wish to find himself immediately entangled in traditional ontological models of philosophy, characterized by the shift from subjective appropriation of the world to an objective dialectic. Having covered *some* stretch of the distance between the Greek logos and the Indian *Vāc*, it would be ill-advised to return on our path. We now have two "Words" to cherish. Both the "logos" and the *Vāc* are part of the totality of what is being spoken in the universe, be it by gods or by men. For the student of myth that possession is both an enrichment and a premonition of possible difficulties. We shall try and meet them as they come along.

Western ontological models have given rise to various disciplines as largely autonomous sciences. It would seem that the recent but as yet insufficiently assimilated shift of looking at the world in terms of relationships and integration, is casting doubt on the methodological approach of traditional ontology. The capacity for integration is a special feature of the approach from consciousness. That is not very evident in the approach through rational analysis. Though both proceed from *knowledge* to the *study* of reality, consciousness takes the thing in all its aspects, while rational analysis takes a particular aspect of the phenomenon apart and studies it in isolation. For rational analysis reality is an object of thought and speech existing by itself. It is to be examined as such and it should not be infused with the subjective impressions of the investigator. Various levels of thoughts should remain distinct. From the point of view of myth, that method of analysis leaves insufficient room for integration and entirety.

Indian metaphysics is until today guided by the *Mahāvākyāni*, the four great statements. These are at the helm of the Indian quest for an integral vision of reality. They show how the human mind, proceeding from one insight to another by means of four principal steps, arrives at an understanding of the meaningfulness of being. Hairsplitting argument among the various Indian metaphysical schools have not threatened the *Mahāvākyāni* as the magna carta of the Indian vision.[6]

In my presentation of the problem of human thought and reality with a view to myth and its consciousness, I try and avoid the seemingly apodictic character of ontological models with the help of the mythical mode. Not because we must at all cost rescue myth. That would mean its philosophical annulment. We have already established that myth has its own mode of looking at reality, its own configuration. Here I shall not be concerned with what myth thinks is reality. I rather wish to rouse delight in the sympathetic mode it displays when letting things happen to its consciousness. Myth shrinks from metaphysical combat. It simply *says* things. The question is: does the philosophical ear have the capacity or the wish to only listen?

I suggest that we now first intentionally disregard ontology—argumentative reasoning *about* being—and, instead, orientate ourselves backwards to what is *before* the rational discourse about being, namely, *experience*. Hence, we now first *condition* ourselves to thought rather than think that we already reflexively think. Because when we think about experience we no longer experience: we think.

6. The *Mahāvākyāni* are: *1. Prajñānam Brahmā*: *Brahman* is consciousness. See: *AU.* 3.5.3. *2. Ayam Ātmā Brahmā*: this *ātman* is *Brahman*. See: *BU.* 2.4.9. *MandU.* 2. *3. Aham Brahmāsmi*: I am *Brahman*. See: *BU.* 4.4.23. *4. Tat Tvam Asi.* That Art Thou. See: *CU.* 6.8.7; 9.4; 10.3. See: John B. Chethimattam, *Consciousness and Reality, An Indian Approach to Metaphysics*, Orbis Books, New York, first published Geoffrey Chapman, London, 1971, pp. 172-181.

My proposal is that we *remain* in sustained experience prior to systematized thought. Why? We must give ourselves time for an intuitive propulsion to extract a confession of receptivity from ourselves. That will enable us to transcend the world of valedictory speech—the realm of logos—when finding ourselves at the gates of perception.[7]

Must we then renounce all desire for rational critical thought when trying to understand reality? Of course not. What we are for the moment trying to seek is if there is a way of grasping reality which is *not primarily* dependent upon rational critical discourse only but which integrates spontaneously induced intuition.

If we attempt to shape our mind and heart together in rationally untranslated receptivity, we find ourselves in a state which may be equalled to the silence of expectation. What then happens is, with a view to the understanding of myth and its consciousness, important. We condition ourselves to the *irruption* of existence into consciousness rather than looking back on it through compartmentalized introduction by rational-critical thought.

The pattern of our thought in our now awakened consciousness by the *irruption* of existence into it, receives a particular character. We are, after our confession of receptivity and by our delight in the surprise of the Universe, now progressively passing *through* experience to its *expression*. What now happens is that our thoughts will not be the observer's model of control and prediction over the World but rather a *mood*. It is a mood of accommodating initiation into reality. The evil we experience will be painful drama. The good will be felt as a celebration.[8] Man and his god will be the centre, not the formula. It is this ritualization of reality which is conspicuous in the Vedic heritage. Be it the shining sun or old age, all things are said as if acted and celebrated in the midst of the effulgence of completion:

Homage to the Sun, the eye of Mitra and Varuṇa!
To the mighty God offer this worship.
To the far-seeing emblem, born of the gods,
Sing praise to the sun, the offspring of Heaven.
May this word of Truth guard me on all sides,
while earth and heaven and days endure.
To its rest goes all else that moves, but never
do the waters cease flowing or the sun rising.

"Just as an overloaded cart lumbers along creaking, in the same way the self in this body, loaded by the Self of wisdom, lumbers along creaking when its breath is

7. The confession of receptivity is an injunction on ourselves to harmonize mind and heart to welcome depositories of what the universe wishes to impress upon us. It can do so only if we willingly receive.

8. Mircea Eliade in, *The Quest*, p. 7 observes that "if the history of religions is to further the rise of a new humanism, it is incumbent on the historian of religions to bring out the autonomous value—the value as *spiritual creation*—of them" (*M.E.*) "To reduce them to socio-political contexts" he says, "is, in the last analysis, to admit that they are not sufficiently "elevated", sufficiently "noble", to be treated as creations of human genius like the Divina Commedia or the Fioretti of St. Francis of Assisi." It is easy for a man of books to ignore the active force of creative interpretation of the universe. The man of learning but perhaps of little living can be readily misled by the purely cerebral discourse of philosophy to assume that because the words of a construct are matched, the experiences to which they refer must be the same.

getting heavy. When he becomes reduced, whether by old age or disease, then, just as a mangofruit or a fig or a pipal fruit detaches itself from its stem, so this person, being released from his limbs, returns to Life to the place whence he has come."[9]

The receptive mood does not superimpose a hard and fast rule. It discovers a *design* which, so we feel in the confession of receptivity, could not have been drawn by what we perceive or what we could possibly have thought. The discovery of a design compells us towards acclamation and cheer rather than mere matter of fact acknowledgement. We need have no fear of disintegration or loss of personality when we emerge from our limited individual or group-memory or from contemporary history. One's "real" age will not be felt to have been reckoned only by the number of times one's eyes have seen the sun encircle the earth. One's age becomes that of the universe. The web of reality just discovered is not that of an individual's private property but a gift in which all men participate.

The ritualization of reality through the conscious passage of initiation into it emerges from a compulsion hardly definable by rational argumentation. It is rather the matrix of the discourse, the logos. It is what is called the mythos. Mythos is awareness of the horizon of intelligibility, the sense of it, behind the rationalized word. Finding words for it will destroy its immediate effects. The disclosure of it will simultaneously mean its enclosure in the rational-critical word.

The universal reverberation, conceived in and through the confession of receptivity, is expressed, in mythos, not by the concept but by the symbol. But symbol here is not a mere epistemic sign of a quantitative equation between subject and object to overcome the split between them. As an outward sign of an inward reality, the symbol here is not equation but interpretation of the peculiar mode of being of the very things we experience. The symbol is not another reality nor the thing as we may imagine it to be in a non-existent ideal realm. It is the thing as it really appears. To no perception and experience can be we attribute existence outside their symbolic form.

Thus the model of rationalized or statistical prediction regarding the world is, in the consciousness of confessed receptivity, from the outset ruled out. The metaphysics of a receptive consciousness is not a system. It is a way of life. It looks at manifested creation with surprise. It is not merely concerned with conditioned and quantitative experience, but with universal possibility. Symbols are both "worlds" and "gods" as levels of reference. Sparks which are neither places nor individuals but states of being realizable within man.

The symbol warns against forgetfulness that the appearance is only appearance. The symbol is not the symbolized. To mistake the symbol for the symbolized is, in Indian thought, ignorance (*avidyā*), confusing appearance with reality. Reality is *Brahman*. *Brahman* is invisible to the eye and inexpressible.[10] Man touches *Brahman* by intuition (*parā-vidyā*). That intuition is flashed by the symbol.

---

9. *RV*. 10.37.1-2: *śam no bhava cakṣusā*. and *BU*. 4.3.35-36. The ritualization of reality excludes the idea of man being the victim of blind cosmic forces nor is he a mere cog in the cosmic wheel. I shall presently refer to the Vedic symbol of the *çakra*, the cosmic wheel. Man is neither an absolute monarch nor a slave cursed with unbearable responsibility. See Part III:8: "*Karma*, the cosmic pilgrimage".
10. *BU*. 3.5.2: ". . .*na dṛṣṭer draṣṭāram paśyeḥ, na śruter śrotāram śṛṇuyāh, na mater mantāraṃ manvithāh, na vijñater vijñātaram vijñāniyāḥ, eṣa ta ātmā sarvāntarah*".

An elaborate discussion with regard to symbols cannot be expected here. The Indian vision of reality, however, gives us some basic ideas of what the symbol intends. That vision could hardly be comprehended without focusing the attention on the concept of *maya* which makes of the Indian vision a phenomenology of the symbol. To know reality does not mean lifting the veil and thus perceiving naked reality. We discover the real by realizing that the veil covers and conceals it. The discovery of that fact establishes revelation proper. The confessed state of surprise at manifested creation makes the disclosure of revelation happen. A rationalized statement would not satisfy our surprise. To reveal in this sense means "to reveal the veil". It is up to man— in the mood of receptivity—to "think" reality made manifest precisely by the veil covering it. We cannot separate the veil from the thing that is veiled. Our own attempt at its discovery is part of the revelation of reality.

The symbol is the punctuation of life as it "as such" comes to us through our confession of receptivity. The symbol, therefore, is never neutral. It asks for commitment from the person to whom it appears. Symbols do not, like signs, merely point at something. They direct our manner of thinking. Symbols operate on the level of the subject. They are not part of our discursive discussion about that which lies outside the self or of our mere intellectual concepts of reality as made up from a series of objects. Symbols are involved in man's subjectivity and in that of the cosmos itself. They are born both in and for an encounter.[11]

Involved as they are in the human condition, symbols are not always obvious. They force us to study life with its manifold complexities and labyrinths as well as with its harmony and syntheses. All these features of life find their level in an orderly design. This design is, in India, known as *Ṛta*.

What then the confession of receptivity of mind and heart results in is the capacity of discovering the universe's most intimate structures as *co-designed* by us through our personal relationship with them in the symbol. We become capable of co-designing the universe by "naming" it. The communication with what we name is not one of command. It is a response to the echo of what has been named. This echo is the symbol enabling us to combine and unify. Hence we learn to see through things and situations. Symbols, as we will later see, make us think. The history of man's use of symbols reflects his changing view of the universe and his relationship to it. Metaphysics which is connected with the nature of ultimate reality is now in many quarters abandoned as impossible. Such a retreat into agnosticism however is unable to satisfy, for without a view of reality within which man can orientate his life, that life becomes meaningless. The necessity of metaphysics is derived from existence and cannot be abandoned. If however, there are no direct means of knowing or stating

11. The wellknown symbols of the *çakra*, the cosmic wheel, the cross, the moon, the swastika and hammer-and-sickle are sufficient evidence of the commitment they evoke in those to whom these symbols speak. Because personal relationships are only accessible in and through symbols, the failure of the symbol for an individual results in his being barred from the attainment of a meaningful orientation towards reality. Psychology has occupied itself extensively with the symbol. Danielou, following Jung's understanding of symbolism, points out that it belongs to the structure of the self so that its use "provokes an intuitive response in the soul." See: J. Danielou, *The Lord of History*, Longmans Green, 1958, p. 133. Also see: Hans Schaer, *Religion and the cure of souls in Jung's Psychology*, Routledge and Kegan Paul, 1951, p. 81.

ultimate truth, man is forced to operate at the level of the symbolic.[12] Symbols turn out to be the only way in which the nature of being may be explored and our relationship with it affirmed.

Symbols speak to the existential anxiety of man since he appears to hold his existence under the threat of non-being. The symbol's validity, therefore, takes place on the level of the person. Its argument refuses defeat by mere rational debate unless the symbol itself is given up.

Since the shaping-force of man and his civilization is the *lived* experience on the cutting edge between suffering and joy, the most significant symbols of human culture speak about just that. The result is *emotionally* experienced meaning and knowledge of reality. The interaction of suffering and joy, man's basic anxiety,—his reality—finds no words of solace and insight except through a meaning behind meaning revealed through symbols.

To conclude we shall have a look at one wellknown and significant symbol, namely, that of the *dharma çakra*, the Wheel of the Law in the Indian tradition.[13]

The *çakra* reveals two concomitant simultaneous movements. The maddening and inexplicable wheel of sorrow of the everlasting round of birth and re-birth, sin, misunderstanding, disease, old age and death; inside that wheel, however, in the very centre, is the deeper, darker, yet more luminous revelation of what in the Buddhist tradition is called the Great Delight, *Mahāsukha*. In Indian tradition the irresistible "point", *bindu*, the stillness of the wheel's hub, will overrule all capricious desire. The pain-bearing aspect of life's experience—the fast and seemingly uncontrollable speeding felly of the wheel—has its counter in the hub where suffering and all there is

12. During the age of rationalism in Europe's nineteenth century and in its nineteenth century's materialism, it appeared to many that the need for symbols had been overcome and that the world could be known as it is. The success of science appeared so overwhelming that the universe's ultimate secrets seemed to be opening up. But efforts to approach reality without recourse to symbols ended in failure. Even metaphysics was doubted until Kant (1742-1804) gave it a new orientation. See: Ernst Cassirer, *The Philosophy of Symbolic Forms*, Vol. 3: *The Phenomenology of Knowledge*, pp. 45-57: "Subjective and Objective Analysis".

13. The wheel in Buddhist iconography is symbolic of the reign of the World Monarch, the Turner of the Wheel, *cakra-vartin*, but also of the teaching of the Buddha, the World Saviour, who, in his first sermon, in the Deer Park of Banaras, set the Wheel of the Law in motion. The image of a spoked wheel, symbolic of the turning world, is attested for India already circa 700 before the Christian era in the *Chāndogya* and *Bṛhadāraṇyaka Ups*. (respectively: 7.15.1 and 2.5.15). The *Praśna Up* 6.6. refers to the Cosmic Person, *Puruṣa*, as "he in whom all parts are well fixed, like spokes in the hub of a wheel: him recognize as the Person to be known—that death may not afflict you". The authors must have been familiar with the spoked wheel of the Aryan war chariot, first appearing in the world in the early second millennium. The *çakra*, therefore, dates from the early Vedic age. An earlier form of it, long antedating the invention of the old Sumerian wheel (c. 3500 B.C.) was the widely known "swastika". Myths, rites and philosophies first associated with these symbols were rather positive with regard to the suffering and joy of existence. But a reversal to the negative took place about 500 B.C. For Pythagoras in Greece and the Buddha in India (563-483 B.C.) life became known as a fiery whirl of delusion, desire, violence, death and waste. The quest for some means of release became urgent and it was found in the hub of the wheel, the centre, where understanding receives clarity. In the classical Greek world the wheel appeared in the meaning of painful discovery of life's apparent defeat and pain rather than its victory and exhilaration. The figure portraying that concept is the mythical Ixion who was bound by Zeus to a burning wheel and sent circling forever through the boundless vault of the universe. The reason for this horrible punishment were the murder of his father-in-law and the rape of Hera, i.e. the punishment for all desire and aggression—recognized in Hindu and Buddhist thought and in modern depth-psychology as creative powers of deadly world-illusion and destruction.

connected with it, is understood, and, hence, sets man free of passion run wild. The hub is part of the wheel. It is experienced suffering which will make man the recipient of understanding how the hub "accumulates" the frenzy of the wheel's felly and yet will not be overcome by it.

What I am here considering for the purpose of our confession of receptivity, is mythologically speaking heaven and earth. Psychologically it is the world of subject and object. From the point of view of *experienced* life it is, to a greater or lesser degree, heaven and hell. All these three aspects together form the world or the cosmos but they are typical of any particularized situation.

To receptively experience the actually turning *çakra* I would like to draw from two sources an example as crude as it is real. The combination of the two sources also brings into focus another significant symbol, the cross, analogous with the *çakra*. Our first source is an astonishing myth in the Hindu *Pañchatantra*, taken from the Buddhist tradition. It is known in the West where it was translated into a number of European languages at an early date. We find in that myth, which I shall presently recount, an awesome reflection on the knowledge of reality, terrible in itself and yet, hiding within itself, the promise of reassurance in the still point of the flash of understanding. For the reader who wishes to know how the lived experience on the cutting edge between suffering and joy can be endured in this present world, I draw from Viktor E. Frankl's amazing book, *Man's Search for Meaning*.[14]

Doctor Frankl bore in his soul and on his head the whole full weight of the wheel during his endless days and nights in the Nazi prison camps. To understand the maddening frenzy of the wheel's felly, some are drawn through the three holes, *khāni*, in the knaves of the chariotwheels through which *Indra* draws *Apāla* "so her skin was shed and she became the "Sunskinned".[15] Such people, having passed to the Sun, "come to know the world-door, progression for the wise, but a barrier for the foolish".[16] Frankl's is, likewise, a testimony to what happens when the symbol,

14. *Pañchatantra*, Book 5, tr. Arthur Ryder, *The Pañchatantra*, Chicago, The University of Chicago Press, 1925. The myth which I shall recount will be found on pp. 434-441. See: Theodor Benfey, *Pañchatantra*, Leipzig: F.A. Brockhaus, 1859, p. 487f: Benfey's study shows the considerable flow of literature from India to Europe in the Middle Ages. The Sanskrit *Pañchatantra* were translated into Arabic in the eighth century, into Syriac in the tenth, into Greek in the eleventh, and into old Spanish, Hebrew and Latin in the early thirteenth century. It found its way into the Grimmcollection and variants have been discovered in every European language where e.g. after long wanderings the fourth seeker comes to a tree and when he wishes for a meal, a set table appears. The Grimmtales also take up motifs from other sources. Viktor E. Frankl, *Man's Search for Meaning: An Introduction to Logotherapy*, New York: Washington Square Press, 1963. Frankl experienced how "the wheel" impairs as well as purifies human speech.

15. The six areas between the spokes of the wheel represent the six realms of the "round of being", *bhavaçakra*. Beginning at the top and revolving clockwise, they are: the gods, the titans, ghosts, hell-beings, animals and men. The felly is bound by the linked chain of the twelve causes of rebirth: ignorance, action, consciousness, name-and-form, the sense organs, contact sensation, desire, intercourse, birth, life, disease, old age and death. Within the hub the motion is communicated by three evercircling beasts which, unless conquered, cause the maddening rush of the wheel's felly. The beasts are: the cock or dove, the serpent and the pig, representing respectively desire, anger and stupidity. For the "Sunskinned" see: *RV*. 8.91.

16. *CU*. 8.6.5: *"lokadvāraṃ prapadanaṃ vidūṣāṃ nirodho vidūṣam"*. Traditions speak of a certain "hesitation"—ultimately every man's hesitation—when it comes to passing through the critical stage towards actually facing the mystery of suffering and joy. Thus e.g. *Agni's* hesitation to become the charioteer of the gods (*RV*. 10.51), the Buddha's hesitation to set the Wheel of the Law in motion and Christ's agony in the garden of Ghetsemane. See: Coomaraswamy: I. *Selected Papers,*

analogous to the *çakra*, the cross, is overruled by greed, passion and pride and the idea of shedding one's own blood instead of someone else's is lost.

Here, then, is the strange adventure of four friends, Brahmins, told in the *Pañchatantra*. They were stricken with poverty and determined to get rich. So they travelled to the *Avanti*-country where they met a magician who was called *Bhairavānanda* which means "Terror-Joy". They asked him to help them in their pursuit. He donated to each a magic feather and instructed them to go further to the Himalayas. Wherever a feather dropped, the owner would find a treasure. The leader's feather of course dropped first. How amazed the four were to see the soil all copper. So he said: "Look here, take all you want". The other three decided to proceed while the first turned back. Next the second leader's feather dropped. He dug the soil, found silver, and returned. The next feather yielded gold. So the fourth and last remarked: "Don't you see the point? First copper, then silver, next gold. There will surely be gems beyond". So he decided to press on.

> "And so this other went on alone. His limbs were scorched by the rays of the summer sun and his thoughts were confused by thirst as he wandered to and fro over the trails in the land of the fairies. At last, on a whirling platform, he saw a man with blood dripping down his body; for a wheel was whirling on his head. Then he made haste and said:" Sir, why do you stand thus with a wheel whirling on your head? In any case, tell me, if there is water anywhere. I am mad with thirst." The moment the Brahmin said this, the wheel left the other's head and settled on his own. "My very dear Sir", said he, " what is the meaning of this?" "In the very same way", replied the other, "it settled on my head". "But", said the Brahmin, "when will it go away? It hurts terribly". And the other said:" When someone who holds in his hands a magic quill , such as you had, arrives and speaks as you did, then it will settle on his head. "Well," said the Brahmin, "how long have you been here?". The other asked: "Who is king in the world at present?" And on hearing the answer, "King *Vinabatsa*," he said: "When *Rama* was king, I was poverty-stricken, procured a magic quill and came here, just like you. And I saw another man with a wheel on his head and put a question to him. The moment I asked a question, just like you, the wheel left his head and settled on mine. But I cannot reckon the centuries."
>
> Then the wheel-bearer asked: "My dear Sir, how, pray, did you get food while standing thus?". "My dear Sir," said the fellow, "the god of wealth, *Kubera*, fearful lest his treasures be stolen, prepared this terror, so that no magician might come so far. And if any should succeed in coming, he was to be freed from hunger and thirst, preserved from decrepitude and death and was merely to endure this torture. So now permit me to say farewell. You have set me free from a sizable misery. Now I am going home. And he went."[17]

The fable as here retold is devoted to the art of getting on and not so much to sainthood. Its hidden import is betrayed in the name of the magician *Bhairavānanda*,

---

Traditional Art and Symbolism, ed. Roger Lipsey, Bollingen Series 89, Princeton University Press, 1977, p. 327.

17. See footnote no. 14.

"Terror-Joy". *Bhairava* is a cult-name of *Śiva* in his most horrific aspect as the destroyer of illusion and consort of the blood consuming black goddess *Kali*, punishing those who assume *Kāla*, temporal time and its values to be eternal Time and Value. Thus *Śiva* as *Kālarūpin* is the destroyer of unduly appropriated time. Time is the universal fatality. In the *Śiva Purāṇa* it is said that

> "the whole universe is caught up in time's mouth and whirls like a wheel through the activities of creation and annihilation."[18]

The Confession of the Sacred: A Second Phenomenology

Through the *confession* of receptivity of heart and mind for the universe's meaningfulness we now have discovered the *possibility* of receptiveness in us for the wholeness of manifested reality inviting surprise and wonder.

> "How does the wind not cease to blow?
> How does the mind take no repose?
> Why do the waters, seeking to reach truth
> never at any time cease flowing?"[19]

Our next question, again with regard to myth and its consciousness, is: how shall we make the transition from the *possibility* of receptiveness to its *reality*? Shall we be able to rise beyond the purely rational critical discourse? But is that not precisely what we have already done by extracting from ourselves a confession of receptivity by which we sustained—purposely disregarding ontological models—the *experience of experience*? We found that we were not so much in need of commenting or explaining. We found ourselves, by the natural rise of symbols out of consciousness, assimilating these living flashes rather than understanding them on a merely mental plane. Our metaphysics, therefore, is now more characterized by what many traditions designate as "the eating of the symbol" than by the dialectical rational digestion of it, useful though this may be.

Through the confession of receptivity for the marvel of manifested reality we discovered the universe to be a design. That may not always be conspicuous in its particulars. Its totality, however, is overwhelming.

The transition from receptivity for the universe to the *actual reception* of it we shall try and achieve by extracting from ourselves another and second confession. That is the confession which the consciousness of the sacred in us makes of the reception of the universe and of existence.[20] Of course, this love for the sacred to try

18. *SP*. 7.1.7.2. See: Stella Kramrisch, *The Presence of Śiva*, Oxford University Press, Delhi, 1981, p. 275. See also Part III *passim*.
19. *AV*. 10.7.37.
20. It is evident that a philosophy or theology of solidarity with and love of the Universe and man in it, cannot be contained in the more or less *dogmatic* canons of a philosophical, philosophical-political or theological system man has known thus far. Their powerlessness to integrate justice, the other side of solidarity and love, conceptually, is nothing compared to their powerlessness to account for the actual position of evil in the world. The concept of "permission" (God "permits" evil but does not "create" it) is a witness to the fact that, to say the least, the *whole* of the Spirit is not contained in dogmatic philosophical, political, and theological schools, systems and religions. Moreover, where there is question not of Spirit but of Mind materialized, the verdict would not be different. To explain away experienced evil by simply reducing it to the sinful nature of man absolves one from personal involvement and hence undermines one's understanding of the multivalence of the

and obtain knowledge of reality cannot take the place of a philosophy of the consciousness of the sacred. It remains to be seen what philosophy makes of it. How does the philosopher incorporate man's consciousness of the sacred into his thoughts? How does he embody it in his argument?

He may fruitfully do so through a dialectic between the *fact* of the finite which he has established and the *possibility* or *necessity* of the infinite. The philosopher cannot accept mere probability. When confronted with the confession by the consciousness of the sacred with regard to human thought and reality, the philosopher must remain true to the penetrating power of the critical-rational argument, the "logos".

Once the diversity and fragmentation of reality is admitted, one must also acknowledge some infinitely resourceful principle unifying the diversity and fragmentation enabling one to know reality. The philosopher will not allow this principle automatically to be called sacred or divine. That is the philosopher's good right. He will rightly insist that the canons of the sacred or the divine be further construed within their own context and limits.

It is at this point that affirmation, denial or doubt concerning the possibility or necessity of a divine principle enters man's discourse. At this point too the ways of humans part. We are here presented with a multilevelled and manyheaded problem. No one in the history of thought has yet proposed a formula sufficiently convincing so that the edge where the spiritual and the earthly, the metaphysical and the moral planes intersect, be eradicated. There has always been a "neither-nor" and a "both-and" unless for the person who says: "I believe". In *believing* confession, thought is freely handed over to Infinite Thought, God. Men and women of all times have thus understood Reality and known It

With Viktor E. Frankl, however, we are able to continue the quest "beyond" when he points to the "logos" as not identical with logic. In a man's attachment to his life—and Frankl knows it—there is something stronger than all the miseries of the world together. Since life then will not conform to reason some call it absurd. Descartes': "I think, therefore I am", would have to be: "I am, but I can't think why!"[21] Frankl's answer to this painful question is:

> "What is demanded of man is not, as some existential philosophies teach, to endure the meaninglessness of life; but rather to bear his incapacity to grasp its unconditional meaningfulness in rational terms. Logos is deeper than logic."[22]

We are here reminded of the *Bodhisattva*, the illumined person in the Buddhist tradition, who is "without thought". Now, if the enactment of the confession by the consciousness of the sacred does not take the place of philosophy to understand reality, where then should it be "placed"? The confession by the consciousness of the sacred falls, nonetheless, within the sphere of interest of philosophy if it is prepared to

---

primordial symbols joining the Universe and the psyche into one totality. Such symbols urge one to follow the path of the "abnormal" in the sense that the study of the Universe and man in it must lead to assimilation of opposites by pouring the good "into" the evil and thus abolish it.

21. The theme of "absurdity" has been worked upon, in the West, by thinkers such as Camus and Sartre. Aldous Huxley's famous novel and fantasy of the future, *Brave New World*, Penguin Books, 1970, satirizes the idea of progress put forward by scientists and philosophers and, as a lesson in pessimism, reflects on some of his theories on the absurdity of existence.
22. Viktor E. Frankl, *Man's Search for Meaning*, p. 187-188.

listen to the scruples of historic investigation and the data gathered by the disciplines of the mind. The consciousness of the sacred and its expression is an utterance by man about himself. Every utterance must be taken up into the philosophical discourse and argument. The philosopher is free to pledge allegiance to the sacred as divine. He is, however, not at liberty to regard it as a mere trifle or, worse, as a dispensable fact in human culture.

The consciousness of the sacred is part and parcel of the structure of man's consciousness, not a mere passing stage of it. The rightful position for the philosopher to take up, is his own sympathetic study of it and see how it contributes to the knowledge of reality.[23]

What path shall I now suggest that we follow after our two confessions: that of receptivity in sustained experience and that of the consciousness of the sacred with regard to the quest for reality? I propose that we now take up more of the "logos" in man's conscious experience of reality and the expression of it. We have, if we remember, at first intentionally disregarded ontology—the word *about* being—when attempting to *condition* ourselves to thought and reality.[24]

Man has always been the contemporary of *different* types of knowledge about the *same* reality: the universe and man in and of it. He enjoys the knowledge of immediate experience with regard to the universe and man and that of rational reflection upon it. In other words: there is the more or less impassioned insight of immediate impact and the cooler analysis of conceptualized thought. These two ways of thought and their expressions ought to be complementary to each other even to the extent of interpenetration—since neither introduces something alien to man.

In India, as in the West, its rich philosophical tradition has generated a spectrum of schools, from extreme materialism to extreme idealism, from absolute monism through dualism to complete pluralism. Numerous and often conflicting theories regarding the nature of consciousness, of reality and the relation between mind and

23. The consciousness of the sacred as a constituent of the structure of man's consciousness has now been generally accepted as a fact proved by research in the fields of archeology, anthropology, psychology and the history of religion and its related sciences as well as by the philosophy of language. Space forbids us to go into the question of "hominization" —the evolution of the human species. If the Paleanthropians are regarded as complete humans, it follows that their proved experience of the sacred—evident from a certain number of beliefs and practices—must be part of the universal human experience of the sacred. In other words, if the question of religiosity or non-religiosity of pre-historic man and all humans after him is raised, it falls to the defender of non-religiosity to bring forward proofs in support of his hypothesis. See: Mircea Eliade, *A History of Religious Ideas,* Vol. I, *From the Stone Age to the Eleusinian Mysteries*, Collins, London, 1979, pp. 3-55. Also see: Andre Leroi-Gourhan, *Les Religions de la Préhistoire: Paléolithique*, Paris 1964, p. 54 and: Karl J. Narr, *Kultur, Umwelt und Leiblichkeit der Eiszeitmenschen*, Stuttgart, 1963. Belief in a survival after death as part of the consciousness of the sacred can be demonstrated from the earliest times. Interesting in our Indian context is the universally distributed use of red ochre as a ritual substitute for blood as a symbol of life. Its use has been known from the earliest beginnings in Central North Africa down to the Cape of Good Hope, the western shores of Europe, Tasmania, Australia, the Americas and in the East. In India one can observe its use daily when the deceased are being carried to the cremation grounds. See: Raymond A. Dart, "The Birth of Symbology" in *African Studies*, 27 (1968) : 15-27 and his, "The Multimillennial Prehistory of Ochre Mining" (1967). pp. 7-13.

24. See the preceding paragraph: "The confession of receptivity: a first phenomenology". It was stressed there that we, with regard to myth and its consciousness, first condition ourselves to thought rather than think that we already think.

matter have been proposed. Indian tradition, which may be called mystical, is not primarily concerned with theoretical concepts. It seeks, above all, ways of liberation by the transformation of consciousness and the change of awareness of one's own existence and of one's relation to human society and the natural world. The knowledge of *Brahman* is the sole way of knowing reality. The wellknown thinker in the *Chāndogya Upaniṣad*, *Svetaketu*, admits that, in spite of the fact that he has studied all the *Vedas*, he "is still lacking the knowledge whereby what has not been heard of becomes heard of, what has not been thought of becomes thought of and what has not been understood becomes understood".[25]

The West shows a different picture. What Heraclitus said in his effort to understand reality, "edizêsamen emeōton", "I have thought for myself", typifies the West.[26] Although this word of Heraclitus' came to maturity only in Socrates, the formula proved to become of immeasurable influence in the Western world. Each of the sciences, successively or in collaboration with other disciplines, assumed the guidance for thought on the problem of man and his approach to reality and determined for longer or shorter periods the line of investigation. The results have been formidable. But two and a half millennia after Heraclitus Max Scheler wrote:

> "In no other period of human knowledge has man ever become more problematic to himself than in our own days. We have a scientific, a philosophical, and a theological anthropology that know nothing of each other. Therefore we no longer possess any clear and consistent idea of man. The ever growing multiplicity of the particular sciences that are engaged in the study of man has much more confused and obscured than elucidated our concept of Man."[27]

That is no consoling word. One would like to think that the ever increasing variety of sources man commands would lead to clear methods combining the range of data into an intelligible whole. Ernst Cassirer remarks:

> "Our wealth of facts is not necessarily a wealth of ideas. Unless we succeed in finding a clue of Ariadne to lead us out of this labyrinth, we can have no real insight into the general character of human culture; we shall remain lost in a mass of disconnected and disintegrated data which seem to lack all conceptual unity.[28]

25. *CU*. 6.1.3: "*yenāśrutam śrutam bhavati, amatam matam, avijñātam vijñātam iti*". Also: *MU*. 1.1.3; *BU*. 2.4.5.

26. Fragment 101, in: Hermann Diels, *Die Fragmente der Vorsokratiker,* ed. W. Kranz, 5th ed. Berlin, 1934, I, p. 173.

27. Max Scheler, *Die Stellung des Menschen im Kosmos*, Darmstadt, Reichl, 1928, pp. 13f, tr. Ernst Cassirer, *An Essay on Man*, Yale University Press, 1962, p. 22. Also the following lines, see *ibid*. The common man suffers repeatedly from this chaotic, confused, and obscured concept of man, reflected, apart from other instances, in misconceptions about himself in e.g. high places of research and learning, administration and planning, responsible for the ordinary running of society. Thus, for example, uncoordinated and ill-conceived town planning giving questionable preference to low-cost highrise flats, carparks, showrooms, shopping centres etc. without integrating playgrounds, flora and fauna as essential to man's being part of the universe, have given rise to a wide variety of major social and psychic disorders in Western society as well as in the "new postcolonial societies". See: e.g. James C. Coleman, *Abnormal Psychology and Modern Life*, D.B. Taraporevala Sons & Co. Ltd, 1981, reprint, Bombay, pp. 144f and *passim*.

28. Ernst Cassirer, *An Essay on Man*, p. 22. In his chapter on "The crisis in man's knowledge of himself" (pp. 1-22) Cassirer stresses the necessity of the teleological character of human life and the theories concerning that life.

The problem of human knowledge and reality belongs to each of the often conflicting fields. We could nowhere dispense with the view of all those fields and lay claim to an autonomous method. What we, however, can do is to try and avoid particular religious and philosophical assumptions of an apologetic and propagandistic nature. We can simply record human experience as a living document. This puts in second place what religionists and scholars think about the matter. There is, in human thought, a psychic and physical continuity, an almost bodily belonging, like the Indian karmic continuity. Is that *belonging* not more important and, for the living human experience, more relevant than doctrinal homogeneity?[29]

What I must now try and examine, with a view to the mythical awareness, is the content of the consciousness of the sacred: what is being *said* there.

Speculation and Myth

The two preceding phenomenologies I have presented we may now combine in view of our query after the nature of the mythical consciousness. I may assume that we can at least *imagine* the receptive consciousness of the sacred. In examining what is being said in that awareness concerning man and his knowledge of reality, we must avoid the temptation to present its most elaborate "philosophic-looking" expressions. To try and flatter the ratio — the logos of conceptual knowledge— in order to rescue the language of the sacred would imply a betrayal of both.

One could be inclined to think that philosophy is challenged to measure itself against the constructs of organized ,and dogmatized religious systems and religious canons of faith with regard to the consciousness of the sacred. Many philosophies as well as popular opinions, both classical and modern, take the dogmatically developed theological systems as their data to assemble and develop their rational-critical argument. By doing so, they reduce the philosophical problem of man's vision of reality, as presented by the consciousness of the sacred, to a critique of systematized religion.[30]

It is, as I said, to the least elaborate, *the least "philosophic-looking"* expressions by the awareness of the sacred that we must now turn. If we do so, we must be convinced from the outset that philosophy too, in its turn, must resist a temptation. It must resist a gnostic pretension to "know" the mysterious aspects there are in the consciousness of the sacred and its particular vision of human destiny. We cannot rationalize the sacred. That would mean to annul it and consider possible remnants as a deposit of a period less human that went before us. Being human is a universal ever since the human came to know of himself as such. This would seem obvious. Nevertheless, it has been made an issue of — and still is — by various scholars as well as by popular opinion.[31]

29. See Part III:8: "*Karma*, the cosmic pilgrimage".
30. I have, in the first chapter, in the paragraph "The idea of the sacred, already referred to the term "religion" as too limited a concept to hold all the experiences of "the sacred. A critique of systematized religion would have to start from different premises, e.g. the phenomenon of censure by its leaders who, in order to keep religion "pure", may cut into precisely the experience of the sacred, show unwillingness towards or lack of understanding of its movement of rupture and resumption, considered dangerous to the integrity of the "deposit". The question of "deposit" has always been a bone of contention in religious systems with regard to the spirit of the sacred. The spirit of the sacred may make someone a religious person but not necessarily a person of religion.
31. Karl J. Narr, "Approaches to the Religion of early Paleolithic Man", *History of Religions* 4, Chicago,

All through the *whole* of man is our postulate. Screening off a constituent of human experience and its expression *as human* leads to pseudo-philosophy, an offence against the rational-critical instinct. Mircea Eliade, discussing the fundamental universal unity of the consciousness of the sacred in quest of understanding of reality writes:[32]

> ". . . beliefs and ideas cannot be fossilized. Hence certain scholars have preferred to say nothing about the ideas and beliefs of the Paleanthropians instead of reconstructing them with the help of comparisons with the hunting civilizations. This radical methodological position is not without its dangers. To leave an immense part of the history of the human mind a blank runs the risk of encouraging the idea that during all those millennia the activity of the mind was confined to the preservation and the transmission of technology. Such an opinion is not only erroneous, it is fatal to a knowledge of man. *Homo faber* was at the same time *Homo ludens, sapiens* and *religiosus* (*M.E.*). Since we cannot reconstruct his religious beliefs and practices, we must at least point out certain analogies that can illuminate them, if only indirectly." [33]

Where does speculation take us when we turn to the confession of the sacred by the receptive consciousness? It takes us, as I said, to *living* experience. But we should not forget that we begun our speculation by promising ourselves to seek what is being *said* in the utterance by the receptive awareness of the sacred. The living experience of the sacred and its expressions cannot be explained through philosophical rational constructions as if these were the very vehicles of the sacred and its utterance. To put it differently: like any mode of human thought, the receptive consciousness of the sacred knows its own deepest crises, resulting in new creations. This is even more true of the mode of the sacred in human thought. Without claiming its superiority, we ought to emphasize its pivotal position in the immeasurable totality of the human experience of the universe and man. In Indian thought, to perform acts of mental sacrifice is often alluded to in the *Upaniṣads*. It is an indication of the heavy responsibility and existential urgency there lies upon the mode of the sacred in human thought. It implies at once a complete objective as well as subjective involvement. "This whole world is *Brahman*."[34] In India, the mode of the sacred in human life resulted

1964, pp. 1 - 29. Also see: Etienne Patte, *Les hommes préhistoriques et la religion*, Paris, 1960, *passim*.

32. In order to understand why scholars have hesitated to admit the possibility of a consistent and complex religiosity — which is different from organized religion — among the Paleanthropians, we must remember that in the second half of the nineteenth century in the West, the term "religion" had a very limited application. Much was called "magic", "superstition", "savagery" etc. The supporters of religiosity and its language, as a language concomitant with other languages of the human species, were accused of idealizing the Paleanthropians because "religion" was taken to mean an ideological complex comparable to Judeo-Christianity, Hinduism or the pantheons known from elsewhere. Such opinions appear now fast on the retreat.

33. Mircea Eliade, *A History of Religious Ideas,* Vol. I, p. 8. For the comfort of the reader unacquainted with Latin : Homo faber : man who fabricates, manufactures. Homo ludens : man who plays, celebrates. Homo sapiens : man who thinks and Homo religiosus: religious man.

34. *CU.* 3.14.1 : "*sarvam khalvidam Brahma*". In another passage the *Chāndogya Upanisad* says: "Containing all works, containing all desires, containing all odours, containing all tastes, encompassing this whole world, without speech, without concern, this is the self of mine within the heart; this is *Brahman*", 3.14.4.: "*sarva-karmaḥ sarva - kāmaḥsarva - gandhaḥ, sarva-rasaḥ, sarvam*

in a series of outstanding creations, such as the *Upaniṣads*, yogic techniques, the message of Gautama Buddha and mystical devotion.

To return to our question: what do we find being *said* by the utterance by the receptive awareness of the sacred? Behind philosophical speculation and *beneath* gnosis and anti-gnostic thought lies the consciousness of the sacred which says something. *What is being said is the myth*. A basic and — if we are true to what factual history offers us — unavoidable discovery. Our discovery of myth and what it says is as of a universal. It is concomitant and contemporary with the consciousness of the sacred and its expression. Myth and its symbols touch and exhilarate centres of life beyond the reach of vocabularies of either reason or coercion. These *are* there "as such" as if come from nowhere. An embarrassing , if not at times painful experience for the philosopher.[35]

Myth is a form of true human thought. Through it the consciousness of the sacred expresses itself as related to the ideas of being, its meaningfulness and truth. What myth *says* it *thinks* of itself as being reality and the transmission of it.

---

idam abhyāttovaky anādaraḥ, eṣa mā ātmāntarahṛdaye etad Brahmā."
Also the *Kauśitakī Upaniṣad* tells us to perform acts of mental sacrifice: "The ancient sages did not offer the *agnihotra* sacrifice, knowing that an endless sacrifice was going on all the while within themselves", 2.5.:-"..*taddhasmaitat purve vidvāmsognihotraṁ na juhavāñcakruḥ*".
The fundamental thought of the whole teaching of the *Upaniṣads* could be seen to be contained in *ṚgVeda* 1.164.46:"*ekam sad vipra Bahudha vadanti*", "To what is one, sages give many a title", although hidden there like a germ. Because this verse asserts that all plurality, consequently all proximity in space, all succession of time, all relation of cause and effect, all interdependence of subject and object, rests only upon words (*vadanti*) or as the *Chāndogya Upaniṣad* puts it, is a matter of words "*vācarambhaṇaṁ vikāro nāma-dheyam*", and that only unity is in the full sense real. An attempt was made, in the first instance, to conceive this unity through the idea of *Brahman*, and finally, without allowing the latter to drop, and by a mere strengthening of the subjective element already contained in it, in the philosophical idea of *ātman*. See: Paul Deussen, *The Philosophy of the Upaniṣads*, Dover Publications, New York, 1966, pp. 398 -399. In the *Upaniṣads*, the universe is the *Brahman* but the *Brahman* is *ātman*. There is no plurality and they are treated as synonyms. See : S.N. Das Gupta, *A History of Indian Philosophy*, 5 vols., Motilal Banarsidass, 1975, vol.1, pp. 28 ff. Also: Paul Deussen, *The Philosophy of Vedānta*, tr. G.A. Jacob, Susil Gupta Ltd., Calcutta, 1957, pp. 10-11.

35. Erich Neumann in his, *The Great Mother, An Analysis of the Archetype*, Bollingen Series, Princeton, 1974, reprint, pp. 75 - 79 discusses the dynamic within the archetype (in his case the Feminine) and the relation of consciousness to it. His observations are of interest to us. Neumann theorizes about the movement along certain axes representing the movement of the ego and consciousness. He speaks of "circles" in that movement, attraction by poles and the shifting of phenomena in the primordial circle of man which communicate different but related aspects. The first circle is the elementary stage of containment, the second that of progress to the transformative stage and finally we arrive at the third circle: spiritual transformation. But it is Neumann's fourth circle that draws the attention here. I quote Neumann: "the fourth circle appears to the ego and consciousness as a borderline experience that plays a significant role in the mysteries of religion in mysticism, but also in the development of the modern individual. The "spiritual transformation" characteristic of the third circle always involves processes that move the whole personality in a direction transcending consciousness. In this sense madness, as well as vision and inspiration, are spiritual phenomena transcending consciousness. Spiritual transformation, i.e. a fundamental transformation and change of the personality and consciousness, occurs only through the crucial emergence of an archetype." (which is what interests us when discussing the emergence of myth, without, however, identifying myth with archetype in the psychological sense. F.B.) Neumann continues:" Negative spiritual change is also archetypally conditioned, and for that reason madness, in mythology, for example, is not simply a loss of consciousness and spirit but a "confusion of the spirit". Yet, madness may be regarded as sacred and taken positively as an inspirational initiation because, behind inundation by the spirit, the world of archetypes appears as the power that determines fate.

As a form of thought myth is itself the discovery of being, its meaningfulness and truth.

Myth, therefore, will not and cannot be left at the mercy of only psychology or be wholly explained by it.[36] Harm to myth's own truth and validity is all too easily caused. The mythical awareness claims for itself a blend of the objective and subjective by virtue of its own configuration in the receptive consciousness of the sacred. That consciousness renders the mythical capable of apprehending and presenting reality. For the sake of both the mythical and the rational - critical mode of thought we may once again take stock of our position. Both modes are constituents of our very humanity and they deserve the most earnest of our attention.

With regard to the question of the objectivity of the mythical mode we may ask: is it possible to transfer that mode from the terrain of a philosophy of the absolute to that of critical philosophy? Does the mythical mode embody both a problem of metaphysics and a problem with regard to the purely transcendental? If we take the concept of the transcendental in the Kantian sense, the problem limits itself to the conditions under which experience is possible. In the context of the critical-rational it will then be asked what kind of experience the mythical is capable of demonstrating if it is to be given the credit of some form of objective truth and validity. Myth's credit would seem to be its psychological truth and necessity. Is the necessity with which myth arises in human culture its only objective content? Speculative idealism formulated the problem exclusively along these lines. Inquiry into the ultimate and absolute foundations of myth was later shifted to the inquiry into its natural cradle of birth. The mytho-genetic zone in man was thus transferred from metaphysics to ethno-psychology. That is for myth too shallow an explanation of itself.

What we in our approach to the mythical form must look for is neither its explanation by means of the essence of the absolute nor its reduction to mere empirical psychological compulsions. A critical analysis of the mythical will take up a position between a metaphysical deduction and a psychological induction. We should try and approach the mythical through the unity of a specific structurally modeling force of the spirit. In other words, we are to seek the unity of the spiritual principle by which the mythical configurations with their vast empirical diversity are governed.

36. Psychology and psychology of religion have contributed substantially to the understanding of religion as well as the experience of the sacred. Freud's discovery of the unconscious encouraged the study of myth and symbols considerably. The historian of religion may be grateful to Freud for proving hat myths have messages, even if the conscious mind remains unaware of the fact. In his presentation of the "archetype" Carl Jung offers invaluable material for the study of myth and symbol. The archetype is not only a dynamic, a directing force, which influences the human psyche, as in religion, for example, but corresponds to an unconscious "conception", a content. In the symbol, i.e., image of the archetype, a meaning is communicated that can be apprehended conceptually only by a highly developed consciousness, and then only with great pains. For this reason the following remark of Jung's is still applicable to the modern consciousness : "Myth is the primordial language natural to these psychic processes, and no intellectual formulation comes anywhere near the richness and expressiveness of mythical imagery. Such processes deal with the primordial images, and these are best and most succinctly reproduced by figurative speech." This figurative speech is the language of the symbol, the original language of the unconscious, and of mankind. See: Carl Jung, *Psychology and Alchemy,* tr. R.F.C. Hull, *Collected Works*, vol. 12. New York, 1953, p. 25. A short allusion to ethnic psychology, W. Wundt's special concern, will be found in the following few lines. For Wundt and his "Völkerpsychologie" see: Jan de Vries, *Forschungsgeschichte der Mythologie*, pp. 335 - 341

This principle is the awareness of the sacred and its receptive acclamation. It will now be clearer why I in the two preceding phenomenologies of the confession of receptivity and that of the sacred with a view to the mythical consciousness did not begin from the godhead as an original metaphysical fact or from mankind as an original empirical fact. What I started from was the subject of a cultural process, our own actual and active human spirit. We remember how we drew ourselves through these processes to condition ourselves. I began from the things we treasure, from our amazement and feeling of surprise.

These few observations may suffice to keep us on our guard in times of temptation or doubt when the truth and the validity of the mythical awareness is concerned. To speak favourably of myth then — for the rational-critical already enjoys many believing friends—: how could myth and its awareness ever rise above the stupor of and escape from captivity in mere material existence if it did not know the differentiation between the "I" and the universe?

But we must return to our new discovery. We found that what is being *said* by the consciousness of the sacred is the myth. Nothing appears more liable, as may be expected, to a direct confrontation with pure rational thought than does mythical thought. Myth causes embarrassment to the rational philosopher. Cassirer writes:

> "The mythical fantasy drives toward animation, toward a complete "spiritualization" of the cosmos; but the mythical *form of thought* (*E.C.*), which attaches all qualities and activities, all states and relations to a solid foundation, leads to the opposite extreme; a kind of materialization of spiritual content. It is true that mythical thinking seeks to create a kind of *continuity* (*E.C.*) between cause and effect by intercalating a series if middlelinks between the initial and the *ultimate* stages. But even these middlelinks preserve a merely material character. From the standpoint of analytical and scientific causality a process is regarded as constant if a unitary law, an analytical function, is demonstrated under which the whole of the process can be logically subsumed and by which its progress from moment to moment can be determined. . . Mythical thinking, however, knows such a unity neither of combination nor of separation. Even where it seems to divide an action into a number of stages, it considers the action in an entirely substantial form."[37]

That is a severe critique. Is it crippling? In metaphysics the mythological process is explained as a particular instance, a specific and necessary phase of the absolute process to be attained by reason. Psychology deduces mythical apperception from the general factors and rules of the production of representations. If we further investigate the mythical awareness and let it be what it simply *is to* the eye and what it simply *says*, should not then the question be asked: are we not in both cases explaining myth and its awareness by referring it and reducing it to something other than what it immediately is and signifies?[38]

That may well be the very question myth itself would like to be asked. As a form of the consciousness of the sacred, myth forces the question by its persistence in

37. Ernst Cassirer, *Mythical Thought*, p. 5.
38. *Op. cit.* p. 12

human culture. For the sake of philosophy we cannot but admit our contemporariness with the language of the sacred.

Nothing seems wider apart than scientific rational truth is from that of myth. But if myth is a way of human thinking it must have its own mode of necessity. And this mode must be in some way demonstrable. If it were purely arbitrary and accidental it could hardly be an object of inquiry. Cassirer, speaking from the idealist point of view, has chosen the correct path to keep the dialogue between myth and rational-critical thought open by his quote from Schelling's magnum opus, *Philosophie der Mythologie*:[39]

> "In this very opposition (the rational-critical and the myth) lies a challenge and a specific task, to discover reason in this seeming unreason, meaning in this apparent meaninglessness, and not as has hitherto been done, by making an arbitrary distinction; that is, by declaring something which one believes to be rational and meaningful to be the essential, and everything else to be mere accident, cloak or perversion. Our intention must rather be to make the form itself appear necessary, hence rational."[40]

In Schelling's opinion myth is recognized for its truth only if it is recognized in its process. That process, repeated in myth in a peculiar way, is the absolute process. Man deals in the myth, not with things but with the powers that arise within consciousness itself. It is these powers that move him. Thus Schelling observes:

> "One could, consequently, maintain that the falsehood of mythology appears only in the misunderstanding of its process or in its imposed fragmentation and particularization. The misunderstanding should in that case be blamed on the observer looking at mythology merely from the outside and not from its own essence in process. It would explain, instead of the falsehood of mythology, the observer's false look at it."[41]

A philosophy of myth cannot cherish the false hope as if the mythical consciousness and its language were the closest to that of argumentative consciousness in terms of its *explanation* of man and the reality he has found. At best the two are complementary and in dialogue. They are, however, distinctly different modes of

39. Friedrich Wilhelm Joseph von Schelling (1775-1854) stands with his transcendental idealism in clear relation to Kant, Fichte and Hegel. He is generally regarded as the principal philosopher of romanticism. Through Coleridge, Schelling's influence on the English romantics has been considerable. His major work, *The System of Transcendental Idealism* (1800), is primarily an attempt to elaborate upon and modify Kant's and Fichte's view of the relation of the self to the objective world. For Schelling, consciousness is the only immediate object of knowledge and knowledge of the objective world arises merely in the form of a limiting condition in the process by which consciousness becomes aware of itself. He argues that in art alone the mind can become fully aware of itself and that philosophical reflection should aspire to the "condition of art". His work on myth caused a new and significant re-orientation which, nonetheless took almost a century to materialize. Schelling defends the "tautogorical" meaning of myth, i.e., the myth must be understood from out of itself: it has to say something and says it. Not its material content is the most important but the intensity with which it lives and with which it is believed, is what counts. See: Jan de Vries, *Forschungsgeschichte der Mythologie*, pp. 172-178.

40. F.W. Schelling, *Einleitung in die Philosophie der Mythologie*, Sammtliche Werke (2 parts, Stuttgart and Augsburg, J. Verlag, 1856) Pt. 2,1,220ff, tr. Ernst Cassirer, *The Philosophy of Symbolic Forms*, part 2, *Mythical Thought*, p. 5.

41. Friedrich Wilhelm Joseph Schelling, *Philosophie der Mythologie*, 2 vols., Wissenschaftliche Buchgesellschaft, Darmstadt, 1976, unaltered reprographic reprint of the original publication, 1856, Vol. I *Einleitung in die Philosophie der Mythologie*, p. 210, tr. F.B.

apprehending the world and its reality.[42]

Mythical reality has been under scrutiny by almost all the theoretical and speculative sciences. Myth does not, as some have thought, explain by means of fables. It is a traditional narrative relating events which happened "at the beginning of time", "in illo tempore". It intends to provide grounds for rites and rituals *now* and it establishes forms of thought and action through which man understands himself in the world. Because the world is in constant change, myth constantly seeks to understand it *as and while it changes*.[43]

The sacred history of Primordial Time which myth narrates is being stressed. Myth narrates how things, and man himself, began to be and, hence, how they now *are*. The realities man experiences have come about as a result of happenings in the realm of the Unseen. Thus man finds himself to be what he is today: mortal, sexed and a cultural being. All that is true history because it deals, for the mythical awareness, with realities intensely *believed*. Myths are a constant reminder of grandiose events which took place in the universe and on earth. This glorious past is, in the mind of the myth, recoverable. The imitation and re-enactment of these remarkable events in paradigmatic acts by the myth- narrative and ritual invites man to transcend his limitations. The mythical elevates man. Myth's consciousness is not a mere common place recapitulation of the past. It is inventive. It constantly creates and re-thinks the past in what is *now* happening. Its freedom from the shackles of mere factual history, of facticity, provides the mythical awareness with a much wider realm to draw its inspiration from.

For the mythical mode of thought, cosmology is true because the universe is there to prove it. The myth is the exemplary model for all significant human

42. Any theory of reality may be called an ideology, a mystification of the real. Each world while being attended to, is real after its own fashion. The reality lapses only with the attention. Thus there is this important aspect of reality: we do not know the real (what Kant called "thing-in-itself: Ding an Sich) because the mind is constitutive of structures that perceive only appearances. Reality therefore is, in a sense, just one "finite province of meaning" as opposed to another. The "Theatre of the Absurd" is a good illustration of this world of meaning. We see there the framing of confusions by the Absurd through a trick, the "Gestalt-switch". It refers to the aspects of seriousness and un-seriousness co-existing on the same plane of meaning. Audiences in the Absurd Theatre are held spellbound to the extent that they loose the faculty of judging whether what they are witnessing is play or the real thing. This frame-analysis has the advantage of enabling us to view reality from both distant and close perspectives. The distant perspective has a greater depth of reach if it has an ideological filter. For ideology is a structured discourse: those who are in the situation do not *create* the definition. It is the inherited social language, the ideological inclinations that find expression. Because of his Hegelian background, Karl Marx formulated the transformational calculus of mutually interdependent categories. He developed the dialectical process of demystification of reality. It had become untransparent because of ideological mystification. Like Kant, Karl Marx asked an inquiry into the conditions for the production of knowledge and those for the production of various systems of mystificatory belief. The relation between reality and ideology is, according to Marx, not a cognitive problem. The split between appearance and reality, which has been talked about since the Greek philosophy, has produced a meaningless epistemological confusion. In *Capital*, Vol. I chapter 19 which is called "The Transformation of the Value of Labour-Power into Wages", Marx spells this out: value of labour-power is the name of real relations and wages is a phenomenal form. The phenomenal form is the basis of all the juridical notions of both labourers and capitalists and the source of all mystifications of the capitalist mode of production. See: Karl Marx, *Capital, A critique of political economy,* tr. Samuel Moore and Edward Aveling and ed. Frederick Engels, Vol. I Progress Publishers, Moscow, reprint, 1977, pp. 501-508.

43. This leads us to the idea of "modernity", discussed in the following paragraph.

activities.[44] It is the philosophers' task to make mythical thinking itself appear necessary, hence rational. Cassirer explains this as follows:

> "In line with the general conception of Schelling's philosophy this basic purpose must be realized in a two fold direction, towards the subject and towards the object, in regard to the self-consciousness and the absolute. As for the self-conscious and the form in which it experiences mythology, this form in itself suffices to exclude any theory attributing myth to pure "invention", for such a theory passes over the purely *objective (E.C.)* existence of the phenomenon it is supposed to explain. The phenomenon which is here to be considered is not the mythical content as such but the significance it possesses for human consciousness and the power it exerts on consciousness. The problem is not the material content of mythology, but the intensity with which it is experienced, with which it is *believed* (*E.C.*) as only something endowed with objective reality can be believed. This basic and fundamental fact of mythical consciousness suffices to frustrate any attempt to seek its ultimate source in an invention — whether poetic or philosophical. For even if we admit that the purely theoretical, intellectual content of mythology might in this way be made intelligible, the dynamic, as it were, of the mythical consciousness — the incomparable force it has demonstrated over and over again in human history — would remain completely unaccounted for."[45]

If the consciousness of the sacred opens the gates of space and time for man so he knows where he was, where he is and where he will be, *belief* is what sets him free from mere cosmic existence: viz. from being a mere thing. That implies a critical awareness and it is rational. Myth speaks reality and the understanding of it. With it freedom of volition and intellect arises. The receptive consciousness of the sacred transcends subjection to the realm of objects.

Myth and "Modern" : India, the Greeks, the West

> "Death is certain for all that is born
> and birth for all that dies.
> Therefore for what is unavoidable
> you should not be distressed."[46]

Can we forget our fleeting and transitory character? We all are "for the moment", for the time being. "Modo"— as the Latins say. To be "modern" is the first thing a man, a woman and a child are. To be "modern" means to be nothing new. Everyone is "modern" for a little while. Our human birth makes us at once "modern". If we add too much to this, "modern" becomes a fad, a fashion, often freakish and full of pranks. Modern man — also the proud Modern Man of the twentieth century—will soon be no longer. And yet, we cannot think of man except in terms of living here and now in this universe. When we think of those that went before us or those still to come we do so in terms of our own "modern" categories.*

---

44. Mircea Eliade, *Myth and Reality*, p.6
45. Ernst Cassirer, *The Philosophy of Symbolic Forms*, Vol. 2, *Mythical Thought*, p. 5.
46. *BG*. 2.27.

* The Idea of "modo" I borrowed from R. Panikkar.

There is no other key to man's understanding of reality than to accept and to realize his "modernness". It is only by accepting the limitations of our concreteness that we can be rooted in truth. Only by being true to our identity—to be "modo", a little while—can we become more universal. Indian tradition has made much of our "little while", the true mode of man. We ought to pass our time as if already are at the gate of passing to the Supreme Person, *Puruṣa*, the great being of the cosmos. What brings us there already now is our acceptance of the passing modernity we are:

> "If at death with steady mind, disciplined in love
> and the power of yoga,
> he located his vital strength between the eyebrows,
> he will reach the supreme person (*Puruṣa*)."[47]
>
> "It is through *samādhi*, steadiness of mind, that we subdue it in the lotus of the heart, *hṛdayapuṇḍarika*. Then, by means of the upgoing *nāḍi*, *suśumnā*, the life-breath of the heart is drawn up and carefully fixed between the eyebrows. By this means the wise man, the *Yogin*, reaches the Supreme *Puruṣa*, who is resplendent."[48]

Our human identity is that of understanding it as being "modo", "for the time being". What else are we in this life, if not a passing moment in the vastness of time and space surrounding us, no matter how intense and laden that moment may be? That awareness, as I said, has something to do with our being simultaneously an inhabitant and a guest in this world. Whatever we see, hear and experience, is only a part of all that is being said, heard and experienced in all there is. True modernity is not a confinement to the commonplace words, thoughts, feelings, duties, concerns and conventions of "our times". What we must settle for instead are tendencies, directions of movement, value and undervalue, the good and the bad, reality and unreality. Even the god we know during our "little while" may be nothing but a god. Modernity is unconventional by virtue of its universal awareness. To be modern is the happy blend of staying here while transient.

In the Indian tradition it is especially *Śiva* who is modern. With the crescent moon in his hair, the trident in his hand, he is *Śiva Mantramūrti*, the immovable, in everlasting thought and contemplation on the mountain. But when he carries the skull, symbol of transience, he points at our cremation-ground. He may appear, wearing the flayed elephant skin only to exchange it, the next moment, for the silken garments of a bridegroom. An encounter with *Śiva* does away with boring and dull conventions which, when god is concerned, all too often create him in the image of precisely those conventions. *Śiva* provokes. He challenges unmindful distinctions between holy and unholy, rich and poor, high and low. Does the mind of the universe approve of disregardful orthodoxy? *Śiva* is often cast outside by the gods, considered a misfit and a bothersome eccentric.[49]

47. *BG*. 8.9-10.
48. *The Bhagavad Gītā, with the commentary of Śrī Śaṅkarāchārya*, Samata Books, Madras, Corrected reprint, 1981, p. 226f.
49. Two very readable as well as scholarly works on *Śiva's* character are: Wendy Doniger O'Flaherty, *Śiva, The Erotic Ascetic*, Oxford Univ. Press, 1981 and Stella Kramrisch, *The Presence of Śiva*, Oxford Univ. Press, Delhi, 1981.

Śiva's position among the gods with their conventions is made clear on the occasion of the sacrifice offered by the pretentious half-god *Dakśa.* Except for *Śiva* everyone had been invited. All the gods and sages, even the rivers and mountains had come. *Dakśa* explains why *Śiva* is not there:

> "What is his lineage and what is his clan? What place does he belong to and what is his nature? What does he do for a living and how does he behave, this one who is drinking poison and who rides on a bull? He is not an ascetic, for how could he then be carrying a weapon? He is not a householder for he lives on the cremation ground. He is not a celibate student, for he has a wife. He is not a *Brahmin* for the Vedas do not know him as one. Since he carries a spear and trident he might be a *Kṣhatriya*, but he is not. Since he delights in the destruction of the world, he cannot be a *Kṣhatriya*, who protects the world from harm. And how can be a *Vaishya*, for he never has any wealth? He is not even a *Shūdra*, for he wears a snake as a sacred thread. So he is beyond the castes (*varṇa*) and the stages of life (*āśrama*). Everything is known by its original source but *Śiva*, the Immovable, has no original source. He is not man because half his body is female. And yet he is not a woman because he has a beard, He is not even a eunuch, because his phallus (*liṅga*) is worshipped. He is not a boy, for he is great in years, that fearsome one, and he is proclaimed in the worlds as beginningless and ageless. How can he be young when he is so ancient? And yet, he is not old, for he is without old age and death.[50]

Śiva falls into no category. He perplexes conventions, including religious conventions. One of his symbols is the many-faced *liṅga*, the *pañçamukha liṅga*, looking into all directions. The *pañçamukha liṅga's* fifth face, on top of the pillar, is generally invisible. It represents the inner realization, by symbolic configuration, of our material and now existing shape which ought to expand into a vision into all directions, into all time and space. Stella Kramrisch draws attention to the circular upper part of the *Liṅga* and its lower part which is square:

> "Once the vision of descending, condensing light strikes the terrestrial base and assumes concrete extension, its volume is situated in space. While the vertical direction of the pillar remains essential, it is ensconced in matter and takes on volumetric extensiveness. Thus the faces hinge on the embodied equation of *mantra* (*S.K.*) and deity, of sacred sound and vision.[51]

The riches of these symbolic equations result from man's being simultaneously an inhabitant and a guest on earth. The fifth invisible face at the pillar's top is the ideal of transcendence and the awareness of one's limitations. Beyond the pillar lies the mythical Perfection in the immeasurable vastness of the universe. Awareness of his limitation in the midst of immeasurable expanse creates a tension in man. That tension expresses itself in speculation and in the arts.

Man is truly "modern" when meditating upon his limits. Awareness of man's limits has always been a property of human culture. Especially the mythical

50. *Kāśī Khaṇḍa (Skanda Purāṇa), Gurumaṇḍala Granthālayā*, No. XX, Vol. 4, Calcutta, 1961.
51. Stella Kramrisch, *The Presence of Śiva*, p. 180-181.

consciousness in its widest distribution excels in acknowledging man's confines. In my reading I met with two youngsters as wide apart culturally as they are in time. Both are equally endearing by their curiosity after the universe's secrets. Their approach differs. Both are welcome participants in our discussion on myth and modern. One of them is *Gārgi*, daughter of *Vaçaknu* of the *Bṛhadāraṇyaka Upaniṣad* of Vedic times. We shall meet her when we take a closer look at India in this paragraph. The other, two thousand years later, is Stephen Dedalus in James Joyce's philosophical novel, *A Portrait of the Artist as a Young Man*. Joyce's work deals with the mythical and the historical and their symbols in the West. Stephen Dedalus was already at a young age interpreting his experience in mythological terms and his mythology in terms of what he saw and what he was able to think.[52]

Stephen Dedalus sat brooding at his classroom desk. He read what he had written on the flyleaf of his geography book: himself, his name and where he was: "Stephen Dedalus-Class of Elements-Clongowes Wood College-Sallins-County Kildare-Ireland-Europe-The World-The Universe". That was what he had written. He read the flyleaf from the end to the beginning till he came to his own name; that was he. But after that? Everything seemed to stop then. How could he, Stephen Dedalus, be the last word to be written? He read again from the beginning to the end and that seemed to make more sense.

The boy had given himself over to a psychological and mythical ambiguity which looked, considering the fact he was still a youngster, quite sophisticated. It had dawned on him that he was both a guest and an inhabitant in the world. His intuition that his story could only be read with sense if read from the beginning to the end, made Stephen Dedalus part of a longstanding tradition of human awareness of our limited mode of existence in the universe. Little did the boy realize that two millennia earlier *Gārgi* had been having the same thoughts. Joyce seeks intelligibility of existence through the often humorous but equally often frightening mix-up of symbols that had come to him from various directions. They had been explained to him in terms of appropriation by a particular opinion or tradition, the very thing symbols do not allow for.

52. The destruction the West faced during and after the first world war (1914-1918) further inspired authors to write their philosophical novels. Among them James Joyce and Thomas Mann are conspicuous. Both authors aim at an intended, carefully controlled opening of associations into the timeless archetypes of the mythical. Their later writings immerse in the realm of myth altogether. The problem they faced was, on the aesthetic level of the modern novel, the heritage of a rationalistic, naturalistic and anecdotal-historical narrative art, inadequate to their understanding of psychology in its universal, mythological as well as individual aspects. On the religious level they faced the related problem of an inherited church tradition, out of touch with the sciences and the actual moral order and the humanistic conscience of the secularized "Christian" nations of the modern West. Joyce, a born Catholic, and Mann, a Protestant, encountered symbols, or the lack of them, incapable of explaining their world. Both attempted the steep climb to an almost inaccessible destination of sorting out the mythical and historical fermentation going on in themselves and their surrounding. They take at times recourse to the East for explanations. See: Thomas Mann, *Der Zauberberg*, Berlin: S. Fischer Verlag, 1924, Engl. tr. H.T. Lowe-Porter, *The Magic Mountain*, New York: Knopf, 1927. James Joyce, *A Portrait of the Artist as a Young Man,* London: Jonathan Cape, Ltd., 1916, p. 40. Carl Jung has given a penetrating description, too long to quote here, of the contrast between Catholic and Protestant thought in regard to their understanding of symbols and myths. See: *The Archetypes of the Collective Unconscious*, tr. R.F.C. Hull, Bollingen Series XX, Vol. 9, New York : Pantheon Books, 1959, pp. 13ff.

Being "modern" has its undeniable limitations in understanding reality. In that sense, being "modern" is as universal as man himself is universal. Stephen Dedalus, brooding at his desk, makes delightful and instructive reading relevant to our inquiry into cosmic awareness in the context of the mythical and the "modern" as here presented. I quote the passage in full:

> "What was after the universe? Nothing. But was there anything round the universe to show where it stopped before the nothing-place began? It could not be a wall; but there could be a thin thin line there all around everything and everywhere. Only God could do that. He tried to think what a big thought that must be; but he could only think of God. God was God's name just as his name was Stephen. "Dieu" was the French for God and that was God's name too; and when anyone prayed to God and said "Dieu" then God knew that it was a French person who was praying. But, though there were names for God in all the different languages in the world and God understood what all the people who prayed said in their different languages, still God remained the same God and God's real name was God. It made him very tired to think that way".

What made Stephen Dedalus very tired was his persistence in rationalizing. Joyce —who is the boy—does so intentionally for he knew himself too well. Vedic *Gārgi's* preparedness, as we shall see, to discontinue her equally critical inquiry and henceforth be silent, shows a different approach. We moderns of the twentieth century are tempted to devaluate the mythical. We find it difficult to establish a link between mythical time and so-called factual historical time. To accommodate mythical places in our geographical space we may find perplexing. The myth is often discarded as a negligible and irrelevant thought, incapable of explaining.

Our questions are quite justifiable. When Copernicus in 1543 published his exposition of a heliocentric universe, sciences began to penetrate into its formerly unknown physical secrets. The ancient cosmological mythic notions of the macro-meso-microcosmic harmony dissolved. Lost was also the ancient concept of the holy arts "making visible in the things that are made, the invisible things of God". The traditional structures by which all things were believed to be held in place crumbled.

One of the functions of myth is to render a cosmology, an image of the universe. Modern man of the rational-critical method turns not to archaic texts but to science. Who can blame man for being curious to know the universe he lives in? The present transition, however, of the image of the universe and its assimilation by our mythic thought to that of scientific empirical query is causing a crisis.[53] The crisis has been more acutely felt in the West than it has been in India until now. Henri Adams

53. Dissatisfied with the Ptolemaic system, assuming that the earth is the fixed centre of the universe, surrounded by concentric spherical shells, Copernicus (1473-1543) revived the heliocentric theory advanced by Aristarchos of Samos. In his work, *On the Revolution of the Celestial Orbs*. 1543, Copernicus used the system of Pythagoras to prove mathematically that the earth is spherical and in uniform motion around the sun. On account of the supposed implications of a discovery that the earth, and hence mankind, would not be at the physical centre of the universe, Copernicus' theory faced violent opposition from the Church.

describes the first upheavals after Copernicus and Galileo who argued in favour of a strict separation of theological and scientific issues as the watershed of the passage to a new era of mankind. In the pursuit of truth and reality whole massive structures of the past were taken down.[54] Adam's crucial point is the naming of the new force and the new theme by which the old, that of unity whether personified or not, was being displaced:

> "The mind should now observe and register forces - take them apart and put them together - without assuming unity at all. "Nature, to be commanded, must be obeyed". The imagination must not be given wings but weights. As Galileo reversed the action of the earth and the sun, Bacon reversed the relation of thought to force. The mind was henceforth to follow the movement of matter, and unity must be left to shift for itself."

The inward vision and outward crude reality seemed to come irresolvably together, forming a knowledge of reality with a bedevilled edge.[55] Our present-day modernity causes concern, if not anguish and at times even panic. It is yet to be assimilated by most in terms of a satisfactory world view. In the whirlwind of change a new stability must be found salvaging the very cosmos and everyone and everything in it. The inherent but disturbed symbiotic linkage of man and nature brings nations to the conference table. Some would seem to be less hopeful with regard to the re-establishment of a sane world-order. Coomaraswamy writes, not without a touch of disillusion:

> "Those who think of their house as only a kind of machine to live in should judge their point of view by that of Neolithic man, who also lived in a house, but a house that embodied a cosmology. We are more than sufficiently provided with overheating systems; but let us not forget that he identified the columns of smoke that rose from his hearth to disappear from view through a hole in the roof with the Axis of the Universe, saw in his luffer an image of the Heavenly Door, and in his hearth the navel of the Earth, formulae that we at the present day are hardly capable of understanding; we, for whom "such knowledge as is not empirical is meaningless". Most of the things that Plato called "ideas" are only "superstitions" to us".[56]

54. Henry Adams, *The Degeneration of the Democratic Dogma,* New York: The Macmillan Company, 1947, re-edition of 1919, p. 287.
55. This adventure has for the West been portrayed by Miguel de Cervantes Saavedra (1547-1616) in his well-known and immortal legend of Don Quixote. Minds had been upset and were obliged to find a new orientation, not without difficulties, as Don Quixote shows us, but yet a new adventure. It was when the winds had risen and, after Copernicus, when the earth began to move and turn around the sun, that Don Quixote went for windmills instead of living with the new. As his servant Sancho Panza ruefully remarked, when he found his master thrown away by the mechanical round of the mill, "Anyone could have seen that these are windmills - unless he had windmills in his head." In his study of the epic of Don Quixote, Ortega Y Gasset remarks: "The poetic can no longer be made to consist of that special attraction of the ideal past,.. now our poetry has to be capable of coping with the present new reality." See: Jose Ortega Y Gasset, *Meditations on Quixote, tr. from the* Spanish by Evelyn Rugg and Diego Marin, W.W. Norton and Company, 1961, pp. 136 - 139. The author further remarks that the discovery of fixed laws regarding the Universe upset people's notion regarding the idea of "possibility" and hence of "adventure" as part of human personality. Cervantes' work aims at showing the need of adventure within the reality of fixed scientific laws. There must be, for man, a way of finding "compossibility".
56. Ananda K. Coomarasway, "The Christian and Oriental, or True Philosophy of Art", in: *Why Exhibit*

The author's concern is understandable. However, change is unavoidable. Both Plato's worldview and that of neolithic man in his cosmic hut were based on experienced observation. They did what they could not avoid doing. So does present-day technical man. Should our attention not be directed to the "still point" of our revolving world and be looked for in the heart rather than in structures? Is it not through *belief* in the restoration of wholeness that cosmological change receives its intelligibility? A particular cosmology may lose its physical truth. It can, however, not lose its own inherent objective, that of finding a place and an orientation for man in the world. This is true for the whole of human history. The world and human culture have always been in constant change and fermentation.[57] Man is permanently modern to the extent he realizes his contingency, his being "a little while". For the purpose of our inquiry we are, therefore, demystifying the notion of "modern" in its popular sense. That notion needs more than ever to be checked especially in its relation to consumerism.

What then is our question with regard to man's mythical awareness in the context of our demystified notion of "modern"? If for neolithic man, for Plato or for us, present-day moderns, myth may no longer be an explanation, does myth thereby lose its validity? Does myth lose its authenticity when its etiological intention stands cancelled? The question is of vital importance for myth. If myth fails to answer it is dead. Shall we say that, in losing its *explanatory* functioning, myth reveals its strength as *exploration* of the meaningfulness of man's human condition in the universe? Its symbolic function is that of its skill in retrieving the bond between man and what he considers sacred. Thus, paradoxically, the myth asserts its very essence and is elevated to the dignity of a symbol when it is demythologized through contact with (scientific) history. In other words: it is in *losing* the myth that we *discover* it.[58] That has always happened to man. The older moderns, those on the archaic level of culture in time, kept the World open by virtue of their receptive consciousness of the sacred and what it says, viz., the myth. There is ample proof of their initiative in counteracting the dead weight of mere historical event.[59] The cosmological myth is concerned not only with

---

Works of Art, London: Luzac and Company, 1943, pp. 32-33.

57. Thus there are, as I shall try and explain in the following subdivisions of the paragraph on "myth and modern," various kinds of "modernities" implying a constant process of demythologization in human cultures and individuals, one more demanding perhaps than another. Because myth is already *word*, i.e, *thought*, it is capable of being re-worded, re-thought. Myth, therefore, has its own dialectic.

58. This happens on various levels of *intensity*. The "loss" of myth and its "discovery" in so-called secularized and historicized cultures is of another amplitude and reach than that in a religious and traditional society. In the West, from the seventeenth century onward, the assertion of linearism and the progressivistic concept of history triumph in the ideas of the evolutionists and in those of Marxism. We now hear of the revival of interest in the theory of cycles, like in e.g., political economy, the revival, in philosophy, of the myth of eternal return by Nietzsche and the philosophy of history by e.g. Spengler and Toynbee, concerning themselves with problems of periodicity. The reappearance of cyclical theories is significant. Marx denied history its transcendental significance in the appearance of the class struggle. Marxism gives a meaning to history in that it is not a succession of arbitrary accidents. There is a coherent structure leading to a definite end, viz., the final elimination of capitalist history, "salvation". Eliade writes: "Here for the militant Marxist lies the secret of the remedy for the terror of history", see: *The Myth of the Eternal Return or, Cosmos and History*, p. 149.

59. I am aware of the absence here of a fuller worked out discussion on the problem of historicism and freedom and history. The following observations may, it is hoped, be considered sufficient to make up for this defect.

the "first time" but also with what happens *after*. The stress often lies not so much on what the gods created but on what happened to them and to man after creation. The mythical awareness employs critical rationality, be it not exclusively, and *causes its own de-mythologisation*. Why? Because the myth and its narration is already *word*, that is, already *thought*. Myths do not try and prove anything. They merely tell us what is for them a truth. One either accepts it or one does not. It either matches an experience of one's own or it does not. The sequence of events is by its very narrative compelling and its philosophy is implicit. This is a basic form of human communication. It makes an immediate contact gathering the hearer into the speaker. The myth narrative is capable of re-wording and re-thinking (see footnote 57). It is its own hermeneutic. Myth's volatility makes it move freely between the beginnings, the now and the end. This is an irksome adventure for the critical rational method. More than once myth is being accused of inconsistency and arbitrariness.

The receptive experience of the sacred keeps man having *ideas* about the world and himself. Its language both challenges and contributes to that of the rational-critical. Thus it adds up to the totality of man's experience of himself and the world.[60] The sacred forces the admission that there is more than rational evidence in living human experience. The revolt of life, of what happens, refuses imprisonment in mere rational argument. Official doctrine and culture have always, often to their dislike and discomfort, known undercurrents of thoughts and activities which, although "impermissible", eventually became eyeopeners to official behaviour. Words, rhythms, images, perfumes, colours and sensations of all kinds have their inevitable associations in symbols which, in being experienced, cannot be subdued by reason alone. Every sight, tactile impression, sound, taste, and smell come to us from some part of space and endure for some time. Space and time are the unavoidable pre-condition of all experience. Where else do we live? All those impressions are linked with the sacred in the receptive awareness shifting the frontiers of reason. It leaves reasoned argument behind by pushing forward beyond it. Paradoxically, for the mythical mind this means to regress to the beginnings.

To understand the myth as myth is to understand what the myth, with its time, its space, its events and personages and its drama, adds to the revealing power of the primary symbols, read by man from the universe. These are first of all the cosmic realities of the sun, the moon, the winds, the earth and the waters. *In* and *on* these primary symbols man reads the sacred as written *in* and *on* them. What man there reads man *says*. That is the myth. What myths say is much more than our often limited idea of what *saying* allows to the myth. Our notion of what the word of the myth is capable of saying is often too narrow.

One of the symbols capturing my imagination is that of *Āpaḥ*, the Waters, in the Indian mythical consciousness. We shall see how these Waters, fanning out into a wide variety of secondary symbols, scan the universe and man, providing a pictorial of

60. The current stress on values of the full human potential is evident in various new movements offering strong opposition to exploitation, fraud, sexism and excessive economic expansion at the cost of man and his environment. Among them must also be counted the holistic view on medical care and education, the latter having already been given attention to by informal educationalists like Steiner and Tagore. Formal education would still seem to lack a combination of rational knowledge and an intuition for the non-linear nature of environment.

their significance and reality. Thus - as an example and as a foretaste of what we may expect in the third part of this book - we find our experience of reality through the primary symbol of the Waters expressed in the *makara* the crocodile, the animal-fish and beast of the deep as well as of firm ground. It lies, in Indian myth narrative and iconography, at the feet of the great Goddess of Nature, the Womb. That Womb is again revealed to us in the rivers. In *Gaṅgā's, Yamunā's* and *Saraswatī's* womb exist both life and death, day and night. Inviting reflection, the goddesses *Gaṅgā, Yamunā* and *Saraswatī* are seated on their thrones at temple gates. Their thrones are entwined by the grapevine, fruit of the earth who is man's solid base and home. Lest man should forget that he is a guest on earth, the grapevines are being matched by the waterjug *(kalaśa),* the vessel of flux and passage. For the Waters not only feed but also envelop and swallow. Thus comes about the harmony of spheres, the totality. Other cultures too, through the medium of mythical depth of thought, have found this profundity of the harmony of spheres. What *Gaṅgā*, *Saraswatī* and *Yamunā* are to the Indian are Demeter and Persephone to the Greeks and to cultures influenced by them.[61] It may already be guessed that the amazing similarity of myths in widely separated geographical areas around the globe, indicates a common origin and a single human consciousness, untrammelled by differences of race, religion, and nationality. The present precarious world situation has in various quarters aroused a renewed interest in myth as a pointer to truth and inspiration. As I said, mythical thought possesses a capacity for problem solving, too little known and appreciated. In the conspectus and conclusion to this work, I shall speak for myth under the caption "symbols make us think".

What the myth says is first of all the happenings of "the beginnings". Not as an external repetition of the same happenings, a cultural immobility. The exemplary model of the creation-myth spurs man on to activity, to recreation of the world, of himself and his surroundings. In the words of Mircea Eliade:

> "Although the sacrosanct models would seem to paralyse human initiative, actually they stimulate man to create, they are constantly opening new perspectives to his inventiveness."[62]

Mythical consciousness is being constantly aware of what happens. It is continuously being "modern". It discovers timeliness and temporality in Eternal Time and the idea of contingency. In that contingence—the world as it actually appears —, man's creativeness and imagination must needs be reviewed by the force of new aspects of contingency forcing themselves upon his consciousness. In as much as the revolt of life cannot be wholly contained in the rational-critical argument, it also resists being imprisoned in a myth grown old.[63] Someone in the community or, as if struck by a

---

61. Hans Leisegang, "The Mystery of the Serpent", in: Joseph Campbell (ed.), *The Mysteries,* Papers from the Eranos Yearbooks, vol. 2, Bollingen Series XXX 2, New York: Pantheon Books, 1955, pp. 250ff.
62. Mircea Eliade, *Myth and Reality,* p. 144.
63. A clear contemporary example - not without its painful implications - is the present process of nation building in independent new Africa. Former colonial boundaries of African countries were not seldom drawn on maps in the West. Political rivalry and economic greed often totally disregarded the ethnic boundaries known to and felt by Africans themselves. On their day of independence many African nations inherited the boundaries forced upon them by their former

flash, the whole community at once is going to ask: Why? The question is born from the "logos" *in* and *of* the "mythos" —not the logos applied from outside—which adjusts man's ideas as he meets the circumstances.[64] Embedded in the midst of our human condition myth does not live in an invented world. But myth is capable of inventions, recapitulation and re-evaluation of circumstances. That is why there is a certain tension between myth and tradition. The continuous human drive in search of an understanding of the world and of man necessarily involves some form of estrangement. There is an epistemological distance in the reality of time as man experiences it viz., the before and the after. Myth tempers the threat of rigidity in the flow of time. In adapting to this contingency the mythical awareness is being constantly rational in its approach towards tradition and set trends. It adjust visions, ideas and concepts of reality. Within the group individual persons let their imaginations be roused by the waking power of the symbol. Its eloquence is expressed in new thoughts. Thus tradition and convention are put to the test. Allowance is made in the group for a certain type of deviant, the visionary, the shaman and the troubadour. Later we shall meet the *yogi*, the *tantric* and the *muni*. The insight of such strangely gifted persons creates myth narrative allowing for fresh thought to circulate in society.

Modernity reveals itself on different levels. Morphological modernity is the deciphering done by parents, teachers, elders, or the more intelligent group members. It usually happens to the younger since they have not yet enjoyed full access to the treasures of their culture. This modernity is often accompanied by a diachronical one when older notions implying ideology and lapse of time must be discussed. One moves from present to past in order to re-interpret, incorporate further or reject. A third modernity is the diatopical when different "places" of myth and philosophy meet. It is important for understanding the developments in the West and the present growth towards a possible global culture.

India

The transition from what had become inflexible ritualism in the *Brāhmaṇas* to meditative inwardness in the *Upaniṣads* altered the perception of the world and its beyond. Automatized sacrifice to external deities shifted to contemplation on the significance of the self. The True Self pervading the universe was found reflected in

---

colonial masters. Many a country faces the problem of mythical tribal and ethnic identities to be moulded into a new nation, cutting across those solidarities and psychic unities. The problem not only concerns boundaries between countries but also internal division in provinces and districts. Thus, for example, the Kikuyu and Luo in Kenya find themselves in a process of painful demythologization in favour of the new Kenyan nation. Likewise, the pastoral Masai people, whose identity of "Origin" spills over into Tanzania and Uganda, find themselves under severe psychological stress. Even though a certain amount of ethnic consideration is observable in the former colonial administration, it betrays the old maxim of "divide and rule" and it was not concerned with solving the problems of "The Origins".

64. A problem connected with this adjustment is the question of "the myth of morals" and "the morals of myth". Even though the question is of importance for the formation of ethical sense and the human conscience, to go deeper into it would take up too much space. Freedom of conscience would seem to depend a good deal on its discovery by un-covering the myths related to the notions of good and evil. R. Panikkar has dealt with the subject provokingly in his, *Myth, Faith and Hermeneutics,* pp. 8 - 55. The idea and the names of the three - fold modernity in the following paragraph and passim I have borrowed from R. Panikkar *op. cit.*

the depth of the soul.[65] *The Chāndogya Upaniṣad* expresses it concisely: "This whole world is *Brahman*" (*sarvam khalvidam brahma*)[66]. Sacrificial self-efficacy yielded to the concept of mental sacrifice beneficial to the acquisition of spiritual knowledge.[67] The subsequent development of monistic philosophy cast a doubt on the belief in some Vedic and Brāhminic gods.[68] Interesting during this time of search for reality within oneself is the "substitution meditation". Certain letters of the alphabet had to be reflected upon as expressions of *Brahman*, some deity or a vital function of the body.

> "These forms of meditation did not mean prolonged contemplation or any logical process of thinking, but merely the simple practice of continually thinking one entity or process or letter as another entity or process."[69]

The emphasis on interiority caused a shift from reality as experienced outside of oneself to its opposite. *The Chāndogya Upaniṣad* puts it tersely:

> "Containing all works, containing all desires, containing all odours, containing all tastes, encompassing this whole world, without speech, without concern, this is the self of mine within the heart; this is *Brahman*."[70]

An interesting philosophical discussion in the *Bṛhadāraṇyaka Upaniṣad* provides us with a picture of the prevailing inward looking mood of upaniṣadic times. One of the participants in the discussion is *Vaçaknu's* inquisitive daughter *Gārgī* whom I introduced earlier. Modern as she was, like Stephen Dedalus, she searched for an attitude to what she saw and experienced of the Universe. The problem she put before the great master *Yājñavalkya* concerns the same question Stephen Dedalus wrote about on the flyleaf of his geography book. This is what *Gārgī* asks:

> "*Yājñavalkya*, as long as this whole world is interwoven lengthwise and crosswise (*ota and prota*) in which are then the waters interwoven, lengthwise and crosswise?" "In the wind, O *Gārgī*." "But then what is it in which the wind is interwoven, lengthwise and crosswise"?
> "In the worlds of the aerial space, O *Gārgī*" "But then what is that in which the worlds of aerial space are interwoven lengthwise and crosswise?" "In the worlds of the stars, O *Gārgī*".

And so it went on: the worlds of gods, the worlds of *Indra*, those of *Prajāpati*, the worlds of *Brahman*:

> "But then what is that in which the worlds of *Brahman* are interwoven lengthwise and crosswise?" "O *Gārgī*, do not question further (*mā ati prākṣīḥ*) so that your head should not burst to pieces by further questioning! You overquestion about a godhead regarding which no further

65. S. Radhakrishnan, *The Principal Upaniṣads*, Allen and Undwin, London, 1953, p. 49.
66. *CU.* 3. 14. 1.
67. R.D. Ranade, *A Constructive Survey of Upaniṣadic Philosophy*, Oriental Book Agency, Poona, 1926, p. 8.
68. R.E. Hume, *The Thirteen Principal Upaniṣads*, Oxford Univ., London, 1971, p. 52.
69. S.N. Dasgupta, *Hindu Mysticism*, Motilal Banarsidass (first edition), Vārānaśī, 1976. p. 19.
70. *CU.* 3.14.4: "*sarva-karmāh sarva-kārmaḥsarva-gandhaḥ sarva-rasaḥ sarvam idam abhyāttovāky anādaraḥ esa mā ātmāntarahṛdaye etad brahma.....*"

> questioning is possible (*anatipraśnyā devatā*); O *Gārgī*, do not question further!" Then *Gārgī*, the daughter of *Vaçaknu*, remained silent.[71]

Stephen Dedalus is living in an age, the twentieth century, and in a culture where autonomy of the student appears a little more pronounced perhaps than it was in *Gārgī's* time. Her silence, however, is no slavish submission to her master. *Gārgī's* Vedic-Indian silence may well be contrasted with a certain lack of it in her counterpart's argumentative thought, that of Stephen Dedalus, and which indeed made him feel tired. The boy's twentieth-century Western environment may indeed be overquestioning the Absolute in terms of critical-rational thought. For that thought to keep silent is a difficult task. *Gārgī's* further questioning with a receptive rather than an argumentative awareness, reveals more her curiosity after the secret of silence than her wish for mere intellectual satisfaction. After a long discourse about the object of knowledge, remaining ever unknowable, her master *Yājñavalkya* says to *Gārgī*:

> "In truth, O *Gārgī*, this imperishable one sees but is not seen, hears but is not heard, comprehends but is not comprehended, knows but is not known. There is besides him none that sees, there is none that hears besides him, there is none that comprehends besides him, there is none that knows besides him. In truth, in this imperishable one is space inwoven and interwoven".[72]

What interests us here, in terms of modernity, is *Gārgī's* and Stephen Dedalus' equal understanding of the *problem* of Absolute Reality namely—that it is unknowable - and their different *attitude* to it. The difference of attitude is reflected in that of their masters. *Yājñavalkya's* exposition is expressed in cosmological mythical language whereas the boy's "master" is the scientific rational conceptual language. Taken for granted by both masters is the concept of all phenomenality as conditioned, through and through, by the organs through which it is perceived. Stephen Dedalus' manner of thinking resembles Kant's words about what *Yājñavalkya* had already made clear:

---

71. The doctrine of "Silence" is an essential part of the Vedic and Upaniṣadic concept of *Brahman* as Reality. It is characteristic of both Hinduism and Buddhism. For the following notes I draw heavily from Coomaraswamy, *Metaphysics,* pp. 198 - 208. *Gārgī* is silent, i.e. "holds her peace", *uparāma.* This is in agreement with the Indian concept of negation which refuses a definition of *Brahman. Brahman* is "*neti-neti*", not this, not this". One may refer to *Śaṅkara* on the *Vedānta Sūtra* 3.2.17, where, after having remained silent twice when asked about the nature of *Brahman, Bhāva* explains when asked a third time" "I teach you indeed, but you do not understand: this *Brahman* is silence". The same significance may be given to the *Buddha*'s refusal to explain what is "*nirvāṇa*". It is "the unspeakable", *avadyam.* The idea of wisdom in regard to *Brahman* is to be a "silent sage", *muni.* Also the *Bhagavad Gītā* 10.38 speaks of *Kṛṣña* as "the silence of the hidden ones", *mauna guhyāṇām.* Access to the knowledge of *Brahman,* Reality, is in Vedic thought made through *dīkṣā,* initiation, and cannot be expressed. The stress on silence accompanying Vedic and later religious activity is significant. Unspoken interiorization would seem almost essential to grasp *Brahman.* Thus it is said in *SB.* 7.2.2. 13-14: "What is silent is undeclared and what is undeclared is everything". *Brahman* is not known in human sound. These few observations are far from doing justice to the notion of "Silence" in Indian thought. Here they may suffice as a reminder.

72. The two passages are, respectively: *BU.* 3.6.1 and 3.8.11 :

    "tad vā etad akṣaram. Gārgī, adṛṣṭaṁ draṣṭṛ, aśrutaṁ, śrotṛ, amatam mantṛ, avijñātam vijñātṛ, nānyad ato' sti draṣṭṛ, nānyad ato'sti śrotṛ nānyad ato'sti mantṛ, nānyad ato'sti vijñātṛ; etasmin nu khalvakṣare, Gārgī, ākāśa otaṣ ca protaṣ-ca."

    See: Paul Deussen, *Sixty Upaniṣads of the Veda,* vol. I, p. 456-464. Deussen observes that the content of these passages has been "emphatically used by Kant".

> "(Herewith) the nature of the highest cause itself remains unknown to me, I only compare its known effect (namely, the constitution of the universe) and the rationality of this effect with the known effects of human reason, and, therefore, I call that highest cause a Reason, without thereby attributing to it as its proper quality, either the thing that I understand by this term in the case of man, or any other thing with which I am familiar."[73]

Intellectual Upaniṣadic thinking explains the world of phenomena as the effect of universal ignorance upon pure consciousness (*Brahman*). Likewise individuality is the effect of individual ignorance on the part of the *ātman* in oneself. For true understanding man needs to draw away from the shores of phenomenality. This, in Indian mythical awareness, is symbolized by immersion into the waters where the shore's borderline disappears.

What *Yājñavalkya* and his pupil *Gārgī* led to the Unknowable but did not *separate* them from it, is the hypothesis of ignorance in phenomenality. The possibility of *identity* with *Brahman* remains open. It is expressed in the four great statements mentioned earlier, the *Mahāvākyas*. The *Chāndogya Upaniṣad* identifies *Brahman* with *ātman:*

> "That which is the subtle essence (the root of all) this whole world has for itself. That is the truth. That is the self. That art Thou, *Svetaketu*."[74]

In India, even its most developed metaphysical speculation never destroyed the symbol of *guhā,* the cave of the human heart, where no sound is heard but that of *Brahman*. It would be a difficult and complicated task to try and explain why this should be so. If morphological modernity — interspersed with diachronical discourse as time elapses in a given human society — mainly takes place within the confines of a given culture, we could hardly avoid a study of the history of India's social, political and economic structures.[75]

Many outside influences notwithstanding, the *guhā,* the cave of the heart, in India remains open. One may argue the intensity of the receptive consciousness of the Indian *guhā* and its true spiritual content. It leaves no doubt that illiteracy and hence the absence of hermeneutical interpretation of the scriptures, have given rise to a good deal of decadence in mythical awareness resulting in superstitions. Also true is the fact that material poverty requires a whole sub-stratum of "myths of redemption" in order to escape "later" from misery "now". Since I am here restricting myself as

73. Immanuel Kant (1724-1804) : *Prolegomena zu einer jeden kunftigen Metaphysik, die als Wissenschaft wird auftreten konnen,* par. 57-58, tr. Joseph Campbell: " Prolegomena to Every Future System of Metaphysics that May Ever Arise in the Way of a Science" in "*Creative Mythology, The Masks of God,* Penguin Books, 1982, reprint, pp. 339 - 340. Kant here starts from a four-term analogy: a is to b as c is to x, which is to be seen "not as an incomplete resemblance of two things, but as a complete resemblance of two relationships between quite dissimilar things" — "nicht etwa, eine unvollkommene Ähnlichkeit zweier Dinge, sondern eine vollkommene Ähnlichkeit zweier Verhältnisse zwischen ganz unähnliche Dingen."
74. *CU.* 6.8.7: "*sa ya eṣo'nima aitad ātmyam idaṁ sarvam, tat satyam, sa ātmā; tat tvam asi svetaketo*".
75. The effort would, in the context of philosophy and myth, certainly have to consider and evaluate the marxist philosophy of history which, too, posits a vision concerning man and reality. The marxist analysis of the history of a country is quite different from the non-marxist one. See, e.g. K. Antonova. G. Bongard-Levin, G. Kotovsky, *A History of India,* tr. Katherine Judelson, 2 vols., Progress Publishers, Moscow, 1979.

much as possible to the "myths of origin", the myths of redemption must regrettably be left untouched.

There is another aspect we must pay attention to in the general context of myth and its awareness. It would be very difficult for the student of myth to find in the Indian mythical consciousness a consistent revolt by man against the highest god, the principle of unity. Any attempt by gods and men in Indian myths to revolt with the express intention to succeed, is thwarted by mythical counter-events that have left telling symbols in everyday Indian life. Thus, when *Brahma,* thinking himself to be the highest god, grew a second head, *Śiva* cut it off. He carried it with him and finally let the skull slip from his hand in *Kaśī,* Banaras, when he took a bath there. Till today there is a site in Banaras, *Kapālamoçana,* to remind us of this "release of the skull bowl" from *Śiva's* hand. Not only in Banaras but[76] all over India, "skull-bowl carriers", *kapālin sadhus,* carry their vessels, also used to collect alms, in token of worship of *the highest Being.* Another symbol revealed to us in the myths is that of ashes, a substance most purified and totally free of blemish. Later we shall meet the sage *Maṅkaṇaka* who, wandering in the forests, is given illumination by the sight of ashes.

If it is true that in the relation between myth and history, myth proves to be the primary and history the secondary and derived factor—because a people's history is implicit in their gods—India will not "as of itself" sever its link with Brahman.[77]

The Prometheus - and Adamic myths account, as we shall see, how the Greeks and the Semites revolted against the Creator. No such revolt is found in the *Prajāpati* cycle.

How India's myths and its modernity will develop can only be guessed. Mass communication media and technology import the *other* of philosophy and myth from different cultural places.[78] India cannot, nor does it wish to escape the emerging global culture. A recent topic of frequent discussion in the media is the erosion of traditional mythical-religious values and ethical norms in especially the more affluent sections of Indian society. Traditional structures, such as the joint-family and marriage, are under stress. The caste—and dowry systems are creating new problems due to misguided increase of capital and exploitative political and administrative management. The questions and doubts many modern Indian students face are often similar to those encountered by students elsewhere.[79]

The age of modern technology and the scientific-rational approach is said to be a

---

76. See : Diana L. Eck, *Banaras, City of Light,* p. 119. *Kapālamochana* "was apparently precisely at the confluence of the *Matsyodarī* and the backward-flowing Ganges. Today the watertank is over a mile to the north of it...".

77. Erst Cassirer, *Mythical Thought*, p. 5-6: looking at myth and history in a broader philosophical perspective, Cassirer maintains that for an individual people as for mankind as a whole there is no free choice by which it can accept or reject given mythical conceptions : "on the contrary, a strict necessity prevails".

78. Two very readable and instructive publications with regard to India's modernization are : Augustine Kanjamala, *Religion and Modernization in India, A case study of Northern Orissa,* Steyler Verlag, St. Augustine/Ishvani, Pune/Satprakashan, Indore, 1981 and: Yogendra Singh, *Modernization of Indian Tradition,* Thomson Press (India) Limited, Delhi, 1973.

79. From the point of view of people's reactions to the wide variety of new modern gadgets, be they imported or manufactured in India itself, there would be little difference between reactions in the West or anywhere else and those in India. And why should they, if indeed we are all humans? Student-joints in the big cities are no different from those in London, Nairobi, Jakarta or Amsterdam.

property of the West. It was so in origin. Its spread to India will no doubt exert its influence on the Indian consciousness. If the Indian remains as convinced of his contingency — his being "a little while" —, as his philosophy and myth tell him, he will take the new adventure in his stride. It is important for our study to remember with the aid of the study of intercultural exchange, that materials carried from any time past to a time present or from one culture to another, shed their values at the cultural port of the recipient. They either become mere curiosities or undergo a major change in the long run through a process of understanding and mis-understanding, reception and rejection in order to be finally broken up and translated into an intelligible possession relevant to the recipient's life. That process is taking its course in the West on a scale for everyone to see. From trackless ways and adventures in the thick of confusion to new embodiments of identity only to return to untrodden paths in search not of a way out but of a way in. Why should such adventures be restricted to the West only? For the new decolonized nations, however, the problem is of special significance. Panikkar writes :

> "To know whether the new modernity of India will imply Westernization is a burning question for two-thirds of today's world."[80]

The question is not rhetorical. One could hardly imagine the dissolution of the Indian spirit. Yet, India ought to be well aware of the forces it faces, the impact of which it might seriously underestimate.

The Greeks

The Greek myth must give us pause. Mircea Eliade writes :

> "Only in the culture of Greece was myth submitted to a long and penetrating analysis, from which it emerged radically "demystified". The rise of Greek rationalism coincides with a more and more damaging criticism of the "classic" mythology as it found expression in the works of Homer and Hesiod. If in every European language the word "myth" denotes a "fiction", it is because the Greeks proclaimed it to be such twenty-five centuries ago."[81]

The transition from the stabilizing influences of nature to a more pronounced concern for inner man through the process of morphological and diachronical modernity was more acutely felt in the Greek culture than it was in comparable processes in India.[82] The Greek question "ti tō ōn?"[83], "what is being?", was linked to rational-critical thought, the sciences and the arts. It was an attempt to uncover the path to knowledge by means of the intelligible "archè" and "entelechies" — pre-existent Idea or Type — of all things of Plato and Aristotle. In Greece, philosophy sought to establish a theoretical view of reality. Confronted not so much by immediate phenomenal reality as by the mythical transformation of it, Greek thought finally shed this transformation in favour of the ratio. Whether or not the Greek thinkers struck on the "archè" all on their own is not a matter for long discussion here. Greek and Egyptian beliefs appear

80. R. Panikkar, *Myth, Faith and Hermeneutics,* p. 104.
81. Mircea Eliade, *Myth and Reality,* p. 148.
82. i.e. the process from the pre-Socratics to the Sophists to Socrates and his disciples Plato and Aristotle.
83. Aristotle, *Metaphysics,* Bk. XII, ch. 8, par. 1074A.

to have been in mutual contact. In Egypt places were named after celestial archetypal fields.[84] Iranian cosmology too was known to the Greeks. The Zarvanic tradition knows each thing under a double aspect, viz. "mēnōk" and "gētīk", a visible and an invisible sky. The earth has its celestial counterpart. Each virtue practised in the visible sky is thought to have its celestial correspondent. In Iranian cosmology the invisible sky precedes the visible one.[85]

Indian cosmology, too is familiar with a two-layered pattern. Liberation is an awakening to, a new consciousness of a situation that existed from the beginning but which one was unable to realize. Ignorance (*avidyā*) is, in the last analysis, an ignorance of oneself. It is the forgetting of the True Self.

For Plato, living intelligently is above all remembering a disincarnate purely spiritual existence, the Idea. Plato's philosophical recollection, the anamnesis, does not recover the memory of events of former lives like traditional Greek doctrine of re-incarnation, but of truths, of structures of the real. It was in seeking the source, the "arché", that philosophical speculation for some time coincided with cosmogony. But it was no longer the cosmogonic myth. It now became an ontological problem. Like in India's transition from the *Brāhmaṇas* to the *Upaniṣads*, in Greece too, religious patterns of behaviour and mythical expressions were not the only subjects of discussion. The Greeks too were involved in psychology and metaphysics.

In Greece, however, that concern seems to have been of a wider distribution than it was in India. The gap between popular expression and philosophical speculation was less wide. The goddess Mnemosyne, the personification of Memory, is the mother of the Muses. She knows past, present and future events. Poets drew from her knowledge. Wandering round the country and singing her praises, they communicated the knowledge of her to all and sundry. Everyone benefitted from access to the "archè". These pre-existent Ideas were manifested in the mythical beginnings and they constituted the foundation of the World. Their being no longer a mere Memory of the past but a knowledge of it embodies the modernity which sprang up in Greece. And what happened to the gods? Mircea Eliade puts it matter of fact:

"For reasons we do not know gods and men decided to part amicably at Mekone."[86]

On the occasion of the primordial sacrifice at Mekone Prometheus appears on the Greek mythical scene. Trying to favour men and deceive Zeus, Prometheus conceals the flesh of the slain ox with its hide—the portion for man—and he offers the bones, covered in fat, to Zeus. Angered, Zeus retaliates by depriving man of the use of fire. Prometheus, however, retrieves it. Zeus, furious, chains Prometheus to a rock and an eagle devours his liver which grows again overnight. Hesoid adds in his narration that from then on men burn bones as an offering to gods, a devaluation of the sacrifice. (Hesiod : Theog. 556).

---

84. Raymond Weill, *Le Champs des roseaux et le champs des offrandes dans les religion funéraire et la religion générale,* Paris, 1936, pp. 62 ff.
85. Henry Corbin, *Man and time,* New York and London, 1957, p. 188. Corbin warns that tne contrast between the Iranian skies and the Platonic scheme is not to be minimized. Plato's opposition between idea and matter is not exactly that of the Iranian invisible and visible sky.
86. Mircea Eliade, *A History of Religious Ideas,* vol. I, p. 255. Eliade uses for his references to Hesiod's Prometheus the edition by M.L. West, *Hesiod's Theogony, edited with Prolegoumena and Commentary,* Oxford, 1966 : Theog. 535.

The Greeks also began eating meat as against the former vegetarian regime. Humanity, in the Greek mind, in the eating of meat, acts religiously. It is a new type of act, that of an independent relationship with Zeus. The later myth of Prometheus' release by Zeus' own son Heracles intends to stress that independence.

To understand the Greek psyche and its vision on the gods, reality and man, I must here recount another myth of essential importance. To man Zeus sent Pandora from whose mysterious jar all evils escape. Left at the bottom of the jar is Hope.

> "But", says Hesiod, "this is precisely what the angry Zeus wanted: to constrain man eternally to hard toil, and that is why he made hope "who feeds the vain efforts of man" enter the vessel".[87]

The Prometheus-myth in Hesiod is not completely emancipated from its theogonic matrix. While giving attention to man, the myth also lies at the origin of things and at the genesis of divine wrath itself. Prometheus does not invent evil: he continues it. His evil is a sequel to the evil displayed in the theogonic combats between the Titans and the earthly elements. It is Aeschylus who transforms Prometheus into a tragic figure, facing Zeus who becomes the hidden god. Prometheus becomes the hero and if not always a human in the myths, he gives, as a demi-god, humanity to man.[88]

Hesiod's account of Zeus' act leaving man with hopeless Hope and Aeschylus' concept of the tragic Prometheus are important to understand the Greek vision. Their combination explains the sudden coming of evil into the world. Evil represents the vengeance of Zeus. This is not the place for a more elaborate theory of evil in Greek thought. I am here merely indicating the instance of its rise and some of its contextual consequences for the Greeks. That will prove useful for our following short discussion on the West in as far as its cultural memory has been influenced by the Greeks. When the Greek civilization declined and the Romans established their hegemony, the Greek heritage came to Europe. A short review of Western cultural physiology is hardly avoidable if I am expected to develop a method of analysis of myth in preparation of my effort, in Part II and III to highlight the Indian mythical awareness of its "Origins".

One observation with regard to evil as represented by the vengeance of Zeus is of particular importance for the understanding of the Greek vision on reality and man. Aeschylus' tragic Prometheus is so only when seen as coincident with the mystery of the iniquitous god. That god provokes, on man's part, what the Greeks call "hubris". "Hubris" is audacity with the colouring of recklessness. Not recklessness in the thought of the moralist prior to Aeschylus when it has the connotation of avoidable immoderation. That is not tragic. Tragedy enters when the immoderation on man's part forces him to prove himself against his wicked god by introducing a human movement, a contrast, a tension into the heart of the mystery. In the face of

87. Mircea Eliade, *A History of Religious Ideas,* vol. I, p. 256. This paragraph on the Greeks owes much to the reading of Eliade's work and that of Gerhard Nebel, *Weltangst und Götterzorn : eine Deutung der Griechischen Tragödie,* Stuttgart, 1951 and Max Scheler, *Le Phenomène du tragique,* tr. M. Dupuy, Paris, 1952. See also Paul Ricoeur's excellent chapter on "The Wicked God and the "Tragic" Vision of Existence" in : *The Symbolism of Evil,* pp. 211-231.
88. I shall come back to the idea of the "tragic" with regard to Indian myth in Part II, where also the idea of "the fault" of creation will be discussed.

the wicked god there *must* be somewhere man's share *where there is no evil.* Were it not so, human existence would be altogether intolerable and unbearable. There must be at least an indication of man's own responsibility where what he does and says is done and said without being of necessity evil. In other words, there must be an opportunity for avoidable fault. Guilt must not be commensurate with human existence. If the wicked god will not allow man a tolerable and bearable existence, man himself will of necessity make it so. The wrath of god will face the wrath of man.[89]

We now have a sufficient base to try and see how the Greeks further developed their vision on reality. Discussing the difference in vision between Homer and Hesiod, De Vries writes:

> "Although informed of the worlds of gods of Homer, Hesiod creates his own genealogies of gods and even conceives of new ones of a generally abstract nature. He does not accept tradition as it comes to him but attempts, by his creations, a profounder search for the beginnings. He shows himself a precursor of the philosopher who is soon to tear down the old faiths."[90]

The Prometheus-myth remains significant when we try and explore areas where man is seen as a result of decisions made "at the beginning of time". It needs to be repeated that it is these beginnings—told in myths but subsequently reshaped by other myths through the process of modernization—which have always activated man's consciousness and driven him further to new vistas. In the effort to cover the epistemological distance between the before and the after, myth creates its own refreshed awareness featuring new receptivities through the power of its own logos. Myth, as we have seen, is *already word and thought*. Each myth narrative comes in fact at the end of a cycle of what has already been thought.

In ancient Greece, its vision on man and his destiny developed into an acute awareness of the precariousness of the human condition. Man found himself in a situation of loneliness like Prometheus. The benefactor of mankind had been chained to a rock. That is the humanity of man. Prometheus suffered because he loved the human race too much. Not only his fatal deceit during the sacrifice but also his theft of the fire, the light and warmth in people's homes, were reasons for Zeus to curse him. Prometheus, however, could never be convinced of his being evil. Thus he becomes the guilty innocent.[91]

Confronted with the impasse of a wicked Zeus in the beginnings, the Greeks pushed forward into man's history on earth. They were compelled to. For them there was no more place with Zeus. In a myth, contemporary with that of Prometheus, we hear how Prometheus' son Deucalion offers Zeus a new sacrifice in the manner his father had done. Zeus now accepts it but, indicates the myth, precisely insofar as distance is maintained.[92] The Greeks began to view reality as that of "Moira"—fate,

89. Guilt as indistinguishable from finiteness has been in various doctrines of predestination a severe theological and psychological problem in Calvinistic and Zwinglian Protestant Christianity.
90. Jan de Vries, *Forschungsgeschichte der Mythologie,* pp. 1-2.
91. For Prometheus as lover of mankind and on the way towards a religion of justice and wisdom if Zeus could be made to understand, see: Louis Sechan, *Le mythe de Promethee,* Paris, 1951.
92. The Greeks no longer felt the express need of the god.

the lot, portion —, allotted to them as evil, represented by *Zeus*. "He is not a man whom Zeus does not send a thousand ills", it was said. Life's symbol became the thread spun by the divinity.[93] Here the vision of the tragic comes in full view. It occurs when the initiative of fault is traced back *into* the divine. To try and theologize that is too terrifying for thought. The Greeks played it on stage to escape its possible reality and to see it *as if* it were true.[94] Hinduism, as I shall try and show, escaped the blinding of man by the wicked god. Did the Greeks? Plato fought the idea with all his might. Yet, the visual portrayal of the tragic *as if* it were life failed to convince the Greeks. What they saw on stage they found all too conspicuously true of life itself. The Greeks, finally arriving at the separation of soul and body as two opposed realities, identified anguish and fear of the beginnings with the wrath of the highest god.[95] Max Scheler offers a valuable suggestion in regard to the problem of the Greek tragedy by arguing that we can *make see* the problem. We can turn our attention to the unique Greek phenomenon of a resolute transaction with the world without the loss of the awareness of the sacred.[96]

The problem of divine justice with its corollary, human destiny, kept the Greek mind occupied from Homer on.[97] Life thrust itself on the Greeks as a reality of human precariousness. They became existentially occupied and the safe company of the gods meant little to them. They could not even hope that prayer could establish intimacy with the gods. What happened in the Greeks' existential situation is the discovery of "the joy of life".[98] They turned the gift of life into a gift to themselves, a most unique and quite amazing process of internal cultural modernization. The Greeks won for themselves true historical awareness of the world. In the human condition man's reality lay for the Greeks on man's end of the beginnings. It proved difficult not to overstep man's imposed limit of excellence in competition with the gods. However, he now turns to his own idea of excellence as assigned to him by his lot. Thus he escapes the accusation of giving himself airs and being proud and insolent. The vision of the tragic gave rise paradoxically to a revalorization of the human condition as reality. Perfection engrafted itself in the *sacredness* of this condition. In other words, the religious sense of the joy of life emerged.

The beauty of the universe, the earth and that of the human body became of value as a way of competing with the gods. Processions, dance, games, sports and the arts are the olympic heroism of man. His initial wrath against the god is transformed into the celebration of the sacrality of joy in the world. In Greece, man authentically secularized. The "saeculum", the here and now of man, is man's own opportunity for eminence. Thus the Greeks became conscious of a religious dimension in man's earthly existence. For them and for those touched by them, a newly discovered

93. To spin someone's destiny is equivalent to binding a person, immobilizing him in a situation that cannot be changed.
94. See Part II, chapter 1.4.1: "Myths of the exiled soul". Acting *as if*, when the presence of the god is concerned, implies the idea of a distance which, so it would seem, in Indian thought is hardly imaginable when "*Brahman* is this whole world".
95. Gerhard Nebel, *Weltangst und Götterzorn*, pp. 11-48.
96. Max Scheler, *Le Phenomène du tragique*, p. 110.
97. Mircea Eliade, *A History of Religious Ideas*, p. 260.
98. The Greek "joy of life" must not be mistaken for what is commonly called secularization. The latter may in principle lose much of the awareness of the sacred.

modernity. It is this bliss of existence, the spontaneity of life and the majesty of the world — together with the split between body and soul as separate realities—which the Greeks carried into emerging Europe when the process of hellenization began.

The West

A pure East-West dichotomy does not exist. The history of peoples is not a patchwork of isolated fragments. Certainly not in presentday history when the destiny of the West may well depend on battles fought in the East and the East may well depend on policies of the West. The Indo-European language-family, for example, unites the Celtic, Germanic, Italian, Greek, Baltic-Slavonic, Anatolian, Iranian and Indo-Arian languages.[99] Philosophical and religious thought cannot be divided into exclusively Eastern or Western ways. There is, however, an *anthropological* category which allows for people to have different approaches to things. It is this category—ultimately simply meaning that all human beings are human beings—which is not surprised to find different cognitive premises. That they may be radically varied, that too does not surprise the anthropological category. It does not cause a *split* between one human being and another. It will be understood that the anthropological category proves its value in the cross-cultural context as for example, in finding a method of analysis of myth.

For a satisfactory understanding of the West we need to be more explicitly introduced to the third instance of modernity, mentioned earlier: the diatopical modernity.[100] This kind of modernity does not only include the sumtotal of morphological and diachronical accommodation. It also encompasses, as the word says, different "topoi", different "places" of understanding reality. It is, as we shall see, an important concept for our understanding of the myth of "memory and forgetting". The distance to be overcome in diatopical modernity is considerable. Not only the temporal distance within the confines of a given tradition or culture must be bridged. Also the gap which may appear between that given cultural reality when it *actually meets* another cultural reality must be covered. What that gap may reveal is not just another or one more philosophy of life or religious outlook but *the other* philosophy or outlook on life. An interesting contemporary example is the much discussed concept of "person" in the West and in India. No well meaning Westerner or Indian will want to say that they are the same. Their discussion may develop into a heated argument. The person-concept, however, will remain different. What their diatopical experience has succeeded in doing is that it has upset the contestants. Both hear opinions different from what they were used to. Diatopical experience adds foreign elements to one's own morphological and diachronical modernity. In that sense the foreign is *the other* and not merely another.

Diatopical modernity is the experience within the self-understanding of a given culture of currents of thought developing their origin of intelligibility and their basic assumptions not in but outside of that given culture. It will be understood that diatopical experience and modernity in our presentday world as a global village may give rise to considerable chaos of various kinds as well as to welcome illumination.

---

99. Heinrich Zimmer, *Philosophie und Religion Indiens,* Suhrkamp Taschenbuch Wissenschaft 26, reprint, 1979, p. 23, footnote I.

100. From the Greek "topos" meaning "place".

Western modernity, from its earliest beginnings, must be viewed from the angle of diatopical experience if we are to understand it at all. Europe's modernity is a long process of interaction, assimilation, absorption, symbiosis, rejection and again re-absorption of four different places of self-understanding and reality.[101]

We find in pre-Christian Europe first the local autochtone mythical consciousness with its pantheon. Second, the Hellenistic spiritual-rational colonization of the European mind on the upper-level of official culture and a simultaneous undercurrent of mythical and spontaneous thought, both Greek and autochtone.[102] Thirdly, Oriental influence in Europe was known already from pre-Christian times. A strong Islamic influence in its southern regions spread from the sixth century onward. Last but not least, Europe was thoroughly influenced by the Semitic-and Christian view of reality and self-understanding through the "historical revelation of Jahweh" and the equally historical revelation of the Saviour, Jesus Christ, the god-man.

Europe's Hebrew-Christian stress on history, as it has understood that revelation, together with the rational scientific approach to the question "ti tō ōn?' "what is being?" - inherited from the Greeks and further developed in Europe, has at present reached a stage inviting criticism on the part of other cultures. Non-Western speculative thought is disenchanted with Europe's (and other Western continents') critical-scientific rationality and its view of history as being only "factual". Non-Western cultures consider this presumptious, if not arrogant. For several centuries European (Western) man has been indoctrinated that his humanity, and consequently his universality, was grounded in critical-rational argumentative reason. Recent historical and philosophical evolution has put Western thought on guard against a form of naive rationalistic optimism. In a short span of time Europe burnt out twice.

In the preceding chapter the West has already featured fairly extensively when I attempted, in the paragraph "Athens, Jerusalem and Mount *Kailāśā*" to frame my European position with regard to my present proximity to the Indian mythical awareness. A few concluding observations concerning the West may here suffice. The intense and multi-facetted diatopical and internal phases of modernity of the European experience from early on provides an interesting picture. When myths and symbols are concerned, a singularly vivid series of clashes and counter-clashes occur leading to the most serious and at times amusing misunderstandings as well as to depths of thought and the uttermost effort on the part of the individual.

---

101. Since, as we have seen, the idea of modernity implies at least some form of human estrangement from tradition, we easily understand that in a culture like Europe's where from the outset all three modernities were found, a more severe form of human estrangement may at times be expected to emerge in its history. Such estrangement is, in terms of modernity, perfectly explainable as a cultural phenomenon rather than as an aberration. It seems to me that political, educational, socio-cultural and Church-institutions are liable to cultural negligence and misunderstanding on this point. Rather than trying to interpret the cultural phenomenon, they appear at times to be given over to moralistic meddlesomeness. In my experience with a substantial number of Western, and of late also Japanese, travelling youths in India over the past nine years, I have observed from their reactions how apparently unconcerned and disinterested the youths' home-institutions can be when the youths' experiences are concerned. Travelling youth may be said to have the wherewithall to do so but they should also be given sympathy. They are often on the move by an impulse related to the context of processes of modernization and modernity under discussion here.

102. Present-day movements in favour of a recovery of ecological awareness and the establishment of peace in all its ramifications are not in the last instance inspired by these undercurrents besides being influenced by also Christian and humanistic values in Europe's cultural physiology.

Europe's later Middle Ages (ca 1200-1650) were a bewildering scene. They witnessed at once the highest peaks of mysticism and a relentless hunt for witches and heretics who could be called so by anyone around, releasing throughout the Christian world a reign of terror. At a certain moment the only well thinking Christian and humanist of the day seemed to be Erasmus (1466-1536) who wrote in his. *The Praise of Folly* :

> "The Christian religion seems to have some relation to folly and no alliance at all with wisdom... there are none more silly, or nearer their wits' end, than those too superstitiously religious.[103]

The learned humanist, who taught in most cultural centres of Europe at the time, failed in his effort to remove from medieval Christianity the view of its being a mere doctrine of salvation and make it see itself as a religion of the spirit. The Church shattered into a number of contending Christianities, all equally opposed to the work of science and reason and yet relying on the ratio for imposing canons of belief that were themselves a mixture of undigested mythical origins.

Where in ancient times, in the Near East, interactions between peoples and their mythical deposits were in process, the Hebrews strongly resisted an assimilation of local mythology from the start. Any contact with other peoples and their cults was forbidden by a singularly strong aversion. It was called no less than prostitution. Never was cosmic religiosity attacked with such ferocity as in Palestine ever since the Israelites' entrance. The prophets finally succeeded in emptying nature of any divine presence.[104] The Hebrews stuck to their desert-based tribal identity, supported by the concept that historical events in their tribal affairs were the work of Jahweh. The prophets' foretellings of Jahweh's inescapable punishment for unbelief were ratified by catastrophes endangering the tribal identity. Historical events acquired religious significance. The prophets interpreted events in the light of strict faith and hence events became "negative theophanies of the wrath of Jahweh".[105] Historical events finally received a value in themselves since they were the will of God. Both the individual and the community stood face to face with Jahweh. Eliade observes:

> "Hence it is true to say that the Hebrews were the first to discover the meaning of history as an epiphany of God, and this conception, as was to be expected, was taken up again and amplified by Christianity."[106]

The Christian God, carried from Israel to Europe, was no longer an Oriental divinity, a creator of archetypal gestures. Thus mythical symbols, as a manifestation of the divine, became for Christian dogmatic theology a problem. The Hebrew-Christian appropriation of history matched well with the Greek Olympian idea of human excellence and its critical view of the "muthos". On Europe's soil the two blended to

103. Desiderius Erasmus, *Encomium Moriae,* tr. John Wilson (1668) *The Praise of Folly,* Oxford : The Clarendon Press, 1913, p. 177.
104. Mircea Eliade, *A History of Religious Ideas,* Vol. I., p. 354f. See: G. Fohrer, *History of Israelite Religion,* Nashville, 1972.
105. Mircea Eliade, *The Myth of the Eternal Return or, Cosmos and History,* pp. 102-112.
106. Mircea Eliade, *A History of Religious Ideas,* Vol. I. p. 356. See: Andre Neher, *L'Essence du prophetisme,* Paris, 1955, pp. 85-178 on the Hebraic framework of prophecy.

become part of its identity. Thus arose, leaving other aspects aside, in the heartland of the European West, the moral initiative in the field of time as accomplished by man. This secular myth is today a guiding force of the spirit in the European West. A classical example is the medieval legend of The Grail, a tribute to man venturing on his own. Westerners themselves, especially those in the more social professions, may not always be aware that this mythical consciousness exists. That the universe and the world are being kept dear and sacred. Theologians and pastors may forget that this awareness often is the only functioning "religious" sentiment. God's initiative is alive in the in-born soul as "intelligible character" of the individual at birth linking him to the cosmos. The freedom to act must thereafter be one's own will. One must be guided by one's own interior voice. This mythical awareness of the self-moving, self-responsible individual in time reveals a depth dimension too, that of transcending time and space. Europe's presentday turn to the East is likely to introduce a new modernity when interiorization of its experience appears to be an increasingly admitted need.

For quite some time now the West has been under the spell of rational-critical thought, especially after Descartes. The hankering after individual effort, however, resists being swallowed by a purely mechanistic existence. Twentieth-century physics has forcefully shown that there is no absolute truth in science and that all our concepts and theories are but limited and approximate. David Bohm's analyses have led him to the idea of "unbroken wholeness."[107] Quantum-processes and thought-processes, in Bohm's opinion, are interlinked.

To conclude our discussion with regard to the West's modernity: most Westerners still are under the influence of traditional Cartesian-Newtonian thought separating — to the exclusion of other possible thought— mind and matter, body and soul. As the distinguished biologist and ecologist Rene Dubos pointed out when observing students' behaviour:

"They usually feel most at ease when the thing they are studying is no longer living."[108]

With those in the West who are aware of the deep-seated reverence for the world in their culture we may ask if Western man should not prepare himself for a more pronounced spiritual pattern of intelligibility of his worldview. We may wonder if the worldview created by the encounter and embrace of rational evidence and historical verification alone, will be able to satisfy Western man's deepest aspirations.

Conclusion

Can we now, at the end of this exercise, *make our own* the Vedic myth of "chaos"— and through it the "idea" of myth— with which we began? I would not have interrogated that myth if it had not challenged us and could not still address itself to

107. David Bohm, *Quantum Theory,* New York : Prentice Hall, London; Constable, 1956, pp. 169ff. Also his, *Wholeness and the Implicate Order,* London: Routledge and Kegan Paul, 1980. For an introduction to the so-called "Systems Philosophy" shifting from objects to relationships between all phenomena, see: Ervin Laszlo, *Introduction to Systems Philosophy,* New York, Harper Torchbooks, London: Gordon and Breach, 1972.

108. René Dubos, *Man, Medicine and Environment*, New York, Praeger, 1968, p. 117. For a descriptive definition of "Western" in geographically non-Western countries, see note in the paragraph on "The idea of the sacred".

us. The myth of "chaos" is seductive. It enkindles our curiosity in the Universe's totality of Perfection. That perfection is *invincible* at the level of man forever in search of meanig, but *unthinkable* at the level of the Universe, already total and complete. "Chaos", if it is there, is with man. One must be in a condition to hear and understand the primordial and incessant act of creation, as of the rush of waters, repeated in every generation and in every awakening from sleep.

> "What *Ṛṣi* put man together?"[109]
>
> "Indra pierced with his bolt the sluices of the streams" and so let loose the "Seven Rivers."[110]

It is an illusion to think that one can make oneself a pure spectator, without involvement, without memory, without perspective and regard everything with equal sympathy by being non-committal. Indifference destroys the possibility of appropriation and keeps shut up from within "the waters in the heart" (*hṛdaya-samudra*).[111]

The result of our undertaking is our discovery *where* one can best listen to, hear and understand what the myths have to *say*. They speak through the pre-eminence of the receptive awareness of the sacred which, full of surprise, not dominates but acclaims. The sacred things man reads *on* the cosmos, he finds, through the symbol, manifested *in* his psyche, his being a human.

109. *AV.* 11.8.14
110. *RV.* 11.15.3: "*vajrena khāni vyatṛṇat nadīnām*". For the "Seven Rivers"; *ṚgVeda, passim*. With regard to our seeing, hearing and thinking etc. see: *JaimUB.* 1.28.29.
111. See: F.B.J. Kuiper, *Ancient Indian Cosmology*, p. 183 for the mythological concept of "*kha-*", aperture, the doors of the mind, those of the primordial hill and those of the heart.

Chapter 3

ANALYSIS OF MYTH: PROBLEM AND METHOD

The Problem

Analysis of myth, its meaning or meanings, is a thorny question. Myth is *lived*. The ensemble of its context is taken for granted. Moreover, myth is *believed*. Believed myth, lived from inside, does not of itself ask to be questioned or to be transcended in search of some ulterior ground. Mythical awareness is a reference point directing man in reality. I have said that, in the context of myth, it is by retracing the unseen that man *sees* where to go. With regard to the myth of origin with which we are mainly concerned, man shifts "the beginnings" through the narration and ritual to the present and thus knows the path ahead which is *as if* of "the beginnings". Panikkar observes:

> "Myth - like the divine - is unseen except from behind, when it has already passed, and then only in vestiges it leaves in the logos."[1]

The one who sees from behind is man. The passage from what he sees — in the mythical realm — to what he believes of the unseen is his criterion of truth. Myth is a passage, a pilgrimage, rooted in a vision. Myth presents facts which it is unnecessary to probe since the facts are truths. The facts are inspired, not by pure intellect but by impulse.

Myth is a basic structure wherein what is believed makes one look over the horizon. That it is the metaphysics of myth. What Kant has called "Ding-an-Sich" is equivalent, as far as it goes, to the *Brahman* of the Indian *Upaniṣads*, "The Void" (*śūnyatā*) of the Buddhists and "The Nameless" of the Tao. From man's side it is believed to be "the yonder shore" (*paramitā*). By the effort to express that shore or, in other words, by the attempt to relate to that shore, man has given rise to myth. Or is it "the yonder shore" giving birth to myth? It is both, not as two ontologically separate movements but as one epistemological flash. The symbol presents its meaning in the transparency of an enigma—evokes it, suggests it—, and not by translation. That is why myths are no allegories. The *donation* of meaning in symbols is not the *translation* of allegories.[2]

Speaking of analysis of myth, my first question is: what is that curious sense of *intention* which, occasionally or more often, comes to one behind those apparent chance-events by which one's life is being directed? In analysis of myth one should be

1. R. Panikkar, *Myth, Faith and Hermeneutics*, p. 20.
2. The kind of symbols in question in our study have nothing to do with that what symbolic logic calls by the same name. For symbolic logic, symbolism is the necessary peak of rigorous formalism. In symbolic logic, in the theory of syllogism, expressions are themselves replaced by letters or written signs which need no longer be spoken and by means of which it is possible to calculate without asking oneself how they are incorporated in reasoning. Thus e.g. the "=" in 2 + 2 = 4 is no longer "pronounced" or "thought" about in the mind. The "is" or "are" become " = " as an element of a calculus.

prepared to rule out chance and see instead a purpose, an intent behind events as of a chain of relationships.

A second matter one ought to keep in mind is clear from the commonly used term "mythological". When the "logos", as rational-critical argumentative word, is applied to the myth, what happens to the myth? It disappears *at that instant* and retreats into its own time and space. In that sense we may speak of the myth as de-mythicized when its ulterior ground is questioned and when the myth is made to answer.

The problem of analysis of myth received its own peculiar and at times irritating feature through the strong claim laid on it by the West once its expansionism began. Myth began to be analysed by the "science of mythology" by a culture calling itself "enlightened", "modern". Western culture seemed the least recognizable for its mythical awareness and sense of the sacred while saying most about it. The European Renaissance subjected myth to a more or less rational reflection. Panikkar writes:

> "Thus that hybrid and even self-contradictory science of *mythology* (R.P.) was born."[3]

Emerging "modern" Europe lost some of its "cosmogonic moment" under the spell of the Ratio precisely at a time when it met, through its expansionism, a wide variety of cosmogonies and convictions of "Origins". In Europe, the search for "the beginnings" shifted to this end of creation, man's end. In as far as this may be called profane, it constitutes a problem with regard to the sacred. In Europe, the conquering of ignorance became equivalent to what was thought to be the mastering of Time. This observation is by no means without its significance. A radical difference between "modern" Western culture and other cultures became conspicuous. It still remains to be seen whether secular thought will be capable of creating a civilization since it is, in view of the whole of human history, a comparatively recent thought. On the other hand, mankind's present historical moment leads us to confrontations, discoveries and possibilities that could not be imagined even fifty years ago.[4] For the present, the West would seem to run the risk of being engrossed in distraction, away from "the beginning". The original joy of life, discovered by the Greeks, augmented by the presence of an Incarnated Saviour, Jesus, and enhanced by an amazing scientific-technological development, would seem to have caused in the Western world a "fall into time". That seems to lead to an ideal of amusement, needing more of it all the time as an escape from precisely that "time" which it had just discovered. The situation is not without its problems.[5]

---

3. R. Panikkar, *Myth, Faith and Hermeneutics, Cross-Cultural Studies,* p. 39. For a rational reflection on myth, see e.g. M.D. Chenu, *La Theologie au douzieme siecle,* Paris: Varin, 1966.
4. See: Mircea Eliade, *The Quest, History and Meaning in Religion*, pp. 1 - 3.
5. For a wide variety of new problematics in modern Western society see: James C. Coleman, *Abnormal Psychology and Modern Life,* passim.. The question of meaningless amusement and the need for time-killing entertainment is being exploited by various quarters in mass communication as, for example, the television program industry, posing problems to social-cultural workers etc. It also causes disquet to the serious humanist and the serious Christian. Both aim at joy in this world but not at the cost of a critical view of the means thereto. In the context of culturally uncreative and mind-numbing time-killing there is an additional difficulty for the Christian, also in theological circles. For it would now not be "Athens *and* Jerusalem" but "Jerusalem *against* Athens" since the Saviour came indeed to bring joy to the world but no dissipation. From the point of view of

Once the trans-human model is left behind, concentration must of necessity be focused on the human condition as human condition. One cannot have secret recourse to a god. Whether such concentration is possible without confession to at least some norms suggested by Life and Cosmos is a point in question. It is, as may be clear from the preceding chapters, an adventure both questionable and exciting: The individual heart as the only honest possibility is a leap indeed.

Western man is now no longer the master of the world. He is no longer managing "natives" but talking to other men. The former "natives" are now active subjects of history—which from their point of view they always were—instead of its former colonial passive objects. Western man should learn and be ready to accept the invitation to a dialogue. It has become necessary to realize that there is no longer any break in the continuity between the "primitive" and "the modern". It would be ridiculous to assert that presentday "modern" man would no longer feel the anxiety of existence-of what it is to live in time and in the human condition. Precisely that anxiety is one of the principle characteristics of mythical awareness in any culture, also that in secular culture.

It is in this new situation of collective consciousness of all humans as humans in this world, in this universe, that a new understanding of one another becomes feasible. Human kind needs a meeting based on solidarity supported by imaginative listening and understanding. No meeting halfway will suffice. In attempting an analysis of myth we ought, then, first to correct the old interpretation of history. History as a straight line, leading from pre-history through antiquity and the Middle Ages to modern times, is no longer accepted. It has given way to a historical consciousness—part of which is the fact that there *is* a mythical awareness—looking at the various successive and co-existent cultures as individualities and not as links in a continuous chain. This view makes it possible to do justice to the individual character of each culture. It is also a symptom of the decline of the ordering principle that had, uptil now, enabled European, Christian mankind to regard itself as the culmination and climax of human development. Once the idea of a universal mankind began to crystallize, the naive Western view of history for which the Near East was quite secondary, while Asia, America and Africa merited hardly any attention, became untenable. Psychology has in no small way contributed to a psycho-historical view of human history. I shall later come back to this when I shall be asked to explain in detail more of the symbol of the Waters *Āpaḥ* in Part III. I may here refer to a recent comprehensive system, integrating different psychological schools, known as "Spectrum-psychology". Its advocate, Ken Wilber, unifies numerous approaches, both Western and Eastern, into a cluster of psychological models and theories reflecting the spectrum of human consciousness. Each of the levels of that spectrum is characterized by a different identity, from the supreme identity of cosmic consciousness to the drastically narrowed identity of the ego. Like in any spectrum, infinite shades and gradations are exhibited, gradually merging one into another.[6] Present day

Church-authorities, however, a moralistic attitude would be out of place. Technology and advance are not anathema.

6. Ken Wilber, "Psychologia Perennis: The Spectrum of Consciousness", *Journal of Transpersonal Psychology*, No. 2, 1975. See also his, *The Spectrum of Consciousness*, Wheaton, Ill., Theosophical Publishing House, 1977.

man's search for the meaningfulness of all there is appears to try and catch up with what in mythical awareness has always been strongly felt: The stress is not on *having* a body but on *being* a body.[7] That, as we shall see, is for the Vedic mind *Puruṣa*, Cosmic Man. The method of analysis of myth which I shall attempt will be conducted along that line.

Method

Various methods of analysis of myth have been developed and applied to Vedic and later Hindu myths, as they were to the myths of other cultures and religious heritages. Whatever the method used, the compelling Indian world view which moulds every image and symbol, every word and idea into a celebration of the belief that the universe is boundlessly various, that everything occurs simultaneously, that all possibilities may exist without excluding one another, that world view must be preserved by the student of Indian myth. Is that not begging the question? I should think not. The student namely must have already read or sensed the susceptibilities of the Indian mythical awareness. But that does not at once clarify the manner in which to deal with them. One of the most intense mythic experiences is the experience of events that make us question our certainty about what is real and what is not. From the Indian point of view the basic condition of human experience is the condition of illusion (*māyā*). If I am to approach that condition as near as possible, I, as a European, may be asked to lower the barrier of rational thought. I cannot ignore assumptions of my own culture but I can at least not be presumptious about them.

The pattern of the Indian myth is clear. Everything, in the end, turns round a "still point" (*bindu, Brahman*). *Bindu* is the condition of power manifesting itself as centres or points of differentiated mass. In statements about *Brahman* there are problems of interpretation. We must think of "It" as only indication and not as signification. *Brahman* has no senses. It is unattached and has no relationships therefore. Yet, *Brahman* is the basic reality underlying all illusory phenomena. Being Truth, *Brahman* is the foundation of all.[8] In the *Bṛahdāraṇyaka Upaniṣad* we are told of the "honey-teaching" (*madhu vidyā*). *Madhu* here means the cause and effect relation between the various categories of objects falling within our experience. To discover that link, one proceeds by seeking the "honey", the spiritual ground or essence of things. Thus the elements earth, water, fire, wind, sun, the quarters of heaven, the moon, lightning, thunder and space, truth and moral law, and the human race itself, are being seen as unifying participants in the essence of things.[9] They all finally lead to spirit where everything finds its final unity.[10]

"This *Ātman* is honey for all things, and all things are honey for this *Ātman*."

---

7. Fritjof Capra, *The Turning Point, Science, Society, and the Rising Culture,* Flamingo, Fontanabooks, *1983, pp. 401 ff.*
8. *BGB*. 13.14: "*sadāspadam hi servam sarvatra sadbuddhyanugamāt*" See for a concise but comprehensive study on *Brahman:* V. George Joseph, *Integral Experience in Advaita Vedānta,* unpublished Ph.D. dissertation, Banaras Hindu University, 1984, pp. 190 - 212.
9. *BU*. 2.5.1 - 14.
10. *BU*. 2.5.15.

In the Vedic and later Hindu question-and-answer myths the questioner is invariably led to *Brahman*. So is, therefore, the student of Indian myth. When one does not arrive at the mystery of *Brahman* one has made a wrong analysis. First to state what an analysis of Indian myth should arrive at and then try and develop a method looks, as I said, like begging the question. But the twentieth-century student of Indian myth is no different from *Gārgī* asking about the world's meaningfulness "lengthwise and crosswise" and finding herself invariably led by her master to *Brahman*. And, also important for the student to remember, "her head did not burst". If the Indian mythical awareness insists on seeing the combination and the convergence of all that the universe encompasses, the chain-symbolism in the one *Brahman*, we cannot avoid taking that insistence as a foregone conclusion when developing a method of analysis of Indian myth.

In the European West, from the sixteenth century until some time into the twentieth, idealists and utopians were infatuated with the "noble savage", thought of as leading a beatific visionary existence in the bosom of nature. True, nature's influence on myth formation should not be denied. For the modern European, however, surrounded by a variety of unnatural things, pure nature became a kind of utopia. Mythical societies in the midst of nature were seen as blissful humanity having escaped the misdeeds of civilization. But the utopians were not always prepared to attribute the same mental capacities and gifts to the "noble savage" they thought they themselves were blessed with. The savage's "innocence" too seemed less desirable if not delightful ignorance.

Whereas European romanticism attributed to the myth a secret and esoteric meaning, the mid-nineteenth-century German School, under the influence of rising positivism, considered the gods principally as personified nature-phenomena. The gods were the result of a form of phantasy. The idea of belief in them received hardly any attention. Cosmogonies were not considered to be also ontophanies. The naturalist school has been partly influenced by the development, in Europe, from philosophically coloured deism to the idea of "the denial of God". Ludwig Feuerbach's lectures, "Vorlesungen über das Wesen der Religion", in Heidelberg (1848-1849) drew large audiences.[11] A reaction to the nature-school is that which, as Claude Levi-Strauss remarks:

> "tried to reduce the meaning of myth to a moralising comment on the situation of mankind.[12]

---

11. The nature-school of myth interpretation originally concerned itself with the Greek myth. Once Indo-Germanistic studies were taken up in earnest, the Vedic and later Hindu myth naturally drew attention. The "Ur-man's" thought was taken to be a soulful contemplation of nature. Ludwig Preller considered nature to be "the motherly ground and beginning of the birth of gods". Alfred de Maury considered both Greek and Indian gods to have taken birth from a "cloud - and weather mythology". Wilhelm Mannhardt, taking the ṚgVeda to be the "Ur-Religion" of mankind, made an extensive comparative study of Indian, Greek and Slavonic names of gods and found phenomena of nature to be underlying all three traditions. Max Müller too belongs to the nature-school, attributing the rise of myth especially to sentiments in man at sunrise and sunset. Müller introduced into his theories elements of language-philosophy. I have elsewhere explained his use of polynomy and synonymy. See: Jan de Vries, *Forschungsgeschichte der Mythologie*, pp. 199-252. Also: Alfred von Hillebrandt, *Vedic Mythology*, tr. Sreeramula Rajeswara Sarma, 2 vols, 1st English language ed. Delhi, 1980, Motilal Banarsidass, Vol. 2, pp. 1-20.
12. Claude Levi-Strauss, *The Raw and the Cooked, Introduction to a science of mythology*, tr. John and

With regard to Indian myth, this would, for example, be the statement that *Rudra* is death and *Kāma* is love. The disadvantage of such an apodictic identification of a name with a quality is the disection of myth into the telling of it and a supposed behavioural norm contained in it. Mythical thought, however, embraces the totality of human existence and its experience which in different ages "demoralizes" one standard of behaviour replacing it by another. Myth must be free to de-mythologize itself in the process of its self-understanding. The mythical idea of *Rudra* and *Kāma*, as we shall later see, is far wider and far more complex to be reduced to only one meaning. Mythical ideas are subject to shades and fluctuations and may at times mean seemingly contradictory things in different cultural contexts. Humans live according to their moral standards without asking for reasons. But the moment the question is asked morals are plunged into crisis. The day they find their reasons morals cease to be moral. It would be presumptuous to think that what we in our times experience regarding changing morals would not have been the case in the lives of people long ago.

Related to the analysis of myth as a moral injunction is the view of myth as a ritual realization in the domain of cult. That attitude towards myth may go at the cost of the light of faith transcending the limits of human rules and regulations materialized in cult. It is for this reason that, for example, the ritualistic *Brahmanas* were relinquished in favour of the interiorizing and freedom inspiring *Upaniṣads*.

The appropriation of history by the West as its exclusive possession has given rise to historical theories of myth on which its analysis was thought to depend. The reductionist view of myth as if it explains the mighty deeds of former national heroes and kings pays little tribute to myth's cosmic awareness and its symbols relating the cosmos to the human psyche. Historical theories may sound sympathetic to former colonized peoples as they would lend a "scientific" air to tales once scoffed at by their colonial masters. Thus, for example, the battle between *Indra* and *Vṛtra* resulting in the release of the Waters, would be said to represent the conquest of the Naga tribes (ca. 1500 B.C.) by the Aryans or, in line with the Marxist vision, the battle representing the supplanting of an agrarian economy by a martial proletariate.

Among many theories of analysis of myth, the theory of archetypes proposed by Jung and based on Freud's earlier findings deserves attention. Human kind, Jung believed, thinks in terms of archetypes buried deep in the collective unconscious. Myths, according to Jung are a projection of those archetypes.[13] Jung's theories are valuable. One obvious difficulty is the disregard of mythical thinking as contemporaneous with rational thinking. Jung's opinions may also fail to do justice to the value of rites and rituals as a volitional correlative of myth.

The value of psychology with regard to analysis of myth is considerable. If mythical awareness is a *form of knowledge of reality* relating the human psyche to the Universe, scientific psychological theories are attractive not only for their sympathy for the mythical awareness but also from the standpoint of the spirit of human solidarity evident in them. As more is being revealed of the deeper levels of human consciousness, individuals and peoples are brought nearer to one another. When

---

Doreen Weightman, New York, 1969.

13. C.G. Jung, *Bewusstes und Unbewusstes*, Fischerbucherei, 1957, pp. 48ff.

different historical cultural contexts meet, cross-cultural relationships improve. In these encounters the mythical awareness receives a double-function: that of knowledge of reality and that of suggesting the unity of the human race. The transcendental and vertical direction of the mythical refers to the beginnings commonly shared by all while its horizontal range results in the meeting of human kind as equally human and equally involved in the human condition.

This is the moment when I ought to admit that the spirit of human solidarity will be my principal guide in an analysis of myth. I must here also admit my sympathy for the sincerity and quality apparent in Mircea Eliade's work in the field of the mythical. Avoiding extremes of philological, historical, metaphysical and symbolic schools on the one hand and the comparatively barren approaches of social anthropologists on the other, Eliade traces common patterns in different mythical systems and probes their roots. He made me more aware that, whenever I cross political frontiers, I am not leaving the hallowed ground of the earth. No one is a foreigner or stranger on earth. Eliade's opus places emphasis on myths as projections of vital experiences of a people. Myths seek to express these vital experiences and they are the only valid medium for externalizing them. That approach offers greater potentialities for my material in Part III when we shall see how the cosmic Waters explore all corners of the Universe and of human existence establishing a pattern of meaningful intelligibility. Commenting on Eliade's profound thoughts, De Vries writes:

> "We have only now come to understand that man has, at any stage of human culture, expressed in his religion as well as in his mythology, the deepest and most essential with regard to his existence in the world. One can even go further: what "primitive" mankind has gained with regard to insight in the world of the gods, namely the symbols through which it has tried to express the inexpressible, all that has been kept for later periods and is alive until today."[14]

With regard to parallels between Indian and non-Indian myths, only seldom referred to considering the aim of this study, I pursue Levi-Strauss's view that diffusion of mythical ideas within the limits of historical probability should be the natural explanation of similarities in myths of different regions. When that fails, the archetype in the collective unconsciousness could be taken recourse to. In Levi-Strauss's own words:

> "If history when it is called upon unremittingly (and it must be called upon first) cannot yield an answer, then let us appeal to psychology or the structural analysis of forms; let us ask ourselves if internal connections whether of a psychological or logical nature, will allow us to understand parallel recurrences whose frequency and cohesion cannot possibly be the result of chance."[15]

My knowledge of Sanskrit is far from sufficient to make use of the text-historical method of analysis of myth explaining a myth by finding its earliest known sources. I am forced to rely on translations and interpretations of texts by scholars whose

---

14. Jan de Vries, *Forschungsgeschichte der Mythologie*, p. 296, tr. F.B.
15. Madeleine Biardeau, "Some more considerations about Textual Criticism, *Purāṇa* X, 2 (July, 1968), pp. 115 - 123.

competence is well known. The text-historical method is useful in determining individual elements of the myth. I felt consoled and encouraged when reading the well known scholar, Madeleine Biardeau's observation:

> "The approach of historical philology will never be suitable for an oral tradition, which has no essential reference to its historical origin."[15]

Wendy Doniger O'Flaherty adds:

> "The historical method of philology is misleading even when it succeeds; for the question to ask is not where the disparate elements originated, but why they were put together, and why kept together. It is when the combination seems most contradictory and arbitrary that it is most rewarding to analyse it as a combination—for only a strong emotional bond can bridge a wide logical gap."[16]

Even if I may have been guilty of wishful reading when presenting their arguments, the authors' opinions with regard to the text-historical method should be considered well-founded. A difficulty related to the historical method is that of chronology in the myths. Indian myths are part of an oral tradition thousands of years old. Ancient thoughts and ideas may have gone lost and been picked up again later. It is not always easy to determine what is earlier and what is later in a mythical tradition. An oral tradition, moreover, resists a rigid regime of chronology. It is of limited value in determining the pattern of a myth as a whole. The narrator may not have included all the details he knew. Thus a later version may have left out an idea which was known in tradition since long. I have in the concatenation of myths of the Waters in Part III followed as much as I could an obvious chronology. One finds, for example, *Brahmā* myths later than those of *Agni's*. But I found it irrelevant to try and locate chronologically *ideas* such as *skambha*, the world axle and *liṅga*. These and many more ideas are of timeless latitude and profundity. They are part of the cosmos' history of both its creation, its maintenance, its exhaustion and destruction in the cycle of eternal return.

After this short review of theories of myth-analysis I may now be expected to propose the method we adopt when confronted with the Indian myths. We must keep in mind that we are looking for what the body of the Indian myth thinks is real and what is not. We should also not forget that from the Indian point of view the basic condition of human experience is the condition of illusion (*māyā*). All Indian philosophies acknowledge that *māyā* is a fact of life, *the* fact of life. Some, the *mokṣa*-oriented, regard it as a negative fact to be fought while others, the *saṁsāra*-oriented, see it as a positive fact to be embraced. While searching for an approach to the Indian myths I have already partly betrayed myself by saying that the spirit of human solidarity will be my principal guide. But it is myth itself, the exteriorization of man's vital human experiences, which is perhaps the fittest expression of that spirit of human solidarity. And if myth also allows us to move quite freely from past to present and to the future and back again, we are in a position saving us from the barriers of a mere material definition of who and where one nation or people is, and who and where another. We find ourselves on the common platform of a single humanity. That

16. Wendy Doniger O'Flaherty, *Siva, The Erotic Ascetic*, p. 12.

will provide us, as part of our method of myth-analysis, with the opportunity to plead for *time to feel* the pulse of another culture's anxiety in the human condition and how that culture clothes that anxiety in the telling of it. We cannot - and should not—of course ignore our own assumptions and preconceptions when reading foreign texts. But if myth itself is a sublime expression of human solidarity, we can, by approaching the Indian myths in that very spirit, try and see what it is that makes us find the Indian texts so puzzling at times. Our puzzlement will not be held against us by the Indian narrator and his myth. Both he and we are partakers of a single human race. We are, therefore, not only looking for *time to feel* the pulse of the Indian myth-narratives, we are also attempting a *leap of faith* if we are to be enlightened by them. We must avoid finding ourselves in an ontological impasse rendering our effort meaningless. The leap of faith will be an imaginative act of creation and discovery. It will help us understand the actual problem set by the Indian texts.

For a satisfying and rewarding analysis of myth, then, we need *incarnational* thinking. That implies *more* than the mere application of the *thought word* to the mythical awareness. The danger of reduction of the mythical to a mere object always lies in ambush. Subjecting the mythical receptive awareness to mere observation makes it elude us. When confronted with another man's myth we cannot but be involved. Levi Strauss writes:

> "I claim the right to make use of any manifestation of the mental or social activities of the communities under consideration which seem likely to allow me, as the analysis proceeds, to complete or explain the myth... You cannot make mythology understood by somebody of a different culture without teaching him the rules and particular traditions of that culture."[17]

Analysis of myth compels us to live in myth itself or at least make an effort to *imagine* the mythical awareness through a personal relationship with it. Myth and its awareness of the sacred cannot be apprehended on a level other than its own. Our relationship with it will not be far removed from a relationship of love. Love without always understanding. If we are asked to give a name to our method of myth-analysis we may call it *incarnational dialectics of myth*.

In the personal relationship, when an analysis of someone else's myth must be made, humans find one another aware that myth cannot be entirely separated from the logos, the applied word, the comment, or better to say, the involved and attentive question. What happens in analysis of myth? Nothing else but the re-enactment of myth itself. I, by trying to live the myth of the *possibility* of human communication, desire to enter someone else's myth. That must be my myth. The possibility of human communication has been revealed to me by the cross-cultural situation I find myself in as a fact. That situation is there by virtue of the plurality of cultures and world views as equally a fact. The cross-cultural situation has been part of human history ever since peoples began to diversify. No scientific empirical science has uptil now convincingly proved when that happened. Human kind's mythical awareness, however, tells us of it whether the reason be jealousy or greed or lack of land to live on or some other reason. If then, through the possibility of human cross-cultural communication,

17. Claude Levi-Strauss, *The Raw and the Cooked, Introduction to a science of mythology*, p. 4.

the potential relationship between persons and peoples can be actualized through contact in the flesh, it only implies the gift to the human race of enunciation of what otherwise was merely its promise.

Our twentieth century offers an increased possibility as well as a need of myths meeting in the flesh. No country, nation or people is any longer only black or brown or white or only Buddhist, Muslim, Hindu or Christian or any other religious tradition. The myth of cultural self-sufficiency has been supplanted by the myth of plurality. Tolerance, respect, solidarity and democracy are now the passwords. These virtues may have been missing, willy-nilly, in earlier efforts of myth analysis. What we are now being asked is that we leave our *status-quo* and our preconceived ideas about someone else's myth.

The method of *incarnational dialectics of myth* is a round-about method of myth-analysis. I must first live my own myth of the possibility of human communication before I can even begin to apprehend another human being's myth. This counts all the more when I meet a person or a people of an "other" cultural situation. Thus, to speak for myself, I must first know how I myself am being "other" to another. I must try and be aware of the cultural implications of being born a European. To be more precise, to be born a Dutchman with a catholic christian background. If that background, to give an example of possible human cross-cultural imagination, has revealed to me Mount Calvary on which the Saviour Jesus Christ died to redeem mankind, then, by virtue of a single but diversified human race, I should be capable of at least imagining another mount where someone else has found redemption. When confronted with the Indian Hindu tradition I find Mount *Kailāśa, Siva's* mount. Panikkar offers a suggestion corroborating the chosen position:

> "(analysis of myth) is not the invasion of the mythos by the logos, reducing the former to the latter, but rather "mythos-legein": telling the myth, saying it, the integral word that is both mythos and logos."[18]

Analysis of myth, therefore, refuses the application of the mere rational-critical word. That is myth's own answer to its analysis. Seen in that context, mythology is not a science. Panikkar observes how recently mythology has given up its pretensions of being a science. We can only "recount". "This is mythology de-mythologised," he remarks.[19]

The Indian philosophic mythical awareness includes within its extensive bounds several concepts quite comfortably compatible with a theory of archetypes. It teaches us that regression is a round-about way of progression and an exploration of our potentialities. In as much as myth may be said to be grounded in the collective consciousness, the regression towards the beginnings calls for a progression of the question where the human race is going in its human condition. That is a most relevant and pressing question in our presentday technological age. Where are we indeed going in the face of obvious scandals of which we are well aware? Have we grasped the fact that our world is finite and our capacity to pollute and destroy it

18. R. Panikkar, *Myth, Faith and Hermeneutics*, pp. 39 - 40.
19. *Ibid.* p. 40. In footnote 9 to his chapter Panikkar refers to O.W. Otto, K. Kerenyi and M. Eliade on the subject. "Mythoslegein" is the Greek word for "reading" or "recounting" the myth.

infinite? The re-immersion in our own archetype and in our own archeism of our personality can be deepened and widened by immersion into the "other", the "different" of another culture's or person's archeism. That will increase our understanding of and solidarity with the human race as a whole. The constant growth of mythical awareness in us is a help to understand archetypal humanity of which we are already part. Myth analysis, through the feeling of and the belief in the *incarnational dialectics of myth*—in other words, mankind's myths meeting in the flesh—is also comforting. We may rest assured that we already belong to the Indian myths, part as they are of humanity's *aimed-at* restoration of the Universe's totality in the mythical consciousness. With regard to myth-analysis Paul Ricoeur urges us :

> "to transport ourselves behind the myth. The myth-narrative is only the verbal envelope of a form of life, felt and lived before being formulated."[20]

It is at this point, the point of pre-formulation, that one can respectfully enter the *other* of a culturally particularized mythical consciousness. One enters another culture's thought in silence, that is, without misgivings. Thus we may the clearer *hear* the myth *say* what it says.

20. Paul Ricoeur, *The Symbolism of Evil*, p. 164.

PART II

THE QUEST FOR HARMONY: *PRAVṚTTI* AND *NIVṚTTI*

Chapter 4

VALUE SYSTEMS IN INDIAN MYTHOLOGY*

Introduction

The *Mahābhārata, Rāmāyaṇa,* and the *Purāṇas* contain a vast repository of myths. The majority are variants of one another. They utilize a common treasure of motifs and imagery. The antecedents to these myths are found in the *Śruti.* True, one meets changes and alterations, even significant ones. In Vedic texts, to give an example, we find the great *Varuṇa,* the universal Lord of the Waters. He bears the title of *Samrāj,* universal king.[1]

"Varuṇa is the warp of the loom,
Varuṇa is the woof of the loom,
of the universe.
Varuṇa is of us, Varuṇa is foreign,
Varuṇa is divine, he is also human
Varuṇa is King."[2]

Varuṇa puts "milk in cows, intelligence in hearts, fire in the waters, in the sky the sun, *soma* on the mountain".[3] He is visible everywhere (*viśvadarśata).*[4] He is many-eyed.[5] He is thousand-eyed, a mythical formula for the stars. He is also one-eyed, his eye is in the sky (*svadṛśa*)[6]. *Varuṇa* sees and observes men.[7] *Varuṇa's* structure as cosmocreator-god is clearly shown. He inspires awe and fear and he notices all malice.[8]

With time, when *Varuṇa* lost some of his earlier grandeur, his all-seeing power and omniscience, becomes his noose. Numerous hymns and rituals mention the liberation of man from the 'bonds of *Varuṇa'.* Not that he became the hangman among gods but he did, at times, become a sinister god with dark associations. Post-Vedic literature refers to him as the Lord of the Waters but these are no longer the

---

* Throughout I have used the term "value system" in a sense akin to "ideology" as an abstract system of ideas, embodying a distinct view of the world. In the Indian context these values are, it seems to me, implicit rather than explicit.

1. *RV.* 1.136.1.
2. *AV.* 4.16.8., tr. Raimundo Panikkar, *The Vedic Experience,* p. 513. Panikkar comments: "The warp and woof of the cosmic loom renders the idea of the *samāṇya* and *vyāṇya,* i.e., extending in length (vertically) and extending under (horizontally)." Nothing escapes *Varuṇa.* He counts the blinks of every eye, *satyānṛta-samīkṣaka, op. cit.,* p. 511, *Varuṇa* is angered at all forms of *anṛta,* lack of righteousness. (*RV.* 7.60.5). Yet, his anger and similar attributes do not overshadow the fact that *Varuṇa* bestows gracious forgiveness.
3. *RV.* 5.85.1-2.
4. *RV.* 4.16.2-7.
5. *RV.* 1.25. 5.
6. *RV.* 5.63.2.
7. *RV.* 7.60.2.
8. *AV.* 1.10.2.

celestial waters. Whatever may be thought of the etymological kinship of their names, it is proper to point out that *Varuṇa* and *Vṛtra* are related to the primordial waters, to the "waters withheld". The great *Varuṇa* "has hidden the sea". His court is beneath or within the waters, surrounded by snakes. It appears that *Varuṇa* was "made" the watergod by the other gods.[9] The sea-animal (*Makara),* serves as his vehicle and he is guardian of the Western quarter, the region of *Yama,* darkness and death.[10] The occasion, referred to in the *Mahābhārata* when, one day, all the gods came and made *Varuṇa* the Lord of the Waters, signifies his sub servience to the rising epic-gods and thus demonstrates *Varuṇa's* change of status in the pantheon's hierarchy.[11]

Literature of all periods of mankind mention an equal myth recurring in dozens of versions. It is interesting to note, with Dimmitt and van Buitenen, that India has no special word for "myth". Closest, perhaps, is *purāṇa,* a "story of old days".[12] These myths are made up of motifs such as the conflict between gods and demons, *Agni's* withdrawal of his flame, the incest of the creator with his daughter, and many others. However, the myths themselves are not subordinate to the motifs. They derive their content from the whole stock of motifs and their particular form from the way the motifs interact.

To grasp the meaning or meanings of these myths, it is essential to know the motifs. One must also penetrate beneath them to the value systems which are expressed through the myths and which also shape the myths. The existence of such value systems becomes clear, it is hoped, after a reading of the myths and the didactic literary material, scattered throughout the texts in which the myths appear.

The *Mahābhārata* and the *Purāṇas* are full of didactic passages. The conduct of people in the various classes and stages of life (*varṇāśramadharma*) receives careful guidance. Also dealt with are cosmogony, cosmology, worship, and many other subjects. Both the myths and the teaching material are concerned with similar topics. Because they belong to different genres, their treatment of the subject-matter is different. The connection may at times be difficult to discover, certainly for one not born and bred in India and reared in a different culture and religious tradition. Yet the attempt must be made to unearth the same set of values beneath both the myths and the passages of guidance.

The Vedic and post-Vedic myths and lessons require "seership". The *Vedas* makes much of this "seership." It is "fearless light" (*jyotir abhāyam*) or "the wide world" (*uruṃ lokam*). There is no question here of "credere" and "scire", faith as against knowledge, as has been the case, for example, in Western Christian theology. The Vedic visionary perception (*Dhī*) or "wise thought and intuition" (*manīṣa*) or even "*Brahman*" in the ṚgVedic prayerful power-meaning of the word, is the source of understanding.[13] Meant here is an all-encompassing vision. The Stoics possessed a

9. *Mhb*. 9.46.
10. *AP*. 51.15.
11. For '*Varuṇa*' see: Sukumari Bhattacharji, *The Indian Theogony, a comparative study of Indian mythology from the Vedas to the Purāṇas.* Firma KLM Private Ltd., Calcutta, 1978. p. 23-47. Mircea Eliade, *A History of Religious Ideas, From the Stone Age to the Eleusinian Mysteries.* Collins, St. Jame's Place, London, 1979, pp. 200-203. See also the index of names and themes in this work.
12. Dimmitt, Cornelia and van Buitenen, J.A.B., *Classical Hindu Mythology, A Reader in the Sanskrit Purāṇas*, Temple University Press, Philadelphia, 1978. p.3.
13. Jeanine Miller, *The Vedas. Harmony, Meditation and Fulfilment,* Foreword by Jan Gonda. B.I.

similar attitude, professing to the maxim "sumpatheia tōn hōlon", "sympathy with the Whole".[14]

Scholars have found different value systems underlying epic and purāṇic mythology. George Dumezil has interpreted the myths of the *Mahābhārata* and seen them from the point of view of a tri-functional ideology, prominent in much of Indo-European mythology.[15] His study has largely been restricted to the first level of epic mythology, that is, to the war between the *Kauravas* and *Pāṇḍavas*. The research has important implications for the second level of epic mythology, viz., that which concerns the gods and the demons, reborn on earth.

The tri-functional ideology is reflected in the figures of *Brahmā, Viṣñu* and *Śiva*. They are the most important gods of the epics and the *Purāṇas*. We can fruitfully make use of this tri-functional ideology as a key to unlock the meaning of the roles these gods perform in the Indian myths. A striking illustration of tri-functionalism in the characters of these deities is found in a passage of the *Kathāsaritsāgara*. The contents of this text is similar to those found in the epics, viz., the *Mahābhārata*, the *Rāmāyaṇa*, and the *Purāṇas*. The gods have arrived to witness a battle and among them are the three principal gods:

> "And *Śaṅkara (Śiva)*, the Lord of everything, came there, accompanied by *Pārvatī*, and followed by the gods, the inferior deities, the spirits and mothers. And the illustrious *Brahmā* came along with *Sāvitrī* and the rest, the personified Vedas, the appendices, the *śāstras* and the great sages. And *Hari (Viṣñu)* a warrior armed with a discus, whose chariot is the king of birds, together with his wives led by *Lakṣmī, Kīrti,* and *Jayā*."[16]

Each god reflects his role in the myths and these roles correspond to one of the three functions. *Brahmā* and his entourage represent the first function. It is the function of priesthood, religion, and the sovereign aspect of kingship. The *Vedas* and the *śāstras* are sources of religious knowledge. Thus it is that *Sāvitrī, Brahmā's* wife, plays a part in the holy-thread ceremony (*upanayaṇa*) and ministers to every male member of the three twice-born classes. The second function, the dynamic aspect of kingship and martial force, is portrayed by the entry of *Viṣñu,* followed by his wives. Characteristic of the third function are the great sages, symbolic of religious learning and wisdom. *Śiva* conforms least of the three to anyone function, but, if any, it should be to the third.

It would be incorrect to understand the roles the principal gods perform in terms of the tri-functional value system only. True, this value system has exercized considerable influence on their position and on the Indian myths in general. The tri-

---

Publications, Bombay, New Delhi, 1975, first Indian ed., p. 10.

14. It is dangerous to apply a Greek or any other philosophic maxim to the most rudimentary beliefs of mankind. The Stoic doctrine, however, of an all-pervading "pneuma", a breath diffused throughout the universe which imparts to all things the tension by which they are held together, shows a clear analogy with the Vedic *dhī* or *manīṣa*.
15. In the first volume of *Mythe et Epopée,* Paris, 1968, pp. 31-257, Dumézil develops Stig Wikander's demonstration concerning the tri-partite scheme in the *Mhb.* On the gods of the Mitanni, see G. Dumézil, *Les " trois fonctions" dans le Rig Veda et les dieux indiens de Mitanni*, Academie royale de Belgique, Bulletin de la Classe des Letters, 5th. ser. 47 (1961); 265-298.
16. *Kathāsaritsāgara,* 8.47.46-48. Somadeva, Bombay, 1930.

functional system, however, does not explain various other ways in which the principal deities appear on the scence. In the first place, each god's activities range right across all three functions at once. This is to be expected. The seers who conceived of the myths were well aware of man's doings on earth and in myths gods and men are never far apart.

In the *Pātalā Khaṇḍa* of the *Padma Purāṇa* we find an entertaining illustration of this.[17] After the construction of images of *Viṣñu* in various centres of worship like *Kāśī, Jagannátha* and *Vṛndāvan,* the assembled *ŕṣis* discussed which of the deities would be entitled to homage by a brahmin. Some suggested *Rudra,* some *Brahmā.* Others proposed *Sūrya* and again others voted for *Viṣñu.* All were agreed, however, that the one, made up of the quality of goodness, ought to be given the honour. So they decided to send *Bhṛgu* to put the gods' character to test. Unable to gain access to *Śiva* who was engaged with his wife, *Bhṛgu* sentenced *Śiva* to the form of the *Liṅga. Śiva* was not to have any offering or worship bestowed on him. His was the property of darkness. The sage then found *Brahmā,* surrounded by wise men. *Brahmā,* however, pleased with his own importance, humiliated *Bhṛgu*. Being made up of the quality of pride, *Brahmā* was excluded from worship. When he arrived at *Viṣñu's* abode, *Bhṛgu* found him asleep. Appalled at the god's sloth, *Bhṛgu* stamped with his left foot on the deity's breast to wake him. *Viṣñu,* instead of being offended, was pleased, grasped the foot of *Bhṛgu* and expressed his pleasure at seeing him. The sage felt so pleased about *Viṣñu's* humility that he proclaimed him to be the only god worthy of worship by gods and men.[18]

Myth is rooted in the great visions of the psyche, establishing secure ground of being and truth. The seers awaken (*bubudhāna*) to a treasure, only to realize that the gods must teach man this treasure. Myth thus provides an outer husk-description of an inner psychological experience. The telling secures light and order for mankind, two basic factors in the civilizing process. The inner psychological experience is, in Indian thought, connected with the inner breath (*prāṇa)*. The Breaths are thought of as streams or rivers of light, sound, and life.[19] They are the very waters and rivers that are released when *Vṛtra* is slain, and are called *nadyaḥ* "because they sounded (*anādata)"*. In the same way the Breath is a noise (*prāṇo vai nādaḥ*) and when it sounds, all else resounds (*saṁnādati)*. With this concept of the Breaths, and indeed of all manifested things, as streams or rivers, we can turn to the contexts in which the doors of the senses are opened.

The Person pierces the openings in man and looks[20] through them. A mythical figure like *Indra* is the answer to the question in *AV*. 10.2.6.11.:

> "Who pierced the seven apertures in the head,
> these ears, the nostrils, eyes and mouth....
> who divided up the Waters for the flowing of
> the rivers in this man?"[21]

---

17. *PP*. ch. 75.
18. H.H. Wilson, *Analysis of the Purāṇas* (ed. Rost, Reinhold Dr. Nag Publishers, Delhi, 1979). p. 60 - 61.
19. *AV*. 10.7.15.
20. *khāni vyaṭṛṇat khāni bhitvā*
21. "The seven apertures": *sapta khāni vi tatarda*, "who divided the Waters" *āpo vy-adadhāt*, "for the

To the question, "What *Ṛṣi* put man together?"[22] the answer is that Indra pierced with his bolt the sluices of the streams and so let loose the "Seven Rivers" by which *we* see, hear and think. This opening up of the treasure that had been hidden by the Vedic Dragon, is the primordial and incessant act of creation and animation, repeated in every generation and in every awakening from sleep.[23]

There is another significant point with regard to the value systems in Indian myth. Each principal god, in his own way, is related to asceticism. Asceticism and themes associated with it, reflect the importance in Indian myth of the values of renunciation.

Underlying much of Indian mythology are two distinct and seemingly opposed sets of values. On the one hand world-renouncing asceticism, on the other values recommended by orthopraxis, in line with the strata found in Indian Hindu society. Orthopraxis observes rules and rituals for the sake of obtaining, preserving or regaining purity. Correct observance has been regarded from the very beginning a source of Indian Hindu *Dharma*. As is often the case with "correct observance", it corrects itself by causing reaction. The epics and the *Purāṇas* have served as abrogative agencies denouncing customs which had become obsolete. They also served as manuals of renewal and updating Indian society in its middle ages. Obsolete and obnoxious customs and usages were tabooed under *Kalivarjya* by the *Brahmā Purāṇa* and the *Āditya Purāṇa*.

The renouncer seeks to attain ultimate release from the bond of *saṁsāra* by giving up the values of orthoprax society. He renounces the emphasis on correct observance, consistent only with a life of action in conformity with stratified society. The renouncer, in fact, abandons society. He becomes an "individual". He no longer derives his identity, his occupation and his marital status as though "given" by birth.

In the Indian myths and the didactic portions of the epics and *Purāṇas* the tension between the two seemingly opposed values shows itself. Especially *Śiva* often experiences great difficulties on the stage of paradoxes and opposites. The *Śaiva Purāṇa* gives an account of his conflict with pleasure, pain, dullness, and lust. Ever in search of an equilibrium, he rarely found it.

Not only the gods, also the elements appear caught between participation and renunciation, creation and destruction. The waters, for instance, both create and destroy.

> "*Śiva* is the seed of everything. During the primeval creation, the seed arising from his *liṅga* was placed in the womb of *Viṣṇu* and in course of time that golden seed became an egg and floated in the cosmic waters for a thousand celestial years. Then a wind split it into two, and the top half became the sky, the lower half the earth, and the yolk the golden mountain. Then, at sunset, the Lord of the Golden Womb was born, and from him all the ascetics appeared."[24]

The waters use their destructive powers during an incident at *Śiva's* wedding with *Satī*. *Brahmā* lifted the veil from *Satī*'s face and was overcome with desire. He spilled four drops of his seed on the ground like a mound of snow, *Brahmā* tried to

---

flowing of the rivers" *sindhu-sṛtyāya*.

22. *AV*. 11.8.14, *samadadhāt*.
23. *RV*. 11.15.13.: *vajrena khāni vyatṛnat nadīnām*. See Part I, ch. 1. "A Phenomenology of "Chaos".
24. *Liṅga Purāṇa*, 1. 20.80-86. Bibliotheca Indica, Calcutta, 1812. See Wendy Doniger O'Flaherty, *Śiva, The Erotic Ascetic*. Oxford Univ. Press, 1981, p. 107.

conceal the drops with his feet but he could not prevent *Śiva* noticing it. Enraged, *Śiva* raised his trident to kill *Brahmā* but, calmed by *Viṣñu*, he instructed the offender to wander on earth in human form to expiate his sin. Then *Śiva* said:

"These four drops of seed will become the clouds of doomsday in the sky."[25]

The two sets of values appearing all through Indian mythology in a wide variety of motifs should be examined further. A clear understanding of each of them would seem indispensable for a correct appreciation of Indian mythology and its view on things of earth and those of heaven.

Pravṛttidharma

Orthopraxis and its sets of values are referred to as *Pravṛttidharma.*[26] Another term for that concept is *pravṛttimarga.* Even a *yoga* of *pravṛtti* (and *nivṛtti*) has been developed.[27] The concepts of *pravṛtti* and *nivṛtti* imply a certain vision or mode of existence. They point to a particular consciousness through which existence is perceived and experienced. Not as a make-do but as a valid way of life. Many an instance in Indian mythology expresses these ideals, one way or another, as rooted in the minds of both god and man.

The literal meaning of *pravṛtti* is 'rolling onwards', or 'act of turning round'. This implies movement and activity. *Pravṛtti* effects a certain life-style. In the following passage from the *Mahābhārata,* the religious differences between the two values are emphasized.

> "*Nārāyaṇa* has said that there is a *dharma,* which is characterized by *pravṛtti,* and on it are based the entire three worlds, moving and non-moving. The *Dharma,* characterized by *nivṛtti* is the unmanifest, eternal *dharma. Prajāpati* has said that there is a *dharma* characterized by *pravṛtti. Pravṛtti* is repeated returning (to *saṁsāra). Nivṛtti* is the highest refuge. The sage who is intent upon true knowledge and always perceives pleasantness and unpleasantness (equally), is completely occupied with *nivṛtti.* He goes to the highest refuge."[28]

Although nothing is said here about action, *pravṛtti* may be understood as characterized by obligatory action (*kārya*) and deriving from *saṁsāra*. Signs of a division in orthodox Brāhminism into two main streams, each stressing different social and religious views, can be found in the *Upaniṣads.* Passages in the *Bṛhadāraṇyaka Upaniṣad* betray a rather critical opinion of those who offer sacrifice and desire worldly acquisitions such as sons and wealth. Those who become ascetics are being exalted. They realize *Brahmān.* Among several instances, the following provides an

25. *Ibid.* p. 42.
26. *Mhb.* 12.210.2-5; 335, 68. In the *Bhagavad Gita* with the commentary of *Śaṅkarāchārya,* (Samata Books, Madras, 1981), *pravṛttidharma* is referred to when the Lord first created the universe and wished to establish order therein. He then caused others, after the *Prajāpatis,* like *Sanaka* and *Sanandana,* to adopt *Nivṛttidharma.* "It is the two-fold Vedic Religion of Works and Renunciation that maintains order in the universe". p. 2. *Nivṛtti,* the antipole of *pravṛtti,* will be discussed in the following paragraph. It would seem that *pravṛtti* and *nivṛtti* are contemporaneous when their 'creation' is concerned.
27. *Mhb.* 14.43.24; *VAP.* 1.6.39.
28. *Mhb.* 12.210.2-5; *KP.* 1.2.61ff. For discussion on the concepts of *pravṛtti* and *nivṛtti* see also Madeleine Biardeau, *Etudes de mythologie hindoue* II, BEFEO, 56 (1978), pp. 81 - 87.

interesting portrait of the ongoing discussion in earlier times. On the instigation of *Janaka,* king of the *Videhas,* the priest asks the assembled Brāhmins from the *Kurus* and *Pāñçālas* to reply to a few vexed questions. Before *Áśvala,* the priest, has been given an opportunity to even begin the argument, *Yājñavalkya* tells his servant to take to his home the cows the king had promised he would present to the one most clever and erudite in his replies. A thousand cows had been promised and to each ten quarter-coins of gold had been fastened. Being rebutted for his obvious cheek, *Yājñavalkya* answers: "We also give respect to the greatest Brahmin but what matters at the present moment is that", he added ironically, "we have the desire for the cows." *Yājñavalkya* is then being put to the test. The priest asks: "As long as this aerial space is, as it were, devoid of steps or rungs (*anārambaṇa*) without support, on which ascending path does the performer of sacrifice ascend upward to the heavenly world?" After some hard arguing *Yājñavalkya* only with difficulty put the questioner to silence. He argued about in-breath (*prāṇa*), out-breath (*apāṇa*) and the intermediate breath of the hymn of praise (*vyāṇa*), through which man gains the earthly world, the aerial space as well as the world of heaven. The master tried to make the assembly see the unity of everything. Whether he was found altogether convincing is not mentioned in the account. One gets the impression that the Brāhmin was lucky to be allowed to keep the cows in his homestead.[29]

Another indication of the divergence of opinions concerning the different value-systems is the distinction made in the *Upaniṣads* between the dead "being led into the worlds of *Brahman,* the *devāyana*, and the dead who return to earth, *pitryana*". The *Upaniṣads* make on several occasions a selection among the dead.[30] The *Chāndogya Upaniṣad* makes explicit mention of those who live in the forest and practice penance. They will be led on the path of the gods. Those who live in the villages saying, "Sacrifice and works of piety are our almsgiving or charity", will return the same way as they came.[31] The distinction between the forest dweller and the villager is symbolic of the ascetic and the man-in-the-world living in society. In more than one passage the *Upaniṣads* assert with considerable force that the efficacy of *pravṛtti* is inferior to austerity as a means towards the realization of release. The *Muṇḍaka Upaniṣad*, for example, distinguishes between higher knowledge of *Brahman* and lower knowledge.[32] In the same *Upaniṣad* we are told that those engaged in action - sacrifice (*karma*) are incapable of understanding truth, affected as they are by impetuous desire (*rāga*). Those free of *rāga* will understand reality and truth (*virāga*).[33]

References to the values of *pravṛtti* and *nivṛtti* are found throughout Indian thought, each boasting its defenders as well as having to put up with its opponents. Thus we find, in the *Mahābhārata*, *Yudhiṣṭhira* proclaiming the excellence of renunciation, whereas *Bhīmasena* ridicules it, insisting on the necessity of a life of strenuous activity.[34]

---

29. *Bhu*. 3.1-10. see Paul Deussen. *Sixty Upaniṣads of the Veda*, tr. V.M. Bedekar and G.B. Palsule, Motilal Banarsidass, Delhi, 1980. pp. 445 -448.
30. *BU*. 6.2.14-16.
31. *CU*. 5.10.1-7.
32. *MU*. 1.1.4-5.
33. *MU*. 1.2.9-11.
34. See respectively *Mhb*. 12.9.26 and 12.10.24-25.

> "If, O King, anybody were to obtain success from renunciation", *Bhīmasena* maintains, "then mountains and trees would surely obtain it. These latter are always seen to lead lives of renunciation. They do not injure anyone. They are aloof from a life of wordliness and all are brahma-cārins."

Efforts to resolve the conflict and find a synthesis between the two paths were made.[35] For some time both ways appear to have been pursued exclusive of each other. While the *Upaniṣads* and the *Gītā* tried to develop a synthesis between the two, the *Mahābhārata* and the *Purāṇas* continue to discuss differences. The problem is presented at considerable length in a dialogue between *Janamejaya* and *Vaiśampāyana* in the *Mahābhārata*. Beginning the dialogue, *Janamejaya* expresses his doubt whether the norms of *nivṛtti* can be at all safeguarded in a life of *pravṛtti*. The speaker maintains that those, engaged in *pravṛtti*

> "do not know the re-absorption, *pralaya,* aimed at by the self. Therefore, they do not dwell on the eternal, stable, and indestructible path. Having conceived of time as their measure, they are engaged in *pravṛtti*. Holding time to be a measure is a great fault of those active ones..."

In reply *Vaiśampāyana* narrates a version of creation, beginning with the *puruṣa* and ending with *Brahmā's* sons creating the universe. The gods ask *Viṣñu* what functions they should perform. *Viṣñu* declares that, for the very maintenance of the universe, *pravṛtti* is indispensable. The universe's support is expressed by sacrifice and action on the part of man and the gods will share in the fruits and honour of these sacrifices and then help man to maintain the worlds. *Viṣñu* says that creation was made by him to last until the end of the *kalpa.*[36] He pleads with the gods to think of the success of the worlds. In view of their role as Lords of men, the gods are followers of the norms of *pravṛtti*, so *Viṣñu* maintains. He declares that the perpetual path of the performance of action is manifest. The 'mind-born' sons of *Brahmā* are the seven sages to whom knowledge has come spontaneously and they abide by the norms of *nivṛtti.* They are the first knowers of *yoga* and they teach the science of liberation, being the founders of the very norms of liberation. The account in the *Mahābhārata* then ends as follows:

> ".....Thus this very fortunate, eternal *Padmanhābha (Viṣñu)* is said to be the one who receives the first part of the sacrifice. Residing in the norms of *nivṛtti*, the way of those who will not die again, he has made the diversity of the world and ordained the norms of *pravṛtti."*[37]

The passage demonstrates that the spatial dimension of *pravṛttidharma* is the triple world (*triloka*) and its temporal dimension is designated by the *kalpa.* We can ask why the dialogue partner *Vaiśampāyana* narrated the creation version, beginning with the *puruṣa.* The question is relevant when we consider how a great number of creation-myths relate the world's origin to its issue from a simple, original thing like a cosmic egg or a tree. Many creation myths tell of the origin of things as formed from a body,

35. See paragraph 4 in this chapter: The reconciliation of *Pravṛtti* and *Nivṛtti*.
36. *Kalpa*: a day of *Brahmā,* equal to one thousand *mahāyugas,* or 4.320 million years of mortals.
37. *Mhb*. 12.327.1 -13; 52cd - 66; 87 - 88.

eacn part giving existence to sea, earth, mountains, rivers, trees etc. It is a typical characteristic of creation myths as is, for example, shown in the Vedic hymn of creation describing how everything comes forth from the parts of *Puruṣa*, the Cosmic Man, offered as a sacrifice by the gods.[38] The Vedic creation hymn is a near perfect example of the epistemological might of mythical thought. Not only is explained the genesis of perceptible, concrete objects but also highly complex, mediated formal relationships. Also the songs, the melodies, and the sacrificial formulae issue from different parts of *Puruṣa.* Stratified society, too, discloses the same concrete material origin.

> "The *Brahmin* was his mouth; of his arms was made the *Rājanya,* the warrior; his two thighs are the *Vaiśya,* the trader and agriculturalist; from his feet the *Śūdra,* the servile class, was born. The Moon was born from his spirit, *manas,* from his eye was born the Sun, from his mouth *Indra* and *Agni,* from his breath *Vāyu* was born. From his navel arose the middle sky, from his head the heaven originated, from his feet the earth, the quarters from his ear. Thus they did fashion the worlds."[39]

Rational thought tries to dissolve all reality into relations and then understand that reality through these relations. Mythical thinking does not do so. It answers the question of origins by reducing even intricate relations such as musical rhythms and caste organization to a pre-existing material substance. In one myth it may be the *Puruṣa*, in another the Waters. Yet another may identify the two. This fundamental form of thought shapes for myth everything into *bodies.*[40] The distinction between the various classes is understandable on the supposition that they contain different substances of the same concrete, material origin. In terms of spatial orientation everything, for the mythical vision, is deducted from "behind", or "in front", the "above" and the "below" of man's intuition of his own body. The world *is* the *Puruṣa.* Myth starts from a spatial-physical correspondence between the world and man and from this correspondence infers a unity of origin.[41]

In myth the whole does not "become" by growing genetically from its elements according to a determinate rule. We find in myth a static relationship of inherence. That however, does not mean that myth is dead. No matter how far we divide, in each mythical part is found the form, the structure of the whole. Each part, each participant has a place, not accidentally but planned, designed from the beginning. Hence, all the relationships in mythical space find their support in original identity. They go back not to a similarity of efficacy but to an original identity of essence.

38. For *Puruṣa* see Part II:5:4.
39. *RgVeda* 10.90 Engl. transl. by Edward J. Thomas, *Vedic Hymns*, London, John Murry, 1923, p. 122.
40. See Hermann Oldenberg, *Religion des Veda,* Berlin. W. Hertz, 1894, 2nd ed. p. 478ff.
41. Paul Deussen, *Algemeine Einleitung und Philosophie des Veda, Allgemeine Geschichte der Philosophie mit besonderer Berücksichtigung der Religionen* (7 vols. Leipzig, 1894-1920), Vol. I, Pt. I, pp. 150ff. For 'Origin' see Part II:5:3. 'The Prestige of Origin'. See Ernst Cassirer, *The Philosophy of Symbolic Forms*, 3 Vols., Yale University Press, 13th ed., 1979. Vol. 2, 83 -104. Cassirer observes: "Both mythical space and perceptive space are thoroughly concrete products of consciousness. Here the distinction between *position* and *content* (E.C.) underlying the construction of "pure" geometric space, has not yet been made and cannot be made. Position is not something that can be detached from content or contrasted with it as an element of independent significance". p. 84.

Unlike in mathematics there is no functional space in myth. In myth space is *structural.* This is one way in which myth creates its own unique civilizing sense of order and understanding through inherent relationship. It is in the measure of one's understanding of this relationship that one can be said to *become.* Comprehending oneself as essentially participating in all that is, is, as we have seen, the intentionality of the myth and its awareness.[42]

For the spatial range of myth *pravṛttidharma* is philosophically a perfectly valid means of existence and a sure path towards the Whole. *Pravṛttidharma* is itself part of the *Puruṣa* and, as such, the acknowledgement of one's identity with created order. In that sense, *pravṛtti* is in Indian philosophical and religious thought truly *dharma* as *Viṣñu* made it clear in the dialogue between *Janamejaya* and *Vaiśampāyana.*

Mythical consciousness, as we observed, whenever it posits a relation, causes the members of that relation to merge. This confluence, concrescence, prevails also in the mythical consciousness of time. The stages of time—past, present and future—do not remain completely distinct. The mythical awareness tends to level the differences and transform them into identity as in the case of mythical spatiality. The idea of time presents language with complex problems. Time is not an immediate intuition. Myth is not satisfied with the intuition of the universe, its parts and forces, as of mere images, mere figures of gods, demons and man. It only begins when a genesis, a *becoming,* a life in time is attributed to these figures. Through action which invites counteraction, the relations grow into a unity, a whole. That is how myth discovers "the history of the gods". Assisted by the rhythm of immediate life unfolding a cycle of birth, sustenance and end, man's mind rises to the idea of a temporal order as a universal order of destiny and purpose. Thus mythical time becomes a potency inherent in gods, demons and men. It is by virtue of this bond that *Viṣñu* in the recorded dialogue consoles the gods, saying that they would be sustained by men in all the sacrifices of the world. The *Vedas,* the sacrifices, and the herbs have *pravṛtti* for their standard, the god declares. Moreover, this relationship in history between god and man will last until the end of the *kalpa.* Here time itself receives a decisive role, through the cycles that dawned upon man, in the cycle of destiny and purpose.[43]

The Indian mythical awareness yearns for the holding together of the worlds (*lokasaṁgraha*).[44] To attain to *lokasaṁgraha* both cosmic conduct and the conduct of each one in society needs to be regulated (*svadharma*). The relationship between the universe, god and man, is symbiotic. Man performs sacrifices and offers shares of these, and acquits himself of his duties. In return the god causes rain to

---

42. It may be observed here that the identity of the "person in the heart" with the "Golden Person in the Sun" is, in Indian thought, a fundamental doctrine in the *Upaniṣads,* e.g. *MU* 6.1 "He bears Himself two-fold, as the breath of life (*prāṇa*) here, and as yonder *Āditya....* Yonder *Āditya* is verily the outer-Essence (*bahir-ātmā*), the breath of life the inner-Essence (*antar-ātmā*)." The incorporeal Essence and the Sun are one and the same.

43. Cassirer in *The Philosophy of Symbolic Forms,* Vol. 2, p. 105 writes: "The true character of mythical being is first revealed when it appears as the being of origins. All the sanctity of mythical being goes back ultimately to the sanctity of the origin. It does not inhere immediately to the content of the given but to its coming into being, not to its qualities and properties but to its genesis in the past. By being thrust back into temporal distance, by being situated in the depth of the past, a particular content is not only established as sacred, as mythically and religiously significant, but also justified as such. Time is the first original form of this spiritual justification."

44. *Mhb.* 12.251.; *BG.* 3.20; 5.1.29.

fall to fertilize the earth. All interests are being served when the earth prospers (*lokasiddhi*).

Nivṛttidharma

Contrary to *pravṛtti*, 'rolling onwards' or 'act of turning around', *nivṛtti* means 'act of turning back' or 'act of returning', thus implying abandonment of earth-bound activity. *Nivṛttidharma* knows no spatial or temporal limits except those which are selfimposed. The adherer to *nivṛttidharma* is propelled by his yearning for pure consciousness (*śuddhabodha-svarūpatva*) of the pure light in the ultimate spiritual reality of *Puruṣa*.[45] *Nivṛttidharma* does not believe that, in life on earth, any transcendence or liberation from human substantiality, both physical and psychic, can be achieved, except that through initiation (*dīkṣā*) and gnosis (*jñāna*). Final emancipation, for *nivṛtti*, comes through that which is behind all experience of the senses and hence must necessarily elude being itself experienced through the senses. Experience is a phenomenal reality belonging to earthly existence. Its essential nature consists of the fluctuations of pairs of opposites (*dvandvas*) and the true state above and beyond the felt presence of the opposites cannot be induced by the fluctuations of experience. The *Bṛhadāranyaka Upaniṣad* exclaims: "How can the knower indeed be known."[46] This upaniṣadic mode of thought continues its trend in that of the *Purāṇas*. Reality (*Pāramārthika)*, even though it is of the nature of consciousness, is beyond empirical experience.

The renouncer's aim is to escape from *saṁsara*. His escape achieves the attainment of freedom and liberation, the most exalted goal in life (*mokṣa*). As a snake is released from its old skin (*vimukta*), so is the arrow of the *Ātman* released from the bow of the mystic syllable *Oṁ* into the target which is *Brahman*.[47] It is freedom to range at will as a bird flies freely through the sky, unobstructed, or as a fish swims in the boundless ocean.[48]

As to the nature of liberation, opinions vary. Standing, philosophically, at the opposite pole from the dualist *Sāṁkhya-Yoga* is the *Advaita-Vedānta*, the philosophy of non-dual reality derived from the *Vedānta* or "end of the *Vedas*", the *Upaniṣads*. We find in the purāṇic myths elements of these trends of thought. *Advaita* or pure monism is only one school of the *Vedānta*. From the philosophical point of view it still is the most important in India. Apart from the intellectual elite, it has exercised a far less profound influence than has the variant *viśiṣṭādvaita*, "differentiated non-dualism". This mode of thought supplies the intellectual framework of the *bhakti* cults with their often highly emotional worship of a personal God. Poles apart though the various philosophical systems may be, they all equally share the conviction of the absolute distinction between the temporal and the eternal. Also considered necessary is the correct use of the intellect when interpreting existence. In the *Muṇḍaka Upaniṣad* (6.34) we are reminded that intellect is for man a means to either bondage or liberation.[49] Bondage if it clings to objects of perception (*viṣayasaṅgī*) and of

45. Seksena. S.K., *Nature of Consciousness in Hindu Philosophy,* Motilal Banarsidass, Delhi. 1971, p.39.
46. *BU* 4.5.15.
47. *MU* 2.2.4.
48. *Mhb*. 12.328.30–31.
49. *kāraṇaṃ bandha-mokṣayoḥ*.

liberation if no attachment to them is found (*nirviśayam*). Thought must be brought to rest in its own source (*çittaṃ svayonāv upaśāmyate*) by the cessation of fluctuation (*vṛtti-kśayāt*).[50]

Once *mokṣa* has been obtained, rebirth is over. At the time of cosmic dissolution (*pralaya*) ascetics move to beyond the triple world.

The world-renouncing ascetic also rejects the spatial limitations of the man-in-the-world. He moves away to an uninhabitable place, jungle or forest, away from the rigorously defined orthoprax society. His is an unbounded area characterized by immeasurability. His move is symbolic of pre-creation conceived of as unlimited potency of being. Withdrawal from society also symbolizes *mokṣa*. *Brahman* is limitless and beyond definition. Man's ego (*ahaṃkāra*), of necessity present in society, imposes limits on his own being. The limits imposed by *ahaṃkāra* may prevent the blossoming of the awareness that

> "there is no 'I' that does, no 'mine' that is the doer, no latent 'I am'."[51]

The text refers to both the objective and the subjective realm. The *ahaṃkāra* is properly speaking a *karmadhāraya* compound. It is not literally the "ego-factor" but the notion of "I am the doer". A verification of its opposite, "not being the doer", can only be made by one who has attained the "point of not being anyone" (*akiñcaññāyatanam*). This "I am not the doer" is a metaphysical position, not a moral one.[52] The renouncer, fleeing from all limitations, cannot escape the real part of him (*ātman*) which he shares with all other beings and to which he is of necessity linked by virtue of being a creature. By renouncing society and its incumbent obligations, the ascetic turns his back on the network of symbiotic relationships governing society and the triple world (*triloka*).

Although the epics and the *Purāṇas* recognize that final emancipation is attainable only through renunciation, there is no explicit injunction on all and sundry to adopt the status of renouncer. Literature refers to a vast number of renouncers, among them women, seen around begging and more than once causing trouble to society while living on the honest bread of the householder and his family. A life of renunciation requires a talent for it and a proper disposition of mind and heart. Not

---

50. India has never found any difficulty in thinking of its greatest and most intellectual exponent of non-dualistic (*advaita*) metaphysics, *Śaṅkarāçārya*, as having been at one and the same time a *bhakta*, a devotee, and a *jñānī*, an enlightened person. His devotional phraseology of certain hymns in V.P. Bhaṭṭa's *Siddhānṭamuktāvalī* (J.R. Ballantyne, tr., Calcutta, 1851) is obvious. Of the *Ātman* we read: "Now that I have gotten Thee, I shall never let Thee go". It is only the academic scholar to whom such an expression of feeling on the part of a Vedantist seems incongruous. The *Bhagavad Gītā* (v. 2-4) plainly affirms that for one perfected in either way, *bhakti* or *jñāna*, one and the same fruit results and this can only be fulfilment in *Brahman* (*brahma-nirvāṇaṃ*).

    The two sharply distinguished paths correspond, on the one hand, to the exoteric, religious, and passively mystical means of approach to God and, on the other, to the esoteric, initiatory, and metaphysical means towards the Supreme Identity. But it would be begging the question to assume that they are to be identified with mutually exclusive paths of dedication (*bhakti*) and of gnosis (*jñāna*).

51. *Saṁyutta-Nikāya* 2.252. *The Book of the Kindred Sayings*, ed. C.A.F. Rhys Davids and F.L. Woodward, 5. vols., London, 1971-1930. *ahaṁkāra-mamaṁkāra—(asmi) mānānusayā na honti*. For the notion of *ahaṁkāra* see also Part III:8: *Karma*, the cosmic pilgrimage.

52. The *Bhagavad Gītā* refers at several instances to the notion of *ahaṁkāra*, e.g. 3.27 where "I am the doer" is inasmuch as the doer thinks that the self of man is "deluded by *ahaṁkāra*".

everyone is capable of leading the life of a renouncer meaningfully and intelligently. Especially renunciation in celibacy was often disadvised (*sannyāsa*).

Confusion concerning an integrated life of *nivṛttidharma* was partly due to the ambivalent attitude in Indian Hindu society towards asceticism. The *Upaniṣads* reveal lipservice being paid to the ascetic. Conventional Hinduism maintained and still maintains a more or less concealed hostility towards renunciation. This may be partly attributed to the paradoxical circumstance that non-castes and low-castes were told to strive after the highest ideals but at the same time forbidden to adopt *nivṛttidharma*. After all, someone has to work and feed the renouncer. Moreover, non-Vedic foreigners aspiring after the high ideal, were identified by Brahminical opinion with the dregs of society such as incendiaries, poisoners, pimps, spies, adulterers, abortionists, atheists and drunkards.[53]

For an understanding of myth formation in India, it will be of help to have a closer look at purāṇic India's social, economic and religious conditions. An eminent scholar in the *Purāṇas*, R.C. Hazra, points to the fact that Brahminical interests influenced the compilation of these scriptures. Puranic myths, therefore, may be expected to show particular characteristics regarding the notions of *pravṛtti* and *nivṛtti*.[54] Purāṇic literature reflects historical trends and developments in Indian Hindu society which throw light on the origin of the myths in these *smṛtis*. Knowledge of the historical background of myths is important. It may guide our understanding of them and the value systems underlying them.

Various anti-Vedic (Buddhism and Jainism), semi-Vedic (Vaiṣṇavism, Śaivism, Brahminism) and non-Vedic (Śaktism) religious movements sprang up in ancient India. Then there were the foreigners who flocked to India. Greeks, Śakas, Pahlavas, Kuśāns, Āhīris, and others who founded kingdoms and settled in the country. They often associated themselves with sectarian groups, suspicious in the eyes of the Brāhmins. A philosophical, theological and social Brāhminic powerstruggle is clearly discernible underneath the purāṇic evolution. After the appearance of Mahavira, Gautama Buddha, a non-Brāhmin like Mahāvīra, preached a message in every way detrimental to Brahminism. Buddhism found its influential patron in king Aśoka, likewise a non-Brāhmin. *Vaiṣṇavas* and *Śaivas* proved unfavourable to orthodox Brāhmin-society which they considered bourgeois. In the *Nārāyaṇīya* section of the *Mahābhārata* we are told of *ṛṣis* who, on mount *Meru*, promulgated a *śāstra* which was on a par with the four Vedas.[55] The treatise was meant for the commoner. As it was to guide and direct him in both *pravṛtti* and *nivṛtti*, it was made consistent with the four Vedas.[56] The directives, therefore, must have successfully passed the scrutiny by Brahmins and was hence considered free of dangerous and novel opinions which might endanger the traditional *varṇāśramadharma*. Casteless foreign races were held in great contempt by purāṇic Brāhmins. They called these outsiders sinners and heretics. Purāṇic authors sounded warnings not to disclose the content of their writings to such people.[57]

---

53. A tirade against the non-Vedic *Vrātya* one finds in *Mhb*. 35.39 – 41.
54. R.C. Hazra., *Studies in the Purāṇic Records on Hindu Rites and Customs*, Motilal Banarsidass, Delhi. 1975, pp. 193-295.
55. *Mhb*. 12.335.27 – 29.
56. *Mhb*. 12. 335.40.
57. *VaP*. 103.69 – 70.

Vaiṣñavas and Śaivas irritated Brahminical society by their unconventional conduct. Women and low-castes were granted access to initiation and personal worship of deities like *Viṣñu*. Likewise the *Śaivas* propagated non-Brāhminical ideas. No wonder then that Brahmins were scarcely able to put up with such insubordinates.

> "One should bathe with the garments on after touching the Śaivas, the Pāśūpatas, the Lokāyatikas, the Nāstikas, the Brāhmins resorting to duties improper to their status and the *śūdras*.".[58]

Understandably not all who worshipped *Viṣñu* and *Śiva* were influenced by uncommon ideas and practices. It appears, however, that the two sects were imbued with doctrines and a manner of behaviour less pleasing to the Brahmins. Apart from doctrinal misgivings, the political supremacy round the year 200 of the Christian era when non-Kśatriyas like the Mauryans and Andhras ruled, was a thorn in the Brāhmin's eye.

The earlier *Purāṇas*, provide a picture of a society in which people often neglected the caste-and *āśrama* regulations.[59] Anti-Brāhmin sentiments persisted in all four castes and *āśramas*. Criticism of Brāhmins was not uncommon those days.

> "Their mind was always occupied with the thoughts of money and they did not hesitate to adopt unfair means to acquire it."[60]

The twice-born, the Brāhmins and the other two higher castes, gave up the study of the *Vedas* and their performance of sacrifices were reserved for "the foolish".[61] Non-Vedic literature was in circulation and many cared little for rules of conduct, mixed with the heretics and became professional beggars.[62]

The spread of Buddhism and Jainism threatened the supremacy of the Brahmins. Their doctrinal authority came to be questioned. People adopted more liberal attitudes. Vaiśyas gave up trade and agriculture and for their livelihood became servants and mechanics.[63] Purāṇic accounts provide information about the considerable political power the Śūdras wielded at the time. Quite a number of kings were of low caste.[64] The records concerning the elevated position of the Śūdras are interesting. Their political supremacy made itself felt in all sectors of public life. They used to drive away Brahmins from their seats and even beat them. Brahmins stooped down to honour them with flowers and those who depended upon Śūdras for their sustenance paid their respects to them in their vehicles and taught them the *Vedas*. Even the best of Brahmins went contrary to the directions in holy writ, turned unbelievers and sold the fruit of their penance and sacrifice.[65] We are told of Śūdras reading the Vedas and performing sacrifice. Buddhism, denouncing the caste-system, naturally attracted them.[66]

---

58. *SmC*. 2.311.; LP.2.
59. *VaP*. 58.; *BP*. 2.31.; *MP*. 144.; *Bhg. P*. 12.2. *VP*. 6.1.; *KP*. 29. See also R.C. Hazra, *op. cit*., p. 208.
60. *VP*. 6.1. 20 – 21.
61. *VaP* 58, 38.; *MP*. 144.38.; *KP*. 1.29.5.
62. *KP*. 1.29.10. – 11.; *VaP*. 58.52.
63. *VP*. 61.36.
64. *MP*. 144.40.; *VaP*. 58.40.
65. *KP*. 1.29. 17 – 23.
66. *MP*. 144.42 – 43.

Thus the *Purāṇas* record a dismal state of affairs in the *Kali-yuga*, the age of decadence, already begun at the time of the purāṇic authors and lasting uptil the present day.[67]

An entire paragraph could be devoted to the relationship between important religious personalities, especially reformers and prophets, and the traditional mythological schemata prevalent among the orthodox religious leaders in purāṇic Indian society. It is possible to reconstruct, at least in part, the impact of the Buddha on the traditional myths. Also Vaiṣṇavism, Śaivism and Tāntrism had considerable influence on the interiorization of the mythical awareness. Despite the fact that these religious movements were at first met with resistance from traditional quarters, they nevertheless succeeded in imposing models or sources of inspiration on the whole community. The surrounding culture, gravitating around myths, was sufficiently receptive of anything embellishing the ideas of paradisial origin already in circulation in the myths. Ecstatic experiences in the new religious movements, for example, enhanced religious imagination. The new movements finally found their allotted place in the purāṇic tradition itself, contributing to its very elaboration as we now possess it in the texts. The historical facts recorded in the *Purāṇas* may, therefore, as to their facticity, be expected to be coloured by a particular conviction or bias of the author. The scope of this chapter does not allow us to discuss these with the attention they deserve. But we can try and discover certain moods in Indian purāṇic times which might clarify the prevalent ideas on the notion of *nivṛttidharma*.

Warnings by orthodox Brāhminism against the threat of heretical Buddhism were no exception. The Buddhists encouraged wandering mendicancy (*pravrajyā*) for the attainment of bliss (*nirvāṇa*.) They also allowed more freedom to women in religious matters, thus advancing their emancipation, a dangerous adventure in traditional Brāhminic opinion. In the *Aṅguttara-Nikāya* (2.232) Buddha is accused of *a-kiriyavāda*, the accuser maintaining that "he teaches that there is no ought-to-be-done with respect to any acts".[68] In the course of the refutation Buddha points out that *akiriya* amounts to an annihilation of the world (*ucchedaṃ. . lokasya*) "of which the very substance consists in the verity, i.e., causal efficacy, of action".[69] Buddha maintains that, as the *Arhat*, he has done what was to be done. This would correspond to the Brāhminical *kṛtakṛtyaḥ*. Misunderstanding of Buddha's doctrine added to a strained relationship with the traditional Brāhmin world. The question of action and non-action always remained a bone of contention.

Even though Tāntrism has a longstanding tradition in Indian religious life, it invites scepticism and often outright contempt on the part of Brāhminism. In the fifth and sixth centuries of the Christian era, Tāntrism became a veritable

67. e.g. scathing remarks on the Śaivite's saffron clothes: *VaP*. 58.64-65., market places marked with tridents: *KP*. 1.29.12, lax morals: *VP*. 6.1.18 – 31.; *VaP*. 58.60.; *KP*. 1.29.14.
68. *Aṅguttara-Nikāya*, *The Book of the Gradual Sayings*, ed. F.L. Woodward and E.M. Hare, 5 vols., London, 1932 – 1939 (PTS). "*sabbakammānam akiriyaṃ paññapeti*".
69. "*kammasacca*", to be understood with respect to any bodily, vocal, or mental activity, *kāya-*, *vācī-mano-sa-mārambha*. When the Buddha says that he has done what was to be done, he does not simply mean "duty done" but "having done what was to be done", i.e., having reduced all potentiality to act and being, therefore, "all in act". The word "*akiriya*", the Buddha implies, is wrongly translated by "inaction". Inaction destroys the world in the sense of "laissez-faire". *Akiriya* means right view in the sense that there is "an *ought not* to be done."

force. Its inculturation in Indian Vedic culture became a fact as time went by. Its treatises and practices, however, also contained non-Vedic elements, one more reason why the doctrine aroused little enthusiasm in orthodox Brahmin circles.

To try and offset lurking dangers, Brahminism extolled the *varṇāśramadharma*. Kauṭilya even promulgated laws regulating the exercise of asceticism. Stories of great men embracing the status of householder, *gārhasthyāśrama*, were made to circulate among the common people.

> "The householder is the source of all three stages of life. It has to be acknowledged as the only means towards *dharma*."[70]

In the purāṇic myths, sages, gods and goddesses are often heard singing the praises of *varṇāśramadharma*. *Dēvi*, *Durga*, when asked how she can be approached by people, says:

> "I am attainable by means of meditation, work, devotion, and knowledge....Practice of *varṇāśramadharma*, I want, with selfknowledge as directed by the Vedas and lawbooks for final beatitude. From *dharma* originates *bhakti* and by *bhakti* is the best knowledge gainded....."[71]

It is clear from the *Purāṇas* that, apart from the honest attempt on the part of Brahminism to keep traditional doctrine free from contamination, it also tried to safeguard its own social and economic vantage point. Even a lukewarm householder might be preferable to an ardent ascetic.

Indian metaphysics, as we are taught it in its six philosophical systems, has a bias towards the realization of man in *Brahman*, the Ultimate Reality. One of the chief characteristics of that realization is its interiority. Realization is a liberation comparable to an "awakening" or a new consciousness of a situation that existed from the beginning but which one was unable to realize. From a certain point of view "ignorance" – which is an ignorance of oneself – can be thought of as a "forgetting" of the true Self. The true Self (*Brahman*) can be realized only in the heart which is its abode.[72] The *Chāndogya Upaniṣad* (8.1.1.) puts it as follows:

> "Now, what is here in this city of *Brahman* is an abode, a small lotus-flower. Within that is a small space. What is within that should be searched out; that is, assuredly, what one should desire to understand."

The progressive transparency of the human mind through knowledge (*jñāna*) of Reality must begin during life. *Brahman* is the eternal Self, being *Sat*, existence, *Çit*, knowledge, and *Ānanda*, bliss. *Sat-Çit-Ānanda* is not a determination, really speaking. *Brahman* is *neti-neti*, not this, not this. Each syllable is the unspeakable Absolute hankered after by man beyond the determinate absolutes of *Sat-Çit-Ānanda*, formulated by man's consciousness. The individual self must, therefore, not only correct for himself his subjective illusion of individuality, not only *wait* for the cosmic illusion of individuality to be corrected, but also contemplate upon all correction

70. R.C. Hazra, *Studies in the Purāṇic Records on Hindu Rites and Customs*, p. 232.
71. See R.C. Hazra, *op. cit.*, p. 232.
72. "*Pure ca veśma rājño yathā tathā tasmin brahmapure śarīre daharam veśma brahmaṇa upalabdhyadhiṣṭhānmityarthaḥ*". *CUB*. 8.1.1.

being itself illusory. The person who realizes his self, hence renounces illusion, is to contemplate liberation, not as something to be reached or effected, but as the Real Self itself, the *svarūpa* of *Brahman*. This is possible because, although illusory, the body is called the empirical city of *Brahman* (*vyāvahārikam brahmapuram*). *Brahman* is attained to in the body. Hence *Brahman* is the support of all empirical reality.[73] In the city of the lotus of the heart (*puṇḍarīkopalakṣite brahmapure*) all one's desires find their fulfilment.

Being part of the fullness, (*Svarūpa*) of The Self, man is already free. Man, however, may not be awake to the fact. It is in the unconditioned turning towards the *svarūpa* whereby illusory action is discontinued, that creature-man recognizes himself. In this sense *nivṛtti* is man's true metaphysic. Its execution through *nivṛttidharma* is an absolute consequence. To make one's earthly village the mainstay of what one *is*, would be like sitting at the villagepond, trying to feed the image reflected in the water. The handful of rice thrown at it will but float aimlessly, unable to still the image's hunger.

We find a delightful illustration of this in the *Dēvī Bhāgavata*. It deserves an abbreviated rendering here. *Nārada*, one of the wisest and most experienced sages of the *Purāṇas*, went to *Mahāviṣñu* to ask him about the secrets of life. "There is nothing called "life". "Life" exists because of *Māyā*, the illusion of the mind", replied the god. *Nārada* insisted. He wished to see *Māyā*. So *Viṣñu* started from his heaven with the sage on *Garuḍa's* back. Crossing forests, villages, cities, mountains and rivers, they finally landed near a lake at *Kānyakubja*. They walked along the lake's shore for some time and *Nārada*, tired as he was, gladly complied with *Viṣñu's* wish that he take a bath. *Nārada* placed his violin and deerhide on the shore and, after first having washed his face and feet and having done *ācamana* with *kuśa* grass, stepped into the water. What a surprise! He was changed into a woman of great beauty. She possessed no memory of her previous birth and coming out of the lake, she stood watching the scenery. King *Tāladhvaja* happened to come that way on horseback and seeing the woman, he began talking to her. He called her *Saubhāgyasundarī*. The king took her to his palace and they spent their honeymoon happily. After twelve years *Saubhāgyasundarī* became pregnant. *Vīravarmā* she called her son. After that she delivered a son every other year. All in all twenty sons she bore. All of them married and in due course begot sons. Thus the king and his wife became the grandparents of a large family and they lived happily. Their happiness was rudely destroyed by enemies who ravaged their land and killed all their offsprings. The *Mahāviṣñu*, disguised as an old Brahmin, came and consoled the weeping queen. On his advice she took a bath in the lake. The water splashed and *Nārada* it was who emerged from the lake. *Mahāviṣñu* was patiently standing near *Nārada's* violin and deerskin and *Nārada*, seeking his violin and deerskin, at once remembered what had happened. But how long had it lasted? *Viṣñu* smiled and said:" Come on, *Nārada*, and finish your bath. What are you thinking about?." In the meantime king

73. *CUB*. 8.1.5.: "*satyam tu brahmapurametadeva brahma; sarvavyavahārāspadatvāt*". The word "heart" signifies the intellect, *buddhi*. *Guhā*, derived from *guh*, to hide, stands for *buddhi*, because in it are hidden the categories of *jñāna*, *jñeya* and *jñatṛ* or the two human goals of enjoyment and liberation (*bhogāpavargau*). The Self realized by man's self is an intellectual conviction: see *TUB*. 2.6.: "*buddhipratyayālokaviśiṣṭatmopalabdhiḥ*".

Tāladhvaja has come home to his palace. Unabled to find his wife he was puzzled to see a bearded *Narada* rising from the place in the lake where the queen had gone to bathe. The king cried loud for he now realized he not only lost all his sons and grandsons but also his beloved wife. "How can human ties be held by *Māyā* which is like water?", asked *Viṣñu*. The king, after doing penance in the forests, attained *mokṣa.*[74]

The rude termination to the king and queen's happiness should not be considered a punishment. No waywardness had found a place in their lives. Their life as householders had been exemplary. The destruction of their kith and kin was the inexorable lot meted out to many a regal couple. The myth tells us expressly that *Saubhāgyasundarī*, when she rose from the lake, did not remember her previous birth. She was her own human self (*ahamkāra*). By a double reversion, when *Nārada* climbed on shore after *Saubhāgyasundarī* took a dip on *Viṣñu's* advice, the myth says that, although there is no inconsequence in the householdership, the metaphysical individuality of *ahaṁkāra* ultimately leads to a life of *māyā*, unless it is pitched towards the eternal *Ātman*, the real Self. Hence the need of *nivṛtti*.

Inversion of themes opposed to each other is one of the characteristics of myth. Myth endeavours a reconciliation of opposites which in the factual and practical world would seem impossible.

The Reconciliation of *Pravṛtti* and *Nivṛtti* Values

Myths of the Exiled Soul

Many didactic passages in the epics and *Purāṇas* reflecting these two sets of values are bitterly controversial. As I have shown, these arguments can be explained in terms of metaphysical, theological and socio-political reasons. Like didactic passages, myths too engage in polemics. In fact, in Indian myths we notice a tendency to increase rather than to minimize the distance between conflicting ideas. Nevertheless, the apparent opposition on certain levels is often taken as the starting point for a series of mediations within the myths. This mediation is necessary to relieve the tension between contrasting cosmic elements and their co-existence within the one given universe, the one given reality. In human terms, contrasting cosmic elements are closely related. In fact, man's experience of himself is that he is *made up* of such contrasts. The tension is there because the complete presence of one of a pair of opposites does not automatically imply the absence of the other. The intense awareness there is in Indian thought of man's temporal existence *in* the totality of *Brahman* will make it difficult, at times, to find in Indian myths a Golden Mean.[75] But myth is first and foremost humble. Like the individual subconscious, myth expresses unconscious wishes which, being in some way inconsistent with conscious experience, cannot be expressed directly. Myth, therefore, can admit failure to comprehend. Its psychological value lies in being able to neutralize oppositions and leave the questioner content with the thought that possibly not everything *can* be answered. It is

---

74. *Dēvī Bhāgavata*, 8th Skanda. See: *Purāṇic Encyclopaedia, A Comprehensive Dictionary with Special Reference to the Epic and Purāṇic Literature*, Vettam Mani. Motilal Banarsidass, Delhi, 1979, p. 784, abbreviated rendering (FB).
75. Wendy Doniger O'Flaherty, *Siva, The Erotic Ascetic*, Oxford University Press, 1981, p. 37.

here that myth may call upon the latent faculty in man to surrender without the feeling of having been cheated. Myth neutralizes opposites by supplying many different versions of one and the same situation without necessarily saying anything new. Hence the sharpness of the polemic in myth is disguised by a multitude of narrative and thematic components. Arguments other than mythical do not necessarily make us either laugh or cry. Myths often do. They release tension. They invite a sigh of relief. One of myth's concerns is to tone down extreme positions by only *imagining* them in order to show that they are untenable. Myth explores the possibility of a solution when the difficulty, in human terms, of reconciling conflicting moral injunctions is perplexing.[76] If, for example, in the instance of *pravṛtti* and *nivṛtti*, one were to deal with them exclusively under the aspects of desire (*kāma*) and asceticism (*tāpas*), they would seem diametrically opposed like black and white. But both can be looked upon as forms of heat with both destructive and generative powers. The notions of *kāma* and *tāpas* seem logically opposed until in them mutually shared elements are discovered. One such element would be "involvement". The mediating third notion softens the two original oppositions and clarifies their interaction until new ones arise and again new mediation is needed. Levi-Strauss has said:

> "The structure of myth is a dialectic structure in which opposed logical positions are stated, the opposition mediated by a restatement, which again, when its internal structure becomes clear, gives rise to another kind of opposition, which in its turn is mediated or resolved, and so on."[77]

As I said repeatedly, man's existence on earth reveals a tension. Mediation in man's human situation is a necessary psychological need. When myth attempts to offer mediation, it offers its philosophy, its wisdom. With regard to the problem of *pravṛtti* and *nivṛtti*, two irreconcilable roles seem to be demanded from man. He could not possibly satisfy both. How could he be a householder and beget offspring and renounce life and seek union with *Brahman*?

In trying to come to terms with the opposites of *pravṛtti* and *nivṛtti*, myth offers us one of its types. This type of myth endeavours to transpose all dualism in man and rationalize it. Meant here is the *anthropological* dualism. In such myths man understands himself as the *same* as his soul and *other* than his body. This type of myth one can call "myths of the exiled soul". They offer a kind of give-and-take between the hard facts of metaphysical and epistemological discipline and the more cloudy and fluctuating experience of everyday life. Myths which try and resolve this "deal" tell about the particular situation of the soul and its liberation by means of knowledge.

Unlike, for instance, etiological myths which pose the question of origin – one myth asking that of the soul and another that of the body –, the "myth of the exiled

76. Claude Levi-Strauss, *The Story of Adiwal*, tr. Nicholas Mann in, The Structural Study of Myth and Totemism ed. Edmund R. Leach, Association of Social Anthropologists Monograph No. 45, London, 1967, pp. 1 – 48.
77. Claude Levi-Strauss, '*The Structural Study of Myth*, in Thomas A. Sebeok, 'Myth" A Symposium', ed. Thomas A. Sebeok. American Folklore Society. Bloomington, 1958. See also: Mary Douglas, '*The Meaning of Myth with Special Reference to La Geste d' Asdiwal*', in Leach, 1967, pp. 49–70. (see footnote 76).

soul" is at the same time a myth of the body. It tells how the soul, divine in its origin, became human and how the body, a stranger to the soul, falls to the lot of the soul. The result is a reasoned experience giving rise to what is called katharsis. Katharsis is, originally, a Platonian and Aristotelian concept. It is a "defeat of the sensations of pleasure". It involves pain. It is a "sacrificial purgation and a purgation consisting in a separation, as far as possible, of the soul from the body".[78] Plato calls it a kind of dying to which the philosopher's life is dedicated; a consequence of existential honesty.[79] The Platonic katharsis implies an ecstasy or a "standing aside" by the energetic, spiritual, and imperturbable self from the passive, merely and solely aesthetic, and natural self. It is a "being out of oneself" in the sense of being in one's right mind.[80] By katharsis, therefore, an attempt is made to avoid unreasoned emotional involvement in the *problem* of body and soul. The aimed-at result, if attained, is a consoling sense of self-purification while experiencing one's existence. Katharsis expels panic and despondency. Katharsis finally comes to express a wholly moral purification by the seemingly *reasonable acceptance* of the very idea of "body and soul", for the simple fact that we *are* such. One cannot be held guilty of what one constitutionally is. How could man be made to suffer moral blemish or stigma because of what he is? Thus katharsis, lifting moral stress regarding the *problem* of man's being body and soul, lends itself to express essential purification, that is, the purification of wisdom and philosophy. The kathartic factor in the philosophy of the "myth of the exiled soul" lies in its speaking of a rupture in the condition of the human being while denying man's division into two realities. The myth of the exiled soul basically provides defence against schizophreny and the fear of being human. The drama of creation it presents does not concern man as a soul. It presents him as an undivided reality. It makes him, as a *whole* being, the seat of the drama and its author, even if only by means of the ritual re-enactment as part of the *aimed-at* restoration of totality. Myths of the exiled soul are, paradoxically, myths of the flesh. Man becomes the inauguration of humanity by the mixture of the two. He becomes the instance, the place where the primordial difference between soul and body is abolished, *as if forgotten*. Thus man becomes the author of the drama of creation not through fear of the division in himself but through love of the whole in himself, for that is what he is. It is well said in colloquial parlance that man, in the face of threat, by instinct strives to keep body and soul together.

As far as our problem is concerned, *pravṛtti* and *nivṛtti* myths of the exiled soul would point to the truth in both, not as more or less peacefully co-existent but as mutually in-existent. They are not two different realities splitting man into two halves. In the *Mahābhārata* we find a lovely instance, the vision of which is precisely that of keeping body and soul together. It is again *Nārada*, venturing into all kinds of situations, who tries to lift, at least partially, the veil of life's mystery.

> "*Nārada* had been born as a worm. On the approach of a chariot, the worm quickly moved away from its route lest the chariot's wheel should crush it to death. The king, seated in the chariot, burst out into laughter, when the worm

---

78. Plato, *Laws*, no. 840c. On 'katharsis' see also his *Sophist*, 226-227 *Phaedrus*, 243AB; *Phaedo* 66-67; *Republic*' 399E.
79. *Phaedrus* 279BC. (80)
80. *Ibid*.

told him as follows: "There is nothing to be laughed at in my action. In every birth the body is much dear to the *Ātman*, soul. Just as you love your body, I also love and protect my body".[81]

The exiled soul – myth may, by transmutation, refer to happenings other than those of man being body and soul. For example, the fertilizing of the earth by rain after a period of drought. The forces of body, symbolized by seed and transmuted to become heavenly rain, fertilize the earth. The earth may be symbolized by the female organ (*yoni*) causing *Śiva* to cast off his phallus (*liṅga*) and, after having restored it to him, promise rain in the cycle of seasons to keep the upper-and netherworld together.

Āśrama

I shall here not be concerned with the history of the antagonism between those professing to *pravṛtti* and others advocating a turning away from the world, *nivṛtti*. It is justified to say that efforts to bring about a reconciliation between the two value systems have accompanied them from a rather early date.[82] Jan Gonda maintains that already the earliest *Upaniṣads* show the beginnings of a revaluation of *pravṛtti* and *nivṛtti*. If man were a mere instrument, what sense is there in any intentional act?[83] Gonda thinks that the theory of *karma* developed in that man himself must act. Did not the gods themselves prove this by their doings?[84] *Nivṛtti* is a matter of inner disposition, whereas *pravṛtti*, an active life of participation in society, should be accomplished in a spirit of indifference as to the fruits of action. Whether success or failure, one's equilibrium of mind ought not to be disturbed. Thus an active life, led in the spirit of *nivṛtti*, became acceptable. The classical form of this reconciliation between the two mainstreams of *pravṛtti* and *nivṛtti* appears early in the *Bhagavad Gītā*. I shall discuss this in a later paragraph.

The *Dharmaśāstras* show a clear and positive appreciation of especially the status of householder.[85] The development of the four *āśramas* made it a matter of course that a man's life would, at different times, conform explicitly to either *pravṛtti* or *nivṛtti* values. There is no mention of the *āśramas* in the oldest Vedic texts. It is in the older *Upaniṣads* that one finds the ground prepared for the appearance of these four significant stages encompassing one's life.[86]

The Brahminical genius for compromise accommodated both sceptics and freethinkers who revolted against the excessive ritualism and sacerdotal theologizing on the part of Brāhminism by promulgating the *āśrama*-system whereby ritualistic activity is progressively eliminated during the last two stages of one's life.[87] The *Āraṇyakas*, besides providing simplified sacrificial rites for the householder, equally sympathized with the forest dweller by offering him relevant religious matter. In the

81. Vettam Mani, *Purāṇic Encyclopaedia*, p. 527.
82. Jan Gonda, *Die Religionen Indiens*, 2 vols. W. Kohlhammer Verlag, Stuttgart, 1960, vol.1, *Veda und alterer Hinduismus*, pp. 297-301.
83. *Ibid.* see *Mhb.* 12.32.13.
84. Jan Gonda, *Die Religionen Indiens*, vol. 2. pp. 285-301. See *Mhb.* 13.6.47.
85. Pandurang Vaman Kane, *History of Dharmaśāstra*, 5 vols. *Ancient and Medieval Religious and Civil Law*, Bhandarkar Oriental Research Institute, Poona, 1974, vol. 2, Part I, p. 416.
86. Jan Gonda, *ibid.*, p. 283.
87. V.M. Apte, *Vedic Rituals* in: *The Cultural Heritage of India*, 5 vols. The Ramakrishna Mission Institute, Calcutta, 1975, Vol. I, pp. 234-263.

Hārita-Dharma-Śāstra it is suggested that both householders and forest hermits make use of the *pañçamāhayajñas* to purify themselves of possible sins.[88] These sacrifices were closely connected with everyday life and they demanded no complicated technical liturgy. In the *Śatapatha Brāhmaṇa* we read:

> "There are five great sacrifices, and they indeed are great sacrificial sessions, – to wit the sacrifice to beings, the sacrifice to men, the sacrifice to fathers, the sacrifice to the gods and the sacrifice to the *Brahman*."[89]

The *Manu-smṛti* envisage a well ordered life in human society by presenting a neatly worked out *āśrama*-system. The law-book renders a philosophical-pastoral treatise guaranteeing salvation to anyone at any stage of life:

> "Neither (the study of) the *Vedas*, not liberality, nor any (selfimposed) restraint, nor austerities, ever procure the attainment (of rewards) to a man whose heart is contaminated (by sensuality)."
>
> "That man may be considered to have subdued his organs, who on hearing and touching and seeing, on tasting and smelling (anything), neither rejoices nor repines. But when one among all the organs slips away (from control) thereby (man's) wisdom slips away from him, even as the water flows through the one open foot of a (watercarrier's) skin."[90]

By its recommendation of equality of all creatures in relation to *Brahman*, the *āśrama* strained the hard and fast rules of Brahminical Hinduism. Practically speaking, however, the idea of *āśrama* as a system further developed the tension of mutually antagonistic castes and sub-castes, weakening its very integrity.

Abhyudaya and Niḥśreyasa

Sanātana Dharma is the establishment of a permanent and eternal way of life. Hinduism calls itself by that name. The goal of life is two-fold: prosperity (*abhyudaya*) and highest bliss (*nihsreyasa*). Together they comprise four values (*puruṣārthas*). Prosperity is the sum of *dharma, artha* and *kāma* or, to put them in reverse order, sense-joy, refined by wealth regulated by law. The achievement of *niḥśreyasa* is the fourth *puruṣārtha* which is final liberation, *mokṣa*. It matters not what value is being given preference. Prosperity, according to the *Manu-smṛti*, is achievable by *dharma, artha* and *kāma* together. Together they culminate in final emancipation. The *āśrama*-system was meant to be of practical help in the actual achievement of prosperity and bliss. Thus Hinduism's all-encompassing *sādhāranadharma* is nothing less than a welfare state in the best sense of the word, enveloping entire creation (*sarvodaya samāj*).

The Hindu calling, described above, is an appeal to the individual. The four fold aspiration of man flows from his basic human desires which he recognizes and acknowledges to be of value. The *puruṣārtha* is of interest as a corroborative attempt

---

88. Pandurang Vaman Kane, *op. cit.* Vol. 2, Part I, p. 697.
89. *SB.* 11.5.6.1: "*pañcaiva mahāyajñaḥ tanyeva mahā satrāṇi bhūtayajño manuṣya-yajñaḥ pitṛyajño devayajño brahmayajña iti*".
90. "*The laws of Manu*", tr. G. Buhler in: *The Sacred Books of The East*, ed. F. Max Müller, Motilal Banarsidass, 1979, Vol. XXV, II, 97-99. The bracketed words are given in the text.

to lend meaning to the *āśrama*. It is a more intellectual understanding of the complementary function of man's basic aspirations being at the same time his valid needs. Man's aspirations are not to be considered irreconcilably opposed one to another. It would seem illogical to give preference to one desire, thereby excluding another from being part of the way of Truth. What else will men request from the gods, when the first rays of the sun appear, if not health, happy feeling, wealth and offspring? Thus we hear in a prayer for general well-being (*rayisaṁvardhana*):

> "Now by the access of that vigour that dwells in all beings of this universe,
> we have come truly to *be*:
> May the wise urge the stingy to give, and may he bestow on us riches and numerous men of valour:."[91]

The theory concerning man's desires (*chaturvarga*) envisages an integral human personality and the cultivation of morality. But man needs to develop a sense of sacrifice and restraint if he wishes to attain peace. Even the ascetic, if he does not live in the spirit of renouncing his very renunciation, is likely to merely seek his own salvation at the cost of a universal vision. Complacent unconcern may cut him off from the company of gods and men.

> "Those men who practise terrific austerities not enjoined by the scripture, given to hypocrisy and egotism, endued with the strength of lust and passion; weakening all the elements in the body – fools they are – and Me who dwell in the body within; know thou these to be of demoniac resolves".[92]

The *chaturvarga* remained largely a matter of theory and speculation. A difficulty seems to have been the uneasiness in linking *mokṣa* with the other three *arthas*.[93] Ultimately the search for an integrated vision remains a matter of its discovery inside the heart, a discovery which has been likened to a sacrificial pole, an axis, descending from above into man and linking the worlds together. Describing the descent of such sacrificial thought, the Vedic poet says:

> "Like swans that flee in lengthened line, pillars have come to us arrayed in brilliant colour. They, lifted up on high, by sages, eastward, go forth as gods to the gods' places.[94]

Thus *abhyudaya* and *niḥśreyasa*, whether they be understood in the framework of either *pravṛtti* or *nivṛtti* or in both together, ultimately point to the realm of a human perfection that, because of its very perfection, would resemble that of the divine. It happens when we are free of fear of being human and when we practice and are surrounded by universal friendship as if alive in one vast shelter (*śaraṇa bṛhantā*).

> "May the atmosphere we breathe, breathe fearlessness in us: fearlessness on earth and fearlessness in heaven! May fearlessness guard us behind and before! May fearlessness surround us above and below."[95]

---

91. Raimundo Panikkar, *The Vedic Experience*, p. 297: *AV*. 3.20.8.
92. *Bhagavad Gītā with the commentary of Sri Śaṅkarāchārya,* Samata Books, Madras, 1981, p. 430. 17.5 - 6.
93. *Mhb*. 12.59.30.
94. *RV*. 3.8.4: "*haṁsā iva Śreniśo yatānāḥ sukrā vasānaḥ svaravo na āguḥ/unniyamānāh kavibhiḥ purastād devā devānām api yanti pātaḥ*".
95. *AV*. 19.15.5, tr. Raimundo Panikkar, *The Vedic Experience*, p. 300.

Bhukti and Mukti

A more interesting conciliatory encounter between *pravṛtti* and *nivṛtti* is one we can gleam from Indian Hindu history in epic and purāṇic times. In the third paragraph of this chapter I have shown how the earlier *Purāṇas* describe the *Kali-yuga* in which we all now live. Indian medieval society grappled with difficulties. The epics and *Purāṇas* were put together during that time.

A strained and often antagonistic relationship between Purāṇic and Tāntric thought kept the *Purāṇas* almost totally free of Tāntric influence until about the year eight hundred of the Christian era. Some of the Purāṇic writings began to recognize the Tantras as an authority on religious matters. Purāṇic religious rites included Tāntric practices through liberal ideas Brāhmins professed. The *Smṛti Nibandhas*, drawing from Purāṇic writing, absorbed elements from Tāntric inspiration.[96] The religious movement embracing both Śaktism, Tāntrism and various cults of the great Goddess, presents an intricate religious complex. Its philosophy and ritual have been a subject of discussion among the best of scholars, probably leaving the tāntric himself quite unruffled. I may call to mind here, quoting Sir John Woodroffe, an essential principle in Tāntrism :

> "It is an essential principle of *Tāntric Sādhanā* that man in general must rise through and by means of Nature, and not by an ascetic rejection of Her. A profoundly true principle is here involved whatever has been said of certain applications of it."[97]

According to Tāntrism, it would be useless in our present *Kali-yuga* age to seek liberation by the methods employed in the ancient Vedic and Upaniṣadic days. Humanity is fallen, Tāntrism admits. It is now a matter of swimming against the stream, starting from the actual darkening of the spirit in the flesh. Tantra appeals, to achieve its aim, to techniques other than those of traditional asceticism and contemplation. It does not renounce the world. It tries to master it, to overcome it. Understanding creation through pure appreciation of it in enjoyment (*bhukti*) is expected to lead to release (*mukti*).

Thus Tantra tries to realize truth in and through the body. It is not abstract, transcending the universe. It is immanent in it. The human body is a true replica of the universe, a veritable microcosmos. A basic Tāntric doctrine is that of divine bi-unity. It points to the Supreme Identity *as an identity of two different principles,*

96. R.C. Hazra, *Studies in the Purāṇic Records on Hindu Rites and Customs*; pp. 260-264.
97. Sir John Woodroffe, *Śakti and Śākta*, Ganesh and Company, Madras, 1975, p. 88. I am aware of the severe criticism Woodroffe has been subjected to by various authors, a.o. Nirad C. Chauduri who writes in his book, *Hinduism*, Oxford Univ. Press. 1979, p. 251: "I myself watched (his i.e. Woodroffe's rehabilitation of Tantra for modern educated Hindus) with interest, but I did not regard it as anything but the hobby of an eccentric. The spectacle of an English judge of the High Court speaking for a form of Hinduism which has always been deprecated by themselves, tickled their national vanity, and they began to think much of Woodroffe and his work on Tantra. The men who would now defend Tāntrism in theory would be the last men to adopt any Tāntric practice. And those who would adopt it would be too well aware of their motives to speak about it:" It is obvious that Chauduri refers to the five M's of Tantra of which sexo-yogic practices are one M. (*Maithuna*). However, if Chauduri fulminates against Woodroffe, other scholars appear to appreciate his work as e.g., Mircea Eliade in his *'Yoga, Immortality and Freedom'* and Jan Gonda in *'Die Religionen Indiens'* See, for example, vol. 2. p. 26 - 52.

distinguishable in all composite things, but coincident, without composition, in the one who is *no* thing. The Identity is that of essence and nature, being and nonbeing, god and godhead. On the other hand, a division between essence and nature, heaven and earth and subject and object, is a *sine qua non* of the existence of created things. Nature recedes from likeness to God but it retains a relationship with the divine being. The idea of God and Godhead includes the idea of masculine and feminine in the Supreme Identity.[98] Henceforth Essence is the Creator and active power while Nature is the means to creation and the recipient of form. Of this the relationship between man and woman is a sacred likeness. The idea of marriage as a sacrament is derived from it. It is an adequate symbol and reflection of the identification of Essence and Nature in the divine. Ultimately all relations between man and woman, if thought of with respect, are such.

The notion of a bisexual polarity in the godhead, as here suggested, has sometimes been regarded as a peculiarity of mediaeval Hindu and Buddhist Tāntric systems. For in these it is clearly enunciated and made the basis of a visual and ritual symbolism, criticized by those who disparage the use of any sexual symbolism and are, therefore, unwilling to recognize it elsewhere. Within the limits of this paragraph it would be impossible to demonstrate the universality of the doctrine of a divine bi-unity. Tāntrism actually finds its theological ground in Vedic tradition where one finds ample evidence of the concept of a divine bi-unity.[99]

The world is created by two polar principles, *Puruṣa* and *Prakṛti*, known by Tantra's followers as *Śiva* and *Śakti*. *Śiva* represents the immovable Spirit. All movement, all creation and life on every cosmic level is due to *Śakti's* manifestation. This manifestation is nature's (*Prakṛti*) innate urge. Deliverance is made possible by the union of the two in the body of the believer and not only in the believer's psycho-mental experience. In Tāntrism the human body acquires an importance and sacrality it never had in the history of India's spirituality. Tāntrism poses a question to Upaniṣadic and post-Upaniṣadic pessimism with regard to the body. Mircea Eliade writes concerning Tāntrism's view of the body: "The body is no longer the source of pain, but the most reliable and effective instrument at man's disposal for "conquering death."[100] Fear of the body, also dismissed by the myths of the exiled soul, is baseless. Although mystical erotism is known from Vedic times, Tāntrism made it into an instrument of salvation.[101] Influences of Tāntrism in the *Upaniṣads* are noticeable in passages like that in the *Bṛhadāraṇyaka Upaniṣad* where the 'Strength-libation' is mentioned, the magical charm cast on the wife's lover:" You have made a libation in my fire".[102] What is meant here is the consummated marital union. Tāntrism never made sexo-yogic practices compulsory for its followers. *Śiva* and *Śakti* are experienced by the inner and subtle body within man (*sūkṣmaśrir*). I shall come

98. We find this idea expressed also in the *Summa Theologica* of St. Thomas Aquinas, Turin Edition, 1932, when mention is made of Natura naturans, Creatrix universalis est Deus. see 1.14. 11 ad 3.
99. e.g. of the Supreme Identity it is asked in *AV*. 8.9.10: "Who knows Her progenitive duality? ", *mithunatvam*, and conversely, "He (Brahman) is a womb", *yoniś ca gīyate*, in *Vājasaneyi Saṁhitā* 1.4.7.27: *The White Yajur Veda*, ed. R.T.H. Griffith, 2nd ed,. Banaras, 1927.
100. Mircea Eliade, *Yoga, Immortality and Freedom*, Bollingen. Series Princeton, 1973, p. 227.
101. *Ibid*., p. 254.
102. *BU*. 6.4.12 in *ibid*., p. 255. Practices of ritual accompanied by sexual intercourse are found in many instances in Vedic and post-Vedic texts as they are in other cultural traditions.

back to Tāntrism in the chapter on the symbolism of water. *Śakti*, the universal Force, plays an important part as She continually creates the world, *pravṛtti*. She is actively present in Woman. Every created being is part and parcel of that world and liberation would be sought for in vain if the Woman-force were not recognized.[103]

In tantra absolute Reality is itself neutral by nature. The two aspects within Reality are *pravṛtti*, the dynamic, positive, and *nivṛtti*, the static, negative. Neither is the ultimate truth. It is only through their union that ultimate perfection, Truth, is achieved.[104] The *Mahānirvāṇa Tantra* exclaims, perhaps with a little overenthusiasm:

> ..."that the *Vedas*, *Smṛti*, *Purāṇas*, and *Itihāsa* are each the sacred books of past ages of the world, whilst for our evil age, the *Kali-yuga*, the Tantras have been revealed by *Śiva* for the salvation of mankind."[105]

Whatever be the opinion concerning the Tāntric vision, one can hardly deny its substantial contribution to India's religious and philosophical history. Tāntrism's popularity has more often than not been accepted reluctantly by the orthodox. Their criticism has not seldom been inspired by the very fear of the body which Tāntrism tried to overcome.

The birth of the Great Goddess, a significant event for Tāntrism, is told in a popular and beautiful myth, the first part of which is as follows in Heinrich Zimmer's rendering:

> "...an unconquerable, sublime warrior-maid, who came into being out of the combined wrath of all the gods gathered in council. The occasion of the miracle was one of those dark moments for the gods, when a demon tyrant was threatening to undo the world. This time not even *Viṣñu* or *Śiva* could avail. The titan was a colossal monster named *Mahiṣa*, in the shape of a prodigious water-buffalo bull.
>
> The gods, under the leadership of *Brahmā*, had taken refuge in *Viṣñu* and *Śiva*. They had described the case of the victorious demon and implored the assistance of the two fold All-Highest. *Viṣñu* and *Śiva* swelled with wrath. The other divinities also swelling with the power of indignation, stood about. And immediately their intense powers poured forth from their mouths. *Viṣñu*, *Śiva* and all the gods sent forth their energies, each according to his nature, in the form of sheets and streams of flames. These fires all rushed together, combining in a flaming cloud which grew and grew, and meanwhile condensed. Eventually it assumed the shape of a Goddess. She was provided with eighteen arms.
>
> Upon beholding this most auspicious personification of the supreme energy of the universe, this miraculous amalgamation of all their powers, the gods rejoiced and they paid her worship as their general hope. In her 'The Fairest Maid of the Three Towns' (*tripura-sundarī*), the perennial, primal Female, all the particularised and limited forces of their various personalities were powerfully integrated. Such an overwhelming signified omnipotence. By a gesture of perfect

103. "*Tantratattva of Śiva-candra*", tr. A. Avalon (Sir John Woodroffe), London - Madras, 1914, Vol. 2, p. 17.
104. Shashi Bhusan Das Gupta, *Some Later Yogic Schools*, in *The Cultural Heritage of India* , 5 vols. Vol. 2, p. 17.
105. *MahanT*. 1.20 ff.

surrender and fully willed selfabdication they had returned their energies to the primeval goddess, *Śakti*, the One Force, the fountain head, from where originally all had stemmed. And the result was now a great renewal of the original state of universal potency. The mother (of all manifestations), Life Energy itself as the primeval maternal principle, had reabsorbed them, eaten them back into the universal womb. She was now ready to give forth in the fullness of her being."[106]

Especially *Śiva* symbolism explores the mystery of the two-in-one more than any other tradition of *Śakti* worship. The history of the Goddess is but partially glimpsed in Purāṇic literature, where She is not being given attention in proportion to her prominence. Without the power and energy of *Śakti, Śiva*, it is said, is a *śava*, a corpse. It is She who embodies the vibrance of both life and death.

Bhakti : The "irrational" solution

The subjectmatter of myth has parallels in philosophy and in cult. Whereas philosophy expresses ideas on an intellectual level, cult does so on that of emotion. Myth combines the two. Myth infuses life simultaneously into both concept and image. In this way the process of thought receives a peculiar colour and character. The image will come alive in action. Whereas philosophy may justifiedly stay indoors without loosing its edge, myth must go out into the streets onto the scene. There it provides in images the action to the plot philosophy conceived. Particular contradictions which could otherwise be resolved only on an abstract level of rationalized ultimates, become tangible on the popular and emotional level by the myth. To clarify problems which cannot be solved rationally with full satisfaction, like the very problem of man's existential situation, myth uses the "resolve" of irrational cult. Emotion achieves what reason cannot.

It is often said that philosophy begins with wonder. Would it be equally valid to say that philosophy starts with suffering? The suffering which man experiences in the complexity of existence makes him wonder why. Such suffering creates a katharsis. That purification may, in its turn, through analysis, reach a solution. In Indian thought this is called *mumukṣu*, an intense desire for liberation.[107] Reason, however, will remain trapped.

One irrational but not unreasonable answer[108] to the complexity of existence is an explicit form it receives in myth. It is *bhakti*, mutual devotion between the worshipper and the (his) God. It is a compelling love which overcomes all rational barriers. It would seem as if *bhakti* is a late solution in the sense that man is inclined first to reason his existence and its significance. Then, finding himself at a loose end, man makes explicit a tendency which has been there from the beginning. He appeals to emotion to satisfy his cry for understanding. *Bhakti*, seen in this way, is almost an excuse.

A fine illustration of how myth may develop *bhakti* as a reply to things difficult to understand, we find in the account of the love relationship between *Śiva* and *Śakti*.

106. *MaP*. 81. 93 in : Heinrich Zimmer, *Myths and Symbols in Indian Art and Civilization*, ed. Joseph Campbell, Harper Torchbooks, The Bollingen Library, New York, 1962, p. 190. See also the index of names and themes.
107. John V. Chethimattam, *Patterns of Indian Thought*, Orbis Books, New York, 1971, p. 99.
108. Another answer is suicide. See e.g. Anderson and Trethowan, *Psychiatry*, Bailliere Tindall, London, 1979, p. 327 where it is said that this act is a cry for help in the face of an intolerable situation.

Śakti, the great Goddess, the Mother of the Universe, as *Kālikā*, resolved to be a mortal on becoming *Satī*, a real woman alive with the spirit in the flesh. She became woman in her own right with thoughts, feelings and understanding not known to a man. *Satī*, now being woman, knew the lust feelings of a man. She too desired *Śiva* who understood a woman's desire. *Śiva*, however, had become a *yogī*, capable of drawing up his seed. Should any man lust after *Sati*, *Śiva* would surely kill him.[109] Being much in love with *Śiva*, *Sati* subjected herself to severe austerities in order to win him as her husband. At one time the seven sages came to her to make her change her mind. Did she know who *Śiva* really was? Being a *yogī*, was he not too inauspicious? Too ugly? He had no home, no lineage, no clothing and he associated with goblins. Why not marry *Viṣñu*, auspicious, wealthy and with many excellent and lordly attributes. This must have happened on Mount *Parvata* because *Satī* here is *Pārvatī*, "Mountain's Daughter".[110] Even though *Śiva* was without the valued things of this world, what use were they when it comes to love? The embellishments and ornaments the world adores are not to be found in the yogic *Śiva*. He is beyond what is merely beautiful and auspicious. Away from the mountain, when *Pārvatī* is *Satī*, she and her lover discussed their relationship. Both seemed uncertain about the steadiness of each other's feelings. They decided to marry. After their marriage, when the trees blossomed and the waters were full of lotus flowers[111] they made love to each other and *Śiva*, the yogī-god, conversed with his wife and gave her knowledge of the real Self.[112] Then, following their long honeymoon, they moved to the Himalayas. There they lived in love for ten thousand years of the gods.[113] But after making love to *Śiva* until satisfied, *Sati* became indifferent. She told her husband that her mind had turned away from the delights of love and passion, although she was happy to have become *Śiva's* wife.[114] She guessed that the Lord had married her out of love, no doubt, but not only out of love for her but also out of love for his devotees. *Sati* and *Śiva* in their immutable selves must be known to the devotees and love and passion was the play of *Śiva* to reach his goal. The Self transcends all that we know on earth about love and passion.[115] *Sati*, although she never felt cheated or done injustice to in her womanhood, doubted. She could at first not understand how devotion might go beyond the love and passion she had known as true. What then was the secret of devotion? *Śiva* explained to her that there was no difference between devotion and perfect knowledge.[116] He meant to say that there was no difference in what is obtained by them. *Śiva's* concern had been his devotees, release from the world and at the same time their happiness in it.[117] *Śiva* had the *Kali-yuga* in mind in which we now live. This dangerous age may obscure the knowledge of ultimate reality and detachment. No other path brings happiness as does devotion.[118] *Satī* felt satisfied as she felt to

109. *SP*. 2.12.34.
110. *SP*. 2.3.26.
111. *SP*. 2.2.21.29.
112. *SP*. 2.2.21.42.
113. *SP*. 2.2.22.
114. *SP*. 2.2.23.1-7.
115. *SP*. 2.2.23.6.
116. *SP*. 2.2.23.16.
117. *SP*. 2.2.23.15 - 17.
118. *SP*. 2.2.23.38.

have been made a participant in the effort to obtain true knowledge, needed especially in the *Kali-yuga*.[119]

Time and again the subject of devotion comes up for discussion between *Satī*, the human on earth, and *Śiva*, the Lord. The *Śiva Purāṇa* makes a passionate plea for devotion as the only means of overcoming doubt and fear. The incarnation of the Great Goddess as *Satī* was her way back to *Śiva* through the failings and sufferings of the human condition that she had chosen. Now she knew that the human mind needs answers satisfying its ever present longing for ultimate knowledge, its need for devotion and the relationship between these needs. She now knew that the human condition is being made bearable only through a passionate clinging to the Lord.

Classical Hindu *Bhakti* makes its entry with the appearance of the *Bhagavad Gītā* revealing *Kṛṣña* as *Viṣñu* incarnate in human form. The *Gītā's* revelation emphasizes the personal self-surrender of man to God whom he is able to love and adore in spite of all vicissitudes of life. The origin and date of the *Gītā*, the last portion of the *Mahābhārata*, has been a subject of heated discussion. The controversy is irrelevant with regard to our subjectmatter. Nevertheless, it is of interest if I indicated a few points. Dasgupta mentions scholars like Lorinser who hold that the *Gītā* was composed under influence of the New Testament of the Christian tradition.[120] Dasgupta himself strongly disagrees with this opinion, claiming the *Gītā* to be pre-Buddhist. The *Gītā* provides no historical clue which would make it easier to determine its date of composition.

The book is, according to Dasgupta, a work by the Bhāgavata tradition.[121] Chaudhury takes a critical view of this. He maintains that the Hindus, in order to make sure that the *Gītā* was thorougly theirs, backdated its origin to Vedic times "without a scrap of evidence".[122]

Whatever its origin, the *Gītā* captured the imagination of the Hindu fold. Various cults sometimes resulted in a bewildering imagery and ritual. It is not clear how many Kṛṣña these are. The *Kṛṣña* of the *Bhāgavata Purāṇa* is different from the ascetically inclined personage in the *Gītā* who is a teacher, intent on speculation and discourse. The other *Kṛṣña* appears more often than not involved in erotic dealings

119. *SP*. 2.2.23.37-38. In her recent publication, *Bānāras, City of Light*, Routledge and Kegan Paul, London, 1983, pp. 157-175, Diana L. Eck discusses the goddesses alive in old and new Kāśī (Banaras). "On the level of popular piety today", she writes, "one often hears that Śiva has turned Kāśī over to the Goddess for governance during the Kali Age. Thus, Annapūrnā Bhavānī, one of the names of Shiva's Queen, is now the real ruler of Kāśī. Similarly, it is sometimes said that during the Kali Age the great gods, Viṣñu and Śiva, are asleep and do not hear human supplication. But a few deities are wakeful in this dark time, and among them are the goddesses".

120. Surendranath Dasgupta, *A History of Indian Philosophy*, 5 Vols. Motilal Banarsidass, Ist Indian ed. 1975, vol. 2 pp. 545-552.

121. "The *Gītā* may have been a work of the *Bhāgavata*-school written long before the composition of the *Mahābhārata* and may have been written on the basis of the *Bhārata*-legend on which the *Mahābhārata* was based. It is not improbable that the *Gītā* summarizing the older teaching of the *Bhāgavata*-school, was incorporated into the *Mahābhārata* during one of its revisions, by virtue of the sacredness that it had attained at the time". p. 552.

122. This was done "by means of a grotesque misinterpretation of verses 2, 4 and 5 of the 125th *Sūkta* of the tenth *Maṇḍala* of the *Ṛig-Veda* (through which) the idea of selfsurrender to a personal deity was sought to be taken to the Vedic age. Actually, in these verses the personified goddess of speech, *Vāc*, only says that she will confer wealth, food and drink, and strength on those who sacrifice to her with devotion". Chaudhury, *Hinduism*, p. 257.

with the milkmaids whom he seduces with the strains of his flute.[123] If we remember that myths portray the unlimited deposit of human experience and if we keep banning fear of sexual symbolism, the controversy would seem less important. The popular *Kṛṣña*, perhaps to curb his lust, became linked with *Rādhā*, his wife. It remains a topic of investigation whether the love which compels *bhakti* in Hindu tradition to this day, is an agape, love in communion, or whether it is more of an eros raised to the spiritual plane. *Bhakti*, it would seem at times, resembles the love a woman may feel when the love for her husband is raised to spiritual heights without loosing its physical footing. It is the love she feels when her husband and lover is also her lord. The position of women is not the subject of our investigation but it appears that many women have felt the need of a form of *bhakti*, involving a lord, to find a solution to the problem of their experienced suppression. They needed, and still need, the incarnation of the Goddess, as for example in *Satī*, providing them their own place and psychological and physical entity. Once these have been secured, the presence of a lord is called upon to safeguard the female identity.

The *Gītā* prides itself on having contributed to Hindu thought the clearly defined notion of *niṣkāma karma*. It can be performed only by a true *Jñanī*, one who knows and who has forfeited all fruits of his actions. The Lord will never let his devotee perish.[124] The doer of good never comes to grief.[125] Man should attain true wisdom by purging his desires. He should perform his customary duties and be faithful to his own *dharma*. The *Gītā's* classical example, upholding the caste-stratification, is *Kṛṣña's* request to *Arjuna* to give up all his doubts concerning the war he was fighting. He was to cling to God as the only protector bestowing liberation. *Kṛṣña* says :

> "the renunciation of works and their unselfish performance both lead to the soul's salvation. But of the two, the unselfish performance of work is better than their renunciation."[126]

The *Gītā* preaches a new orientation to sacrificial action by advocating *niṣkāmakarma*. The "magic" of sacrifice has always been a danger. Where it slipped into theology it often went at the cost of faith and true allegiance to (the) God.

Dharma in the context of the *Gītā* has its own characteristic. It is that of *asya dharmasya*. The *Gītā*, strives after sublime mystical union with God without any thought of "profit". The book, unveiling the notion of *niṣkāmakarma*, is a further revelation of the divine as eminently approachable, a presence to be intimately enjoyed in love. *Niṣkāmakarma* explores a new avenue of passionate involvement in the divine in that it transcends the pantheon of deities and man as if existing by virtue of a relationship of contract, a precarious balance as to the sharing of power. Thus it invites the embrace of God and man, heaven and earth. Such love is not stereotype or quietistic. It is felt to be a grace. As an "over and above" it transcends the relationship between man and the divine as if it were a deal agreed upon in ritual.

---

123. R.C. Zaehner, *Hinduism*, Oxford Univ. Press, 1966, p. 127. reprint.
124. *BG*. 9.31: *"na me bhaktaḥ praṇashyati"*.
125. *BG*. 6.40.
126. *BG*. 5.2. : *Saṁnyāsaḥ karmayogaśca*
niḥśreyasakarāv ubhau
tayos tu karmasamnyāsāt
karmayogo viśiṣyate.

Ignoring an escapist attitude towards the world and action, the *Gītā* promises liberation by true philosophic knowledge of the nature of the mind-body whole (*kṣetra*) based on an understanding of the relation between *prakṛti* and *puruṣa*.[127] Spirituality is not renunciation *of* action but renunciation *in* action, synthesizing both *pravrtti* and *nivṛtti*.

> "He who does actions, offering them to *Brahman*, abandoning attachment, is not tainted by sin, as a lotus leaf by water."[128]

Elevating its view on work, does the *Gītā* make all activity non-moral? Non-morality and total indifference to activity is an opinion held by the *Sāṅkhya* school of philosophy. The *Gītā* would seem to disagree with that view. It rather tries to effect subjective *nivṛtti* or detachment from desire.[129]

127. Surendranath Dasgupta, *A History of Indian Philosophy*, vol. 2, pp. 461, 523.
128. *BG*. 2.10: *lipyate na sa papena padmapatram ivāmbhasā*.
129. Dasgupta, *op. cit*., p. 508.

Chapter 5

FUNCTIONAL ANTECEDENTS IN THE VEDAS

Introduction

True, the title of this chapter is rather clumsy. In any case it is too short. Functional antecedents in the Vedas to what? In the preceding chapter I have attempted to underline the tension there is in man of being simultaneously a guest and an inhabitant in the world by inquiring into the Indian quest for harmony between these mutually opposing sentiments. The Indian quest revolves around the concepts or *pravṛtti* and *nivṛtti*. They find their expression in theories and lifestyles one more or less stumbles upon in India and they are of themselves an evidence of the guest-inhabitant tension in man. The preceding chapter clarified how Indian myths and the didactic material in them and surrounding them, offer the solace of the *reasonableness* of the guest-inhabitant tension experienced in human existence. As I have explained in the first part of the book, I do not undertake a theory of the human condition. I limit myself to myths speaking of that condition. I restrict myself as much as possible to myths that speak of the beginning of things or myths that, "halfway human existence" in the midst of human experience, ask why it is that things are as they are. That is why we, for example, were able to accompany *Nārada* to the lake at *Kanyā Kubja* where *Viṣñu* took him to reveal the secret of life. This limitation will, I hope, be repaid by a more rigorous understanding of the function of myths related to the guest-inhabitant tension in man and the bond between him and what he considers sacred.

With regard to the manner in which the Indian guest-inhabitant of this world experiences his bond with the sacred, I was forced to speak in terms intentionally vague. We have not yet discovered how, in Indian thought, that bond has been expressed in a cluster of principal Vedic myths of origin which may explain why the very notions of *pravṛtti* and *nivṛtti* and the quest for harmony between them could at all have arisen. We remember how in the relation between myth and history, myth is the primary factor and history the secondary and derived factor. Origin myths and what they have to say explain people's behaviour and their reasons for it. They are antecedent and prior in the archaic depth of the human psyche and often also in time.

If we now limit ourselves to the principal Vedic myths of origin exploring man's condition and the bond felt in that condition with the sacred, we will simply succeed in what we aim at: we will understand more of the Vedic and later Hindu worldview and, through that, of man in general. To prepare ourselves for the encounter with the splendour of the chief Vedic origin myths, we shall first examine the setting in which they arose more closely.

The human condition with its anxiety is supremely the crucial experience of either turning towards or turning away from the sacred. Thus ensues the threat of the dissolution of the bond between man and the sacred. If the energies of the sacred are felt to be at the centre of human experience, the myths of origin dealing with them will be at the same time myths of *totality*. What is felt in the profoundest depths of human experience is for myth the experience of origin. The abyss of the human psyche, its archaism, is by myth transported to the origin beyond temporal time. In recounting how the tension between *pravṛtti* and *nivṛtti* began, the myth places the experience of man in an entirety of both orientation and search for meaning. In this way an understanding of human reality as a *whole* operates, through the myth, by means of a reminiscence and, simultaneously, an expectation.

The Vedic vision is strapped to symbolic expressions of the intelligible relation between forms, ideas, similarities, the eternal reason of things and the things themselves in their contingency. Symbolic expressions overstep the boundaries of mere conceptual intelligibility, without necessarily excluding the latter. In the Vedic vision the eternal reason of things is their real name (*nāma*). As existing by virtue of a precarious balance between the *nāma* and themselves, all that exists is *rūpa*. It appears, it figures as if in a play. Now it comes, now it goes. Hence the constant surprise of Vedic man, lifting him above stereotype phraseology.

> "I ask as a fool who knows not his own spirit: where are the hidden traces left by the Gods?"[1]

More than two millennia of surprise have nearly made the surprise itself into a stereotype. Every day at sunrise and at sunset, usually at the moment of the ritual bath, the Vedic surprise is heard all over the Indian continent until today in the most renowned *mantra* of the *Vedas*, the *Gāyatrī*:

> "*OM*
> We meditate upon the glorious splendour of the Vivifier divine.
> May he himself illumine our minds!
> *OM*."[2]

Between darkness and daylight, when the sun (*Savitṛ*) begins its course and between daylight and dark, when it ends its journey through the vault of the firmament, there is for the Vedic mind the thrill of "the many that are one, the one that is manifold" (*viśvaṃ ekam*)," the manifold truth" (*viśvam satyaṃ*), and "the germ of all" (*viśvaṃ... garbham*).[3] *Nāma* and *rūpa* blend at the crack of dawn when man is as yet untrammelled by doubt and possible disappointment in himself and others. Likewise, at the close of day, there is the surprise of survival after the discharge of duties:

> "Steer clear of dice. Till well your own field. Rejoice in your portion and value it highly. See there, O Gambler, your cattle, your wife. This is the counsel of noble *Savitṛ*".[4]

The inherence of *nāma* in *rūpa* and *rūpa* in *nāma*, their concrescence, is mysteriously

---

1. *RV*. 1.164. tr. by Panikkar, *The Vedic Experience*, p. 38.
2. *RV*. 3.62.1 : "*tat savitur vareṇyaṁ*
   bhargo devasya dhīmahi
   dhiyo yo naḥ pracodayāt".
   tr. *op. cit.*, p. 38.
3. Respectively *RV*. 3.54.8; *RV*. 2.24.12; *RV*. 10.121.7. See *SB* 10.5.2.16: "As to this they say, 'Is He then one or many?' One should answer, 'One and Many'."
4. *RV*. 10.34.13 tr. *op. cit.*, p. 502.

felt and experienced at the edge of the waters on the Indian continent when men, women and children take their daily ritual bath:

> "May I be set free as if loosed from a pillar or loosed from the dirt after taking a bath! May all the Gods cleanse me from sin, as butter is pure after passing through the strainer."[5]

The indwelling in the consciousness of a Centre is a means to a "unified density of cognition" (*ekībhūta prajñāna ghana*). The fullness is known (*kṛtsnaḥ prajñāna ghana*).[6] Feeling the throb of the universe the Vedic mind has knowledge of things not derived objectively and *post factum*, but from their prior likeness in the mirror from where things rebounce but *in* which they exist. The waters reflect both the *nāma* and the *rūpa*. They reveal both Being and being-for-a-time:

> "For from the Waters is this universe produced".[7]

> "In the midst of the Waters is moving the Lord, surveying men's truth and men's lies. How sweet are the Waters, crystal clear and cleansing! How may these great Divine Waters quicken me."[8]

Notes on the Vedas

There are no absolute beginnings in human history. Every history has an origin. Every culture starts from a place, a time, from somewhere outside itself. Among what already existed in the world round the year 2000 before the Christian era, there appeared a new encounter like all else before that encounter had at one time been new. When the Aryans, speaking an Indo-European language, met the people already living on the Indian continent, not a new vein in the physiology of the human species was created but an untapped one opened itself. One more vision, one more strand of thought, until then hidden in the potency of the human drive, manifested itself and was laid bare to become part of the human heritage and memory. A few observations concerning the *Vedas* would not be out of place in the context or our inquiry.

Vedas means supreme knowledge. The *Vedas* are the only source of our acquaintance with the oldest history of the Indian people and its thought. *Vedas* also signifies the knowledge of super-human powers and the way to exercize influence over these powers. The *Vedas* have been "seen" by inspired sages, poets (*ṛṣis*). What was "seen" was for the greater part being sung in Brahmin families. Popular beliefs too found a place in these Vedic hymns. So were thoughts and ideas the Aryans brought from where they had come. What their experience remembered and what they had accumulated in the "cave of their heart", the Aryans mingled with the new sounds of the sages and poets. For a long time the hymns were handed over by oral tradition. In all probability the oldest parts of the Vedic tradition have come down to us from North-West India about the year 1200 before the Christian era. This happened when

5. *AV.* 6.115.3 tr. *op. cit.*, p. 503.
6. Respectively : *MandU.* 5; *BU.* 4.15.13.
7. *SB.* 6.8.2.1.
8. *RV.* 7.49.3. tr. *op. cit.*, p. 119.

the Indo-European Aryan people slowly but steadily made their way in different groups through the Kabul valley into the Land of the Five Streams. They settled themselves a little further to the East where they found a habitable place.[9]

The oldest portion of the *Vedas*, the *Ṛg-Veda*, provides a glimpse of the geographical surroundings the people found. To the early Aryan settlers, used to deserts and semi-arid areas, the waters loomed massive and omnipresent. The rivers nourished, their currents opened up communication with other settlements and their routes pointed ever eastward towards some unknown fulfilment. With the flourishing of commerce and agriculture, the waters were called upon as a matter of fact. Who could live without them? It is these waters and their significance in the worldview of the Vedic and later Indian mind which have captured my imagination. Like the search for the Tree of Life, the waters lead one to places sometimes hard to get to. We shall go in search of them in the following part of this work. It is in the myths of the Waters that we will find centres of decision from both ends of man's mixed experience of *nāma* and *rūpa*. In the Waters we find one of the finest revelations of the realism of *nāma* and the phenomenalism of *rūpa* meeting in the consciousness of man:

> "You Waters who rule over precious things and have supreme control of men, we beg you, give us healing balm. Now I have come to seek the Waters Now we merge, mingling with the sap. Come to me, *Agni*, rich in milk! Come and endow me with your splendour."[10]

The *Ṛg-Veda* explains later Indian civilization to a certain extent. Some of its characteristics, however, are not found. There is no evidence of caste stratification, early marriages, temples and images. The urge towards liberation (*mokṣa*) is much less pronounced than it is in later literature. The *Ṛg-Veda* presents a picture of a village and settler culture. Its members are practical, matter of fact people, with an elementary vision about the temporal side of existence. One longs for a long life, happiness, offspring, health, possessions, fame and victory. It is only in the later portion of the *Ṛg-Veda* that we are being invited to philosophic speculation with regard to creation, the origin of the world and life after death. These reflective and introspective thoughts become more frequent in the later portions of the bulk of the Vedas.[11]

A transition from the ritualistic to the philosophic, implying a modernization of thought, are the *Āraṇyakas*, the last part of these being the famous *Upaniṣads*. In the first part of the book I have referred to this transition. It is important from the point of view of myth. The diachronical modernity within a given culture is responsible for new ideas, new myths involving personal decisions concerning one's view of existence. The myth tries to get at the enigma of human existence, namely, the discordance between its fundamental reality — status of being a creature—and the actual modality of man, sinful and less understanding. The myth attends to this situation by means of a narration. It is a narration precisely because there is no deduction, no logical

9. Jan Gonda, *Die Religionen Indiens*, vol. 1, p. 9.
10. *RV.* 10.9.5.9. tr. Panikkar, *The Vedic Experience*, pp. 119-120.
11. Jan Gonda, *Die Religionen Indiens*, vol. 1, p. 10. See also F.B.J. Kuiper, *Ancient Indian Cosmogony*, p. 92f. Kuiper touches upon the point of the wide chronological distance in the formation of the whole of the *Vedas*.

transition between the fundamental reality of man and his present existence, between his ontological status as a being created good and destined for happiness, and his existential or historical status, experienced in some way or another in a condition of alienation. We see this happen in de *Upaniṣads* where the key vision becomes that of "See the Self" *(ātma vā are draṣṭavyah)* from where all further speculation concerning both *nāma* and *rūpa* originates.

Two Vedic etymologistys, *Yāska* and *Āpastamba,* admit only two divisions in the *Vedas,* viz., the *Brāhmaṇas* and the *Saṁhitās,* the *Āraṇyakas* forming only a part of the former.[12] The *Vedas* has been defined as "a book which reveals the knowledge of supernatural method *(alaukika upāya)* for the achievement of the desired object and avoidance of the undesirable."[13] To be able to understand Vedic texts one needs, to create for oneself an ideal situation, the assistance of the *Vedāṅgas*. There are six of them: phonetics (*śikṣa*), ritual (*kalpa*), grammar (*vyakaraṇa*), etymology (*nirukta*), metre (*chandas*) and astronomy (*jyotiṣa*).

There is an important point with regard to various characteristics of the *Vedas* which we must not forget. The Indian search for balance between *pravṛtti* and *nivṛtti* *corroborates* the claim by myth of its *aimed-at* restoration of universal totality. What I have earlier said must now be said with emphasis and a little more elaborate. I am here referring to the necessary "flaw" there is in any break from the Uncreate into the create.[14] In the Vedic mythical beginnings I have failed to observe a "flaw", a "fault" with the connotation of fatality. The myths do not suggest a banishment of man by a fatal indisposition towards The Origin which then consequently shed the human being and withdrew into itself, leaving man alone in a wasteland and given up to inexorable failure. The myths do not show a fatal disobedience, a ruinous and lethal revolt. The transposition of his anthropological dualism has saved the Vedic and later Hindu Indian from an indissoluble complicity — a plot — against The Origin, the a-temporal beyond.[15] No ethical terror can be found in the Indian myths of the beginnings. One is not confronted with anonymous wrath, a faceless violence of retribution. Living without eternal vengeance hovering over it, the Vedic and later Hindu human world is not written in letters of existential absurdity.* *Saṁsāra*, therefore, is not what it is often all too hastily thought to be by non-Indian analysts of Indian myth and philosophy: suffering. The evil of sufffering is synthetically linked with the evil of plotted creational fault. I would, therefore, oppose the translation of *saṁsāra* by "suffering" to an interpretation of it as a painfully felt delay of ultimate reunion with the Self while living on earth.

Fatal complicity against The Origin implies existential defilement incapable of being blotted out and followed by a reign of terror. It could at the most be fought best by hoping for nothing in order to fear nothing. From psychology we learn that ethical terror is close to obsessional neurosis. I do not think that we can discover much of this in ordinary Indian religious life, whether it be in the home or in the temple or in public life.

---

12. Swami Sharvananda, "The Vedas and their religious teaching", in: *The Cultural Heritage of India,* vol. 1, p. 182.
13. Raja C. Kunhan, *Vedic Culture, op. cit.*, p. 199.
14. The notion of "flaw" will be dealt with on more than one occasion in the course of this chapter.
15. See Part II : 4 : 4 (i) *Myths of the exiled soul.*

*Absence of the eternal appears at times to result in a sense of absurdity of existence.

The reason why I ask, in the following paragraphs, to be introduced to the Indian Prestige of Origin is my curiosity how the absence of terror has come about. Myths of other philosophies show less attractive Origins. The plot by Prometheus in Greek thought, as we saw, at the primordial sacrifice at Mekone, initiated a parting between god and man. Prometheus offered to Zeus the bones instead of the flesh of the sacrificed bull. The Greeks eventually escaped the terror of Moira, fate, the wrathful god, by declaring Mount Olympus their own mount of human excellence.[16] Thus the Greeks turned the sacred towards the goal of human optimal performance as a substitute for being like god. Likewise the adamic myth in the Hebrew tradition is one of a fatal fault. It needed a New Testament through the revelation of the Saviour Jesus where ethics could be entered through the new door of love instead of fear.

In dawn and birth, the circling of the seasons, in germination and growth, in the fullness of human existence passing from this world into the other, the Vedic revelation oozes radiance and cosmic refulgence illustrating the Vedic vision of the *lightsome* character of reality. Reality is suffused with light; it is light crystallized from the actual luminous Source. The light within recognizes and "sees" the light without, and vice versa. Creation, then, is not irredeemably blotted by a primordial fatality.

Another Vedic characteristic is that of its vision of an all-encompassing Reality sheltering the divine-human bond. Neither polytheism nor henotheism nor even monotheism can be taken as the keynote of early Vedic thought. Until the appearance of anthropologists like Malinowsky, Levi-Strauss and the psychologist C.G. Jung, a number of Western interpretations mistook the Vedic seer (*ṛṣi*) for a poet simply inspired by primitive awe and wonder for the forces of nature. It is not our aim here to discuss the origin of religion or the most ancient religious belief of mankind. The idea of the sacred as a hierophany is, indeed, a kratophany, a manifestation of force. This led Western scholars to find the origin of religion in the idea of an impersonal and universal force, "mana", after its Melanesian name. The hypothetical identification of the earliest religious experience with the experience of "mana" is now considered a hasty generalization and, scientifically, somewhat ill-founded. It can now be shown that, among the Melanesians and among all other archaic peoples, the notions of personal and impersonal are devoid of meaning.[17]

---

16. Kuiper in his, *Ancient Indian Cosmogony,* presents a chapter "An Indian Prometheus ?" in which he deals with the problem. After a penetrating analysis Kuiper finally "disposes of the 'Indian Prometheus', when it comes to *Agni* stealing the *Soma*. See. pp. 216 - 229. See also Part 1 : 2 : 5.

17. Mircea Eliade, *Myths, Dreams and Mysteries, The Encounter between Contemporary Faiths and Archaic Realities,* Harper Torchbooks, 1975, pp. 126-131. Eliade maintains "that the question (of 'mana') must be put in ontological terms: that which *exists* (M.E.), what is *real* on the one hand, and that which *does not exist* on the other — not in terms of the *personal or impersonal,* nor of the *corporeal or non-corporeal,* concepts which, for the consciousness of the "primitives", have none of the precision they have acquired in more highly-developed cultures. Anything filled with mana exists on the ontological plane and is therefore efficacious, fecund, fertile. One cannot ascribe "impersonality" to mana, for that attribute is without meaning within the archaic spiritual horizon" p. 129.

The opinion that mythical personalities would be nothing but personified forces of nature has long been in vogue in the West. It has been, not without irony, Max Müller's strong conviction. He explained the origin of myths through the linguistic phenomena of polyonymy and synonymy. His opinion concerning the Vedas:" und wenn wir den Hindus sagen wollen was sie anbeten - blosze Namen von Naturphanomenen, die allmählig verdunkelt, personifiziert und vergöttert werden-, so müssen wir sie den Veda lesen lässen. Ihre Götter haben kein gröszeres Recht auf irgendwelche

Another popular pre-animistic hypothesis was forwarded by J.G. Frazer assuming that, in the history of the human race, magic preceded religion.[18] From this theory followed the emphasis on totemism by, for example, Durkheim, Freud and Jung. Religion would have its origin in the tribal king or chief's mana, assuring the well-being of the tribe. One fundamental objection to these theories is the easy assumption that every form of religion is to be reconstructed from the pre-animistic hypothesis.[19] Religious consciousness is man's universal heritage. It is, however, subject to change in time and circumstance.

A more sympathetic and realistic view on traditions like that of the *Vedas* would be to simply suppose that the Vedic people were able to handle their environment instead of being overcome by it. Given the possibility, for example, of a future civilization in outer space, we, present earthlings, would not accept their explanation of us as "primitives" in the derogatory sense of the word as if we were not able to handle our environment or at least to, philosophically, interpret it.

The West is slowly coming back from its ego-trip which has certainly not been without an unwarranted sense of superiority and lack of anthropological imagination. Mircea Eliade deserves special homage for his undaunted effort to bring back things to their proper proportions. Concerning the *Vedas* he says:

> "To read anthropomorphic polytheism and then henotheism and monotheism in the *Vedas* is, to borrow a phrase from *Gauḍapāda*, to see the footprints of birds in the air."[20]

The orthodox Hindu view that the *Vedas* is authorless and eternal is going to the other extreme. The idea originates from a justified desire to purify our relationship with the text and to avoid any kind of idolatry. The connection between a word and its meaning is not an artificial relationship caused by somebody. The intention rather is that, when a word ceases to convey meaning, it is not *Vedas.* It does not convey real knowledge. The concept of authorlessness rescues the *Vedas* from the grip

> "not only of a certain God functioning as a primal scribe, but also of the Hindu tradition, which cannot be said to be the author of the *Vedas*. . . . Only

müssen wir sie den Veda lesen lassen. Ihre Götter haben kein gröszeres Recht auf irgendwelche wesenhafte Existenz als Eos oder Hemera - als Nyx oder Apate. Sie sind Masken ohne Schauspieler, die Schöpfungen des Menschen, und nicht seine Schöpfer; sie sind *nomina* (M.M.), nicht *numina:* wesenlose Namen, nicht namenlose Wesen," quoted in: Jan de Vries, *Forschungsgeschichte der Mythologie,* Verlag Karl Alber, Freiburg/Munchen, 1961, pp. 228-229.

18. J.G. Frazer, *The Golden Bough,* abridged edition, Vol. 2, Macmillan and Co., Ltd., London, 1960. pp. 768-775. The work became a classic and exercised a tremendous influence on a number of fields of scholarship. Frazer's work, *Totemism and Exogamy,* although less popular, became equally important. Without it one could hardly imagine Freud writing his *Totem and Tabu.* For a much more encompassing view on the subject, see: Wilhelm Schmidt, *The Origin and Growth of Religion: Facts and Theories,* transl. H.J. Rose, New York, 1931, pp. 91-102 and *passim.*
19. A.B. Keith, *The Religion and Philosophy of Veda and Upaniṣads,* Vol. I, Authorised Reprint, Motilal Banarsidass, Varanasi, 1976, p. 42.
20. Chandradhar Sharma, *A Critical Survey of Indian Philosophy,* Motilal Banarsidass, Delhi, 1979, p. 16.

**Gauḍapāda* is the author of the *Manḍukya-Kārikā,* the first available systematic treatise on the *Advaita-Vedānta.* According to tradition he was *Govinda's* teacher, who, in turn, taught *Śaṅkarāchārya. op. cit.*, p. 239.

when you become their "author", when through assimilation you are able to utter them, when you yourself are the proper origin, the auctor of the text, do the *Vedas* disclose their authentic and proper authority. The Vedic revelation is not the voice of an anthropomorphic Revealer nor the unveiling of the veil that covers reality."[21]

Sharma writes concerning the *Vedas*:

"the Vedic sages were greatly intellectual and intensely spiritual personages who in their mystic moments came face to face with Reality and this mystic experience, this direct intuitive spiritual insight overflew in literature in the Vedic hymns."[22]

The Vedic revelation unfolds the process of man's becoming conscious, discovering himself along with the three regions, the three worlds and their mutual relationships. It is a message not speaking via a medium, another party. The very progressive illumination itself is the core of its enlightenment. It is the Revelation of the Word as symbol, as the sound-and-meaning aspect of reality itself. Upholding that authority of the *Vedas* makes this writ particularly relevant today, when strong and mutually antagonistic ideologies tend to darken any authentic word coming straight from the first intuition of truth in man's heart and mind. Here, at least, we have a word that has no bias against being enamoured by either God or world.

"That which cannot be seen or grasped, is without family and caste, without eyes and ears, without hands and feet, eternal, omnipresent, all-pervading, most subtle-that is the Immutable, regarded by the sages as the source of being."[23]

Vedic literature is a witness to man's search for identity-in-difference, ultimately transcending even itself. It is an absolutism hardly describable. It holds both monism and pluralism in itself and, again, transcends both. In the *Upaniṣads* this particular identity-in-difference reaches rare peaks. It is one of Hinduism's characteristics which baffles and at times even angers the student of religious philosophy. It is still with us today in Indian philosophy. For the Westerner, willing to train his eye and mind, it is there in everyday life in presentday India. The search for identity-in-difference happens in a spirit of inwardness and religious feeling and not in the sense modern sciences are apt to designate the term. Vedic religion, as Gonda says, is no "Sondergebiet neben andere Kulturbereichen"[24]* To equate, as Hillebrandt does, the mythical form of Vedic thought with mere poetry would lead to error.[25] No doubt poetry is there. In fact, we must be careful not to banish poetry from the *Vedas*. We must resist the temptation to invent a science of our likes and dislikes, a "science of the soul"—psychology substituting psychological explanations for those of poetry.

21. Raimundo Panikkar, *The Vedic Experience*, p. 13.
22. Sharma, *op. cit.*, p. 16.
23. *MU.* 1.1.6 tr. Panikkar, *op. cit.*, p. 84.
24. J. Gonda, *Die Religionen Indiens*, Vol. 1. p. 15.
*"an activity separate or different from other expressions of culture", transl. F.B.
25. J. Gonda, *op. cit.*, p. 23. See Alfred Hillebrandt, *Vedic Mythology*, transl. Sheeramula Rajeswara Sharma, Motilal Banarsidass, Delhi, 1980, first German ed. Breslau, 1891, 2 vols, Vol., 1, pp. 1-20.

Poetry expresses intellectual and emotional interpretation of being. In the Vedas philosophy and poetry, sentiments of art, thinking and living are inseparable.[26]

A function of Vedic myth, like that of myth in other cultures, is its reference to the past when a sacred action was executed for the first time. The action is then repeatedly re-enacted. The myth, therefore, is no pseudo-historical tale. It is the repeated presentation of some powerful event which, for the mythical consciousness, expresses the reality of all there is. In as far as myth describes and also meditates on primeval creation—the cosmogonic and cosmological myth—,it helps to bring primeval reality to life. Thus it is, for example, that for those who are alive to the mythical consciousness, the waters flow because *Indra* made them their bed. The myth keeps reminding us of this daily reality. It is wholesome to realize that in the myth of the beginnings creation is not unconditionally handed over to man as his possession. It is a gift, a treasure to be guarded and cherished. Earlier I observed that myth, and it is one of the Vedic characteristics, is not of a mind of dominance but of proportioned sharing between man and the heavens.

The way nature comes to us in mountains, rivers, stars and planets, in flora and fauna, can be employed, or better to say "seen and felt" ,to express the events of the very beginning. But it must be remembered that myth does not paraphrase natural phenomena.[27] It rather enables man to do what the gods, the heroes and the ancestors "did in the beginning". Thus myth provides man with a foothold, an identity. The language of myth being that of symbol, is capable of representing a reality on a certain level of reference by a corresponding reality on another. Myth assumes that there *are* analogous realities on different levels of reference, that is, that the world is an explicit theophany; the sacred appears in and through it. In other words, "as above, so below". The chariot of the sun, the cart of the divine, drawn by the horses, for example, is an understanding of the sensitive powers of the soul, the body of the chariot being our bodily vehicle, the rider the spirit. Just as there are two minds, divine and human, so there is a fiery chariot of the gods, and a human vehicle, one bound for heaven, the other for the attainment of human ends. Man's identity, the knowledge of his significance, is that his embodiment is a humiliation as well as a royal possession.

Vedic myth is not static nor is it considered a luxury. It is linked with vital urges and needs. Clashes and friction between heaven and earth are evident. So are tensions between god and man and between one human being and another. One god may have

26. Poet is *kavi* from which *kāvya* poetry is derived. The reference to these words in the modern sense is late. In Vedic contexts *kavi* is primarily an epithet of the highest gods with reference to their utterance of words of creative power, *kāvya*, and *kavitva* the corresponding quality of wisdom. Vedic *kavi* being, therefore, rather an "enchanter" than a "charmer" in the later sense of one who merely pleases us by his sweet words. The Indian category of *alamkāra-śāstra,* the science of poetic ornament, is considered to be the art of effective communication.

27. Jan Gonda, *Vedic Literature,* Wiesbaden, 1975, p. 114. A distinction between the subjective symbol of psychological association and the objective symbol of precise meaning implies some understanding of the doctrine of analogy. What is implied by the doctrine of analogy is, in the Platonic sense, that of adequacy. It means that a reality of a certain order can be represented by a reality of an other order, the latter being a symbol of the former. In this sense a symbol is a "mystery". It follows that if we are to understand what expressive writing intends to communicate, or expressive saying for that matter, we cannot take it only literally or historically. We must be ready to interpret it "hermeneutically". See: "Ohne Symbole und Symbolik, gibt es keine Religion", H. Prinz, *Altorientalische Symbolik,* Berlin, 1915, p. 1. Also see: Edgar Dacque, *Das verlorene Paradies,* Munich, 1938, arguing that myths represent the deepest knowledge man has.

to make way for another as time lapses. Minor deities rise to prominence because, their personality may possess the necessary vacuum and flexibility to be filled with suitable traits, fulfilling the need of the hour in a particular period of human life.[28]

On their way to settlement in India, the Aryans and their divine companions had to face seemingly insurmountable difficulties. Often it was a question of survival of the fittest. Some of the Aryan deities have in India uptil today. One of these is *Viṣṇu,* traversing the sky in three steps (*tripādavikrama*) and whose spatial extensiveness and pervasiveness to maintain the cosmos is always needed.[29] He reigned in ancient times, in Purāṇic medieval times and so he will at the end of our aeon (*Kali-yuga*) at the time of dissolution (*pralaya*). *Viṣṇu* will be resting all alone amid the endless ocean on the serpent *Ananta,* Endless.

A typical pastoral people, Vedic society is thoroughly masculine. When the Aryans settled in agriculture, the goddess appears with her symbols of increase—plants, water, foliage, the murmur of streams and her own womb with her different sex and her own passion. She softens the edges and puts a finishing touch to civilization. Myth is not static. It travels along with people, looking back over the shoulder towards when everyting began. In India one must do what the gods did, as it is said in the *Vedas.* Until today in Banaras, where this work took shape, musicians and bards on festive occasions sing about the beginnings on street-corners and in market-places. The artists often make the deities, themselves and the audience participate in India's modern history with a touch of genuine humour.

Vedic antecedents relevant to the study of value systems in Hindu mythology are those that refer to man's search for an answer as to who he is. In *pravṛtti* and *nivṛtti* man *is* inasmuch as he loses himself. He is called upon to abandon the temptation to be a master. Instead, the myth knows him to be a guest and a citizen.

The Prestige of Origin

Myth, being humble, admits failure to comprehend. It does not shy away from a stammer. But myth equally tells marvels without a blush. Even when myth discovers man to be like God or man giving a name to all living things, as is the case in the Hebrew adamic myth, no pride can be detected in myth. Myth simply tells the truth and in truth there is no pretense. The Kulin people in Australia know their mythical origin to be in Bunjil who created the earth, the trees, animals and man. That was the Kulin's very beginning. Bunjil fashioned man from clay, breathing a soul into him through the nose, the mouth and the navel. Then Bunjil withdrew. His son Bimbeal took over the earth and his second child, the daughter Karakarook, looked after the sky.[30]

The god's withdrawal is a common feature in many origin myths. They, however, insist on the speciality of man, not only his biological speciality. It often is the express account of being given a *breath* that must make man special. As if in the breath there is the potency, the possibility of man to communicate, if he wants, with the Breather. We shall later see how this breath creates, in the Indian context, a whole chain of

28. Sukumari Bhattacharji, *The Indian Theogony,* p. 13. See also : L. Renou, *Religions of Ancient India,* Athone Press, 1953, p. 20.
29. *RV.* 1.154.2; 4.5.
30. Mircea Eliade, *Patterns in Comparative Religion,* Sheed and Ward Stagbooks, London, 1979, p. 41.

symbols. In the case of the Kulin in Australia, his speciality was understood by him to be such that no interference with it would be possible. So it is with all mythical specialities of origin in all cultures. From an imaginary point somewhere outside the universe, enabling us to see all cultures at once, the whole of human kind thinks of itself as coming from an origin not merely human. Very often the origin is a being who breathes into man. From our imaginary position it would appear altogether incongruent if we saw one culture, under one pretext or another, deny another culture its mythical origin. It would, so we would think, thereby deny its own origin. Ideally, myth precludes all domination by dint of the very universality it offers in attempting to encompass the totality. But humans tend to forget their myths and hence their real origin. Thus it is that the resistance of aboriginal Australia to white domination should be attributed to the Kulin's knowledge of who he is and who the one who breathed into him is. The Kulin is breathing the Creator's breath. Denying him this, is more than merely denying him his physical breath. It is nothing less than denying him his identity and declaring him a non-human. Not only that, it was Kulin clay that the Creator used. Taking it away from the Kulin is not only theft, it is a sacrilege.

Another interesting example of the prestige of origin is that of the Dayak-peoples on the island of Borneo in Malaysia and Indonesia. The myths follow each other to form a return to the origin which is continuously recovered in the life of the community and in that of the individual. The cultic cabin of the Dayak longhouse found its identity through these myths. Hans Schärer has given a full account of the origin event of the Ngaju Dayak, of which I shall here present Eliade's rendering.

> "At the beginning the cosmic totality was still undivided in the mouth of the coiled water-snake. Eventually two mountains arise and from their repeated clashes the cosmic reality comes progressivley into existence: the moon, the clouds, the sun, the hills and so on. The mountains are the seats of the two supreme deities, and they are also these deities themselves. They reveal their human forms, however, only at the end of the first part of creation. In their anthropomorphic form, the two supreme deities, Mahatala and his attractive wife Putir, pursue the cosmogonic work and create the upperworld and underworld. But there is still lacking an intermediatory world, and mankind to inhabit it. The third phase of creation is carried out by two hornbills, male and female, who are actually identical with the two supreme deities. Mahatala raises the tree of life in the Centre, the two hornbills fly over toward it and eventually meet each other in the branches. A furious fight breaks out between the two birds and as a result the tree of life is extensively damaged. From the knotty excrescences of the tree and from the moss falling out from the throat of the female hornbill, a maiden and a young man came, the ancestors of the Dayaks. The tree of life is finally destroyed and the two birds end by killing each other."[31]

31. Hans Schärer, *Die Gottesidee der Ngaju Dajak in Süd-Borneo,* Leiden, 1946. See: Mircea Eliade, *History and Meaning in Religion,* The University of Chicago Press, 1969, pp. 77-80. See also: Francis Baartmans, "Marriage among the "Lepo' Tau" Kenyah Long Moh, Baram, Sarawak", in : *The Brunei Museum Journal,* reprint, Vol. 2, No. 3, 1971. Also : F. Baartmans, "Kakus Punan MŪD Healing Rites" In: *The Sarawak Museum Journal,* Vol XIV, nos, 28-29, New Series, 1966. Government Printing Press, Kuching, Sarawak.

Although the deities, in this Dayak myth of origin, reveal themselves in three different forms, each manifestation is a totality. The water-snake is also the hornbill and vice versa. The world is a result of the fight between the polar principles. But from death spring the cosmos and a new life. The longhouse is the "centre of the world" where the origin-myth is tirelessly reiterated. The dancers wear the feathers of a hornbill and the fight is brought onto the stage of the longhouse verandah. In the Dayak marriage ritual the re-enactment of creation takes a prominent place. Sometimes it looks as if marriage is the creation of the first human couple. Birth and death are likewise linked with the beginning by a constant memory of it.[32]

This brief resume of the Dayak origin myth enables us to grasp the role that myths of origin play in identity-formation of peoples and of individuals. The depth and complexity of the Dayak's existence are portrayed in their origin myth. The Dayak myth is particularly illustrative of the fact that myths of origin try to grasp at once the complete primordiality and totality. During my research among the Dayak people of Borneo in Sarawak it was not very difficult to notice the particular relevance some holy trees had in the Dayak's mind. When international timber industry began its onslaught on the Dayak and his myth, his worldorder, it proved to be nothing less than dramatic and traumatic. The felling of the "tree of life" meant nothing else than the felling of the Dayak himself.

A mythical account of origin both presupposes and continues the cosmogony, the description of the meaningful event of primal creation. From the structural point of view origin myths can be homologized with the cosmogonic myths. The myth of origin, however, does not make a systematized reflection. It implies a vision which goes beyond and behind the structure of primal creation. The origin-myth teaches man everything connected with *his existence,* his legitimate mode of being. The origin-myth is a vital ingredient of human civilization. It is, if appreciated, capable of regulating behaviour of humans among themselves, claiming "different origins". As I have just said, the myth of origin tries to grasp the complete primordiality and totality and goes beyond the narrative of its cosmogonic structure to the reflection on the significance of man's mode of being. That is why the origin myth transports itself to a level of unlimited thought. It indicates the intimate accord of the man of cult and myth with the whole of being while clearly observing its particularized situations in actual human existence. But against this the origin myth points at an indivisible

32. In his introduction to Kuiper's book, *Ancient Indian Cosmogony,* John Irwin relates how Kuiper came to accept the structural approach to the study of religion "while at the same time disassociating himself from the anthropologists 'claim of' the primacy of society in classification'. (Irwin quotes here Rodney Needham who translated Hans Schärer's book). Schärer's work assisted Kuiper in shaping his new interpretation of the *ṚgVeda.* Kuiper in Irwin's opinion," was especially conscious of what he calls "the curious one-sidedness of the hymns". Prior to this, scholars had evaded the problem. Looking at the history of religion from an evolutionary (Darwinian) point of view, which presupposed an almost obligatory progression from 'primitive' to 'advanced', they based their analysis of the *ṚgVeda* on the fact of its being chronologically the oldest document; and since religion in its 'primitive' stages was thought to have been concerned with worship of 'natural forces', *Indra's* fight with the demon, *Vṛtra* was interpreted as a nature-myth concerned with thunder-clouds and rain. Against this, Kuiper arrives at his view that *Indra's* fight was a Creation myth, and that the dualism of *Deva* and *Asura* was fundamental to its structure," p. 5. It is in this sense that I have followed Kuiper's opinion in my paragraph called "A phenomenology of 'chaos'" in the first part of the book.

plenitude in which the supernatural, the natural and the psychological are not yet torn apart. It is in virtue of the strength of that conviction and knowledge that myths of origin, interpretating the mode of human existence, are capable of bringing peoples and nations together on a common ground of "not being different" when their ultimate search for significance is concerned.

If we now, in the following portion of this chapter, are going to concern ourselves with the Prestige of Origin in Vedic and later Hindu mythical thought, it may already be said that quiet dawns of movements are typical of the Orient. Cultures sprung from within the Vedic contour often speak of the primordial egg, being there as such. Or it may be produced from primordial elements like it is in the history of the great families of Tibet which opens by the birth of the cosmos from an egg. From it limbs grew the five senses, all perfect. It became a boy of such beauty that he was called King Ye-smon.[33] It has already been guessed, perhaps, that the history of a nation and its particular way of dealing with existence may be said to depend a good deal on the character of its myths of origin. Nations and peoples are "made" by their origin myths. If a particular people is to go a different way from what it always understood to be its original way, a laborious process of demythicizing will result. Cultural upheaval is, from that point of view, very well explainable. For an understanding of the historical development of peoples one must look at their myths of origin, at what peoples possess as their Prestige of Origin. In view of this, political rivalry and cultural clashes become more easily explainable. For it is precisely through a loss or partial loss of mythical consciousness that the totality of things is being forgotten. Writing about the character peoples receive from their myths of origin, Ernst Cassirer observes the following:

> "The true character of mythical being is first revealed when it appears as the being of origins. All the sanctity of mythical being goes back ultimately to the sanctity of the origin. It does not adhere immediately to the content of the given but to its coming into being, not to its qualities and properties but to its genesis in the past. By being thrust back into temporal distance, by being situated in the depths of the past, a particular content is not only established as sacred, as mythically and religiously significant, but also justified as such. Time is the first original form of this spiritual justification. Specifically human existence-usages, customs, social norms, and ties - are thus hallowed by being derived from institutions prevailing in the primordial mythical past; and existence itself, the "nature" of things, becomes truly understandable to mythical feeling and thinking only when seen in this perspective. A conspicuous trait of nature, a striking characteristic of a thing or species, is held to be "explained" as soon as it is linked with a unique event in the past, which discloses its mythical generation.... Thus the past itself has no "why": it *is* (E.C.) the why of all things."

Is the myth of origin then lost or does it completely vanish from actual experience when, as is the case, we moderns are apt to apply the critical historical method? For

33. Ariane MacDonald, La Naissance du Monde au Tibet, in : *Sources Orientales,* Paris, 1957, vol. 1, p. 428.

us a myth is *only* a myth because we can no longer connect mythical time with the time of history as we write it nor can we connect mythical places with our geographical space. What could the myth of origin explain to us at all? The question is: is that myth meant to be explanation? The explanation we want may be the empirical scientific solution. It is rather the vision *to exclude* from myth its etiological intention which is the theme of all necessary demythologization. For, in doing so, we grant the myth, by losing its *explanatory* pretension, to reveal its *exploratory* significance. It is by the latter that myth contributes to understanding. This understanding, as I explained in the first part of the book, is its symbolic function. And it is by the symbol that we discover the bond between man and the sacred and between man and his surrounding. Paradoxical as it may seem, the myth, when it is thus demythologized through contact with scientific history and elevated to the dignity of a symbol, is a dimension of modern thought. Hence, apart from other possible motives to study India's myths, for an understanding of modern India and its history, the study of its myths of origin would seem indispensable. We are now sufficiently prepared to encounter the primal myths of origin of India.

India's Primal Origin Myths

The myth of origin gives an account of some new event before the beginning of the world. Or the event may be told because of its direct relationship with the created world. The particular character of India's chief myths of origin has taken a long time to evolve. For their eventful meaning to crystallize itself, a great length of time elapsed. This is the case also in other traditions. The Hebrew heritage, for example, took a long time before Jahweh-God came to be known as Elohim, God with us. By then, the Hebrews had travelled a great distance through barren lands on their way to the promised land of Palestine after fleeing from Egypt.

Once the Aryans had left the Kabul valley, taking their gods with them, it was not till five or six centuries later that they occupied the region of the rivers, the basin of the Upper Indus. Many a battle had to be fought. It was god *Indra* who destroyed the forts (*pur*) of the enemy, viz. the indigenous population. These were described as being barbarians and professing the cult of the phallus.[34]

A symbiosis with the aborigines, nevertheless, began soon. The Aryans took wives from among their women and they were forced to synchronize customs for mere survival. Aboriginal gods began to be revered by the Aryans. Although practising agriculture, their economy was chiefly pastoral. Cattle performed the function of money. Milk and its produce were eaten as well as the flesh of bovines. From the *ṚgVeda* we know that they loved music and dancing. Music instruments they played were the flute, the lute and the harp and a game of dice must have been an addiction of many. An entire hymn is devoted to it.[35] An important fact to know is that the Aryans mythologized their adversaries by making them into demons and sorcerers. The battles that were fought were assimilated to *Indra's* combat against *Vṛtra*, the demonic being who prevented creation by closing in the waters.

The Aryans did what many before and after them did. They made the occupation

34. B. and R. Allchin, *The Birth of Indian Civilization*, Baltimore, 1968, p. 154ff. See: R.C. Majumdar, "The Vedic Age" in: *History and Culture of the Indian People*, London, 1951, vol. 1.
35. *SB*. 7.1.1.1 - 4.

of the territory legitimate by the building of an altar, a centre where they felt the new country to be their own (*gārhyapatya*). They dedicated the altar to *Agni*, the fire-god. *Agni* thereby procured for himself a place among the principal architects of origin of what we now know to be the Hindu tradition.. The *Śatapatha Brāhmaṇa* tells us clearly of the fact:

> "One says that one is settled (*avasyati*) when one has built a *gārhyapatya* and all those who build the fire-altar are established."

Agni: Sacrifice of Fire and Intelligence

The building of *Agni's* altar is a ritual imitation of creation. It is a common fact in the history of conquerers that the occupied territory be first of all transformed from "chaos" into "cosmos". The ritual makes the territory *real*. In linear time, the time of the clock so to say, man's microcreation such as the demarcation of a territory, precedes the myth of origin through which man turns full circle and returns to the final "proof" of validity of his action.[36] Whereas the return is possible in and through spiritual consciousness, it requires a length of time for man to perceive himself and his surroundings. It is in this perception that myth finds a footing. True myth begins when a genesis, a becoming — not a genetical one —, a life in time, is attributed to the figures of demons and gods. When we speak of the "history of the gods", the emphasis as far as its discovery is concerned, is *not on the gods first*, but on man's need for time to discover them. In other words, "primordial time" gradually turns into "real" time for man when he makes (the) god enter into man's own. At the same time man feels secure to have entered into (the) god's own. Cassirer writes:

> "Here again (in the mythical consciousness) the expression of temporal relations develops only through that of spatial relations. Between the two there is at first no sharp differentiation. All orientation in time presupposes orientation in space, and only as the latter develops and creates definite means of expression are temporal specifications distinguishable to feeling and consciousness."[37]

The initiation of the temporal in which "the history of (the) god" can take place is necessary for the full development of the concept of the divine.[38] Without it man cannot determine his "origin" because the historical aspect of (the) god, travelling with

36. It is of interest to note some of the latest large scale examples of this anthropological-mythical "necessity" of man to ratify acts that have a connotation of domination. Western Christian discoverers and colonizers planted their national flag or the cross on the newly discovered or conquered soil to validate their action, thereby often proclaiming the autochtone culture "chaotic", "barberous" by assigning to themselves the duty of "civilizing" the indigenous population. They needed a theology to provide a legitimate "origin" of their action. This was, until recently, found in an exegesis, grown and reared in the West, where the command for the Saviour Jesus to go and baptize all nations validated the conquerer's occupation of foreign lands. In the economic world of multinationals one finds the same need for justification of moving into a new territory and making it into "one's own" by, for example, adherence to the company's name of the country of origin and the creation of a certain identifiable architectural style of building and lay-out of shops. Such acts provide the businessworld with a feeling of coming into their own wherever they go. Their systems and methods of business are felt to be validated. In the ordinary world of man, living in a foreign country, the creation of at least a minimum of "one's own" is an evident psychological need.
37. Ernst Cassirer, *The Philosophy of Symbolic Forms*, 3 vols. Yale University Press, 1977, reprint, vol. 2, *Mythical Thought*, pp. 106 - 107.
38. Op. cit., pp. 83 - 118 *passim*.

man, is a condition of perception which unites the cosmological linear creation with the ontological origin.

Supremely sacred places like altars and sanctuaries are constructed according to canons. The sacrificial fire obligations in Vedic India were laid down in indexes such as the *Āśvalayāna Gṛhya Sūtra* and the *Śrauta Sūtra*. In the last analysis a sacred place is built by the effort to perceive the primeval revelation which discloses the archetype of the sacred space "at that time". The erection of the Vedic altar is instructive with regard to that. A two-fold symbolism may be observed in the consecration of the sacred spot, the sacred space. On the one hand, the consecration is the "consecration of the world", in our case that of the settlement of the newcomers, the Aryans. The clay needed to built an altar was mixed with water, the Water of the Beginning.[39] On the other hand, the building of the altar meant a symbolic integration of time.

> "The altar of fire is the year..... The nights are the stones surrounding it and there are 360 of them... the days are the *Yajusmatī* bricks for there are 360 of them."[40]

The altar thus becomes a microcosmos existing in space and time quite distinct from ordinary space and time. A different kind of understanding is needed, a godly intelligence, to cover the gap there is between the a-temporal and a-spatial and the time and the space felt by human experience where the divine must nevertheless be known to be present. This is why *Agni* is called the "bull-cow", two perfect opposites in the Aryan human experience of being a pastoral people. The "bull-cow" is a bi-sexual deity as large as the cosmos.[41] Only a superhuman power is thought to be capable of portraying the wholeness of pre-existence. In human terms the "bull-cow's" significance is activity (*pravṛtti*) tempered by cessation (*nivṛtti*). Together they blend on the altar as the meeting-place of the temporal and the eternal. The altar event is the event where god and man meet "like before".

Generally, man's mythical intuition of time, like that of space, is altogether quantitative and concrete; not qualitative and abstract. Myth knows no time "as such", or perpetual duration or cessation belonging to time itself. There are, for myth, only configurations of content and meaning which in their turn reveal a certain contour, a coming and going, a rhythmical being and becoming. Thus, in all cultures and religions, there are "holy days" which interrupt the uniform flow of life in space and time and introduce distinct lines of demarcation, ultimately pointing towards the felt distance between the divine and the human. In that sense "holy days" are expressions of metaphysical understanding as well as of respect for the divine. At the same time they affirm man's feeling of exile.[42]

---

39. *SB* 1.9.2.29 etc.
40. *SB*. 10.5.4.10.
41. *RV*. 10.5.2.
42. For the mythical consciousness activity is organized according to definite time intervals, e.g. periods of seven or nine days, weeks, months, years, the movement of sun and moon, which become "critical" for a well-ordered life in temporal existence. Thus hostilities may be put off until the new moon or marriages and other important human activities may be celebrated when the moon or the week "allows" them. The intuition underlying all this is that spacial and temporal intervals and dividing lines are not mere conventional distinctions of thought but processes which possess an inherent quality and, particularly, an essence of efficacy of their own.

On his fire altar *Agni* becomes the messenger "between heaven and earth".[43] He is "eternally young".[44]

> "You alone can discern both the opposites. Before the sacrifice you seize on man but during the sacrifice man seizes you! Like a racehorse you let yourself be reined by the priests!"[45]

In his sacrificial role *Agni* is the priest (*purohit*). He it is who knows the cosmic order (*ṛta*) for he is its firstborn in the earliest aeon.[46] That cosmic order *is* part of the world order made sacred through the sacrificial fire. *Agni*, therefore, is called "the master of the house" (*grihapati*). He dispells darkness and creates order for he "divides goods justly".[47] *Agni* is on man's side. He is terrestrial. Born in the sky, he descends from it in the form of lightning. He is equally in the water, in plants and in wood. There, in the water of creation, the heavenly element of fire mixes with the aquatic element of the waters creating heat and warmth (*tapas*) which gives rise to foliage, all kinds of growth and also to thinking power (*manas*). Herewith man may discover the right proportion, the correct *ṛta*, in all that is. On earth, *Agni* has a place in its navel (*nābhi*). This refers to the hole in the altar in which the fire was deposited:" *Agni* is the navel of immortality".[48]

There is an important concept, connected with *Agni*, which I wish to draw attention to while discussing the "Prestige of Origin" of Vedic and later Hindu thought. It is that of *tapas*. We attempted to trace, in the foregoing chapter, the source of the values underlying Indian thought, especially the manner in which that thought took shape in the later myths. We discovered the double-edged leaning in the myths towards *pravṛtti* and *nivṛtti*. Indian thought reveals a bias towards austerity, one of the meanings given to the concept of *tapas*.

The concept of *tapas* is multivalent.[49] It projects a true vision on things. *Tapas*, says Chethimattam, literally means concentration in oneself.[50] The author discusses the notion of *tapas* in the context of intuition as the basis of Vedāntic metaphysics. The search for and desire to know *Brahman* (*jijñāsā*) is grounded in more than mere curiosity. What man strives after is the vision of *Brahman* by a curb on dissipation and by elimination of the vagaries of passion in every sense in order to establish a state of self-possession in both *pravṛtti* and *nivṛtti* by means of a forward move of consciousness. All that belongs to the force of *tapas*. *Tapas* is known already in the *ṚgVeda*. As we will see in a later paragraph of this chapter, the cosmic god *Prajāpati* heats himself through *tapas* before the act of creation. No wonder then that *Agni*, fire, was close to *Prajāpati* and is identified with "fiery splendour, energy, efficacy, majesty,

---

43. *RV.* 1.58.4.
44. *RV.* 1.52.2.
45. *RV.* 1.189.7: transl. Raimundo Panikkar, *The Vedic Experience*, p. 810.
46. *RV.* 10.5.7.
47. *RV.* 1.58.3. Of *Agni* it can be said that he facilitates syntheses seeking the reduction of multiple and different planes to a single fundamental principle.
48. Arthur Berriedale Keith, *The Religion and Philosophy of the Veda and Upaniṣads*, 2 parts., Motilal Banarsidass, Delhi, reprint, 1976, part 1, p. 155.
49. The conclusion to this chapter will be dedicated to the notion of *tapas*.
50. John Chethimattam, *Patterns of Indian Thought*, Orbis Books, New York, first published by Geoffrey Chapman, London, 1971, p. 99.

and supernatural power" (*tejas*).[51]

Whatever its connotation, e.g. the erotic sexual, the magical, the a-sexual contemplative "heat" of love or the creative imagination, *tapas* lies at the origin of things. The concept of *tapas* has been known from proto-history but the Orient, and the Indian genius not in the last instance, has elaborated and articulated *tapas* to a very high degree.

Agni's birth—one of them for *Agni* has several births—is from two firesticks. The upper is seen as the male, the lower as the female. In mythical thought the sticks are described as *Purūravas* and *Urvaśī*, a well-known pair of lovers. From them is born the son of strength, *Agni*. He is a prototype of union of opposites, a feature which was to become utterly characteristic of Indian thought. Through *Agni* Vedic man related to his "Origin", be it in a less philosophic—contemplative manner than later progressive development in Indian thought shows.

Much is made of the Fire as light for society and for oneself in the *Śatapatha Brāhmaṇa* (2.2.2.8-20). The following is a short summary. The gods and demons were both the children of *Prajāpati*. Both were devoid of any spiritual Self (*anātmanaḥ*) and consequently mortal; only *Agni* was immortal. Both parties set up their sacrificial fires. As expected, the demons performed their rites externally while the gods lit the fire in their inward self (*enam... antarātman ādadhata*). Having done so, they became immortal and invincible. Today too the sacrificer sets up the fire sacrifice within himself. Inspired by inner light and vision he will do right. The link with *Agni* and hence with the "Origin" is pronounced in another pericope in the same *Brāhmaṇa* when it is said that the sacrificer apprehends *Agni* in himself when he builds up the fire-altar.[52] For it is from himself that the sacrificer in his sacrifice brings *Agni* to birth.[53]

The true fire sacrifice is not a rite to be merely performed at fixed seasons. It is within us daily, after the primordial pattern of the thirty-six thousand *Arka* fires that were of mental substance (*manasā*)[54] Thus the *Agnihotra* provides the corrective (*pratividhi*) for the elemental self to rise up and be identified with its Source.

What *Agni* reveals is man's flame of light of self-identification with what is Identity Itself. When man sees *Agni* he will surely understand that it is *Brahman* who breaks man's isolation without disturbing man's need for pensive moods and solitude. It is *Agni* who burns what is already dried up; without him there would be no renewal, no fresh thought or hope, no discovery of where one stands and where one goes. Light is lit so heaven and earth may see each other.

"First *Agni* sprang to life from out of Heaven:
the second time from out of us came *Jātavedas*;
Thirdly the Many-souled was in the waters,
The pious lauds and kindles him the Eternal.

51. *AV*. 7.89.4.
52. *SB*. 7.4.1.1: "being about to build up the Fire-altar, the sacrificer apprehends him in himself (*ātman agniṃ gṛhṇīte*); for it is from himself that he brings him to birth (*ātmano.. adhjijāyate*)" in: *Satapatha Brāhmaṇa* ed. J. Eggeling, 5 vols., Oxford, 1882 - 1900.
53. Ibid.
54. *SB* 10.5.4.16. "by knowledge (*vidyayā*) they descend to where desires have migrated (*parāgatāḥ*' only to Comprehensors this world belongs" in: *op. cit.*

Agni, we know, thy three powers in three stations,
We know thy forms in many a place divided.
We know what name supreme thou hast in secret:
We know that source from which thou hast proceeded.

The Many-souled lit thee in sea and waters, man's
Viewer lit thee in the breast of heaven,
there as thou stoodest in the third high region
the Seers increased three in the water's bosom.

Agni roared out, like *Dyaus*, what time he thunders
he licked the ground, about the plants he flickered
At once, when born, he looked around enkindled,
and lighted heaven and earth within with splendour.

The spring of glories and support of riches,
rouser of thoughts and guardian of the Soma,
Good Son of Strength, a Kind amid the waters,
in forefront of the Dawn he shines enkindled".[55]

Bṛhaspati: The Prayer of Orthodoxy

The *Brāhmaṇas* exemplify a clerical sacerdotal-administrative priesthood. Its ritualism and adherence to law sparked off the later ideal of internalization in the *Upaniṣads*. But the *Brāhmaṇas* also contain inward looking spirituality. These two portions of the *Vedas* should not to be too strongly contrasted. One cannot draw a hard-and-fast dividing line between the two. Vision and the urge to perceive Reality pervaded the whole of the Vedic period. Periods merge imperceptibly. In both *Brāhmaṇas* and *Upaniṣads*, as well as in the earlier Vedas, we find perhaps the earliest speculations by man with regard to his origin, his being a microcosm as against the universe as macrocosm.

The beatific identification, in the bloom of upaniṣadic times, between the human soul (*ātman*) and the Absolute (*Brahman*) develops from the more magical identification of the sacrifice with the world of sense-perception. Magical not in the sense of pre-logical as, in my view, Ernst Cassirer all too easily accepts in his study on myth.[56] I would not think, for example, that the arrangement of the sacrificial firehall in the earlier *Vedas* can be seen as an attempt to usurp divine powers. One was rather concerned with what one knew to be already present in the reality of existence, i.e., the relationship between the seen and the unseen. Thus Vedic liturgy more often than not visualizes a reality believed rather than a reality usurped. Why should early Vedic thought not be considered sympathetically as having risen beyond the level of contenting itself — as magic does — with producing a particular effect? Early Vedic thought clearly orientates itself towards being and becoming and is, be it not always emphatically so, imbued with the intuition of a *whole* of being.[57]

55. *RV* 10.45.1-5. In: *The Hymns of the ṚgVeda*, Ralph T.H. Griffith, Motilal Banarsidass, Delhi, reprint, 1976, p. 563. This hymn to *Agni*, one of many, contains twelve strophes.
56. Earnst Cassirer, *The Philosophy of Symbolic Forms*, vol. 2, Mythical Thought, p. 29 - 59.
57. From the *ṚgVeda* 3.4.4.5 we learn that the sacrificial hall is the house of *Agni* where the fire is nourished by wood and oblations, particularly ghee. The hall was large enough to contain altars,

In the progressive search for a more unifying, personified principle to explain the phenomenal world, the divine architect *Viśakarman* appears. He builds the universe from wood, easily accessible to *Agni*.[58] He promised the earth to tortoise (*Kaśyapa*) who, as lord of the waters, used to be built into the fire-altar.[59] He is also the lord of the sense-organs. He knows man's psyche.[60] As *Tvaṣṭṛ's* other self, he assists pregnant women and thus *Viśvakarman* is involved in the creation of the human being.[61] Although short, his mythological career was successful. He later dwindles into oblivion.

The view has been advanced that *Bṛhaspati* is the forerunner, or a least the prototype of *Brahmā*, the creator-god of the epic-Purāṇic Triad.[63] Possibly *Bṛhaspati* is an apotheosis of the Brāhmin priest and as such *Brahmā's* prototype. It is perhaps more relevant to see in him a representative or embodiment of ritualist values. He is the chief priest of the gods with whom he intercedes for man's good. *Trita's* cry for help out of the well was heard by him.[64] *Bṛhaspati* is the bluetipped golden flame of the sacrificial fire.[65] With his other name, *Brahmaṇaspati*, his appearance is like that of *Agni's*. He is said to have a clear voice, seven mouths, and a beautiful tongue. During the new and full moon sacrifices *Bṛhaspati* is invoked several times. He is the "holy power", a title given to *Brahman*.[66]

Brahman is found in many *ṚgVedic* and later passages as priest or the priesthood as a profession.[67] In these *saṃhitās* the notion of *Brahman* means "holy power".[68] In early Vedic literature *Bṛhaspati* is often associated with concepts tracing their origin back to the root "*bṛh*". The word "*brahman*" as meaning "sacred utterance", is often used of him. He is also called the "prayer" or "hymn". This is also said of the Brāhmin priest. If the Brahmin is thought to possess *Brahman*, then *Bṛhaspati* by virtue of his identity with "prayer" or "hymn" would indeed represent the power of the social class of Brahmins. Their struggle for supremacy among the various groups settling in the new environment needed a protector.

---

fire-places, the materials necessary for sacrifice, the priests, their assistants and above all the honoured guests—gods and the manes.—"*ūrdhvo vāṃ gātur adhvare akāry ūrdhvā Śocīṅṣi prasthitā rajansi/divo va nābhā ny asādi hotā stṛṇimahi devavyacā vi barhiḥ/*". I have taken this note from: Joseph T.F., *The Vedic and the Christian Concept of Sacrifice*, Ph. D. thesis, Banaras Hindu University, 1982, p. 17. The described arrangement of the sacrificial hall by no means stops at living in the present as an isolated point or in a series of such points, a simple sequence of separate phases of action. It would seem to me to turn much more to the contemplation of the eternal cycle of events if we grant that the congregation was aware of what wood and the other oblations and the presence of the honoured guests stood for.

58. *RV*. 10.84.4.
59. *AV*. 19.53.10.
60. *AV*. 19.53.11.
61. *AV*. 6.81.3.
63. Eleven hymns are addressed to him and he is mentioned one hundred and seventy times. See: Sukumari Bhattacharji, *The Indian Theogony*, p. 317.
64. *RV*. 1.105. 17.
65. *MaiS*. 1.8.6.
66. *RV*. 8.29.3.
67. A.A. MacDonell and A.B. Keith, *Vedic Index of Names and Subjects*, 2 vols., Motilal Banarsidas, Delhi, reprint, 1982, vol. 2, pp. 77-78.
68. Arthur Berriedale Keith, *The Veda of the Black Yajus School Entitled Taitiriya Saṁhitā*, 2 vols., Motilal Banarsidass, reprint, 1967, vol. 2, p. 99. When the priest prays that *Bṛhaspati* may "unite the scattered sacrifice" the idea of cosmic unity as aimed-at is expressed. I have discussed this characteristic of mythical thought in the first part of the book.

Bṛhaspati as the lifegiving power behind the sacrificial act is at the same time the lord of its sound; he is *Vācaspati*, the one who owns *vāc*, the word.[69] He is the heavenly archetype of the Brahmin caste, the divine personification of the art of ritual and of the finishing touch of ritual observance. He is known for sudden and prompt ideas and, that too, for fanciful deceit. Thus *Bṛhaspati* embodied the abilities of the Aryan Brahmin elite. His prayer, therefore, is not necessarily the prayer of humility or contemplation. His is more the prayer of power and order in human terms. As *Vācaspati* he resembles himself well: the creative world which calls forth the cosmos out of chaos. "*Bṛhaspati*", it is said, "is for speech".[70] Emphasizing his wisdom the *ṚgVeda* calls him "poet of poets", "inspired" and "sage."[71] His lordship over prayer and his control of the sacred utterance are stressed in the *ṚgVeda* since prayer as invocation is one of the most precious means to gain the favour of the gods. All of that is also characteristic of the Brahmin and *Bṛhaspati* is the Brahmin of the gods. He represents all that is central in Brāhminical tradition of ritual and sacrifice. Hence he is a symbol of orthodoxy in all its ramifications.

The word *brahman* retained its original meaning of "sacred utterance" in the sense the early *Vedas* and the Brahmin class gave to it. In the period of the *Upaniṣads* the word was used in the sense of the Absolute, that is, what remains unchanged in a world of change. This development may be seen as a metaphysical synthesis of *pravṛtti* and *nivṛtti*. The sages have always been at pains to define the *Brahman* as accurately as possible. *Brahman* is both the formed and the unformed, the manifest and the unmanifest, the mortal and the immortal, the here-and-now and the Beyond.

The Perfection of the Beginnings: Sat-Asat (RV. 10.129)

The eight domains or realities (*aṣṭamūrti*) of the manifest cosmos[72] were given by *Prajāpati* the Creator to his son, the sacrificer[73], who is the embodiment of "mind". "Mind" is the form of the sacrificer.[74] "Mind" embodied in man takes a place like that of the stars in the firmament. It is the overlord of the powers of the soul. There is a power in the soul called *manas* which is "as if the (immanent) deities are the breaths, mind-born and mind-yoked, wherein one sacrifices metaphysically".[75] Ultimately *manas* is undistracted by the workings of the powers of perception and action. *Manas*, in a sense, is the manner in which one is "not anyone" and hence free to become and be someone, filled with the forces of intuition, recollection, memory, intellect and proportion. What else is *manas* than

> "The Swan, the bird of golden colour,
> abiding both in the heart and in the Sun,
> the diver-bird of glorious light—
> to him we sacrifice in his fire"[76]

---

69. *TB*. 1.7; 4.7. For *brahman* as "sacred utterance" being used for *Bṛhaspati* see: *RV*. 2.1.2.; 4.50.8.; 10, 141.3.; *SB*. 5.1.4.14; *AB*. 1.19.
70. *SB*. 10.2.3.3.
71. *RV* 2.23.2; 23.7; 25.1.
72. *SB*. II. 6.3.6. *BU*. 3.9.3. *Mhb*. 1.60.17.
73. He is *Brahmā* in the *Purāṇas*.
74. *TS*. 5.1.4.4.
75. *TS*. 6.1.4.5.: "*prāṇā vai devā, manojātā manoyujas, teṣu parokṣaṃ juhoti*."
76. *MaiU* 6.34: transl. Panikkar, *The Vedic Experience*, p. 41.

Where is *manas* from? *Manas* itself does not ask that question. Who is there who ever knew a firmament without the sun? *Manas* then, we say, came into existence when life stirred in the dark void of the primeval Waters.[77] Where else could *manas* come from? For the Waters are the most pertinent; they cover all, support all, have no form of their own except all form, they are visible and invisible, have no limits and pervade everything. They are the first condition of life, the place of the original seed. They are fertilizing milieu.

How could man find a more fitting milieu than the Waters for *manas* to come from? Because for the *manas*, without the contours of a body, everything is one. Thinker and Thought are simply "perfect simplicity" (*ekavṛtatva*) or "sameness" (*samatā*).[78] The *Manas* which does not ask itself is the Intellect that does not intelligize. It is the Eternal Mystery, the Supreme Goal which cannot be taught. In the *Śvetāśvatara Upaniṣad* it is said that

> "The world vortex is merely Thought (*çittam eva hi saṃsāram*), labour then to cleanse it (*sodhayet*); as is the Thought, such is the mode of Being (*yet çittas tanmayo bhavati*): This is the Eternal Mystery (guhyam... *sanātanam*).[79]

Man as mind, as microcosmos, is seen as homologous with the cosmos, the universal *Manas*.[80] Is that perhaps why the Vedic seer of *ṚgVeda* 10.129 perceived the very first stirrings? Was it *Vāyu*, god of wind and breeze, swift as mind, the thousand-eyed, lord of thought, who stirred man's mind to even begin with thought about Thought? We can here only guess and perhaps be only silent.

What we possess of the Vedic seer of *ṚgVeda* 10.129 is a most remarkable and sublime hymn, the well-known *Nāsadīya Sūkta*. It has captured the imagination of many a philosopher and student of religion. It is one of the oldest philosophic speculations in the history of the human race, as far as we know, with regard to the mystery of the origin of "Origin" itself and of that of all manifestation.

"At first was neither Being nor Nonbeing.
There was not air nor yet sky beyond.
What was its wrapping? Where? In whose protection?
Was Water there, unfathomable and deep?

There was no death then, nor yet deathlessness;
of night and day there was not any sign.
The One breathed without breath, by its own impulse.
Other than that was nothing else at all.

Darkness was there, all wrapped around by darkness,
and all was Water indiscriminate. Then

77. *RV.* 10.129.3.
78. *MU.* 3.1.3: "*paraṃ sāmyam*". Here we move on the plane of reference where "Thought does not think" where the first characteristic is the absence of all characteristics.
79. *SU.* 6.22.
80. A further definition of the cleansing of thought in man is implied in *MU.* 3.1.9: "The thought of men is altogether interwoven with the physical functions "—*prāṇais çittaṃ sarvam otaṃ prajanām*. "It is in him who is cleansed (of this contamination) that the Spirit manifests " *yasmin viśuddhe vibhavati eṣa ātmā*.

that which was hidden by the Void, that One,
emerging, stirring, through power of Ardour came to be.

In the beginning Love arose,
which was the primal germ cell of the mind.
The Seers, searching in their hearts with wisdom,
discovered the connection of Being in Nonbeing.

A crosswise line cut Being from Nonbeing.
What was described above it, what below?
Bearers of seed there were and mighty forces,
thrust from below and forward move above.

Who really knows? Who can presume to tell it?
Whence was it born? Whence issued this creation?
Even the Gods came after its emergence.
Then who can tell from whence it came to be?

That out of which creation has arisen,
whether it held it firm or it did not,
He who surveys it in the highest heaven,
He surely knows - or may be He does not!"[81]

Man's perceptive consciousness attempts to express and fathom the perfection of the very Beginning. Often plenitude and force are felt to be at the Beginnings but at once there ought to be, for as perfect as possible a metaphysical location, also void or stillness. In order to conceive of Being it ought even to be "protected" by Nonbeing. To think about Thought man knows he must suspend duration, history as he knows it and sink into a form of silence which is different again from the very silence man thinks he knows.

"Silently (*tūṣnīm*), for what is silent is undeclared (*aniruktam*), and what is undeclared is everything (*sarvam*)..."[82]

Man possesses no words to express the stirring of the unstirred, the breath that breathes without a breath. If man does attempt to express the Unexpressible, he does so by means of symbolic language. Philosophic speculation began with the concept of being and therefore, by deduction, with the concept of non-being. The very moment when these concepts appeared, when man's consciousness awakened to the unity of being as opposed to the multiplicity and diversity of existing things, the specific

81. *RV*. 10.129.1 - 7. transl. Raimundo Panikkar, *The Vedic Experience*, p. 58. Panikkar adds a few notes to his translation of this difficult hymn. It would only do justice to the translator to mention some of them here. Verse 2: "own impulse": *svadhā*, the active principle, has been translated as "by its own energy "(Zaehner), "power" (Mascaro, Macdonell, Edgerton), "Impulse" (Bose), "of itself" (Misch), "strength" (Raghavan), "will power" (Telang-Chaubey). "elan", "initiative" (Renou), "Eigengesetz" (Geldner), just to give an idea of different readings". Verse 3: "Indiscriminate: *apraketā*, without a recognizable sign, undifferentiated, indistinguishable, unrecognizable, referring to the amorphous chaos, the unformed primordial Waters." Verse 5: "Bearers of seed" are considered to be the male force and "mighty forces" the female principle. Cf. *dakṣa* and *aditi* as the masculine and feminine principles, respectively, in *RV*. 10.72.4."
82. *SB*. 7.22.13 - 14; 2.3.3.

philosophical approach to the world and to the non-world was born. But how to find language to describe, let alone determine, the Perfection of the Beginnings and the Origin, the Ultimate Foundation?

Man is able to state the question of the Original Fount. Any answer to the question concerning the supreme universal formulation, however, cannot but make use of symbolic form and derivatives illustrating the Perfection of the Beginning and the Origin. The mystical seer (*ṛṣi*) of *ṚgVeda* 10.129, proposes a particular material quality: "Darkness there was at first all wrapped around by darkness". This is the visionary's materia prima. Then his urge to fathom more of the Origin becomes more "ideal" and the darkness is replaced by the rational explanatory principle of desire and heat (*tapas*). By virtue of *tapas* Thought Itself is able to set its own immanence moving towards emanation. This generative move is conceived of as Being's or Not-Being's total otherness. The germinal heat, the sexual expression of which is characteristic of the created world, derives from "impulse".[83]

In thought about the Uncreated the *tapas*-force appears in myths and visionary experiences often either as sexless or as bi-sexual or even in the form of some "impossible" sexual circumstance like incest or the union of brother and sister, in order to stress the total otherness of the Uncreate. The Vedic visionary perceives the worldseed coming to life by the drive towards selfcreation by the power of *tapas*. It is in that very drive that the Seed is in a situation of being and not-being. It is his own situation which the seer attempts to project and in doing so he has to deny it of the Uncreate.

Who is the Vedic *Ṛṣi*, the seer-sage? What may we expect from him and what is his personality like? The *Ṛṣis* are often identified with the Breaths, the moves of understanding. The Seers, Sages, Prophets or Sacrificers are often referred to in a standard group of seven. These Seers, expressly identified with the Breaths[84] are said to be co-born (*sajātaḥ*), modalities (*vikṛtayah*) or members (*aṇgāni*) of one and the same Person entering into many places. They are called being-makers (*bhūta-kṛt*), sacrificers and lovers of sacrifice through whom vision is obtained. They are said to attend on the "One beyond the Seven *Ṛṣis*", an epiteth obviously referring to the Self or one of the Self's manifestations. Visibly the *Ṛṣis* are the seven lights of Ursa Major in the centre of the sky and invisibly they are the powers of vision, hearing, breathing and speaking in the head.[85] We must restrict ourselves and cannot discuss the astrological and psychological factors that underlie personalities of the *Ṛṣis*.[86] What is important to realize is that the *Ṛṣis* were human beings in search of the Origin of existence. Their very effort, sustained by their mythical consciousness, made them for others into spokesmen of the Voice. They were the visible lights, the seven lights of

83. Panikkar in his, *Myth, Faith and Hermeneutics*, p. 56 explains: "Darkness was there, all wrapped around by darkness" (*RV*. 10.129.3.). The first darkness is the Creator himself (*svayambhū*), the primordial principle, masculine) which envelops (the theme of the incest appears) creation *parameṣṭhi*, the feminine principle, emanation from the Creator".

84. "*Ṛṣi*" is derived from the root "*ṛṣ*": rush, flow, shine *SB*. 6.1.1.1.; 8.4.1.5. and 3.6.; 9.1.1.21; 9.2.1.13. *Nirukta*, 10.26: *sapta-ṛṣīṇānindriyāṇi, ebhyaḥ para ātmā tani asminn ekaṃ bhavanti*.

85. *RV*. 1.164.15; 10.73.1; 10.82.2; *TS*. 5.7.4.3. *AV*. 10.8.5.9.; *SB*. 2.1.2.4.

86. For a short introduction to the topic, see: J. Pryzluski, "Les sept Puissances divines dans l'Inde et l'Iran", in *Revue d'histoire et de philosophie religieuses*, XVI, 1936, pp. 500 - 507 and L.D. Barnett, "The Genius: a Study in Indo-European Psychology", *JRAS*, 1929, pp. 731 - 748.

Ursa Major, in society. Through them society found its link with the Origin. The *Ṛṣis* also possessed literary restraint. The myth which they themselves must have already heard was left untouched. No mere reason was allowed to violate it. Thus they were able to make the Voice incarnate in communicable form conveying the truth of the Origin. Their precise expression lies in the enigma, an inescapable feature of myth. The *Ṛṣis'* voice and whatever came to be written down of it was meant to be significant (*padārthabhinaya*) and liberating (*vimuktida*). The aim of their language was not to amuse but to instruct. The *Ṛṣis'* voice was understood to be much more imaginative than any other tale precisely because it was understood to be more than mere imagination. No one would think their vision to be founded on mere observation, if only because the myth is always true or else is no true myth while facts are only true eventfully.

Philosophical inquiry into the origin and nature of language is as old as the quest after the essence and origin of being. The question of language should not be overlooked. I cannot present here even a brief sketch with regard to the problem of language. For our understanding of the link between the mortal who tries to find words for the Perfection of the Origin, at least a few observations about language should be made.

In the myths narrating the earliest reflections on being and the world, there seems to be no distinction between language and being, between word and meaning. In the Book of Genesis of the Hebrew-Jewish tradition, for example, it is said: "And God said, "Let there be light", and there was light.[87] In the Indian tradition we read: "By the power of the word, the majesty of *Prajāpati*[88] said: "*Bhūḥ*", "earth!", and the earth was".[89] Man too, in his resolve to fathom the depths of the first Vibration (*nāda*) which took place at the commencement of creation, has tried and ventured to create the presence of the divine, the numinous, by mere sound. It is especially in the East that a complete philosophical and theological system has been developed with regard to sound in metres and *mantras*. Most well known and revered in India is the sound *OM*.[90] *OM* is the *Pravaṇa-Dhvani* which sounded when, on the first vibration, there was a stir in *Prakṛti*, the womb of Nature, the fount of all. This sacred sound is the all-encompassing *Mahabīja*, the See-*Mantra*, through which the true *Yogī* hears the true and Subtle Sound.

Language is a necessary condition for reflection. Philosophical awareness arises only in and through language. For the human spirit language is a given reality, comparable to physical reality. From the moment when man first turns his attention to it, language assumes for him the same necessity and hence also "objectivity" as that of the world of things. There is nothing arbitrary in it. A word is not a nomination. It is in itself a part of reality.

Plato, in his effort to systematize language into a methodology of knowlege, conceived of the ideal "Idea" which was to mediate between the expression in language and the object to be expressed. The mythical view of language, it must be

87. The Old Testament, *The Book of Genesis*, 1.3.
88. *SB*. 2.2.4.4.
89. *SB*. 11.1.6.3.
90. Sir John Woodroffe, *The Garland of Letters*, Ganesh and Company, Madras, 1979, pp. 257 - 266. *OM* will be discussed in the following part. See also the index of names and themes.

understood, precedes the philosophical view.[91] It is characterized by the non-difference of word and thing. Who gains possession of the name also receives power over it. Such a process may result in magic. Signs of magic are present in the Vedic sacrificial formulea where the word would seem to call into being the god it represents. There is, however, a difference between calling the god into existence and calling the god into *presence* with man. The problem of magic cannot be discussed here. When myth and rites are concerned it *is* a problem. If we grant that myth as symbol glimpses behind images and representations looking for the secret of existence, it must also be conceded that it is capable of ideal content.[92]

In the *Nāsadīya Sūkta* we inherit a vision which, apart from the vision itself, exhibits an extraordinary use of language. The Vedic *Ṛṣis*' mythical thinking seeks to understand its own activity. Consequently it becomes a form of knowledge. Its mythical view of language develops from the perception of the particular force contained in the formula to the idea of a universal potency possessed by the word as such, that is to say, by the whole of "speech". Here we find *language as a unity*. If we conceive of the word as "speech", involving *manas*, there will be much less reason to accuse mythical language of magic. The phenomenon of the word as "speech" with a signification is observable also in other early speculations. To take again the example of the Hebrew-Jewish tradition: we find in the book of the prophet Jesaja a unity of language rather than a mere sequence of words each denoting a particular reality, when the prophet sees a saviour born from a virgin in the far future. By linking his own and his people's present to a potential salvation in the future, his words have brought about a signification, something magic is incapable of. Magic makes present an immediate "effect".[93]

The spiritual power of speech is one of the *Vedas*' essential founts. As I have tried to explain in the first part of the book, the human word (*vaikhāri*) has a "mark stamped on the inside of it", showing that it is "made" in the higher and secret three quarters of *Vāc*, the Womb of the Universe. That is why I remarked that the *Ṛṣis* are extraordinary. They seek to understand their own activity. At the base of the human word which comes into being and passes away is the eternal, imperishable word, the celestial goddess *Vāc*. If word magic is said to be man's usurpation of the word, magic would indeed be far from the Vedic mind.[94] The vision of speech as a

91. In the first part of the book I have tried to explain how mythical language must be "taken up" by philosophy since that language, like philosophy, is concerned with being. I tried to show how mythical language, springing up in the midst of discourse, warns philosophical language of its contingency.
92. Ernst Cassier in his, *The Philosophy of Symbolic Forms*, 3 vols., vol. 2, Mythical Thought, pp. 38ff denies to myth the category of the idea. He writes:" Where we see mere "representation", myth, insofar as it has not yet deviated from its fundamental and original form, sees real identity. The "image" does not represent the "thing" it *is* (E.C.) the thing...". Cassirer's opinion on myth is not far removed, it would seem, from Levy-Brühl's "mentalité prélogique" and "loi de participation". Paul Radin accuses Cassirer of having paid a disservice to myth. See: Jan de Vries, *Forschungsgeschichte der Mythologie*, p. 350.
93. The Old Testament, *The Book of Jesaja*, 9.5 - 11.
94. The relation between magic and religion is one of the most obscure and most controversial subjects. Frazer was one of the first to try and prove that, even from an anthropological point of view, the two cannot be subsumed under a common heading. They would be entirely different in psychological origin and they tend to opposite aims. see; George Frazer, *The Golden Bough*, (abridged ed.), vol. 1, *The Magic Art and the Evolution of Kings*.

unity one finds illustrated in a passage dedicated to the calestial *Vāc*, the heavenly Speech:

"I travel with the *Rudras* and the *Vasus*, with the *Ādityas* and the All-Gods I wander... . I am the Queen, the gatherer-up of treasures, most thoughtful, first of those who merit worship. Thus Gods have established me in many places with many homes to enter and abide in. Through me alone all eat the food that feeds then, each man who sees, breathes, hears the word outspoken. They know it not but yet they dwell beside me. Hear, one and all, the truth as I declare it."[95]

Judging by ordinary empirical standards of sensory experience, creation in myth cannot but appear "unreal". But the inner freedom of the mythical function has very different conventions. It is not a product of whim or chance. Myth has its own fundamental laws of form. Mythical consciousness lives in immediate impression. It is irresistible because of the truth it experiences. That is the strength of its vision which, in the Vedic context, is the *Dhī* or *Maniśa,* as indicated in the beginning of the second part of the book. The Seers "awaken (*bubudhāna*) to a heavenly allotted treasure".[96] Myth does *not possess* the object by progressively building it up like in theoretical thought . Myth is *possessed by it*. Therefore, it equally knows.

The shining of the Supernatural Sun is as much an "utterance" as a "raying". That Sun indeed" speaks", (*mitro... bhruvāṇaḥ*).[95] It is "that great and hidden name (*nāma guhyam*) of multiple effect (*purusprk*) whereby thou dost produce all that has come to be or shall become."[98] The name or form of that Sun is thus prior, in hierarchy rather than in time, to the Sun itself and is its reason of being, whether as pattern or as name. It is as an expression (*sṛṣṭi*) or utterance (*vyahṛti*) that it itself is manifested or evoked: "in the beginning this universe was unuttered" (*avyāhṛti*).[99]

The "One" in the *Nāsadīya Sūkta* cannot be properly called a concept. It does not allow for a degree of approximation to the fullness that the "One" in itself is. It rather presents the peak of mystical awareness developed later in India in Advaitic philosophy and in the West in Trinitarian theology. In both traditions we find the doctrine, explicit or implicit, that the utterance of a name has creative efficacy linking the "here and now" to That which has no such predicates. If what of the Supreme Identity is manifestable appears to us to be different from variety and multiplicity, the doctrine of creative efficacy of the name shows the relation of this apparent multiplicity with the unity on which it depends. Apart from this unity its being would be a pure non-entity. In as much as the last end must be same as the first beginning, the creative process always proceeds from multiplicity to unity, from semblance to reality.

"The Makers, laying aside the Yes and No, what is blunt and what is veiled of speech, have found their quest; they that were held in bond by names are now

95. Ralph T.H. Griffith, *The Hymns of the RgVeda*, p. 631. On the mythical and religious significance of *Vāc* see Paul Deussen, *Sixty Upaniṣads of the Veda*, 2 vols., Motilal Banarsidass, 1st Indian ed., 1980, especially on *Bṛhadāraṇyaka Upaniṣad* 1.5.3. ff.
96. Jeanine Miller, *The Vedas, Harmony, Meditation and Fulfilment*, p. 21.
95. *RV*. 3.59.1.
98. *RV*. 10.55.2.
99. *MU*. 6.6.

beautified in that which was revealed; they now rejoice in what had been revealed by name, in that in which the host of angels comes to be one; putting away all evil by this spiritual power, the Comprehensor reaches Paradise.[100]

The Birth of His Own Perfection: ***Hiraṇyagarbha*** **(*RV.* 10.121)**

The Vedic Seers became increasingly curious to apprehend the unitary and unifying principle of the universe. The multitude of gods shrank under the influence of growing awareness searching for an explanation. No god became altogether identified with the One Being sustaining the manifold. The function assigned to the god was more important than that god himself. Gods rose to prominence whose names tell of their creation functions as, for example, *Bṛhaspati*, the Lord of prayer. The persistent search for the origin of the universe results in a new departure.

Like in other archaic traditions, Vedic Seers are fond of representing the same thing in different images. Yet, at the same time, they "see" different things in the same image. Thus *Sūrya* may mean the shining sungod (*Tvaṣṭṛ*) or *Savitṛ*, the sungod with his regenerating, revivifying power. The sun shines, creates and renovates; all the three names were able to achieve recognition as three different personalities. The fact, however, that the *Sūrya*-hymns are different in content from the *Savitṛ*-hymns does not contradict the basic identity of these two gods. Mythical consciousness is fond of paradoxes as well as of oppositions. Oppositions in particular are attractive. They have the same basic element underlying them. The basic element in itself is neutral but in the act of fighting itself, it comes to life. From mythical-philosophical speculation a concept of strength or a potency emerges. With regard to gods, these elevate them to personages in the highest heaven.

What is fascinating about the Vedic Sages is not only their piercing exploration of the outer space of being, the very outskirts of reality, but also their plunge into the Beyond beyond, the inscrutable Prelude of Existence from where no human words could possibly resound. The Seers ventured into that limitless enclosure where there is only "That One" (*tad ekam*). Who or what is That One? *Tad ekam* is praised as *Hiraṇyagarbha*, the Golden Germ:

"In the beginning arose the Golden Germ:
he was, as soon as born, the Lord of Being,
sustainer of the earth and of this Heaven.
What God shall we adore with our oblation?

He who bestows life-force and hardy vigour,
whose ordinances even the Gods obey,
whose shadow is immortal life — and death —
What God shall we adore with our oblation?

Who by his grandeur has emerged sole sovereign
of every living thing that breathes and slumbers,
he who is Lord of man and four-legged creatures -
What God shall we adore with our oblation?

---

100. *Aitareya Āraṇyaka* 2.3.8.3.4. ed. A.B. Keith, Oxford, 1909. "what is blunt and what is veiled of speech" i.e., all dialectic is abandoned. See *NU.* 3: "Where all abides in one nest" - *yatra viśvaṃ bhavaty ekanīḍam*. "Blunt" and "veiled" seem to imply *pratyakṣam* and *parokṣam* — all that is formal, no longer significant for one to whom the content of all form is immediately present.

To him, of right, belong, by his own power,
the snow-clad mountains, the world-stream, and the sea.
His arms are the four quarters of the sky.
What god shall we adore with our oblation?

Who held secure the mighty Heavens and Earth,
who established light and sky's vast vault above,
who measured out the ether in mid-spheres —
What God shall we adore with our oblation?

Toward him, trembling, the embattled forces,
riveted by his glory, direct their gaze.
Through him the risen sun sheds forth its light.
What God shall we adore with our oblation?

When came the mighty Waters, bringing with them
the universal Germ, whence sprang the Fire,
thence leapt the God's One Spirit into being.
What God shall we adore with our oblation?

This One who in his might surveyed the Waters
pregnant with vital forces, producing sacrifice,
he is the God of Gods and none beside him.
What God shall we adore with our oblation?

O Father of the earth, by fixed laws ruling,
O Father of the Heavens, pray protect us,
O Father of the great and shining Waters!
What God shall we adore with our oblation?

O Lord of cretures, Father of all beings,
you alone pervade all that has come to birth.
Grant us our heart's desire for which we pray.
May we become the lords of many treasures!"[101]

This hymn and other hymns of the tenth *maṇḍala* of the *ṚgVeda* paved the way for the cosmologies and philosophic doctrines of the *Ātharva-Veda*, the *Brāhmaṇas* and the *Upaniṣads*.

For an analysis of the modality of religious experience it is perhaps best to concentrate on its non-rational aspects. We would at least be in a position to avoid as long as possible a rationally measured definition.[102] We must accept, to begin with, the fact that for man as a believer *the living god is possible*. The living god, therefore, is not always the god of philosophers. Being not merely an idea or an abstraction or simply a

101. *RV.* 10.121. transl. Panikkar, *The Vedic Experience*, p. 71. Notes by the translator: verse I: "The Golden Germ, *Hiraṇyagarbha*, the source of golden light, the Sun-God, the seed of all creation, Cf. *RV.* 10.82.5-6, which tells us of the cosmic egg conceived as a germ by the primeval waters. Verse 4: the world-stream (surrounding the earth) *rasā*".

102. See: Rudolph Otto, *Das Heilige, Über das Irrationale in der Idee des Göttlichen und sein Verhältnis zum Rationalen*, Göttingen, 1917. He also deals with "the sacred" as a fundamental religious category.

story, the living god has been for man a fount of intense joy and freedom. Belief in that god has enabled man to escape the dreariness of convention and cliché making him succeed in rising above the limits of direct environment to a universal vision. Where indifference or even reasoned justice fail to answer the cry of those in pain, it is the living god who inspires charity. The living god may also be wicked and be a terror. The idea of the tragic in the Greek mythical vision made man face a scandalous living god.[103]

What may be said of the divine with human certainty is that the divine is "totally other". It is radically different. Man possesses no language of his own other than the language of immediate intuition to express this "otherness". However, even in this intuition, man expresses himself in terms borrowed from the realms of nature and his profane consciousness. The history of religious consciousness is the discovery of (the) god's manifestation beginning from the most elementary as, for example, in a sacred stone or tree. For the Hindu the most developed manifestation is in that of the *avatāra* or in the sound of the sacred syllable. But there is no real break in the continuity. We find ourselves, with regard to structure, faced with the same mystery: the manifestation of the "totally other". Although "totally other" and of a reality that is not of the human world, divine manifestation appears in things and persons as part and parcel of human experience.

Hiraṇyagarbha, the Golden Seed, generated by its own power into Itself. In the nativity of *Hiraṇyagarbha* no female or any other human element plays any part.[104] It evokes the image of the primordial cosmic egg, nourished by the waters, born from *Brahmā* the Creator.[105] It is said of the egg that it is resting on the waters of the universal ocean, "swollen with beings".[106]

Prajāpati, The Lord of Generation

To the repeated question "What God shall we adore with our oblation?" in the hymn to *Hiraṇyagarbha*, a reply is given in the very last verse. It is *Prajāpati*, the Lord of Generation.[108] Most probably the name of *Prajāpati* is a later addition.[109]

The process of myth narrative formation never rests. Outdated elements it discards or it moulds them into new forms. Such a process is not a cut-and-dry system. It is the result of the restlessness of the human mind, caused by psychological conditions as well as by external factors such as migration, climate, contact with other peoples, changes in the firmament, the power of creative personalities and factions among classes. This is not to say that the mythical-religious consciousness simply *follows* from the empirical content of the social form. It is rather one of the most important agents of the feeling of human community. Myth itself is a spiritual synthesis through which a *verbal* bond, its narrative shape, and a *believed* bond, the

103. Max Scheler, *Le Phénomène du tragique*, tr. into French by M. Dupuy, Paris, 1952.
104. *AV.* 15.1.1-2.
105. *VaSa*. 22. 17 - 22, 30 - 39. *AP*. 17.3 - 8.
106. *Map*. 42.64.
107. *MU*. 5.
108. *RV*. 10.121.10: Griffith in, *Hymns of the ṚgVeda*, mentions in his translation of the hymn the name *Prajāpati*.
109. Jan Gonda. *Vedic Literature (Saṁhitās and Brāhmaṇas)*, Otto Harrassowitz, Wiesbaden, 1975, p. 138.

understood myth, are made possible among a community's members. A relation of kinship is created. The myth is an instrument of crisis forging consciousness on the individual and on the group level by an interpretation of the first indeterminate life feeling. In this process the elements of social and physical existence provide merely the raw material acquiring its form only through certain fundamental spiritual categories, like that of the sacred, not situated in it and not to be derived from it., That is why I said that, when myth and magic are concerned, the utmost reserve must be shown. *Origins and gods are not easily created.* It is above all characteristic of myth that the dividing lines it draws between "inside" and "outside" are of an entirely different kind and quite differently sketched than those drawn by empirical-causal cognition. The difficulty of defining the concept of nationhood shows that there is more to a nation than merely observable and theoretical definitions of demarcation. One feels and knows oneself a member of a nation. The underlying initiative to that consciousness lies in the spirit and in a conviction shared between people convinced of a common origin, a principle beyond the visible demarcations making them into a nation, a group or clan. It is the task of sociology of religion to describe in detail the relations between religious form and social form. I must needs confine myself to these few observations.[110]

The *ṚgVeda*, says one knowledgeable authority, is no "Urmythologie", nor the beginning of Indian mythology.[111] It is a part of a long mythological evolution and it has been subject to scrutiny by influential persons, families and schools. This means to say, and it is as well to remember this, that we shall never know *what has been left out*. The *ṚgVeda*, therefore, is not the deposit of all the thoughts and beliefs of that age. There was no lack of undercurrents and streams of thought of various kinds. I pointed out that some of these streams, e.g. Tāntrism, found a berth among the Brāhminical and later subsequent speculations. Lost ideas may have been taken up by less orthodox thought and reintroduced with modifications into the mainstream.[112]

Of all the gods in Vedic literature it is *Prajāpati* who is the protagonist in most of the cosmogonic myths. He occupies an important place in the *Brāhmaṇas*. He embodies not only values of spirituality but also those of rites and rituals, supervised by the Brāhmin class. It is understandable, therefore, that *Prajāpati* is linked with sacrifice and that a high speculative summit is reached with regard to the theological development concerning sacrifice. Each Brāhminic sacrifice enacts a new creation of the world.[113] Our study of myth and its consciousness of the sacred shows how construction-ritual presupposes a more or less explicit imitation of the cosmogonic act. The imitation of an archetype was revealed for the first time. What happens in

110. It is especially the French sociological school, led by Durkheim who starts from the principle that we can give no adequate account of myth as long as we seek its sources in the physical world, in an intuition of natural phenomena. Not nature but society is the true model of myth. All its fundamental motives are projection of man's social life. Durkheim, however, would seem to neglect the purely spiritual aspect. See: Emile Durkheim, *Les formes élementaires de la vie réligieuse*, Paris, 1912.
111. Alfred Hillebrandt, *Vedic Mythology*, 2 vols., transl. by Sreeramula Rajeswara Sarma, Motilal Banarsidass, first Indian ed., 1980, vol. 1, p. 13.
112. In a Mahārāṣṭri legend the event is told of a large gathering where it was being discussed who was the highest god and what that god's attributes were. See Hillebrandt, *ibid.* p. 356.
113. *SB.* 6.5.1 ff. as an example.

ritual is that the current of profane time is being suspended. The assembly is being projected into the mythical time of the Origin. This is not the occasion for an elaborate theory on sacrifice and rituals but it may be observed that any significant construction—also that in so-called secularized societies— tends to go back to a construction of paradisial shape and meaning and hence actualizes at least a portion of a cosmogony.[114]

If the altar *imitates* the cosmogonic creative act, the sacrifice has another end: it *restores* the primordial unity that existed before creation. *Prajāpati* created from his own substance and once he was "spent", "he feared death".[115] The gods revived him. Without the high Lord of Creation no creation can subsist. Sacrifice renews this creation and hence it restores the "Prestige of Origin".

In the epics and *Purāṇas, Prajāpati's* name becomes one of *Brahmā's* most frequent epiteths. *Prajāpati's* creation is an ongoing renewal and reversal. It is a concatenation, the links of which transmit the past to the future. The memory and the promise of an eternal "now" is always there. Mind (*manas*) and speech (*vāc*) are a procreative couple but it is worth mentioning that it is, in many a mythical account, *Prajāpati* who became pregnant. Sexual images abound in the world of *Prajāpati*. The Indian images of later times show *Brahmā* as pot-bellied, rendering visually the identity in god of creation and procreation. *Manas* and *Vāc* are so closely knitted in the Creator that he carries them in his shape. "He (*Prajāpati*) laid the power of reproduction in his own self" (*SB*. 11.1.6.7). It is this idea which the *Vedas* and *Brāhmaṇas* celebrate: the sublime union of the conjoint principles of *Manas* and *Vāc*.

I have earlier drawn attention to the creative force of *tapas*. The powers generated by this force in Indian creation myths are important. *Tapas* is said to be "the heat of concentration" through which *Prajāpati* propels himself to emanation. The creative god and man equally approach each other through *tapas*. This thrust underlies the Indian world view when actualized in various forms of austerity and concentration on truth (*satya*). It constitutes the link between *pravṛtti* and *nivṛtti* when vivifying the devotee (*bhakta*). In the conclusion to this part of the book we shall consider the notion of *tapas* more elaborately under the title "*Tapas*—discernment and intelligent concentration".

In the paragraph on the *Nāsadīya Sūkta* we were illumined by Being and Not-Being (*Sat and Asat*) generated by concentration and giving birth to the One Potential (*ābhū*). From this Potential develops Desire (*Kāma*) being the first seed of Consciousness (*Manas*), also called The Golden Seed (*Hiraṇyagarbha*). This brief recapitulation should not let us forget that the enigma of the secondary creation of the phenomenal world remains. The Vedic seers were enthralled by various types of cosmogonies. In each of them they found a Prestige of Origin. In the beginnings

114. For theology and psychology the question of paradise and archetype is of importance with regard to the formulation of the concept of "fault" or "sin" in relation to the notion of history. To those living with a paradise or an archetype, time is recorded only biologically without being allowed its corrosive influence of the irreversibility of events upon consciousness. Contrary wise, when history is seen in a manner accounting for personal events, the confession of sins or other evils becomes a necessity. History, however, conceals an aspect of terror when indentified with irreversibility. If history becomes intolerant and allows for no forgiveness, the confession of sins, instead of strengthening man's responsibility, may lapse into magic.

115. *SB*. 10.4.2.2

Prajāpati was the unmanifested reality of the purely spiritual presence of unity and totality; the acme of *nivṛtti*.

At rest in itself, supreme consciousness is simultaneously outgoing. Thus it is said that Fury (*Manyu*) with the bright light of Fire (*Agni*) dwelt in *Prajāpati*. It spent itself in action (*pravṛtti*) resulting in the birth of *Rudra*.[116] *Manyu* and *tapas* are as close to each other as are *manyu* and *kāma*.[117] The creation myth tells us how, overcome by emotion, *Prajāpati* wept. At the eternal end the god wept and longed for company, alone as he was in the immensity of the uncreate. *Prajāpati* wished an opposite end. "More I want to be, I wish to spread", *Prajāpati* cried.[118] And so it is that at *Prajāpati's* opposite end created man's cry for union with *Prajāpati* is heard.

The creative and regenerative power of *Prajāpati* is an ongoing process in the Indian experience of reality. *Prajāpati's* urge to expand into more of himself began aeons before man came to think of it. Man's view of himself as the complementary opposite of the creative god gives him his self-esteem. That self-esteem, however, is true only when directed towards the creative god. Whereas at the divine end of timelessness the god sheds tears for loneliness and breaks into creation, man, at the other end, barely tolerates history and time. He periodically abolishes them in sacrifice and ritual so he may enter into timelessness.[119]

Prajāpati's hot tear fell on *Manyu* and *Rudra* was born, thousand-eyed, hundred-headed, the fierce archer *Sarva*.[120] But now, so we are told, all the gods left *Prajāpati* and they abandoned him.[121] Why? Were they jealous? Unlike *Prajāpati*, the Lord of Offspring, they were mortal. They had not drunk from the moon (*Soma*) the draught of immortality.[122] It so happened that an eagle had stolen *Soma* and a considerable argument had arisen as to who was to enjoy it.[123] But why is it that all the gods abandoned *Prajāpati*? If they were not immortal, their misunderstanding of the move they saw *Prajāpati* make is pardonable. They judged by human standards of behaviour which cannot fathom the moves of the divine. For this is what happened.[124] *Prajāpati* was seen to move in the form of a male antelope towards his own daughter *Uṣas*, Dawn, seen around by the gods in the form of a doe. He made love to her, a terrible act for the gods to see. *Rudra* was at once implored to pierce the Creator but before the arrow struck, *Prajāpati's* seed fell to the ground, the earth, the place of sacrifice.[125] The Creator leapt up to the sky and, in the mind of those who saw the sky at those times, became *Mṛga*, the constellation of the antelope, Orion. The guardian of sacred ordinance *Rudra*[126] took his place as archer, *Mṛgavyādha*, in the firmament. We now

---

116. *SB* 9.1.1.6.; *RV* 1.84.2.
117. *AV*. 9.2.23.
118. *SB*. 2.2.4.; 6.1. 1-9; 11.5.8.1.; *BU*. 1.2.1-7; 1.4.1-5. See: Heinrich Zimmer, *Philosophie und Religion Indiens*, Suhrkamp Taschenbuch Wissenschaft, 1979, p. 272.
119. Mircea Eliade, *The Myth of the Eternal Return or, Cosmos and History*, tr. Willard R. Trask, Princeton Univ. Press, 1974, pp. 51 - 92.
120. *ŚB*. 9. 1.1.6.
121. *SB* 9.1.1.6.; *RV*. 10. 84. 2.
122. For a philological study of the cult of the *soma* plant in the moon image, see: Alfred Hillebrandt, *Vedic Mythology*, vol. I., pp. 200-209.
123. Alfred Hillebrandt, *op. cit*., pp. 190-195.
124. *RV*. 10.61.4.
125. *RV*. 10. 61. 5-7.
126. *AB*. 3. 33.; *SB* 1. 7.4.1-3.

see him in Sirius. *Uṣas* is the star *Rohini*, Aldebaran.[127]

Rudra's shot to prevent the apparent crime paradoxically caused creation when the Lord of Generation spilt his seed. Seeing the totally unexpected move by *Prajāpati* towards his daughter, the gods had said: "*mā dūṣa*"- "pollute not", but the seed had fallen. The seed eventually became *manusa*, man.[128] This happened when, in mythical time, *Prajāpati* became an epiteth of *Brahmā*.[129]

For the visionary mythical consciousness, enlightened by its own search for explanations, the history of creation is written large in the sky. For Vedic man there existed no sharp boundary separating man from the Totality revealing itself in the whole of all living and moving things. The model of the architectural myth recognizes at least three spheres where it looks for an explanation of The Origin. The netherworld, the here, and the upperworld of which the luminaries in the sky form a part. Happenings in the firmament are signals of time and they are important with regard to the sacrifice. Sacrifice unites profane time with sacred time. To equate man's cosmic intuition with a naturalistic outlook would be to deny his capability to indeed link the two. Implicitly one would also deny the possibility of sacrifice.

Myths of creation tend to dramatize the act.[130] From the utter silence of Pure Consciousness to the cosmos where the patter on earth of progeny is heard, is, as Stella Kramrisch calls it "an act of violence that infringes upon the Uncreate, the undifferentiated wholeness."[131] Many creator gods are fecundators. The transition is indeed perhaps best portrayed through the image of the spurt of progenitive seed. It follows from the explosive character of the act of creation that a fissure is implied, a split. Usually one finds a mythical instance of this after the creation myth. An indication of this would be, in my view, the fact that *Prajāpati* claims two different drinks. He enjoys the drink of light (*soma*) and that of darkness (*sura*). *Soma* stands for truth and excellence whereas *surā* points to the opposite.[132] The rupture between heaven and earth, so conspicuous in mythical consciousness, results in a courageous acceptance of consequences which, in the case of Indian mythology, have been handed down to us in fairly great detail. Creation departs from the perfection of the unconditioned state to proceed to the rupture between heaven and earth. In man's view this is nothing but a drama. And so it is from god's end when a bond of friendship and understanding with creation is the divine aim. The "Prestige of Origin", therefore, is admitted to have flawed in the sense that, at the temporal end of creation, man is caught in darkness, misunderstanding and in the pain of being shaded by a fissure, the inexorable split there is between a life divine and a life human. This

127. *AB*. 3.33. See. A.A. Macdonell and A.B. Keith, *Vedic Index of Names and Subjects*, 2 vols., Motilal Banarsidass, reprint, 1982, vol. 2, pp. 171, 174.
128. Sukumari Bhattacharji, *The Indian Theogony*, p. 323.
129. *LP*. 1.41.37-38. In her book, *The Presence of Śiva*, Oxford Univ. Press, Delhi, 1981, p42f, Stella Kramrisch refers to astronomical events pointing to a time when some Vedic myths could have arisen, referring to J. Deppert, *Rudras Geburt: Systematische Untersuchungen zum Incest in der Mythology der Brāhmaṇas*, 1977.
130. Mircea Eliade, *Patterns in Comparative Religion*, Sheed and Ward Stagbooks, London, 1979, pp. 96-111.
131. Stella Kramrisch, *The Presence of Śiva*, p. 1.
132. *SB*. 5.1.2.10.

experience, implying a delay of reunion with the divine, is what is meant by the Indian concept of *saṁsāra*.[133]

With regard to the Indian view of creation, I have already made the observation that it is not one of irreparable tragedy. Precisely because the Prestige of Origin is believed to have its fount in the Eternal Perfection of Origin, Indian myth offers the cosmogonic solace of *Prajāpati's concern* with the earth. His frantic search for the earth is encouraging for man:

> "*Prajāpati* in the form of wind swings on a lotus-leaf on the waters.[134] He thought "this is it upon which it stands." He dived and reached the earth below. He then knocked off a piece and came up. This he spread out on the lotus-leaf. Since he spread it out (*aprathayat*) the earth is called *pṛthivī*.[135] *Pṛthivī* is "she" for she must be fertile. She is *śakti*. *Prajāpati* put her into position."[136]

The *ṚgVeda* concentrates mainly on cosmogony clad in mythical narrative. Later *śruti* are more concerned with a variety of concepts, terms and theories about the origin and structure of the universe. An example would be the framework of thought on the support or cosmic pillar or cosmic axis of creation, *Skambha*.[137]

> "Whoever knows the *brahman* in man, they know the most exalted one; who knows the most exalted one and who ever knows *Prajāpati*, who knows the chief *brāhmaṇa* they accordingly also know the *skambha*."[138]
> "In the *skambha* is all that is possessed by the spirit, *atmanvat*, all that breathes."[139]

"Hence they will be free from darkness and evil".[140] *Śūktas* as these promise a prospect of knowledge and the realization of identity. What is transmitted to us by the myth of *Prajāpati*, especially the drama of the incest-event, is that creation, once brought forth, *tries to free* itself from the Creator. Left to itself, however, it is lifeless and chaotic. The Creator must enter his creation so it may have life. It is only then that creation is real and significant. The solace of the *Prajāpati*-creation myth is the regeneration of time in its eternity by abolishing mere human events as if they were the whole of history.

Like in other myths, in the Indian myth too the sky-god is in the course of time replaced by a god who fecundates and creates. Man's thirst for the concrete, which in mythical consciousness is the divine expansion into the expanse of the visible universe, cannot be content with a sky-god far away. Thus it is that the great Vedic sacrifice (*aśvamedha*) came to be offered to *Prajāpati*. It is he who is closest to the created cosmos in Vedic times. By sacrificing the horse, identified with the cosmos, and offering it to *Prajāpati*, the act of creation was, for Vedic man, reproduced, or rather

133. See. Part II 4-4(i): "Myths of the exiled soul".
134. *TS*. 5.6.4.2.
135. *TB*. 1.1.3.6.
136. *TS*. 5.2.4.2.; *TB*. 3.11.1.1. ff; *MaiS*. 2.13.20.
137. *AV*. 4.1; 7.2; 8.9.10. See: M. Bloomfield, *The Atharva Veda and the Gopatha-Brahmana*, Strassbourg, 1899, p. 89.
138. *AV*. 10.7.17; 1.25.16; 10.8.43.
139. *AV*. 7.8.2.
140. *AV*. 10.7.40.

"done again", thus firmly establishing the fact of the Creator's search for the earth. He found it and spread it firmly on the Waters.[141]

What then, to conclude our discovery of *Prajāpati* as one of India's mythical architects, is the discovery of the creation myth for us? First of all, nowhere in myth do we find a passive contemplation of things. In myth all contemplation begins in and from an attitude, an act of feeling and will. Insofar as the myth condenses into lasting configuration and insofar as it sets before us the stability of an objective world of forms, the significance of this world becomes intelligible to us. And that only if behind it we can feel the dynamic of the life feeling from which the myth grew. Only where this feeling is aroused from inside and where it manifests itself in love and hate, fear and joy and hope, the mythical consciousness creates a world of specific representations. In myth, therefore, intuition, thought, and life are interwoven. This is what makes the mythical mode characteristically self-contained and gives it its pungent imprint. Our world shapes and articulates itself according to the basic forms of pure intuition, that means to say, it breaks down into unity and multiplicity, into a co-existence of objects and a succession of events. The mythical intuition of space and time that thus arises is governed by boundaries, different from what they signify in theoretical thought and the theoretical structure of the objective world. Also the mythical, therefore, claims knowledge of this world. It experiences a division occurring in consciousness where it introduces into man's intuition of the world diverse strata of meaning. Myth knows and approaches this division and fashions unity from multiplicity by a process of reason all its own.

In Praise of Man's Origin: Puruṣa Śūkta (*RV*. 10.90)

The transition from the Uncreate into emerging create, from timelessness into time, is a transition of such magnitude and depth that man cannot fathom it. When he thinks of it in the deepest crevasses of his soul and mind, man often experiences this transition as a danger-zone. By its very magnitude and mysteriousness the transition would seem to involve a risk. Never was there a thinner line drawn, being at once the sharpest demarcation possible, than that between the Uncreate and the create, between *no-thing* and *thing*. These very words, despite their limitation, suggest the moment when the Uncreate and the create touch each other. They also suggest some way of in-existing of the Uncreate and the create. For what is the no-thing without the thing? It would indeed not be. What is the thing without the no-thing? It would indeed be only a thing, not a person, not something that would know and understand. It could indeed be anything with no determination whatsoever. It would altogether lack any consistency. Thus man happens to think of oneness and multiplicity. Doctrinal systems often fear man's thought of everything being one. That pondering by man has often all too easily been accused of pantheism. Would it not at least be more sympathetic to first grant man his desire for a god-man communion in one? To ask the creator-god to stay away in the sky is to deny that god his descent into the Waters in search of the earth and of man and to re-unite with them once the initial fissure of the break from the Uncreate into the create occurred.

Indian mythical belief conceives of the danger-zone between the Uncreate and the create as exhausting. Proceeding from aeon to aeon in perpetual creative motion,

141. See: Mircea Eliadce, *Patterns in Comparative Religion*, pp. 96-99.

the Uncreate surrenders itself in the transmission of life in creation and regeneration. That perpetual transmission shows signs of fatigue, apparent in the slowly diminishing force of life in everything created. We shall later see how in the Hindu vision a totally new beginning, a recharge. after a general dissolution, is inescapable. For how could there be an end? Each end must only be beginning for in one totality there is, so to speak, neither.

> "I thought that my voyage had come to its end at the last limit of my power,—that the path before me was closed, that provisions were exhausted and the time come to take shelter in a silent obscurity.
> But I find that thy will knows no end in me. And when old words die out on the tongue, new melodies break forth from the heart; and where the old tracks are lost, new country is revealed and its wonders."[142]

Without the intrinsic bond between the Uncreate and the create as constitutive of the whole of reality, man would not even be able to contemplate. He would be as frozen in a spiritual ghetto of his own, irrelevant to both himself and his surrounding. To realize the whole in himself, because it *is* there, is the maximum possible assimilation of man's existential and only real situation.

To the mythical awareness the realization of *wholeness into one Body* is a strict necessity. It is a force that seizes upon consciousness. This mythical conviction arises independent from all invention. It is, indeed, opposed to invention both in form and in substance. The conviction issues from a process at once enveloping the totality. In and through this process man discovers himself as co-architect of his own origin by the vital link with the Perfection of Origin. Consciousness may resist this discovery but it cannot deny the truth of it, much less annul it. Philosophy and theology ought to be aware of the relation between myth and history when myth proves to be the primary and history the secondary and derived factor. No one who understands what its myth-narrative means to a people, what inner power it possesses and what reality is being manifested therein, will say that myth-narrative, any more than language, was invented. It is with this knowledge, as Schelling maintains, that philosophy hits upon the actual vital source of mythical thought. Schelling claimed it his special achievement to have replaced inventors, poets and individuals by the human consciousness as the source of mythical conviction and its reality.[143]

It is not then by its *history* that the mythical awareness and its narrative is determined. Its history develops out of its myths and the manner in which the myths shape a particular view of the world, the universe and man in it. This fact is becoming increasingly important in the presentday cross-cultural situation. It would deserve more attention than I have given it here. I have touched upon it in the first part of the book when I tried to explain the phenomenon of an *other* in philosophy and the subsequent problem of analysis of myth.

We must now return to our inquiry after India's mythical primal architects, those ideas, personages and factors long ago who "made" the Indian consciousness

142. Rabindranath Tagore, *Gitāñjalī, Song Offerings*, A collection of prose translations made by the author from the original Bengali, MacMillan, India, 1979, p. 21.
143. Friedrich Wilhelm Joseph Schelling, *Philosophie der Mythologie*, 2 vols., reprint, 1976, Wissenchaftliche Buchgesellschaft, Darmstadt, vol. 2, p. 140 ff, and *passim*.

while at the same time being born in it. We shall now approach the presence of *Puruṣa*, the Cosmic Person. *Puruṣa* is Man and the immortal substrate of the human person.

"Beyond *Puruṣa* there is nothing".[144] *Puruṣa* is identified with the boundless tortoise. His identity, therefore, is that of *Brahman*.[145] *Puruṣa's* micro-essence is the *puruṣa*, as big as a thumb, the individual human being. In the hymn to *Puruṣa* which I shall quote in full, the believing Hindu experiences his stablest joy as well as a sting of pain. He understands himself in the world of perception as *the same as his soul and other than his body*.[146] *Puruṣa* stands at the very cross-roads. Three fourths of *Puruṣa* are eternal life in heaven. One fourth of *Puruṣa* are all creatures. Thus, at one end of *Puruṣa*, exists the infinite possibility for growth in contemplative-metaphysical thought whereas at the other end there is the dark alley where the micro-consciousness "to the size of a mere thumb", man, recounts the telling in the myth.[147]

The world-*Puruṣa* is beheld in man in his diminished size, capable nonetheless of transcending. It is in the small man, the dwarf, that of all existing creation the urge to know his Origin is most apparent. For it is in him that the unity-in-difference takes the form of crises of understanding. The gods have solved theirs for they all eventually received the gift of immortality. Those who did not, disappeared already before, or else, after the churning of the ocean.[148]

Puruṣa is not only the cosmic Man. He is also the personal aspect of the whole of reality. This idea would exclude any isolation or alienation and include an internal, inherent relationship between all there is. *Puruṣa* as cosmic Man safeguards a divine and human ecology by which "environment" becomes shared as possessed by all. It is as large as the universe and ultimately stabilized by that part of *Puruṣa* which is called in the cave of the heart *Brahman*. One partakes of this integral cosmic biology through the sacrifice of *Puruṣa* sharing himself into multiplicity while remaining one. The multiplicity lies at small man's end and it is apparent in the succession of time and events. Thus the cosmic Man ascends and descends into every sphere and realm of being. Through the constant sacrifice of immolation and division, the universe exists in multiplicity while being one totality.

---

144. *KathaU*. 3.2.

145. *TA*. 1.23.

146. See : Part II, ch. 2,4.1: "Myths of the exiled soul". The word *puruṣa*, of uncertain derivation, is probably from the root "*pṛ*", "to fill". That it is properly rendered by and corresponds to "person" can be established by a confrontation of texts. For example: *AA*. 2.2.2-3 "....theirs (mere animals) is an estimative understanding (*abhivijñāna*) merely according to hunger and thirst, they do not speak what has been discriminated...Their becoming is only so far, they have being (*sambhavāḥ*) only in the measure of their understanding (*yathā prajñaṃ hi*). The "person" thus defined is the sea (*sa eṣa puruṣaḥ*) and transcends the whole universe (*sarvaṃ lokam ati*)".

147. *RV*. 10.90.4: "With three-fourths Man ascended high "*ūrdhva udait*". One fourth took birth again down here "*abhavat punaḥ*." From this he spread in all directions "*viśvam vyakramat*." into animate and inanimate things", *sāśanāśane*. (into what eats and does not eat).

The identity of the "person in the heart" with the "Golden Person in the Sun" is, of course, a fundamental doctrine in the *Upaniṣads*, e.g. *MU*. 6.1.: "He bears Himself two fold, as the breath of life (*prāṇa*) here, and as yonder *Āditya* ... Yonder *Āditya* is verily the outer-Essence (*bahir-ātmā*), the breath of life the inner-Essence (*antar-ātmā*)". "*ātman*" is never just "body". "*pratyagātman*" is almost literally "hypostasis".

148. References to the myth of the "Churning of the Ocean", *samūdra manthāna*, will be found in the following part dealing with *Āpaḥ*, the Waters.

If three quarters of Cosmic Man reside above and only one quarter are the things of creation, it is clear that man cannot stand for long on one foot, that is, on the external and empirical realm alone. The point of gravity lies in the heavens. The tender balance is kept by a constant reference to the Whole. The Vedas clarify the situation by referring to the *Aśvattha* tree. In the *Kathā Upaniṣad* this tree is described as:[149]

"Its root is above, its branches below-
This eternal figtree [150]
The (root) indeed is the pure. That is *Brahmā*.
That indeed is called the immortal.
On it all the worlds do rest,
And no one so-ever goes beyond it.
This, verily, is that."

Commenting on the inverted tree.[151] V.S. Agrawala writes:

"Here *urdhva* and *adhaḥ* are not spacial conceptions but *urdhva* signifies the unmanifest immortal source and *adhaḥ* its material manifestation. These are the two relative stages applicable to the cosmos, viz. its existence in the cause and in effect. *Urdhva* is the same as the unborn source called *Avyage*, the imperishable one. The *Aśvattha* tree is said to be the abode of all the gods, each leaf is a divine seat. The implication is that the cosmos is a divine manifestation and all the powers of mind or life or matter are present in each part of the tree..."[152] Thus we witness in the cosmic process a two-fold sacrifice (*yajna*). One primal and divine and the other descending to the plane of matter.[153]

The personal man, woman and child on earth is the temporal extension of the eternal Cosmic Man. *Nivṛtti*, a certain restraint in involvement in things of earth and the constant contemplation of the Cosmic Being, appear a metaphysical consequence. Participation in *Puruṣa's* mere last quarter of earthly appearance is equally a metaphysical demand (*pravṛtti*). For, without its last quarter, the whole of *Puruṣa* would be impaired. The problem of an interpretation of this existential tension in human existence was discussed in the foregoing chapter. In the following part I hope to show how the symbol of the Waters, the liquid form of divine and true human vision, enables man to understand his position and his calling as part of the Whole Man.

Could it be safely said that orthodox traditional Hinduism, judging by the content of its traditional philosophical systems and the day-to-day religious life of its

---

149. *RV.* 7.33.9.
150. This same simile of the world as an eternal fig tree, growing out of *Brahman*, is further elaborated in *Bhag. Gītā* 15.1.3.
151. "*Urdhva mūlam adhaḥ-Śākham*
aśvathaṁ prāhur avyayam."
152. V.S. Agrawala, *Vedic Lectures, Proceedings of Summer School of Vedic Study*, Vārānasī, 1963, p. 104.
153. In the Vedic tradition both *ṛta* and *satya* are spoken of as *yajña*, the first referring to the Supreme mind, the level of pure ideation and the second to the principle of mind manifesting itself in matter. They are mutually related conditions one preceding the other. Only with the potential power of the first which is infinite, universal (*RV*.1.105.12) in nature, the second *yajña* becomes possible. Hence in the *Ṛg-Veda* we read: "*yajñena yajñam, ayajanta devāḥ*" (*RV.* 10.90.16). See: V.S. Agrawala, *op. cit.*, p. 72.

people, approaches reality with a pronounced bias towards the three quarters of Cosmic Man in the heavens? The Hindu does not readily grant inherent significance to the external world unless it be through freedom from it through *mokṣa*. His "Dasein" is fixed on the model of Eternal Permanence.[154] It is there that his "I" is found. The "I" in the objective world is illusory (*ahaṁkāra*). The resulting alienation in the human condition is, as I have tried to show, solved on the level of emotion, grounded in Being, through *bhakti*. It would seem that in tāntric efforts, on the other hand, the process of realization requires selfcompletion in and through the human condition and that emancipation would not be obtainable by methods of negation.[155]

The mythical consciousness cannot be content unless it traces "Origin" beyond temporal time and space. For the individual as well as for the group this "Origin" creates and establishes fulfilling self-identity as indissolubly linked with the One Identity. It is, therefore, in *Puruṣa* that we find one of Hinduism's most able architects of its identity.

Whether we speak of a personalist tradition professing *Prajāpati* to be the origin of all, or of a non-personalist view for which the One comes forth from nothingness, when the Indian Perfection of Origin is concerned, the Creator divides himself into as many parts as are needed to complete the cosmos. There always is the primordial sacrifice, the complete self-giving of the Immortal who creates or rather constitutes the universe. The importal deed has been recounted in many ways in Indian tradition. Thus it is said that *Prajāpati* wished to procreate. This was his desire as he was alone.[156] It was by *tapas* that he became operative and created by emanation (*visṛśisthi*). He created the powerful word (*brahman*). Then he went into the waters

154. In the West the existentialists have concentrated on the conscious human being as the centre of all reality. Conscious man is what Martin Heidegger has called "Das Dasein". See: Martin Heidegger, *Introduction to Metaphysics,* tr. Ralph Manheim, New York, Doubleday. 1961, pp. 45-115.

155. The development of the mythical consciousness in the West has taken a different turn, as I have attempted to show in the first part of this work. Comparing traditional mythical consciousness and mythology as a "great collective faith, prehistoric and historic, pretending to hold encompassed in its ritualized aspect all of the truth ever to be known" to newly inspired creative mythology on a new level of experience of the "I", I do wish to draw the reader's attention to the famous European legend of the Grail, composed about A.D. 1200 in old French known as the Vulgate Cycle. The cycle consists of five works showing a significant development in the magical, mystical and psychological realms of inspiration in medieval Europe, contributing substantially to its later cultural development. For my information I am drawing from a penetrating analysis of the legend of The Grail by Joseph Campbell, *The Masks of God, Creative Mythology*, Penguin Books, reprint, 1982, pp. 530-570. The author maintains that "L' Estoire del Saint Graal "as well as the later "La Queste del Saint Graal" presents The Grail as the symbol of supreme spiritual value. It is, however, not obtained by renouncing the world or even current social custom, but on the contrary, by participation with every ounce of one's force in the century's order of life in the way of ways dictated by one's own uncorrupted heart; what the mystics call the Inner Voice. Trevrizent's observation that a miracle had come to pass, inasmuch as Parzival had forced God by defiance to make his Trinity grant his will, touched the quick of the teaching: the anagogy, the metaphysical 'san', of this exemplary Gothic tale. According to its revelation, sprung from the heart and heartland of the European West, the moral initiative in the field of time is of man, not god; and not of man as species or as member of some divinely ordained consensus, but of each one separately, as an individual, self-moved, in self-consistent action". (p. 564) "The point for now is", writes Campbell, "that the syndrome of ideas presented (in The Grail) as a unit is one of the earliest definitions of the secular mythology that is today the guiding spiritual force of the European West" p. 564. In the doings of the legend's personages Campbell discovers in the self-moving, self-responsible individual actions, "a depth-dimension, transcending time and space". (p. 565). It stands to reason that for a full understanding of this note the reading of the legend is imperative.

156. *SB*. 6.1.1.

and from an egg the earth-developed.[157] Fire, wind, sun and moon arose from his *tapas*. *Uṣas*, dawn, the daughter was there and seeing her, he emitted seed.[158] And from a golden bowl of this creative substance is *Puruṣa*, the Cosmic Person, whose praise is sung in the *Puruṣa Sūkta* (*ṚgVeda 10.90*).

"A thousand-headed is the Man
with a thousand eyes, a thousand feet;
encompassing the Earth all sides,
he exceeded it by ten fingers' breadth.

The Man, indeed, is this All,
What has been and what is to be,
the Lord of the immortal spheres
which he surpasses by consuming food.

Such is the measure of his might,
and greater still than this is Man.
All beings are a fourth of him,
three-fourths are the immortal in heaven.

Three-fourths of Man ascended high,
one-fourth took birth again down here.
From this he spread in all directions
into animate and inanimate things.

From him the Shining one was born;
from this Shining one Man again took birth.
As soon as born, he extended himself
all over the Earth both behind and before.

Using the Man as their oblation,
the Gods performed the sacrifice.
Spring served them for the clarified butter,
Summer for the fuel, and Autumn for the offering.

This evolved Man, then first born,
they besprinkled on the sacred grass.
With him the Gods performed the sacrifice,
as did also the heavenly beings and seers.

From this sacrifice, fully accomplished,
was gathered curd mixed with butter.
Thence came the creatures of the air,
beasts of the forest and those of the village.

From this sacrifice, fully accomplished,
were born the hymns and the melodies;
from this were born the various meters;
from this were born the sacrificial formulas.

157. *SB* 11.1.6.1.
158. *KausB.* 6.1.

From this were horses born, all creatures
such as have teeth in either jaw;
from this were born the breeds of cattle;
from this were born sheep and goats.

When they divided up the Man,
into how many parts did they divide him?
What did his mouth become? What his arms?
What are his legs called? What his feet?

His mouth became the brahmin; his arms
became the warrior-prince, his legs
the common man who plies his trade.
The lowly serf was born from his feet.

The Moon was born from his mind; the Sun
came into being from his eye;
from his mouth came Indra and Agni,
while from his breath the Wind was born.

From his navel issued the Air;
from his head unfurled the Sky,
the Earth from his feet, from his ear the
four directions.
Thus have the worlds been organized.

Seven were the sticks of the enclosure,
thrice seven the fuel sticks were made,
when the Gods, performing the sacrifice,
bound the Man as the victim.

With the sacrifice the Gods sacrificed
to the sacrifice.
Those were the first established rites.
These powers ascended up to heaven
where dwell the ancient Gods and other beings."[159]

---

159. Tr. from Raimundo Panikkar, *The Vedic Experience*, p. 75f. Some of Panikkar's notes are "verse 2: The equation without any further qualification of the *idaṁ sarvam*, "all this "(the universe), with the *puruṣa* has caused this hymn to be labeled pantheistic. Verse 5: The Shining one: *virāj*, "the cosmic waters" (Edgerton), "the cosmic egg" (Raghavan), "Mother principle", "*mahat*", "*yoni*" (V.S. Agrawala). It can be understood as a feminine principle, a kind of "primitive *Śakti*" (Renou), a cosmic source, a womb fecundated by the *puruṣa*. The union of *virāj* and *puruṣa* gives birth to *virāja* (son of *virāj*) Cf. *RV*. 10.72, 4-5. "The theology of *virāj*", Panikkar continues, "might offer a fruitful point of encounter between the different notions of the first uncreated emanations of the Supreme which are to be found in more than one religious tradition: *śakti*, logos, pre-existent Christ etc. The end of this "*ṛc*" can be interpreted thus: He stretched himself further (as God, men etc), then he created the earth and the astral bodies. Verse 6: The trinitarian character of the sacrifice has been stressed time and again by scholars of different ages; the three seasons, the three elements . . . are more particularly, the trilogy of sacrifice, sacrificed, and sacrificer. Verse 12: The first clear mention of the four great social divisions."

We meet here, in the attempt to harmonize the concepts of creation and sacrifice, at once a cosmogony, a theogony and a soteriology. The mythical theme that creation cannot take place except from a living being who is immolated, is widely distributed. Such a being may be a primordial androgynous personage, a mother-goddess or a mythic Young Woman. At the root of the concept lies the fundamental idea that life can be born only from another sacrificed life. For his "origin" to be true, man must be able to refer to the immolation of life, a life resembling his own. From the history of religious traditions an illustration of this belief is found in the fact that people refer their belief's origin back to the immolation "in the blood of martyrs" of earlier believers. Also with regard to ideologies this would be the case.

Although the theory of sacrifice is not my concern in this work, a few observations would obviously not be out of place when *Puruṣa* is concerned. The hymn to *Puruṣa* has upset various theological quarters who, as Panikkar says, labeled the hymn pantheistic. *Puruṣa* reveals himself to be at once immanent, "this world", and transcendent, distinct from the cosmos and yet omnipresent in the cosmic realities. In addition, as *ātman* he inhabits the heart of man, implying identity between man's true self and the universal Being. He who "knows" will know himself to be united with Being, *to be* Being, with all creation and the cosmos. Since *Puruṣa* constitutes at once a cosmogony, a theogony and a soteriology, the question whether or not a real human sacrifice took place when the *ṛṣis* conceived of the hymn, is, for the purpose of our inquiry, irrelevant. According to the *Śatapatha Brāhmaṇa*, sacrifice (*yajña*) i.e. *Puruṣa*, is the very self of all mortal creatures and immortal beings.[160] *Yajña* is ratified as *deva-ratha* wherein all words find their true support.[161]

We must return to the myths. Once the seed of *Prajāpati*, who is *Puruṣa*, had fallen, rumours of creation and all kinds of activities abounded. It looks, in the myths, as if everyone must tell the tale. One hymn tells of the birth of *Aditi*,[162] the Waters and the Earth. The bowl of seed the gods protected with fire,[163] so the seed might not be polluted; "*mā dūṣa*", "pollute not".[164] From it was to be born *mānuṣa*, small man. Then all the animals were made: bovines, antelope-like animals, camel, ass and red beasts came forth.[165] They came from the ashes left over after the burning of the seed, surrounded as it was by the gods' fire guarding it against contamination. Then, as everything was heating up by the Creator's *tapas* and the gods' fire, *Rudra* kindles the Waters through *tapas*. Once life began to stir in them, plants grew from the contact between the Waters and the heat. They feed all living things on earth for they are part of Mother Earth. And now, after the burning of the seed, *Vāstu* was left, a wasteland. *Vāstu* is this earth with a psychological touch: the ground of existence, the place of tears and laughter, the house, the home of man. On it the Golden Seed had fallen and that is why we live here. It is on *vāstu* that human existence must be engineered against all odds.

And thus the thrust from the Uncreate into create was complete. For Vedic man

160. *SB*. 14.3.2.1: "*Sarveṣām vā eṣa bhūtānāṁ/Sarveṣām devānāmātmā yad yajñaḥ*".
161. *KausB*.7.7: "*deva-ratho vā eṣa yad yajñaḥ*".
162. *RV*. 10. 63.2.
163. *AB*. 3.4.
164. *AB*. 3.5.
165. *TMB*. 8.2.10; *AB* 3.34.

and for all those after him a marvel as well as a hazard.[166] *Puruṣa* is at once sacrificial victim and divine sacrifice, at once transcendent and immanent.[167]

The earth, the wasteland (*Vāstu*), becomes the place where the event of creation is being remembered; the site of the sacrifice (*vedi*).[168] Creation as the cycle of temporal time is, as part of *Puruṣa*, also a constitutive element of eternal time. Time in its temporality, however, is felt as a break with the notion of "flaw". Cosmic Man's dismembered being is the perfect Prestige of Origin of small man but in its temporality in human experience it "flaws", "limps". To actualize awareness of the "flaw" and "repair" it, a sacrificial site is set up. That location calls to mind the centre of Being and Significance. The sacred site is its symbolic *whole* presence. Such a centre may take various shapes such as temples and pilgrimages but the altar has been always a conspicuous one. Usually, in archaic traditions, an astrologer is consulted. He indicates the correct place for the altar. In Indian tradition it is the place above the head of the snake, the support of the world. A small wooden peg from the *Kadira*-tree is taken, together with a coconut, and driven into the ground to secure the snake's head.[169] Then, on the very spot, the act of Creation is repeated through sacrifice. That act projects man into the mythical epoch of "The Beginning" and thus the worlds are being held together (*lokasaṁgraha*).[170] Those who supervised conduct and order in Vedic society put the idea into logical thought by expressing it as follows: "*Puruṣa* is *Prajāpati*, *Puruṣa* is the year."[171] "Truly, I have created a pendant of myself,

166. The vexed question of the division of society into the four great groups, *Brāhmins, Ksātriyas, Vaiśyas* and *Śūdras*, is now often being interpreted as a social-theological fact, inspired by conditions prevailing at the time.

"The seers of the early Vedic period know nothing of caste. Delve as much as one might into the literature of this period, one discovers only classes, not castes. The elements which go to form castes were, however, present so that gradually a gulf was created between one order and another. For a long time, however, the conception of social segregation and untouchability was repugnant to the genius of the people who sought unity in variety and dissolved variety in unity. Each class was regarded as an integral part of the fabric of society": R.P. Masani quoted in R. Panikkar, *Hindu Society at Crossroads*, Bombay, Asia, 1955, p. 15. See also: Yogendra Singh, *Modernisation of Indian Tradition*, Thompson Press (India) Ltd., Delhi, 1973, p. 222. Singh writes: "We know that castes did not exist in ṚgVedic times. By 500 B.C. it was in recognisable working order. It has been in existence for perhaps three thousand years." p. 38.

167. R. Panikkar in *Myth, Faith and Hermeneutics*, pp. 311-317, discusses four Archetypes of the Ultimate which, when enumerated one after another, may sound a little awkward: Transcendent Transcendence, Immanent Transcendence, Transcendent Immanence and Immanent Immanence. The first is typified by the author as "masculine". The lofty segregation of God brings forth especially his Force, Power, Glory. Panikkar refers to the Hebrew Yahweh, the Christian Theos and the Islam Allah. The second type would be visibly feminine. "*Brahman* is transcendent because of its own and proper immanence", Panikkar writes. "It is the *matrix*, the *yoni* (R.P.) more like a mother nurturing from below than a command from above". One discovers the *brahman* that is in one or that one is. The third type is no longer masculine or feminine but rather neuter but nonetheless somehow personal, although in a nonanthropomorphic sense. Here, "One has to reduce to ashes everything one can conceive of or think; every idea or imagination of being has to disappear in order that pure nothingness (*śūnyatā*) may emerge, obviously not as something and much less as something else, but as the non-emergence of anything. *Nirvāṇa* is the supreme experience . . . that there is no transcendence other than immanence". The fourth type is the "radically terrestrial attitude. Immanence is not to be transcended . . . no escape from the factual human condition".

168. *RV*. 1. 164.35; 10. 110.4.

169. Margaret Sinclair Stevenson, *The Rites of the Twice-Born*, London, 1920, p. 354.

170. See the foregoing paragraph on "*Prajāpati*, the Lord of Generation".

171. *JaimB* 2.56; *SB*. 6.1.1.5.

that is the year", is *Prajāpati's* own thinking.[172] The joints (*parvam*) of the Cosmic Body are the five seasons of the year.[173] The original idea of sacrifice in the *Brāhmaṇaṣ* is to recreate and rejuvenate the disjointed cosmos. In mythical image it is portrayed by the gods assisting the exhausted *Prajāpati* after creation. Through sacrifice the world is being kept alive, blossoming, and integrated. The repetition of the cosmogony remains a constant demand.

When studying the myth of Origin it is important to remember that it is the *epic* mode of ontogenesis that requires interpretation, a mode of thought according to which the completed order *comes at the end* and not at the beginning. That, for man, is all the more a confirmation that the end towards which the Creator's activity is directed and in which man lives, is of necessity linked with the beginning. Cosmology completes theogony. What what there is to *say* about the world is the result of the *genesis* of the divine. That intention must be recaptured and understood in and also beyond the images of myth.

The idea of primordial man and sacrifice is a possession of not only the Indian tradition. In China, P'an-ku's head, arms and feet have given shape to the four corner-mountains. Sun and moon are his eyes and his breath is in the wind, his voice in the thunder. Likewise Ymir is the cosmic man of mythical Northern Europe, the mythical geography of which is derived from parts of the cosmic being. The sacrifice of origin happens in various ways. Odin, in European myths, they hung on the cosmic tree. This, later, became for Christians a most significant idea.[174] For cultures or religious traditions—its people as a whole as well as each particular individual—to be able to claim a perfect mythical origin, indeed an origin at all, it is of paramount necessity to offer sacrifice, "to repeat what has been done before", according to a primeval model. With the appearance of cosmic *Puruṣa* the Vedic Indian as well as the Hindu Indian today, has been able to cover the way back to the original fount. The sacrifice of remembrance, whatever form it takes, links man to the first spot of sacrifice aeons ago when *Agni*, intelligent Fire, claimed it. We, later men, are scarcely able to imagine the fathomless discovery and gift that first immolation of Cosmic Man, *Puruṣa*, meant for a people and its individuals in the beginning of human history. It is at once also a victory of the practical intellect and psyche of man to be able to interpret himself and his environment (*manasaḥ sattvam*) in relation to what is beyond. Indian myth has its own way in explaining the piercing into the timeless beginnings: it is the time which broke forth when *Rudra's* arrow left the bow and hit *Prajāpati* who was seen embracing his daughter *Uṣas*. It was at that moment that "time" (*kāla*) made its entry. The Uncreate broke into create. The wonder of the initial immolation—Origin, therefore, homage and healin—is being repeated in rite and ritual. It is time and again a new discovery presenting new possibilities of interpreting man and environment for those who *now* believe in the singleness of the universe and the human race. The mythical consciousness could well be a welcome visitor at conferences of importance for the future of the human race by looking at things as they "once were". A projection out of time may be of help to understand time itself.

---

172. *SB* 11. 1.6.13.
173. *SB*. 6.1.2.
174. Thomas Fawcett, *The Symbolic Language of Religion, an introductory study*, SCM Press Ltd., London, 1970, pp. 130-135.

Time in mere temporal movement is profane and hence "without meaning" unless it is, in the widest sense possible, infused by the sacred. The immolation of the Perfection is not to be understood as an incision into profane time. It is rather a renewal, a recharge of the whole. Once the way back to the Origin has been covered, the way forward from there extends into the furture by way of the present. Myth makes the Perfection of Origin movable. Myth is, in principle, not stuck for solutions and visions. Despair is not the mood of myth. It is the mood of man without myth. Schelling writes:

> "Mythology has not merely a religious but also a universal significance, for it is the universal process that is repeated in it; accordingly, the truth contained in the mythological process is a universal truth, excluding nothing. We cannot, as is commonly done, deny the historical truth of mythology, for the process through which it arises is itself a true history, an actual occurrence. Nor can we exclude physical truth from it, for nature is as necessary a period of transition in the mythological as in the universal process."[175]

The Origin's birth through sacrifice by which the co-existence of the opposites of eternal and temporal is made possible, makes man "approach the gods and become one of them."[176] A ritual death, then, is the preliminary condition for attaining to the presence of the gods. At the same time it secures a full life in this world. The *Vedas* and the *Upaniṣads* do not shy away from the forces of life. "Hinduism was not, at this state, a world denying religion", writes Zaehner.[177] The author thinks that under the influence of later classical Hinduism this world as *saṁsāra*, even though not evil in itself, became a place to be avoided.

In the cosmic primal event, wholeness is often portrayed by an androgyny, the bi-sexual being who creates by self-insemination. In the primal state there is neither male nor female, apart and distinct from each other like in the world of perception. In the primal world they are coalescent. *Puruṣa* emanates *Virāj*, the female principle of creation. She is the hypostasis of the universe as a *whole*. Then *Puruṣa* lets himself be born from her as world. Vedic mythical thought, before expressing the concept of divine two-in-oneness in metaphysical terms (*sat* and *asat*), worded it first in biological terms of bi-sexuality. The divinization of man has always been and still is a predominant motive in Hindu spirituality. Through difference-in-identity man has a footfold in eternal Being. Indian yogic and ecstatic tradition, also apparent in esotheric tāntrism, have contributed to the identification of the body with the macrocosm. Through *Śiva-Śakti* one is able to equate oneself with Cosmic Consciousness.[178] The holistic concept of *yantras*, *mantras* and *maṇḍalas* also contributed to the interiorization of the reality of sacrifice, the immolation into the whole of existence. This concept was to be one of the greatest spiritual syntheses of India to come to terms with the world of perception.[179]

---

175. Quoted in: Ernst Cassirer, *Mythical Thought*, p. 9.
176. *SB*. 7.3.1; 3.1.1.8.
177. R.C. Zaehner, *Hinduism*. p. 42.
178. Ajit Mookerjee-Madhu Khanna, *The Tantric Way, Art, Science, Ritual*, New York, 1977, p. 15.
179. Mention may be made here of the *vastu-puruṣa-maṇḍala*, a symbol of wholeness which functions as a paradigm of involution and evolution.

I now conclude our inquiry into the *Puruṣa Śūkta*. Mythical space, in contrast to the functional space in pure mathematics and related sciences, is *structural. Puruṣa* occupies a space in which all the component parts hinge on the original identity of the ultimate. The component parts, therefore, share original *identity of essence*. That explains why the year, a spacial dimension of time regulated by the luminaries in the sky, ceaselessly repeats the cosmogony, creation. Each day is one of the bricks of the altar of the year. Even in the words or sounds in space, the identity of essence is known, like in the holy *mantras*. Often, too, rites, rituals and behaviour are spatially related to society and to the divine at once. Marriage rites, for example, have a divine model. Husband and wife are assimilated to heaven and earth. "I am heaven", says the husband, " thou art earth".[180] Mythical space structures the couple and adorns husband and wife with a temporal-eternal dimension. Thus in mystical erotism the marital act is transformed into a hierogamy, linking the earth with heaven. Whenever myth finds an organically structured whole, like in *Puruṣa*, and hence a foothold in an origin, that origin is not static. It is a fount of life. It is believed and felt to be a fount of life. Those who cannot for one reason or another accept or imagine the mythical consciousness should here perhaps keep a respectful silence.

The methods of thought in myth tend to see the totality in the image and organization of the human body. I have earlier observed that, in terms of spatial orientation, everything for mythical thought is deducted from "behind" or "in front", the "above" and the "below" of man's intuition of his own body. The world is *Puruṣa*. Like any true myth, the *Puruṣa Śūkta* seeks through intuition of space to transform all the distinctions it postulates and model them into coherence. Coherence implies movement. It is a dialectic. There cannot be question of grafting given impressions, like the revelation of *Puruṣa*, onto the world of perception as if from outside. The characteristic achievement of the spirit at work in mythical consciousness begins much earlier than that. Only what is made, *is*. And what *is*, through having been made, cannot but originate from a principle of unity, from a *one*. At a given moment the spirit of myth has no more words for this marvel, unless by repeating it in yet another narrative, expressing the same content. It is, in my opinion, those who, when myth invites to silence, yet dare to speak who all too hastily accuse mythical consciousness of pantheism. For behind the doubtful phrase lies a silence, The Silence. As far as myth itself is concerned, it is not disturbed by the accusation. One might as well accuse it of panathropism. Behind that too lies The Silence. We may remember that *Prajāpati* gave preference to the spirit over the word when a quarrel broke out between them. It is for this reason that the supplicant is admonished to make an offering to *Prajāpati* in a whisper:

The space of *Puruṣa* is a significant symbol of Indian civilization. For India space is neither to pass through nor to remain in. Nor can one conquer it the way scientific man does. India has lived in space ever since its primal Origin. Space, for Indian thought, is not "outside". It does not separate things as if existing in an other space. Space is where *Puruṣa* is and where *Puruṣa* is, I, small man, am.

Finally, the Hindu's death, his ultimate sacrifice, begins at birth. As he moves through earthly life towards final realization, he moves further away from death.

180. *BU*. 6.4.20.

Death exudes no terror. For the non-plussed and sometimes baffled non-Hindu at a cremation-site in India, the music, flowers, incense and ghee, the apparent indifference on the part of bystanders and a certain casualness, at times cause scandal. Possibly the observer is, indeed, only an observer, unaware of *Puruṣa*.

Conclusion: Tapas—Discernment and Intelligent Concentration

Creation—the propulsion by the Uncreate into the create—enters man's perception and his history, in the world through cultic rite and ritual, thoughts and desires which surround man's human activities. Cult is a form of action, not merely a fixed enactment. Cultic activity presents a renewal of the cosmogony by active participation. The expected question will be: how? To be able to answer that question satisfactorily, we must, in the context of our inquiry after India's "Prestige of Origin" and its attitude towards it—*pravṛtti* or *nivṛtti* or their synthesis—, look again at Vedic cosmogony. We must see what role, if any, has been alotted to man in that cosmogony. What is man's role in creation? This role, if discovered, is what is celebrated in man's cult of creation, his *aimed-at* restoration of Wholeness, and the imagery, liturgy and thought accompanying it.

Creator-god *Prajāpati* organizes the world in accordance with *Dharma*, and *Ṛta*. From very early times *Varuṇa* had travelled with the Aryans and before *Prajāpati* had revealed himself as the Lord of Generation, *Varuṇa* had been known as intimately connected with *Ṛta*, the order in the world, at once cosmic, liturgical and moral.[181] Creation has been effected in conformity with *Ṛta*. Also the gods act according to the norms of *Ṛta*. *Ṛta* rules both the cosmic rhythms and moral conduct.[182] *Ṛta* implies inherent harmony and sense of proportion. It also implies the spontaneous rightness observable in the movement of the stars and in the other rhythms of nature. Above all, *Ṛta* is the property of *Sat*, Being. Hence, what emanates from *Sat* is infused with *Ṛta*.[183] *Ṛta*, therefore, is the regular, harmonious and fundamental structure, and nature of the universe. It underlies the cosmic, mundane and ritual events. From it *dhīti*, vision, arises. *Dhī*, "meditative or visionary thought", is connected with *manas*, mind or mental power.[184] Dharmic organization is thrown out of balance by sin, error and ignorance. In myth the inadvertent derangement or the deliberate reversal of *ṛta* or *dharma* is frequently illustrated. The repairwork of correcting *dharma* has in such cases been incorporated into the framework of the *avatāra*-myth. *Prajāpati* is committed to the preservation of *ṛta* and *dharma*. He is "the firstborn of *Ṛta*".[185] *Ṛta*'s opposite is *anṛta*.[186] *Anṛta* is in myth represented by the demons. The myth employs

181. George Dumézil, "Order, fantaisie, changement dans les penseés archaiques de l' Inde et de Rome", Revue Etudes Latines 32 (1957), p. 14. See also Part 2:4:7.

182. *Ṛta* is the past participle of the verb meaning "to fit". In later literature *ṛta* is replaced by the vocable "dharma". *Ṛta* can be derived from the root "r". to go. But it is not the same as the root "gam" which simply means "going". The root "r", clear from other derivations, meant a particular kind of going, "going straight or regularly or via a straight course". Hence *ṛta* in another derivative means "any settled point of time, fixed time, right time". (Monier Williams: Sanskrit-English Dict.) in: Sukumari Bhattacharji, *The Indian Theogony*, p. 29.

183. *RV.* 10.65.5. See Part 2:5:7.

184. Jan Gonda quoted in Jeanine Miller, *The Vedas*, p. 175, see *RV* 1.171.3.

185. *TB.* 2.8.1.3; *AV.* 12.1.61. M. Bloomfield, *A Vedic Concordance*, Delhi, 1964, reprint, p. 610.

186. *Ṛta* is opposed to *anṛta*, disorder, falsehood on the ethical plane. On the cosmic plane it is counterracted or even thwarted by *nivṛtti*, dissolution. Until such time, the gods are guardians of Order, Truth, *ṛtasya gopā* and even the rivers and all other waters and seasons, bodies in the

the motif of conflict between *Ṛta* and its contrary through the conflicts between gods and demons. In the *Śatapatha Brāhmaṇa* we are given an instance of this when, arrogantly, the demons thought: "In whom shall we sacrifice?". They sacrificed into their own mouths and were put to ruin *(anṛta)*. The gods, however, performed sacrifice to one another and *Prajāpati* surrendered himself to them.

Refusal to participate in the interdependent relationship between the worlds according to the idea of *Ṛta* will invariably lead to disaster. No wonder there arose quite a stir among the gods and men when, one day, *Agni* disappeared. It was known that the waters are his resting place. *Prajāpati* was requested to go in search of the loiterer. For how could the sacrifice be performed that regulated the relationship between gods and men? How could, without *Agni*, Fire, destruction be averted? It stands to reason that everyone was relieved when *Agni* was finally found, idling away his time sitting on a lotusleaf.

The cultic renewal of primary creation and active participation in it means, therefore,—for I owe a reply to the question how that is done—participation in the execution of *Ṛta* and *Dharma*. They guarantee, in religious language, the "Total Man". The *āśrama*-system, as we have seen, is based on this concept. *Ṛta* and *Dharma* enable man to grasp the permanence and validity of his specific situation of being in the world. The two concepts constitute the theoretical validity of participation in the reality of perception. Now, although *Ṛta* and *Dharma* establish the base of man's participation—it is even his duty—for Indian thought the world of perception remains an aggregate of images (*māyā*).[187] *Māyā*, the constant flux, stands for man in the way of attaining pure knowledge. In the midst of the dialectic of opposites, the Uncreate and the create, Indian thought hankers after an ideal: the union and fusion of both. Indian thought insists on concrete, experimental knowledge of the true situation of non-duality. It is by the conjunction of opposites, a transcending of the phenomenal world, that abolishment of all experience of duality is accomplished. In the realization of this ideal the Hindu experiences two polar and contradictory forces: that of *saṃsāra*, the cosmic process, and that of *nivṛitti*, the need to arrest this process as illusory flux. One transcends both by the knowledge that the ultimate nature of the phenomenal world (*saṃkleśa*) is identical with that of the absolute (*vyavadāna*). Indian thought, as I had occasion to observe in the paragraph on *Puruṣa*, knows no terror of death at the end of man's earthly sojourn. But one needs all one's insight and strength of conviction not to be overcome by a terror of life, that means to say, if one were not filled with conviction of the identity-in-difference with the Origin.

The return, during life, to the primordial state of non-differentiation is, in Indian thought, painted in a wide variety of images and cultic acts. In *Yoga*, as we have seen earlier, the effort towards unification of sun and moon, represented by the union of the in-breath (*prāṇa*) and the out-breath (*apāṇa*) illustrates the yearning after return to original Unity. Both in *Yoga* and *Tāntrism* the "drawing up of semen" as an afterimage of the shedding of *Prajāpati's* seed, is considered a paradoxical act beyond the normal physiological context. On the bodily plane the act of return ranks as

---

firmamant etc. flow in *ṛta*: *ṛtamarpanti sindhavaḥ*.

187. *Māyā*" from the root "*may*", to change. For a mythical representation of *māyā* see the myth of *Nārada* stepping into the lake, Part II:4:3, *Nivṛttidharma*.

transcendence of the phenomenal world and entry into freedom. Thus it is that the *ujāna sādhanā*, "going against the current", is an essential element in the *yogic* and *tāntric* vision. The *yogic* and *tāntric* tradition are but two paths in the Indian view to try and realize primordial wholeness in the midst of existential fragmentation. Underlying both is a concept of importance in the Indian view of reality. That concept is *tapas*.

Tapas, from the root "*tap*", to heat, to be boiling, is clearly documented in the *ṚgVeda*.[188] The notion of *tapas* belongs to an Indo-European heritage widely distributed in tales of heroism, shamanic feats and magico-religious activities. It is especially the Vedic people who inherited pre-historic techniques of "heating". Ritual "heating" acquired in India an unparalleled variety of depth of meanings from ancient times down to the present day. *Tapas* is creative on at once the cosmogonic, the religious, the physiological and the metaphysical plane. It is multivalent in a disseminated way over a multiplicity of images and symbols.[189] *Tapas* is a permeating, impregnating force. It ignites and kindles, first of all, a vision begotten by spiritual ardour based on the knowledge of Being.

> "By the knowledge of *Brahman*, by ardour (*tapas*) and contemplation he gets everlasting bliss, when "the man in the cart" is liberated from those things with which he was filled up and by which he was overcome, then he attains to conjunction with the real Spirit."[190]

Being's eternal ardour, the unimaginable Fire burning of Its Own, lights up, from the temporal end, man's path of return to the Origin. *Tapas*, says one author who discusses the concept in the context of intuition as the basis of Vedantic metaphysics, literally means concentration of energies in oneself.[191] The desire to know *Brahman* (*jijñāsā*) is embedded in more than mere curiosity. Striven after is a vision of *Brahman* through restraint and a sense of self-possession.[192] Consciousness arising from this discipline is in itself *tapas*, a penetrating intelligence not otherwise obtainable. The cosmic creator-god *Prajāpati* heats himself by *tapas*. That resulted in creation. In the world of the gods, their efforts are often being propelled by the irresistable drive of *tapas*. Thus *Rudra* as a young ascetic kindles the waters with his creative fervour and as a result life began to stir within them. It was *tapas* which made him create humans after his initial failure and when he had in anger torn out his phallus which had proved no use.[193] *Agni* is in the *Vedas* identified with *tejas*, a force comparable to *tapas*. He is "fiery splendour, energy, efficacy, majesty, supernatural power".[194]

---

188. See for example, *RV.* 8.59.6; 10-.136.2; 154.2.4. 167.1; 109.4.
189. A number of references to *tapas* one finds in 2.5.4(v) "*Prajāpati*, the Lord of Generation".
190. *MU* 4.4: "the man in the cart" — *rathitaḥ*. To be carted about used to be a traditional punishment and metaphysically significant as subjection of the free spirit by the senses; while conversely it is a royal procession when the spirit drives the vehicle in a direction it itself wills. "conjunction with the Spirit" — *ātman eva sāyujam upaiti*.
191. John Chettimatham, *Patterns of Indian Thought*, p. 99.
192. Here the notion of self-denial is implied. The ethical aspect of this self-denial is a means to self-realization, not an end in itself. *Tapas*, whether Brāhmiṇical or Buddhist, is never, a "penance", but in its disciplinary aspect a part of that training by which the petty self is subjected and assimilated to the Great Self. In Vedic symbolism it is the steeds that are brought under the driver's control.
193. *Mhb.* 10.17.20-24; *LP.* 1.86.92.
194. *AV.* 7.89.4.

In whatever context, such as the magical, the shamanic, the erotic, the contemplative ardour of love or the creative imagination, *tapas* lies at the origin of things and moods and movements. It also sustains a process and brings it to its destined end. *Tapas*, as I said earlier, has been known from proto-history but the Orient, and the Indian genius in particular, has elaborated and articulated the notion to a high degree. For our purpose, which is to try and retrace the way back to the "Prestige of Origin" of Vedic and later Hindu tradition, we have no need of inquiring further into the shamanic or magical features of *tapas*. In any case, the true pilgrim on earth, be he a *yogi*, a *tapasvin* or an ordinary citizen doing his daily duties, is advised to resist the temptation of such powers and overcome the attractive lure to try and acquire the power to fly or to become invisible, if he is to reach the perfect non-conditioned state of *samādhi*. In him must rather shine the quiet brilliance of *śānti*, tranquillity, peace of soul and absence of passion of whatever kind.[195] The Hindu's life is a continuous pilgrimage of re-integration, like a stream which has its fount in one lake and after coursing through valleys and plains, finally finds rest in another. Yet, both waters are fed by the oceans encircling the earth. By doing what the gods did, man is given a sufficient and clear directive as to how to conduct his life. In the *Vedas Prajāpati* assists the gods in a positive way by revealing to them the knowledge necessary for the correct performance of ritual, the cult through and in which the basic attitudes to life are mirrored. The gods, however, are also taught in a negative way. When the demons are granted a boon they are effectively stopped from accumulating any greater intensity of *tapas*.[196] *Brahmā* in this instance showed himself "composed of *dharma*", absolutely impartial. *Dharma* ought to be considered an absolute norm of behaviour. In the myths one notices that *Viṣñu* and *Siva* are more flexible. Active more in the realms of *pravṛtti* and *nivṛtti*, they appear to understand more of the pinge of the human predicament. Like *Prajāpati, Brahmā's* motivation for assisting the gods is his commitment to the preservation of *Dharma*. *Brahmā* too, when he later takes his place of importance among the gods, is "*dharma* embodied".[197] A little harsh at times, he always appears to have chosen the correct path. He refuses to grant immortality to the demons for reasons that are understandable but his express aim was that the gods be successful with the sacrifice in their relationship with man. For the sacrifice bestows some kind of immortality upon the sacrificer in the sense that it breaks the continuum of repeated death. Demons could never have been granted immortality. That would have overturned the order of *Ṛta*. *Tapas* belongs to the phenomenology of the spirit even though it can operate in the realm of physio-psychology. It does not necessarily involve physical austerities including that of *brahmacharya*, sexual continence, but, as Heinrich Zimmer says, "may refer to mental or vocational activities". "The heat is that of our inner self (*antarātman*). The glow is that of our inward Sun."[198]

---

195. D.J. Hoens, *A Contribution to Ancient Indian Religious Terminology*, The Hague, 1951, p. 177. *Śānti* from the root "*śam*" which originally included the meaning of extinguishing fire, anger, fever or heat provoked by demons.
196. *Mhb.* 3.258.21 where *Brahmā* insists that *Rāvaṇa* and his brothers stop performing *tapas* before being granted a boon.
197. *SB.* 2.3.43.31; *Mhb.* 12.175.34.
198. *JaimUB* 3.32.4. See: Heinrich Zimmer, *Indische Mythen und Symbole, Vishnu, Shiva und das Rad der Wiedergeburten*, Diederichs Gelbe Reihe, 1981, p. 130.

I would like to draw attention to an important characteristic of *tapas* apparent in early Vedic religious tradition and which continues its impact in later Hinduism. The special feature of *tapas* which I wish to highlight here is perhaps best described as *the element of assault* in *tapas*. The "assault" in *tapas* envisages to force a solution to the problem of *saṁsāra* by hard disciplinary measures with a view to acquiring intelligence and power of insight in the human condition. Not only at the temporal end of being, man's world, this "assault" is apparent; the gods, too, appeal to *tapas* to see their plans carried out. The ardour of spirit and the quest for Truth with which his God endowed Mahātmā Gāndhi and with which he cooperated, engendering in himself an extraordinary power of mind and will, resulted in the wresting of India's independence, through *ahiṁsā*, itself a form of *tapas*, from a world dominating power. In contemporary history this feat is one of the most glaring examples of what *tapas* is able to achieve. Indians fight for their rights or what they might think are their rights, by taking recourse, like anywhere else, to strikes. But Indians often strike by organising *satyāgraha*, implying vigils and fasts, even fasts unto death. Hunger-strikes and round-the-clock vigils are considered a respectful but effective means of assault on the powers that be. The austere Indian displays an element of *tapas* not always apparent during similar strikes elsewhere.

The feature of "assault" in *tapas* has been, as I said, a property of not only Indian religious traditions. All traditions glorify their saints and mystics who forced the heavens and received grace and vision in abundance. Man is not naturally attracted by magic so that any accusation to that effect with regard to the element of "assault" in *tapas* should be carefully worded. *Tapas* deserves first of all a sympathetic interpretation. When India's vision of reality is concerned, that kind understanding would be much more in line with its traditional vision of the human condition and that of the gods. A peculiar characteristic of religious language and behaviour is to conceive of the physical world as a fruitful source of symbol, symbolic action and cult. To religious man light and darkness, rivers, seas, mountains, rain, breeze and storm, sunshine etc. communicate the meaning of life. This must have been especially true of so-called pre-scientific religious man before Plato made the effort—the first we know of in recorded human history—, to abstract perception from the perceiver. Physical phenomena are by religious man responded to in a personal way. Contrary to physical science which excludes the personal model and observes nature "apart" from its existential significance to make it subservient and of use to man, religious motivation feels in the physical the touch of life. The breath of "structure" pervades the physical world. In religious vision physical environment is encountered as a "you". It is a souled life. *It is through the symbols man receives from the souled physical world that he learns to speak the language of total man*. Religious man does not speak in formulas, he speaks in language of structure rather than in that of function.

It is the impulse in the physical world, call it *tapas*, which for religious man and for mythical consciousness constitutes the feeling of unity with the very Origin of that impulse. Hence there arises an assimilation of the physical-temporal and the eternal, the primeval mode. This very assimilation is itself *tapas* for it involves concentrated understanding of that unity wherein the eternal and temporal relate to each other as mutually explicative. In Indian thought this relationship is one of unity-in-difference. Rather than indulge in accusations of pantheism, I would prefer to think of the Indian effort to grasp the whole of reality in terms of the excellence of *tapas* as "assault", that is, to break from fragmentation into unity. Then man, in his turn, becomes a creator. In the *Śatapatha Brāhmaṇa* it is said: (the Fire-sacrifice)

> "The true *Agnihotra* is, in fact, not a rite to be merely performed at fixed seasons, but within you daily, after the primordial pattern of the thirty-six thousand *Arka*-fires that were of mental substance and mentally edified by the first sacrificers; mentally were they edified, mentally were the cups of *Soma* drawn, mentally they chanted... These Fires, indeed, are knowledge-built; and for the Comprehensor thereof all beings built up these Fires, even while he is asleep".
>
> "by knowledge they ascend to where desires have migrated; it is not by rewards nor by ignorant ardour (*tapas*)... but only to comprehensors that the world belongs.[199]

By means of the Unity-in-differentiation *tapas* is the common property of the religious experience of the entire Vedic and Hindu tradition. It is not merely the prerogative of ascetics and ecstatics possessing world-consciousness. Theirs is a consciousness which differs from that of others only in degree, not in essence.

Cult and its entourage such as offerings, fasts, vigils, prayers, partial or total abstention from sexual contact, and sacraments (*saṁskāras*) is the physical exteriorization of interior *manas*, force of mind, Eternal Mind, by mean of *tapas* regenerating itself. Thus arises the dialectic between heaven and earth. All Hindu rites and rituals express, on the level of action, the desire to remake the world, repeatedly, and reunite *Prajāpati's* scattered members. The cult is repeated in continuous sacrifice in one form or another in order to restore wholeness to the world and the relationship between the world and eternity. In a transmutation of the myth of *Prajāpati* where he is said to be exhausted after his creative but divisive act[200], *tapas*, from man's end, supplies re-enforcement. The re-enforcement ultimately arises from consciousness and from a concentration on self and The Self.[201]

Closely connected with *tapas* are *yoga* and *tantra* experience. We left these disciplines to orientate ourselves first in a more general way to *tapas*. Like other aspects of Indian thought, these disciplines too, wellknown for their ex-professo practice of *tapas* in the form of physio-psychological austerities, present the foreign student of Indian thought with the proverbial bewildering matter for reflection. In India ascetic practices developed to a degree unknown elsewhere. A very complex system of thought and ideals matured with regard to the notion of *tapas*. A deeper understanding of this notion will prove useful, if not necessary, for our investigation of

199. *SB*. 10.5.4.16: "These Fires are knowledge-built" - *vidyācita eva*. "all beings" i.e. "all the powers of the soul" - *sarvāṇi bhūtāṇi*. "to where desires have migrated - *parāgatāḥ*. "not by rewards nor by ignorant ardour" - *dakṣiṇābhiḥ - avidvaṁsaḥ tapasvinaḥ*. *SB*. 10.4.2.31 declares: "Whosoever as a Comprehensor performs this sacred work, or even one who is a comprehensor (but does not actually perform the rites, puts together again this (divided) *Prajāpati*, whole and complete". Again in *SB*. 13.1.3.22: there is a distinction between those merely "seated at a sacrificial session" (*sattrasadaḥ*) and those "seated in reality" (*satisadaḥ*). The latter "are seated among the very gods "(*satisu devatāsu sīdantah*).

200. *SB*. 8.6.1.10; *TS*. 8.4.2.1.; 6.3.4.7; 6.3.10.2. See also Ananda K. Coomaraswamy, *Hinduism and Buddhism*, New York, 1943, p. 19ff.

201. John Chettimatham, *Patterns of Indian Thought*, p. 99.

the symbol of *Āpaḥ*, the Waters, in the following part of the book. Time and again, as we shall see, *tapas* asserts itself either in opposition to or in conjunction with the Waters.

Yogic and *tāntric* influence on Indian thought remains alive till the present day. Remarkable performance by *yogis* and *tāntrics* are the ordinary run of things. What austerity is able to achieve we are told, for example, in the story of *Vrātya* of the *Atharva Veda* two millennia ago.[202] Perhaps he was one of a consecrated group of peers dressed a little conspicuously in black, wearing a turban and carrying a lance and a bow.[203] Whoever these *Vrātyas* may have been, their sacrifice of the inner self (*vratyastoma*) was accommodated in the cult by the ritualistically inclined Brahmins, unable to resist the truth of the *Vrātyas'* earnest endeavour. The wandering *Vrātya*, so the telling goes, obtained powers through his transforming vision and ardour of spirit. One day, while roving as usual, he faced *Prajāpati*. At once *Prajāpati* saw the Gold within himself. He became aware that he held the Golden Germ, (*Hiraṇyagarbha*).[204] Propelled towards generation, *Prajāpati* brought out the Gold within himself. It spilt from him like seed and fell on the earth, the temporal end of the stream of Golden Seed. It is in that Golden Stream that Vedic man found himself, paradoxically, fragmented on the wasteland of earth (*vāstu*). This is the Hindu's heritage upto the present day. The propelling force of the Golden Seed is still within him. Like *Vrātya*, later *yogīs* and *tāntrics*, no matter their place of prominence in everyday life in India, remain resourceful personalities on the fringe of society. In as far as their progressive *dharma* requires it, it is their vocation. They have a message. Another aspect of their marginal existence in Indian society is that they are being put there. Sound of mind though they are, they are considered eccentrics. That is what they intend to be. They refuse identification with the centre of cult inasfar as it may be governed by ritual and sacrificial orthodoxy. Their ritual interiorization implies, besides mental prayer, a profound assimilation of physiological functions to the life of the cosmos.[205] This feat is pan-Indian and traces of it are to be found in the *Vedas*. "Strictly speaking, however, it is only in tāntrism and largely because of the contribution of *yogic* techniques, that it acquired the coherence of a "system", writes Eliade.[206] I have alreay drawn attention to the homologue of the physical body with the cosmos in the paragraph on the *Puruṣa Śūkta*. It effects the non-dual cosmic consciousness when no longer any support is needed (*samādhi*). The interwoven being has broken through a shell, that of the outer cult. Such holy intent, which may also take the form of *bhakti*, possesses the force of assault. Ultimately it is the intended break-through into cosmic consciousness. Thus it is that the gods—and who else could be expected to be the first to intend cosmic consciousness?—gained immortality through sacrifice as well as by their austerity. It was *Indra* who forced the heavens by *tapas*.[207] *Tapas* is itself sacrifice. When the heat of ardour burns in the form of consciousness of Being, then *tapas* in its turn, being total prayer, makes the physio-psychological functions replace the ritual sacrifice,

202. *AV*. 15.
203. *AV*. 15.2.1.
204. *AV*. 15.1.1.2.
205. Mircea Eliade, *Yoga, Immortality and Freedom*, pp. 111 - 114.
206. *Op. cit.*, p. 112.
207. *RV*. 10.167.1; *TB*. 3.12.31.

libations and objects of the outer cult. Hence we find religious exercises such as the *prāṇāgnihotra*, the "sacrifice of respiration."[208]

The notion of interiorization of the sacrifice has always been a corrrective influence on Brahminical orthodoxy. Being foreign to the recognized canonical liturgy, it was and still is not always given a hearty welcome. Its influence on orthodoxy is two-fold. On the one hand, it launches an attack on the theological supremacy of the sacerdotal class, in our case the Brahmins. On the other hand, orthodoxy, more or less willingly, finds itself with no other option but to accommodate and integrate foreign elements and new visions which often prove to be agents of theologicai and spiritual renewal. Resistance on the part of orthodoxy was nonetheless unavoidable. *Manu* says, warning the Vedāntic: "If he keeps both his organs and his consciousness under subjection, he can attain his ends without further tormenting his body by *Yoga*."[209] *Śaṅkara* too writes a note of warning. "*Yoga*", he says, "leads to the acquirement of extraordinary powers but the highest beatitude cannot be obtained by the road of *Yoga*."[210] Vedāntic metaphysicians usually prefer a more rationalized spirituality to esotheric disciplines. But these practices and doctrines nevertheless did find their way into valid orthodoxy. In the *Vasiṣṭha Dharma Sūtra* we read: "Neither... through the daily recitation of the *Veda* nor through offering sacrifices can the twice-born reach that condition which they attain by the practice of *yoga*."[211]

The dialectic of rejection, accommodation, assimilation, and absorption from the earliest beginnings of Vedic times until the present day, has adorned Hinduism with a tremendous wealth in the field of spirituality, psychology, physiology, mystical experience, metaphysical adventure and ritual activity. Hinduism has also known a lively hermeneutic and the interpretation of the *smṛti* and *srūti* may change according to circumstances. It is sometimes alleged that this is Hinduism's strength as well as its weakness. Its survival in the service of man's search for his true Origin and his proper place on earth will to a greater or lesser extent depend on how far Hinduism will be able to accommodate modern history. This, of course, is, as we know from other major religious traditions, no mean task.

To conclude this second part of the book on the functional antecedents in the *Vedas* with regard to the mutual relationship between the value systems of *pravṛtti* and *nivṛtti* in Indian philosophical-religious thought, I would like to make an observation referring to India's power of concentration on the self (*tapas*) and The Self (*Sat*) in connection with the presence of Christianity and Islam on its soil. Christianity and Islam in India have always feared the assimilative power of absorption in Hinduism. Hindu tradition, in its turn, shows little sympathy for the unaccommodating doctrinal systems of Christianity and Islam. The fact that it has absorbed little of either is partly due to psychological reasons. Religions of colonizers often have the connotation of ungodliness in the minds of those colonized. Until these religions themselves broaden their theological insight, starting from the base provided by anthropology and philosophy, and enrich themselves with the power of *tapas*, one of India's great features

208. *VaikS*. 2.18.
209. *Manusmṛti* 2.100 tr. G. Bühler, *The Laws of Manu*, Sacred Books of the East, Vol. XXV. p. 48.
210. Commentary on the Vedānta-Sūtras, tr. G. Thibaut, *The Vedānta Sūtra with Śankara's Commentary*, SBE. Vol. XXXIV, p. 223. 298.
211. *VDS*. 25.7. tr. G. Bühler, *The Sacred Laws of the Āryas*, SBE., vol. xiv, p. 125.

of identity, and until Hinduism begins to view these religions as equally valid paths towards self, realization in The Self, India will face the constant threat of communalism. A heavy burden and a great challenge rests upon the shoulders of religious leaders to take up the dialogue and forget differences which in every day life may well have been already obliterated. Flogging a dead horse often destroys the dialogue. If, in the context of intuition as a basis for thought, the descriptive definition of *tapas* as concentration of energies in oneself, is valid, then there is, by analogy, a unity-in-difference among all religious traditions as much as there is a unity-in-difference between the believing Hindu and his Perfection of Origin. Christianity, Islam and Hinduism equally draw from a rich heritage of mysticism. Thus I pray with the Hindu, for it is his tradition we are studying, that *Agni*, Fire, bestow upon all India's people as *tapasvins* "the heat of the head", and bless the country with a clear vision.

PART III

THE SYMBOLIC PREGNANCE OF *ĀPAḤ*, THE WATERS

Chapter 6

PRESENTATION OF THE CASE : *PRAVṚTTI*, *NIVṚTTI*, AND *ĀPAḤ*, THE WATERS

Man, be it in temporal time or in the archaic depth of his psyche, is *already a man of division*. Hence the myth can only be an intentional restoration or reinstatement and is in that sense *already symbolical*. To gather scattered fragmentation into some wholeness, man needs "The Pure Water of Understanding" (*yathodakaṃ śuddham*):

"As water descending on mountain crags
wastes its energies among the gullies,
so he who views things as separate
wastes his energies in their pursuit.
But as pure water poured into pure
becomes the self-same - wholly pure
so too becomes the self of the silent sage,
of the one, O *Gautama*, who has understanding.[1]

Symbolization of the world discloses its value and meaning when it no longer operates at random but must struggle and overcome obstacles.[2]

We have arrived at the heart of our investigation. The hypothesis to be tested is the following: In the Vedic-Indian world-view the concepts of *pravṛtti* and *nivṛtti* reveal the reality of man's existential predicament because of his specific mode of being in and of the universe as a creature endowed with intellect, the sumtotal of *vāc*, *prāṇa*, and *manas*. Man's existence is founded upon a balance between two contrasting powers: eternity and finitude. Man, being body and soul, is the concretion of those two. He represents both. Man is a *double entity*, but *one reality* of eternal *jñāna* and fleeting *māyā*. The *possibility* of a balance between the contrasting powers of eternity and finitude is successfully shown in the primary symbol of *Āpaḥ*, the Waters, as Vedic-Indian thought perceives of it through its receptive mythical consciousness. That consciousness of "*Āpaḥ*" and its derivatives in the Vedic-Indian mind is the other complementary side of its rational-intellectual admission that the fundamental law of the Universe cannot be arrived at through only the rational mind.

---

1. *KathU*. 4. 14 - 15.
2. The pathology of speech and action give us a standard by which to measure the distance separating the organic world and the world of human culture, the sphere of things and the sphere of the spirit. The aphasiac or apracitic seems to have been thrown one step backward along this path which mankind had to open up by slow, steady endeavour. Pathological behaviour has in a sense lost the power of the intellectual impulse which forever drives the human spirit beyond the sphere of what is immediately perceived or desired. Pathological behaviour throws a new light on the general movement of the spirit. See: Ernst Cassirer, "Pathology of the Symbolic Consciousness" in: *The Philosophy of Symbolic Form*, Vol. 3, *The Phenomenology of Knowledge*, pp. 205 - 277.

That then could be said to be the thesis of this book. The experience of the Waters corroborates man's understanding of himself as struggling (*saṁsāra*) at this end of all intentionality and experience (*idam*) as distinct from "That" (*tat*)" at the other transcending end. What is more, this would seem to be the ***sole truth*** about man except that the struggle is not a doom.[3] The path of the "wise waters" lies in the realization of essential oneness with the ocean. Their course, however, is through crags and gullies, but lifegiving. At this temporal end of *tat*. Being, man is a creative, active, and unique centre of the universal life-force.

That excellence of man invites, a few observations with regard to myth and the Vedic-Indian concept of sacrifice *yajña* (....). The distance between experience and intention has been recognized by authors who have attributed to myth a biological role of protection against anxiety.[4] Myth-making harbours in itself an antidote to existential distress because the man of myth is already an "unhappy" consciousness. For him, unity, conciliation and re-conciliation are things to be spoken of and acted out, precisely because, as I earlier observed, *they are not given.* Mythical awareness and myth-making imply participation in the Universe's totality as signified rather than experienced.

It is here that the Indian concept of *yajña,* sacrifice, offers comfort to the experience of a "deficiency" of totality by the mythical consciousness. Sacrifice is being praised as the *nābhi,* navel, of the world. In the Vedic tradition a sacrifice is not only the central act of religious belief. It also is the supreme principle of all that is. In the Vedic perspective *yajña* is elevated to a world-principle. V.S. Agrawala writes:

> "....*yajña* forms a complete theoretical statement of the metaphysical viewpoints of the *ṛṣis* and their practical application to human life. If *yajña* is properly understood, everything else in the *Veda* may be comprehended as a matter of course."[5]

Yajña represents the universal creative activity. It is the source of all creation, that of living beings as well as of inanimate existence. The doctrine of the *nābhi* is an important Vedic concept and often mentioned in the *Ṛg-Veda* where the unmanifest source of everything is referred to as *nābhi* and its manifest form as *bandhu.*[6] The former is the father and the latter the mother. Whereas the manifest is mortal because conditioned, the unmanifest is immortal, unconditioned as it is by time and space. Since *yajña* is the navel of the universe, the *nābhi* becomes visible as *bandhu*[7] when man performs sacrifice and thus reaches the ***highest possible*** stage of re-integration. The *Śatapatha Brāhmaṇa* says:[8]

"Navel means centre and the centre is safe from danger". Whether in the

---

3. See Part III:8 "*Karma,* a cosmic pilgrimage" and the conclusion to Part III.
4. In Part I:7:4. "Athens, Jerusalem, and Mount Kailāśa." I have referred to Gusdorf's opinion - and taken a critical view of it - , as if the mythical consciousness is "the spontaneous form of being in the world" at the same time a biological protective role. The mythical consciousness rather is one of man's awarenesses.
5. V.S. Agrawala, *Vedic Lectures, Proceedings of the Summer School of Vedic Studies,* B.H.U. Varanasi, May-June, 1960. p. 146.
6. *RV.* I. 164.33: *"Dyauḥ pitā janitā nābhir-atra, bandhur-me mātā prithivī mahīyam."*
7. *RV.* I.164.35 : *"Ayam yajño bhuvanasya nābhi."* In another text it is said: "the sacrifice is our father.... our Manu": *RV.* 10.100.5: *"yajño manuh pramatirnah pita".*
8. *SB.* 1.1.2.2. see also *SB.* 8.7.3.21: "all beings are settled under sacrifice" it being the all sustaining principle, *SB* 9.2. 3.27.

outward cult or in the interiorized *yajña* in the inner of man's heart, the navel is understood to be the birthplace of all existence where heaven and earth meet.[9]

In manifesting the purely symbolic character of the relation of man to the lost totality, the myth receives, from the theoretical viewpoint with regard to *yajña*, a solace against distress. *Yajña* signifies the emergence of dynamic activity out of the womb of stillness. In the Vedic-Indian view Water is the universal substratum, always in the state of perfect equilibrium where all forces come to rest. It is for the sake of creation that this equilibrium is "disturbed" by time. In the myths this stormy condition is referred to as the churning of the oceans or other symbolical movements such as dance, propulsion, vibration.[10]

By speaking in myth and acting out in cult those happenings of the Waters, man intends to gain a foothold in the totality of Being. Being is, on the one hand, indeterminable (*nirguṇa*), on the other, it is the creative source of all determination (*saguṇa*). The indeterminable Silence and the creative Eloquence are two equally real dimensions of ultimate Reality. Man is the most unique word of the creative eloquence of Being and it is in myth that man attempts his ultimate reply. As Coomaraswamy aptly says:

> "Myth embodies the nearest approach to Absolute Truth that can be stated in words."[11]

That approach to absolute truth by the mythical awareness is corroborated by the metaphysical endeavour of Indian Philosophy. The Śankarite School does not reduce change and flux of life to a pure illusion of the senses. It considers constant change as a particular type, order or level of reality: a pragmatic type of reality (*vyavahāric sattvā*) but real from the point of view of primal ignorance (*māyā* and *avidyā*). Creation cannot be said to fool man. It is man's home, a place of culture and civilization in the making. With *Kṛṣña*, man participates in the eternal battle for righteousness (*dharmayudda*). Thinkers like Tagore, Vivekānanda, Gāndhi and Aurobindo all appealed to the main-spring of Vedic thought for a profound spiritual synthesis, a comprehensive philosophy of life, as the foundation for integrated living. The Indian mythical awareness projecting man as *one reality* promotes such living. We discussed this earlier when reviewing the Indian attempts at a reconciliation between *pravṛtti* and *nivṛtti*. One of the issues was if the Greek myth of the exiled soul could be said to be applicable to Indian thought. That myth, quite solitary, has played a considerable role in Western culture. It presided, if not over the birth, at least over the growth of Greek philosophy. It divides man into soul and body and concentrates on the destiny of the soul which is seen as coming from "elsewhere", and straying here

9. See: J. Gonda, *Aspects of early Viṣñuism*, Utrecht. 1954, p. 87. *Yajña* signifies the emergence of order from chaos. This is, besides its religious significance, the constant activity of the human psyche.
10. The myths of the churning of the ocean and the dance of *Śiva* will be found in the symbolism of *Āpaḥ*. Both myths became in time clear images of the activity of the Divine and its involvement with man. During my studies I have failed to find any literature with regard to the theological incarnational aspects of the Divine hidden in these myths. *Śiva Natarāj*, the Cosmic Dancer, is wellknown. Among the many publications I mention only one: Ananda K. Coomaraswamy, *The Dance of Shiva, On Indian Art and Culture*, Sagar Publications, New Delhi, 1982.
11. A.K. Coomaraswamy, *Hinduism and Buddhism*, Philosophical Library, New York, 1943, p. 33.

below. The cosmological background of other myths was often forgotten on account of it. The Greek myth of the exiled soul — which betrays a connotation of "punishment" — seeks to transpose all *anthropological* dualism and rationalize it. I could now add the observation, left unmentioned before, that for Greek and later Western divinity — another classical name for theology — body and soul are not only two different entities but two different and distinct realities. The Greek myth of the exiled soul needed its invention to make it a paradigm of an originally pure being "out there", but here and now, in man, forced into a " mixture". This Greek adventure of "purification" is related to the myth of tragedy — the wrathful divine — which we also discussed. This is not the place for an argument with regard to the philosophy and theology of guilt and guilt-culture, important though these concepts are in human culture and behaviour.

The Greek "exiled" and "straying" soul would be hard to find in the Indian myth. If an analogue must be found inasfar as the symbolic concept of "alienation" is concerned, we would have to turn, in the Indian context, to the realms of *māyā* and *avidyā*. But again, those concepts involve the whole of the human being. Moreover, in the dialectic between the Uncreate and the create, Indian thought is free to search for the union of both and that union *can be achieved* — be it conditioned — in the experienced created human condition by the attainment of consciousness of *Brahman*. If in the Indian world-view " *Brahman* is this whole world",[12] human existence comes to express an "already moral purification" — katharsis — by the understanding acceptance of the *reasonability* of body-and-soul for the simple fact that man *is* body-and-soul. Man cannot be guilty of what he constitutionally is nor can he be made to suffer moral blemish or stigma on account of it.[13] Inasfar as myth can be said to be the self-representation of man, the Indian mythical view of man does not consider him as just "soul", nor does it reduce man to the dead weight of the "body".

For the self-representation of Vedic-Indian man as portrayed in the myth, we will turn to what we have earlier discovered to be myth's *exploratory* strength. That will be pointing in the direction of speculation that follows it. This we are able to do because we have treated the myth as a rehandling of the fundamental symbols elaborated in man's living experience in this world and the Universe: loss of and a yearning for totality, quest for the beginnings, precarious balance, sense of alienation. The myth *anticipates speculation* only because it is already *word*, an interpretation, a hermeneutics of the primary symbols in which the prior consciousness of loss of and yearning for totality gave itself form. With regard to philosophical speculation, therefore, we must now recall our earlier professed maxim: at one point our principle of *orientation* becomes a principle of *limitation*. We ought now to suspend our theorizing. In other words: uptil now we have thought about myth—now/ myth will think about and for us.

That the myth gives rise again, in its turn, to thought is a consequence of the fact that it itself interprets other symbols. It is thus that we shall seek to understand the myths of *Āpaḥ*, The Waters, reserving for a later investigation — in the conspectus and conclusion — the thoughts which the myths and the symbols *evoke*.

12. *CU.* .14.1: *"sarvam khalvidam Brahmā"* See: *Maitri Up. 4.6* where it is stated: *"Brahmā khalvidam va va sarvam"*.
13. Although an extremely important subject, the question of impurity, defilement and sin must regrettably be left undiscussed.

For the purpose of our investigation into the characterology of the primary symbol *Āpaḥ* and its successful suggestive handling of man's precarious situation between eternity and finitude — *pravṛtti* and *nivṛtti* — we may content ourselves that our typology of the Indian myths ought here not to be confined to a further attempt at classification; we must go beyond the statics of classification to a dynamism that has as its task the discovery of the hidden life of the myths and the interplay of their secret affinities. This dynamism must reveal the way for a philosophic recapture of the myths and the truths they speak.

Here then are *Āpaḥ* the Waters of Life (*ūrje dadhātana*):

"O Waters, source of happiness,
pray give us vigor so that we
may contemplate the great delight.
You like loving mothers are
who long to give to children dear.
Give us of your propitious sap.

On your behalf we desire, O Waters.
to assist the one to whose house you send us-
you, of our life and being the source.

These Waters be to us for drink;
divine are they for aid and joy.
May they impart to us health and strength;

You Waters who rule over precious things
and have supreme control of men,
we beg you, give us healing balm.

Within the Waters, *Soma* has told me,
remedies exist of every sort
and *Agni* who brings blessing to all.

O Waters, stored with healing balm
through which my body safe will be,
come, that I long may see the sun.

Whatever sin is found in me,
whatever wrong I may have done,
if I have lied or falsely sworn,
Waters, remove it far from me.

Now I have come to seek the Waters.
Now we merge, mingling with the sap.
Come to me, Agni, rich in milk!
Come and endow me with your splendor !"[14]

14. *RV*. 10. 9.1-9 in Raimundo Panikkar, *The Vedic Experience*. In verse 1 "vigor" - "*ūrj*" is invigorating and nourishing sap, hence inspiriting, giving spirit, life. Later commentators say that the great

The Symbol of Water

In the beginning things undoubtedly began. That true but dull and colourless statement leaves most people unsatisfied. It neither excites nor gratifies the quest by the human awareness for the whole of the beginnings and their significance. The statement is almost an offense to what we know and feel we are. It almost sounds as if the statement were not true. It does not answer the resounding "why?" and "what?" in the whole of man when he questions the idea of being. Man knows from experience that dawn is not the day and that birth is not the whole of life.

The true beginning are a *be-coming* which is an authentic *coming* to *be*, an unfolding. No one is content to see the lotus in the potential of its stalk. Any thought about the beginnings thrusts us into what follows. Here is what the Vedic *ṛṣi* thought :

> "In the beginning, to be sure, nothing existed, neither the heaven nor the earth nor space in between. So Nonbeing, having decided to be, became spirit and said: "Let me be!"[15] He warmed himself further and from this heating was born fire. He warmed himself still further and from this heating was born light."

The dawn developing into day or birth flowering into life unfold the credentials of reality: anything is possible with the really real that has *come to be*. Thus it is with the beginnings[16] unfolding into the "began". They open up for man the realms and dimensions of time and space, the possibility of movement. Joy as well as terror are made possible by the opening up of the beginnings. One star moves with a fiery trail to another, the stem moves slowly into its flower and one lover approaches another. But likewise one nation moves against another with deadly intent or one man steals the food of another or moves in front, obsessed by money or power. Mankind knows all about the beginnings once they began! Indian thought often likes to think about the expressed beginnings in terms of warming up, heat, *tapas*, in whatever form.[17]

All that, however, concerns the beginnings once they began. Those are the beginnings man knows and is able to handle in some way. They are man's immediate ambience: he needs them, wants them and thinks them so he may be man, whether in success or in failure, in certainty or in doubt.

But what about the beginnings themselves "before" the actual beginning? We cannot say "before" the beginning without falling into contradiction. The beginning is nothing but the beginning. It has no "before". It is beginningless. No matter what way

---

delight is *Brahman*. See Panikkar p. 119-120.

15. *TB*. 2.2.9.1-2 in *ibid*., p. 49. *"tad asat eva sanmano 'kuruta syām iti"*: a condensed text: "so Nonbeing made a resolve of being: may I be". *"san-manaḥ kṛ*: make up on's mind.

16. The first credentials of reality as "begun" give rise to metaphysics as a natural disposition (metaphysica naturalis) of man to think and reason things. If not a fully developed science, "metaphysica naturalis", maintains Kant, is human reason when dissatisfied with the extent and variety of knowledge acquired through an empirical use of reason. It is led by an inner urge to ask questions. See, Immanuel Kant, *Critique of Pure Reason*, tr. Norman Kemp Smith, London: Macmillan & Co., Ltd 1964, p. 56. See also, Bertrand Russel, *The Problem of Philosophy*, Oxford Univ. Press 1980. pp. 93-94.

17. The renewed interest in the phenomenon of myth and the mythical consciousness is not in the last instance due to the fact that the beginnings, once begun and carried by man's responsibility, are in the present tensionful world in danger of an untimely end before our age would have been able to come into full bloom. There is no instance in the mythical world where man has been expressly told by the gods to destroy creation. New awareness of the harm done to the earth's treasures and forces could be categorized under man's mythical awareness.

man turns in thinking about the beginning, he must use a language almost "other" than his own. Yet, in that language man is most himself for he knows he is "after", not "before". His language must needs be one of opposites, paradoxes, affirmation and negation, a language of pictorials. Man must use a language able to hold all imponderables, a substratum which knows of no barriers. Not able to think outside space and time, man finds he is *given* an "expanse" where limits seem to disappear. That expanse is the symbol. Symbols are a spiritual language transcending all confusion of tongues. They are not peculiar to any one time or place when they are traditional symbols, rising from the depth of man's psyche.[18]

For our setting in which to locate the symbol of water, it is of interest and relevance to take note of Oswald Spengler's observation that the concept of infinite expanse, space, is perhaps an exclusively Occidental idea, entirely foreign to Greeks and Romans, as well as to Indians and Egyptians. He writes:

> "What "infinite space", this creative interpretation of the experience of depth by us people of the Occident, and by us alone, tries to express—this kind of dimension, which the Greeks called Nothing, and which we call the All—saturates the world with a colour, which neither the Greek or Roman, nor the Indian or the Egyptian had on its palette."[19]

Spengler, it seems to me, is misinformed besides giving an unwelcome stress on the already well-known Occidental love for expanse! Infinity of space is one of the fundamental ideas of e.g. Buddhism. This is all the more important as it derives its value not merely from philosophical speculation. It is based on direct spiritual experience, achieved by the systematic exploration of the human mind through meditation. Infinity of space, in the most ancient Pali texts frequently alluded to as *ākāśanañcāyatana*, has retained its importance up to the present day. It was known as one of the higher stages of yoga-experience even before the advent of Buddhism.

The word "*ākāśa*" itself is significant. It is derived from the root "*kās*", "to shine". It implies an active movement, vibration or radiation. Even in the negative definition the idea of movement is instinctively associated with the concept of space as the "non-existence of obstruction or hindrance."

The idea of expanse as the "non-existence of obstruction or hindrance "provides and excellent setting for thought on the symbol of water, especially because it is typical of Indian philosophy to affirm by negation. We have already seen how, in the Vedic myth of *Vṛtra*, the Waters were waiting to be released by *Indra* so they might provide expanse and move in freedom.[20] It will be understood that water is a universally distributed symbol. A review of it, however, I must here leave to the reader's own interest.

18. Adequate symbolism may be defined as the representation of a reality on a certain level of reference by a corresponding reality on another. Thus, e.g. no object of meaning in the world is worthier of being made a type of God than is the sun. René Guenon, in Mythes, mystères et symboles, *Le Voile d'Isis* (1935) calls the traditional symbol "le symbolisme qui sait", "the symbolism which knows "and the individual and self-expressive poetic symbolism, "le symbolisme qui cherche", "the searching symbolism". A symbol is a "mystery". It has its own way of being understood.
19. Oswald Spengler, *Der Untergang des Abendlandes*, Munich, C.H. Beck, 1923, vol. 1, p. 234 tr. F.B.
20. See. Part I:1:1" A phenomenology of "chaos". The myth of *Vṛtra* will of course feature in the following chapter on *Āpaḥ*.

Better than any other element, water conveys of itself the idea of non-existence of obstruction. Its work is to precede creation and take it again to itself; it never can get beyond its own mode of existence. It can never express itself in *forms*. It is always in the condition of being a "potential", of seeds and hidden powers. Everything that has form is manifested above, beneath or in the waters as separated from it. On the other hand, as soon as "form" has separated itself from water, "form" loses its potentiality. It will fall under the law of time and life; it will become limited, enters history, shares in the universal law of change and decays. It would finally altogether cease to exist were it not again to go through a "flood" or baptism in order to partake again in "the creation of the universe". Some ritual with water must be there to escape from the "fleeting instant" of the fleeting water. The waters, themselves fleeting, nonetheless stabilize. On their course, the waters restore what had been lost but they also absorb and destroy what had been there. Any use of water with a sacred intention brings together reintegration and creation. Through the coordination of all aspects of the spiritually known universe, the consciousness of a higher dimension is born through the symbol of water. The symbol replaces the concept and intuition takes the place of calculation.[21] What the Waters reveal on their course is a "logic of direction" different from the inorganic logic of material three-dimensional extention. What results is dynamics instead of statics. A statically conceived universe has no reality *behind* it. It is, in Indian thought, *māyā*. The world must be grasped as it "moves about".[22]

That movement is well expressed by the symbol of water. Principle of what is formless and potential, basis of every cosmic manifestation, container of all seeds, water symbolizes the primal substance from which all forms come and to which they will return either by their own regression or in a cataclysm. Water always exists, but never alone. It always is germinative, containing the potentiality of all forms in their unbroken unity. It precedes, upholds and takes in all forms. Hence water appears in a wide variety of names and attributes.[23] Where it is conspicuous through its absence, it makes man all the more think that he *is* water.

Water is intermediate. It is neither air nor earth, yet both are contained in it. When all by itself, its transparency facilitates the fisherman's catch, but mixed with

21. A warning against excessive stress on psychology in this respect would here not be out of place. Jean Gebser in his, *Ursprung and Gegenwart, Fundamente and Manifestationen der aperspektivischen Welt*, Stuttgart, Deutsche Verlage-Anstalt, 1949-53, vol. 1, p. 327, writes : "The present day psychological terminology which postulates an "Unconscious" in contrast to consciousness, becomes thereby guilty of a falsification of fundamental psychosomatic facts. This terminology and the subsequently wrongly structurized phenomena are a typical example of the faulty conclusions which arise from a radically applied dualism "(tr. F.B.). See also, Erich Fromm, *Zen Buddhism and Psychoanalysis*, p. 96.

22. Thus, if we contemplate the Milky Ocean in the starry sky, it is not the present universe alone which we see, but a universe of the past — and what is still more remarkable — a universe of which the different parts have not even existed simultaneously. Some existed a few minutes, others some millions of years ago, although we see them in the same moment. The lived experience of primary symbols leads to prayer and meditation. From them arises a condition of creative tension between the human and the "other", the consciousness of incompleteness and the ideal of completeness. The tension between the present state of ignorance of delusion and the intended liberation results in the awakening from the illusion of separateness to the wholeness of life. The state of prayer is universal depth-consciousness: *ālaya-vijñāna* in Indian thought, not to be psychologized as an enemy of reason and the source of uncontrollable drives as the "Unconscious" of modern psychology.

23. Some of these we will meet in the following chapter, displaying a variety of appearances of the Indian primeval waters, *Āpaḥ*.

earth, the water sends him home empty-handed while it may have protected the fisherman from a monstrous crocodile. Water is free, although it is not supreme. It is immense, fathomless, when it calls itself ocean or sea. But how easy to negotiate it when it murmurs in the stream. Water is everywhere and is needed everywhere, whether it be in the herdsman's life in the Kabul valley in Vedic times or in modern industrial life. Water brings life and is our friend, yet it may be fatal. One of water's latest names is "heavy water" when, through a process of physics, it is part of present day mankind's biggest threat, the nuclear weapon.

Water with its many characteristics emerges as a powerful symbol of the whole of potentiality. At every level of existence water is a source of life and growth, decline and re-birth.

> *Śvetaketu* said to his father, *Uddālaka Aruṇi*:
> "Let me learn even more, sir!"
> "Very well, my dear," he said.
> "Put this salt in the water and come to me again tomorrow morning."
> He did so. Then he said to him: "Bring the salt that you put in the water last evening!"
> When he searched for it, he could not find it, for it was all dissolved.
> "Taste the water on this side! How does it taste?"
> "Salty."
> "Taste from the middle; how does it taste ?"
> "Salty."
> "Taste from that side; how does it taste ?"
> "Salty."
> "Taste once more and come to me!"
> He did so, "it is always the same"
> Then his father said to him: "In the same way you do not perceive Being here, although it is always present."
> "That which is this finest element, the whole world has for its self: That is truth; that is the *ātman*: *that are you, Śvetaketu* !"[24]

24. *CU.* 6.8.13: *"Sa ya eṣo 'ṇima aited ātmyam idaṁ sarvaṁ, tat satyaṁ, sa ātmā: tat tvaṃ asi śvetaketo"*.

Chapter 7

AN EXPERIENCE OF *ĀPAḤ*, THE WATERS, INSPIRED BY VEDIC AND HINDU MYTH

"Hail to you, divine, unfathomable, all-purifying Waters."[1]

1. *Āpaḥ*, the Waters: Where are they from? Either they are uncreated or they find their origin in a peculiar way.

   "The waters are produced from *Vāc*, the Word."[2]

   "What then was that, beyond Heaven and Earth, beyond *Devas* and *Asuras*, which the waters conceived as their first embryo, in which all Gods saw each other?[3]

   "He, the divine Self-existent, *Svayambhū*, desiring to produce beings of many kinds from his own body, first with a thought created the waters, and placed his seed in them.[4]

   "Then *Nārāyaṇa*, desirous of another, once more meditated in his mind. As he stood absorbed in meditation sweat came out of his forehead. It expanded into these primordial waters. In them was born *Tejas* as a golden egg. Therein was born the god *Brahmā* with the four faces."[5]

2. The Waters are *Āpaḥ*: they were set free, pervaded everything, and because they pervaded — "*āp*—", they were called *Āpaḥ*, water. Since they covered everything —" *vṛ*—", they were also called *vāri*, water.

   "Water, thou art the source of all things and of all existence."[6]

   "He who obstructed you is not here for *Indra* has plunged his bolt in *Vṛtra's* mortal spot."[7]

3. The Waters are *ayana*, the first residence, the first motion of *Nara*. Hence he is called *Nārāyaṇa*.

---

1. *TS*. 1.2.2.
2. *SB*. 6. 11.9.
3. *RV*. 10 82.5.
4. *Manu Smṛti*, 1.8.
5. *MahaU*.1.3.
6. *BhavP*.31.14. Eliade uses this text to explain that the waters "are the source of all possible existence", see: *Patterns in Comparative Religion*, p. 188. In the Latin tradition the waters are "fons et origo".
7. *RV*. 8.100.7: *"na iha yo vo avāvarīt ni ṣiṃ vṛtrasya marmani vajram indor apipatat"*: see: Jeanine Miller, *The Vedas*, p. 28:" The implied resulting freedom is expressed at the beginning of the same stanza: "now you can run (or flow down) each in your own separate way" — *pra nūnam dhāvata pṛthak.*

"The waters are called *nārāḥ*, for the waters are indeed the offspring of *Nara*; as they were his first residence, *ayana*, he thence is named *Nārāyaṇa*.[8]

"*Suta* said: we hear that the work *Nara* means waters or sons of waters. He filled the void with waters and made it his resort. Since he lies down in the waters he is known as *Nārāyaṇa*.[9]

4. The Waters are *pratiṣṭhā*, underlying principle, basis, repository, support, standing place, receptacle.

"The Waters are the foundation of this universe"[10]

5. The Waters are *Hiraṇyagarbha*, the womb of the seed of all creation.

"When came the mighty Waters, bringing with them
the universal Germ, whence sprang the Fire,
thence leapt the God's One Spirit into being.
What god shall we adore with our oblation?

This one who in his might surveyed the Waters
pregnant with vital forces, producing sacrifice,
he is the God of Gods and none besides him.
What God shall we adore with our oblation?"[11]

6. The Waters are the womb of *Brahmāṇḍa*, the cosmic egg from where *Brahmā*, the creator, arose.

"Long ago, when all things animate and inanimate were lost in one dreadful ocean there appeared a large egg, source of the seed of all creatures. Lying in this egg, *Brahmā* went to sleep. At the end of a thousand Ages he awoke."[12]

---

8. *Manu Smṛti*, 1.10.
9. *LP*. 70. 119: The *Liṅga-Purāṇa*, tr. A Board of Scholars, *Ancient Indian Tradition and Mythology Series*, 2 vols., Motilal Banarsidass, first ed., 1973. (10). *SB*. 14.3.2.13: see: Panikkar, *The Vedic Experience*, p. 118.
10. *SB*. 14.3.2.13 : see: Panikkar, *The Vedic Experience*, p. 118.
11. *RV*. 10.121.7-8: see *ibid*. p. 72, The Golden Germ, *Hiraṇyagarbha*, the source of the golden light, The Sun-God, the seed of all creation. cf. *RV*. 10.82.5-6 where the cosmic egg is conceived as a germ by the primeval waters. Also, *AV*. 10.7.28; *SB*. 6.1.1.10-11; *CU*. 3.19; *KathU*. 4.6.
12. *VaSa*, 22. 17-22 in: Cornelia Dimmitt & J.A.B. van Buitenen, *Classical Hindu Mythology, A Reader in the Sanskrit Purāṇas*, p. 32. The following verses 30-39 are interesting and of relevance. I quote the authors' translation: "Awake and knowing creation to be lost in this flood, the lord broke open the egg. From it *OṂ* was born; then arose *Bhūḥ*, matchless *Bhuvaḥ* and third the sound *Svaḥ*. Together they are known as *Bhūr-Bhuvaḥ-Svaḥ*. From this arose *tejas* (which is *tat savitur vareṇyam*) *Tejas*, escaping from the egg, evaporated the water. When the residue had been dried up by *tejas* it became an embryo. The embryo, called a bubble, became solid. It is known as *dhāraṇī* because of its hardness and because it is the sustainer of all creatures. The place where the egg rested is lake *Saṃnihita*. That which first came forth from *tejas* they call *Āditya*. *Brahmā*, grandfather of the world, arose in the middle of the egg. The placenta is known as Mt. Meru (mythical identity with Mount *Kailāśa*, F.B.) and the waters of the womb are the oceans and the thousand rivers. The water which surrounds the navel of *Brahmā* is *Mahat*, and by this choice pure water is the great lake filled. In the middle of it, O great-minded one, a banyan-tree stood like a pillar. From it sprang the classes: *brāhmaṇa*, *kṣatriyas*, *vaiśyas* and *śūdras*, who thus arose to do reverence to the twice-born". *Tat savitur vareṇyam*: beginning words of *RV*. 3.62.10, with which the other *mantras* constitute one often used invocation."*dhāraṇi*" means "that which supports" and is

"That which is earlier than this earth and heaven, before the *Asuras* and Gods had being, —What was that germ primeval which the waters received, where all the Gods were seen together? The waters, they received that germ primeval wherein the Gods were gathered all together. It rested set upon the Unborn's navel, that One wherein abide all things existing."[13]

7. The Waters are *janitrī*, the Mothers.

"For you are the most motherly physicians, mothers, *janitrī*, of all that stands and goes."[14]

"May the Waters, the mothers, purify us."[15]

8. The Waters are *ambaḥ*, the flood, one of the four spheres, the flood of the heavenly ocean beyond the heavens, created by *Ātman*. *Ātman* next created the other spheres: *Maricīḥ*, the Light-atom of aerial space; *māram*, the earth as "the death" and *āpas*, the water of substratum, primal base for the structure below the earth.

"Then he created the worlds: The Flood, Light-space, the Death, the Water. That is the flood, beyond it the heaven; the heaven is its bottom;- The light-spaces are the air-space. The death is the earth. What is below it, are the waters."[16]

9. *Āpas*, the ur-water, brings forth the ur-man, primal man, *Puruṣa*.

"He thought: Now there are the worlds. I will now create the world-guardians. Then he brought forth out of the waters a *Puruṣa* (man) and formed him."[17]

---

also a word for "earth".

13. *RV*. 10. 82.5.6, tr. Griffith.
14. *SB*. 6.50.7. tr. Kuiper, *Ancient Indian Cosmogony*, p. 98. Kuiper also refers to *RV*. 10.17.10; 1.23.16. The author refers to an etymological pun in the *Śatapatha Brāhmaṇa* 6.8.2.3, where a *mantra* referring to divine "wives" is explained in the words: "the wives (*janayaḥ*) verily, are the waters, for from these waters this universe is born (*jāyate*)". "Clear reference to the primeval waters", says Kuiper, "are only found in the last and most recent book of the *Ṛg-Veda* in the so-called philosophical hymns." He thinks the primeval waters belong to the old heritage of concepts in the *Yajur-Veda*. Linking this to the fact that the primordial waters are found in cosmogonies all over the world, Kuiper assumes that the idea of the origin of the world from the waters cannot have been the product of later Vedic poets. "These primeval waters are accepted as a given fact about whose origin it would be useless to speculate", writes Kuiper, p.98.
15. *TS*. 1.2.1.
16. *AU*. 1.2: in Deussen, *Sixty Upaniṣads of the Veda*, p. 15. The preceding verse reads: "In the beginning of this world, there was *Ātman* alone: there was no other thing there, which cast up the eyes. He cogitated: "I will create the worlds".
17. *AU*. 1.3: See: Deussen, *Sixty Upaniṣads of the Veda*, p. 15. The concept "ur-" is from the German language. It suggests the very beginning, primeval times but supposes an already arisen existence. Kuiper in, *Ancient Indian Cosmogony*, takes the view "that the Vedic cosmogonical myth comprises two different stages: first, that of an undivided primordial world which consisted of "the waters" and the beginning of the earth floating on the surface of them; second that inaugurated by *Indra's* throwing his weapon, the *vājra*, against the dragon or the mountain itself, which thereby became firmly founded." It would leave no doubt, as Kuiper thinks, that the second stage has been for Vedic man the exemplary cosmogonic myth in the cult and in the effort of thought to restore in

10. From man's psychic-physical organs of speech, in-breath, sight, hearing, hair, *manas*, out-breath and semen come the eight world-guardians of *Agni*, *Vāyu*, *Āditya*, quarters or directions, plants, moon, death, and water.

> "He brooded over him; then he hatched him.
>
> His mouth split, out of the mouth sprang forth his speech. His nose split. . . .
>
> "The generative organ split itself, out of the generative organ sprang forth the semen, out of the semen the waters."[18]

11. The human being is the waters, *āpas*, through the *Ātman*.

> "In man, indeed, lies this (*Ātman*) in the beginning as a germ, because what is his semen, it is its vigour or the strength collected together out of the limbs; then he carries the self itself in it, and he discharges it in the wife, thus he makes him take birth; it is its (of the *Ātman* of the child) first birth."[19]

---

intention the cosmic totality. The often mentioned "breaking of the resistance", *vṛtrahatya*, is a principal mythic event which also points to the psyche of man breaking open into understanding the relationship between itself and a meaningful universe. The idea of "the sacred" which man reads in and on the Universe and his psychic response to it together make up man's understanding of the Universe's meaningfulness and man's existence in it. See Part I: A phenomenology of "chaos" where the release and the flowing of the waters in the Vedic context have been elaborately dealt with. With regard to man's consciousness of his surrounding, psychoanalysis and psychiatry have made extensive research in view of a clearer grasp of the state of the embryo, surrounded by the amniotic water. The state of the ovum between ovulation and fertilization seems, according to the study of pre-natal dream material, to point to what Kuiper calls "oceanic feelings". (*op. cit.*, p. 117). Mythical symbolism not seldom refers to the forceful penetration of the female organ by the penis and the "danger"- moment of it. Science shows how the spermatozoon must overcome a strong resistance by dissolving the hormonal liquids that surround the ovum. Psycho-analytical treatment of people benefits from research in the field of the process and the experience of conception and being conceived with regard to possible shocklike effects on the ovum as well as the "later" human psyche.

18. *AU.* 1.4 in Deusen, *op. cit.*, p.15. In *AU.* 2.1-5 the whole process is reversed when man's psychic-physical organs are again taken up and into the eight world-guardians of the elements. The godheads tumbled into the great ocean and looked for a place to stay. After their refusal to go and live in a cow or a horse, they agreed to live in the human being. We have here a fine example of how the world is the first manifestation, the primordial revelation to man. The elements are the real symbols standing for the ultimate constituents of reality.

19. The central symbolism of the feminine is that of vessel. From the very beginning down to the present we find this archetypal symbol as essence of the feminine. The basic symbolic equation woman-body-vessel corresponds to what is perhaps human kind's — man's as well as woman's — most elementary experience of the Feminine. The experience of the body as a vessel is universally human and not limited to woman. Erich Neumann in his, *The Origin and History of Consciousness*, London, 1954, pp. 28ff, 290ff, lists this expression of the phenomenon of the body as vessel under the category of "metabolic symbolism". All the basic vital functions occur in this vessel-body schema, whose "inside" is an unknown. The vessel symbolism of the body containing the psyche is always alive. We speak of our "inwardness", of "inner" values, and so on, when we mean psychic or spiritual contents, as though they were contained "in" us and came "out" of us. For obvious reasons woman is the vessel par excellence. The sexual act connotes at once the "outside" of the male and the "inside" of the female character. Woman discharges the real meaning of birth and growth and "deeper" understanding. The female personality is the "life-vessel as such" and thus the Feminine occupies an absolute central position in human symbolism. Patriarchal symbolism is "anti-natural" in the sense that it usurps and claims birth and growth in areas where it "is not". Thus e.g. the mythical inverted tree with its roots "above" in various patriarchal and male-dominated cultures is an affront to the female personality from the psychological point of view. Patriarchal cultures often

"It is so, O *Yājnavalkya*; now just tell us about the inner controller!" "He, who dwelling in the waters, is different from the waters, whom the waters do not know, whose body is the waters, who inwardly controls the waters — he is your soul, the inner controller, the immortal one."[20]

12. The Waters are seed.

"Him whom they consecrate (with the *dīkṣā*) the priests make into an embryo again. With waters they sprinkle; the waters are seed. . . ."[21]

13. The Waters as mothers gave birth to *Agni*, fire, and to vegetation.

"Him, duly coming as their germ, have plants received; This *Agni* have maternal Waters brought to life. So in like manner do the forest trees and plants bear him within them and produce him ever more."[22]

14. *Agni*, fire, is *Apāṃgarbha*, the child or embryo of the Waters.

". . . He who begot and will beget the dawnlights, most manly, Child of Floods, is youthful *Agni*. Him, varied in his form, the lovely Infant of floods and plants the blessed wood has engendered."[23]

15. *Agni* is *Rudra-Agni*, the fire of creation and twin of *Soma*, the elixir of immortality. Both were hidden in the primal resistance, *Vṛtra*, before *Indra* slew and broke that inertia and the Waters flowed freely.

"Only a part of the power penetrating the universe is what as it were, shines forth, there in the centre of the sun and in the eye and in the fire; but that

---

distort and pervert the natural character of the symbols. It would be highly interesting and fruitful to trace the effects of patriarchal thought on psychology, philosophy, theology etc and their world-views. Present-day women's movements are re-examining myths and symbols to see how the male mind might have distorted their true meaning in actual scientific and speculative thought and systems. See also: Erich Neumann, *The Great Mother, An Analysis of the Archetype, passim*.

20. The whole passage mentions "him who is different from all the elements", yet "within" them: *apo antaraḥ. . . eṣa ta ātmāntaryāmy amṛtaḥ*. He is the inner controller, the immortal, *antaryāmin*.

21. *AB*. 1.3. The idea here is that in the face of the Universe's totality a certain" anonimity" or self-naughting is essential. All initiations (*dīksā*) and, likewise, Buddhist ordination (*pabbajana*) which as in monasticism elsewhere is a kind of initiation, involve a self-denial. One must be reduced to one's earliest potential in order to grow again, anew. The anonimity is not only a monastic ideal but has far-reaching consequences in societies where the distinction of sacred from profane is more difficult to find than in works written about such societies. *Dīkṣā* is a death and a re-birth, "the initiate is the oblation"- *havir vai dīkṣitaḥ* (*TS*. 6.1.4.5.; *A.B*. 2.3).

22. *RV*. 10.91.6.

23. *RV*. 3.1.12-13. Connected with the preceding nos. 12 and 13. The *Agni*-cycle is vast and complex, here forbidding even a short hermeneutics. Only a few links can here be suggested. "The sacrificer casts himself in the form of seed (represented by grains of sand, F.B.) into the household Fire"- *ātmānaṃ . . . retobhūtaṃ siñcati* (*SB*. 7.2.1.6). He thus ensures his birth in the heavenly world. The text also refers to sexual intercourse, ritually understood, as a kind of *Soma*-sacrifice (*BU*. 6.2.13; 6.4.3.) for the household Fire is identified with the wife from whom one is born again in this life. The sexual act thus is the pouring of oneself — *"siñcati"* — into the divine womb. One, therefore, has two selves, two inheritances, human and divine. The idea of *"Agni* hidden in the waters" is one of the central *ṚgVedic* religious concepts. It is linked with the notion that "the earth lies spread on the waters "- *SB*. 7.4.1.8: *"āpo vai puṣkaram tāsām iyaṁ parṇaṁ, yatha ha vā idaṁ puṣkaraparṇam apsv adhyāhitam, evam iyam apsv adhyāhitā"*: see: Kuiper, *op. cit*., p. 80. The earth again is, in its turn, mythologically equivalent, maintains Kuiper, to the nether world, equated to or localized in the cosmic mountain. Thus *Agni*, the fire of the harmony-making (*Ṛta*) sacrifice on earth is "hidden in the waters", see: Kuiper, *op. cit*., p. 80.

power is *Brahman*, is the immortal one, is the splendour, is *Satyadharma*.

"Only a part of the power penetrating the universe is what is the nectar in the sun (which flows collectively into it out of the *Veda*); but the power, of which also the *Soma* and the vital breaths themselves are sprouts or offshoots, is *Brahman*, is the immortal one, is the splendour, is *Satya dharma*."[24]

16. The *Soma* makes of gods and men one community when the moon-water of the gods streams into the *soma*-juice of men and the sacrifice transforms it into *vasatīvaryah*, the holy waters.

"Forth on their way the glorious drops have flowed for maintenance of Law, knowing this sacrifice's course.

Down in the mighty waters sinks the stream of meath, most excellent, Oblation best of all in worth."[25]

17. *Hiraṇyagarbha*, the Golden Germ, springs from the waters and again enters and fecundates them. Thus Fire, *Agni*, is daily born in them.

"What time the mighty waters came, containing the universal germ, producing *Agni*. Thence sprang the God's one spirit into being. What God shall we adore with our oblation ?"[26]

18. The Waters receive spermatic creative power.

"Water is female and fire is male; life is born from their intercourse."[27]

---

24. *MaitraU.* 6.35 tr. Deussen, *op. cit.*, p. 375. The constituents of the world are "distributed" in the primordial sacrifice where it is asked "how many-fold (*katidhā*) did they divide up (*vy-adadhuḥ*) the Person?". These divisions are alluded to in *RV.* 1.164.15 and are, in fact, of the primordial Waters, "*āpo vy adadhāt*"- (*AV.* 10.2.11), i.e. their release. One idea set forth here is that neither the sun, nor the sun-nectar, nor the sacrificial fire or illuminating chant is the proper object of adoration since they are only a part of the power of the universe- "*nabhaso ntargatasya tejaso "mśamātram"*: see: Deussen, *op. cit.*, p. 375. Kuiper in *op. cit.*, p. 216-229 concerns himself extensively with the Vedic theft of the fire and compares the Vedic myths with the Greek Prometheus-myth which the author denies of the Vedas. Kuiper's observation: ". . . *Agni* and *Soma*", had to be liberated from the primordial world before *Indra* could slay the dragon to found the dualistic cosmos. Many Vedic texts state, indeed, that *Indra* conquered *Vṛtra* with the help of *Agni* and *Soma*", *op. cit.*, p. 218. One must here remind oneself of the "fire of intelligence" and the "illuminating sacrificial drink of *Soma*"- parts of man's psyche - by which man links his existence and that of the Universe in a meaningful relationship. In that sense *Agni* and *Soma* are "prior" to "chaos" and help indeed to slay chaos, personified in *Vṛtra*. The *Agni*- and *Soma*-sacrifices are symbolic self-immolation in exterior or interior cult, giving rise to the elemental self of the comprehensor of the universe's significance.

25. *RV.* 9. 7.1-2. tr. Griffith. As the Moon-god pours down its rain which is like honey for the earth and man, through the sieve of heaven, he is addressed and worshipped as *Pavamāna*, Self-purifying. Nearly all the hymns of *ṚgVeda* 9 are addresed to *Soma Pavamāna*. The rain from heaven is represented by the quickening *Soma*-juice as it undergoes purification by flowing through the wool which is used as a filter or strainer. See: *Muir*, O.S. Texts, V. 258ff.

26. *RV.* 10.121.7 tr. Griffith. Apart from its spiritual significance, the text obviously refers to the rising and setting of the fiery sun-disc. See: Part II:5:4(iv): "The birth of His Own Perfection: *Hiranyagarbha* (*RV.* 10. 121)".

27. *SB.* 1.6.3.23. Stephen G. Darian in, *The Ganges in Myth and History*, Univ. Press of Hawaii, Honolulu, 1978, pp. 79-88 describes "the new vision" that arose from the blending of the Aryan civilization with the indigenous Indian one. The lush vegetation came upon the desert-nomads as a new revelation.

19. *Agni* dwells in the heavens, the clouds, the earth, the plants and the waters, in everything.

> "He is in the stones and within men. He lives in cattle, in the horses."[28]
>
> "Resplendent are the rays of light; loud is thy voice like pressing-stones. Yea, of itself thy thunder goes forth like the roaring of the heaven.
>
> Thus, seeking riches, have we paid homage to *Agni* Conqueror. May he, most wise, as with a ship, carry us over all our foes."[29]

20. *Agni's* twin, *Soma*, elixir of immortality and inspiration, lives in heaven and in the waters and speaks from within the seer, the comprehensor.

> "the seer makes surge the wave from the ocean of his heart."[30]

21. The *Vṛtrahatya* by *Indra*, his slaying of the primal inertia, set flowing the waters of the mind.

> "Ye with your strength (*Indra-Varuṇa*) have pierced the fountains of the floods; the Sun have ye brought forward as the Lord of Heaven. Cheered by this magic draught ye, *Indra-Varuṇa*, made the dry places stream, made songs of praise flow forth."[31]

22. From the Waters comes *Agni* as *Apāṁgarbha*, a guest among men, conveyor of knowledge of the cosmic truth, wisdom, insight and inspiration.

> "*Agni*, inventor of resplendent speech."[32]
>
> ". . .bring the light of inspired speech."[33]
>
> "Verily thou art the well of the cosmic truth."[34]

23. At the sight of the waters, prayer wells within us:

> "*Agni*, thy home is in the waters; into the plants thou forcest way, and as their child art born anew."[35]

---

28. *AV*. 12.1.19 The cult of fire and its interiorization has been an ever-inspiring source for Vedic and Indian thought. One of *Agni's* epithets is: "*viśvacarṣaniḥ*:- the god of all men.
29. *RV*. 5.24.8-9. tr. Griffith. "our foes" refers to the waters withheld by the dragon *Vṛtra*. In *RV*. 6.3.5. *Agni* is said to whet his *tejas* like a point of iron. *Agni* is "*tigma-śocis*", a sharp flame. The word *tejas* may be translated by "fire" or by "fiery energy", the essential quality standing for the essence, the characteristic act for the agent. The thunder's blast and the lightning is like the blast of the Spirit. This prescient Spirit is dispersed in all directions. See, *BU*. 2.1.3; *KausU*. 3.3; 4.20; *MU*. 2.1.1.
30. *RV*. 10.123.2: The guardians of *Soma* are the *Gandharvas* (*RV*. 9 83.4; 4.27.3). A falcon, *Indra* himself, stole the *Soma* from the eternal abode. (*RV*. 1.22.14). The *Gandharvas*' station is beyond the gods and precedes creation. Hence the *Gandharva* is the creative *Soma*-inspiration within the seer in sacred secrecy because when *Soma* speaks, one speaks as if from the "other side" of creation. It is as though the seer is on the border between the as yet unflowing waters and the moment they begin to be released.
31. *RV*. 7.82.3: the mind-loosening draught of *soma* during the sacrifice takes the memory back to whom the waters of thought were as yet withheld by the mountain.
32. *RS*. 2.9.4: *tvam śukrasya vacaso manotā*. See: Kuiper, *op. cit*., p. 182.
33. *RS*. 3.10.5: *vipam jyotiṁṣi bibhrat; op. cit*. p. 182.
34. *YV*. 10.4. The well is the "*utsa*", primordial, cosmic well "abounding in water" – *utsam kavandham udriṇām* (*RV*. 8.7.10) and the same as the "golden well" which is the moon. (*RV*. 9.107.4). See: Kuiper, *op. cit*., p. 37. The moon is *soma*.
35. *RV*. 8.43.9.

"May the gleaming waters who took Fire as their germ be for us blessing and joy."[36]

24. The Waters are *apraketā*, an amorphous chaos, the unformed, unrecognizable. Concealed in their void (*ābhū*) they are also potent (*ābhū*). They are "that One". In them stirred warmth (*tāpas*).

"Darkness was there, all wrapped around by darkness, and all was Water indiscriminate. Then that which was hidden by the void, that One, emerging, stirring, through power of Ardor, came to be."[37]

25. Yet, in the Waters as *apraketā* was Breath, Impulse by its own nature (*svadhā*).

"There was no death then, nor yet deathlessness; of night or day there was not any sign.
The One breathed without breath, by its own impulse. Other than that was nothing else at all."[38]

26. Thus was discovered in the Waters a wonderful Truth: Being in Non-being! Desire and Love (*kāma*) was the first seed of the Spirit (*Manas*).

"In the beginning Love arose which was the primal germ cell of the mind, the Seers, searching in their hearts with wisdom, discovered the connection of Being in Non-being."[39]

27. *Svadhā*, Breath, by its own nature condensed, in the formless Waters (*apraketā*), into proto-cosmic concentration (*tapas*).

"Darkness was there, all wrapped around by darkness; and all was Water indiscriminate. Then that which was hidden by the Void, that One, emerging, stirring, through power of Ardor, came to be."[40]

28. *Tapas* gave birth to Cosmic Order (*Ṛta*) and Truth (*Satya*). This happened in the aeon of pre-creation. No human voice was heard, no twitter of birds, no cry of either joy or pain.

"From blazing Ardor Cosmic Order came and Truth; from thence was born the obscure night; from thence the Ocean with its billowing waves."[41]

29. Avoiding meaningless chaos and designlessness, the ontic *Ṛta* and *Satya* produced the ocean of space and the idea of time, the year.

---

36. *AV*. 1.33. Ib.
37. See: Part II, ch. 5, 4.3.: "The Perfection of the Beginnings – *Sat-Asat*". *Nāsadīya Sūkta*, tr. Panikkar, *The Vedic Experience*, p. 58.
38. *RV*. 10.129.2, see: *Nāsadīya Sūkta*. I indicated in Part II various translations of *svadhā* by scholars.
39. *RV*. 10.129.4. see: *Nāsadīya Sūkta*. In the Vedic hymn of the Origins the symbol of water shows its most emphatic pertinence.
40. *RV*. 10.129.3, see: *Nāsadīya Sūkta*. See note no. 38 for *Svadhā*.
41. *RV*. 10.190.1. tr. Panikkar, *op. cit.*, p. 60. Panikkar writes: "Owing to *Ṛta* this world is not a chaos but a cosmos, not an anarchic mass, but an ordered and harmonious whole. Owing to *satya*, the world is not a haphazard place, an irresponsible game, or an inconsistent and purely fluid appearance. *Satya* is not primarily an epistemic truth but an ontic truthfulness, an ontological fullness, with content, weight, and reality, namely, being", *op. cit.*, p. 59.

"From Ocean with its waves was born the year which marshalls the succession of nights and days, controlling everything that blinks the eye."[42]

30. The *apraketā*, the formless Waters, what else did they conceal? *Dakṣa* and *Aditi,* male and female forces, but organless (*aliṅga*), came to be.

"A crosswise line cut Being from Nonbeing. What was described above it, what below ?

Bearers of seed they were and mighty forces, thrust from below and forward move above."[43]

"Earth sprang from the Productive Power; the regions from the Earth were born. *Dakṣa* was born of *Aditi*, and *Aditi* was *Dakṣa's* Child."[44]

31. What else was there, in the beginnings, in the Waters? The female voice of *Vāc*, the Word.

"On the world's summit I bring forth the Father: my home is in the waters, in the ocean. . . From there I extend to all existing creatures."[45]

32. The Waters are *kāraṇa-salila*, causal fluid without shores or boundaries.

"Where does this Water begin? Where is its middle? And where is its end?"[46]

"Of this universe, it is in truth the Waters that were made first, hence when the Waters flow, then everythings here, whatsoever exists, is produced."[47]

33. In *kāraṇa-salila* rests Being. As Being it is *Sat*, as Consciousness it is *Çit*, as Bliss it is *Ānanda*. That perfect matrix contains both heaven and earth. But these were in the very beginning not yet there. There was only *Satçitananda*.

---

42. *Rv*. 10.190.2., tr. Panikkar, *op. cit.,* p. 60.
43. *RV*. 10.129.5: *Nāsadīya Sūkta*. tr. Panikkar, *op. cit.*, p. 58.
44. *RV*. 10.72.4. tr. Griffith, op. cit., p. 585. According to *SB*. 2.4.4.1-2 *Prajāpati*, in the beginning, desiring offspring, sacrificed. He was *Dakṣa*. The later *Brahmā* made *Dakṣa* the creator of all living beings. The myth refers implicitly to the one where *Rudra-Śiva*, when told to procreate, hides in the waters. He fails to create and cuts off his organ. By creating *Dakṣa* the later Purāṇic *Brahmā* creates himself. The later cycles of creation-myths express in more anthropomorphic terms some of the conflicts which appear symbolically in earlier myths: mental or ascetic creation versus sexual creation, asceticism versus married life, men versus women. *Aditi* here is the world Mother, giving birth to a "mortal egg". The myth competes with that of *Hiraṇayagarbha*. *Aditi* is Infinity or the Infinite (and *Dakṣa* is Force or Power), but personified. See: Griffith, *op. cit.*, p. 585. Also: Kuiper, *op. cit.,* p. 100.
45. *RV*. 10.72.4. tr. Griffith. See: Part I:1:5: *"Vāc* and *Vaikhārī*: The Word and human speech "and" *Vāco Bhāgam*: sharing in the womb of the Word".
46. *RV*. 10.3.8: *RV*. 10.82.1 shows *Viśvakarmā's* creation as a continuous cosmic substance not yet patterned into a granular structure. This is in opposition to *RV*. 10.72.6 (see footnote no.49) where the process of centres of strain appear in the continuity, symbolized by the dance of the gods in the all-pervasive Water. This happening is traceable in other cultures' myths. It represents a fundamental law of creative revolution and constitutes the fundamental riddle how discontinuities first appear in the midst of continuity. See: Woodroffe, *The World as Power*, p. 285f.
47. *SB*. 7.4.1.6. The text may be linked to the myth of *Vṛtra* and *Indra*, referring to the awakening of the mind and the "rise" in the human psyche of the Universe's meaningfulness. The flowing of the Water constitutes a horizon against which man builds. an underlying and conscious picture of the world. Panikkar says in *op. cit.*, p. 115: "Ultimately the intelligible pattern of all human understanding is based on an accepted cosmology. Man cannot get rid of matter, and his material conception of the world is reflected in any of his supposedly spiritual intuitions."

"The Father of the eye, the Wise in spirit, creates both these worlds submerged in fatness. Then, when the eastern ends were firmly fastened, the heavens and the earth were far extended."[48]

34. The Waters as *kāraṇa-salila* begin to show centres of strain and concentration by the dance of the gods, *Devatas*: the seven *Ṛṣis*, the stars of Ursus Major.

"When ye, O Gods, in yonder deep close clasping one another stood, thence, as of dancers, from your feet a thickening cloud of dust arose. When ye, O Gods, like *Yatis*, caused all existing things to grow, Then ye brought *Sūrya* forward who was lying hidden in the sea."[49]

35. The waters reveal not merely the principle of "IS", the cosmic *Puruṣa*, but also the principle of Becoming. She is *Mula*, the root, the fount of things "before"– *pra*– –"creation"– *kṛti*. *Prakṛti* is Nature with her infinite potency of bearing, transforming and nourishing. She is *Saṁyavastha*, equilibrium of energy.

"Before creation this world was devoid of sun, moon and the stars, and without day and night. There was no energy and no distinction of directions. The *Brahmaṇḍa*, the universe was then destitute of sound, touch, and the like, devoid of other forces, and full of darkness. Then but that one eternal *Brahman*, cosmic consciousness, of whom the *Śrutis* speak, and the *Prakṛti*, the Cosmic Force, who is existence, consciousness, and bliss, alone existed."[50]

36. The dormant side of the eternal stillness of *Satçitananda* is *Mūlaprakṛti*. In *spandana*, the first cosmic vibration of *kāma*, Love and Desire, She is *Sakti*, but as yet organless (*aliṅga*). She as *Śakti* is *avyakta*, not yet the person of woman-wife who lets herself be touched. She is the teleological instinct of *Satcitananda* who is outward bound (*pravṛtti*).

"The place of my birth is in the water within the sea: he who knows this, obtains the dwelling of *Dēvi*"

Śiva addresses himself to *Dèvi*:

"Thou art Thyself the *Parā Prakṛti* of the *Paramātmā*."[51]

37. The initial creative movement of *kāma*, Love and Desire, is *Paraśabda*, the first Cosmic Sound. It is hidden in *Vāc*, the Word, and in the Waters.

---

48. *RV*. 10.72.1.
49. *RV*. 10.72. 6-7: See footnote no. 46.
50. Earlier mention has been made of the Archetype of the Feminine in psychology. The archetypal Feminine is preserved in its transformative character, which provides the most numinous of all transformation mysteries: growth. The accent of a symbol depends in large measure on the matriarchal or patriarchal culture situation in which it is embedded. In the latter, for example, the "mater" (mother) character of the symbol "materia" (matter) is devaluated. Matter is then regarded as of small value in contrast to the ideal, assigned to the male-paternal side.
51. *Mahant*. 4.10: *"mama yonir apsvantaḥ samudre ya evam veda sa devīpadamāpnoti"*. See, no. 33 and footnote no.48. Speculation about the Goddess *Dēvi*, for a great part "from outside the Indo-European sphere", as Eliade maintains, comes from earliest aboriginal India. See: Mircea Eliade *Yoga, Immortality and Freedom*, pp. 293-358.

"On the world's summit I bring forth the Father: my home is in the waters, in the ocean."[52]

"I, verily, myself announce and utter the word that Gods and men alike shall welcome. I make the man I love exceedingly mighty, make him a sage, a *Ṛsi*, and a Brahman."[53]

38. Drawn out by *pariṇama*, the ejective process, *Śakti-Mūla Prakṛti* is *Śakti Tattva*. That is power as metaphysical centre or point. That point is *Bindu*, ready and about to evolve the Universe. A symbol of this state is *Maṇidvīpa*, The Isle of Gems in the Ocean of Nectar (*Amṛtārṇava*). The Unfolding of *Bindu* is the Sound *Brahman* (*Śabdabrahman*). In the *Valakhilya* hymn in the *ṚgVeda* we are presented with a glimpse of this vision:

"One is also this and differently all."[54]

"That is full; this is full. The full comes out of the full. Taking the full from the full, the full itself remains."[55]

39. *Brahman* without *Prakṛti* is actionless. *Prakṛti* without *Brahman* is unconscious. Their mutual fecundity enables *Bhairavī* to address *Bhairava*. Creation would now be possible.

"Thou art the Guru of all, I entered into Thy body (*Puruṣa*) and thereby Thou didst become the Lord. There is none but myself who is the Mother to create (*Kāryāvibhāvinī*). Therefore it is that, when creation takes place, Sonship is in Thee. Thou alone art the Father Who Wills what I do. (*Kāryyavibhāvaka*; that is, She is the vessel which receives the nectar which flows from *Nityānanda*). By the union of *Śiva* and *Śakti* creation comes (*Śiva-Śakti-samayogāt jāyate sriṣṭikalpānā*). As all in the universe is both *Śiva* and *Śakti* (*Śivāśaktimaya*), therefore, Oh *Maheśvara*, Thou art in every place and I am in every place. Thou art in all and I am in all."[56]

40. It is in the Divine Waters, *Āpo devīḥ*, that all those truths are contained:

"Ceaselessly they flow from the depths, pure, never sleeping, the Ocean their sponsor, following the channels ordained by the Thunderer. Now may these great divine Waters quicken me!

---

52. *RV.* 10.125.7: this whole hymn, dedicated to *Vāc*, illustrates the constant assimilation of the phenomena of nature to the sacrifice. All that has a voice in nature is embodied in *Vāc*. It is an other expression for the idea of the unity of the world. See also Part I, ch. 1.5 and 6 on *Vāc*. *Vāc* is speech personified, the Word, the first creation and representative of Spirit, and the means of communication between men and gods.
53. *RV.* 10.125.5. See *RV.* 1.164.37: "What thing I am I do not know. I wander secluded, burdened by my mind. When the Firstborn of Truth has come to me, I receive a share in that selfsame Word."
54. *RV.* 8.58: "*ekam va idam vi bahudha sarvam*". See: Part I:1:3: "The Juices of *Saptadvīpas*, the seven islands".
55. *IsU.* Invocation. We have a symbolic but real vision of the universe if we understand the relationship between "basis/reality" (*prāna*) and its "image/symbol" (*pratimā*) in Indian thought. Reality and symbol imply mutuality. Reality does not exist independently of its symbol and no symbol is fully itself except through manifestation of reality. In this sense the Indian world-vision is symbolic. It safeguards the existential character of the "many" without prejudice to the ontic fullness of the "One".
56. *Kulac. Nig.*

Waters may pour from heaven or run along channels dug out by men; or flow clear and pure having the Ocean as their goal. Now may these great divine Waters quicken me!

In the midst of the Waters is moving the Lord, surveying men's truth and men's lies. How sweet are the Waters, crystal clear and cleansing! Now may these great divine Waters quicken me!"

From whom King *Varuṇa*, *Soma*, and all the Deities drink exhilarating strength, into whom the Universal Lord has entered. Now may these great divine Waters quicken me!"[57]

41. The *Bindu* is *Brahman*, – "*aham brahmā asmi*", "I am *Brahman*".

"Not thinkable and not unthinkable, thinkable and unthinkable together, Free from every partisanship, is *Brahman* which he then reaches.

Beginning the *Yoga* with *OM*, meditate wordlessly on the highest one since through wordless meditation, is being attained not mere non-being.

That is *Brahman,* the partless, changeless and without deception; "I am that *Brahman*", so knowing one surely reaches the *Brahman*."[58]

42. In the midst of the ocean the song of *Haṁsa*, the swan, was heard. *Viṣṇu* sang from the lotus. From his navel *Brahmā* was born in a later aeon. His vehicle was to be the swan and his chariot was to be drawn by seven swans (*haṁsārūḍhaḥ*).

"Many forms do I assume. And when the sun and moon have disappeared, I float and swim with slow movements on the boundless expanse of the waters. I am the Gander. I am the Lord. I bring forth the universe from my essence and I abide in the cycle of time that dissolves it."[59]

43. The wild gander (*haṁsa*) exhibits the two-fold nature of all beings. Swimming on the water's surface, the gander-swan is not fettered by it. The homeless free-wanderer between the upper celestial and the lower earthly spheres is at ease in both and not bound to either. When it so wishes it alights upon the waters of the earth, *pravṛtti*; but just as easily it withdraws to the void on high, *nivṛtti*.

For man that gander's flight between the two realms is possible by *prāṇāyāma*, the disclosure of all modalities of consciousness. Thus *Svadhā*, Immortal Breath, stirring in the primeval Waters, is not unknown to man.

---

57. *RV.* 7.49. 1-4, tr. Panikkar, *op. cit.*, p. 118. The Thunderer is *Indra*.
58. *BrahbU.* 6-8. "*aham Brahmā asmi*" e.g. *BU.* 1.4.10.
59. *MP.* 67.13.25. The *Matsya Purāṇa* devotes most of its chapters to aspects of iconography. In the *Viṣṅudharmottara Purāṇa Brahmā* is drawn by seven swans: "*jagatādhāraṁ çaturbhuṁ saptahamse rathe sthitam*". In the *Kathopaniṣad* the swan as residing in the sky is identified with the Sun and ultimately it stands for the Supreme Soul, *Ātman*, who is above all thigns on earth: 2.2.2:" *haṁsaḥ śucisad vasurantarīkṣasad – haṁsaḥ śucisad vasurantarikṣasad hota vediṣad atithirduroṇasad nṛṣadvarasad ṛtasad vyomasad abjā gojā ṛtajā adrijā ṛtam bṛhat*". This verse may be found in *RV*, 4.40.5; *AV.* 10.24; *SB.* 6.7.3.11. Possibly the seven swans are the seven rivers or seven *Rsis*. The seven rivers may be those of bliss, existence, consciousness, Manu, truth, breath and gross body. Aurobindo in, *On the Veda*, p. 138 writes:" The sevenfold waters thus rise upward and become the pure mental activity, the Mighty ones of Heaven. They reveal themselves . . . as the seven Words or fundamental creative expressions of the divine Mind, *Saptavāṇīḥ*.."

"I strike thee (the harp) for the *prāṇa*, the *apāṇa*, and the *vyāṇa*".[60]
"The water, which is drunk, is divided into three parts; that which is the grossest constituent becomes urine, that which is the middling one becomes blood, that which is the finest one becomes *Prāṇa*, vital breath."[61]

44. *Haṁsa* is *Puruṣa-Prakṛti-Tattva*. *ham* is *Śiva*, *sah* is *Śakti*. They are the *Haṁsa*-pair.[62]

"In Thy *Anāhata* lotus I salute the wondrous pair who are *Ham* and *Sah*, swimming in the mind of the great who ever delight in the honey of the blooming lotus of knowledge."

45. This *Haṁsa* reversed is the Vedantic *So ham*, "This (am) I".. The waterbird reminds man of his ego (*ahaṁkāra*). Breathing the *prāṇa*, man concedes to creation and involvement by his very existence (*pravṛtti*). His out-breath (*apāṇa*) however, is the yearning for release (*nivṛtti*).

"(here) follows the instruction about the I-consciousness, *ahaṁkāra*: I (*aham*) am below and above, in the west and in the east, in the south and in the north; I am the whole world. Out of this follows the instruction about the soul (*Ātman*); the soul is below and above, in the west and in the east, in the south and in the north; the soul (*Ātman*) is this great world.

He who sees thus, thinks and knows, rejoicing in the soul playing with it, copulating and enjoying with it, such a one is autonomous (*sva-raj*) and there is freedom to go anywhere for him in all the worlds; but those who regard or think otherwise, are heteronomous (*anva-rājānaḥ*) their blessedness is perishable, and there is no freedom for them to move at will, in all the worlds (*akāmacāraḥ*)."[63]

46. *Haṁsa* sports in the World-lotus sprung from *Mohāpaṅka*, the Mud of Delusion in the Lake of Ignorance (*avidyā*). *Haṁsa*'s *pakṣitva*, its "birdness", dissolves when it becomes unworldly (*niṣprapañca*). Thus the *Sa-ham Ātman* is established, "I am *Ātman*".

"*Gautama* spoke: "Now we will impart precise information over the *Haṁsa* and the *Paramahaṁsa* for the Brahman-student who is passionless, restrained and devoted to the teacher:

With the sound "*haṁ-sa haṁ-sa*" (out-breathing and in-breathing) it (the breath) stays continually in all bodies, filling them completely as the fire in the fuel or the oil in the sesameseeds. Ḥe who knows it does not fall in the hands of Death.

". . . one should meditate on the essence of the *Hamsa* in the eight-petal lotus-flower which is in the heart. (One may think of him in the form of a bird, as *Haṁsa*, a goose:) *Agni* and *Soma* are his wings, the *OṂ*-sound his

60. *Sāṇkhāyana Śrauta Sūtra* 17.
6I. *CU*. 5.2., tr. Deussen, *op. cit.*, p. 164.
62. *Ānandalahari* 39. See: Sir John Woodroffe, *The Garland of Letters, Studies in the Maṇtra-Śāstra*, Ganesh & Company, 1979, pp. 165-174. The universe is made of and informed by the *Haṁsa*-pair (*Haṁsa-dvandva*) who are *Puruṣa* and *Prakṛti* and iṇ all the latter's varied forms (*Pumprakrtyātmako hamsas tadātmakam idam jagat*), *op. cit.*, p. 165.
63. *CU*. 25.1. 2-2, tr. Deussen, *op. cit.*, p. 188.

head, the *anusvāra*-point his eye, his mouth; *Rudra* and *Rudraṇī* his hands and feet, *Kāla* and *Agni* his both sides: "sees" and "homeless" are his two remaining sides above and below."[64]

47. The following then are the holy words the *Haṁsa*-student speaks:

"To the sun: *om sūryāya hṛdayāya namaḥ*.
to the moon: *om somāya śirase svāhā*.
to the spotless one: *om nirañjanāya śikhāyai vaṣaṭ*.
to the lustreless one: *om nirabhāsāya kavacāya hum*.
tanu-sukṣma: *om tanusūkṣma netratrayāya vaṣaṭ*.

and *pracodayāt: om pracodayāt astrāya phaṭ*, and with addition (every time): to *Agni* and *Soma vaṣaṭ* "the constituent aphorisms are laid as a diagram on the heart. . ."[65]

48. Thus, in the most renowned *mantra* of the *Vedas*, the *Gāyatrī*, man is the whole of the Universe:

"*OM*
We meditate upon the glorious splendour of the Vivifier divine.
May he himself illumine our minds!
OM."[66]

49. The Vedic concept of the universe is based on a cosmic dichotomy: Heaven-Earth; Day-Night; *Devas-Asūras*.

"Two-fold indeed is this universe, there is no third."[67]

50. The Golden Germ (*Hiraṇyagarbha*) hovers over the Waters and when entering them as *skambha*, the Cosmic Pillar, it makes them into "world".

"Men recognize the Golden Embryo as the unutterable, the Supreme. Yet, it was the Support who in the beginning poured forth upon the world that stream of gold."[68]

---

64. *Haṁsa Upāniṣad* Ib. 2 and 6.
65. *Haṁsa Upāniṣad* 5. Verse 7 reads: "And this *Haṁsa* (i.e., the individual soul) is that *Paramahaṁsa* (the highest soul), which shines like ten million suns and pervades the entire world.". tr. Deussen, *op. cit.*, pp. 718-720.
66. *RV*. 3.62.10: "*tat savitur vareṇyaṁ bhargo devasya dhumahi dhiyo yo naḥ pracodayāt*". The *Maitri Up*. gives an account of the *Gāyatrī's* symbolism and introduces us to the *Sāvitrī* as follows: "The Swan, the bird of golden colour, abiding both in the heart and the Sun, the diver-bird of glorious light-to him we sacrifice in this fire." (6.34).
67. Kuiper in *op. cit.*, p. 52f discusses the dual conception at length. The famous "third stride" of *Viṣñu* has, Kuiper says, "never been expressly stated (in its mythical) significance". The creation-myth knows two worlds "the Waters and the earth being uncovered by Indra's "propping up" the sky. *Viṣñu's* first stride corresponds to the nether world, his second to the upper, but his third step is a mystery, not perceptible to the human eye, for it corresponds to the totality of the opposed moieties, just as the thirteenth month stands for the totality of the preceding twelve months. As compared with the *thesis* (*K*) of the primordial world, and the *antithesis* of *Indra's* creation, *Viṣñu's* third step is the *synthesis*". Kuiper quotes *RV*. 1.154.4 (p. 52) where *Viṣñu* is said to hold in a three fold way Earth and Heaven, *all* that exists": *ya u tridhātu pṛthivīm uta dyām eko dadhara bhuvanāni viśvā*.
68. *AV*. 10.7.28, tr. Panikkar, *op. cit.*, p. 65.

"How does the wind not cease to blow? How does the mind take no repose ? Why do the Waters, seeking to reach truth never at any time cease flowing?

A mighty wonder in the midst of creation moves, thanks to Fervor, on the Waters' surface. To him whatever gods there are adhere like branches of tree around a trunk.

Tell me of that support, who may he be? In him exists no darkness, no evil. In him there are the lights, including the three that are in the Lord of Life. The one who knows the Reed of Gold standing up in the water is truly the mysterious Lord of Life."[69]

51. The Cosmic Pillar (*Skambha*) standing in the Waters makes possible man's discovery of "surrounding", both spiritual and material.

"Through whom men know the worlds and what enwraps them, the waters and Holy Word, the all powerful in whom are found Being and Non-being – Tell me of that Support – who may he be?

By whom Creative Fervor waxing powerful upholds the highest Vow, in whom unite Cosmic Order and Faith, the waters and the World – Tell me of that Support – who may he be ?"[70]

52. The earth, then, was in the beginning lying upon the Waters a little forsaken. The boar *Ādivarāha* who had propped it up apparently left it there, afloat on the Waters. Who among us knows exactly what has happened? Some say that the earth was the primordial hill itself and the Waters were flowing underneath it. So when *Indra* pierced the hill, a "second" earth appeared.

Prajāpati, The Lord of Generation, took care of the earth. He was seen around swinging on a lotus leaf in the Waters.

"In the beginning this universe was the waters, the ocean, *Prajāpati* became the wind and moved in the ocean. He saw the earth and became a boar and seized her; he became *Viśvakarman* and stroked her, spreading her out so that she became extended; she became the earth, and so the earth is called *Pṛthivī* ("The Extended"). *Prajāpati* exhausted himself in her and he produced the gods, *Vasus, Rudras*, and *Ādityas*."[71]

"In the beginning the earth was only the size of a hand-span. A boar raised her up, and he was called *Emūṣa*; he was *Prajāpati*, her husband, and she was his mate, his dear abode."[72]

---

69. *AV.* 10.7.37-38, 40-41, tr. Panikkar, *op. cit.,* p. 66.
70. *AV.* 10.7.10-11. The whole hymn of *AV.* 10.7 is dedicated to the philosophy of the *Skambha.*
71. *TS.* 7.1.5.1 in: *Hindu Myths, A Source-book translated from the Sanskrit*, with an introduction by Wendy Doniger O'Flaherty, Penguin Books, reprint, 1982, p. 185. See also: *RV.* 1.61.7; *SB.* 7.5.1.5.; 14.1.2.11.; *TB.* 1.1.3.5; *TS.* 6.2.4.2. For notes on the two boars (*Prajāpati* and *Viṣñu*) see: Kuiper. *op. cit.*, pp. 100-101 Also see: Part II:5:4 (v) "*Prajāpati,* the Lord of Generation". The boar-*avatar* was originally a part of the *Brāhmaṇas*. On account of its symbolism the myth was easily assimilated to *Viṣñu* who helps *Indra* to retrieve a sacrificial boar.
72. *SB.* 14.1.2.11a. in *Hindu myths*, p. 185. For a discussion see: Gonda, *Aspects of Early Viṣñuism*,

"Realizing that the earth was within the waters when the universe had been made into a single ocean, *Prajāpati* wished to raise it. He made another body; as at the beginning of previous aeons he had made the fish, the tortoise, and others, so now the eternal, constant, supreme soul, the soul of the universe, *Prajāpati* took the body of a boar, a form composed of the Vedic sacrifice, in order to preserve the whole universe."[73]

Thus *Pṛthivī*, the factual geographical earth, came about. The earth upon which man lives and works, loves and suffers is *Bhūmi*. She knows man's condition. She can also be hurt by man.

53. Those not content with *Prajāpati's* concern with the earth, found solace in another more mysterious explanation for its origin:

"Water was this in the beginning, a great flood that impregnated as a wave another wave. Thence arose two golden cups, *kukṣi*."[74]

The *Chāndogya Upaniṣad* takes up that theme in a meditative-philosophical mood:

"The sun is the *Brahman*, such is the directive for adoration. About that is this explanation. This world was in the beginning non being; this non-being was the being. The same originated. An egg then developed itself. It lay there as long as a year. Thereupon it split itself; of both shells of the egg, the one was silver, the other was of gold.

The silver one is the earth, the golden one is the heavens above. The outer membrane (*jarāyu* = chorion) are these mountains; the inner membrane (*ulvam*, amnion) – (this membrane closing the foetus) are here the clouds and the mist, the vascular arteries are the rivers, the feeding water within is the ocean."[75]

54. Whether he conceives of the earth's creation in a mechanical fashion or in that of the embryo, man wishes to know and understand where he lives. He needs security. In the ritual speculations *Indra* was known to have secured the earth so man could go to sleep with a quiet heart. How could man live otherwise?

"Thou art firm (*dhruvam*) do thou make the earth firm (*dṛḍha*)"[76]

"He (*Indra*) then brings pebbles. Now the gods and the *Asuras* both of them sprung from *Prajāpati*, once contended for superiority. This earth was then trembling like a lotus-leaf; for the wind was tossing it hither and thither; now it came near the gods, now it came near the *Asuras*. When it came to the gods, they said, "Come, let us steady this resting place and when firm and steady let us set the two fires on it; whereupon we will xclude our

pp. 129-145.

73. *VP*. 1.4.3.11 in *Hindu Myths*, p. 186. The sacrifice as intended restoration and as psychological concept of meaningfulness of the universe has been discussed earlier in this work on various occasions.

74. *JaimUB*. 1.56.1.

75. *CU*. 3.19. 1-2.

76. *VajS*. 1.17.

enemies from any share in it. Accordingly in like manner as one would stretch a skin by means of wooden pegs, they fastened down this restingplace; and it formed a firm and steady restingplace."[77]

Thus the earth was taken care of by the gods and wrested from the exclusive power of the *Asuras*, the demons.

5. Just then, from the centre, when the dual universe was being created, *Viṣṇu* rose. Just as the pillar (*skambha*) connects heaven and earth, *Viṣṇu* forms part of both worlds. *Viṣṇu-Śeṣa*, the "Serpent-*Viṣṇu*", supports the world-axis from below but in three strides he covers the whole of what is.

"I will proclaim the mighty deeds of *Viṣṇu* who measured out the earthly regions and propped the heavens above, accomplishing in his course three mighty strides.
The marks of his three strides are filled with honey imperishable; each is cause of joy. Alone he supports the three spheres – Earth and Sky and all things living.
May I attain to *Viṣṇu*'s glorious mansion where the faithful rejoice, where, close beside the Strider, within his highest foot step springs the well of purest honey!"[78]

6. Heaven and Earth, though far apart, are linked by *Viṣṇu* and *Indra*. They remind man of the *Soma*-sacrifice climbing the illustrious *skambha* to the divine regions, linking them with the world of man. *Viṣṇu-Indra* are like the precious *Soma*-bowl (*kalasa*) holding the sacrificial juice.

"This your deed, *Indra-Viṣṇu*, must be lauded; widely you strode in the wild joy of *Soma*. You made the firmament of large compass, and made the regions broad for our existence.
Strengthened with sacred offerings, *Indra-Viṣṇu*, first eaters, served with worship and oblation, fed with holy oil, vouchsafe us riches; you are the lake, the vat that holds the *Soma*."[79]

7. In *Viṣṇu's* highest footstep springs the well of the water of wisdom and immortality (*madhva-utsaḥ*). The god holds the waters, the earth and everything else together in three strides.

"May I attain to that, his well-loved mansion where men devoted to the

---

77. *SB*. 1.1.8-10 tr. Julius Eggeling. It is important to note that in the *ṚgVeda* and the *Brāhmaṇas* the notion of a stable earth is clearly emphasized. Combining the various data of the Vedic creation-myth, Kuiper concludes that "since the mountain was the cosmic centre, the central point of the earth, the whole earth become thereby "firm and steady" (*dhruva, aśithila*). Thus the cosmic mountain not only was the origin of the earth but also came to function as the "peg" which secured the earth a firm support (*pratiṣhṭha*). This idea still survives in the later Mount *Mandāra* as the cosmic pivot, called Indra's peg (*Indrakīla*)", *op. cit.*, p. 108f.
78. *RV*. 1.154.1.4.5 tr. Panikkar, *op. cit.*, p. 152. The "honey" may refer to *Soma* since the third step is transcendent, filled with the nectar of immortality; See footnote no. 67.
79. *RV*. 6.69.5-6. tr. Griffith, *op. cit.*, p.329. These verses are exemplary of what I earlier called the *aimed-at restoration* of totality in myth and cult. Man's breakthrough beyond the immediate horizon offers a perspective and deeper dimension capable of shaping a vision of the universe's totality.

gods are happy. For there springs, close akin to the Wide-Strider, the well of meath in *Viṣñu's* highest footstep."[80]

58. Thus *Viṣnu* is the god of *pravṛtti* or cosmic progression, in each and everything at all times. He is, as *Brahma*, especially involved in creativity. However, as *Viṣñu Jala-Sayin*, sleeping on his serpent-couch *Ananta*, Endless, *Viṣñu* is in each and everything the god of regression (*nivṛtti*) especially at the end of times.

"When the waters come to rest, having reached the realm of the seven seers, then this single ocean completely covers the three worlds. Wind blown out of *Viṣñu's* mouth makes the clouds disappear in a hundred years. When the eternal lord, fashioner of all creatures, inconceivable, the condition of creation, the beginning of everything who has no beginning himself, has entirely consumed the wind, then, reposing on *Śeṣa* in the single ocean, the lord, first creator, rests in the form of *Brahmā*, praised by *Sanaka* and others, the seers who went to *Janaloka*, and also meditated upon by those who went to *Brahamaloka* seeking freedom. Resting in meditative sleep, in the divine form of his own illusive power, *Viṣñu*, destroyer of *Madhu*, concentrates on the form of himself calls *Vāsudeva*. This is the dissolution called occasional, O Maitreya; the occasion is that *Hari* (*Viṣñu*) rests in the form of *Brahmā*. When the soul of all awakens, then the world stirs. When the imperishable one has gone to his bed of illusion, it falls completely asleep. A day of *Brahmā*, born from the lotus, lasts a thousand periods of four Ages; a night, when the world is destroyed and made into a vast ocean, is of the same length. At the end of the night, *Viṣñu*, unborn, having awakened, takes the form of *Brahma* in order to create, as it has already been told to you."[81]

59. Already in pre-*Indra* aeons when *Vṛtra* obstructed the waters, *Varuṇa*, the Lord of the Waters, had been known. Knowing all that happens both in heaven and in the oceans, he is near man.

"He knows the path of birds that fly through heaven, and sovereign of the sea. He knows the ships that are thereon.

True to his only law He knows the twelve moons with their progeny: He knows the moon of later birth. He knows the pathway of the wind: He knows Gods who dwell above. *Varuṇa*, true to holy laws, sits down among his people; he, most wise, sits there to govern all."[82]

60. *Varuṇa*, whose eye is in the sky, is the Sun who sees all (*sarvadarsī*). Sitting in the waters on earth and rising from there, the human world is not foreign to *Varuṇa*.

"This earth is his; to him belongs the lofty boundless sky above. *Varuṇa* contains within his body both the oceans, and yet he is also contained within one droplet."[83]

---

80. *RV*. 1.154.5. tr. Griffith p. 103. "Highest footstep" – *pada parama*", also understood to be the transcendent abode of *Viṣñu*.
81. *VP*. 6.3.14 – 41 and 4.1 – 10 in: Dimmitt & v. Buitenen, *op. cit.*, p. 43.
82. *RV*. 1.25.7 – 10, tr. Griffith, *op. cit.*, p. 15.
83. *AV*. 4.16.3. tr. Panikkar, *op. cit.*, p. 512.

"Emerging resplendent from the bosom of the mornings, he ascends, heart's delight of all the singers, This is the god I hail as Vivifier! He never infringes the Order's harmony."[84]

"If I totter along, O wielder of thunder, like a puffed-up wineskin, forgive, Lord, have mercy!"[85]

61. Hence *Varuṇa* is also the god of the netherworld, an important spot. In the netherworld *Varuṇa* watches over *Ṛta*, Cosmic Order. *Ṛta* is said to be "fixed and hidden where they unharness the horses of the sun."[86]

62. *Varuṇa* is *nṛcakṣaḥ*: he sees and observes all.

"He puts milk in cows, intelligence in hearts, fire in the waters, in the sky the sun, soma on the mountain."[87]

63. While setting in the western quarter's ocean, the sun becomes the god of the netherworld where the seat of *Ṛta* is found and where its light guides man's behaviour:

"Firm is this new wrought hymn of praise, and meet to be told forth, O Gods. The flowing of the floods is Law. Truth is the Sun's extended light. Mark this my woe, you Earth and Heaven."[88]

64. When from the earthly oceans the Sun rises in the morning, it rises from the seat of *Ṛta*, setting man into motion according to a design. The Sun not only causes consciousness of the morning but also bestows mature vision of reality and an aim in life, a point, like the Sun's zenith in the sky.

"*Agni* is wakened; *Sūrya* rises from the earth. Mighty refulgent Dawn has shone with all her light. The *Asvinis* have equipped their chariot for their course. God Savitar (the great cause of life) has moved the folk in sundry ways."[89]

"He lights up all things, guards each holy ordinance. None can deceive him, the great God, the radiant. He has stretched out his arms to all earth dwellers. Maintaining his own laws he runs his course."[90]

65. At the bottom of the Cosmic Axis, *Varuṇa* supports the cosmic spaces of heaven and earth.

"He is an Ocean far removed, yet through the heaven to him ascends the worship which these realms possess. With his bright foot he overthrew their magic, and went up to heaven.

---

84. *RV*. 7.63.3. tr. Panikkar, *op. cit*., p. 822.
85. *RV*. 7.89.2. tr. Panikkar, *op. cit*., p. 517.
86. *RS*. 5.62.1. in: Kuiper, *op. cit*., p. 67. Kuiper discusses the question how a "heavenly idea" such as cosmic order could be said to be seated in the netherworld. For our purpose it will be sufficient to say that the Sun, being heavenly, but setting in the waters, is everywhere. For the mythical mind there would be no mental and abstract division between heaven and earth when an important "feeling" of harmony in life is needed for man to feel secure. Kuiper quotes *Naighaṇṭuka* 1.12 where the "womb of the *Ṛta*" – *ṛtasya yoniḥ* – is said to be equivalent to "water" see p. 67.
87. *RV*. 5.85.1-2.
88. *RV*. 1.105.12. tr. Griffith.
89. *RV*. 1.157.1 tr. Griffith. *Surya* from "*su*–" meaning to impel, to enliven, to beget. The Sun not only gives physical light but also inspires man's heart and mind.
90. *RV*. 4.53.4. tr. Panikkar, *op. cit*., p. 197.

Ruler, whose bright far-seeing rays, pervading all three earths, have filled the three superior realms of heaven. Firm is the seat of *Varuṇa*: over the Seven he rules as King. Who, after his decree, overspread the darkness with a robe of light; Who measured out the ancient seat, who pillared both the worlds apart as the Unborn supported heaven. Let all others die away."[91]

66. *Viṣñu's* position at the centre associates him with the cosmic pillar guarded from underneath by *Varuṇa*. But *Viṣñu* occupies a more central position already at an early date. His three strides (*trivikrama*) cover the whole distance of the pillar from below along the middle to beyond. The power of *Viṣnu* is a disguised one since he belongs to the whole length of the cosmic axle and is friend with everyone. After a period of lesser prominence in the *ṚgVeda*, he becomes constantly identified with sacrifice in the *Sāma Veda* and the *Śatapatha Brāhmaṇa*:

"*Viṣñu* is the sacrifice."[92]
"much have they given us, who gave us that which has the same size as the sacrifice."[93]

That "size of the sacrifice" refers to *Viṣñu's* revelation of his *trivikrama*, his "three strides". The story is delightfully told in the *Puraṇas*: *Bali*, king of the *Asuras*, performed sacrifice. Present was *Vamana*, who was *Viṣnu* in the form of a dwarf. Against other advice, *Bali* adhered to the rules of hospitality and offered *Vāmana* as much land as he could cover in three steps. At once *Viṣñu* revealed himself and covered in three steps the whole of the universe. The cultic act by man aims by sacrifice to restore the universal fullness in himself. He does what the gods did.[94]

67. The *skambha*, standing in the waters of the netherworld and linking them to the heavens, has from the *ṚgVedic* beginnings been understood to be the Tree of Life, transmitting the flow of rhythm between the two worlds.

"*Varuṇa*, King, of hallowed might, sustains erect the Tree's stem in the baseless region. Its rays, whose root is high above, stream downward. Deep may they sink within us, and be hidden."[95]
"This Bull's (the sun) most gracious far-extended favour existed first of all

91. *RV*. 8.41.8-10. tr Griffith.
92. *SB*. 14.1.1.6.
93. *SB*. 1.2.5.5.
94. *VaSa*. 10.1-9; 33-66; 85-87. See also BhgP. Kuiper in *op. cit*., p.48 refers to *Viṣñu's* important and at the same time ambiguous position – a role in other mythologies attributed to the "divine trickster" (Josselin de Jong) – because *Viṣñu* cannot take sides with anyone because everything is part of his essence. For *Viṣñu* and *skambha* also see; *Mhb*. 5.101.2; 8.69.48.
95. *RV*. 1.24.7. tr. Griffith. The Cosmic Tree in Indian thought and iconography is commonly held to be the *Aśvattha*, the fig tree (Ficus Religiosa). The *nyagrodha*, banyan tree, figures in secondary and derived realms. Earlier I mentioned the "inverted tree" as a problem in natural symbolism with regard to the Feminine. However, unless the male spirit is able to construct a purely abstract world, it must make use of the nature-symbols. The matriarchal character of the nature-symbol always asserts itself. See: Neumann, *The Great Mother, An Analysis of the Archetype*, p.50.

in full abundance. By his support they are maintained in common who in the *Asura's* mansion dwell together.

What was the tree, what wood, in sooth, produced it? The wood from which they fashioned forth the Earth and Heaven? These two stand fast and wax not old for ever: these have sung praise to many a day and morning."[96]

68. As the upperworld was related to day and the netherworld to night, the night-sky as heavenly ocean was equated to the primordial Waters, *Āpaḥ*, enveloping all that is.

"This everlasting fig tree, whose roots are on high and whose branches are below, is the Pure, the *Brahman*, what is called the Immortal. In that all worlds are established and nothing passes beyond. This in truth is that!"[97]

69. Through the homologue of the world-axle with the Tree, the idea of fertility and growth comes more in focus.

"This earth is his (*Varuṇa's*); to him belongs the lofty boundless sky above. *Varuṇa* contains within his body both the oceans, yet he also is contained within one droplet."[98]

"*Varuṇa* lets the big cask, opening downward, flow through the heaven and earth and air's mid-region. Therewith the universe's Sovereign waters the earth as the shower of rain bedews the barley.

When *Varuṇa* is fain for milk he moistens the sky, and earth to her foundation. Then straight the mountains clothe them in the raincloud; the rains, putting forth their vigour again disperse the clouds. None verily has ever let or hindered this the most wise god's mighty deed of magic.

If we have sinned against the man who loves us, have ever wronged a brother, friend or comrade, the neighbour ever with us or a stranger, O *Varuṇa*, remove from us the trespass"[99]

"Draw the great vessel up, let it spill over, let the flood-waters burst forth and flow far. Saturate both heaven and earth with fatness; give to the cattle fair thirst-quenching pools."[100]

70. The casket poured out by *Varuṇa* is also called the "Golden Well" of *Soma Pavamana*, the Moon. The moon, her bright radiance reflected in the waters, moves in them like a bull moves among cows and impregnates them. The moon's water is semen and produces fertility, whether it be as rain on the lands or as sacrificial juice for man's mind and heart.

"Let us sing praise to the Gods; sing loudly, send the *Soma* forth for mighty riches. Let it flow, sweetly flavoured, in the filter and let our pious one rest in the pitcher."[101]

96. *RV.* 10.31.7.
97. *KathU.* 6.1. tr Panikkar, p. 568.
98. *AV.* 4.16.3.
99. *RV.* 5.85.3-4; 6-7. tr Griffith.
100. *RV* 5.83.8. tr. Panikkar, p. 275.
101. *RV.* 9.107.4. It is an ancient belief-not only in India-that the moon is the lord of the waters. The *Purāṇas* state that the moon's chariot consists of water. In *AB.* 8.28.15: "the rain comes from the

". . .you impregnator of the waters."[102]

71. Down at the base of the centre of the cosmos is *Varuṇa's* court (*antaḥsalila*) "beneath or within the waters". It is surrounded by watersnakes (*nagas*). The *nagas*, of the family of *makara*, the monstrous animal-fish, are reminders of *Vṛtra*, the monster who held back the flowing waters. They also remind us that land and sea, earth and heaven, belong together. The waters will finally receive all creation back into their bosom when the aeons have come to completion. They are the living receivers of involution of creation (*nivṛtti*).[103]

72. *Varuṇa's* vehicle is *makara*, the serpent-crocodile, guardian of the western quarter. That quarter is the region of *Yama*, darkness and death. *Varuṇa* and *makara* together stand for the return to the Uncreate,. to original perfection at the time of dissolution (*pralaya*) which is always present and in progress. In Indian iconography the *makara* appears with a small human figure (*gana*) in his mouth, an image of the inherent tendency in creation to return to the Waters.[104]

73. *Makara's* dual nature receives affirmative symbols when vines grow out of its mouth. *Makara's* serpent brothers and sisters live in trees moistening them with water. Once, so the myth goes, *Sita* was carried away by *Mādhavī Devi*, goddess Earth. The *nagas*, however, to be able to hide *Sītā*, made divine Earth rise on a seat, carried by them. It also happened that a crocodile was dragged from the water and transformed into a beautiful girl decked with ornaments.[105]

74. While *Varuṇa's* court is down at the base of the central world-axle, from the very centre itself which is the lotus in *Viṣṅu's* navel, rises forth *Brahma*. He is four-faced and himself the centre of all directions.

"At the end of the last aeon, when the worlds were in darkness, there was nothing but a solitary sea, not gods, no seers. In that undisturbed isolation slept the God *Nārāyaṇa* (*Viṣnu*) supreme person, lying on the bed that was

---

moon "– *candramaso vai vṛṣṭir-jāyate*. *RV*. 9.86.39: "O moon, you are placed in the worlds as the semen bearer" – *retodha indo bhuvanesa-arpitaḥ*. *RV*. 9.74.5:" *dadhati garbham aditer upastha ā yena tokaṃ ca tanayaṃ ca dhamāhe*". The terrestrial *Soma* is a replica of the celestial one. Both rest in the womb of the waters. For "*Soma*" see: Alfred Hillebrandt, *Vedic Mythology*, vol. 1, pp. 121-266.

102. *RV*. 9.36.8: ". . . impregnator of the waters" – *apām peru*. The moon is the bull who moves in the middle of the herd. e.g. *RV*. 9.16.6: *śuro ha goṣu tiṣṭhati*.

103. *Mhb*. 9.46.

104. *AP*. 51.15. I am avoiding here Coomaraswamy's wellknown study chiefly dealing with the *makara's* vegetal affinities, although in the following numbers vegetal affirmations will be found. See: A. Coomaraswamy, *Yakṣas*, 2 vols., Delhi, 1971. The *makara* points to the fact that all passages from one state of being to another involve a kind of "danger". One finds their statues and images placed over door-ways and templegates. Thus the *kāla-makara* head is in India called both "*makara* face" (*makara-vaktra*) and the "lion's jaws" (*siṃha-mukha*). Universally, the fundamental element in the dragon's powers is the control of water. Both in its beneficial and destructive aspects, water is regarded as animated by the dragon.

105. *Mhb. Ādi-Parvan* 218. For the happening to *Sītā*, see: *R*. 7.97. The *nāgas* bore *Situ* down to the depths: *rasātalam*.

the serpent *Seṣa*. . .Once during his sleep there arose in play from his navel a pure lotus, wondrous and divine, core of the three worlds. . . "Who are you?", the universal soul, *Hari* (*Visnu*), although he recognized the great yogin, asked *Puruṣa*, the creator. Beginning to laugh, the lord *Brahmā*, keeper of the *Vedas*, with lotus-eyes, replied in these polished words: "I am creator and ordainer, the self-existent great-grandfather; in me is everything established. I am *Brahma* who faces in all directions. "Hearing this, *Viṣnu*, whose power is his truth, took his leave and entered into the body of *Brahmā* by *yoga*. Seeing all three worlds with gods, demons and men in the belly of the god, he was astonished. . . Then the one born from a golden egg, the four-faced *Brahma* who had entered therein by the power of *yoga*, displayed himself on the lotus. Lord *Brahma*, self-existent, the Grandfather, womb of creation lustrous as the inside of a flower, shone there radiantly, resting on a lotus."[106]

75. In the first aeon after the break from the Uncreate into the create, *Svadhā*, the Breath over the oceans, had said: "I want to be many". The position and condition of all created things was still to be clarified and organized further. That happened in the centre. Already in the *ṚgVeda* we hear of the *Aśvinıs*, celestials, who swung the Cosmic Tree in an effort to free *Saptavadhri*, the personified celestial fire.

"Tree, part asunder like the side of her who brings forth a child. You, *Aśvinīs*, listen to my call: loose *Saptavadhri* from his bonds.

For *Saptavadhri*, for the seer affrighted when he wept and wailed, you, *Aśvinīs*, with your magic powers rent up the tree and shattered it."[107]

76. More happened in that first aeon of the break into creation. So we are told by purāṇic tradition. The significant event of the Churning of the Ocean (*samudra-manthana*) took place. Gods and demons met to settle various matters after creation had come to be. Some say that the event took place in the Milky Ocean in the sky. The gods did not do well in their fight with the demons whose strength persisted undiminished. They had been given the power of resuscitating those who had fallen in battle. *Kāvya Ūṣanas* had received that power from *Śiva*. The worried gods asked *Brahmā* for his advice and he told them to cooperate with, rather than to fight, the demons. It was agreed that together they should churn the ocean for *amṛta*, the drink of immortality.[108]

Using the cosmic pivot, mount *Mandara*, as their churning-stick, the contestants held the rope, the serpent *Vasuki*. At one end, holding its tail, stood the gods. At the other, the demons. Not surprisingly, *Viṣñu-Śeṣa*, guardian of the *skambha*, was seen around.

106. *KP*. 1.9.6-29. in: Dimmitt & v. Buitenen, *op. cit.*, p. 30f. (abreviated rendering, F.B.). *Brahmā* is represented with a sacrificial ladle (symbolizing his essence as *Puruṣa* or *Prajāpati*, the sacrifice), a book (he can be known through wisdom), the rosary, *Kamaṇḍalu* (the jug symbolic of the mendicant's life) and the bull-mount, connecting him with *Śiva*. Elsewhere he has *Garuḍa*, *Viṣñu's* bird. He also has a swan (*haṁsa*) as a vehicle, like his daughter *Saraswatī*.

107. *Rv*. 5.78. 5-6. See: A. Bergaigne, *La Religion Védique*, vol.2., p. 467.

108. *MP*. 249.3-22.

"So directed by the god of gods, all the gods joined with the demons in a combat to produce the nectar. After gathering various herbs, the gods, *Daityas* and *Danavas* threw them into the water of the ocean of milk whose glow was as clear as the sky in autumn..."[109]

77. *Viṣñu* deceitfully made the churningstick *Mandāra* rest on *Kaśyapa*, Tortoise, one of his water-animal self-revelations. His move betrayed his intent. From the outset it was to be clear that nothing but the divine could claim immortality.[110]

"In the middle of the milky ocean lord *Hari* himself appeared in the form of a tortoise to support the rotating mountain while it was churned, O great seer. *Keśava* appeared in one form in the midst of the gods, bearing mace and discus; in another form he pulled the snake-king with the *Daityas*; and in a third gigantic form, unseen by gods and demons alike, he strode up the mountain, O *Maitreya. Hari* then infused the serpent-kind with strength, and in his original form invigorated the gods with power."[111]

78. Wonderful things came up from the ocean. The accounts differ as to which of them came first. Those present were too amazed at seeing all the wonders. Among the gifts which appeared was *Viṣñu's Kaustubha* gem.

"This divine jewel *Kaustubha* came up in the middle of ghee and stayed in the breast of *Viṣñu* spreading its rays everywhere."[112]

"Out of the middle of this ocean of milk that was being churned by gods and demons, there first arose *Surabhi*, source of the oblation, honoured by the deities. Both gods and *Dānavas* were delighted, great seer, their minds excited, their eyes unblinking. Even as the heavenly *Siddhas* were thinking, "What is this?", the goddess *Varuṇī* appeared, her eyes rolling with intoxication. Next from the whirling milk ocean came the *Pārijata* tree, perfuming the world with its fragrance and delighting the wives of the gods. And then, *Maitreya*, a most marvellous throng of *Apsaras*, endowed with the virtues of beauty and nobility, sprang up from the milky ocean."[113]

---

109. *VP*. 1.9.2-116. in: Dimmitt & v. Buitenen, *op. cit*., p.96. (the whole event is here recounted as one of various versions and interpretations, scattered over several sources) see. e.g. *Mhb*. 1.16.6-32; *MP*. 249. 23-82.

110. *VP*. 1.9.88-90.

111. *VP*. 1.9.2-116 in: Dimmitt & v. Buitenen, *op. cit*., p. 97.

112. "The churning of the ocean is the classic image of creation by means of chaos – the disruption of the serene primeval waters in order that all the opposing pairs may emerge and meet in creative conflict. In the course of this process, the agents (the gods and demons) become differentiated. At first they are united in their task, but later they are opposed. The basic symbolic dialectic is that of liquids. The neutral water is transmuted into various elixirs – human (milk), ritual (butter) and divine (mead, ambrosia, or *Soma*) as well as into the reversal of all elixirs – poison. According to Hindu cosmology, the earth is ringed by several concentric oceans – first the salt ocean, then oceans of sugar-cane juice, wine, clarified butter, milk, whey, and fresh water....The structural force of this dialectic is so powerful that almost every essential element of the myth is duplicated: the ambrosia itself is obtained twice, and there are two snakes, two mountains, two eclipses, and two rains-one creative and one destructive", in: *Hindu Myths*, Penguin Books, 1982, p. 273f. The salt ocean comes first because salt soil is valued in a pastoral society since cattle thrive on it.

113. *VP*. 1.9.2 – 116. in: Dimmitt & v. Buitenen, *op. cit*., p. 97. *Vāruṇī* is *Varuṇa's* wife and also the name of an intoxicating drink. See also: Part I:1:3: "The juices of *Saptadvīpa*, the seven islands"

In the *Mahabharata*-account the gods are said to have been extremely tired when churning. They needed *Viṣñu's* special encouragement:.

> "Then from the ocean there arose *Soma*, the calm moon, with its cool rays, and the sun of a hundred thousand rays. And immediately after this the goddess *Srí*, dressed in white, appeared from the clarified butter; then the goddess of wine; then *Uccaiḥsravas*, the white horse of the sun; and then came the divine *Kaustubha* gem for the chest of the blessed *Narayaṇa*, blooming with rays, born of the ambrosia. And the great elephant *Airāvata*, with his enormous body and his four white and shiny tusks, came forth and was taken by the wielder of the Thunderbolt."[114]

79. But then disaster threatened. Again the accounts differ as to when the gods' and demons' churning seemed to turn into ill fortune. In their avid greed, obviously misplaced, for the nectar of immortality (*amṛta*), the gods and demons caused the ocean, or perhaps it was *Vasuki*, the serpent-rope himself, to throw up a vicious mass of stinking venom (*kalakūta*). The *Rāmāyaṇa* says *kālakūta* came first.[115]

80. The venom burnt like doomsdayfire and the gods knew that death had come about. It's name is *Kāla*, time. The *nāgas* took possession of it. Thus, at the base of *skambha*, the cosmic pillar, where *Varuṇa* sat in the waters, *Kāla*, time, joined the seat of cosmic order, *Ṛta*. The elements of rhythmic spacial and time-bound change of years, months, days, nights, moments and modifications of man's thoughts and feelings had come about.[116]

81. *Siva*, in the *Viṣṇu-Purāṇa*, had kept away when everyone was helplessly looking for a means to dispose of the foul smelling *Kālakūta*, vomited up by the ocean or, perhaps, *Vasuki*. *Siva* took to himself the moon, newly born from the waters. Ever since, we see *Siva* flaunting the moon in his hair. It is the crescent moon.

Prajāpati had revealed himself as the embodiment of the annual cycle of vegetative life when he played his part in the very dawn of the beginnings. That earliest dawn signified, mythically, the beginning of time as such and that of creation. Ritually it meant the beginning of sacrifice and the altar as event and place of restoration and remembering. *Prajapati* is the sacrifice. The altar layers were understood to be the seasons. Thus sections of time were equalled to spacial extent. In the mind the concept of time precedes its symbols in the seasonal segments. In the language of myth, Time is the father of *Prajāpati*.[117] He has brought forth the past and the future.[118] Time is thus the source of immortality of all beings. Even though time is only time, it harbours in itself the timeless Time. Timeless Time had spontaneously flowed into creation.

---

114. *Mhb*: 1.15.5-13; 1.16.1-40; 1.17.1-30: in: *Hindu Myths*, Penguin Books, 1982, p. 276f. Also: *MP*. 250. 1-5.
115. *MP*. 250. 14-61 and *R*. 1.
116. *VP*. 1.9.97
117. *AV*. 19.53.8, II See Part II:5:4 (v): "*Prajapati*: The Lord of Generation". The year, *Prajāpati*, was renewed each spring at the vernal equinox, when a star was seen to rise before the sun.
118. *AV*. 19.53.3.

Neither violence nor sin accompanied its descent. Time in man's life deserves respect.

Siva now placed the moon in his hair. Everyone present at the churning of the ocean realized – and we humans too, realize – that "time" with its seasonal moon-tides is an indelible part of creational existence. *Siva*, the divine, is beyond waxing and waning. Unlike the fisherman and the sailor, *Śiva* is not dependent upon the tides of the sea. Nor are births of his seed dictated by the menstrual cycle of woman. Although *Siva* played no part in the hymns of Time in the *Atharva Veda*, the *Śvetasvatara Upaniṣad* knows him to be time's master:

> "Higher and other than time . . . is he from whom the world revolves."[119]
> "He is the beginning, the impulse of the causes . . . beyond all time, and without separate parts."[120]
> "He is the maker of time" (*kālakāra*).[121]

82. The moon in *Śiva's* hair is said to be the sixteenth segment of the moon (*candrasya ṣoḍasī*). It is the transcendent completion of all waxing and waning. The sixteenth *Kala* of the moon is the immovable stillness, the eternal quietude beyond the brightly lit and dark days and nights of the terrestrials, looking up to the moon in the sky.

The believing human being experiences existence through the devout devotion of the *Cāndrāyaṇa*-fast: the daily quantity of food, consisting of fifteen mouthfuls at full moon, is diminished by one mouthful every day during the dark fortnight until it is increased in like manner during the bright fortnight.

> "O excellent sages, devotion results from thousands of *Cāndrayaṇa*, hundreds of *Prajapatyas* monthly fasts and other holy rites. Those who lack in devotion to the lord fall into a mountain cave and undergo the results of their *Karman*. A devotee is liberated through his devotional emotion . . ."[122]
>
> "If one diminishes one's food daily by one mouthful during the dark half of the month and increases it in the same manner during the bright half, and bathes daily at the time of three libations (morning, noon, and evening) that is called a lunar penance (*Cāndrāyaṇa*)."[123]

---

119. *SU.* 6.6.
120. *SU* 6.5
121. *SU* 6.2.16.
122. *LP.* 10.32-37.
123. *Laws of Manu* 2.217. *SCN.* 46. "Here is the excellent supreme sixteenth *Kalā* of the Moon. She is pure, and resembles (in colour) the young Sun. She is as thin as the hundredth part of a fibre in the stalk of a lotus. She is lustrous and soft like ten million lightning flashes, and is downturned. From Her, whose source is the *Brahman*, flows copiously the continuous stream of nectar (or, She is the receptacle of the stream of excellent nectar which comes from the blissfull union of Parā and Parā"—
"Atrāste sisusuryasodarakalā candrasya sā soḍaśī
śuddhā nırajasukṣmatantuśatadhabhagaikarūpā parā.
Vidyutkotisamanạkomalatatanurvidyotitādhomukhī
nityānandaparamparātivigalat-pıyuṣadhārādhārini". *in:*
John Woodroffe, *The Serpent Power, being the Ṣaṭ-Cakra-Nirupaṇa and Pādukā-Pañcaka*, Ganesh & Co., Madras, 9th ed., 1973, p. 443. Some of Woodroffe's notes: "*Parā* and *Parā* are the Bindu-

83. Elsewhere, in the telling of the churning of the ocean, *Śiva* complies with *Brahmā's* request to protect everyone from the deadly poison. *Śiva* swallows it. It left a dark blue spot on *Siva*'s throat and hence he came to be called *Siva Nīlakaṇṭha*, the blue-throated. It looked as though the purple-necked peacock had kissed him and *Śiva* is seen accompanied by the bird.[124]

84. The poison purified the throat of the meditative *Śiva Mantramūrti*. It became the centre of purity (*viśhuddha cakra*): the fifth centre of subtle energy in the yogic human psycho-physical body, unseen by medical science.[125] Lying in the region of the human throat at the junction of the spinal column and the medulla oblongata, it is the seat of the *udāna*-breath and of the *bindu*.

> "In the throat is the Lotus called *Viśuddha*, which is pure and of a smoky purple hue. All the sixteen shining vowels on its sixteen petals, of a crimson hue, are distinctly visible to him whose mind (*Buddhi*) is illumined. In the pericarp of this lotus there is the Ethereal Region, circular in shape, and white like the full Moon. On an elephant white as show is seated the *Bīja* of *Aṁbara*, who is white of colour...."[126]

85. Withdrawing to his cave on Mount *Meru*, *Siva Nīlalohita*, the blue-red god, waved the honours bestowed on him for swallowing the world-poison (*kālakūta*). It was no poison at all when compared to mundane existence. The real poison is desire and attachment (*pravṛtti*) which must be overcome by detachment (*nivṛtti*). That is freedom.[127] *Śiva* warned everyone.

> "O Lord, the bull-bannered Lord, the terrible poison *kala kūta* has been neutralized by you. Hence everything has been stabilized by you."
>
> On hearing their words, lord *Nīlalohita,* the *Atman* of the universe, smilingly said to those sages, *Sanandana* and others "O excellent brahmins, of what consequence is this? I shall mention another more terrible poison. He who nullifies that poison is really efficient. Of what avail is this? The mundane existence is two-fold in accordance with one's rights and duties. In regard to men of deluded minds, the mundane existence is very terrible and burdensome. O sages of good holy rites, creation is caused by ignorance due to the effects of malice and attachment. It is certainly due to these that virtue and evil befall everyone. O brahmins, even in regard to things not

---

rupa *Śiva* and *Śakti*. *Ānanda* is the joy which arises from the union of the two, and from such union flows the nectar of which *Ama-kalā* is the receptacle. The sixteenth *Kalā* of the moon is the *Amā-Kalā*. This is said to be the *Urdhva-śakti-rūpā*, or the upward (towards the *Brahman*) moving *Śakti*.

124. *MP*. 250.14 – 16; *Mhb*. 1.16.38. *Śiva* as transcendental Time is *Mahākāla* and as *Kāla* he is forever at work, changing at every moment the living bodies that he consumes through the process of time. Temporal time, left to itself, is like poison of darkness without any perspective or dimension beyond the directly measurable. For the peacock, see e.g. *SkP*. 5.2.14.9. As *Mṛtyuñjaya*, the conqueror of death, (*SkP*. 1.1.10.68), *Śiva* absorbed in himself its deadly darkness, *kāla*, the destruction of phenomenal existence. "We strove for immortality", said the gods, "but found death" (*SkP*. 5.2.14.5).

125. *SS*. 5.90- 91.

126. *SCN*. 28-29. in: Woodroffe, *op. cit.*, p. 384. In the *Viśuddha Cakra* the Word which is the body of the universe becomes manifest.

127. *LP*. 1.86. 4-20.

near at hand, the scripture creates desire for them even in the minds of good men in the world merely by hearing of it. Hence, the perceptible world and the world of Vedic tradition and rituals both should be echewed with great effort. He then becomes *Virakta* (unattached person) altogether."[128]

86. At last, from the ocean, *amṛta* appeared. *Dhanvantari* held it in a water-jar full of nectar. After a fierce battle the gods won it. They left it with *Viṣñu* for safekeeping.

"...next from the whirling milk ocean came *Dhanvantari* himself, clad in white, carrying a water-jar full of nectar, whereupon all the mindful *Daityas* and *Dānavas* became joyful, *Maitreya*, along with the seers....But the *Daityas* led by *Vipracitti*, forsaken by *Lakṣmī*, were dismayed. So they stole the jar full of potent nectar that was in *Dhanvantari's* hand. Whereupon *Viṣñu* fooled them with an illusion. Assuming the body of a woman, the Lord took the cup from the *Dānavas* and gave it to the gods..."[129]

87. About *amṛta*, the nectar of immortality, it is said:

"To one result leads the impermanent, they say, to another the permanent. Thus we have heard from the wise who explained it to us. The man who understands both the impermanent and the permanent, holding the two in tension together, by the impermanent passes over death and by the permanent attains immortal life."[130]

88. The multi-layered myth of the churning of the ocean is based on the annual cyclical movement of the sun. Its rising and setting was seen as due to the gyrating of heaven and earth. Because gods speak in terms of human emotion and conscience, the battle in the cosmic oceanic centre was repeated in the Great War, the mythical-geographical centre of which was *Kuruksetra* near the rivers *Yamuna* and *Gaṅgā*. *Kurukṣetra* represents the cosmic orientation right versus left.

The "right-hand" *Yamunā* is *Kālindī*, the daughter of the Sun who, as *Agni*, dwells in the masculine, in blood. The "left-hand" *Gaṅga* flows from the moon onto *Siva's* forehead and she is equalled to the feminine lifegiving qualities of the moon, engendering growth and semen. *Hastināpura*; the elephant-city, animal of the netherworld, lies on the banks of *Gaṅgā*. The city of the *Pāṇḍavas, Indraprastha*, is situated on *Yamuna's* bank. Thus, in *Kurukṣetra* and in the middle region of *Madhyadeśa*, the battle to vindicate the right understanding of *dharma*, righteousness, is fought. The victors turn out to be king *Yuddhiṣthira* and *Arjuna*.

Arjuna said: "My heart contaminated by the taint of helplessness, my mind confounded about *Dharma*, I ask Thee: Tell me what is absolutely good. I am Thy pupil. Instruct me, who have sought Thy grace."[131]

128. *LP*. 86.6 – 13.
129. *VP*. 1.9.2 – 116.
130. *IsU*. 13 – 14.
131. *BG*. 2.7. Also see: Kuiper, *op. cit.*, p. 33f.

89. *Kurukṣetra* where true understanding of *dharma* was revealed, is known for its holy bathing-place, *Varāha-Tīrtha*. *Viṣñu* is said to have stayed in that spot for a while in the shape of *Varāha*, the Cosmic Boar who had propped up the earth from the ocean.[132]

90. *Viṣñu*, poised as *Kaśyapa*-Tortoise between the two parties of gods and demons at the *samudra-manthana* had occupied a pivotal position. Now *Kṛṣña*, standing between the two deadly enemies, speaks the immortal *Bhagavad Gītā* from *Arjuna's* chariot.

> "Then seeing the people of *Dhṛtaraṣṭra's* party regularly marshalled, while the discharge of weapons began, *Arjuna*, the son of *Paṇḍu*, whose ensign was a monkey, O King of earth, took up his bow and said thus to *Kṛṣña*: "O *Achyuta* (Immortal), place my chariot between the two armies, that I may just see those who stand here desirous to fight, and know with whom I must fight in this strife of battle."[133]

> "Abandoning all righteous deeds (*dharma*), seek me as thy sole Refuge; I will liberate thee from all sins; do not grieve."[134]

91. The fifteenth discourse of the *Bhagavad Gītā* deals with the immanence of the Lord:

> "Penetrating the earth I support all beings by My Energy; and having become the watery moon I nourish all herbs."[135]

The *amṛta*, drink of immortality, is said to be drunk from the moon, the vessel of the beverage of life. The *Soma Pavamāna* becomes resplendent in gods and men. In the *Viṣñu Purāṇa* we read:

> "In the clear starry sky the moon is shining with its full disc like a *yogī* with his last body and spirit in the company of the good."[136]

92. The moon-vessel changes its shape cyclically thereby moving within her own limits. She is the mystic container wherefrom the gods, the ancestors, and the dead drink *amṛta*, the ever-refilling water of life:

> "The moon increases in force in the beginning of the bright half and is stationed in the way of the sun. Day by day it gets refilled till the end of that half. The sun develops and nourishes it. It is drunk up by *Devas* during the dark half. It is being drunk in continuity for fifteen days by *Devas*. The sun refills it part by part by his single ray *Suṣumna*: Thus the physical body of the moon is developed and nourished by the vigour of the sun.

132. *Mhb. Vana Parva*, ch. 83.88.
133. *BG*. 1.20-22. in: Alladi Mahadev Sastry, *The Bhagavad Gītā*, with the commentary of Śrī Śaṅkarāchārya, Samata Books, Madras, 1981, p. 12.
134. *BG*. 18.66. *op. cit.*, p. 499. "Righteous deeds" including unrighteous deeds (*a-dharma*) since *naiṣkarmya* or freedom is taught here.
135. *BG*. 15.13.
136. *VP*. 5.10.7: *tārakāvimale vyomni rarajakhaṇḍamaṇḍalaḥ / candraś caramadehātma yogı sadhu kule yathā*. In the *Brahmavaivarta Purāṇa Kṛṣña's* face is: *śaratpārvaṇacandrābhaṃ sudhapurnaṇanam*.

On the full moon day it appears with its full white disc. Beginning with the second and ending with the fourteenth day in the dark half, *Devas* drink up the moon that was nourished and developed day by day during the bright half. They drink the watery honey and nectar that had been accumulated in the course of half a month, thanks to the splendour of the sun. They sit near the moon for a single night on the full moon day for drinking up the nectar from the moon, along with the sages and the *Pitṛs*."[137]

93. The crescent moon in *Śiva's* hair is not only a reminder of transcendent tranquillity and equilibrium. She is also a symbol of the renewal of vegetative life, recurrent time and the abode of the dead. The moon is *Soma*, the juice of the plant used at the Vedic sacrificial altar. The plant *soma* (Sarcostemma Intermedium) contains an acidulous milky juice just before and during the rainy season. When the lifegiving rain juices come down from the moon, from the earth *soma*-oblations are offered in return for the boon of growth and of medicinal plants. The plants are live comrades of man. That sentiment is conspicuous in Indian literature as well as in art.
Darian writes:

"(they) are concerned with the concept of *Dhvani* or reverberation, the repetition of a theme in subtle and unstated ways. Aside from the plant motif, we find that *Agni* is often portrayed as a jackal because of his rapacious nature. Like *Agni*, the giant fig tree is called *vanaspati* – Lord of the Jungle – from its habit of growing on other trees and eventually strangling them."[138]

"May waters gathered near the Sun, and those wherewith the Sun is joined, speed forth this sacrifice of ours. I call the Waters, Goddesses, wherein our cattle quench their thirst; Oblations to the streams be given.

Amṛta is in the Waters; in the Waters there is healing balm: Within the Waters – *Soma* thus has told me –, dwell all balms that heal."[139]

"A month is a day and a night of the *manes* (the dead). But the division is according to fortnights. The dark fortnight is the day of active exertion, the bright fortnight is the dead's night for sleep."[140]

"The burnt-oblation offered at a sacrifice to the *manes* must not be made in a common fire; a *Brāhmaṇa* who keeps a sacred fire shall not perform a sacrifice of funeral except on the new-moon day. Even when he, after

137. *LP.* 56.4-10a.
138. Steven G. Darian, *The Ganges in Myth and History*, p. 82. The vegetal rhythm in Vedic-Indian literature and art is self-evident as it is in any universal consciousness. Its ecological sense serves as an excellent example of integrated human living. Humans and animals mix well together in Indian streets and one may wonder whether a change "for the better" could be introduced. The lack of animals in industrialized life certainly seems an impoverishment of life. To blame animals for road accidents is a poor excuse for man's dominating attitude and nervous quest for gains that, from the Universe's point of view, are "not there" or if there, at least in a manner which cannot go at the cost of forms of life. Without minimizing possible problems of sanitation, a clean animal cannot be said to be "dirtier" than a motor vehicle.
139. *RV.* 1.23.17-20.
140. *Manusmṛti* 1.66.

bathing, satisfies the *manes* with water, he obtains thereby the whole reward for the performance of the daily *Śrāddha*."[141]

94. To *Indra-Soma* who set the Waters free and makes him feel the throb of his vegetal essence, man sings:

"How great, O *Indra* and *Soma*, is your power! It was you who performed those first and mighty exploits. It was you subdued the Sun, subdued the Sky and chased away all darkness, all the ribald. *Indra* and *Soma*, you make the dawn to glow and cause the Sun to rise in all his splendour. You have propped up the Sky with a supporting pillar and spread out Mother Earth in all directions.

Indra and *Soma*, you smote the serpent *Vṛtra* who sought to obstruct the waters. To you the heavens yielded their load, you pierced the river torrents as with a lance and filled full many a sea. Within the cows udder, unprepared, it was you, O *Soma* and *Indra*, who placed the milk. You held the cream-hued unimpeded stream within the multicoloured moving creatures.

Great are the riches you grant, O strong Ones, which free from fear and pass to children's children. With many powers you invest the sons of man that they may be victorious in the battle."[142]

95. The "single sun-ray *Suṣumṇā* that refills the moon part by part" is a mystery gift. It is found in the *naḍi*, vein or artery, in the "lotus of the heart" in man's mystical and Universe-conscious physiology. *Nāḍī Suṣumṇā* is the seat of *Citta* for, concentrating on it, the *yogī* becomes conscious of consciousness.[143]

96. *Suṣumṇā* is the *brahmanāḍī*. It is the *māhapatha*, "The Great Way". It is also the *śmaśāna*, the cemetary. It is *Sambhavi* (= *Durga*). Another name for it is *madhyamārga*, "The Middle Way". Finally it is *Śaktimārga*, the way of *Śakti*. Such is the flow in the arteries and veins of microcosmic man, making him understand the structure of creation and the Universe in and with the Self, *Ātman*.

To the right and to the left of the spinal column which is the centre *Meru*, are found *nāḍī piṅgala* – sun, the masculine –, and *nāḍī iḍā* – moon, the feminine. *Suṣumnā*, the sun's single ray, lies in between those two. She is the form of Moon, Sun, and Fire.[144]

"In the space outside the *Meru* placed on the left and the right, are the two *Śirās* (*Nāḍī*), *Śaśī* (moon) and *Mihira* (Sun). The *Nāḍī Suṣumna*, whose substance is the three-fold *Guṇas*, is in the middle. She is the form of Moon, Sun and Fire. Her body, a string of blooming *Dhaturā* flowers, extends from the middle of the *Kāṇḍa* (root) to the Head, and the *Vajrā* inside her extends, shining, from the *Meḍhra* (penis) to the Head."[145]

---

141. *Manusmṛti* 3.282-283.
142. *RV*. 6.72.
143. *YS*. 1.36.
144. *Hath. Ypr*. 2.46.
145. *SNC*. 1. in: Woodroffe, *op. cit*., p. 320.

97. The *Meru* in the micro-cosmic human mystical physiology cannot be seen with the physical eye. Nor can the *Skambha*, the world-axle, with its theocosmological significance. It is the transcendent and explanatory ground holding the waters and the sky together, both as a unity and as a Tree the branches of which are Being and Non-being. Faith, worship, sacrifice, all that transcends the level of empirical experience are in the *Skambha*, manifest but hidden. In the hymn to the *Skambha* we hear :

> "Through whom men knew the worlds and what enwraps them, the Waters and Holy Word, the all-powerful in whom are found both Being and Nonbeing – Tell me of that Support – who may he be ?
>
> By whom Creative Fervour waxing powerful upholds the highest Vow, in whom unite Cosmic Order and Faith, the waters and the Word – Tell me of that Support – who may he be ?
>
> On whom is firmly founded Earth and Sky and the air in between; so too the fire, moon, sun, and wind, each knowing his own place – Tell me of that Support – who may be he ?
>
> The branch of Nonbeing which is far extending men take to be the highest one of all. They reckon as inferior those who worship your other branch, the branch of Being."[146]

98. Man "sees" the Pillar by discovering its traces in creation:

> "Homage to him whose in-breath and out-breath is the Wind, whose eyes are the *Aṅgirasas* whose wisdom consists in the cardinal points. Homage again to this supreme *Brahman*.
>
> How does the wind not cease to blow? How does the mind take no repose? Why do the waters, seeking to reach truth, never at any time cease flowing? To whom the Gods always with hands and feet, with speech, ear, and eye bring tribute unmeasured, in all well-measured place of sacrifice – Tell me of that Support – who may he be?
>
> In him exists no darkness, no evil. In him are all the lights, including the three that are in the Lord of Life. The one who knows the Reed of gold standing up in the water is truly the mysterious Lord of Life."[147]

99. When the traces of the pillar in created experience are found by man, he finds one quarter of Cosmic *Puruṣa*, the Cosmic Man.

> "From him *Viraj* (the Waters) was born ; again *Puruṣa* from *Virāj* (the Waters) was born. As soon as he was born he spread eastward and westward over the earth."[148]

100. Cosmic *Puruṣa* is *Prajāpati*. In him takes place the *Devayajña*, the Sacrifice of God, the dismemberment of *Puruṣa*. Dismemberment and distribution are

---

146. *AV*. 10.7.10-12; 21-22. in: Panikkar, *op. cit.*, p. 62f.
147. *AV*. 10.7.34.37.39-41. in Panikkar, *op. cit.*, p. 65f.
148. *RV*. 10.90.5 in Griffith. See: Part II:5:4: (vi): "In praise of man's Origin: *Puruṣa Sūkta* (*RV*. 10.90)"

another instance of creating order out of chaos: a re-arrangement, the base of which is *Ṛta*, cosmic order.

> "With this sacrifice the gods sacrificed; these were the first *dharmas*. And these powers reached the dome of heaven where dwell the ancient *Sadhus* and the gods."
>
> "In the beginning, to be sure, the Lord of creatures, was One only. He reflected: "How may I be propagated?". He kindled his own ardour, performing this very act with fervour. He generated the First born from his mouth therefore the Firstborn is a consumer of food."[149]

101. To *Prajāpati's* aid came the Waters, offering him the *Agnihotra*, the fire-sacrifice. Signified by them is the perpetual process of death and resurrection:[150]

> "In the beginning, to be sure, this world was water, nothing but a sea of water. The waters desired: "How can we be propagated?" They kindled their own ardour, performing this very act with fervour. While summoning their creative energy, they warmed up and a golden egg was produced. At that time, to be sure, the year was not yet existing. This golden egg floated about for as long as a year."[151]

102. The generative force and glow of Fire was diffused into the formless waters as *apraketā*. Because the waters are said to reassemble *Prajapati* in the sacrifice which is the Year, the cycle of day and night shapes itself into months and years.

> "Water is female and fire is male; Life is born from their intercourse."[152]
>
> "And so they say: all other sacrifices have an end but the *agnihotra* does not come to an end. All that which lasts for twelve years is indeed limited; the *agnihotra* is nevertheless unlimited; for when a man has offered in the evening, he looks forward with confidence to offering in the morning . . . Thus the *agnihotra* is unlimited and, hence, from its unlimitedness, the creatures also are born unlimited. Whosoever knows the unlimitedness of the *agnihotra* is himself unlimited in prosperity and offspring."[153]

103. *Prajāpati* is *yajña* which is the year. The year is both part and counterpart of *Prajāpati*, the year being the indication of man's terrestrial temporality. The Waters therefore are not only the generative principle of the cosmic sacrifice but

---

149. *RV*. 10.90.16. See: Part II:5:4 (v): "*Prajāpati*, the Lord of Generation".
150. *SB*. 2.2.4.1. The notion of *Ṛta* is that of direction which can of itself not lead to indirection: see *AB*. 3.43: "His before and after are the same "– *yad asya pūrvam aparam tad asya*.
151. *SB*. 9.1.6.1. in: Panikkar, *op. cit.*, p. 79. Notes given by the author: "May I be propagated": *prajāyeya* which is the passive of "*pra-jan-*" optative to express possibility or probability in the near future, to be born, to be begotten and born again, to be propagated. The waters said "How can we be propagated?": *tā akāmayanta kathaṁnu prajāyemahi*. In *SB*. 9.1.1.1 *Prajāpati* is identified with *yajña* and this latter with the year (*Agni*, death, and time) In *SB*.11.1.6.13, *Prajāpati* considers himself to be the counterpart of the year. The waters are also the result of a sacrifice" Although such texts may seem outdated, they essentially relate to human consciousness which is constantly in search of principles of unity and intelligibility.
152. *SB*. 1.6.3.23; 1.1.1.20.
153. *SB*. 2.3.1.13.

also the result of the sacrifice "back" to *Atman*, the immutable counterpart of the changing cycle of time. Man, unable to return to the beginnings along a temporal line, returns to them through the symbol and thus pierces into Eternity, the core of which is not "time" but consciousness.[154]

104. The primordial cosmic Man (*Puruṣa-Prajapati*) is not a historical beginning like that of terrestrial man. It is an ontic beginning, a principle. The *Upaniṣads* reflect on the beginning of human consciousness, the first experience of which is the same loneliness *Prajāpati* experienced when being alone in ontic time:

> "In the beginning there was nothing whatsoever. All this was swayed in Death – in Hunger, for hunger indeed is death. Then he resolved to himself: "Would that I had a self". So he moved around in worship. While he was worshipping, water was born."[155]
>
> "In the beginning this was the Self alone, in the form of a Man. Looking around he was nothing whatever except himself.
>
> He said in the beginning: "I am" and thence arose the name "I". So, even today, when a man is addressed, he says in the beginning "It is I", and then adds any other name he may have . . ."[156]
>
> "He was afraid; so even today, one who is alone is afraid. He thought to himself: "Since nothing exists except me, of what am I afraid?". Thererupon his fear vanished, for of what must he be afraid? It is of a second thing that fear arises."[157]
>
> "He found no joy: so, even today, one who is all alone finds no joy. He yearned for a second. He became as large as a man and a woman locked in close embrace. This self he split into two; hence arose husband and wife. Therefore, as *Yajñavalkya* used to observe: "Oneself is like half of a split pea". That is why this void is filled by woman. He was united with her and thence were born human beings."[158]

105. *Prajāpati*, so the *Upaniṣads* further reflect, finally pushed man to the forefront with a task. He called man "the protector of the world".

> "He thought again to himself: "Let me now create the protectors of the world". He raised a man from the waters and conferred a form upon him. Once this was done, a mouth broke open, similar to an egg. From the mouth the Word came out and from the Word fire."[159]

---

154. *SB*. 9.1.6.13. 9.1.1.1.
155. *BU*. 1.2.1. The idea – also applying to the following two texts – of selfhood and the consciousness of it, creates its own potentiality for sustaining and developing it. *Āpaḥ* serve as an excellent primary symbol of that potency. Also in psychology, the experience of solitude, when gone through to the very end, may lead to the overcoming of it.
156. *BU*. 1.4.1.
157. *BU*. 1.4.2. The question of identification of the "I" and "some" origin or principle plays an important part in the psychiatric treatment of people with involutional depression where the idea of "self-uselessness" is violently manifested, See e.g. William Sargant and Eliot Slater, *An Introduction to the Physical Methods of Treatment in Psychiatry,* E.S. Livingstone Ltd., Edinburgh and London, 1969, e.g., p. 64.
158. *BU*. 1.4.3.
159. *AU*. 1.1.3-4, in: Panikkar, *op. cit.*, p. 83.

106. And here then is man. Man in his humanly understood existence, his anthropological existence. That existence, so the preceding texts tell us, is androgynous. Man is man and woman. Man is also water and fire. In fact, so we have been told, man is heaven and earth. Man *is* things rather than that he *has* them. To be truly human means *to be* rather than to have.

Thus, when man blesses his house, he does not bless it as its "proprietor". Man has and needs a house only in order to be. The Vedic house is part of man. He *is* his house, he does not possess it. In it he is part of creation. It is natural for man to live in a dwelling. To say that a human being has a right to a house has become a sad necessity because one human being may refuse another a house. One human being is capable of denying another his being a human. *Man's problem is the problem of being and having.* Every man, woman and child is called to pray the *salapratiṣṭha*, the blessing of the house:

> "Here do I fix my dwelling. May it stand firm, flowing with melted butter! May we approach you, O House, with all our people, sound in heart and limb.
>
> Bring forward, woman, this full jar, a stream of ghee, mingled with life's elixir. Anoint those who drink, with immortality. May our votive offerings ever protect this house.
>
> I bring this water free from all impurity, I bring this immortal fire, With these I set my foot within this dwelling and take possession to it."[160]

107. With regard to *being* and *having*, the Waters show the true perspective. When they claim and when they apparently destroy, it is only with a view to regenerate and bestow new being. The Waters create the sacrifice. What comes from the Waters goes back to the Waters only to re-appear again. In the changing cycle of man's time as he experiences it, to be possessive is a negation of his own existence and that of others.

Each sacrifice is a cosmic expansion (*pravṛtti*) drawn out by an understanding between the Universe and man (God and man) in man's liturgical year, the year of *kalā*, a moment. It is the remembrance of the burst from the Uncreated into the created. But each sacrifice – in its widest sense, each sensible thought – is also a reminder of the cosmic *nivṛtti*, the return from the created to the Uncreated. Thus in sacrifice, i.e., in true thinking, man is his true self.

> "Day by day, man offers sustenance to creatures; that is the sacrifice to beings. Day by day a man gives hospitality to guests, including a glass of water; that is the sacrifice to men. Day by day a man makes funerary

160. *AV.* 3.12.1.8-9. in: Panikkar, *op. cit.*, p. 289. See Part I.1: "Breaking the boundaries" where I discussed the consumer attitude and that of the consecrator with regard to consciousness of the Universe. Everyone in his senses is well aware of the enormous injustice in the presentday world caused by unbridled consumerism institutionalized in economics and politics at the cost of millions of human beings exploited by a few.

offerings, including a glass of water; that is the sacrifice to the ancestors. Day by day a man makes offerings to the Gods, including wood for burning; that is the sacrifice to the Gods.[161]

108. In the fire-sacrifice, the link between Cosmic Man and small man is maintained. It is the ontic experienced *satya*, the truth of unity and harmony. In fire sacrifice and in all sacrifice man becomes mortally immortal.

Here is part of a conversation between *Naciketā* and *Yama*, Death:

"You know, O Death, the fire which secures heaven. Explain it to me who listens to you in all faith! Immortal are they who stay there in heaven, — I choose this as a second gift. *Yama*: "Well, I will explain to you the fire which secures heaven; listen to it with understanding. The fire which leads to the attainment of, and is the foundation of, that eternal world — know it lying in a hiding place."[162]

109. In the same *Upaniṣad*, the "hiding place" is *Ātman*, "truly, this is that".

"He was there already before *Tapas* – he, who was there already before the primeval waters –, Him one sees dwelling in the cavity of the heart – one sees him here through all beings. Truly, this is that!

Concealed in the rubbing fuel-sticks, the knower of beings, just as the foetus (lying concealed) is well protected by the pregnant woman."[163]

110. It is fire that builds the world. That means: the world signifies maintenance of all necessary correct relationships. Where they are lacking there is not "world" really speaking but chaos and nonsense. In other words, a consciousness of the Universe's presence, a true religiosity, is the mainstay of existence and of the meaningfulness of the Universe.

"Possessing three *Naciketā*-fires, possessing three bonds i.e. relations with father, mother and teacher. Doing three kinds of work, sacrifice, study and charity, one strips oneself of birth and death. Knowing God who knows what *Brahman* creates, laying or arranging the fire, one enters into serenity for ever."[164]

111. Preparing the ground for the fire and laying the *apanabhṛt*-bricks, the first of five layers of bricks for the fire-altars, Vedic society prayed as follows:

"I place thee in the going of the waters; I place thee in the rising of the waters; I place thee in the ashes of the waters; I place thee in the light of the waters; I place thee in the movement of the waters.

Sit on the billows as thy place of rest; sit on the ocean as thy place of

161. *SB*. 11.5.6.2. in: Panikkar, *op. cit.*, p. 394. The sacrifice "with the mind as instrument" – *manasā* – or "mentally" occurs very frequently in the *ṚgVeda*, e.g. 1.172.2: *stomo...hṛdātaṣṭau manasā*; 2.40.3., *rathaṃ . . . manasā yujyamānam*; 7.64.4, *gantaṃ manasā takṣat* etc. The true idea of sacrifice a mere mechanical operation sloer not allow for.

162. *KathU*. 1.13.14. in: Deussen, *op. cit.*, p. 277.

163. *KathU*. 4.5 and 6. in: Deussen, *op. cit.*, p. 292.

164. *KathU*. 1.17, in: Deussen, *op. cit.*, p. 278.

rest; sit on the stream as thy place of rest; sit on the abode of the waters; sit on the seat of the waters.

I place thee in the seat of the waters; I place thee in the dwelling of the waters; I place thee in the dust of the waters; I place thee in the womb of the waters; I place thee in the stronghold of the waters."[165]

112. The digestive fire of food which comes from the waters is homologized with the *agnihotra* in the *Prāṇāgnihotra*: the ritual feeding and cleansing of one's body is said to lead to the intellectual sacrifice, the sacrifice made by the mind (*manasa yajña*). Sacrifice *is* man, taking place within man and therefore not necessarily dependent upon rite and ritual. Sacrifice is not an isolated unity, disconnected from or taken out of environment, least of all one's body. To obtain *mokṣa*, lived liberation, *Upaniṣadic* texts sometimes almost go as far as ridiculing ritual.

"Tottering and unsteady are these sacrificial rites, the eighteen ones in which the inferior ritual finds expression, the fools, who greet it as the better one – they again sink into old age and death.

Meandering in the depth of ignorance, imagining themselves as the wise and the learned, the fools knock about aimlessly hither and thither like the blind men, whom, one who himself is blind, leads..."[166]

113. About the *Praṇagnihotra* and the metaphysical interpretation of food, thereby interiorizing the sacrifice, we read:

". . . and then he (as it were) clothes (*paradadhati*) the *Atman* with water (through the rinsing of the mouth). After he has rinsed the mouth with water and made an offering of food to the *Atman*, he should reflect over the *Atman* with the two verses respectively beginning with – "*Prāṇa*, fire, you are ", "you are *visva*, the universe". Before it he has said: To the *prāṇa, svaha!* (Hail!) To the *apaṇa, svahā!* To the *vyāṇa, svāhā!* Thus he makes an offering with these five invocations with food to himself".

"As life, as fire, the highest self rests in me as five breaths. He, the all-consumer, himself gratified, – may he gratify (the universe) all!"

"You are *Viśva*, the Universe, you are *Vaiśvānara*. You maintain the universe which is born from you; May all the flowing sacrificial obligations find place in you; Where you are, there is life and living creatures, – You, the immortal animator of all."[167]

"Now, therefore, let us explain the sacrifice in one's own body, the body-sacrifice which forms the essence of all the *Upaniṣads*, which is helpful for knowledge of the *Saṁsāra*, which is studied, and which has food for its authority."[168]

165. *TS.* 4.3.1. in: A. B Keith, *The Veda of the Black Yajus School, entitled Taittiriya Saṁhitā*, p. 327.
166. *MU.* 1.2.7-8. in: Deussen, *op. cit.*, p. 575.
167. *MaitraU.* 6.9. in: Deussen, *op. cit.*, p. 35.
168. *PranagniU.* 1. in: Deussen, *op. cit.*, p. 646.

114. For the *jñānin*, the knower, the *Praṇagnihotram* supersedes all ritual and rite and philosophical speculation. It constitutes purifying interiorization through the understanding of the primary meaning and force of water and of fire, elements present at the very Beginning before man came to speak of them.

"The (immanent) deities are the breaths, mind-born and mind-yoked, in them one sacrifices metaphysically."[169]

"Liberation from *Saṁsara* is possible in this present human body, even without the *Agnihotram*, and without the *Sāṁkhya* and *Yoga*. In this belief one puts down food on the ground, each according to the prescription applicable to him, and consecrates it with the three stanzas: "The herbs which are in *Soma's* realm", and with the two verses: "Give us, O Lord of food".

The herbs, which are in *Soma's* realm, Many different in hundred ways, which *Bṛhaspati* created in the past, They should protect us from fear.

Those that bring fruit and those fruitless, Not blossoming and blossoming, Which *Bṛhaspati* created in the past, They should protect us from fear.

....

By waters may the earth be purified, Purified, may she make me pure! By *Brahmaṇaspati, Brahman*, Purified, may she make me pure !

....

O Water, you are *Amṛtam* (ambrosia, nectar) you are bed of *Amṛtam*, I offer *Amṛtam* in the *Praṇa*! In us, O ward, you are fed!

Svāhā to the *Praṇa*, the most pre-eminent! – *Svāhā* to the *Apāṇa*! – *Svāhā* to the *Vyāna*! – *Svāhā* to the *Samana*! – *Svāhā* to the *Udāṇa*!

With these words he offers with the little finger and the thumb to the *Prāṇa*, with the nameless (ring) finger to the *Apāna*, with the middlefinger to the *Vyāṇa*, with the forefinger to the *Samāna*, with all fingers to the *Udāna*. Then he silently makes an offering to the *Ekarṣi*, the sun, two to the *Āhavanīya* (in the mouth), one to the *Dakṣiṇa* fire (in the heart), one to the *Gārhapatya* (in the navel), one to the All-atonement fire (below the navel).

Then he says to the water: "You are the covering. For immortality I superimpose you!", and therewith he rinses out the mouth, takes once more of it and rinses out once more. Then he takes the water in the left hand, lays hold of the heart therewith and murmurs:

"The breath-fire, by five winds, Encircled, who is the highest *Ātman*, Who gives peace to all the creatures! I shall not be born anymore! You are all, all-human, multiform, You sustain the universe born out of you....."[170]

115. The drinking-sacrifice (*Vājapeya yajña*), a "sacrifice of victory" in the fruit-season, is transposed to the begetting of a son as the continuation of the

169. *TS*. 6.1.4.5. in: Keith, *op. cit.*, p. 489: "*prāṇā vai devā, manojata manoyujas, teṣu parokṣam juhoti.*"
170. *PrāṇāgniU*. 1. in: Deussen, *op. cit.*, p. 647-648.

sacrificial duties of the father. The procreative act is spiritually assimilated to the All-atonement fire of the *Praṇagnihotram.* That fire below the navel comes from the moonlight which, in man's mystical physiology, is the lunar disc situated on the forehead. It flows down as the water of semen through the arteries and veins (*naḍi*). Through the procreation-limb the semen falls into the sacrificial fire-pot. The body therefore consists of *Soma*-juice and *Agni* and is a constitutive element of the Universe. The procreative act in its cosmic framework under the symbol of the creative *Soma*-juice is candidly explained:

"Indeed the essence of the created beings is the earth, the essence of the earth is water, the essence of the water is the plant, the essence of the plant is the blossoms or flowers, the essence of the flowers is fruit, the essence of the fruit is man, the essence of man is the semen.

Once *Prajāpati* thought: "Well, I will prepare a dwelling-place for this semen", and he created the woman. After he had created her, he sat down near her to copulate. That is why man should adore the woman in the lower parts below (the reproduction as an act of religious adoration) – And he stretched out for inserting this *Soma*-pressingstone which was directed and erect in front and created with it.

Her genital parts is the sacrificial altar, her hair the *Kuśa* grass (*barhis*), her skin the *Soma*- pressing, her reproductive organ the fire in the middle. The world which the performer of the *Vājapeya*-sacrifice gains – the world as wide as that, is gained by him who having this knowledge practises this pleasurable (sexual) act; he wins the fruit of the good actions of these women for himself. But he, who, without having this knowledge, practises the pleasurable act – (the fruits of) the good actions of such a man are gained by the women for themselves. . . .

"When anybody, in sleep or in waking state, spills his semen, he should touch it or (without doing so, without touching it) chant the following verse:

"That semen which spilled out of me today on earth, – That semen flowed into the plants and water; I take it back to me; my strength (virility) should come back, back again, like the fire back into the fireplace, in its abode, it should again be:".[171]

171. The following verse (5b) is irrelevant in the total context of the cosmic significance of the procreative act which belongs to both the man and the woman as equal creators and partners, claiming equally significant mystical physiology and psychic participation. The verse, however, – as are other verses mentioned below –, is important with regard to presentday feminist thought and its effort to re-evaluate the position of woman in official society, including that of sexual mores over which woman, so it is maintained, would often seem to be denied personal authority. The verse reads:" With these words, he should take a part of the semen and rub it between the breasts and between the eyebrows of the woman". Although the lines have meaning within the archetypal Feminine and the symbols of transformation and of growth where no distinction is made between the mystical significance of the symbol and its domination by patriarchal cultures, the symbol, as observed earlier, becomes "anti-natural" and offensive to the woman's psyche. Verse 7 reads:" If yet she (unresponsive to his will) does not deliver herself to him, then after having struck her with a stick or with the hand, he should pay no heed to her (*atikrāmet; Śaṅkara* reads *"abhikrāmet"* "should go to her") and say "With my virile strength and glory I take (*ādade*) the glory from you:".

Further, if one looks at himself in the water, he should chant the following words: "The splendour and virility, glory, power and good actions, let these abide in me!"[172]

116. The wish and prayer for a son (*putrakāma*) takes the prospective parents back to the origins when *Prajāpati* of the Waters created through Ardour (*tapas*).

"(the wife): I saw you as within your mind grew insight, born from Ardour, strengthened through Ardour. Bestowing here offspring, bestowing treasure, produce now, desirous of a son, a progeny!

(the husband): I saw you meditating within your heart, your body being afflicted at the season. Rise now to meet me! Be a young woman! Produce now, desirous of a son, a progeny![173]

(*Prajāpati*): It is I who have placed in every plant a seed; it is I who have placed in all creatures a seed; it is I who bring forth children on the earth. I will forever henceforth produce sons in women!"[174]

117. The fire sacrifice, performed in the morning when the sun rises from the waters and again in the evening when the sun sinks into the waters, provides man with two precious moments when he is able to assert himself and join the timelessness of the cyclical circle of day and night. In the *agnihotra* man adds his share towards the maintenance of cosmic order (*Ṛta*). At dawn and dusk there is the *sandhyā*, the "holding together" of all there is, seen and unseen.

". . . The *agnihotra* is nevertheless unlimited, for when a man has offered in the evening he looks forward with confidence to the morning; and when he has offered in the morning he likewise looks forward with confidence to offering in the evening. Thus the *agnihotra* is unlimited and, hence, from its unlimitedness, creatures also are born unlimited. Whoever knows the unlimitedness of the *agnihotra* is himself unlimited in prosperity and offspring."[175]

To him, *Agni*, –, the wise Ordainer, ancient and glorious, a song I offer. . . By holy Law they kept supporting Order, by help of sacrifice, in

---

Then she will become devoid of glory and splendour". The appropriation of the mythical awareness by a particularized partiarchal (or matriarchal) culture may account for a certain decadence of myth narration with regard to, e.g. birth, growth, transformation and their sexual implication in a patriarchal society when the feminine psyche is concerned. For a general study of "decadence of myth" see: Mircea Eliade, *Myth and Reality*, pp. 139-193. Feminist literature with a view to the study of woman in myth is abounding. One of the earlier critics is the English author D.H. Lawrence in his whole work. Lawrence, Mann and Joyce, contemporaries, busied themselves much with symbols and myth. For a penetrating study on Lawrence's work on the occasion of his first centenery (11th Sept. 1985) see: Jaap T. Harskamp, "D.H. Lawrence, De Schepping van een oevre" in the Dutch literary journal *Bzzlletin*, Den Haag, 12th vol. no. 117, June, 1984, pp. 53-76 and 80. Also see works of e.g. Renate Rubinstein with regard to feminism. For example her book: *Liefst Verliefd*, Meulenhoff, Amsterdam. ("De Schepping van een oevre" – The Creation of an opus "–"Liefst verliefd "–"In love, preferably").

172. *BU*. 1.1-3.5a.6. in: Deussen, *op. cit.*, p. 534.
173. *RV*. 10.183. 1-2. in: Panikkar, *op. cit.*, p. 172.
174. *RV*. 10.183.3. in: Panikkar, *op. cit.*, p. 172.
175. *SB*. 2.3.1.13. in: Panikkar, *op. cit.*, p. 363.

loftiest heaven, – they who attained with born men to the unborn, men seated in that stay, heaven's firm sustainer."[176]

118. *Sandhyā* is man's assertion as well as his admission of being "seasonal". Man knows birth, growth, and death, drought and humidity, heat and cold like those of the seasons and the earth. *Sandhya* is the cross-roads between *Ṛta*, order and harmony, and *Ṛtu*, the season, on the one hand, and *anṛta*, darkness and chaos on the other. At twilight (*prātasandhya*) and dusk (*sāyamsandhyā*) the human and divine manner of dealing with reality encounter each other. They discuss with each other meaningfulness of all there is.

"Where do the half months and the months proceed in consultation with the year? Where do the seasons go, in groups or singly?"[177]

"Your circling seasons, years, nights, succeeding days, your summer. O Earth, your splashing rains, your autumn, your winter and frosty season yielding to spring – may each and all produce for us their milk!"[178]

119. Actually, what happened was, so the myth remembers, that the two *Sandhyās* were put there by the sun while the whole *Sandhyā* was still burning in the sacrificial fire in which she had thrown herself. *Sandhyā*, namely, had felt hurt when *Brahmā*, her father, had looked upon her with desire. The myth is a later reminder of the one, aeons earlier, when *Prajāpati* had moved towards his daughter *Uṣas*, Dawn, and had not been able to contain his seed. Creation is a break-away, not without its dramatic aspects. After the morning-and evening-twilight had risen from the fire, *Sandhyā* herself too rose from it in the form of *Arundhatī* which was to say that on no account righteousness was to give way to obstruction. The cosmic order (*Ṛta*), splitting up in the ever recurring cycle of day and night and the seasons (*Ṛitu*), shall not be subject to arbitrariness.

Arundhatī, now found in the sky as a star (Cassiopeia of the Pleiades), became an example to women by her authentic womanhood and feminine personality. During the marriage-ceremony of (Brahmin) Hindus, the bridegroom says:

"Now from the fetter of *Varuṇa* I free you, wherewith most blessed *Savitā* has bound you." In law's seat, to the world of virtuous action I give thee up uninjured with thy consort" (*RV.* 10.85.24). Then he causes her to step forward in north-eastern direction seven steps with the words: "may you take one step for sap, second step for juice (vigour), third step for the thriving of wealth, fourth step for comfort, fifth step for offspring, sixth step for seasons, may you be my friend with your seventh step". Then, bringing the heads of the bride and the bridegroom together, the *açarya* sprinkles water of them from a water-jar . . . When she has seen the Pole Star, the star *Arundhatī* and the seven sages (Ursa Major), let her break her silence and say: "May my husband live and may I secure offspring."[180]

---

176. *RV.* 5.15. 1a-2 in: Griffith.
177. *AV.* 10.7.7. in: Panikkar, *op. cit.*, p. 786. See also *AV.* 10.7.5.
178. *AV.* 12.1.36. in: Panikkar, *op. cit.*, p. 786.
180. Kane, *History of Dharmaśāstra*, vol. 2, Part 2, pp. 529-530.

120. *Sandhya,* the Twilight of each ritual and seasonal day of man, is in her cosmic form *Uṣas,* Dawn. *Uṣas* is said to be born in *Ṛta*, Cosmic Order, and as kinswoman of *Varuṇa* she is aware of the happenings of the very beginnings. Had she not seen her own father, *Prajāpati*, the Lord of Generation, approach her? She is also said to have been present when *Indra* opened the gates of the Waters. *Uṣas*, in her turn, opened in the rock the doors of the Waters.

"Sister of *Varuṇa*, sister of *Bhāga*, first among all, sing forth, O joyous Morning.[181]

"Blest were these Dawns of old, shining with succour, true with the truth that springs from holy Order: With whom the toiling worshipper, by praises hymning and lauding, soon attained to riches.

Hither from eastward all at once they travel from one place spreading in the selfsame manner. Awaking, from the seat of holy Order the Godlike Dawns come might like troops of cattle."[182]

"Bright leader of glad sounds our eyes behold her; splendid in hue she has unclosed the portals. She, stirring up the world, has shown us riches: Dawn has wakened every living being."[183]

"Bestow on us, O Dawn, that ample bounty which thou did send to those who sang thy praises. Thou whom with bellowings of a bull they quickened; thou didst unbar the form-set mountain's portals."[184]

121. Cosmic *Uṣas* mediated in the arrangement of the seasons according to *Ṛta*. Hence she has overcome the powers of the netherworld and is Goddess Dawn, and mother.

"Which among these is eldest, and where is she through whom they fixed the *Ṛbhus* (seasons) regulations?"[185]

"She, everlasting, born indeed of old, she, ancient, encompassed all; the

---

181. *RV.* 1.23.5. in: Griffith. *Uṣas* as "born from *Ṛta*", see 1.118.12: *ṛtejaḥ*. In 1.49.1 *Uṣas* is the daughter of Heaven and said to come from the sky. "*uso bhadrebhir a gahi divas cid recanād adhi*. "The daughter of Heaven" 7.75.1.: *divajāḥ*. Kuiper in *op. cit.*, p. 159 stresses the fact that "the mythical identity of the *nocturnal* (K) sky with the netherworld has scarcely ever been clearly stated causing fundamental misunderstandings about Vedic mythology". *Uṣas* has a role in the cosmogony. The seasons have been arranged by her : *RV.* 4.51.6: *kva svid āsāṁ katama purāṇi yayā vidhānā vidadhur ṛbhūnām*. In *RV.* 58.2.: "Only one Fire is kindled manifold, only one Sun is present to one and all, one only Dawn illumines this All; that which is only one becomes this All" *ekaṃ va idaṃ vi babhūva sarvaṃ*. One may relate this verse to the well-known "mental chant" *manasā stotra* - of *RV.* 10.189, addressed to the Serpent Queen Sarparājñī who is at once Dawn, Earth and Bride of the Sun. The "mental chant" means that it is within the power of the intellect (*manas*) not merely to encompass this *imām* i.e. this finite universe in a single moment, but also to transcend it. Man's intellect not only is able to contain (*paryaptam*) but also to environ (*paribhavitam*). In this way, by means of pronouncing the beginnings in symbols, both worlds are possessed and understood mentally.
182. *RV.* 4.51.7-8. *ṛtasya devīḥ sadaso budhānā gavaṃ na sargā usaso jarante*. (see Kuiper, *op. cit.*, p. 160).
183. *RV.* 1.113.4.
184. *RV.* 7.7.9.4.
185. *RV.* 4.51.6a.

great goddess of the dawn, shining forth, she looks forth by every one who winks."[186]

122. *Uṣas'* graceful appearance in the morning represents the victory of light over darkness, of vigour and energy over apathy and inertia. From man's end, however, those boons, although given by *Uṣas*, are not obtained effortlessly, without the experience of strife between good and evil. The Aryans used to organize contests in the early morning, expressing the day's expectancy and the possible danger of its failing.

Uṣas, always there somewhere in the universe, but each morning for man opening up a new real day, is *Puramdhī*. She is the Cosmic Present-giving. She opens up the goods of life.

"Young woman of old, O Goddess, bestowing all treasures, thou keepest thy pledges as *Puramdhī*."[187]

123. At dawn everything seems primal, unblemished, unhurt. The dawn by itself promises joy. If there are tears at dawn, they come from the preceding night or day. Yet, facing the dawn or standing in her midst, man fears — no matter "how carefully *Uṣas* comes, fostering all creatures, stirring to life all winged and creeping things" (*RV.* 1.48.5.). Man is aware of his inclinations towards diminishing the light of dawn. At dawn man is in two minds: staying with *Uṣas* and keep away from involvement *(nivṛtti)*? Or moving with *Uṣas* into the light of day and start to stir *(pravṛtti)*? At dawn one hardly sees where the sky ends and the earth begins. What line of action is man to take each day at dawn? The dawn has a message, a feeling of hope that darkness may not come until the evening. Each day at dawn, man once again cuts from eternity into time. Man cannot say: "Dawn, do not come".

"This maiden infringes not the Eternal Law, day after day coming to the place appointed."[188]

Uṣas does not inspire fear. If there is fear, it is because one man hates another, one family threatens another or one nation battles with another. Man at dawn is stirred to action not swiftly but advertently, ready to believe that *Uṣas' Ṛta* drives off wicked spirits and dread darkness. Man must at dawn decide if the light, as far as he is concerned, will dispel darkness or if the darkness will have the upperhand.

"Arise! The breath of life again has reached us. Darkness has fled and light is fast approaching. She leaves a pathway for the Sun to travel. We have arrived where life will again continue.

Whatever wondrous gifts the Dawns convey as blessing to the offerer who

186. *AS.* 10.8.30. in: Kuiper, *op. cit.*, p. 161: *eṣa sanatnī sanaṁ eva jātaiṣa puruṇı pari sarvaṁ babhūva mahī devy uṣaso vibhāti saikenaikena miṣata vi caṣṭe.*

187. *RV.* 3.61.1. in: Kuiper, *op. cit.*, 161: *purāṇi devi yuvatiḥ purandhir anu vrataṁ carasi visvavure.* Kuiper presents in his work a scholarly and enlightening discussion on *Uṣas* (pp. 150-176). His work could hardly be overlooked by the student of myth.

188. *RV.* 1.123.9.

shows himself zealous in worship, that may *Mitra* and *Varuṇa* grant to us, and *Aditi*. The Sacred River, Earth and Heaven."[189]

124. Where else ought man to be found in the morning but at the waters over which the dawn ascends? And where may man be found when the sun returns from his course into the waters? It is at the waters that man is part of cosmic *nivṛtti* and *pravṛtti*.

But those thoughts were perhaps not always foremost in the Aryans mind when they, tracking eastward, came upon rivers which faced them with obstacles as well as with blessings. The rivers for them were a matter of life and death. In the *ṚgVeda* the rivers are said to yield themselves to the Aryans' chariots as they travelled towards their new home.

"Yea, we will listen to thy words, O singer. With wain and car from far away thou comest. Low, like a nursing mother, will I bend me, and yield me as a maiden to her lover.

Soon as the *Bharatas* have fared across thee, the warrior band, urged on by *Indra*. Then let your streams flow on in rapid motion. I crave your favour who deserve our worship."[190]

125. As the Aryans advance and procure for themselves a foothold in their new homeland, settlements and towns appear on the river banks, such as Kampilya between Hastināpura and Kauśambi.[191] From about 800 B.C. we also hear about Rājghāt (Banaras). The city of the *Mahabharata* has, so we are told, broad streets and public squares and in honour of *Kṛṣña's* visit the streets are decked with jewels.[192] As trade and administration begin to flourish, *Indra*, who accompanied the Aryans from their former abode, also becomes the patron of trade.

"I stir and animate the merchant *Indra*, may he be our guide, chasing wild beasts and highway-men; may be bring me riches. Let us find favour in selling and bartering, may this exchange of goods enrich me."[193].

126. Slowly adapting themselves to agricultural settlement, vegetation and soil-produce acquired for the Aryans increasing importance. The relationship between vegetative life and the waters enters into the framework of their theology of sacrifice and is clothed with religious significance and sentiment. The sap of plants is equated to all life-sustaining liquids.

"Rise up with life, unite yourself with life, rise up with the sap of plants."[194]

The face of *Agni* has entered the waters, the child of the waters guarding against the demons, power, in each home do thou offer the offer of kindling-stick, O *Agni*; let thy tongue seek the ghee.

189. *RV*. 1.113. 16.20 in: Panikkar, *op. cit*., p. 167.
190. *RV*. 3.33.10.11 in : Griffith.
191. *VajS*. 23.18. See: Steven G. Darian, *The Ganges in Myth and History*, p. 56.
192. *Mhb. Ādi parvan* 128; *Udyoga parvan* 89, 94; *Śānti parvan* 9; *Aśramavāsika parvan* 5. See: Darian, *op. cit*., p. 56. Also see: Keith, *op. cit*., p. 66.
193. *AV*. 3.15.1.2.5.
194. *AV*. 8.7.9. Plants are being endowed with a semblance of immortality.

"In the sea is thy heart, within the waters; Let the plants and the waters enter thee; With the offerings of the sacrifice, O Lord of sacrifice."[195]

127. One of the Aryans' dearest memories was *Saraswatī*, the stream whom they were forced to leave behind and who lost herself in the desert sands. There are numerous descriptions of her in the *ṚgVeda*. Later, by transformation, *Gaṅgā* receives all her qualities while *Saraswatī* becomes her mythical, unseen but ever present and much loved companion.

"Aid us, divine *Saraswatī*, thou who art strong with wealth and power; like *Puṣan* give us opulence. Yea, this divine *Saraswatī*, terrible with her golden path, Foe-salyer, claims our eulogy".

Whose limitless unbroken flood, swift-moving with a rapid rush, comes onward with tempestuous roar.

Yea, she most dear amid dear streams, seven-sistered, graciously inclined, *Saraswatī* has earned our praise."[196]

128. From their former Indo-European and Indo-Iranian memory, the Aryans also brought with them to the Indian sub-continent their allegiance to *Varuṇa* and *Mitra*. Besides a host of other responsibilities allotted to them, they are also the gods of the water streams on earth as well as those in the sky.

"Ye Twain, who rule in heaven and earth, the region, clothed be your clouds in robes of oil and fatness. . . .

Kings, gods of mighty everlasting Order come hitherward, ye Princes, Lords of Rivers. Send us from heaven, O *Varuṇa* and *Mitra*, rain and sweet food, ye who pour down your bounties."[197]

129. The Aryans called their new region—the basin of the Upper Indus—the Land of the Seven Rivers (*sapta sindhava*). They moved there about 1500 B.C. The Seven Rivers are said, by the Aryans, to have been set free after the *Vṛtrahatya*, the slaying of *Vṛtra*, by *Indra*.

"(*Indra*) who stilled the quaking of the mighty earth and set at rest the agitated mountains, who measured out the middle regions of space and gave the sky support: he, men, is the Lord !

Who slew the dragon and loosed the seven rivers, who drove the cattle out of *Vala's* cavern, who brought forth fire from between the rocks, victorious ever, he, men, is the Lord."[198]

---

195. *TS*.1.4.45. (The *Dakṣina* Offerings) in: Keith, *op. cit.*, p. 66.
196. *RV*. 6.61.6.10. tr. Griffith.
197. *RV*. 7.64.1a-2. tr. Griffith. For *Varuṇa* and *Mitra* see: Mircea Eliade, *A History of Religious Ideas*, Vol. 1, pp.. 200-208. Also: Sukumari Bhattacharji, *The Indian Theogony*, pp. 1-47, especially p. 41, footnote.
198. *RV*. 2.2-3. in: Panikkar, *op. cit.*, p. 202. The "*Vala*-myth is the counterpart of that of *Vṛtra*. *Indra* split open *Vala*, see: *RV*. 8.14.7: *abhinad valam.* In 1.52.4-5: *Indra*, the *Vṛtra*-killer (*vṛtrahatya*) broke through *Vala's* enclosure (*bhinad valasya paridhīn*). Miller, in, *The Vedas*, p. 29, notes a "significant variation" in the *Vala*-myth when in *RV*. 2.24.3 not *Indra* but *Bṛhaspati* pierces through *Vala* by prayer, driving the cattle out. The meaning is: darkness dispelled, heaven's splendour discovered. (p. 29) Kuiper in *op. cit.*, p. 138ff points to the idea of *Vala* as recepticle holding many goods. It is pierced like a *kosa*, a pail, full of water. See: *RV*. 4.20.6: The frightful one pierces the *Vala* as a solid

130. The rivers are the dawn's companions when she emerges from the night. Together, with their waters and light, they adorn the Earth, the home of man: *Bhūmi.*

"Whatever wondrous gifts the Dawns convey, as blessing to the offerer who shows himself in worship, that may *Mitra* and *Varuṇa* grant to us, and *Aditi,* the Sacred River, Earth and Heaven!"[199]

"(Earth) on whom are ocean, river and all waters, on whom have sprung up food and ploughman's crops, on whom moves all that breathes and stirs abroad—Earth, may she grant to us the long first draught !

On whom the flowing Waters, ever the same, course without cease or failure, night and day, may she yield milk, this Earth of many streams, and shed on us her splendour copiously!"[200]

131. The waters are renowned for their lifegiving properties. They make it possible for Earth to be a home for man. Each one of us is linked with the waters. Numerous are the tellings of gods and men born from the rivers. So, for example, that of *Tansu.* For twelve long years king *Matinara* performed sacrifice on the banks of the river *Saraswati* until she appeared to him in the form of a woman. Together they had a son, *Tansu.*[201] One of his descendents, *Sandanu*, married *Gaṅgā* and had children by her. Likewise, *Kārttikeya* was born from *Siva's* seed cast into the Ganges.

Couples, eager for children, invoke the rivers for the blessing of offspring. In the *Jātakarma,* birth-ceremonies, the waters and "the wise forms of water, butter and honey" are praised:

"At the birth of a son, the child's father, before anyone else touches him, should feed with a golden spoon a little butter and honey in which a trace of gold-dust has been mixed and say:" I feed you with the wisdom of honey, I feed you with ghee, the gift of God, the beautiful. May you have long life, protected by the Gods, may you live in this world a hundred cycling years."[202]

Near the child's navel or right ear he says softly:

"The Lord is full of life; through firewood he is full of life. By this vital power I make you full of life: through herbs he is full of life. . . .
By this vital power I make you full of life. The ocean is full of life: through the rivers it is full of life. By this vital power I make you full of life."[203]

On the spot where the child was born he says:

---

enclosure crammed with goods like a pail (*kośa*) (full of) water" - *ādartā vajraṃ sthaviraṃ na bhīma udneva kośaṃ vasuna nyṛṣṭam*. The underworld as a recepticle of goods is known in other traditions too. The Seven Rivers are said to be: *Gaṅga* (Ganges), *Yamunā* (Jamnā), *Saraswatī* (Sarsutī), *Śatadru* (Satlej), *Parushani, Marud-Vridha, Arjikāyā* (the Vipāsā Hyphasis Byās) in: Mohammed Israil Khan, *Brahmā in the Purāṇas,* Crescent Publishing House, Ghaziabad, India, 1981; p. 86. See also Griffith. *op. cit.,* p. 587. It is not always certain what rivers are meant and traditions vary.

199. *RV.* 1.113.20. in : Panikkar, *op. cit.*, p. 167. *Aditi*, the Goddess of the Infinite - *aditer anīkam* -, also associated with light.
200. *AV.* 12.1.3.9 in : Panikkar, *op. cit.*, p. 124.
201. *Mbh. Ādi-parvan*, 95.
202. *AGS.* 1.15.1-2.
203. *PGS.* 1.16.6.

"I know your heart, O Earth, that rests in heaven, in the moon, the vessel of waters, I know your heart; may it know me! May we see a hundred cycling years, may we live a hundred cycling years."[204].

Then he prays over the mother.

"You are *Iḍā*, the daughter of *Mitra* and *Vāruṇī*. You, a courageous woman, have born a vigorous son. May you be blessed with vigorous children, you who have blessed us with a vigorous son"

He places a jar of water near her head.

"You, O Waters, are co-watchers with the Gods, As co-watchers with the Gods, watch over this mother, who is now confined, and also her child."[205]

132. No Vedic-Indian *Grihya-Sūtra*, domestic ceremony, is performed without ample use of water. In the *Saṇkhāyana-Grihya-Sutra* the teacher introduces the young student to the *brahmakārya* as though into a second birth:

"He fills the two hollows of his own and the student's joined hands with water and then says to him: "What is your name?" "I am N.N. sir", says the other. "Descending from the same *Ṛṣis*?", says the teacher. "Descending from the same *Ṛṣis*, Sir", says the other. With the words *"Bhūr, bhuvaḥ, svaḥ"* the teacher sprinkles thrice with his joined hands water on the joined hands of the student. . . and says: "By the impulse of the God *Savitār,* with the arms of the two *Aśvinīs*, with *Puṣan's* two hands I initiate you. . ."[206]

133. The river waters reminded the Aryans and their Hindu posterity until today of the time when the boons of creation (*puramdhī*) were set free from the mountain and monster *Vṛtra*. The might of *Saraswatī* too is said to have been assisting.

"She with her might, like one who digs for lotus-stems, has burst with her strong waves the ridges of the hills."[207]

134. *Saraswatī's* glory keeps being remembered in later times in the *Purāṇas*. One of her origins is from the *Plakṣa*-tree, the fig-tree, in the middle of *Plakṣa*-island, one of the seven islands and surrounded by the sea of sugarcane-juice. Some of *Saraswatī's* legacy was transferred to *Gaṅga* who falls from on high, sweeping the mountain crest and as *Gaṅgā Bhagirathī* she falls from *Śiva's* hair.

"The world was about to be burnt by *Baḍavāgni* when Indra requested *Saraswatī* thus;"Oh, *Devi*, you should deposit this *agni* in the western ocean: or else the world will be cosumed in its flames". Then she appeared at the *āśrama* of *Uttanka* under the *Plakṣa* tree in the presence of the *Devas*. Just as *Śiva* carried *Gaṅgā*, the *Plakṣa* tree bore. *Saraswatī* and immediately did *Śiva* give to her *Baḍavāgni* in a pot. She went towards the north with the pot and came to Puṣkariṇī, and she stopped there to forgive the sins of people.

204. *PGS*. 1.16.7.
205. *PGS*. 1.16.19.22.
206. *SGS*. 2.2.4.-12.
207. *RV*. 6.61.2a, tr. Griffith.

It is believed to this very day that those who drink water from the *Puṣkara* will attain *Brahmaloka*."[208]

"On becoming king, *Bhagīratha* handed over the reigns of government to his ministers and began efforts to bring down *Gaṅgā* to earth. He did *tapas* for thousand years on the slopes of the Himālayas when *Gaṅgā* asked him to please *Śiva* first as he alone could face her fall on the earth. . . *Śiva* agreed to receive *Gaṅgā* on his head. With a terrific noise *Gaṅgā* come down on *Śiva's* head."[209]

135. As the Aryans proceeded further eastward, slowly but steadily, *Vṛtra* recedes into the past. The mountain holding the Waters, the rain, the rivers, *soma-amṛta* and all lifegiving liquid becomes that of *Himavat*, the Himalayas, in epic and puranic times. The mountain in the cosmos of Hindu myth is the centre of that cosmos; on its heights dwell the great gods. *Śiva* dwells on *Kailāśa* and also favours *Mandāra*. These mythic sites on high, seen from below, are assigned to the north, the Himalayas. They signify, cosmically and symbolically, the region of the Pole Star. Mythically, the *Himavat*-region is the Pole Star's proxy on earth. Its king is *Parvata* (Mountain) whose eldest child is *Sandhyā*, the twilight or dawn. In Hindu thought the *Himavat* brings the anthropomorphic representation of the pre-cosmic past. Things celestial and those of the mind come from *Himavat*.[210]

136. Along with all the waters, *Gaṅgā*, *Saraswatī*, *Sindhu* and *Yamunā* flow down from the slopes of *Himavat*. From *Himavat* come all boons and structures of thought. It was when *Parvata's* daughter, *Kuṭilā*, made difficulties when asked to conceive of a son who could slay *Mahiṣa*, the monster, that *Brahmā* said:

"Because you pay no attention to my words, vile *Kuṭilā*, you will be burnt by my curse to dissolve into water!" Cursed in this manner by *Brahmā*, O seer, *Himavat's* daughter became water, a river in spate that inundated *Brahmaloka*. When he saw her waters overflowing, the Grandfather bound her firmly with fetters made of words, namely the *Ṛg*, *Sāma*, *Yajur* and *Atharva Vedas*. Thus contained, the little daughter of the mountain remained in *Brahmaloka*."[211]

137. And now we know why the lineage of *Vṛtra* was continued in king *Parvata*, Mountain, of the Himālayas. *Parvata* is as old as the rocks and the *ṚgVeda*. Who can tell him news? In the *ṚgVeda* he has been invoked together with the Waters, the Rivers, Heaven and Earth, *Indra*, *Savitṛ* and all others who have some connection with the Waters and the Light. *Parvata* always guarded the Waters and the Light zealously as if afraid that the unblemished state of Uncreatedness—so well manifested in his shape of the Himālayas—would lose its integrity by being broken open by the flow of *amṛta* and the seed of *Prajāpati*. It was *Rudra*, the bowman, who tried to prevent the seed from flowing when *Prajāpati* had approached his daughter *Uṣās*, Dawn. Now *Parvata* resisted any attempt to

---

208. *PP. Sṛṣṭikhaṇḍa*, in : Vettam Mani, *Purāṇic Encyclopaedia*, p. 695.
209. *R. Bāla Kāṇḍa* 43.44. See also : *BP*. 97; *VP*. 2.2; *VmP*. 11 .4; *SkP*. 1.35.25; *MaP*. 56.6.
210. See. e.g. *VP* 2.2.; 2.8; *BhagP*. 5.17; *KP*. 1.44.28-33 etc, etc.
211. Part of *VaP*. 25.1-75 relating *Pārvatī's* birth, in: Dimmitt & v. Buitenen, *op. cit.*, p. 157f.

release the beginnings of life.

"Sweet be this song of mine to *Ahibudhnya*, *Parvata*, *Savitār*, with Floods and Lightnings; Sweet, with the Plants, to Gods who seek oblations. May liberal *Bhaga* speed us on to riches."[212]

"I will declare the manly deeds of *Indra*, the first that he achieved, the Thunderwielder, He slew the dragon, then disclosed the waters and cleft the channels of the mountain torrents.

He slew the dragon lying on *Parvata*: his heavenly bolt of thunder *Tvastr* fashioned. Like lowing cattle in rapid flow descending, the waters glided downward to the ocean. Impetuous as a bull, he chose the *Soma*, and in *Maghavan Indra* grasped the thunder for his weapon and smote to death this firstborn of the dragons."[213]

"The mountain, for thy glory (*Bṛhaspati*) cleft itself apart when he opened the stall of cattle (waters). .. he did hurl down water-floods which gloom had compassed round."[214]

138. *Rudra* held back, in the very first of aeons, the Uncreate in its blissful and unblemished state by aiming his arrow at *Prajāpati* when he was about to shed his seed in *Uṣas*, Dawn, his daughter. Before the arrow of *Rudra* reached its aim, the seed had fallen. The arrow was a fraction too late. *Prajapati's* seed caused creation just then. Now time had come about and the hustle of creation on earth. It irritated *Siva*, the yogi on Mount *Mandāra*, turning away from the world's anxieties. The myth of *Prajapati* and *Uṣās* is transposed to that of *Śiva* and *Pārvatī*, the daughter of *Parvata*, when *Śiva* opposes the incestuous relationship between mother and son and injures his own son, born from him and *Pārvati*. Their son was born blind (*Andhaka*). What *Śiva* meant was the blindness of those who had made the world-poison (*kālakūta*) make itself throw up from the ocean: unless the relativity of things created is understood, they are as venom. Greed creates ugliness and monstrosities.

"Once in the past on Mount *Mandāra*, *Pārvatī* closed the eyes of the god with braided hair, the god of fierce attack, and she did it in play, as a jest, closing his eyes with her two lotus hands that shone like newly sprouted choral and golden lotuses. When *Hara's* (*Śiva*) three eyes were shut, total darkness fell in a moment. But from the touch of her hand, the great lord shed the liquid of passion. A drop of that copious water came forth and splashed on *Sambhu's* forehead, and it was heated. It became an infant. . . ungrateful and full of anger, strange, deformed, disfigured, a dark, hairy man with matted locks and a beard. . . *Pārvatī* asked: "My Lord, who is this deformed creature? And by whom and whose son he is? When *Hara* heard the words of his beloved, he replied: "This child whose heroic power is

212. *RV*. 6.49.14. tr. Griffith.
213. *RV*. 1.32.1-3. tr Griffith.
214. *RV*. 2.23.18. tr Griffith. The Waters flow from the mountain in four directions in the shape of rivers. ("*aśmavraja*" 10.139.6)

marvellous and fierce was born when you closed my eyes; he was born of sweat and is named *Andhaka*, blind."[215]

139. The drop of copious water, referred to as the liquid of passion and which produced, through uncontrolled heat, a deformity, points to the image of fire placed in water. That image, in the Indian mythical awareness, expresses the need of control of excess energy. The forces of fire and water must be kept in balance like it was in the aeon of the uncreated. The fire, in Indian thought, almost always emerges intact, at time controlled or transformed by the combination with water. The fire suspends its power and must come to rest.

It is especially *Śiva's* lust feelings, as a symbol of uncontrolled *pravṛtti*, that must be tempered by immersion in water to obtain control and transformation of desire. The cycle of the *Śiva Kāma* (desire)-myths in the *Purāṇas* rages as a battle back and forth on various magical, mental, and physical levels.[216] For a sound vision of controlled desire in whatever form, a thought-process of "cooling" is indispensable. "Let a man in whom passion has arisen enter the water."[217] The true power of desire lies in its transformation. A complex interpretation of the symbols of *Agni* and liquid is given in the *Śiva Puraṇa*:

> "*Agni* is the glorious form of *Śiva* and *Soma* his calming form. The *tejas* form is sun and fire; the liquid form is *Soma* and water. Everything is made of a combination of *tejas* and liquid. From fire *Soma* arose, and fire is kindled with *Soma*. Fire flows upwards and *Soma* downwards. The universe is periodically burnt by the doomsday fire and reduced to ashes, the seed of fire. Then this seed of fire is again flooded with *Soma*."[218]

The balance between *pravṛtti* and *nivṛtti* is precarious, difficult to establish and to maintain. Time and again *Śiva* takes recourse to the waters to quench apparent unquenchable lust. He is heard pleading with *Pārvatī* to draw him out of *Kama* as out of fire. At other times the balance is portrayed, as we will see, under the symbol of sexual forces when *liṅga* rests, without shedding seed, in *yoni* (*ūrdhvaliṅga*).

> "*Śiva* was overcome with desire and he wandered over the earth sprinkling his body with water, finding no peace. One day he saw the *Yamunā* river and he plunged in, trying to assuage the torture of his heat, but the water of the river became black by contact with the fire of *Siva* and *Kama*. . . He fell into the *Kālindī* river and the waters were burnt up and became as dark as collyrium, but still he found no peace."[219]

140. The theme of "ordered desire" finds expression in the person of *Pārvatī*, daughter of the Mountain and his wife Mena, "the Woman". *Parvati* is "woman" in her own right. She longs for *Śiva* the *yogi*, the Supreme Lord. She also yearns for a child

215. *SP*. 4.4-26. Shutting the inner third eye refers to spiritual blindness. See: *RV*. 1.164.44 where man from a "round-about-seer" (*paridraṣṭṛ*) may come to "see everything", (*viśvam. . . Abhicaṣṭe*).
216. For example, see: Wendy Doniger O'Flaherty *Siva, The Erotic Ascetic*, p. 148ff. p. 148ff.
217. *Mbh*. 12.207.13.
218. *SP*. 7.28,3f
219. *SkP*. 6.58.1-4; 33.26.1-5; *VP* 6.30-31.

as men and women do. At the same time she is not averse to the joy of union with her husband for personal fulfilment without the promise of offspring.

> "(*Jaimini* said): This whole universe is filled everywhere with descendants of *Brahma* and *Viṣnu*; tell me about the descendants of *Śiva*. The sage replied: *Śiva* is man and *Parvatī* is woman; they are the causes of creation. All men have *Siva* as their soul, and all women are *Parvatī*. *Siva* has the form of the male sign, *liṅga*, and the Goddess has the form of the female sign, *yoni*. The universe, moving and still, has the form of the sign of *Śiva* and the Goddess. Long ago *Pārvatī* made a request of *Śaṅkara* (*Śiva*) for she wished to have progeny, even though, being the Goddess, she dwells in all progeny: "Unite with me this very day and beget a natural son". But he said: ". . . I have no death, Goddess, so I have no use for a son. ... you are woman and I am man; let us enjoy being the two causes from which progeny arise and rejoice in the pleasures of men and women; without progeny, let us always sport, taking pleasure in ourselves". *Parvatī* said: "Lord god of gods, blue-necked, three-eyed, what you have said is indeed true, but nevertheless I do wish for a little child. When you have begotten a child, you can do your *yoga*, great lord; I will bring up the son and you can be a *yogī* quite properly. An excessive yearning for the kiss of a son's mouth has arisen in me. If you wish, the son will be averse to marriage, so that you will not have a son and grandson and subsequent descendants."[220]

Earlier *Parvatı* had been born as *Satī*, daughter of *Dakṣa*, one of *Prajāpati-Brahma's* "mind-born sons". *Dakṣa* was to create humans by sexual power but had failed. He had gazed on *Satı*, immensely offending her. She had thrown herself in the fire, leaving behind her grieved and angry husband *Śiva*, the true creator and comprehensor. The episode reminds us of the "danger-zone" which is the break from the Uncreated into the created.[221]

But now *Satı* had returned as *Pārvatī*. She, by her understanding of *Śiva Mantramurti*, the inward-turned *Śiva*, and his ideals and by her reasoned affection for the creational world, reveals the possibility of equilibrium.[222]

> "*Gautama* spoke: The awakening of the *Brahman*-lore which is familiar with all duties, which comprises the contents of all texts, Through what, O Sir, is it effected? *Sanatjujata* spoke: Pondering over all the *Vedas* and grasping firmly their content, *Śiva* explained to *Parvatı* the Truth; learn it from me. Indescribable and shrouded, equally, is the mystery of the *Yogins*, which spreads out the path before the *Haṁsa*, Bestows joy and the fruit of liberation."[223]

---

220. Part of *BrhadP*. 2.60.1-4, 7-79, 106b-8. in: *Hindu Myths*, p. 262f.
221. The distinction is not of one "man" from another, but of the two forms *Prajapati-Brahmu* (and *Siva* now identifying himself with, now distantiating himself from either the one or the other or both). The forms are "immortal and mortal", "undesirous and desirous", "uncircumscribed and circumscribed" etc. (*SB*. 4.7.5.2; *BU*. 2.3. *MU*. 6.36)-and of "two minds, pure and impure" (*MU*.6.34.6). The Pure Mind is the *daivaṃ manas* of *BU*. 1.5.19, identified with *Brahmā* in *BU*. 4.1.6.- "*mano vai saṃrāt paramam brahma*"-and with *Prajāpati* in *TS*. 6.6.10.1. or *SB*. 9.4.1.2.
222. *KP*. 1.13.61.31.; *Mhb*. 154.52.60-61.
223. *HaU*. 1. in: Deussen, *op. cit*., p. 718.

141. *Brahma* himself assisted at the conception of the "idea" of *Pārvatī*. To let *Purvatī* be born, *Brahmā* invoked the goddess of the lustful feelings of the night (*Rātri*) to infuse herself into *Menā*, *Parvata's* (the Mountain) wife, so *Parvatī* would be born black as the night. Why? Perhaps it was meant to show the dark, destructive side of createdness. Delusion of the mind is part of the mind of those who do not see, caught as they are in *maya*.

> "You are like lust itself to the sensuous, you are the play of those who are playful, the delusion of the mind, and you are *Kalaratri*, the Night of Demons, and the destroyer of all that exists."[224]

Thus *Brahma* had praised the goddess Night.

142. When *Menā's* womb opened, *Pārvatī* was born at midnight. *Parvata* was perplexed by *Parvatī's* indescribable beauty and radiance. Once again, on *Parvata*, the Mountain, the beginnings reiterated themselves because in *Parvatī* the Great Goddess appeared. *Parvata*:

"Who are you? I do not know you, my child."[225] In the centre, mount *Parvata*, surrounded by *Apaḥ apraketa*, the formless Waters, the Self-existent Goddess had appeared. *Parvata* praised her with a thousand names.[226]

143. *Śiva*, the Self-existent, was happy with *Pārvatī*. She was *Maheśvarī*, half of *Śiva's* body to the eyes of man who cannot comprehend totality except by the unison of opposites like that of male and female. *Pārvatī* is *Prakṛti*. She is the highest *śakti* or power of *Mahesvara*, the Great Lord. *Parvata*, the Mountain, abided by *Pārvatī's* wish and she marrried the Great Lord, *Śiva*, [227] who has no beginning and is unborn.

At the marriage of *Siva* and *Parvati* a host of gods and beings were present, every one of them called by name in the *Liṅga Puraṇa*.[228] Silence fell and *Brahma* spoke:

> "The universe is created by the cosmic forms of this lord *Rudra* since the lord has the eight forms of earth, fire, water, ether, wind, moon, sun, and the *hota*. Still, at the instance of the lord of the mountains as well as at my instance this unborn *Prakṛti* of black, white, and red colour should be given to *Śiva*. You too are the *Prakṛti* (he said to *Siva*). The alliance with the king of the mountains is conducive to your welfare as well as mine. In the *Padma Kalpa*, I was born of your umbilical lotus. Hence you are my father and an ancestor to this mountain who is a part of mine."[229]

> "Then *Viṣñu* washed the feet of the lord with his own hands. He sprinkled the water thereof on his own head as well as those of *Brahmā* and the lord of mountain, *Himavan*. "This daughter of *Mana* and my younger sister now

224. *MP*. 154.78-84.
225. *KP*. 1.11.56-61; 1.66.68: 1.1.21.
226. *KP*. 1.1.211.
227. *KP*. 1.11.316.
228. *LP*. 103.4-36.
229. *LP*. 103.42-45.

is married to you". Saying thus, he dedicated the goddess to the lord of *Devas* with the water. *Viṣṇu* too offered himself to the lord along with water. All bowed down to him. The hair on their skins stood on end due to pleasure."[230]

144. Thus the Mountain proclaimed the truth of the undistinguishable beginnings which can be seen only by the contemplative *yogic* mind. The ancient and at times less appreciated orders of the *Kāpālikas*, wearers of skulls, and the *Aghorīs*, who wandered in cemeteries, united themselves with *Pārvatī*, The Woman, thereby also carrying sexual practices and ritual to the extreme. Mystical erotism received a valid place in *yoga*. Both in marital union as well as in contemplative thought, the union of heaven and earth, hierogamy, became visualized.[231]

145. On Mount *Himavat* lives *Parvata's* other daughter, *Gaṅgā*, of whom *Siva* himself sings:

> "She is the source of redemption.... Heaps of sin accumulated by a sinner during millions of births are destroyed by a mere contact of a wind charged with her vapour.... As fire consumes fuel so this stream consumes the sins of the wicked."[232]

146. *Gaṅga Kutīla*, the curvacious one, is the prototype of all India's rivers. "Beautiful as the rays of the moon", she is freed from the Himalayas, the northern region of the Pole Star. Both that mountain range and the star are proxies of the Cosmic Axis, Mount *Meru* or *Mandāra*. Released from near the moon, her powerful fall first caught in *Śiva's* matted hair adorned with the sixteenth segment of the moon, *Gaṅgā* flows down over the earth.

> "This river follows the path of the luminaries. It is frequented by groups of luminaries, and by thousands and crores of stars of the sky."[233]

147. *Gaṅgā* rides *makara*, the water-animal. Here ambivalence is inescapable, for waters create and dissolve and make man face his position between this temporal end and the timeless end.

> "May Mother *Gaṅgā*, the mother of the universe, stationed in the world of *Rudra*, a delighted devotee of *Siva*, dispel my sin."[234]

148. *Gaṅga's* descent from heaven (*Gaṅgavatarana*) has given rise to many tellings of wonder. It was in the waters where the *Kālakeyas* lived, allies of the monster *Vṛtra*, that order (*Ṛta*) was absent. The devils pestered the world. They were finally killed when *Viṣnu* commanded his descendent *Agastya* to drink the ocean. Left without water the world withered. It was *Bhagīratha*, the king-yogi, who, through sheer ardour and ascetic willpower, accomplished the nearly impossible.

---

230. *LP*. 103.48-51.
231. See: Mircea Eliade, *Yoga, Immortality and Freedom*, passim.
232. *BrahmavaiP*. 34.13f.
233. *LP*. 52.4.-8. "as beautiful as the rays of the moon". See: *Vāmaṇa Purāṇa*. *Mhb*. 3.108. 1-6; *R*. 1.37-43; *BhavP*. 9.8.8-31; *SP*. 5.38.48-57.
234. *LP*. 82.88.

That is what man may learn through concentration and wise judgment: to restore order where it has been disturbed. In Mahāballipuram near Madras, a rockrelief pictures *Bhagīratha* who uplifts his arms doing penance. It was his willpower which persuaded *Siva Maṇtramūrti* to help *Gaṅga* come down from the mountain. Thus *Gaṅgā*, refilling the ocean, was instrumental in restoring water to the earth.[235]

149. The regenerative property of water is praised in countless instances. To *Ṛṣi Chyavana* youth is restored when his wife takes him to a pool to bathe (*SB.* 4.1.5.1-12). *Gaṅgā's* water is brought in golden jar for *Rama's* consecration in *Ayodhyā* (R. 2.14-15). The river waters sanctify the believer:

"As *amṛta* is to the gods, even so is *Gaṅgā* water to human beings."[236]

"*Indra* leads *Yudhiṣṭira* to the netherworld during his exile; "Here is the celestial *Gaṅga* sanctifying the three worlds. Enter it and you will find your rightful place."[237]

150. The rivers, with *Gaṅgā* as their prototype, possess a wide experience of all the worlds. Through them the worlds relate, and man, through the rivers, is related to all the worlds and continents. In the heavens *Gaṅgā* is called *Mandakinī*, i.e. gently flowing. On earth she is *Gaṅga* or *Vegavati* and she is *Bhogavatī* in the nether-world for she purifies the dead.

151. *Gaṅgā's* sister-river *Yamunā* is *Yama's* sister: *Yama,* the god of death. She is the underworld's river in its traditional foreboding image. Riding on a tortoise and carrying a waterpot in her hand, *Yamunā* is the daughter of the Sun when her name is *Kālindi,* black. She sets with the sun in the region of the western quarter, the region of death. *Yamuna Kālindī* figures conspicuously in the *Bhāgavata Purāṇa* in a scene which serves as a reminder of the primordial *samudra manthana* when gods and demons churned the ocean for *amṛta* but, instead, first saw the world-poison *kālakūta* rise up from the waters. The people in the realm of the snakes had agreed that each month an offering be presented to the snakes under a tree to keep all trees alive. *Suparṇa, Viṣñu's* bird *Garuḍa,* used to receive a portion of the offering. It so happened that *Kaliya*, the son of *Kaśyapa*, tortoise, and *Kadru*, progenitor of the race of *nāgas,* ate the fish allotted to *Garuḍa.* After a fierce fight *Kalīya* hid in *Yamunā* where he lived in an environment of poison. It is when greed enters the Waters, the substratum of creation, that creation turns into poison. One day *Kṛṣña* wandered in *Vṛndāvana* when he saw cows and their shepherds fall lifeless on *Yamunā's* banks after drinking from *Yamunā's* waters.

"There was a pool in the *Kālindī* into whose waters, which boiled with the fire of *Kaliya's* poison, fell birds which were passing overhead . . . and all creatures who came to its banks died. When *Kṛṣna* who had become

235. *R.* 1.38-44, *Mhb*. 108-109 *Vana Parva*.; *Bhag* p. 9.9.
236. *Mhb*. 13.26.
237. *Mhb*. 79.

incarnate to restrain the wicked, perceived that the river had been polluted by that serpent whose poison was so virilent and swiftly active, he climbed a very high *Kadamba* tree . . . and plunged into the poisoned water. The mass of water in that pool was swelled by the poison and now shaken by the vigorous dive of the Man and it overflowed. *Kalīya* slithered out and enveloped angrily with his coils and bit in his vital spots that boy whose feet were like the inside of a lotus, who was bright as a cloud. In the coils of the serpent he appeared motionless and all were greatly distressed. The cows and bulls and calves lowed in their misery. There were calamities on earth, in the heaven and in the body. When the lord *Bala* came to search for his younger brother he came to the banks of the *Yamuna*. And *Kṛṣna,* seeing that his own village was so miserable because of him, and knowing that it had no other refuge other than him, conformed to the way of mortals and, staying for a moment, rose up from the serpent's grip. The serpent's hoods were tortured by the expanding body of *Kṛṣna,* and he released him... When *Kalīya* finally turned conscious again he folded his palms and said to *Kṛṣña*: "We are evil from our birth... ordain for us grace or punishment as you think best". "You must not stay here, serpent", said *Kṛṣña*, "go to the ocean, let this river be enjoyed by cows and men"... and thus the *Yamunā* became free from poison, its water like ambrosia".[238]

152. Both *Gaṅgā* and *Yamunā*, coming from the region of Mount *Kailāśa* in the Himalayas, are said to rest, in the figurative geography of the *Purāṇas,* in *Mansarovar* - The Lake of the Mind -, near the foot of *Kailasa*. From there the mighty northern rivers are said to flow onto the sub-continent.

"On the summit of Mount *Meru - Kailasa-* is the vast city of *Brahma* . . . enclosed by the river Ganges which.... falls from the skies, and after encircling the city, divides into four mighty rivers flowing to the ends of the earth."[239]

153. From their abode in the Himalayas, especially *Gaṅga* from her cradle in *Siva's* matter hair adorned with the crescent moon, both sisters, *Gaṅgā* and *Yamuna*, were well-acquainted with *Śiva Nīlakaṇṭha,* the blue-throated, who had swallowed *Kālakūta*, the world poison thrown up at the churning of the ocean. They had attentively listened to *Śiva Nīlalohita's* discourse on the poison of attachment and ignorance. They had heard *Śiva*'s plea to be un-attached (*virakta*). Time, in its manifestation, unfolds innumerable illusions, while he from whom this world is born is beyond and other than time.

---

238. *BhagP*. 10.17.2-12; 10.15.47-52; 10.16.4-34,51-67. in : *Hindu Myths*, pp. 223-228. The "idea" of *Śeṣa* (= *Yad aśiṣyata*) is all-encompassing. It is *Ananta*, Endless, the Ender, the World Serpent, the Swallower in whom all possibilities whatever are latent and from whom all possibilities of manifestation are extracted. In that sense to be "headless, footless, sightless and recumbent" - *apaśyam amukhaṃ śayanam* - is applied in the positive to those who, like *Brahman*, have no ends like the eternal Serpent. See: *TS*. 7.3.1.4. "*anto nāsti yad Brahmā*". Those who are ignorant and slaves of time are equally "headless, footless etc" but on the negative end of the Serpent. *Yamunā,* this river springs in the Himālayas among the Jamunotri peaks, flows for 860 miles through the plains before it joins the *Ganges* at *Prayāga* (Allahabad).

239. *VP*. 4.2.

"He is higher than the world-tree, than Time and all forms, out of him originates the unfolding panorama of the world."[240]

Gaṅga and *Yamunā* are well-educated in all cosmic experiences, coming, as they do, from on high while at the same time harbouring the sands and the waters of the earth in their riverbeds. What of human life would escape them when they touch so many villages and cities along their banks? *Yamunā* knows her brother *Yama* who is *Rudra* who is *Kala,* time. *(Mhb. 13..16.51).* Time is the universal fatality. It is *Śiva Kālarūpin,* the shape of time. It is the antithesis of *Siva* the *Yogin. Śiva* the *Yogin* means to say that the Uncreated is restored in its integrity. *Yoga* knows the contingency of things and defines them within the limits of created being.

Kala, time, is relentless, slowly bringing to an end everything, be it by *Nityapralaya,* the daily decay or destruction of all animate and inanimate things or by *Prakṛtipralaya* at the end of times when *Viṣñu* will rest upon the cosmic waters on Serpent *Ananta*, Endless.[241]

Gaṅgu retains her benevolence towards both the living and the dead. She sits in *Śiva's* hair, she feels the movement of *Śiva Nataraj*, dancing his cosmic dance on the "non-being" of all that exists.

"The whole universe is caught in *Kaľa's* mouth and whirls like a wheel through the activities of creation and annihilation."[242]

"Obeisance to one who is stationed in between *Brahma* and *Viṣñu* in the midst of waters; obeisance to the splendour, the protector, the destroyer, the perpetual maker and the Death. Obeisance to Lord *Śiva.*"[243]

"Obeisance to one who facilitates easy crossing of the ocean of mundane existence, obeisance to the splendid one, obeisance to one having two forms, to one of hundred forms, to one devoid of forms and to one holding a banner."[244]

154. Vedic-Indian speculations on the origins say that there are doors in man, opening him towards the Origin. The door is associated with the Waters.

"*Agni* bestows a blessing on each pious man, and opens wide the doors for him."[245]

"*Agni* and the Waters, the first door to divine order"

240. The Highest is spoken of as "nestless" *aniḍaḥ*: *SU.* 5.14; *RV.* 10.55.5-6 -, it is not a tree where creatures nestle in "time".
241. The Endless (*Ananta*) Residue (*Śeṣa*) is *Brahman*, the *Akṣara,* the accent, who, now that all semblance of otherness is discarded, remains the same World Serpent "for that both his ends meet" (*AV.* 10.8.12: *anantam... antavac ca samante).* Thus we can better understand *KU.* 5.1.4" "When this immanent *unstrung* body-dweller is released from the body, what survives?" (*asyavisraṇsamānasaya śarīrasthasya dehinaḥ dehād mucyamanasya*) - the answer is" "That" i.e. "That are you." We are ourselves, if we take away from our person all that is not-self.
242. *SP.* 7.1.7.14.
243. 18.18.1.
244. *SP.* 18.15.
245. *RV.* 11.24.5; 1.128.6.

"Wide be the doors, the godesses, throw open, easy to pass, invoked through adoration.[246]

The guardians, the waters and the goddesses are drawn into the same compass. The First Principle, *Atman*, reflects on his labours thus:

"Here are now worlds, let me create world guardians (man). Right from the Waters he drew forth and shaped a person."[247]

The portal of ascent in man, when he understands the body, is the vein *Iḍà,* to the left of *susuṃnā. Iḍā* is *Gaṅgā*, the outbreath (*apāṇa*). That is "moon"; that is "woman". *Piṇgalā* to the right is *Yamunu*, the inbreath (*prāṇa*). It is "sun". It is male. In a yogic text from about the fifteenth century we read:

"The goddess *Gaṅga* is *Iḍa* (referring to the *Soma* qualities) the river *Yamunā* is *Piṇgalā* (of the *Agni* traits). Between them lies the *Kuṇḍalini* (the untapped source of spiritual energy resting at the base of the spinal cord)."

"*Yoga* brings about the confluence of the three rivers, flowing in the three channels, *Iḍa, Piṇgala,* and the centre channel, the *Susuṃnā*, and carries the mind to *Kedara* (*Kedarnath,* the Himālayan shrine marking the confluence of the *Alakanandā* and the *Mandakini,* two of the three original tributaries of the *Gaṅga*)"[248]

155. To unloosen the *kuṇḍalini*—energy, the coiled up or sleeping force of the soul, and to stimulate it towards consciousness, the *yogī* must keep the *kuṇḍalinī* in the median canal (*suṣumnā*) and make it rise through the *lotus-çakras* to the top of the head (*sahasrara-çakra*). Through *āsanas, prāṇayama* and *mudra,* the person searching for knowledge should try to immobilize the outbreath and in-breath, his thought and the seed, thus obtaining harmony between the opposite forces. These forces are *Iḍā* which is of the essence of *Śakti-Śiva,* the moon and semen, and the force of *Piṇgalā* which is of the essence of *Śakti,* the sun and the ovum.[249]

"When *Prāṇa* is passing through *Iḍu,* assume *Padmāsana* and then lengthen the *Akusa* of 12 points by 4 - that is, as an exhalation *Prāṇa* goes put in 16 measures, and in inhalation comes in 12, inhale for 16 and thus gain power. Then, holding the sides by each hand, stir up *Kuṇḍalini* with all one's strength from right to left fearlessly for 48 minutes. Draw the body up a little to let *Kuṇḍalinī* enter *Suṣumnā.* The *yogī* does a drawing-up movement in which the shoulders are raised and dropped. *Praṇa* enters of itself with Her. Compressing above and expanding below, and vice versa, *Prāṇa* rises."[250]

---

246. *AV.* 9.3.22: *RV.* 2.3.5. In the Vedic tradition the Sun, the Truth, is the Portal of tne Universe and Heaven's only Opening, Cleft, (*loka-dvāra, divās-chidra).* It is as it were the hub of the Wheel (*rathasya kha*) passing through which the comprehensor is wholly liberated - *atimucyate.* See: *CU.* 8.6.5.; *IsU.* 15.16. Christ too spoke of himself as the Door.
247. *SGS.* 3.3.2.9.
248. *Hath. Ypr.* 3. 106; 2.23. See: Mircea Eliade, *Yoga, Immortality and Freedom,* passim.
249. *Gorakṣasiddhāntasaṁgraha.* See: Mircea Eliade, *op. cit.* p. 239.
250. *YogkU.* I. See also the *Ānandalaharī,* verse 32.

"Like a tortoise he draws within, the hands and feet and the head, while the breath still plays around the gates. Then it is called "Fill in ! Fill in ! When, after closing the nine gates, He seeks to breathe out and in like a torch in a jar without wind, that is called "detaining."[251]

156. Thus the human physiology is made into a cosmos. It lies within the reach of each and every earnest seeker after knowledge and the Truth. For the *Tāntric* this cosmosization is further realised through sexo-yogic practices. On the non-orgastic union of the *Sadaka* and the *Yogini* spiritual nectar (*amṛta*) flows. It runs in ambrosial streams through the body to the *muladhāra,* flooding the *Kṣudra-brahmāṇda* or microcosm. The union of the *Sakti-Kuṇḍalini* with *Siva,* in the body of the *Sādaka*, is that coition (*maithuna*) which "is the best of all unions for those who have already controlled their passions".[252]

"They with the eye of knowledge see the stainless *Kāla* united with *Cidānanda* on *Nāda.* He is the *Mahādeva,* white like a pure crystal, and is the effulgent Cause, *biṃba-rūpa-nidāna,* and She is the lovely woman of beautious limbs that are listless by reason of her great passion".[253]

157. The ten ducts or veins (*nāḍīs*) where the *yogī* in maditation retains the five breaths, form the *nādīçakra.* Through the *nādīçakra* travels Life by the physical-spiritual control of breaths. That is the *prāṇayāma.* Man's breath lying above the *Iḍā, Piṅgala,* and *Suṣumnā,* is the Day (*prāṇa ahar*). The out-breath is Night (*apāṇa*).

The *praṇayama*, practised with the breath contained in the centre of the body is of the essence of the moon (*Çandragrahaṇa*). But that which supersedes physical principles is of the essence of the sun (*Sūryagrahaṇa*). It is through this *Praṇayama* that the formless soul may be experienced.[254]

"With the body erectly threefold and symmetrical, with *manas* and the senses locked in the heart, the wise man must cross, with the boat of *Brahman,* all the frightful flood of waters of birth and death."

158. Breath, Life and Wind are a triad. For presentday modern man the triad may have been torn asunder. In the Vedic-Indian vision it is experienced as a whole. Breath discloses the intimate union between life and matter. When life and matter become too noisy, as may be the case in modern man's life, breath becomes strained. When man must shout to make himself understood, breath suffers. Breath must be heard as of itself, it is everywhere. It is the most natural movement of creation. In and through it man stands at the threshold of immortality for he breathes Eternal Breath. His breath is like the waters, ever flowing towards the gathering ocean.[255]

251. *YUp.* 12-13. in: Deussen, *op. cit.*, p. 715.
252. *YT.* 6. See: Woodroffe, *The Serpent Power,* p. 240: *Sahasrāropari bindau kuṇḍalya milanam shive, Maithunaṃ paramaṁ dravyaṁ yatinaṁ parikīrtitan*. Also: pp. 181-256.
253. *Brh. Sri.* v. 5.
254. *AP.* ch. 214. See; S.D. Gyani, *Agni-Puraṇa, A Study,* Chowkhamba Publications, the Chowkhamba Sanskrit Studies, Vol. XLII, Vārānaśī, 1964, *passim.* e.g. p. 30. 148. Also in the *Bīja* of "water" which is *Vaṁ* the soul may be experienced.
255. *SU.* 2.8. in: Deussen, *op. cit.*, p. 309.

"Praise to the Breath of Life! It rules this world, master of all things, on which all things are based.

When Breath of Life the broad earth with rain bedews, the cattle exult : "We shall have plenty", they say.

The plants converse with this Breath, drenched by its moisture; Our life is prolonged for you have made us all fragrant. Praise to you, Breath, when you come and praise when you go when you stand up when you sit still, to you praise.

Breath of Life is death, is fever, revered by the Gods. In the highest world he sees the man who speaks the truth.

Breath of Life is Queen, is Guide, revered by all things; breath is sun, is moon.

The two breaths are rice and barley, Breath the ox that pulls. In barley resides in-breath; out-breath is called rice.

A man breathes, breathes out and in within the womb. Quickened by you, to birth he comes once more.

Breath of Life, do not forsake me. You are, indeed I. In the Embryo of the Waters I bind you to me that I may live.[256]

159. Whereas in art the mode of the Self (*Brahman*) is stone, in sacred thought it is water. The realization that all embodied forms are but a moment's inflection of *Brahman,* the formless essence of matter, almost forces man to the waters to try and fathom" true form". Man does not pray to water but to the life within it. The waters are the tangible form of *Brahman.* At once the purifier and the origin of the mystery, water is the real and spiritually conceived source of life and the reminder of fleeting existence.

"He who was born of old was born of water. Right from the Waters the Soul drew forth and shaped a person."[257]

"Golden in form is he, like gold to look upon, the Son of the Waters."[258]

160. The Indus civilization and its legacy bestowed on water a sacred character. From the prominence of the Great Bath building at the archeological site at Mohenjo-daro, we understand the importance of the bath in Hindu life today. Research has proved that the Harappa civilization knew the cult of the Great Goddess. Also animal worship, phallism, the cult of trees and that of water are evident in the Harappa civilization. All those elements later entered the Hindu synthesis.[259]

"Any sin we have committed, consciously or unconsciously, deliver us from it, O Gods one and all! From whatever sin I, a sinner, committed, awake or asleep, may both past and future set me free, as if from a stake to which I was fastened!

256. *AV.* 11.1.5.6.7.11.12.13.14.26. in: Panikkar, *op. cit.,* p. 206.
257. *KU.* 4.6.
258. *RV.* 2.35.9-10.
259. See; Steven G. Darian, *The Ganges in Myth and History,* pp. 39-47. Also: Ernest Mackey, *Early Indus Civilizations,* London, 1948, p. 16.

May I be set free as if loosed from a pillar or loosed from the dirt after taking a bath! May all the Gods cleanse me from sin, as butter is pure after passing through the strainer!"[260]

161. To be set free from all sin and impurity (*papamocana*) is the natural prayer of the faithful when taking a cleansing bath. The deeper meaning of the purifying bath, however, is the yearning for the discovery of *jnana,* saving and purifying knowledge. What matters is an insight into the nature of evil. The inner purification of the whole man-*manas, vāc, prāṇa* or *śarīra-,* both the outer and the inner body, should be accomplished. The secret of the waters guides the *jnanin,* the knower of the Self to a state beyond good or evil. What matters is the state of harmony with all beings (*Ṛta*). How could man not realize that he is part of a flux where all things receive a touch of transience, when he contemplates the waters and stands in the midst of them? Would not any thoughtless rush or a hankering after *Having* be radically against the *Being* of the waters? The grabber looks ridiculous in the midst of the waters. How can man sell himself or his neighbour to greed when he really does not *possess* anything?

"What then, O God, is my greatest transgression for which you would ruin your singer, your friend? Tell me, O God, who knows all and lacks nothing, so that, quickly prostrating, I may sinless crave pardon.

I question myself on my sin, O *Varuṇa,* desirous to know it. I seek out the wise to ask them; the sages all give me this answer: "The God, great *Varuṇa,* is angry with you."[261]

"I seek the Lord of the Waters of golden appearance. May he hear our entreaty and grant us a place of ablution! Whatever food I have taken in the house of the wicked, whatever gift I have received at the hand of the crafty, whatever sin of thought or word or deed I have committed, from this may *Indra, Varuṇa, Bṛhaspati,* and *Sūrya* cleanse me again and again! If I have eaten or drunk to excess, or consorted with people of violent ways, may king *Varuṇa* wipe it all away!..."[262]

"Water, verily, is greater than food. Therefore, when there are no good rains, living beings are afraid that food will be scarce. But when there are good rains, living beings are happy, there will be much food. It is water in its different forms which is the earth, the atmosphere, heaven, the mountains, Gods and men, animals and birds, grass and trees, wild beasts, worms, flies and ants. All these forms are only water. Meditate on water!.[263]

162. Sin and purification are more than individual processes. They also move in a realm which is more and larger than merely moral or ethical. The inextricable maze of good and evil fills the universe from man's end. It is the cause of the cycle of *saṁsāra.* From that the *Jñānin* seeks release through *jñāna-śuddhi.*

260. *AV.* 6.115.
261. *RV.* 7.86.3-4.
262. *TA.* 10.1.12.13.
263. *CU.* 7.10.1. in: Panikkar, *op. cit.,* p. 680.

"May the Waters purify the Earth, May this Earth, purified, purify me! May the Lord of the Holy Word purify me, May Earth, purified by *Brahman*, purify me!"[264]

163. The purifying bath (*snana*) has been from the beginning one of the most important duties of Vedic Indian and later Hindu traditon. The holy and cleansing bath has been accorded a central place in the theology of God's salvific purpose and of man's attempt to understand his existence and to reach liberation (*mokṣa*). The holy bath is the hallmark of the India's Hindus, carrying the country's fame and its religious genius to all corners of the world. It is the sacred rivers of India which lend unity of purpose and meaning in life, each and every day in the year of *Prajāpati*, to the Hindus and others in this land.

"O cleansing Bath, cleansing as you flow, may I wipe out with the help of the Gods such sin as I have committed against my fellowmen..."

"Having put on fresh clothing, they step out of the old. Even as a snake sloughs off its skin, so does the penitent slough off his sin; there is not in him even as much sin as there is in a newborn child."[265]

164. Of the *nitya-snāna,* the obligatory daily bath, one finds different descriptions in different *sūtras, smṛtis* and treatises. The *naimittika*-bath is to be performed on certain occasions while the *kanya* is a bath which the *snataka,* bather, takes when he desires certain rewards. *Manu* (6.6.) prescribes only one bath a day for *brahmacārins,* celibates, and two baths for hermits. Elsewhere *Manu* stipulates three baths for the hermit (6.22). Over the centuries, the general rule for all Hindus has come to be one bath a day. No bath should be taken at night except on the occasion of an eclipse or when the sun passes into the zodiacal signs of Cancer and Capricorn. On the occasion of a marriage too, a birth or death or when a vow is taken, bathing at night is permissible. Only when natural water or a tank in the vicinity of a temple is unavailable, may a bath be taken in water belonging to an individual by first removing some handfulls of clay.

For those sick or otherwise disabled, provisions to bathe in the courtyard using water drawn in a vessel, have been made. The *Gaṅga* and her waters have come to be considered one of the holiest, if not the holiest, of India's waters.

264. *MahanarU.* 317-318. in: Panikkar, *op. cit.*, p. 524. The prophetic moment in the consciousness of evil is the revelation in an infinite measure of the demand that the Universe (or "God") addresses to man. It is this infinite demand that creates an unfathomable distance between the Universe (or "God") and man. That distance causes distress for it cannot be wholly healed unless man discovers in himself the latent or dormant totality. Thus sin moves in the realm of the *aimed-at totality* which is beyond the mere individual self or, in Indian terms, the *ahaṁkāra.* Sin is blotted out once the state of *jñanin,* the knower of the Self, is reached. Such knowledge makes one sinless, even if there are acts that have the "externals" of imperfection. To act in perfect conscience implies that one has reached perfect consciousness. One is on the way to that state. It is the effort of putting together what had been dismembered—*sandhyā samdha*—and the building up—*Saṁskār*—of another and unitary Self, different from *ahaṁkāra,* that wipes out sin and evil. The effort therefore less depends on "codes of behaviour" than on "being concerned with the Self". Purification, says *PrasnU.* 5.5 does not depend on a purifying bath or any sacred action, but on meditating on *Puruṣa,* Cosmic Man, as the fruit of *Jñāna.*

265. *SB.* 4.5.22-23. in: Panikkar, *op. cit.*, p. 520. What is left behind is the *śeṣa*, residue, so one receives the character of *brahmavit* or *brahmabhūta*.

"Let him always bathe in rivers, in ponds dug by the gods themselves, in lakes and in waterholes or springs."[266]

165. The procedure of the holy bath may here in a few words be indicated. The *Viṣñu Dharma Sastra* gives the following guidelines:

"Having removed the dirt from his body with water and loose earth, the bather should plunge in water, invoke the water with three verses *apo hi ṣṭha* (*RV.* 10.9.1-3), with these four verses *hiraṇyavarṇaḥ* (*TS.* 5.6.1.1-2) and with the verse *idamāpaḥ pravahata* (*RV.* 1.23.22 Or 10.9.8.). Then, while still plunged in water, he should thrice mutter the *Aghamarṣana* hymn (*RV.* 10.190.1-3) or he may mutter *tad viṣñoḥ paramam padam* (*RV.* 1.22.20) of the *Drupada Sāvitrī* verse or the *anuvaka* beginning with *yuñjata mana* (*RV.* 5.81.1-5) or the *Puruṣasukta* (*RV.* 10.90.1-16). Having bathed, he should, with his garments still wet, perform *tarpan* of gods and *Manes* while still in the water. But if he has changed the clothes, then he may do it after coming out of the water".[267]

The *Snānasūtra* of *Katyayana,* prescribing the daily bath, describes the way in which the bather, filling his joined hands with water, utters a number of verses and then immerses himself. In all ritual prescriptions we find the following recitation of the creation-hymn:

"From blazing Ardor Cosmic Order came and Truth; From thence was born the obscure night; from thence the Ocean with its billowing waves.

From Ocean with its waves was born the year which marshals the succession of nights and days, controling everything that blinks the eye.

Then, as before, did the creator fashion the Sun and the Moon, the Heaven and the Earth, the atmosphere and the domain of light."[268]

166. In modern times the bath and the ritual surrounding it, including that of *sandhyopasana,* the prayer at twilight, also draws from the *Purāṇas* and the *Tantras.* There is ample scope to express one's personal devotion by means of *mantras* and *mudrās* to obtain the grace of purity and a proper disposition. For many the *praṇayama,* restraint of breath, has become part of the ritual bath. Underlying the *praṇayama* is the philosophical and spiritual vision of the *Yoga-sūtra.* That *sutra* expounds the deeper meaning of the three components of each breath: the *puraka,* inhaling the outside air, the *kumbhaka*, the arrest of the breath, and the *recaka,* exhaling air from the lungs.

The aim of breath exercise during the bath is its interiorization. The spiritual bath, in fact, may be taken any time by *prāṇāyāma* for it does not absolutely require the presence of physical water. The cosmic polarity of sun and moon continues on the human plane where *prāṇa,* ascendent breath, is assimilated to the sun and *apaṇa,* descendent breath, to the moon or the lunar

266. Kane, *op. cit.,* p. 316.
267. Kane, *History of Dharmasāstra,* Vol. 2, part 1, p. 659.
268. *RV.* 10.190.1-3. in: Panikkar, *op. cit.,* p. 60. "as before"– *yatha-purvam* – can be considered an expression of a dynamic process.

essence. The *sandhyā*, the twilight-prayer, contemplates the deity *Āditya*, represented by the sun's orb. That orb's Intelligence dwells in one's heart. Likewise, rinsing the mouth before and after meals is seen as a bath. The *Upaniṣads* refer to water as the garment of *prana*.

One of *Yoga's* significant contributions is the control of psychosomatic mechanisms by the regulation of the breath. The breath, a constant factor of personality, is a vital point of contact between the self and the body. The *praṇayama* is perhaps one of the most ancient and most important consciousness developing techniques for controlling the human body's forces, manifesting themselves as *Prāṇa*. It purifies the nerve circuits and provides vitality to the subtle centres of the body. Its major intention is to stimulate the centre of paranormal consciousness. That centre, the brain, is called upon to arouse the *Kuṇḍalinī*. To achieve yogic bathing of the body and the human personality, *yoga*-discipline has developed a systematic technique, with special emphasis on location, duration, speed, depth and rhythm of breathing. Man's normal breathing, if not otherwise trained, is irregular and lacks harmony. Under those circumstances the current of energy flowing downward to strike *Kuṇḍalinī* is inadequate, leaving it unawakened. An excellent opportunity to cleanse the body and purify the mind is then lost.

> "One who has external cleanliness should practise internal cleanliness too. The holy bath should be conducted in accordance with the injunctions. It is threefold: 1. *Agneya*, fiery. 2. *Varuṇa*, watery and, 3. *Brahma*, consisting of *Brahman*.
>
> It is only after he has practised the external bath that he should practise the internal. If he is devoid of internal purity, he is still dirty even as he applies clay over his body and plunges into the waters of the *tirthas*. O excellent brahmins, the moss, the fishes, the sharks and the animals that prey upon fishes, remain ever in water. But are they pure? Internal cleanliness should always be pursued in accordance with the injunctions."[269]

> "Internal cleanliness is mentioned as follows: One should apply the holy ashes of detachment (*nivṛtti*) with a feeling of devotion. One should take a holy dip in waters of knowledge of the soul. This is how one can attain purification."[270]

167. For the *tāntric* the bath does not remove ignorance. It rather creates a general background for inner equilibrium. Through the bath purity of mind (*naimālya*) is acquired, purging the identity between the Ego and the body. Baths are an immersion—

> ". . . immersion into the "eight" bodies, *mūrti*, which are the eight *nagas* corresponding to planets. The devotee hopes to assume their capabilities."[271]

168. To obtain liberation through the union of opposites (male-female, microcosm-macrocosm, sacred-profance, *Śiva-Śakti*), is a persistent *yogic* theme. For the

---

269. *LP*. 32-35.
270. *LP*. 8.36. in: Kane, *op. cit.*, p. 316 (also 268).
271. *SvT*. 7.46. and commentary. See: Woodroffe, *op. cit.*, pp. 235-256.

purpose of union of opposites, *yoga* has developed an elaborate and subtle geography of the body that must be learned, controlled, and ultimately resolved into unity. *Tantrism*, while availing itself of yogic discoveries, is more ritually inclined. In the *Vamaçara Sadhanā* the quest for knowledge and purity takes a particularly dramatic form. The *sādhaka* undertakes the ritual known as *pañça-tattva*, that of the five "forbidden" fruits and considered to be a purifying bath. The *pañça-tattva's* aim is to overcome the distinction or duality of clean and unclean, sacred and profane, in order to dissolve the bondage by an artificially fragmented world. Five ritũal ingredients, beginning with "M", apart from the literal meanings, are reminders of yogic processes.

Construed into a streamlined mental configuration, the ritual becomes a "right-hand" tāntric practice (*Dakśiṇāchāra*) accessible to a wider public than when its five ingredients are gone through in their literal context. Thus *madya,* wine, becomes the symbol of "intoxicating knowledge"; *māṃsa*, meat, implies the control of speech; *matsya*, fish, represents the two vital currents moving in the *Iḍā* and *Piṅgalā* on each side of the *Suṣumnā*; *mudrā*, parched cereal, symbolizes the yogic state of contemplation and, finally, *maithuna*, sexual union, symbolizes meditation upon the primal act of creation. The "right-hand" practitioner uses material substitutes for the five "M" s. Wine is substituted by coconut juice while meat finds its representative in ginger. *Mudrā* is replaced by rice, wheat or grain and *maithuna* by two types of flowers: *karavi* representing the *liṅga*, the male organ, and *aparajitā* symbolizing the *yoni*.[272]

169. Common to all tantric and yogic tradition is the aim to establish enstasis (*samādhi*). This "inexistence" will be achieved by meditating on the subtle aspect of matter (*sūkṣma*). *Samadhi* in its liberating and most perfect form is the *asamprajñāta samādhi*, the undifferentiated state when the flow of impressions is being completely arrested by the inner spiritual bath. The *yogin* reaches his true Self.[273]

272. The intricate yoga-and tāntric mystical, mystical-erotic and "intentional" language has been excellently presented and commented upon by Mircea Eliade in: *Yoga, Immortality and Freedom,* passim. It would be impossible to discuss the topic satisfactorily here. Ultimately all the ideas express a desire to effect the *coincidentia oppositorum*, the reintegration of polarities. The same motifs are found in the mythologies and iconographic symbolism of many archaic cults. The coincidence of the ultimate and the proximate – *para* and *apara* – *Brahman* in the *Upaniṣads* is that of *Mitra-Varuṇa* in the *Vedas*. The Supreme Identity is equally bipolar whether one thinks of "It" as masculine or feminine. With respect to the Great Mother, Creative Nature one asks:" Who knows her progenitive duality" – *mithunatvam*, *AV*. 8.9.10. And conversely, "He (*Brahman*) is the womb", – *yonis ça gīyate YV*. 1.4.7.27. If the conjoint principles are considered in their reciprocal relation, it is the manifested Identity ("God") that is the masculine and unmanifested Godhead that is the feminine power, as being the inexhaustible reservoir of all possibility, including that of manifestation. See: *Kṛṣña* who "deposits the embryo in the Great *Brahman*, my womb. . . my ultimate Nature, *parā prakṛti*, the womb of all existence"– *BG*. 14.3; 7.5.6. Also: *RV*. 9.74.5.: Into the womb of the Infinite that *Soma* puts the embryo". This is in accord with *RV*. 10.121.7: "Waters wherein was laid the universal embryo" which is the "Golden Germ", *Hiraṇyagarbha*. See: Part II:5:4: (iv) "The birth of His own Perfection: *Hiraṇyagarbha* (*RV*. 10.121)". The union of opposites also refers to that of "the intercourse by Intellect with the Voice" – *manasā vācam akrata*, *RV*. 10.71.2, which in *SB*. 6.1.2.9. "makes *Him* pregnant" – *sa manasaiva vācam mithunaṃ samabhavat, sa garbhy abhavat*. Thus *Prajāpati* divides the Voice (which had been his "Silence") from himself: *BU*. 6.4.2: "He separated the Woman" – *striyam asrjata*.

273 *Yogasāra Saṃgraha*. See: Micrea Eliade, *op.cit.*, p. 84. Also in this book: part II:4:4(i) "Myths of the exiled soul".

170. Reflections on conjoining principles of polarity, ultimately signifying one unity, are for the mythical awareness excellently expressed by the confluence of rivers. The *sangam* joins various themes. Especially the confluence of rivers at *Prayag* (Allahabad) is reminiscent of the riverwaters coursing in the three realms of space, thus uniting them into one world.

Nāga Vāsuki, who offered his services during the churning of the ocean, dwells in *Bhogavatı*, the river of the underworld. She is sometimes referred to as *Saraswatī*. Possibly because *Saraswatı* has lost herself in the sands and the Aryans had to leave her waters behind. *Vāsuki's* bathing-site, *Bhogavati*, appears on earth at *Prayag*. It is famous for its spiritual benefits.

Descending from heaven and passing through *Siva's* matted hair, *Gaṅgā* sets the dead free in the underworld as *Bhogavatī*. Meeting her sister *Saraswatī* there, both travel together to *Prayāg* where they are met in loving embrace by their common sister *Yamuna*. The confluence of sacred waters and cosmic forces reaches near perfection at *Prayag*.[274]

171. Without a visit to *Vasūki's* famous temple at *Prayag*, a bath in the sacred confluence would be incomplete. It would fall short of all its cosmic implications.

> "... the merit of bathing at the sacred confluence of *Gaṅgā* and *Yamunā* is not complete until (the batther) visits the temple of the King of Serpents."[275]

172. Southern India's sacred riverwaters have their own specific origins and excellence. Narmadā, " pleasure-giving", for example, who as goddess stays in *Varuṇa's* palace, worships him. Having knowledge of *Ṛta* which has its seat in Varuṇa's realm, Narmadā bestows gifts on all who bathe in her. Once she offered her banks to *Indra* to drink *Soma*, the drink of immortality.[276] When lord *Viṣñu* appeared in his avatar-form of the fish and was preparing to submerge the earth and everything in water, *Manu*, the Man, asked him how many years the destruction would last and how he, *Manu*, was to protect the world. And *Viṣñu* replied:

> "Then take this boat of the *Vedas* and place the essences and seeds of all living creatures upon it; and by attaching the ropes as I have taught you, fasten the boat to my horn, and you will be protected by my majesty. You

274. *Mhb. Śalya parvan* 37; *Vana parvan* 85, 86; *SkP*. 3. 111-115. Diana L. Eck in, *Bānāras, City of Light*, p. 292, writes; "Prayāga is one of India's most famous *tīrthas*. The name means "The Sacrifice", and it reminds us of the way in which pilgrimage to a sacred place came to be considered the primary substitute for Vedic sacrifical rites. Known as the "King of *Tīrthas*" Prayaga is located at the confluence of the Yamunā and the Ganges Rivers, about fifty miles as the crow flies from Bānāras. (Today it bears the Muslim name Allahabad, City of Allah). According to the Hindu tradition the mysterious, sacred underground river, the *Saraswatī*, is also said to emerge there, at the confluence called the *Trivenī*, "Where Three Rivers Meet". Bathing at this confluence, it is said, is always auspicious. Sins from countless lives begin to "tremble like trees struck by a great wind "(*Kāshī Khaṇḍa*, 22.64), when one prepares to go to Prayāga. Especially during the month of *Māgha* (the wintermonth, F.B.) people come to Prayaga to bathe, and every twelve years they come by hundreds of thousands to India's greatest *Mela*, the *Kumbha Melā*.

275. From a Pilgrim's account: *Kaśīnāth* "Serpent Worship", Indian Antiquary 2 (1873): 124 in: Steven G. Darian, *op. cit*., p. 63. According to *Mhb. Śalya parvan* 37, *Vāsuki*'s home is on the river *Bhogavatī*, a name sometimes referring to the *Saraswatī* (*Mhb. Śalya* parvan 37).

276. *Mhb. Vanaparvan* 121.19. The *Narmadā* is the modern Nerbudda.

alone will remain when even the gods have been burnt. The moon and the sun, I and *Brahma*, together with the four World-protectors, the holy river *Narmada*, the great sage *Markaṇḍeya*, *Bhava*, the *Vedas* and *Purāṇas* and subsidiary sciences - all of these will remain with you during the interval of destruction of the era of *Manu Cakṣuṣa*, when all is a single ocean...When the time arrived as it had been foretold, *Viṣñu* appeared.... and a serpent in the form of a rope come to *Manu*'s side. Then the sage who knew *dharma* gathered together all creatures and placed them on the boat, and by the technique of attachment he tied the boat to the horn of the fish with the rope that was a serpent..."[277]

173. For those more spiritually aware, the confluence at *Prayāg* where *Gaṅgā*, *Yamunā* and *Saraswatī* meet, a bath at *Trivenī* unites man with the forces of *Iḍā* and *Piṅgalā*: *Gaṅga* and *Yamunā*, the forces of the mellow moon and the flaming fire of alternating life and death. In the *Hevajra-tantra*, the *Buddha* (*Bhagavān*) proclaims that, without a perfectly healthy body, one cannot know bliss. *Yoga* and *tantra*, with regard to the body, oppose Upaniṣadic and post-Upaniṣadic pessimism and asceticism. They project the concept that sanctity can be realized in a "divine body" receptive of all cosmic forces.

"Here (within this body) is the Ganges and Jumnā. . . here are Prayāga and Banaras—here the sun and the moon. Here are the sacred places, here the *Pīṭhas* and the *Upa-Pīṭhas*. I have not seen a place of pilgrimage and an abode of bliss like my body."[278]

174. It was from the Milky Ocean - during the creation of the world - that the divine healer *Dhanvantari* offered the cup of immortality to *Jayanta*, regent of paradise. This nectar, churned up from the ocean at the beginning of time, is said to have come down and splashed the earth in four places as it was whisked away to heaven by the gods: *Prayāg*, *Hardwār*, *Nāsik* and *Ujjain*, the four sites of the *Kumbha Melā* pilgrimage. These four sites are centres of pilgrimage for all times and in all seasons.

As the Aryans obtained a foothold in the regions of the Ganges basin, their civilization, like its succeeding Indian Hindu civilization, became known by its rivers and human life centering along their banks. A new world was being shaped, drawing its rhythm from rains and rivers, the dry heat of summer and the sustenance from plants and trees and the harvests of the earth. The heartbeat of mother earth began to be more felt. The cosmic elements enter into the sacrifice, the renewal of creation. At the offering of the *Soma*-sacrifice the people invoked the waters and the plants:

"O ye, divine, vast, all-soothing waters, the water of the rain are the divine,

277. *MP*. 1.11-34; 2.1-19: together these pericopes make up the episode of *Viṣñu's* becoming a fish to save *Manu* from dissolution. The fish's expansion had first frightened *Manu* like *Viṣñu's* cosmic form had made *Arjuna* afraid or *Kṛṣña* his mother. The fish becomes a destructive force to be disposed of like *Siva's* seed, transferred from one body of water to another until it rests in the ocean. See: *Hindu Myths*, pp. 181-184.

278. *HevT*. in: Eliade, *op. cit*., pp. 228ff.

vast, all-soothing waters; if the priest said not that praise, the divine waters would descend in anger on this world.[279]

"Let the waters bless us; may the plants be auspicious" Rise up with life, unite yourself with life, rise up with the sap of plants."[280]

175. The pitcher with water from the river, being carried home after the daily bath, reflects many cosmological ideas and revelations from Vedic times. In the beginning there was water wherein *Prajapati* wished to have a firm foothold (*pratiṣtha*). He created the earth and consolidated it and hence it was called *Pṛthivī* because it became "established" (*Jain B*.3.318). The earth is also a receptacle of the subterranean waters. As a receptacle, the earth is *pātra*. Carrying home his pitcher, man is part and parcel of the firmness of the earth on which he lives and of its fleeting temporality.[281]

176. The pitcher with water also reminds us of *kalasa*, the *Soma*-bowl in which the sacrificial juice is offered. The sacrifice being the establishment of the link between heaven and earth is not some magical connection that can be done or undone at will. It is the link that maintains the whole of reality in truth and order. If man were to see only the limits of his house, his village or city, or if for him the world would stop at the frontiers of his country or even the uttermost horizon of the earth, would he not soon feel imprisoned and wish to go further afield? The centre where everything happens cannot be pointed at by man's finger as though he could claim it. The link with that centre (*skambha*) is the link *prohibiting* exploitation of the earth as well as the usurpation of the heaven. The *skambha* is renowned for its length, breadth, width and depth. It is in the ocean, the sea, it is on the land and in the air, in each country and in each home and heart. It is in the pitcher with water after the bath.

"*Mahāmeru*, the tender sporting ground of *Śṛkaṇṭha* is eighty four thousand yojanās high. Lord *Śiva* is seated there together with *Umā* and the chiefs of his *Gaṇas* and also sports about there for a long time. The auspicious river of holy waters circumambulates the mount *Meru*, the worldaxle.

With the water agitated by the wind and by its own velocity, the river flows down and all the four inner peaks of the *Meru*. After going beyond all the mountains partially, it enters the great sea at the behest of lord *Śiva*.

There are hundreds and thousands of rivers branching out from this, which flow through all the sub-continents as well as the mountains therein . . .[282]

279. The holy places, the "Seven Cities "(*saptapurī*) are known all over India. In the North there is *Ayodhyā*, the capital of Lord *Rāma; Mathūra*, *Kṛṣṅa's* birthplace; *Hardwār*, the Ganges-gate; *Kāśī* (Bānāras) the city of *Śiva*. In central India *Ujjain*, sacred to *Śiva*. In the West *Dvārakā*, *Kṛṣṅa*'s capital. In the south *Kāñchī*, sacred to *Śiva* and *Viṣṅu:* See: Diana L. Eck, *op.cit*., p. 284.

280. *AV.* 8.7.9.

281. *SB*. 6.7.1.17;—*tasya pa eva pratiṣṭhā/apsu hime lokāḥ. partiṣṭhā*. *SB*. 12.5.2.14: *apo va asya sarvasya pratiṣṭhā*. I here follow Kuiper's assumption that the thoughts about the waters being *pratiṣṭhā* and the earth *pātra*, are old cosmological ideas: see: *op. cit*., p. 138-139.

282. *LP*. 52. 8b-11. Without straining the psychological implications too much, we may connect the idea of receptacle and *skambha* with the "Sun" as the "Eye", constantly assimilated notions in Vedic

177. From Mount *Meru* where *Siva* dwells flow the waters over the whole world into all realms of life. It is *Gaṅga* who comes from *Śiva's* hair and who comes from the inner peaks of Mount *Meru*. She is the one who knows *Śiva's* intention with creation. She is mentioned in one of the earliest descriptions of the religious bath, found in the *Matsya Purāṇa*. From the account it is evident that the bath was common to all classes and groups of people.

If possible one should bathe with water drawn in a vessel or pitcher from a well or a stream. The bather should invoke *Gaṅgā* to be present. Then, uttering the names of the great sages, the bather will be encompassed by *Gaṅga* flowing in the three worlds.[283]

178. The water pitcher is not only *pātra* or *kalaśa*. It also is *kumbha*. *Kumbha* represents the deity. The vessel as *kumbha* expresses the formless *Brahman*. Carrying the *kumbha* home after the bath, man attests to the prayer of the dying person wishing to be united with *Brahman* by requesting the Sun to disperse its rays, veiling the Truth. The dying person is waiting to receive his true form.

> "With a bowl, made entirely out of gold, the mouth of Truth is covered over; Open this for me, O *Pūṣan*, in order to proclaim it to me as I am faithful to the truth!
>
> O *Pūṣan*, the only seer, O *Yama*, the sun-god, *Prajapati's* son, disperse your rays, withdraw together your splendour; Yes, I see it, your lovable form; and that one there, I am that one himself!
>
> May now the breath be one with the wind, be one with the immortal and may this body end in ashes..".[284]

179. What else could be a most significant meaning of *kumbha* than that of "as woman" from whose pregnance birth and growth flows forth? In the *kumbha*-vessel, filled with water when I return from the river, I am — although contained in it—, open to all that is possible. I may be scattered in dissipation and un-truth, swung around on the Wheel's felly, but in the vessel *(kumbha)* I carry my own truth home. Potentially exposed to being either scattered or gathered, in the *kumbha* I am, as in the womb, unified and whole.

> "Unified am I, quite undivided, unified my soul. Unified my sight, unified my hearing, unified my breathing—both in and out—unified is my continuous breath.
> Unified, quite undivided am I . The whole of me.
> Under the impulse of the divine Impeller, with the Powers for arms and the Spirit for hands, I, impelled, grasp hold of you!" [285]

There are numerous instances of the womb of the rivers giving birth to gods and humans. Both *Gaṅgā* and *Saraswati* themselves were born from *Brahmā's*

---

mythical awareness. The Sun as the Eye is there also in me so I may feel and know myself to be directly related to the centre.

283. *MP*. 102. I - 8.

284. *BU*. 5.15.1. in; Deussen, *op. cit.*, Without going into further exegetical details one may say that *Pūṣan* is the Spirit, the one who is with me on my way, on my path. The Spirit who is my guide as I go along and must choose where to go. *Pūṣan* is with the traveller.

285. *AV*. 19. 51.1-2. in : Panikkar, *op. cit.*, p. 340. *Spirit is Pūṣan.*

waterjug. In art the goddess is often found depicted as a vase, the vessel of life. She features in the ceremony performed prior to the building of a temple.

> "(The sacrificer) shall carefully excavate a hole in the centre... and place the pitcher in the midst thereof, the hole with the pitcher in it, standing as it were, for the impregnated womb.... Worship the earth-goddess in a lotus-shaped copper receptacle."[286]

180. The rivers and the vegetation along their banks became for the Aryans their very sustenance. The rivers are *Aditi*, the mothers. They are assimilated to the mother-goddess under the symbol of lush vegetation produced by the waters. There is a relationship between the tree, the goddess and the waters. *Saraswatī*, on her course down from the Himalayas, is said to come from a fountain at the foot of the *Plakṣa*-tree. The *Vāmana Purāṇa* attributes her birth to a fig tree (II. 3). The *Śiva Purāṇa* repeats this theme of *Gaṅgā* flowing from the branches of an *Udambara* (fig)-tree. (*Koṭirudra Saṁhita*, 27.4)

During their journey to Mount *Kailāśa* the *Puṇḍava* brothers of the *Mahabharata* came upon *Viṣṇu Narāyana's* hermitage, filled with celestial trees and flowers:

> "the rounded trunk of a great jujube-tree. It was fresh and shining and by the gigantic jujube-tree the *Bhagirathı*, (the Gaṅgā) of graceful descent, with stairs of rubies and chorals."[287]

181. The mythical motif of a bathing woman, arousing passion, identifies the woman with the fertilizing powers of the waters or the seed of the waters. The woman's power and gift of fertility is at once creative and destructive. The sexual aspects of the bathing woman usually point, in mythical portraits, to the extraordinary way the gods deal with situations. Thus *Śiva's* son *Skandha*, who plays important roles in many aeons, cannot be expected to have a normal birth. Once, when *Śiva* and *Pārvatī* made love and were disturbed in the act of coition, half of *Śiva's* seed was taken by *Agni*, the intruder. But given to the gods, it tore up their bodies and the seed spilt like a lake of golden fluid.

> "... and hearing of this, *Parvatī* was full of curiosity and went there to play in the water. Then, wishing to drink the sweet water, she said to the six *Kṛtikkās* who were bathing there : "I want the water that you have taken up in that lotus-petal and are bringing home." They said to her: "If we give you this water, a child will be born from it. . ."[288]

182. The rivers, drenching the earth with fertility, transmit their motherhood to the fertile earth who herself receives the name of mother. At a cremation people say:

---

286. *AP*. 41. 17 -20. See also Steven G. Darian, *op. cit.*, pp. 114-134, The Image of *Gaṅga* in Indian art. The body-vessel scheme with regard to the Feminine has been earlier discussed. Body - vessel and mother - child situation are the positive elementary characters of the Feminine.

287. *Mhb. Vana parvan* 144. *Aditi* is also World-Mother who gave birth to seven gods and, as the eighth, to a "mortal egg", *Mārtaṇḍa*. See: Kuiper, *op. cit.*, p. 100.

288. *MP*. 158. 27-50; *PP*. 5. 41.110. See: Wendy Doniger O'Flaherty, "Agni, the Erotic Fire" in *op. cit.*, pp. 90-110.

"Crawl to the earth, your mother."[289]

"Thou, who art earth, I place thee in the earth. The earth is a Mother. I am the son of the Earth, my father is *Parjanya.* born of thee, mortals return in thee."[290]

"Instill in me abundantly, O Mother Earth, which emanates from you and from your plants and waters, that sweet perfume that all celestial beings are wont to emit, and let no enemy ever wish us ill !

Your fragrance which adheres to human beings, the good cheer and the charm of men and women, that which is found in horses and in warriors, that which is in wild beasts and in the elephant, tne radiance that shines about a maiden — O Earth, steep us, too, deeply in that fragrance, and let no enemy ever wish us ill !"[291]

183. Numerous are the myths in which the waters are bearing seed and act as arbitrators creating both good as reward and evil as punishment. The power of the riverwaters is direct. It is assimilated to that of the gods, quick to act and everywhere present.

The Waters and the Earth differ in character. Swift, quick to enter and again to withdraw, at times impatient, the Waters are robust. The Earth is slower, silenter, careful and attentive and, producing from her own substance, constantly reproducing herself while producing for others. The Earth is conspicuous because she is more silently at work. The Earth does not argue her prominence when man sleeps, sits and stands on her all day and all night and could not be without her for even a second without falling into empty space and loosing his direction.

"Earth is composed of rock, of stone, of dust; Earth is compactly held, consolidated. I venerate this mighty Earth, the golden-breasted, O purifying Earth, I invoke you!

O patient Earth, by Sacred Word enhanced, bearer of nourishment and strength, of food and butter, O Earth, we would approach you with due praise! Pure may the Waters flow over our bodies, That which defiles — I fling it upon our foes, I cleanse myself, O Earth, as with a filter."[292]

184. Latencies and seeds in water may spend several cycles before they become manifest and emerge from the water. But of the Earth it may be said that it never rests. She gives birth ceaselessly to all species and to all individuals of each species. Mother Earth is near to all as the breast is to the baby.

"Your regions, Earth, to eastward and to northward, southward and westward, may they receive me kindly whenever on their paths I travel. Never, when standing on your surface, may I totter!

289. *RV.* 10.18.10.
290. *AV.* 12.1.11.14. See: Mircea Eliade, *Patterns in Comparative Religion*, p. 252.
291. *AV.* 12.1.23.25 in: Panikkar, *op. cit.*, p. 125.
292. *AV.* 12.1.26.29.30. in: Panikkar, *op. cit.*, p. 126.

Whether, when I repose on you, O Earth, I turn upon my right side or my left, or whether, extended flat upon my back, I meet your pressure from head to foot, be gentle, Earth, you are the couch of all!

Whatever I dig up of you, O Earth, may you of that have quick replenishment, O purifying One, may my thrust never reach right unto your vital points, your heart!

Your circling seasons, nights succeeding days, your summer, O Earth, your splashing rains, your autumn, your winter and frosty season yielding to spring — may each and all produce for us their milk !

This cleansing Earth, who trembles before the Serpent, who guards the fires that dwell within the waters, who castigates the god-insulting demons, has chosen for her mate *Indra*, not *Vṛtra*, surrendering herself to the powerful one, the potent.

May the Goddess Earth, bearer of many a treasure and of wealth stored up in diverse hidden places, the generous sharer of riches, impart to us, in addition to gold and gems, a special portion of her favour !

O Earth, O Mother, dispose my lot in gracious fashion that I may be at ease. In harmony with all the powers of Heaven set me, O Poet, in grace and good fortune!"[293]

185. The Waters are there at the beginning and end of every cosmic cycle. They inspire awe in man and open up unspeakable vistas. The earth is present at the beginning and end of each one's life.

"In the boundless waters in the centre of the universe on the back of the firmament, greater than the great, having suffused with his splendour all the lights, the Lord of beings stirs within the womb.

He who is the guardian in the centre of the universe, He who (bestows) the worlds to virtuous people, and the golden glow of death, that golden light established in heaven and earth, may he bestow on us that light! The cosmic waters glow. I am light! The light glows. I am *Brahman*!"[294]

"May Earth, who bears mankind, each different grouping maintaining its own customs and its speech, yield up for me a thousand streams of treasure, like a placid cow that never resists the hand.

Peaceful and fragrant, gracious to the touch, may Earth, swollen with milk, her breasts overflowing, grant me her blessing, together with her milk!"[295]

186. Everything emerges into being above the surface of the Waters. Yet, everything is once again reduced to its primal formlessness. It is taken back into the formless Waters (*Apaḥ apraketā*) as the result of a historical disaster or a cosmic

293. *AV.* 12.1.34-37.44.63: *Bhūmi Sukta*, Hymn to the Earth. in: Panikkar, *op. cit.*, p. 123 ff.
294. *MahanarU.* 1-2; 152-156: in: *op. cit.*, p. 335.
295. *AV.* 12. 1.45.59: *Bhumi Sūkta*, in: Panikkar, *op. cit.*, p. 129.

end (*mahāpralaya)*. Water *precedes* every creation and every form, whereas earth *produces* living forms.

The mythical destiny of water is to open and close cycles. That of the earth is to stand at the beginning and end of every biological form and share in the history of man's dwelling. The earth herself is that dwelling. Thus the earth mediates between man and the waters. She belongs to both and has a stake in both camps. That is why the earth knows her involvement in man's history while she is at the same aware that her life too depends on the term allotted to her by the waters. The earth is of herself a place of *pravṛtti* and *nivṛtti.* That is in her nature. And so is living on the earth. Man's living on the earth is of itself involvement in tilling the earth's soil while at the same time waiting for the waters. Man's double responsibility makes him a man of both worlds, that of the Gods and that of Men.

"In the ocean without shores, in the midst of the Universe, on the ridge of the heavens, greater than the great, with his splendour penetrating the world lights, the stars, he tarries as *Prajāpati* in the mother's womb.

Into him the world disintegrates and then unfolds itself, upon him all the gods are founded. It is that, what was already there and will be. It is in the syllable in the highest space.

In it, the space with earth and heaven is enveloped, the sun outshines with splendour and sparks. In the ocean itself the poets weave their poems. And in that highest syllable there are all the creatures.

It procreated the creatures of the world. It, through water, created forth the living creatures on the earth, and itself entered into plants, animals and human beings, into the mobile and the immobile beings."[296]

"May Earth, the stage where mortals sing and play with various shouts and noises, which resounds with cries of war or beatings of the drum, drive far my foemen and rid me of all rivals!

In village or forest, in all the places where man meets man, in market or forum, may we always say that which is pleasing to you!

The Maker of the world thought the earth with her oblations when she was shrouded in the depth of the ocean. A vessel of gladness, long cherished in secret, the Earth was revealed to mankind for their joy."[297]

187. When a form emerges from the waters, every direct organic bond between them is broken. The emerging of form from the waters is a declaration of self-existence (*pravṛtti*) on the form's part as against its former unevolved state (*nivṛtti)*.

Emergence from the waters is a danger-zone, a break-away from the Uncreated. Where is the path between the Uncreated and the created?[298]

296. *MahanarU.* 1-4. in: Deussen, *op. cit.*, p. 249.
297. *AV.* 12.1.60.56.41: *Bhūmi Sūkta,* Panikkar, *op. cit.*, p. 127.
298. An image of the danger-zone is e.g. *JaimB.* 1.173-175 where the Sacrificers are on their way to heaven and ask:" Who shall be able to swim away out of the open jaws of the crocodile?" referring to "the crocodile standing in the one and only way, against the current, with open maw "- *ekāyane siṃsumārī pratīpaṃ vyādayatiṣṭhati.* It is clear that the motion of the sacrificers themselves, on the one way, is downstream to the sea; the crocodile, who is *siṃśumārin-makara-mṛtyu-sūrya*, is the keeper of the Gate which is in this case the "mouth" of the river as far as man is concerned.

There is no such danger-zone between the earth and the forms she gives birth to. The forms remain bound to their source and the relationship is one of intimacy and solidarity. A vision concerning the earth as if she is antagonistic to the forms existing through and on her is to injure the feelings she has towards all the forms she constantly gives birth to. On the earth all forms are allowed by her to work out their *pravṛtti* and *nivṛtti* as their two strands of their one texture. On earth all forms experience reality. An overstress of one strand at the cost of the other gives rise to *maya,* illusion, a state of unreality. A form's unbalance on the earth is a refusal to exist. It is an affront to both the earth and the waters from whose womb the earth herself emerges.[299]

The sympathetic bond between the earth and all forms springing from her-whether animate or inanimate-, receives flesh and blood when all forms find themselves together in the same and commonly shared "place" on earth which is "time". All the earth's forms share in-breath and out-breath. Their unity is biological through the warmth of the womb of the earth and it is metaphysical by virtue of the womb of the Waters as the mothers (*Aditi*), ground of existence.

> "Impart to us those vitalizing forces that come, O Earth, from deep within your body, your central point, your navel; purify us wholly! The Earth is Mother; I am son of Earth. The Rain-giver is my Father; may he shower on us blessings."[300]
>
> "For from the Waters is this universe produced."
>
> "Of this universe it is, in truth, the Waters that were made first. Hence, when the Waters flow, then everything here, whatsoever exists, is produced."[301]

188. The Waters are Mothers (*Aditi*). They are "woman" with her own personality and sex. The waters' organ (*yoni*) is not biological. As mother-goddess, the Waters are *Aditi* as co-matrix of creation and indispensable partner of the androgyne, *Ardhanarisvara;* the bi-sexual principle of the beginning of things. The Waters are "woman" in her own right, deciding upon the fate of the earth.

The Earth, so we are told in the *Viṣhñu Purāṇa,* approached the gods for help when she felt she was being harrassed by demons who disturbed the mortals on her surface. *Viṣñu* agreed to be born from *Devakī,* wife of *Vāsudeva* to undo the evil. He became incarnate in the eighth pregnancy of *Devakī.* Once *Viṣhu* was incarnate, the planetary bodies moved in brilliant order in the heavens. The seasons were regular and genial. Goddess Earth was splendid.

> ". . . no person could bear the gaze upon *Devakī,* from the light that invested her. . . "Thou", said the divinities, "art that *Prakṛti,* infinite and subtle, which formerly bore *Brahma* in its womb: then wast thou the

although it is rather the mouth of the sea into which the river pours. See: Coomaraswamy, *A New Approach to the Vedas,* London, 1933, p. 45f.

299. See: Part II:4:1, introduction, where *Varuṇa* is said to be the warp and the woof of the loom of the universe; - *samamya* and *vyāmya.*

300. *AV.* 12.1.12. in: Panikkar, *op. cit.,* p. 124.

301. *SB.* 6.8.2.3; 7.4.1.6 in: Panikkar, *op. cit.,* p. 118.

goddess of speech, the energy of the creator of the universe, and the parents of the *Vedas*. Thou, eternal being, comprising in thy substance the essence of all created things, wast identical with creation . . . As *Aditi* thou art the parent of the gods; As *Diti* thou art the mother of the *Daitas,* their foes. Thou art light whence day is begotten. Thou art humility, the mother of true wisdom. Thou art kindly policy, the parent of order. Thou art modesty, the progenetrix of affection. Thou art desire of whom love is born. Thou art contentment whence resignation is derived. Thou art intelligence, the mother of knowledge. Thou art patience, the parent of fortitude. Thou art the heavens and thy children are the stars. And from thee does all that exist proceed. Such, goddess, and thousands more, are thy mighty faculties. And now innumerable are the contents of thy womb, O Mother of the universe.[302]

The whole earth, decorated with oceans, rivers, continents and cities, village hamlets and towns; all the fires, waters, and winds; the stars, asterisms and planets; the sky crowded with the variegated chariots of the gods, and ether, that provides space for all substance; the several spheres of earth, sky and heaven; of saints, sages, ascetics and of *Brahmā;* the whole egg of *Brahma,* with all its population of gods, demons, spirits, snake-gods, fiends, ghosts and imps, men and animals, and whatever creatures have life, comprised in him who is the eternal lord of them, and the object of all apprehension. They are now with that *Viṣnu* in thee.

Thou art *Swaha,* thou art *Swadhā;* thou art wisdom, ambrosia, light and heaven, Thou hast descended upon Earth for the preservation of the world. Have compassion upon us, O goddess, and do good unto the world. Be proud to hear that deity by whom the universe is upheld..."[303]

189. *Ardhanansvara,* the androgyne, male and female in a single unity, is therefore not alone or lonely. Each being the half of the One, is His and Her own. That is *Atman,* total completion and true bliss and truth. He was afraid in the beginnings, so it is said, but had no reason to be so since there was no one to fear. Yet, there were two — but they were and are One — the organless Male and Female. They have no procreative association. In their immediate closeness there is desire. That is why, in the pre-creative state of "the time of *Apaḥ,* the Waters, there is no feeling of lust. The undivided male-female is not split up into a male and female separate entity. Hence there is no enjoyment as of a man and a woman. Likewise there is no abuse of a man by a woman or of a woman by a man.

"In the beginning, the *Atman* alone was this world in the form of a man. He glanced around himself, then he saw nothing else than his own self. In the beginning he then exclaimed: That I am"

Then he was afraid; that is why, when one is afraid, one is alone. Then he thought: "Why should I be afraid?". There is no one else except me. Consequently his fear fled away because, of whom should he have been

302. *Apas* is a feminine noun declined in the plural.
303. *VP.* 5.2.

afraid? Because there is fear only in front of or in the presence of a second one."[304]

190. But being alone and having no fear, the *Atman* felt no delight. No delight in seeing creatures, no delight in creating creatures through the delight of sexual fulfilment. The speculative myths concerning the essence of the Self-fulfilled divine and the sexual aspect of man, woman and creation abound and intersect. It is said that all *Śaktis,* all female powers, spring from the Great Goddess. Hence *Brahma* asked *Śiva* to give him the power to create woman.[305] He implored the mother of the universe to be born as the daughter of *Dakṣa,* his son. The supreme goddess who is *Śiva,* the *Śakti* of *Śiva,* consented. From the middle of her eyebrows a *Śakti* came, equal in glory to herself. She became *Satī.*[306] Procreation could now be sexual because *Satī* is "The Real".[307] *Satī* is the image of the universal Goddess whom *Siva* was to know as his wife in the universe. In the image of *Ardhanārīśvara* the All-Encompassing manifested now the signs of sexes as the cause of creation. All creatures carry these signs.[308] Thus, when *Satī* was born, the great god and the great goddess stood face to face. *Satī* was able to be the woman in the life of *Śiva* and *Śiva* was able to be the man in the life of *Sati.* And so, in *Satī* and *Śiva,* women and men participate in the mystic play where they are called to be:

> "The sanctifiers of living beings in the entire universe; the couple whose bodies are devoid of birth and death and who have taken the bodies of an excellent man and a youthful maiden."[309]

In the complexities of the divine play and its creation the great goddess *Sakti-Prakṛti* stepped out of *Ardhanarisvara* of her own free will. She stepped out of the sex-less male-female unity of the beginning of the Waters. She became *Satī,* the woman with desire the way her personality wished, thereby creating the male desire in response to hers.

The creation of carnal humanity as divine in the form of the throb of flesh and blood, is through woman in the context of Mother Earth where there is the delight of the senses. On earth both woman and man are to enjoy their otherness but now implying the danger of abuse and misunderstanding. The delight of the senses can be forcibly claimed when the inherent unity of *Ardhanārīśvara,* inherent from the beginning in each being, is forgotten or disregarded. The forces of sex are now in human hands and so is the relationship between man and woman. Good sense is needed on earth:

> "This is the truth: From him comes force with its fuel, the sun; from the moon rain, thence plants on the earth. The male pours seed into the female; thus from the Person creatures are born."[310]

---

304. *BU.* 1.4.1-2.
305. *SP.* 3.3..7.20.
306. *SP.* 3.3.21-27.
307. *LP.* 1.70.326-327. See, Stella Kramrisch, *The Presence of Śiva,* pp. 202-210.
308. *Mhb.* 13.14.
309. *SP.* 7.1.15.35.
310. *MU.* 2.1.5. in Panikkar, p. 735.

"The creatures of your forest, O Earth, dwellers in woods, lions, tigers, man-eaters that prowl about, hyena and wolf, misfortune stalking around, demons both male and female, chase them far!

All evil spirits, male and female alike, drive them far from us, O Earth, the ones that grab and the ones that devour, all vampires and all demons! Drive each and everyone to distant realms!

May she in whom the bright and also the dark, the day and the night, associate, though separate, the far-fung Earth, oft by rain made fertile, graciously settle each one in his well-loved abode!

Heaven and Earth and the space in between have set me in a wide expanse! Fire, the Sun, the Waters, the Gods, have joined to give me inspiration!"[311]

191. It is after the establishment of the self-identity of man and woman on earth and after the created differentiation of sex that awareness of order is experienced and the need of respect for what is "other", for what is "not mine". In all things and animals and human beings exists the initial *ardhananrisvara* of the primal origin, the male-female in one. In every man there is woman, in every woman there is man. So it is in every tree and plant and beast. To claim, to usurp, to subjugate, to torture is truly non-being. Disturbance of the initial *ardhanārīśvara* is sin. Sin was never in the *ardhananrisvara* of the primal *Āpaḥ*, the Waters. They carry sins away. Nor is there any sin in the Earth. Sin in *on* the Earth, brought onto her by beings who claim what is not theirs. Sin is the overstress of being *of* the Earth. It is *pravṛtti* overstretched.

The dichotomy between an ethical and cosmic order is foreign to Vedic-Indian thought. They exist as embedded in the anthropocosmic order and thus include both the ethical and the cosmic in one.

"Whatever sin is found in me, whatever evil I have done, if I have lied or falsely sworn, Waters, remove this stain from me."[312]

"Sin of the mind, depart far away! Why do you utter improper suggestions? Depart from this place! I do not want you! Go to the trees and the forests! My mind will remain here along with our homes and our cattle!"[313]

192. On earth, man and woman represent through their union as authentic partners the metaphysical ontic unity of *ardhanarisvara* of the pre-created state of the Waters. In mythical language human marriage is equál to that of the Sun with the Moon.

In the hymn of praise to the Sun's marriage, the authenticity of the human marital union is shown when *Viśvavasu,* the spirit who uptil the girl's marriage has been with her, is asked to make room for the husband.

"Get up from here, *Visvavasu*! We entreat you now with the due respect, Seek another willing girl and leave the wife alone with the husband.

---

311. *AV.* 12.1.49-53 tr. Panikkar, *op, cit.,* p. 123ff; the *Bhūmi Sūkta,* Hymn to the Earth.
312. *RV.* 1.23.22. tr. Panikkar, *op. cit.,* p. 486.
313. *AV.* 6.45. 1-2. tr. Panikkar, *op. cit.,* p. 489.

I free you from the fetter of *Varuṇa* with which the kindly *Savitār* secured you. Unharmed within the bosom of Order I set you, along with your husband, in the world of goodness."[314]

193. The Earth-Mother's human representative is the woman. The man is accorded his rightful place. In many cultures and religions the sacred marriage between heaven and earth is the model of fertility of the soil and of human marriage. In the *Vivāha,* the marriage-ceremony, bride and bridegroom are being compared to earth and heaven. During the "grasping of the hand" ceremony:

"The Heaven am I, the Earth thou. Come, let us marry. Let us unite our sperm. Let us beget offsprings. Let us acquire many sons and may we reach old age. Loving, bright with genial minds, may we see a hundred autumns, may we live a hundred autumns."[315]

In the *Asvalāyana-gṛhya-sūtra,* among other texts, the greater or lesser fitness of a partner is judged by making the partner choose from a number of lumps of clay taken from different spots, each lump representing a particular moral quality, either good or bad.

194. In anthropological and ethnological circles there is little doubt that agriculture in

---

314. *RV.* 10.85. 22.24. tr. Panikkar, *op. cit.,* p. 254.

315. *HGS.* 1.1.6.20.1. See, Kane, *History of Dharmaśāstra,* vol 2, part 1, p. 230. A note with regard to the increasing crisis in Indian marriages would here not be out of place. The definition of womanhood in the traditional Indian marriage as it emerged from India's early and later Middle Ages has come under severe criticism, not in the last instance from national and international women's organizations. Indians in general only grudgingly admit the fact of a rapid increase in the number of divorces and remarks concerning the dowry-systems are often dismissed as irrelevant or "disrespectful" towards Indian tradition when they come from foreigners. No one, however, can reasonably disown the fact that, for example, the dowry-system and its abuses has become a national worry as well as a scandal. The media give much publicity to the various crises in the man-woman relationship in presentday India. In an article by Suneet Vir Singh in *The Times of India,* Sunday, December 2, 1984, p. III, entitled "Take back your wedding ring", the author writes: "The much extolled stability of the traditional Indian marriage rests solely on the willing shoulders of the *pativratā* wife. In the North they call it *stri dharma,* in the South it is called *karpu.* Whatever the region, whatever the language or the religion, Indian culture offers only one definition of the *dharma* of a wife: to merge her identity with that of her family, to seek fulfilment in the service of her husband, her in-laws and her children. *Sītā,* Kasturbā Gāndhī, Kamalā Nehru — each one of them accepted this definition of womanhood. Their marriages endured because in each case the woman ungrudginly devoted herself to the cause of her husband's happiness. *Sītā* followed her husband into exile, Kasturbā cleaned latrines because of her husband's love for Harijans, Kamalā emulated her husband's example and coveted imprisonment. These women had little opportunity to develop an individual personality distinct from the role of a wife. It is no coincidence that Mirā Bāi, the Rānī of Jhānsi and Indirā Gāndhī, women who left a mark on history, were first liberated from the constraints of being a wife before they became achievers. Though presentday feminists decry the slow spread of female literacy, in recent years there has been a tremendous explosion in women's education. It is this factor more than any other which is responsible for creating a new consciousness of individuality among our women. Even the women who are not educated are influenced by the example of those who are. And so today's bride enters matrimony with an additional burden - her individual personality." Women's economic and social dependence prevents many from escaping marital bondage and sexual exploitation. Barring the problem of how to deal with the dowry as part of an economic exchange-system, the obvious greed on the part of prospective husbands is becoming increasingly irritating to the younger generation of India's women. Foreigners who have lived for some time in India will have experienced how families approach them for "western made goods" to please future husbands' requests.

its first stages was discovered by women, affiliated as they are through their mental and physical constitution to the centres of cosmic fertility, the earth and the cycles of the moon. In many civilizations the woman is identified with the furrow, the man with the seed and with instruments working the soil. The male and female characteristics of fertilized soil are assimilated to human fertility. Thus we find, for example, the identification of agricultural labour with the act of generation in the myth of the birth of *Sīta,* the heroine of the *Rāmāyaṇa.* Her father *Janaka,* progenitor, found her in his field while ploughing and he called her *Sītā,* "furrow" (*R.* ch. 66).

"This woman is coming as a living soil: sow seed in her, ye men."[316]

"May woman be looked upon as the field and the male as the seed."[317]

195. A most noble vegetal symbol of integrated living on earth came to the Aryans from India's original inhabitants. It is *padma,* the lotus.[318] Having its root in the mud of the waters, its stem resting in the waters and its petals emerging from them and facing the Sun's light, *padma,* radiating her quiet beauty, encompasses all movement and non-movement. The lotus is the symbol and image of all spatial extension, also in the spiritual sense, and thus puts the earth of man in a true perspective in the cosmic reality;

"What is the lotus, and of what sort ? What this lotus is, is Space; the four quarters and four inter-quarters are its constituent petals."[319] *Padma* is wise. She knows the things of earth as well as those of heaven. Holding her petals clasped round her heart and opening them towards the light, *padma* reveals the mystic vision of things unseen. She is radiance and cosmic refulgence. She is ever the same. In Indian thought, *padma* remains the spiritual ground of Non-Being, dismissing, as it were, all unduly stressed temporal forms. She is involution. (*nivṛtti*) but also suggests as yet unmanifested potential (*pravṛtti*).

"(and *Satyakama,* the teacher, said:) Your face shines, my dear one, as of one who knows the *Brahman.* Who has taught you? And the pupil practised simulation and said:" Who should have taught me? These here, indeed, look such and also those others." Thus he spoke and pointed at the fires-" What have they told you, my dear one".

And he replied to him: "thus and thus". Then the teacher said: "They have only told their world-spaces. But I personally will telll you: as the water does not cling to the leaf or petal of the lotus-flower, so also no base

316. *AV.* 14.2.14. in: Mircea Eliade, *Patterns of Comparative Religion,* p. 259. For a discussion on anthropo-telluric comparisons in other cultures, see *op. cit.,* pp. 259-260.
317. *Laws of Manu,* 9.33.
318. The lotus features in many myths. Also the Buddha-like all Enlightened Ones - is represented as sitting on a lotus-throne. The *padma* is the proto-type of all *maṇḍalas* (symmetrical polygons and diagrams, awakening the consciousness of man's identity with the Universal Consciousness) and of all *çakras* and psychic centres in which the chaos of unconscious forces is transformed into a meaningful cosmos and in which individual existence finds its fulfilment in the final realization of Enlightenment, the state of completeness and perfect equilibrium between the Waters and the non-Waters. The lotus-*sādhanā* in *yoga* portrays that state in the human physical position.
319. *MaitraU.* 6.2. tr. Hume, *The Thirteen Principal Upaniṣads.*

act sticks to one who knows this."- And he, the pupil said: "The venerable teacher should tell it to me!"[320]

196. It is in the nature of the Supreme Being to take delight and be at rest in Itself. Out of Its cosmic body, resting on the Waters, a lotus is put forth, having a thousand petals of pure gold. The lotus is the statement of the singleness of the Supreme. The mythical portrait of that statement has taken shape in a composite being such as *Svayambhu,* combining various themes of Vedic and Hindu mythical truths. In the *Satapatha Brahmaṇa* it is said *Brahman Svayambhū* offers himself in creatures and the creatures offer themselves in His Self (13.7).[321] The result is the *Sarvamedha* sacrifice. *Brahma* is usually described as rising out of a lotus in *Viṣñu's* navel. Strictly speaking he is *Svayambhu*. *Svayambhu* is a late epiphany of *Brahman.* It is *Svayambhu* who, in the *Mahabharata,* created a luminous lotus in which *Ahaṃkara* appears, composed of five elements (12.175.14-16). This *Svayambhu* is *Viṣñu.* Since he is self-created, *Brahma* is so too. Thus the lotus combines several notions concerning Divine Eternity.[322]

197. The lotus is considered the gate, the opening of the womb of the universe. *Padma* expresses the manifestation of the cosmos, the appearance of forms. *Padma* manifests to man that creation actually did take place for it would almost be an offence to *Padma* to attribute to its radiant splendour a mere fantasm. Her splendour pierces all appearance. When man looks in amazement at *Padma,* he is consoled to know that his surroundings are firmly established above the Waters. The lotus is the highest aspect of the firmess and security of Mother Earth.

Padma especially, among all floral symbols, expresses the joyful rightfulness of being on Earth. But let each one remember that *Padma*-lotus stands in the waters. Its root is *nivṛtti,* its bloom is *pravṛtti. Padma* is the Goddess Moisture. She is the Goddess through whom the Absolute moves into creation. As mother of created beings (*prajanam bhavasi matā*) she is called *Kśamā,* Earth.

The Aryans learnt to know her from the vegetative soil in their newly found homeland where the original Indian inhabitants were already long since acquainted with *Padma.*

Soon *Sri Lakṣmī,* who had been born of the foam at the Churning of the Ocean in the beginning, is praised as *padmavarṇa,* lotus-coloured. She is also *padmākṣī,* lotus-eyed and *padminī* and *puskariṇi,* abounding in lotuses.

Lakṣmi represents the feasibility of ethical thought before greed which, in the form of world-poison (*kālakūta*), destroys the best there is in creation. Before *Lakṣmi-lotus* any thought of grabbing or avaricious appropriation looks vane and meaningless.

"Then, seated on a lotus, Beauty's bright Goddess, peerless *Śrī* rose out of the waves; and with her, robed in white, came forth *Dhanvantarī,* the gods'

---

320. *CU.* 4.14.2-3. tr. Deussen, *op. cit.,* p. 129.
321. From man's end the sacrifice makes him collect himslef-*saṃharati.* His self, as it were, is emptied out - *SB.* 3.8.1.2: *rircana ivatma bhavati.*
322. See: Sukumari Bhattacharji, *The Indian Theogony,* p. 342: By a gradual process the neuter *brahman* (nom. *Brahmā*) is changed into masculine (nom. *Brahmā*). See also p. 333.

physician. High in his hand he bore the cup of nectar, Life-giving draught-longed for by gods and demons."[323]

198. *Lakṣmı Karṣiṇi* is the Earth-Goddess cherishing earth's moisturous soil. Her sons are *Kardama,* mud, and *Ciklīta,* moisture. They contribute to *Lakṣmı's* earthy gifts to man. The possibility of cultured growth and beautification of earthly existence is a gift from *Śrī Lakṣmı* rising on *Padma* out of the Waters. Men and women of taste thank her for the gift of the sense of proportion and enchanting forms. As Daughter of the Ocean of Milk[324] *Lakṣmī* is the goddess of beauty, of intelligence, of ecological thinking, of wealth and of all prosperity *(kśīrasāgarakanyakā).* She is the counterform of *Kālakūta* which is greed, boorishness, platitude and all forms of discourtesy. Egoism and provincialism is superseded by *Lakṣmī's* personal and civic responsibility, seated as she is on the lotus of Space. The racist, fascist or communalist has no place with *Lakṣmı* on her lotus-petals.

> "*Śrī*, the bride of *Viṣñu,* the mother of the world, is eternal, imperishable; as he is all-pervading, so she is omnipresent. *Viṣñu* is meaning, she is speech; *Viṣñu* is polity, she is prudence; *Viṣñu* is understanding, she is intellect; he is righteousness, she is devotion; *Śrī* is the earth, *Hari* (*Viṣñu*) is its support. In a world of gods, animals and men *Hari* is all that is called Male; *Lakṣmī* is all that is termed Female; there is nothing else than they."[325]

199. *Mahālakṣmī,* Daughter of the Milky Ocean, carrying a lotus in her right and a bilva-fruit in her left hand, completes the quartet of the goddesses of excellence. She joins *Gaṅga,* seen in the form of a lotus-umbrella, *Saraswatı,* playing her stringed instrument and seated on a lotus or a swan, and *Yamuna,* riding on a tortoise.

> "At the instant there came *Lakṣmı,* the consort of *Viṣñu,* slowly and smilingly. She was bedecked with ornaments of diverse kinds. She was accompanied by experts in the science of instrumental music and by those who were conversant with the function of the lute. They were charming in the use of sweet words..."[326]

200. The imperturbable lotus, standing in the waters between heaven and earth, holds those worlds together. *Padma* is assimilated to the relation between the Mountain and the Waters. From the lotus rises Mount *Meru,* the primeval mountain and world-axle which holds the Waters and lets them flow to pervade everything.

---

323. *VP*. 1.9.; *R*. 1.45.40-43.
324. *Dēvī Bhagvata* 9.
325. *VP.*
326. In the *Vāyu Purāṇa* 72. 46. *Saraswatī* presents *Skandah* with a great *Viṇa-* stringed instrument at his birth. The *padma-pātra,* the vessel made of lotus-leaves, was used by the *Gandharvas* in the incident of the "milching" of the earth (*VaP.* 62.187-188). The *Gandharvas* love the lotus as their homestead. The *Gāndharva-vidyā,* i.e. the Science of Music, is included in the list of eighteen *vidyās* such as the *Vedas, Mımāṁsa, Nyaya, Ayurveda* etc. The names of *Gāndharva, Ṛṣabha, Ṣaḍaja, Madhyama, Vairājaka, Niṣāda* and *Pancama* are names of *Kalpas,* one of them also at times called the *Padmakalpa.* The names are directly associated with the *svaras* (tones) of the Indian musical scale. See: Devendrakumar Rajaram Patil, *Cultural History from the Vāyu Purāṇa*, p. 96-99.

Like the *liṅga,* the worldpillar, standing in the womb of the Waters *(yoni), Padmā*-lotus stands between Uncreatedness and createdness. She, a symbol of both , stands in the divine and earthly overflow. She, indeed, made an excellent cradle for the Supreme to be born in, the lotus rising from *Viṣṅu's* navel.

"Who is it whose semen was offered in the sacrifice in the beginning of the world ?.. Is the golden mountain *Meru* made of any other semen ?..See how the world bears everywhere the signature of the *liṅgam* and the *yoni.*"[327]

"The lotus is the Waters."[328]

201. The role of *Brahmā,* born from the lotus in *Viṣṅu's* navel and himself the "lotus-eyed", is entrusted to men and women of perception and concentration. Commenting on the *Yoga-Sutra, Vyāsa* refers to concentration and universal awareness in relation to "the lotus of the heart" (1.36).

"Everything that exists, the whole world, whatever is visible, whatever is audible, Everything, external and internal, *Nārāyaṇa* encompasses and penetrates.

Endless, eternal, full of wisdom, by his vastness the end of the sea, bringing all-round well-being; as heart, similar to the lotus-cup becoming pointed towards below.

He lives in a short space below the neck, a few spaces below the navel, where he shines in a wreath of rays, he is the great fulcrum of the universe.

He lies suspended downward, encompassed by arteries, almost like a flowercup. Inside him there is a small cavity in which the whole universe rests."[329]

202. Inside the lotus of the heart is *guhā,* the heart-space. The gaze that lies within it holds the key to the knowledge of all.

"(Then the pupil will say to the teacher:) The teacher says: Here in this *Brahman*-city, the body, is an abode, a small blooming lotus, the heart; inside it is a small space; one should investigate into what in it is, he should try to know the true....

Then the teacher shall reply: Truly, this space inside the heart is as great as this world-space; in it are resolved both, the heaven and the earthboth, the fire and the wind, both the sun and the moon, the lightning and the stars and what one below here possesses and does not possess, everything is resolved therein."[330]

---

327. *Mhb.* 13.14.
328. *SB.* 7.4.1.8.
329. *MahanarU.* 11.5-8. tr. Deussen, *op. cit.,* p. 258. The "lotus of the heart "corresponds to the Earth-lotus in the Vedic tradition which blooms on the surface of the primordial Ocean in response to the down-shining of the light above., We find a similar idea in the Greek tradition where the Sun perceives a fertile land, Rhodos, the Rose, rising from the seas' depths. Analogy is also found in the Hebrew "Tree of Jesse". All three are the Great Mother. It is interesting to note that in many traditions the Mother of God is a "flower".
330. *CU.* 8.1.1-3. tr. Deussen, *op. cit.,* p. 191. In the heart-lotus are to be realized all the possibilities of our being. See, *RV.* 6.9.6.: "What is ours here" i.e. human goods (*mānuṣa vitta*) known sensibly

203. In yogic and tāntric spiritual thought, *Padma*-lotus is a symbol of the unfolding of the deepest self and of expanding consciousness. Just as the lotus grows in the darkness of mud and, finding its way upward through the waters, bursts into blossom on the waters' surface, so the inner self transcends and transforms itself beyond its corporeal limits.

In *yantra*-patterns a ring of lotus-petals generally means a stage in the actualization of the spiritual process. It signifies a wave of optimism. In the symbolism of the *Çakras,* the psychic centres of the human body, "lotus" means all the experience of the upward movement of energy in successive stages, each petal signifying the blossoming of a quality or mental attribute. Finally one reaches the acme of spiritual perception, symbolized by the thousand-petalled lotus placed above the head, the *Sahasrāra Çakra.* The lotus-symbol of the *çakra* is a kinetic symbol.

The *Çakras* are : *Muladhara,* red lotus with four petals; *Svādiṣṭhana,* vermilion with six petals; *Maṇipura,* blue with ten petals; *Anāhata,* twelve golden petals; *Visuddha,* sixteen petals of a smoky purple; *Ājnā,* two white petals resembling the shape of the famous third eye, and finally, the *Sahāsrāra Çakra.*

The lotus also represents the ubiquitous subtle element of space. The infinity of space and consciousness are identical.

> "Verily what is called *Brahman,* pure consciousness, that is what the space outside the person is...that is what the space inside the person is..."[331]

204. The lotus as the "womb" duplicates the *yoni,* the foundation of the *liṅga,* the phallus (*SB.* 10.5.2.7-8). Probably the *liṅga* came to the Aryans from India. The most important form of *Śiva's* cult is the worship of the *liṅga.* The practice can be traced back to the pre-Vedic societies of the Indus-civilization circa 2000 B.C.[332] It first appears in Indian iconography in the second century B.C. Myths explaining the origin of *liṅga*-worship occur in the latest layers of the epics. Widespread as they are, they probably met a need to justify the non-Vedic aspects of the gods who had been only recently assimilated. In ancient times phallus-worshippers were kept away from the sacrifice (*RV.* 7.25.5) *Indra* slew them (*RV.* 10.99.3). For the Aryans it must have been an uneasy transition from sacrifice to *liṅga*-worship. It is one of those modalities of a given hierophany which may be lived and interpreted quite differently by the religious elite and the rest of the community. Among those who worship *Śiva's liṅga,* many would see it only as an archetype of the generative organ.[333]

(*cakṣuṣā*)." what is not ours here", i.e. of the world above (*daiva vitta*) known intelligibly (*śrotrena*). This reminds us of *Indra,* who is an immanent deity and who "crushes and rends *Vṛtra's seat (yoni)*', the seat being the womb as in *MU.* 2.1.8. wherein the sense-powers are hidden, *guhāśaya nihitāḥ.*

331. *CU.* See: Woodroffe, *op. cit., passim.* The book also beautifully presents the *Çakras* in colour. See also, Mookerjee and Khanna, *The Tāntric Way, passim,* equally well illustrated.

332. See: Steven G. Darian, *op. cit.,* p. 110.

333. If seen as an archetype of the penis, the *liṅga* implies the concept of vulva (*yoni)* and especially so the *liṅga into* the *yoni,* rather than *in* or *out of* it. To understand the *liṅga*-worship in Indian tradition, some notions need to be clearly perceived to avoid unnecessary misunderstanding on both the physical generative, psychological, philosophical and the theological level. I quote Stella Kramrisch in, *The Presence of Śiva.* p. 242: "The *liṅga* in the *yoni* is a paradoxical visual symbol... The mythical account of the entry of the *liṅga* into the *yoni* related in the *Śiva Purāṇa* reduced the

In earth-symbolism, the identification of the furrow with the *yoni* leads to a further assimilation of the phallus with the spade or plough, the semen with the seed or the act of tilling the soil.[334] Both the *liṅga* and the *yoni* move in the physical-generative as well as in the metaphysical ontological realm.

205 The *liṅga-yoni* symbolism is directly related to man's existential anxiety of being simultaneously an inhabitant of and a guest in the world. The basic duality in unity of *pravṛtti* and *nivṛtti* becomes problematic once the equilibrium between them is disturbed. Control and transformation of desire in its widest meaning is the ultimate necessity to establish balance.

The attempt to control and transform desire appears in Vedic and Hindu thought in a wide variety of themes and motifs under the *liṅga-yoni* symbol. Their purely physical interpretation is, although significant, one of several.

The word "*liṅga*" has various meanings, such as "mark" or "attribute", "essence", "nature", "the inner man" or "physical organism". As *liṅgaṃ nīrāśrayam* it stands for the physical organism diverted from the external world:

> "What is unconscious, dwells in consciousness, unthinkable and full of mystery, therein one should immerse consciousness and the *Liṅgam*, deprived of any support."[335]

206. The myth of the origin of the *liṅga* (*liṅgobhava*) opens with the familiar primeval situation. There were only the waters the interval between dissolution and creation. On the Waters rested, lying on his cosmic serpent, *Viṣñu Anantasayin*. He is the anthropomorphic embodiment of the lifeless fluid holding all potentiality.

Surprisingly, *Brahma* too appears on the scene and the two get involved in a fierce argument: Who is the greater? While they contest each other's claims, a towering *liṅga* emerges from the Waters. As the two contestants explored it, it

---

cosmic dimension of the *liṅga* to its basic function as penis. The reduction in meaning as conveyed by the myth, however, was in line with the naturalism of the shape of the earliest *liṅgas* set up for worship. Between the explicitly phallic shape of the earliest *liṅgas* and the later, abstract pillar shape of the *liṅga* lay the symbolic saturation of this vertical sign with ontological meaning. Between the abstract pillar shape by itself and its setting in the *yoni* lay a return to the primary phallic meaning. If the early "naturalistic" shape was shown turgid with life-giving power in which inhered all the possibilities of generation and modalities of existence, the *liṅga* in the *yoni* focuses on the sexual situation of coitus, introducing into it, however, the paradox of the *ūrdhvaliṅga* (the non-orgastic, "seed drawn-up" *liṅga*, F.B.) as a sign of *ūrdhva retas* (Cha. 1.3). The latter connotes the retention, ascent and transformation of the seed within the body of the lord of *yogis.* The abstract, geometrical shape, however, of the *ūrdhvaliṅga*, the repository of the onthology of existence, placed on the *yoni* as its pedestal, rises out of the *yoni,* the womb; it does not enter it. The "*liṅga* in the *yoni*" emerges from the *yoni;* it does not penetrate it. This paradox in the coital proximity of the sexual symbols is consonant with and amplifies that of the *liṅga* itself."

334. A much misunderstood symbolism—to the disadvantage of the place of woman in society and the feminine spirit and psyche—is the erect male member in agriculture iconography. It is first a symbol of war-like ecstasy and not fertility. There is no contradiction between them. The masculine phallic principle is necessary for the preservation of life as experienced by the matriarchate. The woman is dependent of the "war-like" male who bloodily opens the female. She is identical with the ploughed field. She gives herself however to the fecundating male, of whom she indifferently makes use. Here the male remains inferior to the Feminine in that it confronts him as a power of destiny. See: Neumann, *The Great Mother*, pp. 281-336.

335. *MaitraU.* 6.19 tr. Deussen, *op. cit.*, p. 110.

grew and expanded and finally *Śiva* appears from it, claiming his supreme power over the universe.

The sex-charged symbol shows at once the "possessor of seed", goal of ascetics. In his ontological stature *Śiva Liṅga* is not the polarity of sex with its pleasure and pain, but controlled desire (*tapas*) leading to liberation.

". . . above it (*liṅga*) *Viṣṇu* saw the lord *Śiva* like the pure crystal. It was the fourth entity, devoid of attributes, nectarine, unsullied, undisturbed, devoid of mutually clashing opposites, unique, void, without an exterior or an interior but still endowed with exterior and interior, as it was stationed both without and within. It was devoid of beginning, middle and end, it was the cause of bliss."[336]

207. In the enumeration of *Śiva's* thousand names in the *Liṅga Purāna*, *Śiva's* first two names are: *Sthira*, steady, and *Sthānu*, pillar, The *Śivatoṣiṇī* commentary understands by *Sthānu*, "the abode of the universe".[337] *Śiva's* exuberant pillar is but a complement of his appearance as *Śiva Sthānu*, the motionless.

He invokes here the image of his eternal embrace of *Pārvatī*, Mountain (*Parvata's*) daughter. It seems an antithetic image. But *Pārvatī* is *Prakṛti*, the eternal female half of the one all-comprising Essence. The sexual symbol of embrace is consonant with the idea of cosmic totality on Mount *Meru*. Of that unity *Śiva Mantramūrti* is the expression. *Śiva* and *Pārvatī's* eternal embrace is the image of inherent cosmic satisfaction (*nivṛtti*) on the level of myth. It would, unless activated (*pravṛtti*) not result in procreation. In one theme of the myth *Śiva* and *Pārvatī* do not procreate. In the motionless Eternal Embrace of totality the seed is drawn up (*urdhvaliṅga*) because Love is not identical with the sexual act. It is under the symbol of the carnal phallus that procreation of the human race is guaranteed.

"*Śiva* and *Pārvatī* made love for a thousand years, every day, but *Pārvatī* did not become pregnant by *Śiva*. The gods became worried and said: " Just as *Kāma* is attached to *Rati*, so is *Śiva* to *Pārvatī* but our need is not fulfilled because the embryo keeps flowing out. We must see to it that their love play (*rati*) does not recur. . ."[338]

208. Between the abstract pillar shape of the *liṅga* rising from the Waters by itself and its setting in the *yoni*, lies the primary phallic meaning. To preserve the ontological characteristic of existence, however, the idea of *ūrdhvaliṅga*, the erect *liṅga* indicating continence, is introduced. The seed is held. It must, however, not be held motionless but must be rechannelled and made to ascend and be absorbed in the body.

---

336. *LP*. 17. 52-55.
337. *LP*. 64, 54b-168: "*Sthānuḥ—tiṣṭhanty asmin*" *ST*. Refer to: *saṁsāramaṇḍapasyāsya mūlastambhāya sambhave* - cited in *Śivatoṣiṇī's* commentary, *Śiva's* name as *Liṅgam* occurs in the enumeration under no. 917. *Śiva's* names under the symbol of water are e.g. *Payonidhi* storehouse of water, milk *Vāryakṣa*—one who has the eyes in water. *Mahārṇavanipātavid*-one who knows the fall into a great sea.
338. *VmP*. 28.61. See: Wendy Doniger O'Flaherty, *op.cit.*, ch. 8, "The Control and Transformation of Desire" where a.o. the question of the separation of fertility and eroticism in the *Śiva* cycle of myths is discussed, pp. 262-267.

The upward motion of seed, rechannelling the life forces, represents the distinction between the false ascetic, remaining in the state of withdrawal without further involvement and love, and the true *yogī*, coming into withdrawal and emerging out of it through solidarity with existence. This is in keeping with the mythical concept of power which cannot be destroyed but must be set in motion in a valid direction.

The state of the "*liṅga* in the *yoni*"[339] is the presentation of the union of opposites to portray the immovable and eternal tranquillity of the state of pre-creation, the divine. On the human level that tranquillity is the realization of equilibrium between *pravṛtti* and *nivṛtti*. Thus the *liṅga* is the object of the greatest sanctity, more sacred than any other anthropomorphic image. Cosmic in its dimension, it is at once intelligible to terrestrial man.

The praise of the cosmic form of *Śiva*, is sung in the *Liṅga Purāṇa*:

"The ray named *Harikeśa*, belonging to the lord in the form of the sun, is the cause of development and nourishment of the stars.

The ray named *Viśvakarman*, belonging to the lord in the form of the sun, nourishes *Budha* (Mercury).

The ray of the trident-bearing lord in the form of the sun that is called *Viśvavyaca* is the nourisher of *Śukra* (Venus).

The ray that is known as *Samnyadvasu*, belonging to the trident-bearing lord in the form of the thousand-rayed sun is the nourisher of Mars.

The ray that is known as *Arvāvasu*, belonging to the *Pināka*-bearing lord in the form of the sun, develops *Bṛhaspati* (Jupiter) always.

The ray known as *Svarat* . . . nourishes *Śanaiścara* (Saturn) by day and by night.

The ray known as *Suṣumnā* belonging to the lord, the consort of *Umā*, the source of origin of the universe and solar in form, develops the moon always.

The lunar form of the lord, the slayer of Death, is stationed in all embodied beings in the form of the semen.

The physical form of the lord, named *Soma*, is the most excellent among the bodies in all living beings. It is stationed in the form of the nectarine digit in sixteen parts."[340]

"The water that is within and without the universe and the water that is within the physical body of all living beings constitutes the great (physical) form of the lord *Śiva*.

The nectar-like water of the rivers and the streams and the ubiquitous water of the oceans constitute the physical form of the consort of *Umā*."[341]

"The *Liṅga* shall be made with great assiduity in accordance with the injunction. A *Liṅga* shall be made of rock.

---

339. See footnote no. 334, quoting Stella Kramrisch ..., *The Presence of Śiva*.
340. *LP*. 12 11-12.
341. *LP*. 12.30-31.

It shall be identical with *Brahmā*, *Viṣṇu* and *Śiva*. . . It shall have its pedestal (*yoni*) and the exit for water. . .

Lord *Brahma* resides at the root; lord *Viṣṇu* in the middle. The unborn *Rudra* (*Śiva*), *Paśupati*, the lord of all the most excellent one resides at the top...."[342]

209. Several *Purāṇas* mention the entire Asian river-system as flowing from the sacred region of *Śiva's* Mount *Meru* to the world's corners. They first separate themselves from Gaṅgā. From that wealth of myth-information emerges the correspondence between the rivers and the holy places (*tīrthas*) on their banks.

The word *tırtha* means the palm of the right hand by which water is taken. For example, in the *acamana*, the sipping of water during the morning— and evening ablutions (*sandhyopasana*). *Tirtha* has come to mean a holy place or bathing place for religious purposes. In India, a pilgrimage to a sacred bathing site has from early times been considered part and parcel of one's religious life. Each bathing place showers its special benefits upon the bather which is not to say that the sacred waters always automatically guarantee salvation.

"He would get salvation whose limbs, mind, knowledge, austerity and fame are under his own control. He who lives clean in body, without egoism contented and never accepting gifts for services done, would get salvation if he visits holy places. He who would fast if he did not get food, whose organs of sense are all under control.....He who is righteous, free from anger, treats all animate objects like himself, would get salvation if he visits a holy place...."[343]

210. One of the most celebrated *tīrthas* on the Indian subcontinent is *Kāśī* (*Vārāṇasī*), the city of *Śiva*. The benefits coming from *Kāśī* on *Gaṅgā's* banks to the pilgrim-visitor are endless. The few philosophical terms used to describe *Brahman* are also applied to *Kāśī*: it is *paramātman*, the "supreme soul"; *chidānandamayī*, "made of consciousness and bliss"; *nisprapañca*, "without expansion"; and it is *anakhyeya*, the "unspeakable".[344]

The splendour of Bānāras as the city of liberation is almost indescribable. Some even take a vow never to leave it (*kśetra sannyasa*).[345]

In the *Matsya Puraṇa, Śiva* says of Bānaras:

"Because I never forsake it, nor do I let it go, this great place is, therefore, known as *Avimukta*."[346]

---

342. *LP*. 47.6.11.
343. *PP*. 2. Mention of *tīrtha* is made in e.g. *VP*. 2.2.; 2.8; *BhagP*. 5. 17; *KP*. 1.44.28-33.
344. *Kasi Khaṇḍa* 99.6 and *Kāśī Rahasya* 2.97.
345. The book by Diana L. Eck, *Banaras, City of Light*, Routledge and Kegan Paul, 1983, is a must. The author, at present professor of Indian Studies at Harvard University, appears an excellent scholar as well as a writer. The book is beautifully illustrated and contains six appendices with an enormous wealth of information. Banaras is one of the oldest living cities in the world, as old as Jerusalem, Athens, and Peking. For over 2,500 years this city has attracted pilgrims and seekers. Sages, such as the *Buddha*, *Mahāvīra*, and *Śaṅkara* have come to Banaras to teach. The city's life reaches back to the sixth century B.C. in a continuous tradition. The author writes: "If we could imagine the silent Acropolis and the Aghora of Athens still alive with the intellectual, cultural, and ritual traditions of classical Greece, we might glimpse the remarkable tenacity of the life of *Kası* , *op. cit.*, pp. 4-5.
346. *MP*. 180. 54.

According to the city's mythology, Bānāras is the place where the *liṅga* of *Śiva* was first established and worshipped on earth as the symbol of the Lord's perpetual presence. Even during the periodical general destruction (*pralaya*) the city will be held above the floodwaters by *Śiva*, lifting it up on his trident.

211. In the *Maitrāyaṇa Upaniṣad* it is said:

> "Reality is luminous. The core of all things is the divine light in which we like water in Water, like air in Air."[347]

In Bānaras-*Tirtha* one receives that light:

> "Then *Atri* said to *Yājñavalkya*: That infinite, unmanifested *Ātman*, how can I perceive him? And *Yājñavalkya* said: "That indestructable, infinite, unmanifest, having perfect bliss as the only taste, spiritual *Ātman*—this infinite, unmanifest *Ātman*, he is to be found in the *Avimuktam*.
>
> But where is the *Avimukta*-place to be searched for? It is to be searched between the *Vāraṇā* and the *Nāśī*—But what is the *Vāraṇa* and what is the *Nāśī*? *Vāraṇā* is so-called because it wards off (*vārayati*) from the *Ātman* all the faults committed by the body-organs; *Nāśi* is so called because it destroys (*nāśayati*) all the sins committed by the body-organs. But where is the place of this *Avimuktam*? - It is the meetingplace between the eyebrows and the nose. For this is the meetingplace between the heavenly world and the highest world of the *Atman*. Therefore, the knowers of *Brahman* worship this connection as the union-time (twilight). For in *Avimuktam*, so they know, one should revere *Ātman*. He who knows thus, proclaims his knowledge as *avimuktam*, "unforgettable".
>
> And *Yājñavalkya* further said to him voluntarily:
>
> "In *Kāśī Rama's* formula
> Was muttered by the bull-bannered (*Siva*)
> Through thousands of Manu-ages
> With worship, offerings and prayers.
>
> Whoever dies in *Maṇikarṇı* pond
> In my temple, or on *Gaṅgā's* bank,
> Grant him liberation!
> Nothing further remains for me to wish."[348]

The interiorization of the pilgrimage, such as in the concept of *Avimukta*, never had the canonical status it enjoys in the tantric and yogic traditions under the name of *pıṭha*, the seat of the goddess. The number of *pīṭhas* varies. One Vedic myth with regard to *pīṭha* crystallizes in the *Mahabharata's* account of *Dakṣa's* sacrifice. The mother-goddess *Śati* had, like her husband *Siva*, not been invited to that sacrifice. *Śati* decided to attend her father's sacrifice uninvited and found

347. *MaitraU.* 6.34.
348. *RuttU.* 4, tr. Deussen, *op. cit.*, p. 884. *Maṇikarṇī* pond is famous in Bānāras for *Pārvatī* bathed there and left one of her ornaments behind, so the myths says. See: Diana L. Eck, *op. cit.*, p. 245-251.

herself insulted by him. *Śiva* enraged, decapitated the culprit and, for grief of *Śati* who had immolated herself after the insult, carried her body round the world, dancing and bursting forth in wild and uncontrolled lament. To prevent *Śiva* from disturbing the world, the gods cut up *Sati's* body. The places where her severed limbs fell became the *pīṭhas*.[349]

The *pīṭha* may be interiorized through hypostasis in the body. The *pīṭha* will then, as *Śakti*, the mother-goddess, take possession of the searcher to liberate him.

212. Almost all sacred bathing sites pride themselves of their sacred temples. The Hindu temple is thought to be the mountain and the centre as a reminder of the captured Waters in the first aeon when *Indra* slew *Vṛtra*. Entrance into the temple signifies cosmic participation.

In terms of symbolic architecture, the primary units of the temple include the building, the altar, the door and the guardians, especially *Gaṅgā* and *Yamunā*. In the innermost sanctuary the stylized representations of *liṅga* and *yoni* are set up in every *Śiva* temple and in many other temples too. *Liṅga*, rising from the ocean, is reflected by the water place in or near the temple and in the performance of the rites. Many pillars, supporting temple gates, feature the serpent of the waters coiled round their base, while tree spirits are seen frolicking on the pillars' upper portion. Elaborate instructions with regard to the planting of trees in the temple compound and the lay-out of watertanks and ponds are found in lawbooks. The relationship between the vegetative, earthy and watery life underlies the entire temple concept. Each temple portion stands in meaningful relationship to the other, the whole being designed as an aid towards contemplation (*dhyāna*) and realisation (*samādhi*). The theme of the Hindu temple states and repeats the primordial beginnings.

> ". . . to the east of the *maṇḍapa* of a temple fruitbearing trees should be planted, to the south trees that contain milky sap, to the west a reservoir of water with lotuses should be constructed and to the north a flowergarden and sarala—and tala trees. . ."[350]

213. The sapling, the tumulus, the stone slab, and the pillar—the announcement of the place of the dead—come to house the departed spirit and eventually the deathless god himself, embodied in the *liṅga*. That mark of potency stands in the centre of the temple, the centre of the world-mountain. Surrounding the central point is the ring of stones—the shape of mother earth, the lotus, the waters—evolved into the *yoni* giving birth to everything. The temple parts are conceived in apposition and embellish a single theme: the merging of dualities—male and female, left and right, fire and water.

In the *Saivite* tradition the river goddess appears at the temple door as its guardian. *Gaṅgā* water, poured on the *liṅga*, often flows from above through an opening shaped like a *makara*, the water beast—*Gaṅgā's* vehicle—or a cow.

349. *Mhb.* 12. 282-283.
350. *MP*. 270. 28-29 in Kane, *op. cit.,* 895. Kane mentions a number of heavy fines for those who wrongfully cut any fruit—or flower trees, grass or herbs in the temple compound.

Gaṅgā has her origin at *Gomukh*: "the mouth of a cow".[351] In a song, devoted to the house or to the sacrificial building, we hear :

> "Facing you, O House, who are facing me, I approach you peacefully; sacred Fire and Water are within, the main doors to Cosmic Order.
>
> I bring here these waters free from disease, destroyers of disease. In this House, together with Fire immortal, I take up my abode!"[352]

214. There is no human life and no true love in disjunction from the big house of man, the world in which all men live together. Humanity (*manuṣyatā*) has its own home (*manuṣyaloka*) where exists a constitutive relationship between all things and all animals and all men, women and children. How can man push someone out of this world by pushing him out of his house or off his land or exile him from his country? How can one insist on *having more* of this world than another? Would one, as the Vedic seer says, not be like a puffed-up wineskin, bursting at the seam? Applying himself to the world (*pravṛtti*) and caring for it (*dīkṣā*) man knows the world as a part of the whole (*Puruṣa*).

The relationship between man and his surrounding—nature—is not a technical one. It is not one of domination or exploitation as if nature and all of man's surrounding were an article to be traded by man. When man begins to trade the basics of true humane living—food, drink, house, land, the woods, playgrounds, the lakes—and equals them with something that they are not —money—then the rooftop may come down on him instead of opening itself to set him free. The temple pillars will not support his prayers. True human life is one of partnership and collaboration.[353]

> "We, with the Lord of the Field as our friend and helper, obtain for our cattle and horses, food in plenty, that they may be sleek and well-fed. May he graciously grant us his favour!
>
> O Lord of the Field, like a cow yielding milk, pour forth for us copious rivers of sweetness, dripping honey like nectar and pure as pure ghee (butter). May the Lord of the Law grant us mercy.
>
> Sweet be the plants for us, sweet be the heavens, sweet be the waters and the air of the sky! May the Lord of the Field show us honey-like sweetness. May we follow his furrow unharmed !
>
> In contentment may the ploughshare turn up the sod, in contentment

---

351. Mention may here be made of the Buddhist *arhat* who "flies up in the air, cleaving the roof-plate of the palace" towards freedom—*ākāse uppativā pāsādakaṇṇikam dvidhā katvā*. in: *The Jātaka, or Stories of the Buddha's Former Births*, ed. EB. Cowell, 6 Vols. Cambridge, 1895-1907.

352. *AV*. 9.3.22.23 tr. Panikkar. *op. cit.*, p. 292. The idea of any dwelling, the house of life, the spatial world of experience, is above all a half-way house. It is a place of procedure from potentiality to act, not a place to hide in, away from environment. A house, lacking promise of potentiality, is like a dead man's grave.

353. I am here obviously referring to those forms of political, economic, philosophic and religious capitalism which condone the fact that one is by law allowed to possess a *surplus* of goods at the cost of the basic needs of others. Where "religion" allows itself to be allied with such system, one often finds that "the other, later, and" more blissful "life" separates itself from "this life" in a manner that one is promised to gain the former independent of works in this world. This world is as a result abandoned and left to "its destiny" or to those who exploit it. The exploited are being promised "the other life". It is here that religious position shows its ambivalence.

the ploughman follow the oxen. Celestial Rain pour down honey and water. Ploughshare and Plough, grant us joy!"[354]

215. Respect for the earth with her produce as given by *Kśetrapati*. The Lord of the Field saves man from an overbearing attitude towards his natural surrounding.

"Brimful of sweetness is the grain, brimful of sweetness are my words; when everything is a thousand times sweet, how can I not prosper?

I know one who is brimful of sweetness, the one who has given abundant corn, the God whose name is Reaper-God; Him we invoke with our song.

As a spring gushes forth in a hundred, a thousand, streams and yet stays inexhaustible, so in a thousand streams may our corn flow inexhaustibly."[355]

"You have poured down the rain; now withold it, we pray you! You have made the deserts fit for travel. To serve as food you have made the plants flourish. Receive (O Rain) from us in return grateful praise."[356]

216. On the sustenance by the waters all vocations of man and beast depend, whether they be smiths, fathers or mothers, carpenters, priests, doctors or a frog.

"From the fountain whose bucket is well prepared with good strong ropes, where water flows freely—from this copious fountain we draw, inexhaustible."

"We all have various thoughts and plans and diverse are the callings of men. The carpenter seeks out that which is cracked, the physician the ailing, the priest the *Soma*-press. Flow, *Soma*-juice, for the sake of the Lord!

The smith with his store of seasoned plants, with his feathers of birds and stones for the tips, enkindles the flame to make arrows and then seeks out a client bulging with gold! Flow, *Soma*-juice, for the sake of the Lord!

I am a singer, my Dad a physician, my Mummy's task is to grind the corn. Diverse are our callings but we all aim at wealth; we run in its wake like a cowherd trailing cows. Flow, *Soma*-juice, for the sake of the Lord!

A horse desires to draw a light cart, gay hosts to evoke a laugh and a jest, a male desires his mate's approach, a frog a flood to plunge within. Flow, *Soma*-juice, for the sake of the Lord!"[357]

217. In a holistic perspective, viewing man and cosmos as a dynamic unity, a spirit of maintenance of the world emerges (*lokasaṁgraha*). To be actually involved in *lokasaṁgraha* is man's true calling. This means that man acts truly humanly when his actions have a cosmic as well as a social reverberation. His involvement must "have in view"—as the word *saṁpaśyan* suggests (*BG*. 3. 20)—the welfare and coherence of the world. That welfare and coherence is not to be identified with what man calls "results" and "success". To reach the fulness of cosmic and

354. *RV*. 4. 57 1-3-8 tr. Panikkar, *op. cit.*, p. 271.
355. *AV*. 3.24 1. 2a. 4. tr. Panikkar, *op. cit.*, p. 273.
356. *RV*. 5. 83.10 tr. Panikkar, p. 275.
357. *RV*. 9. 112. 1-4. tr. Panikkar, p 279.

social reverberation in one's doings, one must be disattached from the idea of having to *have* result or success.

True action and hence true knowledge are in the *Bhagavad Gīta* dealing with that topic in a special manner, compared to an "all-spreading flood of water" existing side by side with one's doings as their true reservoir.

> "What utility there is in a reservoir by the side of an all-spreading flood of water, the same utility there is in all Vedas for an enlightened Brāhmana."
>
> *Śaṅkara* comments: "Whatever utility of bathing, drinking and the like, is served by a well, a tank, and many other small reservoirs of water etc., all that utility is only as much as the utility which is served by an all-spreading flood of water; that is, the former utility is comprehended in the latter. . . wherefore, for a man who is qualified for works it is necessary to perform works, which stand in the place of wells and tanks, before he becomes fit for the path of knowledge."[358]

218. The secret of an integrated human life is action and involvement in a cosmic setting (*karmayoga*). Ultimately leading to the realization of *Ātman* in one's life, cosmic awareness implies the intelligence how to relate the forces of life to the order there is in the whole. The relationship with the totality of the universe results in the ability to mould indiscriminate forces into a unity.

> "In the boundless waters in the centre of the universe, on the back of the firmament, greater than the great, having suffused with his splendour all the lights, the Lord of beings stirs within the womb.
>
> He who is the guardian in the centre of the universe, he who bestows the worlds to virtuous people, and the golden glow of death,
> that golden light established in heaven and on earth, may he bestow on us that light!
> The cosmic waters glow. I am Light! The light glows.
> I am *Brahman*!"[359]

219. The basis of that cosmic *Ātman*-realization in one's life is the Vedic *soma*-spirituality. In the *Vedas* the process of extracting that life-giving juice from the *soma*-plant is described in great detail. *Soma* is immortality, on earth already pre-lived through cosmic consciousness. *Soma's* earthly origin is said to be in the mountains on Mount *Mujavat*, yet another name for the cosmic pivot holding the worlds together (*RV* 10. 31.1). Its true origin is in the realm above where it is extracted from its mythical source, the moon, who is the "controller of the waters". *Soma*, therefore, is "the child of heaven" (*RV*. 9.33.5). It is "heaven's

358. *BG*. 2.46. See also *BG*. 3.20 where the wise *Janaka* is praised for his active dedication in a spirit of unattachment (*sattvaśuddhi*) with a view to set an example to the world. The manner in which, in the *Rāmāyāṇa*, a child is given to *Janaka* shows how true "*possession*" of the world depends on a harmonious cosmic integration with environment: "At a time when *Janaka* had no issue, a girl emerged from the furrows of the ploughed earth and Janaka felt a desire to bring up the child as his own daughter. This daughter was *Sītā*" (*R. Ayodhya Khaṇḍa*).

359. *MahanarU*. 1-2, 152-156. tr. Panikkar, *op. cit.*, p. 335..

milk" (*RV.* 9.51.2). *Soma* is the "offspring of the heavenly waters."[360]

The *Soma*-juice from on high is, in its earthly liquid form, said to be the rain. The rain showers fertility upon earth by the power of the spirit-fertility of its life-giving sister. *Soma*. *Soma* is the "Lord of the Rivers and Child of the Waters".

Soma is the vehicle of immortality. The way there is not one of escape from the material world in cowardice but rather one of assimilation of earthly realities. True *nivṛtti* is realised in and through *pravṛtti*. The equilibrium is a matter of appreciative involvement in the human condition. Such involvement is, like *Soma Pavamāna*—linking the worlds together—"flowing clear". It purifies by its effects. True involvement never separates man from the Truth. On the contrary, it has healing power. It makes the lame walk and the blind see (*RV* 8.79.2).

Someone who is able to relate the worlds one to another is the person of balance for whom the question of *pravṛtti* and *nivṛtti* is no problem. That person is the man or woman of excellence, of radiance, kindness and absolute solidarity with the world and its inhabitants. Such a man or woman is called a *somya*.

> "I have tasted, as one who knows its secret, the honeyed drink that charms and relaxes, the drink that all, both Gods and mortals, seek to obtain, calling it nectar.
>
> Once penetrated within my heart, you become *Aditi* and appease the Gods' wrath, O Drop, who enjoy *Indra's* friendship, convey to us wealth, like a seed who is bridled, obedient.
>
> We have drunk the *Soma* and become immortal! We have attained the light, we have found the Gods! What can the malice of mortal man or his spite, O Immortal, do to us now?
>
> This drop that has penetrated our hearts, this *Soma*, immortal deep within us mortals, him would we honour with our oblations, desirous of becoming possessors of riches.
>
> O Guardian Gods, pronounce on us a blessing! Let sleep not overtake us nor useless talk! May we forever be dear to *Soma*. Having won the mastery, let us speak wisdom!"[361]

---

360. Compare *RV.* 9. 31.5, where it is said of *Soma Pavamāna*: *tubhyam gāvo ghṛtaṃ payo babhro duduhre akṣitam / varsiṣṭhe adhi sanavi*, Also: *RV.* 9.5 : *tā abhi santam astṛtam mahe yuvānam adaduḥ /indum...* The relationship between rain and *Soma*-juice is close and it keeps changing in a wide variety of imagery. e.g. *RV.* 9.106.9. "Stream opulence to us, ye drops of *Soma*, pressed and purified, pouring down rain from heaven in floods and finding light "(Griffith): *ā nahsutāsa indavaḥ punānā dhāvatā rayim/ vṛṣṭidyāvo rītyāpaḥ ṣaḍvidhaḥ* /. Another image speaks of the drop which grew in the waters: *RV.* 9. 85.10: "*apsū drapsaṃ vavrdhānam samudra ā* / and *RV.* 89.2: "*apsu drapso vavṛdhe syenajūto*. The ninth *maṇḍala* of the *ṚgVeda* is full of ideas that envisage the relationship between *Soma*, the rainwaters, the cosmic waters and the moon as holder of those waters.

361. *RV.* 8.48.1-3,12,14., tr. Panikkar, p. 367. *Soma*-spirituality is based on fullness and not on want. Many traditional spiritualities seem to stress want, guilt, penance, renunciation, and a general flight from the world and from pleasure. Often such religious forms come from those in stress, hardship, hunger and thirst. And rightly so. When man suffers want he needs solace to be able to survive and somehow protect his human dignity. Earlier I referred to the ambivalence of religions when fullness is preached to the oppressed, the hungry and the homeless but when action is not taken. Such

220. One of the central problems of man's experience in his human condition is the experience of sorrow, pain, suffering, decay and death. Those are experiences not merely sociological or psychological but experiences in depth. Man in his concrete existential situation in and of the universe and creation often seems to starve from the lack of the very thing that is most abundant around him. Is there not the universe's totality and the fact that everything has been provided for in inexhaustible fullness? The earth, the waters, the plants, the animals, the air and space, they are all there offering surplus and surprise all the time. Yet man often experiences himself thirsting for more. Man appears not to *be* all that superabundance. A and by trying to grab creation's gifts he appears incapable of adding more of *being* them. In the midst of the shaped waters, taking the countless forms of the variety of creation, man feels his inexorable path back into the waters as if swallowed up by them:

> "Let me not pass to the house of clay, King *Varuṇa*, as yet. Forgive, Lord, have mercy! If I totter along, O wielder of thunder, like a puffed-up wineskin, forgive, Lord, have mercy!
>
> If by ill chance in the dullness of my wits, I went straying, forgive, Lord have mercy!
>
> Thirst is plaguing your worshipper, even when he stands surrounded by waters, forgive, Lord, have mercy!"[362]

221. The Indian upaniṣadic tradition not seldom seems to radicalize the nature of sorrow and destruction. It often looks like the only remedy is a fast escape into another form of existence. On the other hand, sorrow and destruction are considered a contribution to the awareness of the transcendent.

> "Because plutrality here is only inward, it is so in the state of wakefulness too; Here, as there, is only imagination, locked up within us, here as there.[363]
>
> There is no dissolution and no becoming, no bound one, nor an aspirant, no seeker of emancipation, no emancipation, in truth. . ."[364]

222. The notion of suffering (*dukha*) and its reality is mythically explained by the *Indra*-myth of the creation of the dual organization of the cosmos as upper—and netherworld thereby rendering the possibility of realized totality increasingly difficult. The anti-dote to that distress has been provided for in many ways since myth is the *aimed-at restoration of totality*. One of those anti-dotes is *Viṣñu* arising as the personification of the unity of the two worlds, that is, of cosmic completion. *Viṣñu* controls the stability of *stambha*, the worldpillar standing in the midst of the Waters. He acquires for this reason in later times two vehicles: *Garuḍa,* the celestial bird, and *Śeṣa*, the underworld water- snake.[365]

---

religious education is not worthly of the name and it is no *Soma*-spirituality. Spirituality presupposes a human being satisfactorily fed, clothed and housed and respected. They are the first things. I—and my neighbour—need to be human.

362. *RV*.7.89.
363. "*samvrtatve na bhidyate*"
364. *MU*.2.4.32. tr. Deussen, *op. cit.*, p. 617.
365. For *Garuḍa* see: pp. 5.44.40-70.79-110.

223. In Vedic times *Indra* was continually invoked to repeat his primordial exploit and to reiterate his creation act, wresting heaven and earth from the Waters.

> "Thou from the curse didst free the mighty Waters and as their only God didst watch and guard them. O *Indra* cherish evermore thy body with those which thou hast won in quelling *Vṛtra*.
>
> Heroic power and noble praise is *Indra*: yea, a song worships him invoked of many. *Vṛtra* he quelled, and gave men room and freedom: *Śakra*, victorious, has conquered armies."[366]

224. Vedic spirituality and its ritual suggest that *Indra*'s conquest of *Vṛtra* was reiterated at the beginning of each new year. It was mythically and ritually re-enacted and re-lived when a progressive "degradation" of the cosmos was thought to have reached a serious dangermark. The limitless aeons from the Perfect Beginnings down to man's coming to be are poured for man into a measure that is intelligible to him. During the course of a year man witnesses and is part of the changing *ayus*, lifespan, and the *ṛhbus,* the seasons.

The implication is that in the days preceding the new year the world had fallen back into a state of indiscrimination and threatening chaos corresponding to the primordial world of the formless and indiscriminate Waters (*apaḥ apraketā*). Intelligently interpreting his human condition, Vedic man, in fidelity and faith (*satyaṃ śraddheyaṃ*), recognized his existence to be that of the Waters:

> "*Janaka* of Videha once asked *Yājñavalkya*, "What is used for the *agnihotra*. Can you tell me?" "I can, O king", he replied. "What is it then?" "Milk", he said. "If there were no milk, what would you use for the offering?" "Rice and barley". "And if there were no rice and barley, what would you use?" "Some other herbs". "And if there were no other herbs, what would you use?" "I would use wild herbs", he said. "And if there were no wild herbs, what would you use?". "Some fruit". "And if there were not any fruit, what would you use?" "I would use water" he said. "And if there were no water, what would you use?" "Then indeed ", he said, "there would be nothing at all, and yet an offering could be made—truth with faith ".
>
> *Janaka* then said: "You know the *agnihotra*, *Yājñavalkya*; I give you a hundred cows."[367]

225. In the *Brāhmaṇas* and especially in the myths of the *Purāṇas*, the Indians sedulously developed gigantic systems and theories of reiteration of time. They are the world—ages (*yugas*). At the end of the *yugas* the whole universe and all the gods will be destroyed. The only one remaining will be *Viṣñu* asleep on his snake *Śeṣa* on the surface of the primordial waters.

In all probability the theory of the destruction of the world (*pralaya*) was known already in Vedic times. Like at the end of times when *Viṣñu* gathers all to

366. *RV.* 10.104.9-10. tr. Griffith.
367. *SB.* 11.3.1.2-4.

himself, he is also present at their beginning. During the Churning of the Ocean *Viṣñu* occupies a pivotal position between gods and demons in his tortoise-*avatār* and he was also seen enthroned on the crest of Mount *Mantana*, the world-centre. In the *Taittirīya Saṁhitā Viṣñu* is invoked as follows when a spot for the high altar is selected:

"I shall proclaim the mighty deeds of *Viṣñu* who meted out the spaces of the earth. Who established the highest abode, Stepping three times, the far-goer. Thou art the forehead of *Viṣñu*, thou art the back of *Viṣñu*, ye two are the corners of his mouth. . ."[368]

226. The idea of humanity and all creation returning to the Waters from where they had come and the concept of a new era and a new humanity is common to more than one culture and religious tradition. Deluge symbolism points to man's yearning for the state of paradise where things are as he knows they should be. In many myths the Flood is connected with the concept of "fault" like, for example, in the Christian idea of original sin. In the Indian tradition the experienced "flaw" is that of the break of the Uncreated into the created resulting in a danger-zone. There is in creation a feeling of uneasiness as if being "outside" of its Beginning, its Creator, the Absolute. Man's lack of total and complete wholeness, his shortcomings and the decrepitude of the world are the chief causes for an end of the World in the past and for an end in the future. The Flood opens the way towards a recreation of the World and regeneration of humanity.[369]

In other words, the End of the World in the past and that to take place in the future, both represent the mythical-ritual system and cycle of the sacrificial Year with all its festivals and commemorative rites. These are projected on the macro-cosmic and universal scale, thereby receiving an unusual degree of

---

368. *TS.* 1.2.13. Also e.g. *AV.* 10.8.39-40. See for a discussion Mircea Eliade, *Myth and Reality*, pp. 54-74. The "Gathering unto Itself" of all that is: the Silence of *Brahman*. It is the state where Intellect and Voice are one as Unuttered: *RV.* 10.27.1: "Beyond this here, assuredly, there is another sound"— *śrava id ena paro anyad asti.* Also: *MU.* 6.34: "The mind must be brought to a stop" —*mano nirddhavyam.* It is only when Mind and Voice are divided, when heaven and earth are pillared apart by the axis of the universe (*skambha*) that Intellect and Voice "poles apart" (cf. "poles of the Vedas"— *vedasya āṇī,* AA. 2.7), i.e. celestial and earthly, have come to be. Then Being and Non-being take on an ethical qualification as of Life and Death, Good and Evil, divided from each other as the "here" from the "there" by the width of the universe. It is only from his position "below" that man prays: "Lead us from Nonbeing to Being, from Darkness to Light "(*BU.* 13.28) Creation and slow cosmic fatigue are not merely the necessary means towards freedom but also the very antithesis of the last end, which can only be the same as the beginning." The Voice that went away from *Prajāpati* must return to him" and in *RV.* 1.20.2 where the Ṛhbus, the seasons (called "the artists of the gods") "work by joining together Intellect and Voice"—*vacoyujā tatakṣur manasa.*

369. In part I on myth in general I observed how restoration of the state of paradise is considered possible on earth in mythical-ritual thought. The restorative feature is one of the main characteristics of myth and ritual. The "intention to restore" and consequently to act upon it, is an indelible part of human endeavour to make the world "as it should be". The political "right" and "left" movements for the betterment of the human condition, etc. are part of man's consciousness, a "portion" of which is mythical. I attempted to argue that myth belongs to the psychic-religious constitution of the human species. When so-called "secularized myth" is concerned one may argue its definition, but it is in any case myth. Mirroring oneself against a Perfection is the motivation of all human ideals and ideologies whether they be experienced as "good" or "evil" in the moral-ethical order.

intensity in the theory of the *yugas* and the different kinds of *pralayas*. Among the many exegetical texts presenting the Indian visions, the following from the *Viṣñu Purāṇa* may be quoted:

> "At the end of a thousand periods of four Ages, the earth is for the most part exhausted. A total death then ensues, lasting a hundred years and in consequence of the failure of all food all beings become languid and exanimate and at last entirely perish. The eternal *Viṣñu* then assumes the character of *Rudra*, the destroyer, and descends to reunite all his creatures with himself. He enters into the seven rays of the sun, drinks up all the waters of the globe, and causes all moisture whatever, in living bodies or in the soil, to evaporate, thus drying up the whole earth. The seas, the rivers, the mountain-torrents, and springs are all exhaled and so are the waters of *Pātāla*, the regions below the earth.
>
> Thus fed, through its intervention, with abundant moisture, the seven solar rays dilate the seven suns, whose radiance glows above, below, and on every side, and sets the three worlds and *Pātāla* on fire. The three worlds, consumed by these suns, become rugged and deformed throughout the whole extent of the mountains, the rivers, and seas; and the earth, bare of verdure and destitute of moisture alone remains, resembling in appearance the back of a tortoise. The destroyer of all things, *Hari* in the form of *Rudra*, who is the flame of time, becomes the scorching breath of the serpent *Śeṣa* and thereby reduces *Pātāla* to ashes. The great fire, when it has burnt all the divisions of *Pātāla*, proceeds to the earth and consumes it also. . ."

227. In mythical thought the construction of cosmic time by means of a repetition of primeval creation is principally done through the symbolism of sacrifice and other offerings. Rites and rituals mark a new creation of the World. In the Vedic sacrifice the water with which the clay is mixed, is the primordial water; clay represents the earth when used as the base of the altar; the side-walls are thought to be the atmosphere. Each stage in the building of the altar is accompanied by verses which mention the cosmic region that has just been re-created. Unless man makes these gestures of re-creation, he falls apart in meaninglessness and misunderstanding of the basic structure of universal order, *Ṛta*.

> "Day by day a man offers sustenance to creatures; that is the sacrifice to beings. Day by day a man gives hospitality to guests, including a glass of water; that is the sacrifice to men; day by day a man makes funerary offerings, including a glass of water; that is the sacrifice to the ancestors. Day by day a man makes offerings to the Gods, including wood for burning; that is the sacrifice to the Gods. And the sacrifice to *Brahman*? The sacrifice to *Brahman* consists of sacred study."370

370. *SB*. 11.5.6.1-3 tr. Panikkar, *op. cit.*, p. 349. The "five great sacrifices", *pañcamahāyajña*, constitute the central act of worship. They are also in the list given by *Manu* 3.69-72 (note by Panikkar).

228. If the raising of the altar imitates the cosmogonic act, rites and rituals and especially sacrifice have also an other purpose: to restore the primeval unity existing before creation. *Prajāpati* created the cosmos from his own substance; once he had given it forth "he feared death" (*SB*. 10.4.2.2) and the gods brought him offerings to restore and revive him.

To prevent barrenness of sacrifice, the *Upaniṣadic* and *Yogic-tāntric* visions attempt the "interior sacrifice". The human condition, subject to exhaustion, is in need of rejuvenation and renewal and a reproduction of the primordiality of *Prajāpati*.

> "Thus whosoever, knowing this, performs this holy work, or he who but knows this without practising any ritual makes up this *Prajāpati* whole and complete."[371]

229. The conscious effort to re-establish the primordial unity, the whole that preceded creation, is a conspicuous characteristic of the Indian spirit. Its thirst for primordial unity implicitly grants the deterioration and cosmic fatigue of which man himself is a part.

Man's experience of death and dissolution expresses the point of view of the Waters with regard to human and all other created life. All life, in the mind of the Waters, is fragile. It must periodically be engulfed since it falls to the lot of all forms to be dissolved in order to re-appear. Unless forms are regenerated and periodically dissolved in water, they will crumble as far as the human condition is concerned. Mankind would eventually be completely deformed by wickedness, emptied of its seeds of life and creative powers. Instead of permitting a slow regression into sub-human forms, the floods effect an instantaneous dissolution.

Both the sacrifice on the instant level of daily human experience and the dissolution on the level of myth are, in Indian thought, eternal time materialized. Since time materialized is being renewed to become immaterial Time, Eternity itself, of which creation is a part, a wheel of continuous destruction and creation emerges. Such is man's universal experience. It could, in Indian thought, not be otherwise. The Source at rest (*nivṛtti*) from where everything evolves (*pravṛtti*) calls everything back to Itself by a process of involution:

> "*Prajāpati* is the year."[372]

---

371. *SB*. 10.4.3.24ff. Kuiper in *op. cit.*, p. 167 is of opinion that in the Vedic New Year festival, besides the idea of the renewal of life, also the idea of present-giving and victory over opponents was celebrated. cf. *RV*. 3.8.1 where the sacrificial tree is erected as a *yūpa:* "God-serving men, O Sovereign of the Forest, with heavenly meath at sacrifice anoint thee, grant wealth to us when thou art standing upright as when reposing on this Mother's bosom earth. . . driving far from us poverty and famine, lift thyself up to bring us great good fortune "*-añjanti tvām adhvare devayanto vanaspate madhunā daivena/yad urdhvas tiṣṭhā draviṇeha dhattād yad vā kṣayo mātur asyā upasthe.*" Removal of personal of social evil at the New Year is a common cultural possession. Slaves are given freedom, debts are paid off, prisoners set free etc. The Israelites celebrated special Renewal Years every seven, twelve, twenty-five or fifty years. The later Christian tradition continued the Hebrew custom by the pro-clamation of special Renewal Years in the Christian Church. In cultures and religious traditions the removal of personal and social evil is equated with a near-perfect state approaching that of the Beginnings.

372. *AB*. 7.7.2. tr. Eggeling.

"and the year is the same as Death; and whosoever knows this Year to be Death, his life that year does not destroy."[373]

"That fire-altar also is the Year—, the nights are its enclosing stones, and there are three hundred and sixty of these, because there are three hundred and sixty nights in the year; and the days are its *yagushmatī*-bricks, for there are three hundred and sixty of these, and three hundred and sixty days in the year."[374]

230. The World proces is thus divided into three stages: *sṛṣṭiḥ*, creation; *sthiti*, maintenance, existing and *laya*, dissolution. The World process is the passage from a state of homogeneity (*laya*) to one of heterogeneity (*sṛṣṭiḥ* and *sthiti*), and back again to homogeneity in an unending series of evolution with periods of rest in between.[375]

The three stages should not be thought of as following chronologically one upon the other. Evolutionary processes and involution are contemporaneous with *sthiti*. Thus the daily decay of all animate and inanimate creation is called *nityapralaya*. It is the immediate personal experience of temporality resulting in earthly death. Daily decay, resuscitation and once again decay is man's closest experience of the Eternal Cosmic Cycle. At one moment man may feel the pulse of life's exuberance and know himself on top of a situation like a stork perched on the rooftop. At another he lifts his imploring arms to the heavens like the branches of a mango-tree.

It is at that level that each creature is personally confronted with the view the Waters have of creation. The Waters show what human life and all other forms of life may be worth to a mind other than the created human mind. In rituals and rite and the daily carrying of the dead towards the river banks, the Hindu affirms the mind of the Waters. Symbolic participation in the cosmic cycle is expressed, for example, in the ritual immersion of oneself after cremating a deceased relative or friend:

". . . They should collect the bones. . . and they must throw them into water (from the Ganges) and then immerse. . ."[376]

231. Concomitant with and congenial to *nityapralaya* is man's experience of himself and all surrounding creation as existing in universal passing time. In Indian thought that universal swallowing time is mythically conceived of as being a series of Ages (*yugas*). Through the experience of increasing deterioration in measurable time man becomes part of the collective consciousness of creation which, so the myths show, points to a gradual degradation of

373. *SB.* 10.4.3. tr. Eggeling.
374. *SB.* 10.5.4.10. tr. Eggeling.
375. "Creation" or rather "expression" - *sṛṣṭiḥ*—is typically thought of as a "determination" or "measuring out"—*nirmāṇam*-, the Measurer who is the measure of all things remaining "unmeasured among the measured"; *AV.* 10.7.39. The "measures of fire and breath and intellect", mortal in themselves, must proceed from and again return to the Immortal but as measures they are nonetheless "the gods within you" of the *Upaniṣads*.
376. *VDS.* 19. 6; 10-11.

standards. The presence of ontic fatigue and the very presence of destructive evil have been apparent from the very first *yuga,* i.e. the *Kṛta-yuga.* Although considered to be the perfect age, its perfection became at once stained if assessed in human terms. It began with the fall of the Creators's seed, the fall from Uncreation into creation.[377] The rise of greed in the form of *kālakūta,* the world poison vomited up from the ocean, is one of the direct "results" of creation. Its potential threat became part and parcel of creation and man has to deal with it to the best of his ability. If not successful, he will time and again fail in coming to terms with himself and his environment in his human situation.[378]

232. The concept of *yugas* and the destruction following them on the macro-cosmic scale should not be considered as mere incapacity of man to deal with his situation. In a more positive sense the *yugas* express man's search for restoration and the attempt at integral living. The *yugas* are the macro-cosmic portrayal of the human year with its vicissitudes in an inflated manner. Man's cry for an understanding of his human condition might be more clearly heard and given attention to. His attempt at restoration succeeds well, psychologically and religiously, when temporal time is infused with Eternal time. Time is called the father of *Prajāpati (AV.* 19.53.8). It is the "highest heaven; Time beyond time (*AV.* 19.53.3). That transcendent time, according to the *Atharva Veda,* flowed spontaneously into creation. Neither violence nor sin accompanied its descent, the myths say. Of this the Hindu is aware, although perhaps not always consciously, as much as he is aware of his being part of that Time which, in the *Śvetāśvatara Upaniṣad,* is called *Brahman*:

> "Some teachers speak to us about Nature, others about Time; they are completely wrong. No, it is the god's omnipotence which makes that *Brahman*-wheel revolving in the universe. Through it he reigns.
>
> He who continually envelops the universe. He is the spirit, the creator of Time, the possessor of *guṇas,* the all-knowing one; this work of creation unrolls itself and exhibits itself as earth, water, fire, air and ether.
>
> He is higher than the world-tree, than Time and all forms. Out of him unfolds the panorama of the world.
>
> The one swan in the midst of the universe, he entered as fire in the billows of water. Only he knows the escape from the realm of Death, there is no other way to go.
>
> The lord of the primeval matter, *pradanam,* of the individual souls and of *guṇas,* he brings about a standstill condition, *sthiti,* a transmigration, deliverance and bondage."[379]

---

377. In the Churning of the Ocean-myth, the multi-layered in-sight into the danger-zone resulting from Uncreation falling into being creation is evident. The myth is based on the diurnal annual cyclical movement of the sun. Its rising and setting was seen as due to a churning of heaven and earth (*RV.* 10.24.4). Other Vedic myths provide for healers in the event of disaster in the persons of the *Aśvinīs.* The inescapable presence of greed is more strongly shown in Indian consciousness in the later *Purāṇas.* But also there, *Śiva* and *Viṣṇu* save man from harm.

378. *VP.* 1.9.17.

379. *SU.* 6.1; 2.6.15.16.

233. To be in small time, the time of our daily life with its joys and pains, means to be related to Transcendental Time (*Mahākāla*). *Śiva* is *Mahākāla*. *Śiva Mahākāla* is time in its infinite vastness, wholly quiet and serene as if standing still like a mountain lake without a ripple Descending into everything created, *Mahākāla* consumes all created substance from within, imperceptibly perhaps but surely and steadily. In created substance *Mahākāla* is fractured into moments (*kṣaṇa*) composing the years, months, days and the seasons experienced by man and beast. Also the plants and the rocks know *kṣaṇa*. Broken into segments *Mahākāla* is *Kāla*. As *Śiva Kālakāra*, "the maker of time", *Śiva* hands time to man and makes him propel into action and movement. But created time is like an arrow leaving the bow. It progresses with declining force. Time as time in the world of man becomes a physical entity. It erodes of necessity the substance in which it lives. That is *Śiva Kālāgni*, burning up creation. But consuming time is not a doom or condemnation. It permeates everything we do and it makes all our separate acts unique, unrepeatable and different from one another. *Kāla*, small time, is a great possession in man's hands. It gives him his past, his present and his future framing him into the Universe. Man is not left forgotten in a nook where he could not seek to extend his joy or shorten his pain. He may do today what was left undone yesterday and make plans for tomorrow.

> "Higher and other than time is *Śiva* from whom the world resolves. . . He is the beginning, the impulse of the causes. . . beyond time, and without separate parts. Into him, in the beginning and at the end the universe is gathered.[380]

234. The Indian mythical awareness and its metaphysical-religious vision describe *Kāla* as breath (*prāṇa*). *Prāṇa* on the human level is subject to universal fatality. It is being swallowed by *Śiva Kālarūpin*, relentlessly and unilinearly active in the shape of time.

> "The whole universe caught in its mouth whirls like a wheel through the activities of creation and annihilation."[381]

> "From Time came into being the Waters, from Time the Holy Word, Energy, and the regions. By Time each day the Sun arises, in Time he goes to rest again.
>
> By Time blows the cleansing wind, through Time the vast Earth has her being. The great Heaven has his post in Time."[382]

---

380. The problem of "time" has never abated but moves through the whole history of metaphysics and epistemology. To try and master the concept of time by subordinating it to a universal concept has, in the history of Western philosophy, been first done by St. Augustine in his Confessions. In space it would seem possible to conceive of the "here" as independent of the "there". For "time", however, such a separation is not even abstractly possible. Every moment immediately implies temporal relations and temporal intentions. The present, the now, obtains its character as present only through the reference to past and future comprised in it. Any attempt to separate content and representation, existence and symbol, would, if successful, destroy the vital nerve of temporality. It would also destroy the ego-consciousness which combines into a unity past, present and future and recognizes them as such through the I-concept making all three phases comprehensible: See: Ernst Cassirer, *The Philosophy of Symbolic Forms,* vol. 3, p. 170. Text reference: *SU.* 6.6.; 6.5; 4.1. *Mhb.* 13.16.51; 13.17.31-32.

381. *SP.* 7.1.7.2.

382. *AV.* 19.54. tr. Panikkar, p. 219.

235. The shape of time, says the *Kurma Purāṇa*, swallows everything. It has the quality of darkness (1.10.82). Mythically, darkness finds its concrete form in the formless Waters (*āpaḥ apraketā*). Darkness (*tamas*) betrays itself by a tendency towards disintegration, inherent in creation. Whatever came to exist returns to shapeless form; to non-form. The return to non-form will be in reverse order. The earth with all her properties will dissolve into water. Fire devours the water; fire is dissolved in wind; wind in space; space in sense-organs. *Ahaṁkāra*, the principle of individuality, is dissolved in *mahat*, the cosmic intellect. That is dissolved in *Brahman*. Then *prakṛti*, the cosmic substance, is separated from *puruṣa*, the spirit. *Prakṛti*, the womb of the world, is without consciousness because only *Puruṣa* is consciousness. *Purusa* remains. The only One.[383]

236. The macro-cosmic disintegration is in man's consciousness his expression of yearning for a land-without-evil. Not only later but here and now. How could man wish for evil to happen in his home, his street and his country? How could he want it to happen to his neighbour? Man likes to believe the possibility to live with at least as little as possible evil. He does not easily deny that solidarity is feasible. The myths and their thoughtful narrative are produced, treasured and controlled by the collective desire of the whole community for a land-without-evil. The myths of the land-without-evil thrive on the ever renewed consent by successive generations. They are being re-thought and re-charged with new meaning by an anonymous creative process having a name nonetheless. It is the wish of the god and of man. A community cherishes an intuitive hope for paradise to happen, also that on earth.

Hence religious insights are not the only visions underlying the Indian concepts of *pralaya* and *yuga*. Social initiatives too are clearly discernible. Myths allow for no compartments. The *Viṣñu Purāṇa* expresses the hope that destruction and subsequent paradise will come once the newly found land is rid of the evil of invaders and oppressors. The doctrine of *laya* and *yuga* thus receives an earthly characteristic.

Of *Viṣñu*'s *avatars*, the final one, *Kalkin*, is the only one yet to come in the future, so the myths say. He will appear at the end of this present *Kāli-yuga*, the age of decadence. It is not improbable that the idea originated with the invasion of India by the Parthians in the first centuries of the Christian era. *Kalkin* himself has the form of an invader: like the Scythian and Parthian intruders, he comes riding on a white horse. His purpose is to destroy them. He uproots the wicked cities of intruder-kings and lays waste to the heretic's home including the Buddhists whom he himself had just produced in his last but one incarnation. When *Viṣñu* challenges the *Kāli-age*, the tides turn. He acts as a cog in the wheel of time.

> "Unable to support their avaricious kings, the people of the *Kāli*-age will take refuge in the chasms between the mountains and they will eat honey, vegetables, roots, fruits, leaves, and flowers. . . No one will reach twenty-three years, and thus without respite the entire race will become destroyed in the *Kāli*-age. . . . When Vedic religion and the *dharma* of the law-books

383. *KuP*. 2.44.13-24.

have undergone total confusion and reversal of the *Kāli*-age is almost exhausted, then a part of the creator of the universe, of the *guru* of all that moves and is still, without beginning, middle, or end, who is made of *Brahmā* and has the form of the soul, the blessed lord *Vāsudeva*—he will become incarnate here in the universe in the form of *Kalkin* endowed with the eight supernatural powers, in the house of *Viṣñuyaśas,* the chief *Brāhmin* of the village of *Śambala*. . . . Immediately at the conclusion of the *Kāli* age, the minds of the people will become pure as flawless crystal, and they will be as if awakened at the conclusion of a night. And these men, the residue of what is left of mankind, will thus be transformed, and they will be the seeds of creatures and will give birth to offsprings conceived at that very time. And these offsprings will follow the ways of the *Kṛta* Age."[384]

237. The Indian doctrine of *yugas* as it developed in later Hinduism resembles, to some extent, the older *Vedic* and *Upaniṣadic* concept of the sacrificial annual renewal of the World. There are, however, some important differences. The later Indian *yuga*-theory may give a false impression as if man plays no part in the periodic recreation of the World or that eternal renewal is unwelcome. As if Man's goal would be to try and escape the cosmic cycle.[385]

The gods too do not appear to be actual creators. They rather resemble agents through whom the cosmic process is accomplished. What the *yugas* mean to say is that the End has no meaning except for the human condition. Man is able to halt the process in which he would otherwise be blindly carried along. He can personally share in the creative process of which he is, by virtue of *Puruṣa,* a part.

238. Man's target, in Indian mythical thought, is to transcend the limits of individualized consciousness. From the viewpoint of the Waters that target is made possible through union with Transcendent Time by a spiritual flood (*Atyantikapralaya*). Spiritual dissolution signifies man's self-limitation in relation to the eternal I. The *aimed-at union* between them comes true when the realized person can say in truth "*aham brahman*," I am *Brahman*.

"In the ocean without shores, in the midst of the universe, on the ridgetop of the heavens, greater than the great, with his splendour penetrating the world lights, He tarries as *Prajāpati* in the mother's womb. Into him the world disintegrates and then unfolds itself. It procreated the creatures of this world. It, through water, created forth the living creatures on the earth. And Itself entered into plants, animals and the human beings, into the mobile and immobile beings.

Indeed, it is *Agni,* it is *Vāyu.* It is *Sūrya,* it is *Çandrama*, it is pure, it is immortal. It is *Brahman,* it is the water and *Prajāpati.*

All the parts of time sprang out of *Puruṣa,* minutes, hours, and seconds. Days and nights, all of them. Half months, months, seasons and year—may they be contained in it. It milks the water out of both—out of the aerial space and the heavens there.

384. *VP*. 4.24.25-29 in *Hindu Myths,* p. 235.
385. See the following chapter on *Karma*.

The form of that one is not to be seen. Nobody sees it with his eyes. Only one who is spiritually ready in the heart, the mind and the spirit sees it; — They who know it become immortal."[386]

239. The *Atyantikapralaya* reveals a rationale explained by the concept of *Puruṣayajña*: Man *is* sacrifice (*SB*. 1.3.2.1a). What else is man to do but to allow creational experience to circulate in himself? Today's joy may be crushed by tomorrow's sorrow, yesterday's rejection by a friend may be today's loving embrace. The circulation of the tides of existence in man brings him face to face with responsibilities. Must he not with *Śiva Kālakāra* sculpture his past, present and future into an pleasing frame for himself and his neighbour? It is only by being circulation that man can possess the constitutive bond holding the worlds together. They are the worlds of the gods, the sages, the ancestors and man's neighbour. The fifth bond of the five great sacrifices (*pañcamahāyajña*) is sacred study. Attentive listening to one's innermost intuitions, we may say. For, not everyone is a lover of books. These five responsibilities towards the gods, the sages, the ancestors, the neighbour and to one's own creative intuition imply surrender and immolation. They place man in the web of relationships which make up the wholeness of all there is. Not that man fulfils his five responsibilities grudgingly. They are free gifts to man which he shares with his surrounding. No one's life is exclusively one's own.

The *Puruṣayajña* and the *Pañçamahāyajña* are the Vedic magna carta of intelligent behaviour and true human existence. There is a debt to be paid to the God, to the community, to the sustenance of intellectual and religious talent, to family life and to the neighbour: they are the tides of the cycle of man's daily life.

"When a man is born, whoever he may be, there is born simultaneously a debt to the Gods, to the sages, to the ancestors and to men.

When he performs sacrifice it is the debt to the Gods that is concerned. It is on their behalf, therefore, that he is taking action when he sacrifices or makes an oblation.

And when he recites the Vedas it is the debt to the sages which is concerned. It is on their behalf, therefore, that he is taking action, for it is said of one who has recited the Vedas that he is the guardian of the treasure store of the sages.

And when he desires offspring it is the debt to the ancestors which is concerned. It is on their behalf, therefore, that he is taking action, so that their offsprings may continue, without interruption.

And when he entertains guests, it is the debt to man which is concerned. It is on their behalf, therefore, that he is taking action if he entertains guests and gives them food and drink. The man who does all these things has performed a true work; he has obtained all, conquered all."[387]

240. The five debts of man must not be thought of as the elimination of the individual person. It rather means, from man's end, the healing of the Universe by putting

386. *MahanarU.* 1.2a.4.7-9.11 tr. Deussen, *op. cit.*
387. *SB* 1.7.2.1-5. tr. Panikkar, *op. cit.*, p. 393.

together again (*sandhyā*) what had been dismembered and by building up (*saṁskār*) the true unitary Self. That effort allows for no egoism of any kind. Man's true perspective is that of a healer. The cosmological *Puruṣa*-myth is man's dream of paradise. It need not remain a dream. By paying off the five debts he has to his surrounding, man unloosens the fetters of an otherwise imprisoned human predicament.

From the point of view of personal liberation man ought to be aware that he is the lower *Brahman* (*apara*) and as such a wanderer (*saṁsarati*).[388] The *yogic* Indian mind attempts to achieve the pre-creation state by retracing time backwards, by swimming upstream (*pratiloma*). Underlying this psychic-religious effort is the hope of escape from senseless transmigration. Yogic texts express the idea often in no uncertain terms:

> "The breasts at which he once drank, later he squeezes lascivously. On the womb which once gave him birth, he sates his carnal desires. Thus in the rotation of *Saṁsāra* like a bucket on the water-wheel. running round, he is once more born in the mother's womb."[389]

What is needed for one's liberation from the bondage of created limitation is the re-enactment in one's own being of the process of cosmic reabsorption. One must proceed against the current (*ujāna sādhanā*). In the spiritual exercises set forth in the *Śivasaṃhitā*, one "sees" the element Earth become subtle and dissolve in the element Water and so on until all is reabsorbed into the *Brahman*. From the human end that state is called *nirbīja samādhi*, dissolution without seed, without any support.[390]

The Indian vision is not one of destruction of surrounding since whatever is, is a platform of the Eternal Breath extended into creation. Man is the temporal domain or garden, a mirror of the Bliss of Self.[391]

"The sacrifice is man. It is man who offers it because it is man who spreads

---

388. The "higher" (*para*) *Brahman* is that "One, the Great Self, who takes up his stand in womb after womb (*yo yonim yonim adhitiṣṭhati ekaḥ, mahātma*). . . as the omniform Lord of the Breaths (*viśvarūpaḥ. . . prāṇādhipaḥ*). That Self wanders about in the conceptual notion of the "I am" of the small self of man. The embodied Self receives functional forms in the human person." (*SU.* 5.1-13) See *MU.* 6.26: "As rays from the Sun, so from him (*Brahman*) his Breaths and the rest come forth continually here in the world in due order"—*tasya prāṇādayo vai punar eva tasmād abhyuccarantīha yathākramena.* In *BG.* 15: The flowing Breaths that proceed from and return to the *Brahman*-heart are the fount in all elements (*kṣaraḥ*) and "unflowing". (*akṣaraḥ*) in *Brahman's* own eminence. The Breaths are like the Winds and the Waters which ever return upon themselves and hence flow without the possibility of exhaustion (*JUB.* 1.2.5ff)

389. *YUp.* v. 3 and 5.

390. *SS.* 1.69f.

391. Man and his body is the domain or garden (*arāmā, BU.* 4.3.14) or platform (*adhiṣṭhānam, CU.* 8.12.1) of the unseen, incorporeal, and impassilke Self. The "Platform" concept is regularly employed in connection with the "mounting" of the psycho-physical vehicle by the Spirit (*ātman*), e.g. *AV.* 10.8.1.: (*Brahman*) *śarvam..adhitiṣṭhati. "adhiṣṭhā"* implies the idea of management, administration and its application to the extension of the Eternal Breath on earth implies action and involvement in a positive sense. See: *MU.* 11.6f where the Person who makes things intelligible (*manomayaḥ puruṣaḥ*). *Prajāpati*, awakening as if from sleep, divides himself fivefold in the senses to awaken his lifeless offspring (*pratibodhanāya*). The Creator is said "to eat of the sense-objects" in creation (*visayan atti*): the cognitive powers are his "rays", the organs of action are his steeds. Impelled by him the body spins like the potter's wheel when in a state of consciousness.

it out, in being spread out, it assumes exactly the same stature as man. For this reason, the sacrifice is man."[392]

Man, therefore, cannot here on earth desire only heaven. He is in some way already in heaven by living on earth. Whether earth will indeed be like heaven depends on whether man is prepared to take up his five responsibilities, his five debts. If he is not, earth will be like hell. The earth's destiny has fallen into man's hands. Man cannot heap responsibility for the earth on some impersonal fate or on a god made to answer for problems man prefers not to face. In the cosmic process man has a rectifying and an invigorating spirit.

241. The primordial beginnings and all that henceforth happened, is happening and still is to happen, are contained in *Āpaḥ*, the Waters.

"In the boundless Waters in the centre of the Universe on the back of the firmament, greater than the great, having suffused with his splendour all the lights, the Lord of beings stirs within the womb. The consmic Waters glow. I am Light! I am *Brahman*!"[393]

Now, of all that has been said here of the life, the movement and the thoughts of *Āpaḥ*, the Waters, there is nothing that needed to be said. All that is contained in the imperishable Sound-Form "*OṂ*".[394]

"Speech recedes along with the mind unable to attain him. He is expressible through the single syllable *OṂ*, which is the Divine order, the supreme cause, truth, bliss, nectar, the supreme *Brahman,* greater than the greatest. Out of that single syllable "*OṂ*" the syllable "a" is *Brahmā*; "u" is *Viṣṇu,* and "m" is *Rudra-Śiva.*

"a" is the cause of creation, "u" of illusion and of bliss it is "m".[395]

242. The reward of meditation upon *OṂ* is the unfolding of the lotus in the heart, opening up the secret of the Waters.

"The lotus flower, that occupies the space in the heart, calix down, the stalk on high, dewing down, Therein the *Manas* has its seat.
With the a-sound it becomes luminous
With the u-sound it opens out

392. *SB.* 1.3.1.2. tr. Panikkar, p. 393.

393. *MahanarU.* 1-2.156.

394. *Mantra* is primarily a concentrated "thought form" composed of nuclear syllables based on the esoteric properties believed to be inherent in sound vibrations. *OṂ*, the most powerful of all sounds, is the source of all *mantras* and a key to realization. It is made up of three sounds a, u, m, which symbolically represent the three ultimate tendencies or *guṇas,* i.e. creation, preservation, dissolution, and encompass all the knowledge of the different planes of the universe. It is the quintessence of the entire cosmos. The "period" (dot) does not stand like a tombstone in Sanskrit. It adds vibration to the dull sound. It is especially significant in that it raises "o" from the chest vibration to the *OṂ* sound in the head, the higher sphere. It raises the physical sound to the *çakra* of consciousness, the "*ājñā*"—*çakra* between the eye-brows, and gives it meaning. In *MU.* 6.4: "The three-quarter *Brabman* (i.e. the Tree as extended within the cosmos from earth to the sky) has its roots above. Its branches are the air, ether, fire, water etc. This *Brahman* has the name "One tree" To it belongs the Sun and the imperishable sound *OṂ*. In *AV.* 10.7.21: "*OṂ*" is Brahman's "One Awakener"-*eko'sya sambodhayitṛ*.

395. *LP.* 17.56-62.

With the m-sound it resound,-

Motionless is the half sound.-"[396]

243. In the sound *OṂ* lies the reverberation (*dhvanī*) of true understanding.

"Long drawn like a drop of oil, long humming like the sound of a bell,
Silently reverberates the tip of *OṂ*.
Who knows it has the knowledge.
Making one's body the friction-wood, with the *OṂ*-sound as the upper stick.
Through meditation's friction one sees God like the fire hidden in the wood.

Pursing one's lips like a lotus stalk, one is accustomed to drink water, One should similarly draw in wind also, when as a *yogin* one practises the *yoga*.

For the forehead between the brows, where there is the root of the nose, is the perennial dwelling place, the great resting place of all."[397]

244. "Everything existent and non-existent will be grasped by pronouncing *OṂ*!."[398]

245. "*OṂ*! This syllable is the whole world. Its explanation is as follows: The past, the present and the future, all this is the sound *OṂ*. And besides, what still lies beyond the three times, that also is the sound *OṂ*!"[399]

246. "The *Brahman* created *Brahman* in a lotus-flower. The latter deliberated: "Which is the one word by which all desires are obtained and all worlds, gods, Vedas, sacrifices, rewards of the sacrifices, everything movable and the immovable is known ?" — And he practised *Tapas*. After he had practised *Tapas* he saw that syllable, which consists of two letters and four *moras*, which is all-encompassing, all ruling, ever new, the *Brahman*. Through the first letter he perceived the water, *āpas*, and the acquisition (*āpti*); through the second the fire and the light.

The first *mora*, the "a" sound, is the earth and the fire, the plants, the *ṚgVeda, bhūr*, the *Gāyatrī*. . The East, the spring, and with reference to the self, the language, the tongue and the speech.

The second mora, the "u" sound, is the atmosphere and the wind, (the *YajurVeda*), *bhuvaḥ*, the *Triṣṭubh*. . . the West, the summer, and with reference to the self the breath, the nose and the smell.

The third *mora*, the "m" sound, is the heaven and the sun, the *SāmaVeda*, *svar*. . .the North, the rainy season, and with reference to the self the light, the eye and the sight.

The fourth *mora*, the *Anusvāra*, is the water and the moon, the *AtharvaVeda*, *janas*. . the South, the autumn, and with reference to the self the heart, the knowledge and the known.[400]

---

396. *YUp.* 9-10.
397. *DhyanabU*, 18.20.21-22.23. tr. Deussen, *op. cit.*, p. 703.
398. *MaP.* 39. 6-16.
399. *MU.* 1.1.1. tr. Deussen, *op. cit.*, p. 611. See also *CU* 1.1.1. for the same expression. Also *MU.* 6.4.5. where *OṂ* is said to be both the "*para*" and the "*apara*" *Brahmin.*
400. *PranU. I.* tr. Deussen, *op. cit.*, p. 925.

247. "In the ocean without shores, in the midst of the Universe, on the ridge of the heavens, greater than the great, with his splendour penetrating the world lights, he tarries as *Prajāpati* in the mother's womb.

Into him the world disintegrates and then unfolds itself. Upon him all the gods are fonded. It is that which was already there and what will be, it is in the syllable in the highest space. In it. the space with earth and heaven is enveloped. The sun outshines with splendour and sparks. In the ocean itself the poets sing. And in the highest syllable *OṂ* there are all the creatures."[401]

248. "It is *OṂ*, it is the Waters, it is the essence of light, the immortal *Brahman*. *Bhūr*, *Bhuvaḥ*, *Svar*, OṂ!"[402]

249. And *Çitra* taught *Gautama*, the father of *Śvetaketu*, about what happens to the man or the woman who is searching. And then, when the searcher meets *Brahman*:

"Then *Brahman* asks him: "Who are you? Then he will reply: I am the season, I have sprouted forth from the season, I am born out of ether as my cradle, as the seed or sperm of my wife, as the splendour of the year, as the self of every being. You are the self of every being; what you are, I am.

And he asks *Brahman*: "Who am I then?" Then *Brahman* will say: the truth".

"How, in what manner, tne truth?"

"What is different from the gods and the corresponding living organs, that is "true"; but what the gods and living organs are, it is (true) "ness". It is expressed through the one word "truth". This comprehends the whole world, you are the whole world".

He then will speak thus.

It is signified by the verse:

With *Yajus* as belly, *Sāman* as head, with *Ṛc* as body, as the everlasting one
He is to be regarded as *Brahman*
The great wise sage, full of Brahman
The *Ṛṣi* who arises

And he asked him:

"Through whom do you comprehend my masculine names?"

"Through the *Manas*."

"Through whom, my female names?"

"Through the *Vāc* (Speech)."

"Wherewith my smells?"

"With the breath."

"Wherewith my forms?"

"With my eyes."

"Wherewith my sounds?"

---

401. *MahanarU*. 1.3 tr. Deussen, *op.cit.*, p. 249.
402. *MaitraU*. 6.35, tr. Deussen, *op. cit.*, p. 376.

"With the ears."

"Wherewith my juice of nutrition?"

"With the tongue."

"Wherewith my actions?"

"With the hands."

"Wherewith my pleasure and pain?"

"Through the body."

"Wherewith my bliss, sex-pleasure, and procreation?"

"Through the organ of procreation."

"Wherewith my movements from place to place?"

"With the feet."

"Wherewith my thoughts, that to be known and my wishes?"

"With intelligence, (*prajñā*)."

Thus then he will reply.

Then he will say to him: "The primeval waters are, indeed, my world (as *Hiraṇyagarbha*) and it is yours!."/indeed, every conquest of *Brahman*, every unfoldment of *Brahman*—he who has such a knowledge acquires this conquest, unfolds himself with this unfoldment—he who has such knowledge."[403]

250. *OṂ* We meditate upon the glorious splendour of the Vivifier divine.
May he himself illumine our minds! *OṂ* [404]
It is *OṂ*
it is the waters,
it is the essence of light, the immortal *Brahman*.
***Bhūḥ bhuvaḥ svaḥ OṂ*.[405]**

403. *KausU*. 1.6-7, tr, Deussen, *op. cit.*, p.29.

404. *RV*. 3.62.10. The *Gāyatrī* is the most renowned mantra of the *Vedas*. It is addressed to the divine life-giver, symbolized by *Savitṛ*, the Sun. It is recited daily at sunrise and at sunset, usually at the moment of the ritual bath. "*OṂ tat savitur vareṇyaṁ bhargo devasya dhīmahi dhiyo yo naḥ pracodayāt OṂ*."

405. *MaiU*. 6.35.5

Chapter 8

KARMA: THE COSMIC PILGRIMAGE

The reciprocal relationships between man and the Universe, established in the mythical consciousness, I have thus far—by asking *Āpaḥ*, the Waters, to speak, regarded essentially in the form they assume in the mythical-religious world of *ideas*. As I said before: symbols give rise to thought.

I now have the task to widen the field of inquiry. The mythical-religious spirit has its true and deepest root *not* in the world of *ideas* but in the realm of *feeling and will*. Feeling and will actually underscore the believed reality of all the ideas of the mythical-religious awareness. Feeling and will relate to language and being. I have had occasion to point out that in the myths narrating the earliest reflections on being and the world, there is no distinction between language and being, between word and meaning. "By the power of the word, the majesty of *Prajāpati* said: "*Bhūḥ*", "earth", and the earth was."[1] Feeling and will of the Creator underline the reality of the idea of creation. Creation *is*. The world in it *is*. The Hindu's equally affirmative reply to "*bhūḥ*" is the *Praṇava-Dhvanī*, the primal sound: *OṂ*.[2]

Every new relationship with reality man experiences is expressed not solely in his ideas and beliefs but also in his volition and action. And herein man's attitude towards the vastness in which he finds himself, and the Hindu finds himself also *in Brahman*, must inevitably be more clearly manifested than in the figures and images of his mythical structures. Consequently, we find true objectivation of the fundamental mythical-religious feeling not in the bare image of the gods but in the action devoted to them. In action is man's active relationship with his gods or (the) God to be found.

The mythical account is itself for the most part only a reflection of that immediate relationship of action. And so the naturalistic approach to myth comes under severe criticism for it can be clearly shown that a vast number of mythical motifs had, and still have, their origin in the intuition of "what is to be done" or "having done what was to be done". Such intuitive obligations are a reconfirmation of

1. *SB*. 11.1.6.3. See, Part II:5:4(iii): "The Perfection of the Beginnings: *Sat-Asat* (*RV*. 10.129)" I have in that paragraph made mention of the difficulties there are with regard to the philosophical inquiy into the nature and origin of language. The idea of mythical language as "pre-logical" language, both in temporal as well as in psychic archaism, is becoming obsolete. Mythical language and its awareness is contemporaneous with other forms of human consciousness. Mythical language as mirroring itself in "some" perfection cannot be said to be the earliest language of mankind as if it would have given itself over to another and "better" language in later times. The mythical word and its awareness, creating a reality, are an indelible part of contemporaneous human awareness, now less, now more pronounced. We find its clearest example in the expressions of volitional emotion, also, therefore, in so-called secularized culture. When lovers express their volitional emotion by saying "I love you", the words actually create "love" and between them it is. Likewise, "I hate you", "I believe you", when volitionally expressed, create hate and belief.
2. See, *ibid*., p. 307. Also see the water-myths nos. 241-250 in the preceding chapter where the *OṂ mantra* manifests itself clearly as an affirmative answer to the reality of creation resulting from *Prajāpati's* volitional word.

the perfection of the beginnings. "What is to be done" has its root in an Example. Mythical motifs are not exemplified in any physical thing or event but in an activity, be it of Being or of man or both. That activity is explicitly represented by the motifs in myth.

It follows that denial of action is, in mythical-religious consciousness, philosophically impossible. To say it more emphatically and more clearly framed within the context of this inquiry: *pravṛtti* is not only inescapable, it also is the necessary and valid human existential reply to the Creator's will and intention. And herewith we are once again back in our Indian philosophical environment and world view.

If one unqualifiedly escapes *pravṛtti* one becomes an anomaly. It is in that perspective that *Kṛṣña's* revelation in the *Bhagavad Gītā* must be understood:

> "Actions are done in all cases by the energies of Nature. He whose mind is deluded by egoism thinks "I am the doer."[3]

Here the qualification attributed to action is the egocentric approach. The same characteristic of egocentrism is given to the action by him "whose mind is deluded by egoism (and who thinks) 'I am the non-doer". Performance and non-performance are equally an illusion if the agent does not put himself in a true perspective with regard to his being in the world and the fruits of action and non-action. The question of action and non-action is related to that of the nature and the cause of things. Man ought to be aware that what he does or leaves undone, has something to do with what the Lord *Kṛṣña* says:

> "Time am I, world-destroying and mature."[4]

---

3. *BG.* 3.27. This text is intimately linked with the intuitive obligations: "what is to be done" or "having done what was to be done": *krtakṛtya, kata karaniya, katakicca*. The one who understands does not think of "himself as the doer of anything", the word for "doer", *kartṛ*, meaning equally "maker" or "creator". "The energies (*karma*) of Nature" that are the cause of actions wrought have a purpose that lies beyond a temporal definition, steering one within the totality of the design inherent in the Universe. In the *Bhagavad Gītā* 18.20 it is expressed as: "Bound by the working (*karma*) of a nature that is born in thee and is thine own, even that which thou desirest not to do thou doest willy-nilly". We are nothing but a link in a causal chain of which we cannot imagine a beginning or an end. There is nothing here that the determinist can disagree with. The metaphysician, however, who is not, like the determinist, adherer to the idea of "no-mores", merely points out in the text that only the working of life, the manner of its perpetuation, can thus be causally explained; that the existence of a chain of causes presumes the logically prior possibility of this existence. In other words, it presumes a first cause which cannot be thought of as one among other mediate causes, whether in place or time. One may call this "inherent fatality" but not in the sense that it does away with personal responsibility. *Karma* is not an inescapable fate. One understands *karma* perhaps better by the simple analogy that one does not conceive that one can move to and fro as one wills but knows that one is getting older every day, whether one likes it or not. But at no point in ageing man thinks of himself as not free. In the sacrificial interpretation of life—the putting together of the fragmented cosmos—acts of all kinds are reduced to their paradigms and archetypes, and so referred to the One from whom all action stems. When the notion" that I am the doer "(*ahaṁkāra, karto'ham asmīti*) has been overcome and acts are no longer "ours", when we are no longer "anyone", then we are no longer under the law because we are "all action". That requires that the sacrificial act of creation (*karma, sṛṣṭi*) in the centre of our individual being coincide with the centre of the wheel, the extension of the wheel no longer involving us in only local motion but in the entire universe's circuit, thus making us into "round-about-seers" (*paridraṣṭṛ*)" overlooking everything. We can then speak of "rationalizing" our conduct by acting "to the point" (*sādhu*) and "in good form" (*pratirūpam*).
4. *BG.* 11.32.

The nature and cause of things are not monodimensional, merely to be interpreted from man's end. Action and non-action lie in the mind of the "Author of time, possessor of all qualities, omniscient" (*SU.* 6.2). It is the discovery of the Non-temporal which gives meaning to what should or should not be done on earth.

> "Some say that inherent nature, others that time is this world's cause. Both are mistaken. It is the grandeur of God within this world by which this wheel of *Brahman* is made to turn.
>
> By whom the universe is ever encompassed, the Knower, the Author of time, possessor of all qualities, omniscient. Ruled by him, the world of creation unfolds—that which is regarded as earth, water, fire, air, and space.
>
> Having begun with works accomplished by the qualities he assigns a destiny to all existent beings. So soon as these cease to be, the work done is destroyed. At the work's destruction he continues, essentially other."[5]

We may examine the nature of action in Indian tradition a little more closely. The proposal is that we do so, as may be expected, by means of the myth. There is a lovely myth in the *Mahābhārata* to which I would like to draw the attention. It all happened in *Kurukṣetra*, the place where good and evil were pitched against each other, the "middle of the world", to the south of the river *Saraswatī* where lakes and sacred places abound. There were *yakṣas* and *yakṣīs* around.[6] They are potent presences who give wealth to the soil and who are responsible for the nourishing strength in the plants. There is a sacred spot there, called *Śākambharī*, dear to *Dēvī*, the Great Goddess, and full of nourishment and embodying the warm fullness of the earth.[7] She, *Śākambharī*, had lived there for more than a thousand heavenly and blissful years, subsisting on plants alone. The benefits one obtains by visiting that sacred spot are countless. One is infused, for example, with true knowledge if one fasts there only three nights and lives on a diet of plants. One discovers, so it is said in the myth, another dimension of time. So naturally many a pilgrim and searcher for truth visited that hallowed spot from the earliest time. Among the pilgrims was *Maṅkaṇaka Ṛṣi*. He had absorbed in himself the nourishing plants of earth and even the *Soma*-juice itself. It would seem *Maṅkaṇaka* was well on his way to realization. The plant juices retained their purity in his body, filling him with understanding of solidarity with all surrounding (*jñāna-śuddhi*).

Once, when he roamed the earth, he cut his finger by accident with a blade of *kuśa*-grass. How amazed *Maṅkaṇaka* was when plant juice oozed from the wound. Filled with boundless joy over the waters of nature in his veins, *Maṅkaṇaka* danced and everyone around danced with him. Their dance made the earth shake. *Maṅkaṇaka* felt freed from the bondage of blood and saw his transformation into solidarity with creation come true.

What had the *Ṛṣi* done so that his blood had changed into the watery juice of plants? How was it that he was reborn? Reborn in creation while still being *Maṅkaṇaka*? Was it through someone else that he now existed? Had creation, the universe changed him?

---

5. *SU.* 6.1.2.4. tr. Panikkar, *op. cit.*, p. 222.
6. *Mhb.* 3.81.175-178.
7. *Mhb.* 3.82.11-13. See: V.S. Agrawala, *Matsya Purāṇa, A Study*, Vārāṇaśī, 1963, p. 200.

Maṅkaṇaka's human condition, his temporality, had come to be framed in the proper perspective. At least, so he felt. He had evolved (*pravṛtti*) into a state of involution (*nivṛtti*). Two seemingly opposed and paradoxical processes had blended in him through *Jñāna-śuddhi*.

Maṅkaṇaka's evolution into involution should not be said to be the statement of a process of *formation*—which is the way Western philosophies conceive of evolution. To *Maṅkaṇaka*, nature's juice dripping from his finger, his evolution was an *explanation* of his being. The universal Energy of which he was part had now broken through in him. At least, that is what *Maṅkaṇaka*, the searcher for truth, thought. And everyone else thought so with him.

But now something happened and the *Ṛṣi's* exuberance was very much toned down. No sooner had he begun to dance then *Śiva* appeared. "It is against the *dharma* of sages to dance with the lust of passion or to sing and dance, as is pleasnt to young women, and break the *tapas* of a *Brāhmin*", *Śiva* said.

> "*Maṅkaṇaka* explained the reason for his dance, but *Śiva* merely laughed and struck one of his thumbs against the other, and ashes pale as snow flowed from his wound. When the sage saw this he was ashamed, seeing such a miracle of asceticism, and he said: "You must be *Śiva*, for no one else has such power. Forgive me for what I did in ignorance, dancing and so destroying the *tapas* amassed for many years." *Śiva* was pleased and told *Maṅkaṇaka* that, as a special boon, his *tapas* would be increased rather than destroyed, if he worshipped the *Liṅga*."[8]

Elsewhere in the epic *Śiva* is a little more metaphysical: "One's own body is only made of ashes". The *Śiva* whom *Maṅkaṇaka* met in that sacred spot *Śākambharī*, was *Śiva Bhasmabhūta*, "*Śiva*, made of ashes."[9] It takes indeed the maturity of complete self-integration to fully appreciate the reality and intrinsic value of the world—the world of space, time and manifold individuality—as a field of ever new creation and value emergence. Without that maturity one gets easily bogged down in cliches and in stereotype thought and behaviour. One needs the throb of a high intensity of *tapas*, fervour and ideal, to understand and be transformed.[10] Only through understanding man becomes creative enough to have at his disposal constant correctives (*pratividhi*) to keep him from becoming as hollow as a tomb. Concentration on the world pillar (*liṅga*), the essence of the Universe and keeping the worlds together, is *Śiva's* valuable advice.

Ashes usually symbolize the spirit of renouncement. They are disgusting and anti-erotic. When they flowed from *Śiva's* body, he revealed the result of burnt *kāma*, irrational lust and love of appearances. Ashes are utter purification. *Śiva Bhasmabhūta's* ashes are his life-force, his *tapas*, rather than the funeral pyre wherefrom they are derived. Here the ashes suggest life because they manifest

8. *Mhb.* 3.81.98 - 118; 9.37.34 - 50. See also *Pādma Purāṇa*, 1.27.1-15; 5.18.132.
9. *Mhb.* 13.17.29.
10. *MU.* 4.4 speaks of the knowledge of *Brahman* by fervour, *tapas*, when "the man in the cart" (prisoner) is liberated from those things with which he was filled up. He attains conjunction with the Spirit—*ātman eva sāyujam upaiti*. The prisoner set free by the Spirit can now drive the vehicle to a destination that he himself wills. cf. the idea of "*ātmayājī*", the "one who knows" and whose new body has been integrated (*saṁskriyata*) because it has been superimposed by the body of the sacrifice, i.e. the totality of the cosmos gathered together.

transformation. *Śiva* had looked with sympathy on *Mańkaṇaka's* efforts. In the last aeon which is yet to come, *Śiva* will scatter the ashes of destruction over the world when he will dance his wild *Tāṇḍava* dance as *Śiva Kāla Mahākāla*, the Time-swallower.[11]

It is clear from the lesson *Śiva* taught that *Mańkaṇaka* had exulted too soon. He had not yet sufficiently well understood his existence. He still lacked sufficient understanding of who he was. His I (*ahamkara*) had not yet been fully transformed. He had not yet come, to say it the Hindu way, under the law of the Universe (*karma*). *Karma* is the Hindu way of expressing the human condition and the temporality of man.

Contemporary man, more than ever perhaps, reflects on his historical conditions, measured in moments of time. Especially Westerners who pride themselves of rationality, tend to consider historicity a characteristic almost peculiar to them. A particular interpretation of the Semitic—and later Christian culture—as understood by the West, seems to add to their dominating attitude with regard to history. For our purpose it is sufficient to say that what is called "historicity" in the West, may be called "the theory of *karma*' in Indian thought, although we ought to be aware that neither concept covers the other perfectly.

It is interesting to observe how Westerners tend to be attracted to *karma* as what they think is the theory of re-incarnation as the survival of the identical individuality. One gets the impression that it is the extinction or dissolution of the individuality—of that mental and physical and at times rather nervous composite which I call "myself"—which is hard to abandon for many in the West. Certain trends in Western philosophy have pitched the "I" too much against the "thou" of Being and of surrounding creation. It also seems unbearable for many in the West, too enamoured of life and in the midst of a surplus of this earth's material wealth, that the dissolution of the I simply *is* inexorable. *Karma* for them is an opportunistic and welcome escapist move. It is the promise of "my" survival and re-appearance that is the great lure![12] A deeper reason for what often appears to be an insufficiently studied approach to *karma* is perhaps less the overstress on the I than the loss of "self" which lies at the heart of solipsism. The transcendent and theological implications of "self" in Indian thought hardly allow for solipsism as it is found in the West. The assumed link between the mind of man and The Mind rescues Indian thinking from a shattering loneliness, even if there have been philosophical solipsists in India. There is also the assumed relation between the body of small created man and that of Cosmic Man (*Puruṣa*). The break of the Uncreate into the create, resulting in some form of logical loneliness, does not cause

11. *KP*. 2.4.33: "I am the originator, the god abiding in supreme bliss. I, the *yogī*, dance eternally". In *tāntric* tradition ashes are used to signify the further purification of love, the transcendence of mere carnal erotic love. The sap from *Mańkaṇaka's* finger, according to one interpretation of the myth, is the *Soma*, whereas the sap from *Śiva's* thumb is *Agni*. Both are essential for creation and transformation. See: V.S. Agrawala, *Vamana Purana, a Study*, Banaras, 1964, p. 72.
12. The fear of death and illness has created problems in the West with regard to medical, social, and pastoral care. Not being sufficiently well integrated into the "ordinary" course of human life many suffer from various kinds of traumas. The death ritual is often mechanized and taken over by outsiders who are supposed to dispose of the dead in a clean and fast manner. Children and teen-agers are prevented from being present at death beds for a number of "psychological" reasons. Death and illness are thought of as intruding agents rather than as forces that are natural and part of a continuum.

worry to the believing Hindu. It is when, for many in the West, the create is left without a vital link with the Uncreate, that a haunting fear of loneliness may arise on the emotional level for which a soothing balm must be found. The shallow understanding of what *karma* is may be attributed to a lack of "ashes", in other words, a posture of dominance needing ever more insurances to protect it.

In India too, many misunderstand the theory of *karma*. Their opinion of it causes individualism and groupism screening them off from the five responsibilities or debts to be paid (*Pañçamahāyajña*). Those who have been given the boon of a bearable existence, or who have taken it for themselves, would like to keep their riches and attribute their "luck" to the workings of *karma* which is thought to have predestined them to live in affluence while the next-door neighbour battles with dire poverty. The latter equally appeals to *karma* as the hope for a "better" incarnation in times to come. Often, when discussing social problems, I have found the discussion untimely terminated by a shrug of the shoulders, the burden being shifted on *karma*. There are also those who, by a misconception of what justice is, condemn the poor and the handicapped to a former life of sin which they would now be expiating.

Karma, from the root "*kṛ*", means "action". It is a widespread concept in most Asian traditions. Among all the possible interpretations of *karma* it is important to remember that it is an anthropocosmic concept. *Karma* tells us of the experience of man in creation, in the Universe, in Eternal Time as broken into fragments of temporality. In the *ṚgVeda*, the other *Veda*, and in the *Brāhmaṇas*, *karma* means action and especially sacred action, sacrifice.[13]

> "Look on *Viṣñu's* works, whereby the Friend of *Indra*, close allied, has led his holy ways be seen."

Sacred action in the *Vedas* and *Brāhmaṇas* is necessary to enjoy human plenitude and salvation. Sacrifice is the world and it is five-fold according to the five debts that all of us must pay so that harmony and attention for the Universe and all that is in it may blossom. One can never excuse oneself and shed one's responsibility to pay attention to all five debts by appealing to *karma* as if it were a fate making that attention impossible. The five debts are a call on man to contribute to the Universe's totality.[14] It is for that reason that the *Upaniṣads* initiated the significant transition from the *Brāhminic* ritualistic attitude to the interiorized and conscientisized view of

13. *RV*. 1.22.19; 9.88.1; 1.55.3; 1.61.13; 101.4; 1.112.2; 1.121.11; 3.33.7; 9.96.11.
14. Philosophically, the enigma of fate is impossible to resolve unless by a formula as that of Schopenhauer, according to which, when viewed from outside, logically or scientifically, the world's events can be recognised as governed to such a degree by the laws of cause and effect as to be inexorably determined. Experienced from within, however, from the standpoint of an acting subject, living yields an experience of choice. These contradictory views are only the functions of mankind's alternating modes of conditioned knowledge, i.e. the world as "idea" or the world as "will". Both fail as to the ultimate answer with regard to a man's becoming and being. It is of interest to note that in Buddhism *Karma* is a strictly psychological and not a metaphysical term. It has not the meaning of irrevocable fate or destiny, but of "Action". The Buddha's words in *Aṅguttara-Nikaya* 6.63: "*cetanaham bhikkave kamman vadami*" "Volition, O monks is what I call action" point to consciously motivated and intended exercion as true "karmic" action, and only such action has character-forming consequences. See *BU*. 4.5.4.: "As he acts, as he conducts himself, so he becomes; what he wants. . . that he attains" *yathākāri yathāKārī tathā bhavati. . . sa yathākāmo bhavati. . . tad abhisamadyate*". Such action is then "this person is what he does, he is the *Brahma*-world": *karma kṛtam ayam puruṣo brahmaṇo lokaḥ*. (AA.2.1.3.).

participation. Ritualism often stifles the personal aspect of the human act and is liable to protect vested interests and exercize censorship. The sacrificial act is not a ready-made act, over and done with. It gathers the members into community imposing a renunciation of the I.[15] My I is not the owner of my life. My life as this life does not begin with me. It was given to me, as it was given to her or to him. I did not find life. Life found me. In that sense some of the universal totality was entrusted to me. I am part of the Universe's commitment to me. I am acting it out for the very fact that I am alive. That is *karma*. The *Upaniṣads* unveiled an essential feature of sacrifice by raising it beyond the level of a magical world view. Sacrificial action is not a mere technique. Immediate environment and universal wholeness cannot be drawn into the privacy of the I. They cannot be manipulated or traded. They can at the utmost be conquered by sharing in them. The *Upaniṣads* covered the first step of *karma* as a cosmic pilgrimage. Man's power in the realm of feeling and thinking is subject to an empirical limit. By action, however, man is free to identify ever more with the Universe and its sustaining principle (*Ātman*). In a ritualistic environment there is no dialectic. While attempting to prescribe the correct ritual behaviour, the very content of the ritual may have evaporated.[16] Legalmindedness in ritual easily breeds a mentality of measure for measure. As expressed in a *Vedic* formula: "Give me, I give to Thee; lay down for me, I lay down for Thee. Do offer me sacrifice. I offer Thee sacrifice".

Business mentality in action, also in sacred action, is overcome once the I sees itself as indeed more than the I. In discovering the real I man finds out that his I is nothing less than the Absolute Wholeness looked from a unique point of interest. Related herewith is the question of re-birth understood as reaping in another life the fruits of a previous one. We find the idea in the *Bṛhadāraṇyaka Upaniṣad* summing up a longer development of thought. Man's ethical and moral stewardship receives ontological proportions implying a universal responsibility making it both possible and necessary to re-trace one's steps. Action devoid of ontological consciousness is a shortcoming in the most literal sense of the word. It has consequences both for me and for others, those implied in the all encompassing five-fold debt to be paid to the totality of existence (*Pañçamahāyajña*). When I do not come home in the Universe, my realm of pilgrimage, and when the path is not completely covered by me I come short of wholeness. Thus re-birth is needed from the point of *quality* of the Universe in as far as it has personified itself partly in me.

15. See. *MU*. 2.2.6: "Welfare to you in crossing over to the further shore of darkness!": *savasthi vaḥ tamasa parastāt*. Limitation of the "I" has moment of psychological darkness.
16. Ritualism is not limited to the sphere of the sacred only. It operates equally in institutionalized politics, social and economic behaviour and in educational systems of various kinds. With regard to liturgy it may result in, e.g. the imposition of symbols foreign to the community of faithful, often resulting in misunderstanding of the basic tenets of a particular religious truth. Ritualistic approach often tends to regard environment as hostile and hence fosters "privacy". The problem is acute with a view to encouraging the meeting of religions on a common platform. To exclude the "unbeliever", often made out to be so by the "believer", from participation in sacred action is a common ritualistic approach. Political ritual shows the same inclination thereby complicating a possible approach between different parties. Earlier I have observed that the building of a "centre" is a valid anthropological human need. It may take on perverse contours as when, e.g. multinationals establish "their own" centres in any country without due regard for the local population and their rightful claims.

The vision the Waters project with regard to existence is that of quality. Quality needs re-charging to keep its vitality:

"He who dwelling in the waters, is different from the waters, whom the waters do not know, whose body is the waters, who inwardly controls the waters—he is your soul, the inner controller, the immortal one."[17]

To maintain the Universe's quality and even to attempt to embellish it by caring for its immensely colourful manifestation is the meaning of the Indian concept of *lokasaṁgraha*. The *lokasaṁgraha* requires transcendence of egocentric motives by seeing the self as part of everything. That is the humanness of universal solidarity. One is not to be identified quantitatively with this or that substance in the Universe claiming it as one's possession as if one had created it. In that sense one is to be like *Brahman*: *neti*, *neti*, not this, not this, and yet be everything.

"Indeed, thus self is the *Brahman* consisting of knowledge of mind (*manas*), of life breath (*prāṇa*, of eyes, of ears, of water, of wind, of ether, consisting of fire, and not consisting of fire, consisting of desire and not consisting of desire, consisting of anger and not consisting of anger, consisting of righteous law and not consisting of righteous law, consisting of all.

According as one, now, consists of this or that, according as one does, according as one behaves, according to what he is born: he who does bad things is born a bad man. He who has done good things is born good. He becomes holy through holy works, base through base works.

That is why it is, indeed, said: "The man is wholy fully formed of desire (*kama*) according to what his desire is, his intelligence, *kratu*, is according to it; according as he does work, it produces according to it."[18]

But then *Ṛtabhāga*, for we are listening to a dialogue between him and *Yājñavalkya*, puts the question: "When a man dies, what is there that does not leave him?"[19] And the other replies:

"The name, because unending is the name".

He then goes on to disclose the cosmic law of the conservation of all the elements of the universe:

"his speech enters into the fire, his breath into the wind, his eyes into the sun, his *manas* into the moon, his ears into the quarters, his body into the earth, his

---

17. *BU*. 3.7.3. Participation of the human person in the Universe must be one of "resounding" like the Universe of itself resounds through innumerable voices of life in so many forms. Man's breath, therefore, must be like the Breath. The breaths are thought of as streams or rivers (*nadyaḥ*, *sindhavaḥ*) of light, sound, and life. They are in fact the very waters and rivers that are released when *Vṛtra* is slain, and are called *nadyaḥ* "because they sounded (*anadata*)" when released. (*AV*. 3.13.1; *TS*.6.1.2.). The released and sounding waters are one's break-through of consciousness when one's speech is a flowing (*kulyā*), originating in the pool of the mind, (*JaimUB*. 1.58.1). Thus the senses are opened like sluices pierced by the Inner Power (*Svayambhū*): *khāni vyatṛnat khāni bhitvā*." Who pierced the seven openings (*sapta khāni vi tata:*) in the head, the ears, the nostrils, eyes and mouth, who divided up the Waters (*āpo vy-adadhāt*) for the flowing of the rivers in this man? "(*AV*. 10.2.6.11).
18. *BU*. 4.4.5. tr. Deussen. *op. cit*., p. 495.
19. *BU*. 3.2.12

> *ātman* into the world-space, his hair on the body into the plants, his hair on the head into the trees, his blood and semen into the water. . ."[20]

Ṛtabhaga then asks: "What happens to the man, to the person?" The wise man takes the questioner by the hand and both discuss *karma* "among themselves alone, not in the assembly."[21] What they discuss about that mysterious *karma* is almost disappointing for its all too matter-of-fact truth: "Indeed one becomes good by doing good works and base or sordid by doing base or sordid works." And *Ṛtabhāga* remained silent.

Is it indeed wiser to be silent about *karma*? For indeed many absurdities in many assemblies have been said about it. How could *karma* be true *karma* if its interpretation would go at the cost of even one human being or animal or flower or forest or sea? The law of the Universe is best loved and served only when appreciated without lustful greed (*niṣkāma karma*). What we gather from *Yājñavalkya's* secret words is that *karma* is the core that remains of the person transcending all individuality. Negatively *karma* is my destructive action left behind once I am no longer. The wounds inflicted by me on the Universe will be of consequence for others, causing their *karma*, their inherited world, to be less a reason for exultation and peace. Positively *karma* is to cure oneself and the community of the deteriorating and destructive force of temporal time in us.

Unfortunately humanity's human condition appears to allow for its spookish ability to be a conspicuous agent of destruction. Although progressive deterioration is inherent in creation, it is not creation's direct aim. There remains the remembrance of *Prajāpati-Puruṣa's* original act, breaking himself into creation while in himself remaining whole. Forgetfulness of the singleness and simplicity of the Origin makes man play havoc with his present and his future.

Thus understood, action (*karma*) is the return to the beginnings as a conscientization of what is to be done in the now and later after the beginnings. That puts man in a relationship of responsibility for his surrounding (*lokasaṁgraha*). Man is blessed with an intuition of how things ought to be. Is that intuition perhaps grounded in what *Yājñavalkya* explained to *Ṛtabhāga* "about the name not leaving the person and remaining"? There is more to the human condition and to the human person than meets the eye. We all have a name prior to the one we are called by while on earth. The utterance of our name—"protectors of the world" *Prajāpati* called us—opens the door to a creative efficacy extending our earthly individuality into a universal personality. From there we shall understand the Wheel of the Year fragmented into four ninety-day seasons, as the *ṚgVeda* explains:

> "He by the names of the four has set in motion his ninety coursers, as a rounded wheel."[22]

> "(it is) Thou, Mighty *Indra*, (who) hast four supremest natures with which thou hast performed thy great achievements."[23]

---

20. *BU*.3.2.13.
21. *BU. ibid.*
22. *RV*. 1.156.6.
23. *RV*. 10.54.4: *asuryāṇi nāmādābhyāni. . yebhiḥ. . karmāni cakartha.*

Man's mythical awareness attributes to the Creator's utterances of names the simultaneous appearance of the worlds. Between "let the earth be" of *Prajāpati* and "the earth was" there is no temporal succession of events. Likewise, it is after hidden names that the maker of all things creates angels and it is by man's recourse to *Agni*, the fire of creative imagination, that these angels "receive for themselves those names by which they are worshipped sacrificially and thus receive their own well-born embodiment."[24] Thus it is that in ritual re-enactment man's name, like that of celestials, is projected as truth into eternity. That is why man has an intuition of the paradisial state as a possible *donation* to his world.

Now, and this is the point, if *karma* is the cause and dynamic of this world as a *possible* replica of "that world", man is responsible for using it properly. That is the motif of *karma*. And thus the judgement according to one's deeds is clear. The popular understanding of *karma* has often emptied it of its meaning by an egoistic interpretation of it. Its popular concept is dominantly ethical but not of a very exalted kind. All too often it is that of a mechanism from which *gain* is supposed to flow. It will be easy to understand how, for example, when the higher castes in earlier times gave themselves over to grabbing lust for power, the castes came to be theologized through an abuse of the concept of *karma*. It became an external sanction to "virtue", a code, a trade balance between the temporal and the non-temporal. One's birth through *karma* came to be viewed as either an exaltation or a condemnation. If it is sometimes said of India that it has a negative approach to the world, it is by that abuse of the notion of *karma*. If the Indian mythical awareness shows at no point, as I contended earlier, a "fatal flaw" when the Uncreated broke into created, then a negative approach to creation is hardly defendable. The negative attitude apparent in the psychological and material situation of despair of the impoverished is not a metaphysical negation of creation. The negative attitude on the part of the affluent is likewise due not to a metaphysical negation of existence. Often it is a fear of the poor rising up in arms against them. Both parties are not seldom kept equidistant from a solution to the problem by an erroneous theological and superstitious concept of *karma*. The problem lies at our end of creation and hence lies in our own hands.

The true concept of *karma* in Indian thought does not allow for tragedy. There is no question on an over-charge of fate or an inexorable defeat. *Karma's* intention is the surrender of the claim by man as if he were capable of creating an island for himself in the Universe. Such an attitude leaves no room for and no thought of "ashes". Where there are no ashes there is an absence of fire (*Agni*) as a constitutive element of creation. The watery plant juice dripping from *Maṅkaṇaka's* finger was apparently not sufficient to qualify him for full participation in the Universe. One also needs *Agni*, the fire of intelligent concentration. It is ashes suspended in water that qualify us for true human and humane partnership. How can one human recognize another unless by sharing with him food and drink? How can the animal recognize man unless by his gentle stroke and the morsel given? The flower feels well when allowed to decorate man's home and the tree is happy when people sit in its shade. The god feels content when people sing songs to the heavens and the stars. The clearance of our debts to the Universe, as the Indian *pañçamahāyajña*—the five offerings—explains, is the coming true of *karma*.

24. *RV*. 1.72.3: *nāmāni..dadhire yajñiyāny, asūdadyanta tanvaḥ sujātāḥ*.

Our inquiry is all the more important because the notion of *karma* may be seen to be the result of a historical process of true secularization away from the *Brāhminic* clerical elitist concept to the general understanding of life itself as an offering. Life itself is a rite conducive to salvation. The sacred is henceforth shifting from the altar to the realm of human existence. This is an evolutionary move (*pravṛtti*) of consciousness. It is when the sacred is transported into the world that man becomes truly "body" and hence historical. Consequently he will recognize the Universe as "body". If thereby the spirit is confessed to man will come full circle. Spirituality without body is an overstatement of man's being. It would imply an unwarranted claim to the realm of divinity. In the human situation spirituality without "body" sense is escapism and hence devoid of historical implication. In the human condition, return to the source (*nivṛtti*) is accomplished through a historical *karmic* involvement (*pravṛtti*). They are mutually inclusive.

The move from the altar to man's daily life, without thereby denying the community's need of a common place of sacrifice, marks an intense step in each man's and in each community's understanding of the creative divine. This conscientization of one's inherent universal identity cannot be measured in artificial and arbitrary strategies in regard to the world. There is no way of trying to deceive the personality that the world is. The process of participation in creation represents the essence and fundamental character of life itself as a qualitative unity.

It is, therefore, not merely the mediated and reflected expression of his own being that man finds in the world of his neighbour, in that of the sun, the moon, the stars, plants, animals, earth, oceans and rivers, in passing away and decay, in sprouting and growth. In his surrounding, man apprehends himself immediately and with full certainty. In it he experiences his own destiny. The fundamental mythical feeling is the idea of life as the centre. Life itself as the very pivot of everything impels man to burst through the barriers of his genetic and individual particularity separating him from the universe of living people and things. It is to the degree that one intensifies one's life feeling that one liberates oneself.

Karma designates both the wheel of existence and that what is being burnt and transformed by it. It is a journey towards fulfilment of the Universe through active participation. That sharing consists of a network of relationships between action and re-action. Their convergence will direct the newly arisen situation one way or the other, good or bad. It is each man's responsibility to see to it that the new situation contributes to growth. Thus *karma* is the earthly reality of built-in universal causality. It is, quite simply, the know-how of dealing with life. *Karma* does not reveal what things are but how they work.

Karma does not reveal the essence of things because it is not *Brahman*. *Karma* is "all this" (*idam sarvam*), all that falls within the range of experience of man's situation in the world. What lies outside that realm lies in the sphere of the absolute. It is when I reach the realm of the absolute that I am (*aham asmi*). *Karma* as the experienced human condition can be said to be more in the line of what I have. What kind of "having" is that?

Indian philosophy defines the I of the *karma*-condition as *ahaṁkāra*, "the maker of I". The more I make of *ahaṁkāra*, the more I shall indeed have of it for *ahaṁkāra* signifies individuality and particularity.[25]

These are different from the idea of person. The notions of having and making imply that of individuality as material content. Individuality has something numerical about itsef. It is in the *karma*-condition of man that the *ahaṁkarā*, the principle of individuality, ought to be lifted through universal awareness, not to more of *ahaṁkāra* but to the state of *aham asmi*, I am. *From having to being is man's goal*. Where man's actions inflate his *ahaṁkāra* he is liable to usurp time and space not allotted to him. And who is not aware of man's inclination to force another out of the way? The inflated *ahaṁkāra* claims rights where there are none. Privileges taken by man are in that sense meaningless if not ridiculous. A material concept of oneself as I, makes of one, as an Indian text expresses it, a puffed-up wineskin.

Man then appears to be more than the singular, particular individual. Through what he is in *karma* he is called to what he was and is from the beginings: *Puruṣa*. Humanity's growth, each man, woman and child of it, consists of increasing intensity of participation in the work of gathering the members of Cosmic Man, *Puruṣa*, scattered in creation. That task of gathering (*karma*) is a philosophy of history allowing for no discord in the common pursuit of awareness of the interdependence of all created forms.

That awareness, it is said in the *Kathaka Upaniṣad*, finds its origin in The "Pure Waters of Understanding" (*yathodakaṃ śuddham*):

"As water descending on mountain crags
wastes its energies among the gullies,
so he who views things as separate
wastes his energies in their pursuit.
But as pure water poured into pure
becomes the selfsame—wholly pure,
so too becomes the self of the silent sages,
of the one, O Gautama, who has understanding."[26]

Conclusion

The experience of the Waters has taught us their capacity to resume, on multiple levels of creative interpretation, an old theme: that of primordial wholeness. The primary symbol reflects in an infinite variety the human psyche's constant quest for clarification of the meaningfulness of the human condition. The exemplary model of the Waters, being always open, reveals a profound dimension of human existence: *it is open*. Implied in the projection of values as they come to man through his myth, is that the mythical awareness *creates history*. As I said earlier, the world must be grasped as it *moves about*. The modality of the beginnings is not frozen. The sacrificial will and feeling of the Originator from whom all action stems makes man veer around

25. The Indian view of *ahaṁkāra* which is its spiritual and its psychological therapy against an overstress of the ego, warns against such an overstress by the idea that there is no "I" that does, no "mine" that is the doer, no latent "I am"—*ahaṁkāra mamaṁkāra—(asmi) mānānusayā na honti*. The notion of "not being the doer" can only be grasped by one who has attained the state "of not being anyone": *ākiñcannāyatanam*. The "I am not the doer" is a metaphysical position, already referred to earlier, and not a moral one. It is, therefore, not a matter of indifference of whether one does good or evil or whether one can shed one's responsibility.

the sacrificial interpretation of life. When the notion "I am the doer" has been overcome, and acts are no longer "ours", when we are no longer anyone, then we are no longer "under the law". It is in this sense only, and not by vainly trying to do nothing, that the causal chain of *karma* is broken; not by any miraculous interference with the operation of these causes, but because *we* are no longer part of them. The reference of activity to the creative Origin is what we ought to mean when we speak of giving an account of our conduct. If we cannot give an account—ratio, logos—of our doings it will mean that our actions have been reckless (*asaṁkhyānām*) rather than in good form (*pratirūpam*). Once we are conscious of the sacrificial implication of our life, we are leading not a life of our own in this world but a transubstantiated life. There will be no compulsory pattern but an opening towards the completion of wholeness where it is lacking in man's condition. If true to his Originator whose organs he is, man is by nature original. That may be called man's calling.[27] Man's kārmic pilgrimage is to cover incongruous distances between him and (the) god, between him and his neighbour, between justice and injustice, peace and war, riches and poverty.

---

27. Bede Griffiths, *Marriage of East and West*, Collins, Fount Paperbacks, 1982, pp. 30-31.

PART IV

CONSPECTUS:
THE EXEMPLARY HISTORY OF *ĀPAḤ*, THE WATERS

Chapter 9

SYMBOLS MAKE US THINK

One thing that we may have acquired, at the end of our exercise, is a conviction that the myths of origin reveal the ethical dimension of the myth of tension, "interwoven lengthwise and crosswise" in man's awareness of his dual status as guest and inhabitant in the world.[1] For indeed we have discovered a new myth—or better to say, uncovered an old truth—: the myth of tension. Man's dual status as guest and inhabitant in the world is his only valid and reasonable tension. We may at times be unhappy about our status and wonder as to where it leads us, but we cannot be existentially disgruntled and sulky about it. That tension is the *sole truth* about us. To try as if it were not there would mean the refusal to be a created man or woman.

The Churning of the Ocean (*samudra-manthana*) took place to settle various matters after creation had come to be.[2] And indeed a number of pressing affairs were dealt with. It is clear from *Viṣṇu's* behaviour that the gods were going to win the cup of immortality (*amṛta*). They had to. God or gods *are* immortal. The *samudra-manthana* merely—and justifiedly—gave them their due.. And because they receive their rightful immortaliy, man *did not* receive it. True, man may be *made* immortal by the grace of (the) God or gods, but he is *not of himself* so from his mother's womb. If he had been so, at times we have wishful dreams, no word about the mythical awareness could have been written. There would not have been that intuition of "guest and inhabitant" and hence no myth. The rise of myth is from man's end, not that from (the) God's or gods, and goddesses. Without the tension there would have been no poetry, art, philosophy or religious quest.[3] There would have been no need of an *intention*, of an *aimed-at* restoration of wholeness.[4] We would have *been* that wholeness, the Universe's plenitude. There would have been no quest to attempt to relate to an *other* dimension of reality *in order to be human*.[5] There would have been no myth therefore and no cult.

At the end then of our double approach—through the abstract description of the "guest-inhabitant"-tension in us and its intended re-enaction in the experience of *Āpaḥ*, the Waters, as origin, maintenance, destruction and again origin—the question arises: *How shall we continue*? The rift between pure *reflection* on the tension in man and the *confessed* acknowledgement of it in the experience of *Āpaḥ*, drawing us this way or that, now created, now immersed, now re-created, is clear. Pure reflection makes no appeal to any myth or symbol and is, in that sense, a direct lesson in rationality. That is why the waters were invoked to speak because the ultimate ground of the human meaningful situation which cannot be attained by only the rational

1. See *Gārgi's* debate with her master *Yājñavalkya* concerning reality: Part I:2:5: "Myth and "modern".
2. See Part III:7: myths nos. 76-94.
3. See Part I:1:1: "A phenomenology of "chaos".
4, *Ibid*. Also 2:1: "Myths are no allegorics".
5. See. part 1:1:2: "The idea of "the sacred".

intellect. The rational intellect is not the whole of man's mind.[6]

With regard to the question: "How shall we continue?"—Continue with what? With the book or with the human meaningful situation? I have always tried to keep the two in their closest proximity. The direct connection between the symbolic myth and the mythical symbol helps us here to grasp the paradoxical mythical suggestion that man's inherent tension while on earth is to be released by the *believed* enactment *as if* he is lifted above it. In fact, the earth is to be lifted above itself. If the earth is supported by a lotus, it is because the peculiar temperament of the lotus is to rest upon the waters; the lotus is universally and not in any local sense a ground. All cosmic possibilities, not only her own, are at the earth's choice. Earthly man is free to further stress the cosmic choice by sitting and dwelling on the lotus (*padmāsana*) like the divinities. By lifting themselves up, through the lotus attitude, the earth and man cannot be unnerved or lose sight of each other.

The earth has been propped up by *Prajāpati* from the deepest layers of midmost ocean's stability and then spread on a lotus leaf.[7] If thereby *Prajāpati* broke himself into creation, the earth and man have become altogether real and significant. The assuring solace of the *Prajāpati* creation myth is the generation of temporal time with a touch of eternity whereby the mere human events—the "all-too-human" events—are abolished as if they were the whole of history. Were they the whole of history, there would be no escape—in hope and in fact—from the dictator usurping power or the landowner claiming yet another spot at the cost of the defenceless or from the senseless torturer in prisons. As it is, both the dictator, the greedy landowner and the torturer have—through the possibility offered by the lotus attitude—history against them.[8]

All through our inquiry the *whole* of man has been our postulate.[9] To screen off one constituent of human experience and its expression *as human* leads to pseudo-philosophy, an offence against the rational-critical instinct.[10] Leaving out the receptive consciousness of the sacred as a constitutive contribution to the understanding of reality liquidates the affective relationship with it, wounding the grasp of reality incurably. For the mythical awareness to screen off even one ingredient of man is impossible.

---

6. "*Manas*" is multivalent and difficult to describe with regard to the range of its activity. In the *Saṁhitās* and *Brāhmaṇas*, and also at times in the *Upaniṣads*, *Manas* is the Pure or Possible Intellect, at once a name for the Ultimate Reality and that in us by which that Reality may be grasped. Thus, for example, in *RV.* 1.139.2 we "see the Golden one by our eyes of contemplation and of intellect": *apaśyāma hiraṇyaṃ dhībhiś cana manasā svebhir akṣibhiḥ*. *RV.* 10.181.3 points to intellectual speculation as the Godward path—*avindam manasā dīdhyānā. . . devayānam*. In Part II:5:4(iv): "The birth of His Own Perfection: *Hiraṇyagarbha* (*RV.* 10.121)" we contemplated that which was in the beginning neither Non-being nor Being. In *SB.* 10.5.3.1-4 it is identified with Intellect (*Manas*). There are, on the other hand, expressions implying the distinction between a "mature" and an "immature" Intellect as, for example, in *MaiU.* 6.34 where the Intellect must be arrested in the heart - *mano niroddhavyaṃ hṛdi*. Important for an understanding of *manas* is *MaiU.* 6.34 where Intellect is for man a means of either bondage or liberation - *kāraṇaṃ bandha mokṣayoḥ*. *Manas* in man is not a science, but an opinion—involving *buddhi*, wisdom and insight, as distinguished from empirical or dialectic reason. Objects of perception, *viṣayasaṅgi*, are just that and nothing more.
7. See Part II:5:4(v): "*Prajāpati*-The Lord of Generation".
8. *Ibid.*
9. See Part I:2:4: "Speculation and myth".
10. *Ibid.*

To avoid both pseudo-philosophy and an unbearable burden on myth, we must remind ourselves of our promise to shape mind and heart together in rationally untranslated receptivity and thus find ourselves in a state which may be equalled to the silence of expectation.[11] That exercise conditions us to the *irruption* of existence into consciousness rather than looking back on it through a compartmentalized introduction by rational-critical thought.[12] The pattern of our thought will receive a particular colour: not that of the observer's model of control and monopolizing prediction over the world—dangerously proximate to domination—but that of a *mood* rather, ritualizing the world. We become participants. The evil we experience will then be painful drama and the good will be felt to be a celebration.[13]

And here we may find an answer to our question at the end of our inquiry: *How do we continue*? We may continue—as I have already furtively tried to suggest with regard to all-too-human events "having history against them"—by volitional action engendered by the original enigma of the primary symbol such as that of *Āpaḥ*, the Waters. In other words: by *promoting its meaning in our psyche* and thereby evoking *commitment* to (the) God, god or goddess and to man and the whole Universe. That commitment is the substance of what *Vedic* Indian thought knows to be the *mahāpañcayajña*, the five debts to be paid to the economy of universal totality and integrated living (*lokasaṁgraha*).[14]

> "There are five great sacrifices, namely, the great ritual services: the sacrifice to all beings, sacrifice to men, sacrifice to the ancestors, sacrifice to the Gods, sacrifice to *Brahman*.
>
> Day by day a man offers sustenance to creatures; that is the sacrifice to beings. Day by day a man gives hospitality to guests, including a glass of water; that is the sacrifice to men. Day by day a man makes funerary offerings, including a glass of water; that is the sacrifice to the ancestors. Day by day a man makes offerings to the Gods, including wood for burning; that is the sacrifice to the Gods.
>
> And the sacrifice to *Brahman*? The sacrifice of *Brahman* consists of sacred study."[15]

Our volitional action—which in ordinary language means, "Yes, I'll do something about it"—when embedded in the primary symbol, will be free of theological, philosophical and psychological nervosity. It will, with regard to creation, not be on the look-out for a stress on the opposition between *pravṛtti* and *nivṛtti*, but rather be pleasantly surprised at their mutual complementarity. Surprise comes when things, initially thought to be totally or partly opposed, happen to match. In other words: we continue, not as obsessed by our dual status of guest and inhabitant in the world, but as humans set free by the awareness that *that* state is what we are.[16] Our dual status

11. See Part I:2:2: "The confession of receptivity: a first phenomenology".
12. *Ibid.*
13. *Ibid.*
14. See Part III:8: "*Karma*, The Cosmic Pilgrimage" *passim*. See also Part I:1:1: "A phenomenology of "chaos".
15. *SB*. 11.5.6.1-3. tr. Panikkar, *op. cit.*, p. 394.
16. See Part II:2:4: "Myths of the exiled soul", On various occasions I have referred to the cathartic effect of the experience that man cannot be made guilty of or be stigmatized for what he constitutionally is.

makes wanderers of us, travellers—now at home, now not yet at home. We are mythically exemplified by the wild gander-swan (*haṁsa*). At home in both the upper and the nether regions of the Universe.[17] Both the shore and the waters are ours.

The *Vedic*-Indian mind discovered in *Āpaḥ,* the Waters, as the substratum of all potentiality, their very release from their seclusion "within", in *Vṛtra,* the monstrous mountain. Reading the Waters' release *on* the Universe in the symbol—"thing " of water, the *Vedic*-Indian mind recognized the released Waters to be manifested *in* the psyche, the effect being a broken-open mind, communicative with and receptive of the relationships of all there is. [18]

Āpaḥ, the Waters, reveal man's identity. Manifested in the human psyche they cause the release of unwarranted tension between *pravṛtti* and *nivṛtti* by, as I already said, the surprise of their complementarity. It is surprise which creates both drama and celebration.

Thus there may be—and hopefully there is because surprise goes hand in hand with commitment—celebrating wonder about the marvels of nature or tearful questioning about its senseless destruction. The merciless uprooting of nature, often merely for the sake of faster motorized traffic—to where?, is a blatent proof of man's forgetfulness of the beginnings. And it is clear nonsense to call a child a blessing if after its birth among humans it is but doomed to hunger and thirst or to be enlisted among the millions working as cheap labour, and to condone that fact. The dissenter, armed with the vision and tenacity of his myths, has a perfect right to object, I ought to inform the reader that I am here fulfilling a promise. While I was preparing this book in India's holy city of Banaras, many Western and other travelling young people, in their backpacks their myths, encouraged and helped me to write in exchange for my promise to let their anguish and love for creation be known. There is nothing in the Waters that suggests obvious present day scandals to be part of the cycle of birth, decay and rejuvenation. An increasing number of Indian students too is less impressed with their country's much advertized leap into technology if firsts do not come first.

The promotion of the primal symbol to its capacity to make us think allows us to advance between two hazards. It is not possible to simply put reflection *next* to the confession by the receptive awareness of the sacred and say: here myth ends, there rational discourse begins. Rational discourse must be consistent to the very end. It must try and understand everything, also the receptive awareness of the sacred. But it is also impossible to have a "clear" and rational transcription of the receptive consciousness of the sacred and its symbols. We must insist—as I have tried to make acceptable—that the symbolic myth does not hide any lesson that could be unmasked by the rational-critical instinct so that the myth and its symbol may be conveniently dropped.[19]

Faithful to the gift of both the rational-critical mind and that of the intuitive and cognitive impulse sparked off by the symbol, *I venture to believe in the possibility* of the realization of an ideal: where is there more fruitful thinking than that which is caught

---

17. See Part III:7: "An experience of *Āpaḥ*. . . myth nos. 42-47 and corollary no. 48.
18. See Part I:1:1: A phenomenology of "chaos". *passim*. Also see Part III - Index under *Vṛtra*, *Āpaḥ* and *Indra*.
19. See Part I:2:1: "Myths are no allegories".

in the act of reflection as instructed by the symbolic myth? Thought, instructed by the myth, arises at a certain moment in reflection on the level of the Universe and will begin to wish that its plenitude were true in the human condition. And thus the historical moment of symbol-thought begins, guaranteeing the inquiry after the *whole* of man.

BIBLIOGRAPHY

Primary Sources

Aitareya Āraṇyanka. Edited by Arthur Berriedale Keith. Oxford: 1909.

Aitareya Brāhmaṇa. Edited and translated by Martin Haug. 2 vol. Bombay: 1863.

——— ṚgVeda Brāhmaṇas: The Aitareya and Kauśitaki Brāhmaṇas of the ṚgVeda. Reprint, Vārāṇaśī: Motilal Banarsidass, 1971.

Atharva Veda Saṁhitā. Translated by Maurice Bloomfield. Sacred Books of the East, Vol. 42. Reprint of 1st ed., Delhi: 1964.

Bhagavad Gītā Bhāṣya of Śaṅkarāchārya. Gorakhpur: Gītā Press, samvat 2028.

Bhagavad Gītā with the Commentary of Śri Śaṅkarāchārya. Translated by Alladi Mahadeva Sastry. Corrected reprint, Madras: Samata Books, 1981.

Brahmā-Sūtra-Bhāṣya of Śrī Śankarāchārya. Translated by Swāmī Gambhirānanda. Calcutta: Advaita Ashram, 1977.

Bṛhadāraṇyaka Upaniṣad Bhāṣya of Śaṅkarāchārya. Gorakhpur: Gītā Press, samvat 2029.

Chāndogya Upaniṣad Bhāṣya of Śaṅkarāchārya. Gorakhpur: Gītā Press, samvat 2019..

Classical Hindu Mythology. A Reader in the Sanskrit Purāṇas. Edited and translated by Cornelia Dimmitt and J.A.B. van Buitenen. Philadelphia: Temple University Press, 1978.

Haṭhayogapradīpikā of Svātmārāma. With two commentaries. Reprint of 1st ed., Bombay: 1962.

Hindu Myths. A Source book translated from the Saṅskrit with an introduction by Wendy Doniger O'Flaherty. Edited by Betty Radice. Penguin Books, 1982.

Jaiminīya Brāhmaṇa. Edited by Raghu Vera and Lokesh Chandra. Saraswatī-Vihāra Series 31. Nagpur: 1954.

Kāśī Khaṇḍa (Skanda Purāṇa). Gurumaṇḍala Granthamālāyā no. xx, vol. iv. Calcutta: 1961.

Kāśī Rahasya (Brahmavaivarta Purāṇa Pariśiṣṭa). Gurumaṇḍala Granthamālāyā no. xiv, vol. iii. Calcutta: 1957.'

Kathāsaritsāgara. The Ocean of Story. Translated by C.H. Tawney and edited by N.M. Penzer. 10 vols. Reprint of 2nd ed., Delhi: 1968.

Liṅga Purāṇa. Translated by "A Board of Scholars" and edited by J.L. Shastri. 2 vols. Ancient Indian Tradition and Mythology Series 5-6. Motilal Banarsidass, 1973.

Mahābhārata. Translated by P.C. Roy. 13 vols. Calcutta: 1883-1896.

——— Translated by J.A.B. van Buitenen. 3 vols. completed. Chicago: University of Chicago Press, 1973-1978.

Nighaṇṭu and Nirukta of Yāska. Translated by L. Sarup. Oxford: 1921.

Pañchatantra. Translated by Arthur Ryder. Chicago: University of Chicago Press, 1925.

Rāmāyāṇa of Valmīki. Translated by Hari Prasad Shastri. 3 vols., 2nd ed. London: 1957-1962.

Śatapatha Brāhmaṇa. Translated by Julius Eggeling. 5 vols. Sacred Books of the East, vols. 12, 26, 41, 43, 44. Motilal Banarsidass, 1963.

Ṣaṭ-Çakra-Nirūpaṇa. Translated and with introduction and commentary by Sir John Woodroffe. In: The Serpent Power. Madras: Ganesh & Co., 1973.

Siddhāntamuktāvali. Translated by J.R. Ballantyne and edited by P. Bhaṭṭa. Calcutta: 1851.

Śiva Purāṇa. Translated by "A Board of Scholars" and edited by J.L. Shastri. 4 vols. Ancient Indian Tradition and Mythology Series 1-4. Delhi: 1973.

Sixty Upaniṣads of the Vedas (by Paul Deussen). 2 vols. Translated by V.M. Bedekar and G.B. Palsule. Motilal Banarsidass, 1980.

Śrimad Bhāgavata Mahāpurāṇa (Sanskrit text with English translation). 2 vols. Translated by C.L. Goswami Sāstrī. Gorakhpur: Gītā Press, 1971.

The Srīmad-Bhāgavatam of Krishna – Dwaipayana Vyasa. Translated by J.M. Sanyal. 2 vols. Delhi: Munshiram Manoharlal Publishers, 1973.

Taittirīyopaniṣad Bhāṣya of Śaṅkarāchārya. Gorakhpur: Gītā Press, samvat 2033.

The Book of the Gradual Sayings (Anguttara-Nikāya)). Edited by F.L. Woodward and E.M. Hare. 5 vols. Pali Text Society Translation Series. London: 1932-1939.

The Book of the Kindred Sayings (Saṃyutta-Nikāya). Edited by C.A.F. Rhys and F.L. Woodward. 5 vols. Pali Text Society Translation Series. London: 1917-1930.

The Hymns of the ṚgVeda. Translated by Ralph T.H. Griffith, edited by J.L. Shāstrī. Reprint, Motilal Banarsidass, 1976.

The Laws of Manu, Translated by G. Buhler. Sacred Books of the East, vol. xxv. Motilal Banarsidass, 1979.

The Sacred Laws of the Āryas. Translated by G. Buhler. Sacred Books of the East, vol. xiv. Motilal Banarsidass, 1978.

The Thirteen Principal Upanisads. Translated by R.E. Hume. London: Oxford University Press, 1971.

The Veda of the Black Yajus School entitled Taittirīya Saṁhitā. Translated by Arthur Berriedale Keith. 2 vols. Harvard Oriental Series, vol. xviii. Motilal Banarsidass, 1967.

The Vedic Experience, Mantramañjarī. An Anthology of the Vedas for Modern Man and Contemporary Celebration. Edited and translated with introduction and notes by Raimundo Panikkar. Pondicherry, India: All India Books, 1983.

Vedānta Sūtras (with the commentary by Śaṅkara). Translated by G. Thibaut. Part I and II. Second Reprint, Motilal Banarsidass, 1968.

Vedānta Sūtras with the Commentary by Śaṅkarāchārya. Translated by G. Thibaut. Sacred Books of the East, vol. xxxiv and xxxviii. Delhi: Motilal Banarsidass, 1970.

Viṣñu Purāṇa, H.H. Wilson. Text in Devanāgarī, English translation and notes verse wise. 2 vols. Nag Publishers, 1980.

Other Sources

Adams, Henry. The Degeneration of the Democratic Dogma. Re-edition of 1919, New York: Macmillan Company, 1947.

Agrawala, Vasudeva Sarana. Vedic Lectures. Proceedings of the Summer School of Vedic Studies, Banaras Hindu University. Vārāṇaśī: May – June 1960.

—— Matsya Purāṇa – a study. Vārāṇaśī: 1963.

—— Vision in Long Darkness. Bhārgava, India: 1963.

—— Vedic Lectures. Proceedings of the Summer School of Vedic Studies, Banaras Hindu University. Vārāṇaśī: 1963.
—— Vāmana Purāṇa – a study. Banaras: 1964.
Allchin, B. and R. The Birth of Indian Civilization. Baltimore: 1968.
Altekar, A.S. The Position of Women in Hindu Civilization. Reprint, Motilal Banarsidass, 1978.
Anderson and Trethowan. Psychiatry. London: Bailliere Tindall, 1979.
Antonova, K., Bongard-Levin, G., Kotowski, G. A History of India. Translated by Katherine Judelson. 2 vols. Moscow: Progress Publishers, 1979.
Apte, V.M. Vedic Rituals. In: The Cultural Heritage of India. 5 vols. Calcutta: The Ramakrishna Mission Institute, 1975.
Aquinas, Thomas. Summa Theologica. Turin Edition, 1932.
Aristotle. The Metaphysics. Translated by Huge Tredennick. Loeb Classical Library.
Aurobindo, Sri. On the Veda. Pondicherry: 1956.
Avalon, A. Tantra tattva of Śiva-candra (Translation). London-Madras: 1914.
Baartmans, Frans. Kakus Punan MŪD Healing Rites. In: The Sarawak Museum Journal, vol. xiv, nos. 28-29 (1966), New Series, Government Printing Press, Kuching, Sarawak.
—— Marriage among the "Lepo' Tau" Kenyah Long Moh, Baram, Sarawak" In: The Brunei Museum Journal, vol. 2, no. 3 (1971), reprint.
—— Traditie en Transitie in Zwart-Afrika's stam-en familieverband. Meezoeken naar menselijk welzijn rond Lake Baringo, Kenia. Doctoraal-scriptie for the University of Nijmegen, the Netherlands, 1977.
Barnett, L.D. The Genius: A Study in Indo-European Psychology. In: Journal of the Royal Asiatic Society, 1929.
Benfey, Theodor: Pantschatantra. Leipzig: F.A. Brockhaus, 1859.
Bergaigne, A. La Religion Védique. 4 vols. Paris: 1963.
Beyer, Stephan. The Cult of Tāra. Magic and Ritual in Tibet. University of California Press, 1978.
Bhattacharji, Sukumari. The Indian Theogony. Calcutta: Firma KLM Private, 1978.
Biardeau, Madelaine. Some more considerations about Textual Criticism. In: Purāṇa X, 2 (July 1968).
—— Etudes de mythologie hindou. In: Bulletin de l'École Francaise d'Extrème Orient 58 (1971), 63 (1976), 65 (1978).
Bijeen. A monthly concerning international collaboration in the field of religion and development, no. 3 (March 1983). Gent/Mariakerke, Belgium: L. Vanmelle.
Bloomfield, M. The Atharva Veda and the Gopatha-Brāhmaṇa. Strassbourg: 1899.
—— A Vedic Concordance. Reprint, Delhi: 1964.
Bohm, David. Quantum Theory. New York: Prentice-Hall, 1951. (London: Constable, 1956.)
—— Wholeness and the Implicate Order. London: Routledge & Kegan Paul, 1980.
Campbell, Joseph. The Masks of God: Creative Mythology. Reprint, Penguin Books, 1982.
Cassirer, Ernst. An Essay on Man. An introduction to a philosophy of human culture. Yale University Press, 1962.
—— The Philosophy of Symbolic Forms. 3 vols. Yale University Press, 1977.

Capra, Fritjof. The Tao of Physics. Fontana Books, 1976.
—— The Turning Point. Science, Society and the Rising Culture. London: Fontana Books, 1983.

Chaudhry, Nirad C. Hinduism, a Religion to Live By. Reprint, Oxford University Press, 1979.

Chenu, M.D. La Théologie au douzième siècle. Paris: Vrin, 1966.

Chethimattam, John B. Consciousness and Reality. An Indian approach to Metaphysics. New York: Orbis Books, 1971.
—— Patterns of Indian Thought, New York: Orbis Books, 1971.

Coleman, James C. Abnormal Psychology and Modern Life. Reprint, Bombay: D.B. Taraporevala Sons & Comp., 1981 (by arrangement with Scott, Foresman & Comp.).

Coomaraswamy, Ananda K. A New Approach to the Vedas: An Essay in Translation and Exegesis. London: 1933.
—— Hinduism and Buddhism. New York: Philosophical Library, 1943.
—— The Cristian and Oriental, or True Philosophy of Art. In: Why Exhibit Works of Art. London: Luzac & Company, 1943.
—— Yakṣas. 2 vols. Delhi: 1971.
—— I. Selected Papers. Traditional Art and Symbolism. Edited by Roger Lipsey. Bollingen Series 89. Princeton University Press, 1977.
—— The Dance of Śiva. On Indian Art and Culture. New Delhi: Sagar Publications, 1982.

Corbin, Henry. Man and Time. New York and London: 1957.

Cowell, E.B., ed. The Jātaka or Stories of the Buddha's Former Births. Translated from the Pali by various hands. 1st ed. London: 1895. Reprint, Delhi: Cosmo Publication, 1973.

Dacque, Edgar. Das verlorene Paradies. Munchen: 1938.

Danielou, J. The Lord of History. Longmans Green: 1958.

Darian, Steven G. The Ganges in Myth and History. Honolulu: The University Press of Hawaii, 1978.

Dart, Raymond A. The Birth of Symbology. In: African Studies 27 (1968).

Dasgupta. Shashi Busan. Some later yogic schools. In: The Cultural Heritage of India. 5 vols., Vol. I. Calcutta: The Ramakrishna Mission Institute, 1975.

Dasgupta, Surendra Nath. A History of Indian Philosophy. 5 vols. Delhi: Motilal Banarsidass, 1975.
—— Hindu Mysticism. 1st ed. Vārānasī: Motilal Banarsidass, 1976.

Deppert, J. Rudras Geburt: Systematische Untersuchungen zum Inzest in der Mythologie der Brāhmaṇas. Wiesbaden: 1977.

Despagnat, Bernard. Conceptual Foundations in Quantum Mechanics. Benjamin Inc., 1976.

Deussen, Paul. Allgemeine Einleitung und Philosophie des Veda. In: Allgemeine Geschichte der Philosophie mit besonderer Berucksichtigung der Religionen. 7 vols., Vol. I. Leipzig: 1884-1920.
—— The Philosophy of Vedānta. Translated by G.A. Jacob. Calcutta: Susil Gupta, 1957.
—— The Philosophy of the Upaniṣads. New York: Dover Publications, 1966.

Diels, Hermann. Die Fragmente der Vorsokratiker. Edited by W. Kranz. 5th ed. Berlin: 1934.

—— Die Fragmente der Vorsokratiker. Translated by Kathleen Freeman. In: Ancilla to the Pre-Socratic Philosophers. Cambridge: Harvard University Press, 1948.

Dimmitt, Cornelia and van Buitenen, J.A.B. Classical Hindu Mythology (edited and translated). A Reader in the Sanskrit Purāṇas. Philadelphia: Temple University Press, 1978.

Dubos, Reńe. Man, Medicine and Environment. New York: Praeger, 1968.

Dumézil, George. Ordre, fantaisie, changement dans les penseés archaiques de l'Inde et de Rome. In: Revues Etudes Latines 32 (1957).

—— Mythe et Epopee. Paris: 1960.

Durkheim, Emile. Les formes élémentaires de la vie religieuse. Paris: 1912.

Eck, Diana. Banaras: City of Light. London: Routledge & Kegan Paul, 1983.

Eckermann, Johann Peter. Gesprache mit Goethe in den letzten Jahren seines Lebens, 1823-1832. Berlin: Deutsches Verlagshaus, Bong & Comp., 1916. In: Oswald Spengler. The Decline of the West. Translated by C.F. Atkinson. vol. i.

Eliade, Mircea. The Quest. History and Meaning in Religion. University of Chicago Press, 1969.

—— Yoga, Immortality and Freedom. Bollingen Series LVI. Routledge & Kegan Paul, 1973.

—— The Myth of the Eternal Return or, Cosmos and History. Bollingen Series XLIV. Princeton University Press, 1974.

—— Myth and Reality. London-New York: Harper Colophon Books, 1975.

—— A History of Religious Ideas. vol i., From the Stone Age to the Eleusinian Mysteries. London: Collins, 1979.

—— Patterns in Comparative Religion. London: Sheed and Ward Stagbooks, 1979.

Erasmus, Desiderius. Encomium Moriae. Translated by John Wilson (1668). The Praise of Folly. Oxford: The Clarendon Press, 1913.

Fawcett, Thomas. The Symbolic Language of Religion, an Introductory Study. London: SCM Press, 1970.

Freud, Sigmund. The Psychopathology of Everyday Life, In: A.A. Brill. The Basic Writings of Sigmund Freud. New York: The Modern Library, 1938.

Fohrer, G. History of Israelite Religion. Nashville: 1972.

Frazer, J.G. The Golden Bough. 2 vols. Abridged ed., London: Macmillan & Co., 1960.

Fromm, Erich, Suzuki, D.T. and De Martino, Richard. Zen Buddhism and Psychoanalysis. New York: Harper & Row, 1969. (London: Souvenir Press, 1974.)

Gebser, Jean. Ursprung und Gegenwart. Fundamente und Manifestationen der aperspektivischen Welt. Stuttgart: Deutsche Verlagsanstalt, 1945-1953. Gonda, J. Viṣṇuism — Aspects of early Viṣṇuism. Utrecht: 1954.

—— Die Religionen Indiens, 2 vols. Stuttgart: W. Kohlhammer, 1960.

—— Vedic Literature, Saṁhitās and Brāhmaṇas. Wiesbaden: Otto Harrasowitz, 1975.

Greene, William C. Moira: Fate, Good and Evil in Greek Thought. Harvard University Press, 1944.

Griffiths, Bede. The Marriage of East and West. Collins, Fount Paperbacks, 1982.

Guenon, René. Mythes, Mystères et Symboles. In: Le Voile d'Isis XL (1935).

Gusdorf, G. Mythe et Metaphysique. Paris: 1953.

Gyani, S.D. Agni Puraṇa. A Study. The Chowkhamba Sanskrit Studies, vol. xlii. Vārāṇaśī: Chowkhamba Publication, 1964.

Harskamp, Jaap T. D.H. Lawrence, De Schepping van een oevre. In: Bzzlletin, 12th vol., no. 117 (June 1984). Den Haag.

Hartmann, Heinz. Ego Psychology and the Problem of Adaptation (1939). In: David Papaport. Organization and Pathology of Thought. Columbia University Press, 1951.

Hazra, R.C. Studies in the Purāṇic Records on Hindu Rites and Customs. Delhi: Motilal Banarsidass, 1975.

Heidegger, Martin. Introduction to Metaphysics. Translated by Ralph Manheim. New York: Doubleday, 1961.

Heisenberg, W. Physics and Philosophy. London: Allen and Undwin, 1963.

Hillebrandt, Alfred von. Lieder des RgVeda (German translation). Göttingen und Leipzig: 1913.

—— Vedic Mythology. Translated by Sheermula Rajeswara Sarma. 2 vols. 1st English language edition. Delhi: Motilal Banarsidass, 1980.

Hoens, D.J. A Contribution to Ancient Indian Terminology. The Hague: 1951.

Huxley, Aldous. Brave New World. Reprint, Penguin Books, 1970.

India Today. vol. viii (May 1983).

Jones, Roger. Physics as Metaphor. London: Sphere Books, 1983.

Joseph, George V. Integral Experience in Advaita Vedānta. Unpublished Ph.D. thesis for Banaras Hindu University. Vārānaśī: 1984.

Joseph, T.F. The Vedic and Christian Concept of Sacrifice. Ph.D. thesis for Banaras Hindu University. Vārānaśī: 1982.

Joyce, James. A Portrait of the Artist as a young Man. London: Jonathan Cape, 1916.

Jung, C.G. Psychology and Alchemy. Translated by R.F.C. Hull. Collected Works, vol. 12. New York: 1953.

—— Bewusstes und Unbewusstes. Frankfurt: Fischer Bucherei, 1957.

—— Psychology and Religion: West and East. Bollingen Series. New York: 1958.

—— The Archetypes and the Collective Unconscious. Translated by R.F.C. Hull. Collected Works, Vol. 9.i. New York: 1959.

—— The Structure and Dynamics of the Psyche. Translated by R.F.C. Hull. Bollingen Series xx, 8. New York: Pantheon Books, 1960.

—— On the Nature of the Psyche. In: The Structure and Dynamics of the Psyche. Collected Works, vol. 8. New York and London: 1960.

Kane, Pandurang Vaman. History of Dharmaśāstra. 5 vols. Poona: Bhandarkar Oriental Research Institute, 1974.

Kanjamala, Augustine. Religion and Modernization in India. A case study of Northern Orissa. St. Augustine: Steyler Verlag/Pune: Ishvani and Indore: Satprakashan, 1981.

Kant, Immanuel. Critique of Pure Reason. Translated by Norman Kemp Smith. London: Macmillan, 1964.

—— Prolegomena zu einer jeden zukunftigen Metaphysik, die als Wissenschaft wird auftreten können. In: Joseph Campbell. The Masks of God: Creative Mythology. Penguin Books, 1982.

Keith, Arthur Berriedale. The Religion and Philosophy of the Veda and Upaniṣads. 2 vols. Reprint, Delhi: Motilal Banarsidass, 1976.

Khan, Mohammed Israel. Brāhmā in the Purāṇas. Ghaziabad, India: Crescent Publishing House, 1981.

Kramrisch, Stella. The Presence of Śiva. Delhi: Oxford University Press, 1981.

Kuiper, F.B.J. Ancient Indian Cosmogony. Essays selected and introduced by John Irwin. Vikas Publication House, 1983.

Laszlo, Ervin. Introduction to Systems Philosophy. New York: Harper Torchbooks/London: Gordon and Breach, 1972.

Leisegang, Hans. The Mystery of the Serpent. In: Joseph Campbell (ed.). The Mysteries. Papers from the Eranos Yearbooks. vol. 2. Bollingen Series xxx, 2. New York: Pantheon Books, 1955.

Leroi-Goushan, André. Les Religions de la Pré-Histoire: Paléolithique. Paris: 1964.

Lévi-Strauss, C. La Pensée sauvage. Paris: Plon, 1962.

—— Structural Anthropology. New York: 1964.

—— The Story of Adiwal. Translated by Nicholas Mann. In: Edmund R. Leach (ed.). The Structural Study of Myth and Totemism. Association of Social Anthropologists, Monograph no. 45. London: 1967.

—— The Raw and the Cooked. Introduction to a Science of Mythology. Translated by John and Doreen Weightman. New York: 1969.

MacDonald, Ariane. La Naissance du Monde au Tibet. In: Source Orientales, vol. i. Paris: 1975.

—— and Keith, A.B. Vedic index of names and subjects. 2 vols. Reprint, Delhi: Motilal Banarsidass, 1982.

Mackey, Ernest. Early Indus Civilizations. London: 1948.

Majumdar, R.C. History and Culture of the Indian People. London: 1951.

Mann, Thomas. Der Zauberberg. Berlin: S. Fischer, 1924. English translation by H.T. Lowe-Porter. The Magic Mountain. New York: Knopf, 1927.

Marx, Karl. Capital, critique of political economy. Translated by Samuel Moore and Edward Aveling and edited by Frederick Engels. vol. i. Reprint, Moscow: Progress Publishers, 1977.

Miller Jeanine. The Vedas. Harmony, Meditation and Fulfilment.

Mookerjee, Ajit. Khanna Madu. The Tāntric Way, Art, Science, Ritual. New York: 1977.

Muir, J. Original Sanskrit Texts. Reprint of 1873 ed., Delhi: 1976.

Narr, Karl J. Kultur, Umwelt und Leiblichkeit der Eiszeitmenschen. Stuttgart: 1963.

—— Approaches to the Religion of early Paleolithic Man. In: History of Religions 4. Chicago: 1964.

Nebel, Gerhard. Weltangst und Gotterzorn. Eine Deutung der Griechischen Tragödie. Stuttgart: 1951.

Neher, André. L'Essence du prophétisme. Paris: 1955.

Neumann, Erich. The Original History of Consciousness. Translated by R.F.C. Hull. Bollingen Series xlii. London: 1954.

—— The Great Mother. An Analysis of the Archetype. Bollingen Series. Princeton: 1974.

Nietzsche, Friedrich Wilhelm. Gotzen-Dammerung. Leipzig: A. Kroner, 1919.

O'Flaherty, Wendy Doniger. Siva, The Erotic Ascetic. Oxford University Press, 1973.
Oldenberg, Hermann. Religion des Veda. 2nd ed. Berlin: W. Hertz, 1894.
Ortega y Gasset, Jose. Meditations on Quixote. Translated from the Spanish by Evelyn Rugg and Diego Marin. Norton & Comp., 1961.
Otto, Rudolph. Das Heilige. Uber das Irrationale in der Idee des Gottlichen und sein Verhältnis zum Rationalen. Gottingen: 1917.
—— The Idea of the Holy. Translated by John W. Harvey. Penguin Books, 1959.
Ouspensky, P.D. Tertium Organum. New York: Knopf, 1959.
Pandey, Raj Bali. Hindu Saṁskāras, Socio-religious study of the Hindu Sacraments. Delhi: Motilal Banarsidass, 1977.
Panikkar, Raimundo. Hindu Society at Crossroads. Bombay: Asia, 1955.
—— Myth, Faith and Hermeneutics. Bangalore: Asian Trading Corporation, 1983.
Patil, Devendrakumar Rajaram. Cultural History from the Vāyu Purāṇa. Reprint, Motilal Banarsidass, 1973.
Patte, Etiénne. Les hommes prĥehistoriques et la religion. Paris: 1960.
Plato. The Collected Dialogues of Plato, including the Letters. Edited by Edith Hamilton and Huntington Cairns. Bollingen Series lxxi. Princeton: 1961.
Prinz. H. Altorientalische Symbolik. Berlin: 1915.
Pryzluski, J. Les sept Puissances divines dans l'Inde et l'Iran. In: Revue d'histoire et de philosophie religieuse, xvi (1936).
Radhakrishnan, S. The Principal Upaniṣads. London: Allen and Undwin, 1953.
Radice, Betty (ed.). Hindu Myths. A Sourcebook translated from the Sanskrit, with an introduction by Wendy Doniger O'Flaherty. Penguin Books, 1982.
Ranade, R.D. A Constructive Survey of Upaniṣadic Philosophy. Poona: Oriental Book Agency, 1926.
Renon, L. Religions of Ancient India. Athlone Press, 1953.
Ricoeur, Paul. The Symbolism of Evil. Boston: Beacon Press, 1969.
Rubinstein, Renate. Liefst Verliefd. Amsterdam: Meulenhoff, 1984.
Russell, Bertrand. Introduction to Ludwig Wittgenstein's Tractatus Logico-Philosophicus. Translated by D.F. Pears and B.F. McGuiness. New York: The Humanities Press, 1961.
—— The Problem of Philosophy. Oxford University Press, 1980.
Sagan, Carl. Cosmos. The story of cosmic evolution, science and civilization. London: Futura, McDonald & Co., 1983.
Sargant, William and Slater. Eliot. An Introduction to Physical Methods of Treatment in Psychiatry. Edinburgh and London: E.S. Livingstone, 1969.
Schaer, Hans. Religion and the cure of souls in Jung's Psychology. Routledge & Kegan Paul, 1951.
Schärer, Hans. Die Gottesidee der Ngaju Dayak in sud-Borneo. Leiden: 1946.
Scheler, Max. Die Stellung des Menschen im Kosmos. Darmstadt: Reichl, 1928.
—— Le Phĕnomène du Tragique. Translated into French by M. Dupuy. Paris: 1952.
Schelling, Friedrich Wilhelm Joseph. Philosophie der Mythologie. 2 vols. (Unaltered reprographic reprint of the original publication, 1856.) Darmstadt: Wissenschaftliche Buchgesellschaft, 1976.
Schmidt, Wilhelm. The Origin and Growth of Religion: Facts and Theories. Translated by H.J. Rose. New York: 1931.

Sēchan, Louis, Le Mythe de Promethēe. Paris: 1951.
Saksena, S.K. Nature of Consciousness in Hindu Philosophy. Delhi: Motilal Banarsidass, 1971.
Sharvananda, Swami. The Vedas and their religious teaching. In: The Cultural Heritage of India. 5 vols. Calcutta: The Ramakrishna Mission Institute of Culture, 1975.
Sharma, Chanddradhar. A Critical Survey of Indian Philosophy. Delhi: Motilal Banarsidass, 1979.
Simclair, Stevenson and Margaret. The Rites of the Twice-Born. London: 1920.
Singh, Yogendra. Modernization of Indian Tradition. Delhi: Thomson Press, 1973.
Spengler, Oswald. Untergang des Abendlandes. Munchen: C.H. Beck, 1923.
—— The Decline of the West. Translated by C.F. Atkinson. London—New York: Knopf, 1928.
Stevenson, W.T. History as Myth. New York: Seabury Press, 1969.
—— History and Myth: Some implications for History and Theology. In: Cross Current XXI (winter 1970).
Tagore, Rabindranath. Gītāñjalī, Song Offerings. A collection of prose translations made by the author from the original Bengali. India: MacMillan, 1979.
The Jerusalem Bible. London: Darton, Longman and Todd, 1966.
Thibaut, G. Commentary on the Vedānta-Sūtra (transl.). The Vedānta-Sūtra With Śaṅkara's Commentary. Sacred Books of the East, vol. xxxiv. Motilal Banarsidass.
Thomas, Edward J. Vedic Hymns. London: John Murry, 1923..
Update, a quarterly on New Religious Movements. Published by the Dialog Centre, Klvermarksvej 4, DK – 8200 Aarhus, Denmark.
Van der Leeuw, G. Religion in Essence and Manifestation. 2 vols. New York: Harper Torch Books, 1963.
Vettam, Mani. Purāṇic Encyclopaedia. Motilal Banarsidass, 1979.
Washburn-Hopkins, E. Epic Mythology. Reprint, Motilal Banarsidass, 1974.
Weill, Reymond. Le champs des roseaux et le champs des offrandes dans la religion funeraire et la religion gēnērale. Paris: 1936.
West, M.L. Hesiod' Theogony. Edited with Prolegomena and Commentary. Oxford: 1966.
Whorf, Benjamin Lee. The Relation of Habitual Thought and Behaviour of Language. Language, Culture and Personality. Wisconsin: Menasha, 1941. In: International Journal of American Language, vol. 16, no. 2 (April 1950).
Wilber, Ken. Philosophia Perennis: The Spectrum of Consciousness. In: Journal of Transpersonal Psychology, no. 2 (1975).
—— The Spectrum of Consciousness. Wheaton. Ill.: Theosophical Publishing House, 1977.
Wilkins, W.J. Hindu Mythology: Vedic and Puranic. Reprint, Calcutta: Rupa, 1980.
Wilson, H.H. Analysis of the Purāṇas. Edited by Reinhold Rost. Reprint, Delhi: NAG Publishers, 1979.
Woodroffe, Sir John. The Serpent Power. Madras Ganesh & Company, 1973.
—— Śakti and Śākta. Madras: Ganesh & Company, 1975.
—— The Garland of Letters. Madras: Ganesh & Company, 1979.

—— The World as Power. Madras: Ganesh & Company, 1981.
Zaehner, R.G. Hinduism. Reprint, Oxford University Press, 1966.
Zimmer, Heinrich. Philosophie und Religion Indiens. Reprint, Frankfurt: Suhrkamp Taschenbuch Wissenschaft, 1979.
—— Myths and Symbols in Indian Art and Civilization. Edited by Joseph Campbell.
—— Indische Mythen und Symbole. Viṣṅu, Śiva und das Rad der Wiedergeburten. Köln: Diederichs, 1981.

INDEX OF NAMES AND THEMES IN PART III

RIVER: and *Mitra* and *Varuṇa* 128; and earth and sky 128; and *Ṛta* 128; and *Saptasindhava* 129; and *Vṛtra* 129; and *Uṣās* 129; and *Bhūmi*, the inhabited earth 130; rivers and earth differ in character 183,184,185; see also under *Gaṅgā, Narmadā, Saraswatī, Yamunā, saṅgam, Himavat, Meru*, bath.

ṚTA: Cosmic Order, born from *tapas* 28; and *Satya*, Truth 28; and space and time and the year 29; and *Varuṇa*, watching over *Ṛta* 61; Sun rising from *Ṛta* 64; and *Sandhyās*, twilight and dusk 118, 11; and *Agnihotra* 117; and *Arundhatī* and *Ṛtu*, the season 119; and self-identity of sexed man and woman on earth 191; and concept of sin 191; and ethics and morals 191.

ŚAKTI: as *aliṅga* and *avyakta* 36; and *Mūla-Prakṛti* 36; and *nivṛtti* 36; as first cosmic vibration of *Kāma*, Love, Desire 36; as the teleological instinct of *Sat-cit-Ānanda* and outward bound, *pravṛtti* 36; and *Śiva* 36; as power as metaphysical centre and her names 38; and "the isle of gems" 38; and *amṛtārṇava*, the ocean of nectar 38; and *Sabdabrahman* 38; and *kuṇḍalinī* 156; and non-orgastic coition 156; and *Ardhanārīśvara* 190; and *Satī* 190; see also under *Śiva, Pārvatī*.

SAMĀDHI: enstasis attained by meditating on the subtle aspect of matter, *sūkṣma* 169; and *asamprajñāta samādhi*, the undifferentiated state 169.

SANDHYĀ: the "holding together" of the worlds at dawn and dusk 117; and *Ṛta* 117; as man's "seasonal" being 118; as time of choice for man 118; as goddess 119; as woman abused 119; as danger-zone 119; as *Arundhatī* 119; and man and woman 119; and marriage ritual 119; as cosmic *Uṣās* 120; and *Varuṇa* 120.

SAṀSĀRA: and *Prāṇāgnihotra* 113,114; and *yoga* and *Sāṁkhya* 114; and *mokṣa* 114; and karma 162; and *Jñāna-śuddhi* 162; and dissolution 240.

SAMUDRA-MANTHANA: Churning of the Ocean 76; and *amrta*; and Mount *Mandara* 76; and *Vāsuki* 76; and *Viṣñu-Śeṣa* as guardian of *skambha* 76; and *Viṣñu* 77; and *Kaśyapa*, tortoise 77; and moon and *Soma* 78; and *Lakṣmī* 76; and *Kaushtubhā* gem of *Viṣñu* 78; and *Śiva* 81, 82, 83; and *kālakūta*, the world-poison 79,80,81; and the moon 81,82 and *Cāndrāyana*-fast 82; and *Śiva* swallowing the poison – *Śiva-Nīlakaṇṭha* 83; and *Dhanvantarī*, the divine healer 174, 86; and *Haridwār, Nāsik, Ujjain* and *Prayāg* 174; and *yuga* 225,231; and *pralaya* 225; and *Viṣñu* 225; and deluge-symbolism 226.

SAṄGAM: confluence of rivers and its themes 170; and *Prayāg* 170,173; and *Iḍā* and *Piṅgalā* 173.

SAPTADVĪPA: the seven islands 134, 137.

SARASWATĪ: the mythical river in the Aryan memory 127; and *Gaṅgā Bhāgīrathī* 134; and *Gaṅgā* 127; and *Himavat* 136; and birth 131; as born from *Plakṣa*-tree 134, 180; and *Gaṅgā* 170,179; and *saṅgam* at *Prayāg* 170; and *Yamunā* 170; and *Vāsuki* 170; and *kumbha* 179; as born from *Brahmā's* water-jug 179; and *Aditi* 180; and *Vṛtra* and *Puramdhi* 133; also see under *Gaṅgā, Yamunā*.

SAT: as Consciousness 33; and *kāraṇa-salila*, the waters as causal fluid 33; and *Cit* 33; and *Ānanda* 33.

SAT-ÇIT-ĀNANDA: and its dormant side, *Mūla-Prakṛti* 36; and *nivṛtti* and *pravṛtti* 36; and *Śakti* 36.

SATĪ: the Great Goddess in one of her forms and *Śiva* the *Yogi* 140; and *Pārvatī* 140; and *Śiva Mantramūrti* 140; and *Ardhanārīśvara* 190; as "The Real" with her own

when approached by her father *Prajāpati* 120; present when the waters were released 120; and *Prajāpati* 138; and *Ṛta* 120,121; and *Ṛbhus*, the seasons 121; represents energy over apathy 122; is *Puraṃdhi*, the Cosmic Present 122; and man's task 122; and *pravṛtti* and *nivṛtti* 122,123; her association with *Rudra* concerning creation 137; *Prajāpati* and *Uṣās* as transposed to *Śiva* and *Pārvatī* 138; her role in the creation of time when *Rudra's* arrow hit the target late 138; and man's choice with regard to the day 123.

VĀC: The Word, producing the waters 1; as the female voice present in the waters 31; the first Cosmic Sound, *Parasabda*, hidden in *Vāc* 37; makes one a seer 37.

VĀRI: the all-pervading waters 2; and *Vṛtra* 2; and *Vṛtra's* mortal spot 2.

VARUṆA: and *Vṛtra* 59; and *Agni* 60; and *Ṛta* 61; and nether world, the "seat of *Ṛta*" 63; and *skambha* 65; and Tree of Life 67; is all-seeing 62-69; and *Soma-Pavamāna* 70; and his court *Antaḥ-salila* in the nether-waters 70; and *nāga* 71; and *makara* 71,72; and *Vṛtra* 71; and *Vāma* 72; and *pralaya* 72; and *Narmadā* 172; and *Ṛta* 172; and *Indra* and *Soma* 172; and man's human situation 220.

VĀSUKI: the serpent serving as rope during the contest at the churning of the Ocean 76.

VIṢÑU: present at the creation of the dual universe, heaven and earth 55; as part of both worlds 55; as *Viṣñu-Śeṣa* he supports world-axis from below but is in three strides on high 55; and *Indra* 56; the well of wisdom springs in his highest footstep 57; as god of cosmic *pravṛtti* or progression 58; antithesis of *Viṣñu-Jala-Śāyin* as god of cosmic *nivṛtti*, involution 58; his central position when *Brahmā* rises from his navel 74; with *Varuṇa* guarding *skambha*, the world-axle 74; his central position at the *samudra-manthana* 76; his Mount *Mandāra* 76 77; and *Vāsuki* 76; and *Śeṣa*; 76; and *Kaśyapa*, tortoise, *Viṣñu's* avatar 77; and moon 78; and *Kashtaubhā* gem 78; as personification of unity 222; and *stambha* 222; his vehicles *garuḍa* and *sesa* 222; and *kāla*, time 153; his pivotal role at cosmic dissolution when he rests on the waters 153.

VṚTRA: The mountain, monster, obstacle preventing the waters from release 2; overcome by *Indra* 2; and the waters 59; and *Indra-Soma* 94; and *Varuṇa* 59; and Puramdhi 133, 137; and *Saraswatī* 133; and Mount *Himavat* 135; and *amṛta* 135; and Mount *Parvata* 137; and *Prajāpati* and *Uṣās* 137; and *Gaṅgā* 148; and *Ṛta* 148; and *Gaṅgā vataraṇa* 148; and the waters 212.

VṚTRA-HATYA: the slaying of *Vṛtra* by *Indra* 21; as primal inertia 21; and *Varuṇa* 21.

WATERS (THE): see under *Āpaḥ*.

YAJÑA: the sacrifice, immolation of *Purusa* 100; as creation of order out of chaos 100; as *Ṛta* 100 and *Prajāpati* 100, 103; and dharma 100; and *Ātman* 103; and the waters as cosmic substratum understood in the fire-sacrifice 101,102; is man 112; and *mokṣa* 112; and *prāṇāgnihotra* 113, 115; as the year being assembled in *Prajāpati* through ritual 103; and water-offering 113; and *saṁsāra* 113; and *vājapeya-yajña* 115; and the fruit-season 115; as transposed to the birth of a son 115; and semen 115; semen of the arteries 115; and *liṅga* and *yoni* 115; and cosmic elements 174; and renewal of creation 174; and vegetative essence of man, construction of time, water-ritual and the year 227, 228, 229; and *pralaya* 238; and *pañca-mahāyajña*, the five debts to be paid to all surrounding 238, 239.

YAMUNĀ: and *Gaṅgā* 151, 152, 153; as *Kālindī* 151; and *Saraswatī* 151; and *Kālīya* hiding in *Yamunā*, a reminder of *Vṛtra* and the waters 151; and Mount *Kailāśā* 152; and *Mānassarovar*, the lake of the mind 152; and *Śiva-Nilakaṇṭha* 153; and *Kāla*; and *Rudra* 153; and *Nitya-pralaya* 153; is *piṅgala*, is sun, is *prāṇa*, is male 154; and saṅgam at prayāg 170; and temple architecture 212.

YANTRA: and lotus 203; and *cakras* 203.

YOGA: and the breaths during the bath 166; the interiorization of the bath 166; and *tantra* and *naimālaya* 167; and *mokṣa* 168; and the "right hand" tantric practices 168.

YONI: see under *liṅga*.

YUGA: and *Vishñu-Śeṣa* 225; and *pralaya* 225; its symbolism 126; and *samudra-manthana* 231 232; and *Prajāpati* 232; and its concept 236; and *Viṣñu* 236; and *pralaya* 236; and its concept 237.*

*The index does not mention names and themes occurring in the footnotes to the myths.